Conference on Empirical Methods in Natural Language Processing (EMNLP 2021)

Systems Demonstrations

Punta Cana, Dominican Republic and Online
7-11 November 2021

ISBN: 978-1-7138-9162-8

Printed from e-media with permission by:

Curran Associates, Inc.
57 Morehouse Lane
Red Hook, NY 12571

Some format issues inherent in the e-media version may also appear in this print version.

Printed with permission by Curran Associates, Inc. (2024)

Association for Computational Linguistics
209 N. Eighth Street
Stroudsburg, Pennsylvania 18360

Phone: 1-570-476-8006
Fax: 1-570-476-0860

acl@aclweb.org

Additional copies of this publication are available from:

Curran Associates, Inc.
57 Morehouse Lane
Red Hook, NY 12571 USA
Phone: 845-758-0400
Fax: 845-758-2633
Email: curran@proceedings.com
Web: www.proceedings.com

EMNLP 2021

The 2021 Conference on
Empirical Methods in Natural Language Processing

Proceedings of System Demonstrations

November 7 - 11, 2021

Preface by the System Demonstration Co-Chairs

Welcome to the proceedings of the system demonstrations session. This volume contains the papers of the system demonstrations presented at the 2021 Conference on Empirical Methods in Natural Language Processing, which was held on November 7–11, 2021.

The system demonstrations session includes papers describing systems ranging from early research prototypes to mature production-ready software. We received 130 valid submissions, of which 42 were selected for inclusion in the proceedings after review of the program committee, achieving an overall acceptance rate of 32%.

We thank all authors for their submissions, and the 105 members of the program committee for their timely and thoughtful reviews.

Heike Adel and Shuming Shi
EMNLP 2021 System Demonstration Co-Chairs

Organizers:

Heike Adel, Bosch Center for Artificial Intelligence, Germany
Shuming Shi, Tencent AI Lab, China

Program Committee:

Alan Akbik, Zeynep Akkalyoncu, Akari Asai, Eleftherios Avramidis, Wei Bi, Georgeta Bordea, Ari Bornstein, Aljoscha Burchardt, Eric Charton, Hai Leong Chieu, Simone Conia, Danilo Croce, Montse Cuadros, Marina Danilevsky, Pradipto Das, Victor Dibia, Chenchen Ding, Carsten Eickhoff, Kshitij Fadnis, Nicolas Rodolfo Fauceglia, Anthony Ferritto, Dimitris Galanis, Yang Gao, Stefan Grünewald, Xianpei Han, Jialong Han, Michael A. Hedderich, Leonhard Hennig, Tom Hope, Ales Horak, Kasra Hosseini, Takumi Ito, Peter Jansen, Sai Muralidhar Jayanthi, Haiyun Jiang, Sudipta Kar, Mamoru Komachi, Lukas Lange, John Lee, Jing Li, Marina Litvak, Changsong Liu, Zhengzhong Liu, Wei Lu, Wolfgang Maier, Benjamin Marie, Stella Markantonatou, Ivan Vladimir Meza Ruiz, John Morris, Hamdy Mubarak, Philippe Muller, Preslav Nakov, Diane Napolitano, Pierre Nugues, Yusuke Oda, Tsuyoshi Okita, Daniel Ortega, Sebastian Padó, Sean Papay, Oren Pereg, Stelios Piperidis, Christopher Potts, Prokopis Prokopidis, Fanchao Qi, Carlos Ramisch, German Rigau, Pablo Ruiz Fabo, Irene Russo, Niloofar Safi Samghabadi, Saurav Sahay, Sebastin Santy, David Schlangen, Fabian David Schmidt, Hendrik Schuff, Sanuj Sharma, Liang-Hsin Shen, Michal Shmueli-Scheuer, Sameer Singh, Amy Siu, Konstantinos Skianis, Mohammad Golam Sohrab, Yuanfeng Song, Michael Stewart, Duyu Tang, Juan-Manuel Torres-Moreno, Natalia Vanetik, Andrea Varga, Ivan Vulić, Yan Wang, Longyue Wang, Changhan Wang, Rui Wang, Leo Wanner, Moritz Wolf, Deyi Xiong, Qiongkai Xu, Tae Yano, Seid Muhie Yimam, Dian Yu, Wenhao Yu, Liang-Chih Yu, Rongsheng Zhang, Ningyu Zhang, Guangyou Zhou, Imed Zitouni

Table of Contents

Conference Program

MiSS: An Assistant for Multi-Style Simultaneous Translation

Zuchao Li[1,2,3,†], **Kevin Parnow**[1,2,3], **Masao Utiyama**[4,*], **Eiichiro Sumita**[4], **Hai Zhao**[1,2,3*]
[1]Department of Computer Science and Engineering, Shanghai Jiao Tong University
[2]Key Laboratory of Shanghai Education Commission for Intelligent Interaction and Cognitive Engineering, Shanghai Jiao Tong University, Shanghai, China
[3]MoE Key Lab of Artificial Intelligence, AI Institute, Shanghai Jiao Tong University
[4]National Institute of Information and Communications Technology (NICT), Kyoto, Japan
charlee@sjtu.edu.cn, {mutiyama, eiichiro.sumita}@nict.go.jp, zhaohai@cs.sjtu.edu.cn

Abstract

In this paper, we present **MiSS**, an assistant for multi-style simultaneous translation. Our proposed translation system has five key features: highly accurate translation, simultaneous translation, translation for multiple text styles, back-translation for translation quality evaluation, and grammatical error correction. With this system, we aim to provide a complete translation experience for machine translation users. Our design goals are high translation accuracy, real-time translation, flexibility, and measurable translation quality. Compared with the free commercial translation systems commonly used, our translation assistance system regards the machine translation application as a more complete and fully-featured tool for users. By incorporating additional features and giving the user better control over their experience, we improve translation efficiency and performance. Additionally, our assistant system combines machine translation, grammatical error correction, and interactive edits, and uses a crowdsourcing mode to collect more data for further training to improve both the machine translation and grammatical error correction models. A short video demonstrating our system is available at https://www.youtube.com/watch?v=ZGCo7KtRKd8.

1 Introduction

With the increasing technological development of the world and the acceleration of globalization, people from different languages and cultural backgrounds communicate more and more, and the needs of translation are becoming more and more important and diverse. Although traditional manual translation works well, with the increasing frequency of international communication, traditional manual translation far from meets demand, and machine translation has correspondingly risen in popularity (Hutchins and Somers, 1992). Recently, Neural Machine Translation (NMT), especially Transformer-based NMT, has emerged as a promising approach with the potential to address many of the shortcomings of traditional rule-based or statistics-based machine translation systems (Sutskever et al., 2014; Bahdanau et al., 2015; Vaswani et al., 2017). This has significantly improved the performance of machine translation and other related tasks (Huang et al., 2018; Li et al., 2018a,b).

Although neural machine translation has made tremendous improvements and is relatively high-performing, because human language is so complex, machine translation is often still only used as an assistance tool rather than the sole entity responsible for translation. There are several popular and large existing commercial machine translation systems that provide users with effective translation (e.g., Google Translator, Bing Translator, Amazon Translate, and Baidu Translate). As NMT is still very imprecise, however, these web services fall short, as they do not provide sufficient information to users in how good each translation is, which is particularly pertinent to those who have not mastered the target language. VoiceTra[1] included back-translation in the machine translation system to alleviate this deficiency; however, this practice requires users to perform additional manual evaluations, which brings new usage costs.

In mainstream machine translation systems, sentences or paragraphs are used as the units of translation, which means that it takes a relatively long time to provide users with translated content. Simultaneous machine translation, translating sentences in real-time while the user speaks or types, can significantly reduce this translation time, but its performance lags behind that of standard NMT. Although some commercial machine translation systems such

*Corresponding author. †This paper was partially finished when Zuchao Li was a fixed term technical researcher at NICT. This paper was supported by Key Projects of National Natural Science Foundation of China (U1836222 and 61733011).

[1]https://voicetra.nict.go.jp/

Proceedings of the 2021 Conference on Empirical Methods in Natural Language Processing: System Demonstrations, pages 1–10
November 7–11, 2021. ©2021 Association for Computational Linguistics

as Google and Baidu have introduced simultaneous translation feature, due to the integration of simultaneous translation and whole-sentence translation, users cannot easily control whether the system uses simultaneous translation or whole-sentence translation, and the automated control of commercial systems sometimes does not follow the user's wishes.

Since user input errors are unavoidable for any human-computer interaction system, the quality of NMT system also has been shown to significantly degrade when confronted with source-side noise (Heigold et al., 2018; Belinkov and Bisk, 2018; Anastasopoulos, 2019). The previous grammatical error detection and correction work focused on computer-aided writing systems. Some existing computer-aided writing systems (Grammarly[2] and Pigai[3], Write&Improve[4], and LinggleWrite[5]) detect and correct grammatical errors; however, systems such as these have had little attention when considered in the context of input error detection or correction for commercial machine translation systems, as their main focus is generally post-translation editing.

High quality domain specific machine translation systems are in high demand whereas general purpose MT has limited applications because different machine translation users want to generate translations that can be used in the scenario. On the one hand, general purpose translation systems usually perform poorly (Koehn and Knowles, 2017). On the other hand, appropriate translation is also a very important goal to pursue. There are two typical methods to achieve this goal. One is to use the domain adaptation method to obtain a domain-specific model from the existing general machine translation model through transfer learning. The other is to adopt an conditional translation decoder to integrate various domains into the same model and generate translations according to different input conditions (Keskar et al., 2019). At present, the commercial machine translation system mainly adopts the former one, but it also brings the additional deployment cost.

Considering the deficiencies of existing systems, the new needs of users, and the current development of natural language processing, we developed a web-based machine translation demonstration system **MiSS**. In this system, we tried to integrate several new features to provide better services for users. With **MiSS**, users can get real-time translations while writing, flexible control in switching between real-time translation and whole-sentence translation, informative back-translation feedback and scoring, and input error detection and revision suggestions. In addition, the system also supports user interactions that modify the translations or inputs, which provides crowdsourced data for further improving the performance of our machine translation and grammatical error correction. Notably, there were also several interactive translation systems in the past, such as CASMACAT (Alabau et al., 2014), (Knowles and Koehn, 2016), (Peris et al., 2017), and INMT (Santy et al., 2019). The distinctions lie in the abilities of the systems and the features to adapt to the latest user needs.

2 The MiSS System

There are 5 features in our MiSS translation system: simultaneous translation, back-translation for quality evaluation, grammatical error correction, multi-style translation, and crowdsourcing data collection. The system is available at `http://miss.x2brain.com/` until November 12, 2021. We show a screenshot of the system in Figure 1. In the following subsections, we will describe each component of the system.

2.1 Basis: Transformer-based NMT

Transformer (Vaswani et al., 2017) is an attention mechanism-based network. This architecture introduced the innovative self-attention network (SAN) that computes the relationships between all tokens in the source sequence. (Hassan et al., 2018; Läubli et al., 2018; Li et al., 2020a, 2021) observed that Transformer-based NMT has achieved performance similar to human-level performance on some benchmarks, and because of this tremendous performance, this model has been widely used in the field of machine translation. Given the excellent performance of Transformer-based NMT, we use it as the basis for our system. The model includes an encoder and a decoder, which are respectively used for incrementally processing the source and target sentences. Both the encoder and decoder are stacks of L Transformer blocks.

2.2 Feature #1: Simultaneous Translation

Simultaneous NMT has attracted much attention recently. In contrast to standard NMT, where the

[2]https://www.grammarly.com
[3]https://www.pigai.org
[4]https://writeandimprove.com
[5]https://f.linggle.com

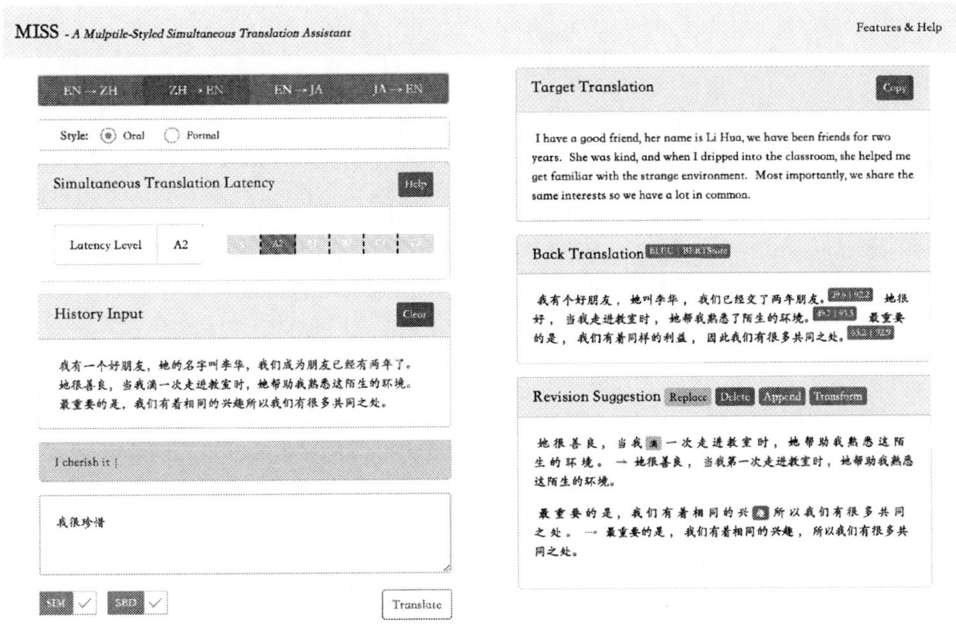

Figure 1: The screenshot of MISS system.

NMT system can access the full input sentence, simultaneous NMT can only utilize the current state of an input sentence (which may be incomplete). Because of this, the translation task entails more uncertainty and consequently, more difficulty. Current simultaneous NMT systems model the task as a prefix-to-prefix problem. Among them, *wait-k* inference (Ma et al., 2019) is a simple yet effective strategy for simultaneous NMT. In *wait-k*, the decoder is asked to generate the output sequence k words behind the input words. Specifically, the *wait-k* strategy is defined as follows: given an input $x \in X$, the generation of the translation y is always k tokens behind reading x; that is, at the t-th decoding step, we generate token y_t based on $x \leq t - k + 1$. We thus adopt a Transformer-based NMT model with the *wait-k* strategy, aiming for balance between translation performance and efficiency.

2.3 Feature #2: Back-translation for Quality Evaluation

A machine translation model on its own is unable to evaluate the quality of its generated translations, as typical translation quality metrics require reference sentences. This lack of obvious evaluation can cause users to mistrust the translation system and doubt whether it accurately expresses a sentence's true meaning. Back-translation – the 're-translation' of a translated sequence back into its original language – is a potential method of generating reference sentences for comparison that utilizes the duality of direction in translation (He et al., 2016). Back-translation is currently mainly used as a data-enhancement method for supervised NMT systems (Edunov et al., 2018) and as a crucial training method for unsupervised NMT systems (Conneau and Lample, 2019), though it has been more controversial as a method of assessing translations. According to (Behr, 2017)'s conclusion, while back-translation can give some evaluation of the translation, it often raises issues not noted by human assessors, and more importantly, is less reliable in general, as many problems remain hidden. These shortcomings are mainly are a result of commonly used automatic evaluation methods (like BLEU) using only surface-level similarity; they do not strictly measure , Semantic Equivalence (SE), which is the true goal. Thus, we adopted BERTScore(Zhang et al., 2019), a language generation evaluation metric based on pretrained BERT contextual embeddings, for semantic equivalence assessment and the evaluation metric BT-BLEU (Li et al., 2020b) (also described in (Nguyen et al., 2021) as reconstruction BLEU) for translation quality evaluation. Furthermore, recent work (Fomicheva et al., 2020) mentions various other unsupervised quality evaluation methodologies, we will include it into the follow-up updates and provide a better reference indicator in our system.

2.4 Feature #3: Grammatical Error Correction

Detecting potential grammatical errors and offering corrective suggestions for them sentence is also a very important feature in MISS. We chose the tag-based modeling approach for this feature based on the fresearch field's latest achievements (Omelianchuk et al., 2020) and our recent work (Parnow et al., 2020, 2021) in the Grammatical Error Correction (GEC).

Specifically, the g-transformations developed by (Omelianchuk et al., 2020) were included in our system in the hopes of providing learners more specific suggestions (i.e., the edit type of an error) to revise the users' input. Predicting edits rather than tokens also increases the generalization of our GEC model. G-transformations are based on several basic transformations: $KEEP (keep the current token unchanged), $DELETE (delete current token), $APPEND_t1 (append new token t1 next to the current token), and $REPLACE_t2 (replace the current token with another token t2). From these basic transformations, further, more task-specific transformations are hand designed (such as $CASE (fix the casing of a word), $MERGE (merge the current token and the next token into a single one) and $SPLIT (split the current token into two new tokens)) and empirically learned (e.g., $REPLACE_cause, which replaces certain words with "cause," and $APPEND_for, which adds "for" when it is needed), resulting in a total tag vocabulary size of 5000.

We train our tag-based GEC model with a multi-stage strategy using the same model architecture and pre-processing script as (Omelianchuk et al., 2020). We use the same synthesis strategy as in (Parnow et al., 2020) to synthesize pseudo data for pre-training in the first stage before fine-tuning on a small, high-quality human-annotated GEC dataset.

2.5 Feature #4: Multi-style Translation

In linguistics, the "style" of a text denotes "the aggregate of contextual probabilities of its linguistic items" (Enkvist, 1964) and can be seen as referring to its deviation from textual norms (Huang, 2015). Machine translation requires generating translated text with different styles, leading to what are known as as domain adaptation tasks (Koehn and Knowles, 2017). In these tasks, there are two main approaches (the data-centric approach and the model-centric approach), but though these approaches produce more powerful in-domain models (i.e., domain-specific models) for their given domains, they bring extra overhead to deployment.

Recently, large-scale Transformer-based language models have shown promising text generation capabilities, as seen with GPT-2 (Radford et al., 2019) and GPT-3 (Brown et al., 2020), which demonstrated strong generation performance with the Transformer decoder. (Keskar et al., 2019) sought to make a more malleable model and released CTRL, a 1.63 billion-parameter conditional Transformer language model, demonstrating that with enough model capacity, and compute power, language models can adapt to and be successful in multiple domains. Inspired by CTRL's use of control codes, which governed the style and other apsects of its generation, and GPT's use of Transformer decoders, we made a simple modification to the decoder of a Transformer-based NMT model, making this decoder also conditioned on a variety of control codes (Pfaff, 1979; Poplack, 2000). We call our system CTRL-NMT. Formally speaking, the target distribution of CTRL-NMT can be decomposed using the chain rule of probability and trained with a loss that takes the control code into account:

$$p(y|x) = \overbrace{\prod_{i=1}^{n} p(y_i|y_{<i}, x)}^{\text{NMT}} \rightarrow \overbrace{\prod_{i=1}^{n} p(y_i|y_{<i}, x, c)}^{\text{CTRL-NMT}},$$

where x is the source language input, y is the target language translation, and c is the control code.

In CTRL-NMT, the control code uses natural language terms (words) instead of separately defined tokens, so it can share the word embedding and has the ability to continue to expand to more codes. There is little change to the model in comparison to our standard NMT model, so CTRL-NMT can be initialized with the checkpoint of our standard NMT model. Additionally, since we only use a single model, deploying multiple styles will not be more costly.

2.6 Feature #5: Crowdsourcing Data Collection

In machine translation, grammatical error correction, and Semantic Similarity calculation, high-performing models rely on large-scale data, particularly high-quality, manually labeled data. Producing large scale annotated data is an onerous task requiring intensive human effort. This is especially true for machine translation, which requires bilingual speakers. "Crowdsourcing" (Howe, 2006) refers to a data collection method that involves obtaining work, information, or opinions from a large group of people who typically submit their data via internet services. Our MISS system adopts crowdsourcing data collection as a method of further improving model performance, making MISS an active learning system.

Specifically, when a user begins to input a sentence, the system responds with translation, back-translation, and revision suggestions. The user's decisions in response to these suggestions will then constitute the data that we collect.

Operation	NMT	GEC	SE
Acc. Trans.	✓		✓
Edit Trans.	✓	✓	✓
Edit Source		✓	
Acc. Trans.Rv.	✓	✓	✓
Acc. Source.Rv.		✓	

Table 1: User operations used for our crowdsourcing data collection in our MISS system.

3 Implementation and Training

The full system consists of 4 neural models: (1) a multi-style NMT model, (2) a simultaneous NMT model, (3) a grammatical error correction model, and (4) a BERT model. In our current MISS release, we translate between three languages (English (EN), Chinse (ZH), and Japanese (JA)) for demonstration.

For the multi-style NMT model, we implement CTRL-NMT using the public fairseq (Ott et al., 2019) toolkit. In our system, we adopt the Transformer (big) setting as in (Vaswani et al., 2017). We did not choose a deeper or wider Transformer (Wang et al., 2019; Sun et al., 2019) model because we wanted to balance performance and efficiency. As in (Li et al., 2019), we used a data-dependent gaussian prior objective (D2GPo) during the NMT model training process for better generalization. Due to resource constraints, our currently deployed model does not perform back-translation of larger sentences. Table 2 lists all our training corpora and their sizes.

For the simultaneous translation model, we implemented the *wait-k* strategy and replaced the bidirectional attention in the encoder side with unidirectional attention. We also used the Transformer model implemented by fairseq as a base for this. Inspired by (Wu et al., 2020), we used beam search for partial tokens during simultaneous translation to obtain better translation sequences. We wanted to emphasize efficient inference, so we adopted a Transformer (Base) setting with fewer parameters. The training data used was the same as that in the multi-style NMT model.

	Provider	Style	Num.
EN-ZH	WMT20	Formal	28.3M
	AI Challenger18	Oral	12.9M
EN-JA	WMT20	Formal	17.7M
	TED+BSD	Oral	0.25M

Table 2: All NMT training data

We formulated the GEC task as a sequence labeling problem and thus adopted a neural sequence tagging model to handle the task. We followed (Omelianchuk et al., 2020)'s model architecture, which was an encoder consisting of a pre-trained BERT-like transformer stacked with two linear layers with softmax layers on the top - one for error detection and one for error labeling. As in (Awasthi et al., 2019), the architecture uses an iterative correction strategy in which predicted transformations are applied to the input sequence successively. After errors are detected and predicted, a modified Levenshtein distance guides the generation of a corrected sentence. We limit the maximum number of inference iterations to 4 to speed up the overall correction process while still maintaining good correction accuracy. The training data we used for GEC is shown in Table 3. We trained our English GEC model at the word level and our Chinese and Japanese models at the character level. We used pre-trained language models for initialization; namely, XLNet-large-cased in English, BERT-base-chinese in Chinese, and BERT-base-japanese-char in Japanese.

For translation quality evaluation, we measure the semantic equivalence using BERTScore, an automated evaluation metric that computes token similarity using contextual embeddings. We use RoBERTa-large, BERT-base-chinese, and BERT-base-japanese-char as the respective initial embedding sources for our English, Chinese, and Japanese evaluation models. As (Zhang et al., 2019, 2020) observed that fine-tuning the pre-trained con-

	Provider	Num.
EN	PIE-synthetic Lang-8 NUCLE FCE W&I+LOCNESS	9M 947K 56K 34K 34K
ZH	NLPCC2018-GEC HSK+Lang8 CGED	1.3M
JA	Lang8	3.1M

Table 3: The GEC training data

	PrLM	Dict	P	R	$F_{0.5}$
EN	–	Word	53.46	37.45	54.22
	+XLNet	Word	76.92	41.03	65.47
ZH	–	Word	38.72	15.07	29.47
	–	Char	45.06	19.55	35.73
	+BERT	Char	50.34	33.46	45.72
JA	–	Word	36.83	20.52	31.78
	–	Char	45.68	16.49	33.74
	+BERT	Char	46.56	27.34	40.82

Table 5: The performance of our GEC models

Models	EN→ZH	ZH→EN	EN→JA	JA→EN
	separate training			
Transformer-big	37.6	28.0	33.5	18.7
	30.8	28.6	23.2	11.5
	joint training			
Transformer-big	36.9	27.2	33.4	18.5
	28.9	28.0	26.9	15.6
CTRL-NMT	37.5	28.4	33.8	19.2
	31.4	29.1	28.9	16.8
	joint training			
Transformer-base	35.4	25.8	31.7	17.0
	27.5	26.7	25.7	14.6
Sim-NMT (k=3)	31.1	23.3	30.2	16.1
	24.0	23.5	23.2	13.3

Table 4: The performance of our NMT models. Each model presents two lines of results - the top one for formal language and the bottom one for oral language translation.

textualized models on a related task can lead to better evaluation, we fine-tuned the pre-trained contextualized language models using our collected data.

4 Evaluation

We conducted empirical experiments on our models to evaluate the performance of important components in our system. For the NMT component, we chose the WMT2020 test set *newstest2020* as the evaluation set for formal EN-ZH and EN-JA translation and the development set of the AI Challenger 2018 competition as the evaluation set for oral ZH-EN translation. In ZH→EN and JA→EN translation, we used Multi-bleu as our evaluation metric, and we adopted the moses tokenizer for word tokenization, while in EN→ZH and EN→JA, we used character-level Multi-BLEU to remove the influence of different segmenters on BLEU score. For the standard and simultaneous machine translation components, we used the same evaluation sets and metrics.

For the GEC component, we followed common practice in the GEC task (Rei and Yannakoudakis, 2016; Omelianchuk et al., 2020) and used precision (P), recall (R), and $F_0.5$ to evaluate our models on all three languages. We evaluated English at the word level and Chinese and Japanese at the character level. We chose the test set of the CoNLL-2014 shared task as our evaluation set for our English GEC model. For Chinese and Japanese, we extracted 5000 sentences from the original training set for the development set and 5000 sentences for the test set and used the rest as the training set. ERRANT[6] was used to convert parallel files to the `m2` format for subsequent scoring with the M^2Scorer (Dahlmeier and Ng, 2012).

The results of our models for standard NMT and simultaneous NMT are shown in Table 4. First, for the evaluation results of standard NMT, we found that the joint training of multiple styles of data does not bring performance improvement compared to separate training, especially when the corpora sizes of the two styles are similar. The translation performance gap between different styles demonstrates that the level difficulty of translation in different styles is different. Since style essentially refers to deviation from standard textual norms, the greater the deviation, the greater the translation complexity is, which explains why different styles will have different levels of difficulty in comparison to standard translation.

In CTRL-NMT, through the incorporation control codes, we found that the translation performance for specific styles using the single model was equivalent to or, in some cases, better than that of training separate models. This shows that the Transformer-based model sufficiently accommodates the generation of multiple styles of language, and leveraging the language commonalities between different styles can bring additional im-

[6]https://github.com/chrisjbryant/errant

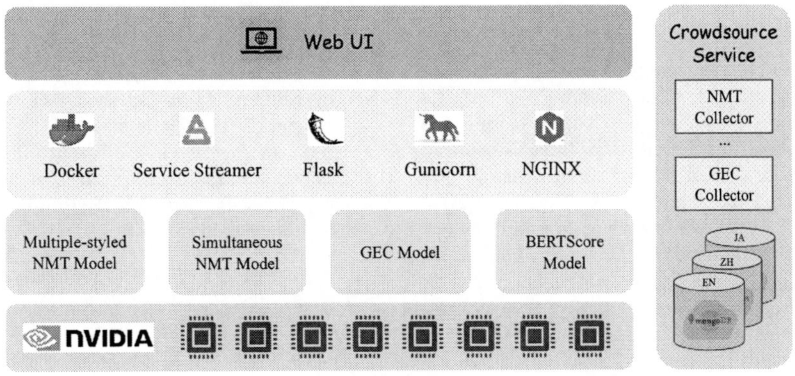

Figure 2: The deployment architecture of MISS system.

provements.

The results of simultaneous NMT and standard NMT, however, do show that the performance of simultaneous NMT still lags behind that of standard NMT when using the same architecture, as there is less information available to the model during simultaneous translation. Despite this, simultaneous NMT is likely to further approach standard NMT's performance in the future through the use of greater contextual information and input prediction facilitated by a specific input module.

We show the evaluation results[7] of the GEC models in Table 5. The results show that pre-trained language models (PrLMs) can bring large performance improvements. Additionally, comparing Chinese and Japanese models at the word and character levels shows that in tag-based GEC modeling, character-level models outperform their word-level counterparts because of the character-level models' smaller tag sets.

5 Deployment

The architecture diagram of our deployment of the MISS system is shown in Figure 2. Since modern GPUs can bring good inference acceleration for deep neural network models, we choose NVIDIA GPUs as the basis for model deployment. There are four models in the system: the multi-style NMT model, the simultaneous NMT model, the GEC model, and the BERTScore model. We use Docker to install and isolate the environments of each model and use service_streamer to assemble scattered user requests to form a mini-batch to make full use of the GPUs in parallel. Flask and Gunicorn are used to wrap the model into a microservice interface for external calls. NGINX is used to distribute static resources and balance load. We use a basic Web UI to make our service accessible to users. In addition, Mongodb is adopted to store the users' logs, which the system collects.

6 Conclusion and Future Work

In this paper, we presented a translation system, MISS. This system supports multi-style machine translation, simultaneous machine translation, grammatical error detection and correction, and back-translation-based quality evaluation. Our goal in developing this system is providing users with a more fluid machine translation experience. Using the research of the NLP community, we were able to introduce a variety of translation and translation-related tools to help users. In addition, we leverage the user's operations and feedback in the system as a source of crowdsourced information to potentially use in further improving the performance of the system. Compared with existing commercial translation systems, our system can provide a more comprehensive experience.

With this work, we also lay out steps to take to further improve the machine translation user experience: improve the consistency of translation by integrating document-level context, enhance the performance of models by incorporating back-translation using monolingual data, include more language styles such as academic translation, and explore the data collected through crowdsourcing for further improving overall performance.

[7] In our results, since the evaluation sets of Chinese and Japanese are self-split and character-level, they are not directly comparable to other work.

References

Vicent Alabau, Christian Buck, Michael Carl, Francisco Casacuberta, Mercedes García-Martínez, Ulrich Germann, Jesús González-Rubio, Robin Hill, Philipp Koehn, Luis Leiva, Bartolomé Mesa-Lao, Daniel Ortiz-Martínez, Herve Saint-Amand, Germán Sanchis Trilles, and Chara Tsoukala. 2014. CASMACAT: A computer-assisted translation workbench. In *Proceedings of the Demonstrations at the 14th Conference of the European Chapter of the Association for Computational Linguistics*, pages 25–28, Gothenburg, Sweden. Association for Computational Linguistics.

Antonios Anastasopoulos. 2019. An analysis of source-side grammatical errors in NMT. In *Proceedings of the 2019 ACL Workshop BlackboxNLP: Analyzing and Interpreting Neural Networks for NLP*, pages 213–223, Florence, Italy. Association for Computational Linguistics.

Abhijeet Awasthi, Sunita Sarawagi, Rasna Goyal, Sabyasachi Ghosh, and Vihari Piratla. 2019. Parallel iterative edit models for local sequence transduction. In *Proceedings of the 2019 Conference on Empirical Methods in Natural Language Processing and the 9th International Joint Conference on Natural Language Processing (EMNLP-IJCNLP)*, pages 4260–4270, Hong Kong, China. Association for Computational Linguistics.

Dzmitry Bahdanau, Kyunghyun Cho, and Yoshua Bengio. 2015. Neural machine translation by jointly learning to align and translate. In *3rd International Conference on Learning Representations, ICLR 2015, San Diego, CA, USA, May 7-9, 2015, Conference Track Proceedings*.

Dorothée Behr. 2017. Assessing the use of back translation: The shortcomings of back translation as a quality testing method. *International Journal of Social Research Methodology*, 20(6):573–584.

Yonatan Belinkov and Yonatan Bisk. 2018. Synthetic and natural noise both break neural machine translation. In *International Conference on Learning Representations*.

Tom B Brown, Benjamin Mann, Nick Ryder, Melanie Subbiah, Jared Kaplan, Prafulla Dhariwal, Arvind Neelakantan, Pranav Shyam, Girish Sastry, Amanda Askell, et al. 2020. Language models are few-shot learners. *arXiv preprint arXiv:2005.14165*.

Alexis Conneau and Guillaume Lample. 2019. Cross-lingual language model pretraining. In *Advances in Neural Information Processing Systems*, pages 7059–7069.

Daniel Dahlmeier and Hwee Tou Ng. 2012. Better evaluation for grammatical error correction. In *Proceedings of the 2012 Conference of the North American Chapter of the Association for Computational Linguistics: Human Language Technologies*, pages 568–572, Montréal, Canada. Association for Computational Linguistics.

Sergey Edunov, Myle Ott, Michael Auli, and David Grangier. 2018. Understanding back-translation at scale. In *Proceedings of the 2018 Conference on Empirical Methods in Natural Language Processing*, pages 489–500, Brussels, Belgium. Association for Computational Linguistics.

Nils Erik Enkvist. 1964. *Linguistic and Style: On Defining Style; an Essay in Applied Linguistics; and Approach to the Study of Style*. Oxford University Press.

Marina Fomicheva, Shuo Sun, Lisa Yankovskaya, Frédéric Blain, Francisco Guzmán, Mark Fishel, Nikolaos Aletras, Vishrav Chaudhary, and Lucia Specia. 2020. Unsupervised quality estimation for neural machine translation. *Trans. Assoc. Comput. Linguistics*, 8:539–555.

Hany Hassan, Anthony Aue, Chang Chen, Vishal Chowdhary, Jonathan Clark, Christian Federmann, Xuedong Huang, Marcin Junczys-Dowmunt, William Lewis, Mu Li, et al. 2018. Achieving human parity on automatic chinese to english news translation. *arXiv preprint arXiv:1803.05567*.

Di He, Yingce Xia, Tao Qin, Liwei Wang, Nenghai Yu, Tie-Yan Liu, and Wei-Ying Ma. 2016. Dual learning for machine translation. In *Advances in Neural Information Processing Systems 29: Annual Conference on Neural Information Processing Systems 2016, December 5-10, 2016, Barcelona, Spain*, pages 820–828.

Georg Heigold, Stalin Varanasi, Günter Neumann, and Josef van Genabith. 2018. How robust are character-based word embeddings in tagging and MT against wrod scramlbing or randdm nouse? In *Proceedings of the 13th Conference of the Association for Machine Translation in the Americas (Volume 1: Research Track)*, pages 68–80, Boston, MA. Association for Machine Translation in the Americas.

Jeff Howe. 2006. Crowdsourcing: A definition.

Libo Huang. 2015. Style in translation. In *Style in Translation: A Corpus-Based Perspective*, pages 17–30. Springer.

Yafang Huang, Zuchao Li, Zhuosheng Zhang, and Hai Zhao. 2018. Moon IME: Neural-based Chinese Pinyin aided input method with customizable association. In *Proceedings of ACL 2018, System Demonstrations*, pages 140–145, Melbourne, Australia. Association for Computational Linguistics.

William John Hutchins and Harold L Somers. 1992. *An introduction to machine translation*, volume 362. Academic Press London.

Nitish Shirish Keskar, Bryan McCann, Lav R Varshney, Caiming Xiong, and Richard Socher. 2019. Ctrl: A conditional transformer language model for controllable generation. *arXiv preprint arXiv:1909.05858*.

Rebecca Knowles and Philipp Koehn. 2016. Neural interactive translation prediction.

Philipp Koehn and Rebecca Knowles. 2017. Six challenges for neural machine translation. In *Proceedings of the First Workshop on Neural Machine Translation*, pages 28–39, Vancouver. Association for Computational Linguistics.

Samuel Läubli, Rico Sennrich, and Martin Volk. 2018. Has machine translation achieved human parity? a case for document-level evaluation. In *Proceedings of the 2018 Conference on Empirical Methods in Natural Language Processing*, pages 4791–4796, Brussels, Belgium. Association for Computational Linguistics.

Zuchao Li, Jiaxun Cai, Shexia He, and Hai Zhao. 2018a. Seq2seq dependency parsing. In *Proceedings of the 27th International Conference on Computational Linguistics*, pages 3203–3214, Santa Fe, New Mexico, USA. Association for Computational Linguistics.

Zuchao Li, Shexia He, Jiaxun Cai, Zhuosheng Zhang, Hai Zhao, Gongshen Liu, Linlin Li, and Luo Si. 2018b. A unified syntax-aware framework for semantic role labeling. In *Proceedings of the 2018 Conference on Empirical Methods in Natural Language Processing*, pages 2401–2411, Brussels, Belgium. Association for Computational Linguistics.

Zuchao Li, Rui Wang, Kehai Chen, Masao Utiyama, Eiichiro Sumita, Zhuosheng Zhang, and Hai Zhao. 2020a. Explicit sentence compression for neural machine translation. In *The Thirty-Fourth AAAI Conference on Artificial Intelligence, AAAI 2020, The Thirty-Second Innovative Applications of Artificial Intelligence Conference, IAAI 2020, The Tenth AAAI Symposium on Educational Advances in Artificial Intelligence, EAAI 2020, New York, NY, USA, February 7-12, 2020*, pages 8311–8318. AAAI Press.

Zuchao Li, Rui Wang, Kehai Chen, Masso Utiyama, Eiichiro Sumita, Zhuosheng Zhang, and Hai Zhao. 2019. Data-dependent gaussian prior objective for language generation. In *International Conference on Learning Representations*.

Zuchao Li, Zhuosheng Zhang, Hai Zhao, Rui Wang, Kehai Chen, Masao Utiyama, and Eiichiro Sumita. 2021. Text compression-aided transformer encoding. *IEEE Transactions on Pattern Analysis and Machine Intelligence*.

Zuchao Li, Hai Zhao, Rui Wang, Masao Utiyama, and Eiichiro Sumita. 2020b. Reference language based unsupervised neural machine translation. In *Findings of the Association for Computational Linguistics: EMNLP 2020*, pages 4151–4162, Online. Association for Computational Linguistics.

Mingbo Ma, Liang Huang, Hao Xiong, Renjie Zheng, Kaibo Liu, Baigong Zheng, Chuanqiang Zhang, Zhongjun He, Hairong Liu, Xing Li, Hua Wu, and Haifeng Wang. 2019. STACL: Simultaneous translation with implicit anticipation and controllable latency using prefix-to-prefix framework. In *Proceedings of the 57th Annual Meeting of the Association for Computational Linguistics*, pages 3025–3036, Florence, Italy. Association for Computational Linguistics.

Xuan-Phi Nguyen, Shafiq R. Joty, Thanh-Tung Nguyen, Kui Wu, and Ai Ti Aw. 2021. Cross-model back-translated distillation for unsupervised machine translation. In *Proceedings of the 38th International Conference on Machine Learning, ICML 2021, 18-24 July 2021, Virtual Event*, volume 139 of *Proceedings of Machine Learning Research*, pages 8073–8083. PMLR.

Kostiantyn Omelianchuk, Vitaliy Atrasevych, Artem Chernodub, and Oleksandr Skurzhanskyi. 2020. GECToR – grammatical error correction: Tag, not rewrite. In *Proceedings of the Fifteenth Workshop on Innovative Use of NLP for Building Educational Applications*, pages 163–170, Seattle, WA, USA â†’ Online. Association for Computational Linguistics.

Myle Ott, Sergey Edunov, Alexei Baevski, Angela Fan, Sam Gross, Nathan Ng, David Grangier, and Michael Auli. 2019. fairseq: A fast, extensible toolkit for sequence modeling. In *Proceedings of NAACL-HLT 2019: Demonstrations*.

Kevin Parnow, Zuchao Li, and Hai Zhao. 2020. Grammatical error correction: More data with more context. *The International Conference on Asian Language Processing (IALP)*.

Kevin Parnow, Zuchao Li, and Hai Zhao. 2021. Grammatical error correction as GAN-like sequence labeling. In *Findings of the Association for Computational Linguistics: ACL-IJCNLP 2021*, pages 3284–3290, Online. Association for Computational Linguistics.

Álvaro Peris, Miguel Domingo, and Francisco Casacuberta. 2017. Interactive neural machine translation. *Comput. Speech Lang.*, 45:201–220.

Carol W Pfaff. 1979. Constraints on language mixing: Intrasentential code-switching and borrowing in spanish/english. *Language*, pages 291–318.

Shana Poplack. 2000. Sometimes i'll start a sentence in spanish y termino en español: Toward a typology of code-switching. *The bilingualism reader*, 18(2):221–256.

Alec Radford, Jeffrey Wu, Rewon Child, David Luan, Dario Amodei, and Ilya Sutskever. 2019. Language models are unsupervised multitask learners. *OpenAI blog*, 1(8):9.

Marek Rei and Helen Yannakoudakis. 2016. Compositional sequence labeling models for error detection in learner writing. In *Proceedings of the 54th Annual Meeting of the Association for Computational*

Linguistics (Volume 1: Long Papers), pages 1181–1191, Berlin, Germany. Association for Computational Linguistics.

Sebastin Santy, Sandipan Dandapat, Monojit Choudhury, and Kalika Bali. 2019. INMT: Interactive neural machine translation prediction. In *Proceedings of the 2019 Conference on Empirical Methods in Natural Language Processing and the 9th International Joint Conference on Natural Language Processing (EMNLP-IJCNLP): System Demonstrations*, pages 103–108, Hong Kong, China. Association for Computational Linguistics.

Meng Sun, Bojian Jiang, Hao Xiong, Zhongjun He, Hua Wu, and Haifeng Wang. 2019. Baidu neural machine translation systems for WMT19. In *Proceedings of the Fourth Conference on Machine Translation (Volume 2: Shared Task Papers, Day 1)*, pages 374–381, Florence, Italy. Association for Computational Linguistics.

Ilya Sutskever, Oriol Vinyals, and Quoc V Le. 2014. Sequence to sequence learning with neural networks. *Advances in neural information processing systems*, 27:3104–3112.

Ashish Vaswani, Noam Shazeer, Niki Parmar, Jakob Uszkoreit, Llion Jones, Aidan N Gomez, Łukasz Kaiser, and Illia Polosukhin. 2017. Attention is all you need. In *Advances in neural information processing systems*, pages 5998–6008.

Qiang Wang, Bei Li, Tong Xiao, Jingbo Zhu, Changliang Li, Derek F. Wong, and Lidia S. Chao. 2019. Learning deep transformer models for machine translation. In *Proceedings of the 57th Annual Meeting of the Association for Computational Linguistics*, pages 1810–1822, Florence, Italy. Association for Computational Linguistics.

Xueqing Wu, Yingce Xia, Lijun Wu, Shufang Xie, Weiqing Liu, Jiang Bian, Tao Qin, and Tie-Yan Liu. 2020. Learn to use future information in simultaneous translation. *arXiv preprint arXiv:2007.05290*.

Tianyi Zhang, Varsha Kishore, Felix Wu, Kilian Q Weinberger, and Yoav Artzi. 2019. Bertscore: Evaluating text generation with bert. In *International Conference on Learning Representations*.

Zhuosheng Zhang, Yuwei Wu, Hai Zhao, Zuchao Li, Shuailiang Zhang, Xi Zhou, and Xiang Zhou. 2020. Semantics-aware BERT for language understanding. In *The Thirty-Fourth AAAI Conference on Artificial Intelligence, AAAI 2020, The Thirty-Second Innovative Applications of Artificial Intelligence Conference, IAAI 2020, The Tenth AAAI Symposium on Educational Advances in Artificial Intelligence, EAAI 2020, New York, NY, USA, February 7-12, 2020*, pages 9628–9635. AAAI Press.

Automatic Construction of Enterprise Knowledge Base

Junyi Chai, Yujie He, Homa Hashemi, Bing Li,
Daraksha Parveen, Ranganath Kondapally, Wenjin Xu
Microsoft Corporation
juchai,yujh,hohashem,libi,daparvee,rakondap,wenjinxu@microsoft

Abstract

In this paper, we present an automatic knowledge base construction system from large scale enterprise documents with minimal efforts of human intervention. In the design and deployment of such a knowledge mining system for enterprise, we faced several challenges including data distributional shift, performance evaluation, compliance requirements and other practical issues. We leveraged state-of-the-art deep learning models to extract information (named entities and definitions) at per document level, then further applied classical machine learning techniques to process global statistical information to improve the knowledge base. Experimental results are reported on actual enterprise documents. This system is currently serving as part of a Microsoft 365 service.

1 Introduction

Massive knowledge bases constructed from public web documents have been successful in enriching search engine results in Bing and Google for over a decade (Noy et al., 2019). There is growing interest in automatically constructing a similar knowledge base for each enterprise from their internal documents (e.g., web pages, reports, emails, presentation decks; textual contents in natural language form are all referred to as documents in this paper). Such knowledge base can help an enterprise to better organize its domain knowledge, help employees (users) better find and explore knowledge, and to encourage knowledge sharing.

Mining knowledge from enterprise documents poses unique challenges. One challenge is that the system needs to be fully automated without per enterprise customization or existing (semi-) structured sources. Knowledge base construction from web documents is often based on bootstrapping entities from human-curated sources such as Wikipedia with customized extraction rules (DBpedia: Auer et al., 2007, Freebase: Bollacker et al., 2008, YAGO2: Hoffart et al., 2013), or the existence of a prior knowledge base (Knowledge Vault: Dong et al., 2014). Maintaining such Wiki site and keep it fresh is costly for enterprise. Another challenge is that most training data for natural language processing (NLP) models is from public documents. Enterprise documents can have different writing style and vocabulary than the public documents. The data distributional shift (Quiñonero-Candela et al., 2008) is a challenge as (a) we need model to generalize better to enterprise domain and (b) we need test metrics to reflect the actual performance on enterprise documents to guide model development.

On the other hand, enterprise domain brings new opportunities. For search engines, the knowledge base must be extremely accurate. This requirement limits the usage of NLP models to extract information from unstructured text as few models can achieve the required precision with meaningful coverage. In enterprise domain, we can relax the requirement on accuracy as enterprise users are expected to spend more time to absorb and discriminate information. In addition, users can curate and improve the automatically constructed knowledge base, which is not an option for search engine users. The relaxation on accuracy requirement makes it possible to perform knowledge mining on unstructured text by heavily relying on NLP techniques.

In this paper, we present the first large-scale knowledge mining system for enterprise documents taking advantage of recent advances in NLP such as pretrained Transformers (Devlin et al., 2019) as well as traditional NLP techniques. It is in production since February 2021 as part of a Microsoft 365 feature (Microsoft Viva Topics[1]). For an enterprise that enables this feature, our system will build a knowledge base from its internal documents that already exist in Microsoft cloud and will keep it

[1]https://www.microsoft.com/en-us/microsoft-viva/topics/overview

Proceedings of the 2021 Conference on Empirical Methods in Natural Language Processing: System Demonstrations, pages 11–19
November 7–11, 2021.

fresh without the need of any customized intervention. At the core of our knowledge base are entities mined from documents that are of interest to the enterprise, such as product, organization and project. These entities are loosely referred to as topics to the end users (not to be confused with topic modeling in NLP). The knowledge base is a collection of "topic cards" with rich information: properties that help users understand the topic (such as alternative names, descriptions, and related documents), or enable users to connect with people who might be knowledgeable about the topic (related people) or explore related topics.

The contributions of this work are as follows:

- We demonstrate a system in production that performs knowledge mining in large scale: hundreds of millions of documents, thousands of organizations.
- We apply state-of-the-art deep learning models in two NLP tasks named entity recognition (NER) and definition extraction. We discuss the challenges and how we improve our system to reach the desired performance.

2 System description

The overall system architecture is depicted in Figure 1. In this section, we discuss at length the knowledge mining system that works "offline". The system works in a semi-streaming mode: whenever there's a document update, the content of the document is sent to the NER and description mining components. The NER component extracts entities then updates information in the topic candidate store. The topic ranker periodically pulls the topic candidates store to select the top N topics. The topic card builder then builds topics cards with various attributes. Note that this is a simplified view of the actual system. For example, there is another component that conflates information from other sources using techniques described in Winn et al. (2019).

2.1 Named entity recognition for enterprise

NER is the typical first step in information extraction (Jurafsky and Martin, 2009, Chapter 22). Based on our study on enterprise customers' demand and an analysis of Bing's Satori knowledge graph, we define 8 entity types that are of interest to the enterprises while covering most of real-world entities. Among them, "person", "organization", "location", "event", and "product" are the common NER types in various public datasets (CoNLL03: Tjong Kim Sang and De Meulder, 2003, OntoNotes: Hovy et al., 2006; WNUT 2017: Derczynski et al., 2017), while "project", "field of study", "creative work" are less common but are also of high interest to enterprises. These 8 types cover about 85% of entities in Bing's Satori knowledge graph. The remaining entities are mainly biological organisms.

Our NER model is based on Transformers with the pretraining-finetuning paradigm (Devlin et al., 2019). State-of-the-art results on several NER benchmarks are achieved with Transformers (Yamada et al., 2020; Li et al., 2020). To make data collection easier, we train our model on public data but apply it to enterprise domain. The distributional shift between training and testing can cause a significant performance drop (Quiñonero-Candela et al., 2008). To measure model's true performance under distributional shift, we construct a test set from actual internal documents within Microsoft. The size of this test set is comparable to CoNLL03 test set (Tjong Kim Sang and De Meulder, 2003).

To mitigate the distributional shift issue, we divide model training into multiple stages, with the first stage training on large amount of automatically annotated data using Wikipedia, which has been shown to help the system generalize better to a new domain (Ni and Florian, 2016). Entities are identified by wikilink, and we use Bing's Satori knowledge graph to find out the corresponding entity type. We selected paragraphs with at least 10 wikilinks, which gives us ~1 million paragraphs. Finally, we use an entity linking tool NEMO (Cucerzan, 2007, 2014) to annotate entities without wikilinks and get $\sim 50\%$ more entities.

The benefit of Wikipedia training data lies in its size, but it comes with low annotation quality. After training on it, we continue training on smaller data with high quality human annotation. In the second stage, we use OntoNotes 5.0[2] data set and mapped their types to our 8 types. This stage is mainly beneficial for the common NER types, but it does not help our additional "project" and "field of study" type. In the last stage, the training data is a combination of a small number of web documents with 8 types annotation (size is ~1000 paragraphs) and CoNLL03 data with "MISC" type being reannotated to one of our 8 types. This last stage of

[2] https://catalog.ldc.upenn.edu/LDC2013T19

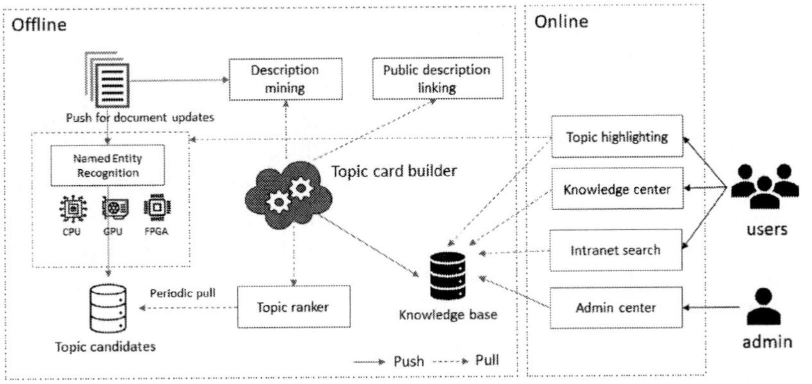

Figure 1: An illustration of the knowledge mining system.

	O	B-per	B-fos	B-wrk	B-prj	I-per	I-fos	I-wrk	I-prj
Turin	0.18	5.8	3.75	4.33	-0.15	0.14	0.17	0.75	-1.19
##g	0.04	-1.3	-0.75	-0.97	-1.64	4.69	3.39	4.8	0.6
Test	0.37	-1.22	-0.6	-0.29	-1.64	2.98	3.5	5.69	0.2

Figure 2: Scores for selected tokens and selected types from the sentence "The history of NLP dates back to the 1950s when Alan Turing proposed a simple test (the "Turing Test") to determine ...". The abbreviations in use are: per for person, fos for field of study, wrk for creative work, and prj for project.

training data is most aligned with our NER type definition.

To illustrate the effect of multistage training as well as additional improvement techniques, we consider BERT-base with cased vocabulary finetuned only on the last stage of training data as a strong baseline. The F1 metrics of our model, baseline, and ablation experiments on our test set from internal documents are shown in Table 1. The baseline 56% F1 is much lower than the reported F1 > 90% on CoNLL03 test set (Devlin et al., 2019), which shows the challenge from the distributional shift (we also test our baseline model on CoNLL03 test set and get F1 > 90%). The most common entity type in our test set is product, which can be more difficult to detect than the most common entity types (person, location, organization) in CoNLL03. Also our test set is noisier than CoNLL03 as internal documents are often less formal than public documents such as newswire articles. Our best model achieved an F1 of 71.1%. In ablation study, multistage training improves F1 by 5.4% from the baseline. We find additional techniques that can robustly improve model performance:

- *Data augmentation*: we find two most useful data augmentation methods out of many methods we have tried. One method is simply lower casing the training data. This method has been shown to increase NER performance on uncased text significantly, and even improve performance on cased text when train and test on different domains (Mayhew et al., 2019). The second method is to replace an entity mention with a randomly selected entity of the same type. This is motivated by our observation that the distribution of entities roughly follows the Zipf's law. Randomly replacing entities can give more weights to tail entities. In combination, data augmentation provides a 0.6% F1 lift.

- *Focal loss*: NER is an imbalanced classification problem as most input tokens are not entities. We test loss functions suitable for imbalanced dataset: Dice Loss (Li et al., 2020), Am-Softmax (Wang et al., 2018), and Focal Loss (Lin et al., 2017). They all provide similar improvement. We report focal loss (hyperparameter gamma=1.6) results here with an additional 1.5% F1 lift.

- *Viterbi decoding*: as there is no hard constraint on the sequence of labels from BERT, the sequence can be invalid under the standard BIO tagging scheme (Lample et al., 2016). Figure 2 shows such an example. The scores for tokens ("Turin", "##g", "Test") give an invalid label sequence of B-per, I-wrk, I-wrk (per stands for person, wrk for creative work) using greedy argmax decoding, which we correct to O, O, O in the baseline setting. We observe that the correct sequence B-wrk, I-wrk, I-wrk has highest sum of scores among

Experiment	Config	F1	P	R
Best model	UniLMv2-large: all techniques	71.1%	72.2%	70.2%
Baseline	BERT base: single last stage	56.0%	54.0%	58.2%
Ablation	BERT base: multi-stage	61.4%	60.7%	62.1%
	+data augmentation	62.0%	60.6%	63.4%
	+focal loss	63.5%	62.7%	64.4%
	+Viterbi decoding	65.4%	65.8%	65.1%

Table 1: NER results on internal test set.

all valid sequences, for example B-per, I-per, I-per. Based on this observation, we use Viterbi algorithm to find the valid path under BIO scheme with the maximum sum of scores. This provides a 1.9% F1 lift. We have also tried adding a CRF layer on top of BERT, training jointly or separately. We do not see additional gain (though CRF layer can further improve 1-layer student model).

- *Bigger and better pretrained model*: BERT is pretrained on English Wikipedia and BookCorpus, which have limited writing styles. Enterprise documents can be more diverse, less formal and noisier. Therefore, pretraining on more diverse corpora may help our task. We switched from BERT base-cased to UniLM v2 large-cased, which is pretrained on additional 144GB corpora including OpenWebText, CC-News, and Stories (Bao et al., 2020). This provides a 5.7% F1 lift.

For production, we distill knowledge from the 24-layer UniLMv2 teacher model into a 3-layer student model, which is initialized from the weights of the first 3 layers of the teacher model (Hinton et al., 2015). We use 1 GB Wikipedia data for distillation. The student model suffers a 5.6% F1 drop. Though not used in production, we experiment continuing distillation with only about 50MB of internal documents. This small amount of data reduces the gap between student and teacher models to 0.9% F1, which suggests the usefulness of using in domain data for knowledge distillation.

Knowledge distillation gives us ~6x speed up for inferencing a single input sequence on Nvidia V100 GPU with f32 precision. On top of student model, we get another ~14x speedup by (1) exporting model from Pytorch to ONNX (Ning, 2020), (2) switching from Python to C#, and (3) running inference in f16 precision and batch mode.

2.2 Topic ranker

In the NER step, tens of millions of topic candidates could be detected. The goal of topic ranker is to pick the top tens of thousands most salient topics while reducing the number of noisy topics. We achieve this in two stages by first simply ranking topics by their total number of times being detected by NER (referred to as NER frequency) to produce a short list of topics. Then we rerank the short list by scores from a binary classifier. The classifier is trained to distinguish between good and noisy topics. It uses features such as NER frequency, document frequency, topic-in-title frequency (number of times the topic appears in the document title) and the ratios of these counting features.

This classifier is effective as it uses global statistical information not available during NER stage. For example, the word "Company" could be mislabeled as an organization by the NER model. Although the probability is small, it could still make into the short list as this word appears very often. The classifier would filter it out as the ratio (NER frequency/document frequency) is very small.

Our training set contains 6000 annotated topics detected from about 0.5 million Microsoft internal documents. Using a single feature NER frequency as a baseline, the AUC is 0.54. We train a gradient boosting trees classifier (Ke et al., 2017) using 5-fold cross validation and achieve an average validation AUC 0.67.

In the production system, as the number of topic candidates scales up, the topic ranker could play a more important role as much lower percentage of topics will be selected. To evaluate its true usefulness, we apply the classifier in the end-to-end system to process all Microsoft documents. We randomly sample a subset of topics before and after applying the classifier. We observe a 9% reduction in noisy topics with the classifier.

2.3 Definition mining

A succinct and accurate description is a crucial attribute of a topic. Such descriptions come from two sources: (1) for some topics such as "field of study" type, their descriptions exist in public knowledge and therefore we retrieve this information from Bing's Satori knowledge graph using an existing context aware ranking service, which is in use for Microsoft Word's Smart Lookup feature; (2) more importantly, we build a description mining pipeline to extract private definitions from enterprise documents. This pipeline consists of the following steps:

1. Split a document into sentences.

2. A deep learning model classifies each sentence into one of 5 categories. Pass a sentence in the "Sufficient Definition" category to the next step.

3. Extract topic from the sentence using a list of patterns, for example: topic is defined as description text.

4. Remove sentences with negative opinion (or sentiment) based on lexicon match. We use the Opinion Lexicon from Hu and Liu (2004).

A large corpus contains definition-like sentences with a wide range of ambiguity beyond a binary classification task can capture. Therefore, we make the task more granular and define 5 categories most common in enterprise domain: Sufficient, Informational, Referential, Personal and Non- definitions. Detailed schema is included in the Appendix.

To collect training data, we need to first collect sentences with a relative high chance of being a description. In addition, we want to collect more hard negative examples such as opinions (e.g., "Caterpillar 797B is the biggest car I've ever seen.") than easy negative examples. Using query log from Bing, we achieved these two goals: we collect search results for queries that match patterns such as "what is {term}", "define {term}" as the results are highly related to definitions. The search results also have the advantage of being more diverse than a single corpus. From the search results, we create a set of 42,256 annotated sentences, which is referred as public dataset. As we will show, a model trained on the public dataset suffers a significant performance degrade on enterprise documents due to distributional shift. Therefore, we construct a second dataset from our internal documents that have been approved for use after compliance review, which is referred as enterprise dataset. The model trained on the public dataset is used for identifying candidate sentences for annotation during the construction of the enterprise dataset. Using the enterprise dataset involves many compliance restrictions. For example, we need to delete a sentence if its source document is deleted or our access expires; the model is trained within the compliance zone and stays within it. Details for these two datasets are shown in Table 2, which also includes the DEFT corpus for comparison (Spala et al., 2019). Roughly 15% of the data from the two datasets is withhold from training for testing.

Dataset	# of sentences	# of positive
Public dataset	42,256	10,927
Enterprise dataset	58,780	49,017
DEFT (Spala et. al. 2019)	23,746	11,004

Table 2: Datasets for definition classification task.

Model	Train data	Test data	F1/P/R
Bert-base	Public	Public	0.82/0.76/0.89
		Enterprise	0.64/0.55/0.77
BERT-base	Enterprise	Enterprise	0.73/0.68/0.80
BERT-large			0.72/0.70/0.77
UniMLv2-large			0.75/0.71/0.80
Rule based	N/A	Public	0.48/0.40/0.60

Table 3: Results for definition classification.

Similar to our approach in NER, we consider BERT-base (with cased vocabulary) as a strong baseline. First we train BERT-base model on the public dataset. When testing it on public and enterprise datasets, we get F1 results of 0.82 and 0.64 respectively, as shown in Table 3. This performance degradation again exemplifies the challenge from distributional shift. Then we train on the enterprise dataset and compare BERT-base with BERT-large and UniLMv2-large. UniLMv2-large achieves the best result with F1 of 0.75, which may again benefit from the bigger pretraining corpus (Bao et al., 2020). In Table 3, we also add the result from rule-based classification, which directly uses the list of patterns in Step 3 (e.g., "is a", "is defined as", "refer to") to identify definition. It is evaluated as a binary classification task: "Sufficient Definition" vs Others. We get F1 of 0.48 with an even lower precision of 0.40. This shows the necessity of model-based classification in Step 2 in our definition extraction pipeline.

For production, we distill our best model into a much smaller BiLSTM model. The embedding of the BiLSTM is initialized from 50-dimensional Glove vector (Pennington et al., 2014) with a reduced vocabulary size of 0.12 million. The hidden dimension size is 300. We follow similar knowledge distillation approach as in Tang et al. (2019). The student model reaches F1 of 0.72 while achieves about 30x speedup vs. the 24-layer teacher.

2.4 Topic card builder

Topic card builder builds topics cards with rich information by aggregating information like definition and acronym from other components. More importantly, it computes the relatedness between topics, documents and users. Using relatedness, it links the top related topics, documents, and users to each topic. By adding related users to a topic, we enable the "expert finding" scenario, which is important for enterprise users to explore expertise. Topic card builder also conflates two topics if their degree of relatedness exceeds a threshold and they pass additional checks to prevent over conflation.

To compute relatedness between any two items, we build a dense embedding vector for each topic, document and user. We apply SVD to decompose the topic-document matrix M into topic and document embeddings, where $M_{i,j}$ is the BM25 of topic i in document j. This is a classical algorithm in collaborative filtering (Koren et al., 2009) and semantic embedding (Bellegarda, 2000; Levy et al., 2015), but the challenge is the size of the matrix M in the j dimension as it can be on the order of tens of millions. We improve a randomized SVD algorithm that iterates on smaller batches of documents so it can solve problem of our scale on a single machine under 8 GB memory limit (Halko et al., 2011). User embedding is represented as the average of embeddings of the documents that the user has authored. Relatedness is computed as the dot product of two embedding vectors. Top K topics and users most related to a given topic are added to the topic card in this manner. For related documents, embedding is used as a recall-oriented step to select candidate documents, and we apply an additional reranking step using additional signals.

To evaluate the overall quality of the system, we conduct human evaluation on the quality of generated topic cards (70K) mined from Microsoft internal documents (40 million). We ask users (Microsoft employees) to judge the overall quality of randomly sub-sampled topic cards by considering all the information. A good topic card means that it has sufficient information to help users understand the topic. In this study, we achieve 85% good rate.

3 Use Cases

The detailed user guide and licensing information can be found on Microsoft Viva Topics website[3]. Here we briefly introduce two ways user can interact with the knowledge base. Figure 3 shows the topic highlighting feature. Topic mentions in documents get automatically linked to the knowledge base. User can hover over the topic mention to see

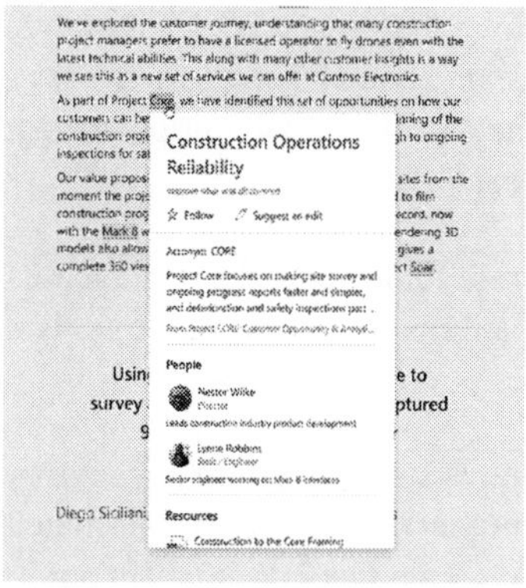

Figure 3: Snapshot of an example topic card impression in enterprise web document.[4]

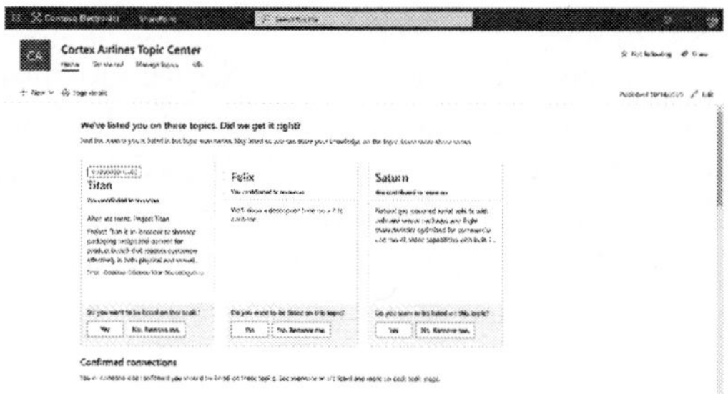

Figure 4: Snapshot of a personalized topic center homepage.[4]

the topic card and click the link in the topic cards to checkout more information. Figure 4 shows an example topic center homepage. The view is personalized as the related topics for a user is presented for the user to confirm. Users can also checkout all the topics from Manage Topics page.

4 Conclusion

Organizing resources inside an enterprise into one centralized location facilitates knowledge and expertise sharing and improves productivity. We present a system that automatically constructs a knowledge base from unstructured documents to help enterprises achieving this goal. The system is built upon a combination of deep learning models and classical techniques. We show the challenge of applying NLP models in enterprise domain. We also discuss how we improve the models and the whole system to meet our requirements with detailed experiment results. Finally, we show two typical use cases. We hope our experience can benefit researchers and practitioners in this field.

[3] https://docs.microsoft.com/en-us/microsoft-365/knowledge/

[4] The contents (company name, topic information) are not real internal information but are created for demo purpose.

References

Sören Auer, Christian Bizer, Georgi Kobilarov, Jens Lehmann, Richard Cyganiak, and Zachary Ives. 2007. DBpedia: A Nucleus for a Web of Open Data. In *The Semantic Web*, pages 722–735, Berlin, Heidelberg. Springer Berlin Heidelberg.

Hangbo Bao, Li Dong, Furu Wei, Wenhui Wang, Nan Yang, Xiaodong Liu, Yu Wang, Jianfeng Gao, Songhao Piao, Ming Zhou, and Hsiao-Wuen Hon. 2020. UniLMv2: Pseudo-masked language models for unified language model pre-training. In *Proceedings of the 37th International Conference on Machine Learning, ICML 2020, 13-18 July 2020, Virtual Event*, volume 119 of *Proceedings of Machine Learning Research*, pages 642–652. PMLR.

Jerome R. Bellegarda. 2000. Exploiting latent sematic information in statistical language modeling. *Proceedings of the IEEE*, 88(8):1279–1296.

Kurt Bollacker, Colin Evans, Praveen Paritosh, Tim Sturge, and Jamie Taylor. 2008. Freebase: A collaboratively created graph database for structuring human knowledge. In *Proceedings of the ACM SIGMOD International Conference on Management of Data*, pages 1247–1249, New York, New York, USA. ACM Press.

Silviu Cucerzan. 2007. Large-scale named entity disambiguation based on Wikipedia data. In *Proceedings of the 2007 Joint Conference on Empirical Methods in Natural Language Processing and Computational Natural Language Learning (EMNLP-CoNLL)*, pages 708–716, Prague, Czech Republic. Association for Computational Linguistics.

Silviu Cucerzan. 2014. Name entities made obvious: the participation in the ERD 2014 evaluation. In *Proceedings of the first international workshop on Entity recognition & disambiguation - ERD '14*, pages 95–100, New York, New York, USA. ACM Press.

Leon Derczynski, Eric Nichols, Marieke van Erp, and Nut Limsopatham. 2017. Results of the WNUT2017 shared task on novel and emerging entity recognition. In *Proceedings of the 3rd Workshop on Noisy User-generated Text*, pages 140–147, Copenhagen, Denmark. Association for Computational Linguistics.

Jacob Devlin, Ming-Wei Chang, Kenton Lee, and Kristina Toutanova. 2019. BERT: Pre-training of deep bidirectional transformers for language understanding. In *Proceedings of the 2019 Conference of the North American Chapter of the Association for Computational Linguistics: Human Language Technologies, Volume 1 (Long and Short Papers)*, pages 4171–4186, Minneapolis, Minnesota. Association for Computational Linguistics.

Xin Dong, Evgeniy Gabrilovich, Geremy Heitz, Wilko Horn, Ni Lao, Kevin Murphy, Thomas Strohmann, Shaohua Sun, and Wei Zhang. 2014. Knowledge vault: a web-scale approach to probabilistic knowledge fusion. In *The 20th ACM SIGKDD International Conference on Knowledge Discovery and Data Mining, KDD '14, New York, NY, USA - August 24 - 27, 2014*, pages 601–610. ACM.

N Halko, P G Martinsson, and J A Tropp. 2011. Finding Structure with Randomness: Probabilistic Algorithms for Constructing Approximate Matrix Decompositions. *SIAM Review*, 53(2):217–288.

Geoffrey Hinton, Oriol Vinyals, and Jeffrey Dean. 2015. Distilling the Knowledge in a Neural Network. In *NIPS Deep Learning and Representation Learning Workshop*.

Johannes Hoffart, Fabian M. Suchanek, Klaus Berberich, and Gerhard Weikum. 2013. YAGO2: A spatially and temporally enhanced knowledge base from Wikipedia. *Artificial Intelligence*, 194(November):28–61.

Eduard Hovy, Mitchell Marcus, Martha Palmer, Lance Ramshaw, and Ralph Weischedel. 2006. OntoNotes: The 90% solution. In *Proceedings of the Human Language Technology Conference of the NAACL, Companion Volume: Short Papers*, pages 57–60, New York City, USA. Association for Computational Linguistics.

Minqing Hu and Bing Liu. 2004. Mining and summarizing customer reviews. In *Proceedings of the 2004 ACM SIGKDD international conference on Knowledge discovery and data mining - KDD '04*, volume 65, page 168, New York, New York, USA. ACM Press.

Daniel Jurafsky and James H Martin. 2009. *Speech and Language Processing (2nd Edition)*. Prentice-Hall, Inc.

Guolin Ke, Qi Meng, Thomas Finley, Taifeng Wang, Wei Chen, Weidong Ma, Qiwei Ye, and Tie-Yan Liu. 2017. LightGBM: A highly efficient gradient boosting decision tree. In *Advances in Neural Information Processing Systems 30: Annual Conference on Neural Information Processing Systems 2017, December 4-9, 2017, Long Beach, CA, USA*, pages 3146–3154.

Yehuda Koren, Robert Bell, and Chris Volinsky. 2009. Matrix Factorization Techniques for Recommender Systems. *Computer*, 42(8):30–37.

Guillaume Lample, Miguel Ballesteros, Sandeep Subramanian, Kazuya Kawakami, and Chris Dyer. 2016. Neural architectures for named entity recognition. In *Proceedings of the 2016 Conference of the North American Chapter of the Association for Computational Linguistics: Human Language Technologies*, pages 260–270, San Diego, California. Association for Computational Linguistics.

Omer Levy, Yoav Goldberg, and Ido Dagan. 2015. Improving distributional similarity with lessons learned from word embeddings. *Transactions of the Association for Computational Linguistics*, 3:211–225.

Xiaoya Li, Xiaofei Sun, Yuxian Meng, Junjun Liang, Fei Wu, and Jiwei Li. 2020. Dice loss for data-imbalanced NLP tasks. In *Proceedings of the 58th Annual Meeting of the Association for Computational Linguistics*, pages 465–476, Online. Association for Computational Linguistics.

Tsung-Yi Lin, Priya Goyal, Ross B. Girshick, Kaiming He, and Piotr Dollár. 2017. Focal loss for dense object detection. In *IEEE International Conference on Computer Vision, ICCV 2017, Venice, Italy, October 22-29, 2017*, pages 2999–3007. IEEE Computer Society.

Stephen Mayhew, Tatiana Tsygankova, and Dan Roth. 2019. ner and pos when nothing is capitalized. In *Proceedings of the 2019 Conference on Empirical Methods in Natural Language Processing and the 9th International Joint Conference on Natural Language Processing (EMNLP-IJCNLP)*, pages 6256–6261, Hong Kong, China. Association for Computational Linguistics.

Jian Ni and Radu Florian. 2016. Improving multilingual named entity recognition with Wikipedia entity type mapping. In *Proceedings of the 2016 Conference on Empirical Methods in Natural Language Processing*, pages 1275–1284, Austin, Texas. Association for Computational Linguistics.

Emma Ning. 2020. Microsoft open sources breakthrough optimizations for transformer inference on gpu and cpu. cloudblogs.microsoft.com.

Natasha Noy, Yuqing Gao, Anshu Jain, Anant Narayanan, Alan Patterson, and Jamie Taylor. 2019. Industry-scale knowledge graphs: Lessons and challenges. *Communications of the ACM*, 62(8):36–43.

Jeffrey Pennington, Richard Socher, and Christopher Manning. 2014. GloVe: Global vectors for word representation. In *Proceedings of the 2014 Conference on Empirical Methods in Natural Language Processing (EMNLP)*, pages 1532–1543, Doha, Qatar. Association for Computational Linguistics.

Joaquin Quiñonero-Candela, Masashi Sugiyama, Anton Schwaighofer, and Neil D. Lawrence, editors. 2008. *Dataset Shift in Machine Learning*. MIT Press.

Sasha Spala, Nicholas A. Miller, Yiming Yang, Franck Dernoncourt, and Carl Dockhorn. 2019. DefT: A corpus for definition extraction in free- and semi-structured text. In *Proceedings of the 13th Linguistic Annotation Workshop*, pages 124–131, Florence, Italy. Association for Computational Linguistics.

Raphael Tang, Yao Lu, Linqing Liu, Lili Mou, Olga Vechtomova, and Jimmy Lin. 2019. Distilling task-specific knowledge from BERT into simple neural networks. *arXiv*.

Erik F. Tjong Kim Sang and Fien De Meulder. 2003. Introduction to the CoNLL-2003 shared task. In *Proceedings of the seventh conference on Natural language learning at HLT-NAACL 2003 -*, volume 4, pages 142–147, Morristown, NJ, USA. Association for Computational Linguistics.

Feng Wang, Jian Cheng, Weiyang Liu, and Haijun Liu. 2018. Additive Margin Softmax for Face Verification. *IEEE Signal Processing Letters*, 25(7):926–930.

John Winn, John Guiver, Sam Webster, Yordan Zaykov, Martin Kukla, and Dany Fabian. 2019. Alexandria: Unsupervised High-Precision Knowledge Base Construction using a Probabilistic Program. In *Automated Knowledge Base Construction (AKBC)*.

Ikuya Yamada, Akari Asai, Hiroyuki Shindo, Hideaki Takeda, and Yuji Matsumoto. 2020. LUKE: Deep contextualized entity representations with entity-aware self-attention. In *Proceedings of the 2020 Conference on Empirical Methods in Natural Language Processing (EMNLP)*, pages 6442–6454, Online. Association for Computational Linguistics.

A Appendix

Category	Description	Example
Sufficient Definition	Can uniquely define and can only define this term.	Statistics is a branch of mathematics dealing with data collection, organization, analysis, interpretation, and presentation.
Informational Definition	Informational but cannot uniquely define this term or can also apply to other terms.	Statistics is a branch of mathematics.
Referential Definition	Is a definition but does not contain the term but instead a reference ("it/this/that").	This method is used to identifying a hyperplane which separates a positive class from the negative class.
Personal Definition	Associated with the name of a person.	Tom is a Data Scientist at Acme Corporation working on natural language processing.
Non-definition	Does not fall in the other categories. It can be an opinion (hard negative) or not related to definition at all (easy negative).	The Caterpillar 797B is the biggest car I've ever seen. "Effective Date" means the date 5th May 2020.

Table 4: Schema for definition categories.

LightTag: Text Annotation Platform

Tal Perry
LightTag
tal@lighttag.io

Abstract

Text annotation tools assume that their user's goal is to create a labeled corpus. However, users view annotation as a necessary evil on the way to deliver business value through NLP. Thus an annotation tool should optimize for the throughput of the global NLP process, not only the productivity of individual annotators. LightTag is a text annotation tool designed and built on that principle. This paper shares our design rationale, data modeling choices, and user interface decisions then illustrates how those choices serve the full NLP lifecycle.

1 Introduction

Building supervised learning models is like operating a manufacturing plant. Raw materials(data) need to be refined and processed(annotated) as a precursor to final assembly. Some manufacturing plants rely on a supply chain (outsource annotation) while others are vertically integrated (annotate in house). According to the theory of constraints (Goldratt and Cox, 2016), a manufacturing process should optimize the global throughput and not any individual sub-process .

LightTag is a text annotation tool built on the premise of global optimization by addressing annotator as well as project managers and data scientists who manage the work and enforce production quality. LightTag is a commercial offering with an unlimited free tier for academic use [1]. LightTag is unique not only in philosophical outlook but also in it's technical implementation and user interface choices, which we share in this paper.

The remainder of this article is structured as follows. Section 2 describes prior art. Section 3 analyzes requirements and user personas to derive LightTag's goal. Section 4 describes novel user facing features. Section 5 highlights LightTag's data model and it's implications. We conclude with a number of case studies from industry and academia.

2 Related Work

Emacs (Stallman, 1981) was (shockingly) used to annotate the Penn Treebank (Marcus et al., 1993). Afterwards a series of standalone annotation tools emerged such as Salsa (Erk et al., 2003) and ITU (Eryiğit, 2007) for treebanks or BOEMIE (Fragkou et al., 2008) and ABNER (Settles, 2005)for the biomedical domain. This generation of tools is notable for being standalone software as opposed to the later web-based tools. DUALIST (Settles, 2011) stands out as an influential system due to it's inclusion of active learning and feature labeling.

The following generation of annotation tools were the first to leverage the browser as a user interface platform and include the Brandeis Annotation Tool (Verhagen, 2010), GATE Teamware (Cunningham and Bontcheva, 2011), BRAT (Stenetorp et al., 2012) and WebAnno (Yimam et al., 2013). These also leveraged a client-server architecture to enable multi-user annotation projects and server side automation. The recent trends and ubiquity of NLP, along with improved web development frameworks and simplified delivery mechanisms, have inspired a new generation of tools which cater to data scientists as opposed to academics and emphasize ergonomics. This generation of tools, of which LightTag is a contemporary, include the open source Docanno (Nakayama et al., 2018) as well as the commercial Prodi.gy (Montani and Honnibal, 2018) which focuses on annotator productivity via active learning, and TagTog (Cejuela et al., 2014) which optimizes for bio-medical annotation.

LightTag's generation of annotation tools offer roughly the same set of capabilities as the previous generation, that of WebAnno, INCEpTION and BRAT. Yet the current generation of tools enjoys a measure of commercial success, despite established and free alternatives. We posit that the cur-

[1] Academic free tier avalible at https://lighttag.io/signup/academic

Proceedings of the 2021 Conference on Empirical Methods in Natural Language Processing: System Demonstrations, pages 20–27
November 7–11, 2021. ©2021 Association for Computational Linguistics

rent generation of tools has a stronger focus on user experience, ease of use and integration with the end users goals and systems. Thus, despite the similar feature sets between the two generations, we offer the commercial success of LightTag and it's contemporaries as proof of innovation that satisfies previously unmet needs.

3 Goals and Design

In designing LightTag, we relied on the manufacturing metaphor mentioned above and identified three user personas and five broad needs that need to be served to optimize the overall "NLP process" as opposed to the local-maxima of individual annotator.

We assume that the end user's goal is to solve a business problem with NLP and that text annotation is a bottleneck in that process (Sambasivan et al., 2021) . We distinguish between the rate at which labeled data is produced, and the rate at which labeled data propagates through the end user's NLP process and optimize for the latter.

3.1 Requirements Of An Annotation Tool

Expressivity An annotation tool should allow the user to express the kinds of annotation they need to carry out. LightTag supports span annotations, single and multi-label document classification and relationship annotation, including dependency and constituency grammars. LightTag also emphasizes working with "text in the wild" and supports RTL languages, unicode, and very long documents such as legal contracts and electronic medical records.

Productivity In our taxonomy, productivity is the rate at which an annotator can express the required annotation. All else being equal, the desired productivity is "As much as possible."

Coordination Larger annotation projects need to coordinate the work among the annotators. This can be as simple as sending out N examples to be labeled by K annotators such that M annotators annotate each example. More complex requirements include sending out tasks to subsets of annotators (based on language or security clearance) or dynamically scheduling work based on agreement levels.

Review and Quality Control As in manufacturing, the quality of an annotation needs to be reviewed before delivery. The ability to efficiently review annotations from multiple annotators and/or models is required for larger annotation projects.

Analytics Project managers and data consumers need to know what is happening. That can include the project's progress, inter-annotator agreement, or annotator accuracy.

3.2 User Personas

Modern annotation projects have multiple, distinct, participants whose requirements from an annotation tool differ. LightTag recognizes three primary user personas annotators, data scientists, and project managers

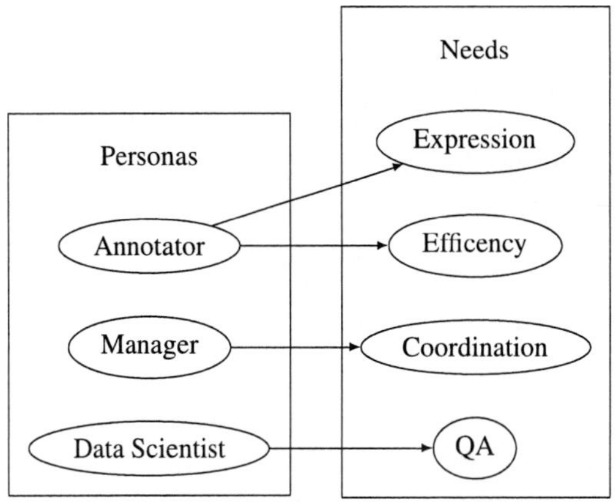

Figure 1: A visualization of the mapping between user personas and their requirements. An annotation platform caters to multiple personas who have different needs.

Annotators have three primary needs from an annotation tool. First, they should express the required annotation (an entity, a document class, relationships). Second, the tooling should help annotators avoid errors such as mistakenly annotating trailing whitespace. Third, the annotator's throughput should be maximized subject to their other requirements.

Project Managers need to control what work is being done and understand the project's cadence and productivity. A common best practice (Hovy and Lavid, 2010) is to have more than one annotator annotate each example. However, coordinating and distributing the work is complex, and the effort scales with the number of annotators while being constrained by the availability of the project manager. LightTag resolves this issue by automating the distribution and management of work according to a project manager's configuration.

Data Scientists are the final consumer of labeled data and are responsible for assessing it is quality and suitability. LightTag minimizes their heavy lifting by calculating inter-annotator agreement, precision and recall (based on reviewed data), and other metrics. This allows data scientists to spend more time in differentiated data science instead of joining excel files.

4 User Interface and User Facing Features

In this section, we present user interface decisions and user-facing features that are, to our knowledge, unique to LightTag.

4.1 Annotation Features

Contextual Display: Conversational annotation requires preceding messages in order to interpret and properly annotate their followers. LightTag supports this ability through "contextual display," whereby a project manager can configure to display all examples with a particular metadata attribute (such as conversation_id) at once and sort the items by a separate attribute (such as timestamp). Thus annotators can see the entire conversation but annotate each message individually.

Drag And Drop Relationship Annotation: Relationship annotation is a common feature of text annotation tools. To our knowledge, all text annotation tools that offer this functionality implement it as arcs drawn between entities in text, implemented with Scalable Vector Graphics (SVG).

LightTag implements relationship annotation via the dragging and dropping of entities onto each other and visualizes a full tree in a separate pane. Inspired by the Trees3 program Phillips (1998), users can annotate partial trees and drag and drop branches to annotate richer structures.

Of note is the ability to annotate constituency grammars by defining non-terminal nodes. This feature is often used to "group together" related nodes in a "container" such as in resume annotation, where a title, company and dates are all constituents of a single job.

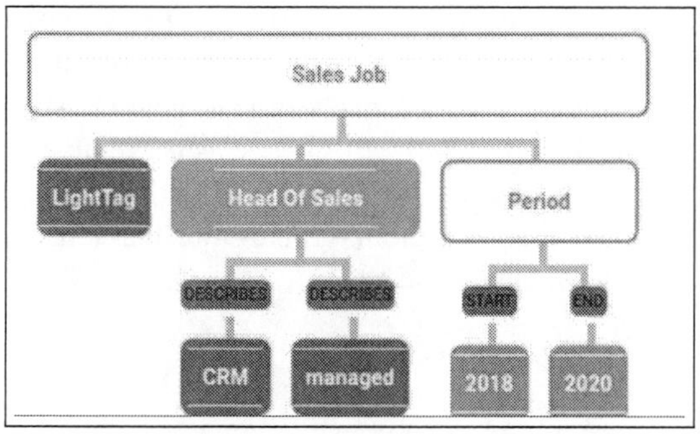

Figure 2: Relationship annotation of a resume with a constituency grammar. The "Sales Job" and "Period" nodes are user defined non-terminals while the other nodes are entities from the text

Large Taxonomies: Annotation starts with a taxonomy, the collection of concepts that will be annotated. Some projects are based on taxonomies with hundreds or thousands of classes or entity types. In these cases, it is infeasible to display the entire taxonomy in a static list. Long lists slow down annotators and introduces an availability bias (Tversky and Kahneman, 1973) where annotators are more likely to select entities that are visible and at the top of a list, thus biasing the resulting data.

LightTag resolves this issue by providing a searchable field for classes and entities, allowing the annotator to quickly find the correct class by searching.

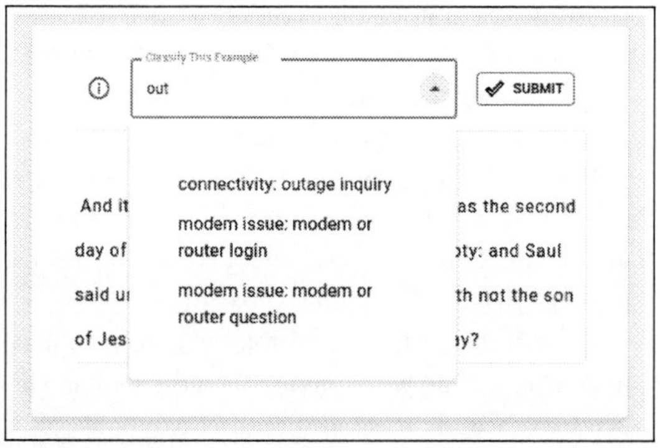

Figure 3: The user can search a taxonomy of a few thousand classes to quickly find the most relevant class, without scrolling through a list

Unobtrusive Pre-Annotations: Many annotation tools offer pre-annotations to increase annotator productivity. The efficacy of pre-annotations depends on both their accuracy and how the user interacts with them, particularly when the pre-annotations are incorrect. If a user must make an action for every pre-annotation, incorrect ones risk increasing the total number of actions and diminishing productivity.

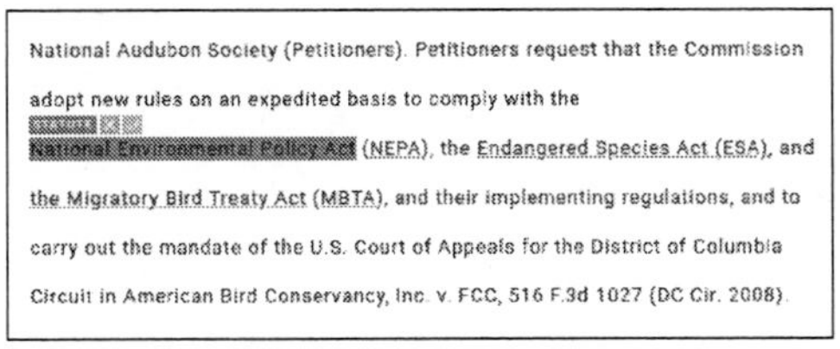

Figure 4: Unobstrusive pre-annotations are displayed as colored underlines. When the user hovers over a pre-annotation they can accept or reject it. A batch accept butto (not displayed) allows users to save clicks by accepting all at once.

LightTag displays pre-annotations in as an unobtrusive underline. The user can ignore them (and thus take no action) or accept/reject them by hovering over a pre-annotation and clicking. LightTag offers a batch accept button allowing users to accept many pre-annotations at once.

We find that this mode of interaction has a significant effect on annotator productivity, with a near doubling of annotator throughput achieved when only 50% of pre-annotations are accepted.

Annotating With Search Like other annotation tools, LightTag defaults to displaying examples to annotate one at a time. However, many datasets are sparse with respect to the classes or entities that users need to annotate. In such cases having annotators annotate each example, where the majority are irrelevant, is ineffective.

To address this issue, LightTag follows Attenberg and Provost (2010) by offering a "Search Mode" in which the entire dataset is displayed in an infinite scroll, and the user can narrow it down using search queries.

LightTag's implementation of search is noteworthy because it is operationally simple while remaining fast at scale. Cox (2012) demonstrated the use of tri-gram indices to speed up plain text and regular expression search and Korotkov (2012) introduced an implementation to Postgres. Leveraging these, LightTag can offer users very fast regular expressions search with minimal operational overhead.

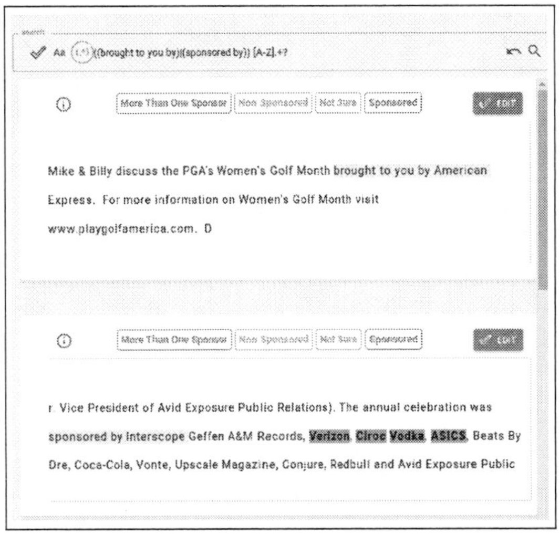

Figure 5: Annotating with search. Users can write search queries or regular expressions to narrow down the set of documents to work on. In this example, documents from the Federal Registar are annoted for mentions of foreign policy.

4.2 Review

Project managers and data scientists want to review annotations produced by both annotators and, later, by models. LightTag's Review mode displays all annotations made in a selected example and consolidates agreements and conflicts. Reviewers can narrow the scope of review to human or model annotations and automatically accept all annotations that meet a certain agreement threshold.

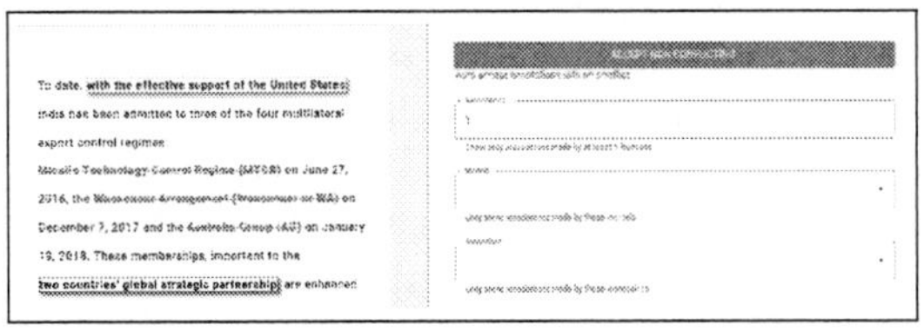

Figure 6: Agreement detection powered by the relational model. Conflicts are easily detected by the system and visually displayed during review. A reviewer can click on the button to accept all annotations meeting a specific criteria

4.2.1 Batch Lexical Review

We observe that the distribution of annotated entities is Zipfian. Rather than having reviewers review every case of trivially correct or incorrect annotations, LightTag offers a batch review function where every instance of a particular lexical form can be seen and reviewed in either a stream or in one click.

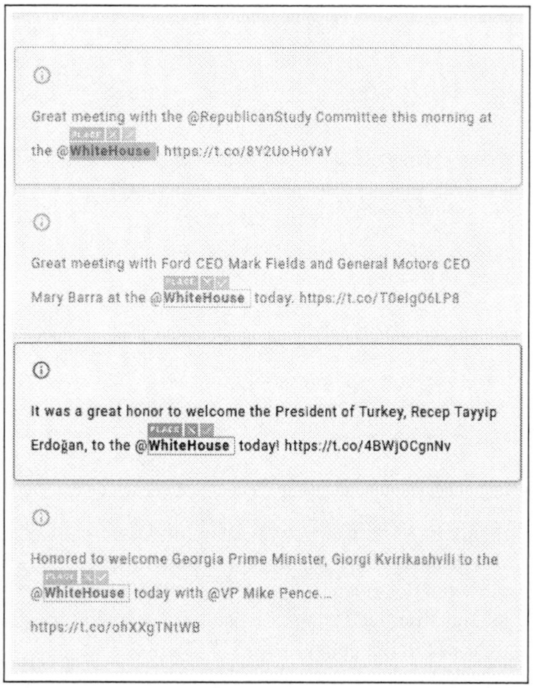

Figure 7: All instances of the form "White House" labeled as place are displayed. The user can review them one by one or batch accept/reject them with one click.

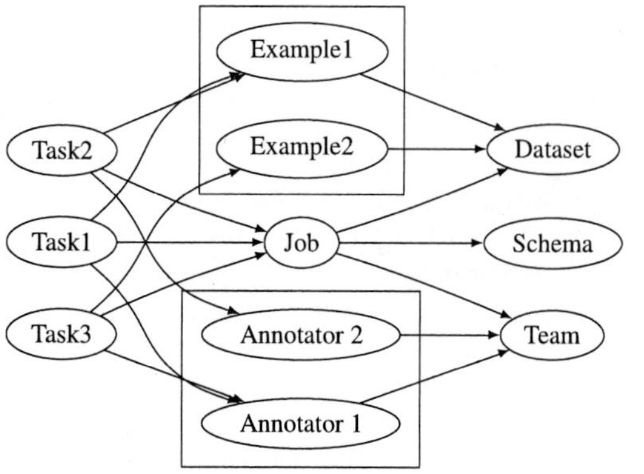

Figure 8: A graphical display of the relation between data entities describing three tasks carried out by two annotators as part of a job

5 Backend and Data Model

LightTag's focus on project management and quality assurance requires a rich data management structure. LightTag's backend is a relational database using Postgres and makes heavy use of relational design theory Codd (2002). In this section, we provide an overview of LightTag's data model and elaborate on useful implications.

5.1 Relational Data Model

A project manager in LightTag may define a Job comprised of the Dataset to annotate and the concepts (entity tags or document classes) with which to annotate. N annotators should annotate each Example in the Dataset of a Job. A project manager may wish to have the same Dataset annotated with the same Schema in two Jobs, where a different Team executes each Job. The definition and assignment of work as described above fits neatly into a relational model.

The natural extension of a relational data model is that annotations are stored separately from the Example being annotated. LightTag takes this idea a step further and separates the Platonic Ideal (Plato, 1961) of annotation from the event that Annotator A made Annotation X, thus brining the database to third normal form. For example, the "Ideal" that "Document X is classified as class Y" is stored in a distinct table with id Z. A separate events table would then store the event "Annotator 1 made classification Z during Task x". Storing every possible ideal would be inefficient, thus LightTag stores the ideal of an annotation the first time it is manifested via annotation.

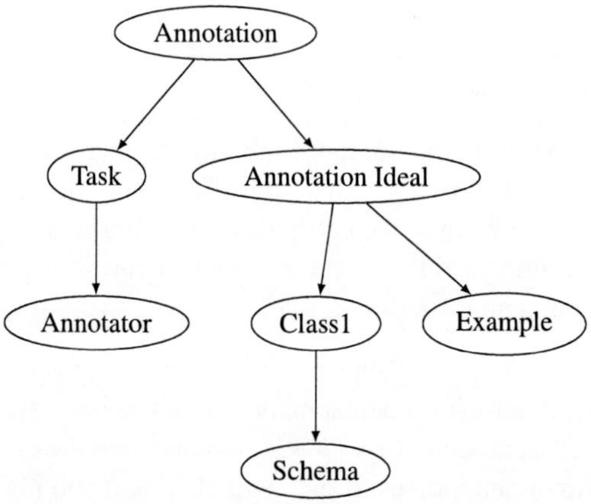

Figure 9: A graphical depiction of the relations defining an annotation. Each node corresponds to a row in the respective table. The annotator that worked on the Task made the annotation represent by the Ideal of an annotation that the Example is classified as Class1

5.2 Relational Data Implications

A notable implication of this design is batch functionality during review. For example, automatically accepting all annotations with a majority vote is displayed as a button to the user and is implemented by aggregating over the "Annotation Ideal table" id, counting and comparing with the number of users that saw that example (derived from the Tasks table).

Measuring Negative Annotations When annotating with a larger team, we can not assume that every team member annotated every example. Thus when calculating metrics such as inter-annotator agreement, a particular annotator even saw the particular example needs to be accounted for. The relational model makes this easy by implicitly providing a list for each annotator of the Examples they worked on (by aggregating on the Task table).

Majority Vote During a quality assurance process, it is common practice to automatically accept annotations with a majority or unanimous vote automatically and manually review annotations in a conflicting state. By separating the Ideal of an Annotation from the Event that annotation was made and recording the particular Job under which the annotation was made, LightTag can provide the reviewing user with a one-click functionality to accept all annotations that meet some agreement criteria.

Transitive Annotation Rejections LightTag's quality assurance functionality assumes only one correct answer for an annotated span or a document classification[2]. When a reviewer marks an annotation as correct, the system rejects any conflicting annotation automatically, be it a difference in class, an entity tag, or span range. If annotations A and B overlap and A is correct, then B must be incorrect. The relational model allows executing the transitive rejection in $\mathcal{O}(1)$ time instead of scanning the entire annotation table. More importantly, doing so in a single database transaction ensures that the data is never in an invalid state.

6 Case Studies

6.1 Detecting Foreign Policy With Search

The Federal Register is the official journal of the federal government of the United States that contains government agency rules, proposed rules, and public notices. A team of researchers from Harvard Law wished to annotate every mention of foreign policy across over 100,000 rules spanning 2.1 Million paragraphs. A team of 15 undergraduate law students was assembled, and the data was loaded into LightTag. Using LightTag's search mode, subsections of the dataset were assigned to subsets of annotators who then searched over the corpus to find and annotate over 60 thousand distinct mentions of foreign policy in the corpus.

6.2 Sponsorship Detection in Podcasts

Thoughtleaders (TL). a provider of marketing analytics created a corpus of podcast transcripts to detect which brands sponsored each podcast episode (Kassuto, 2021). TL trained a BERT-based model to recognize brands and distinguish between casual brand mentions and mentions of a podcast sponsor. To create a training corpus with LightTag, TL first created pre-annotations with regular expressions and then had their team validate those and annotate missing entities.

Within a week, they had generated over 20 thousand human-annotated entities and trained a model that met their requirements. To validate the model's performance, they loaded model predictions from data outside of the training set into LightTag and used the review functionality to verify model predictions and establish performance metrics manually.

6.3 Multi-Lingual Malware Detection

CS is a provider of Malware analytic and early detection systems. To serve their customers, they develop custom NLP models to detect the sale of zero-day exploits on the dark web. Due to the multi-lingual nature of the data, they needed to manage multiple teams and projects, each specializing in a particular language (Mandarin, Russian, English, etc.). LightTag's workforce management solution enabled them to minimize project management overhead, while pre-annotations and review functionality allowed the team to validate both annotations and candidate model outputs, reaching production grade models and their market faster.

6.4 Mentions In Other Publications

Sarkar (2020) created a corpus for emotion detection in musical lyrics. Vasilyev et al. (2020) generated a corpus of text-summary quality on a five-point scale across five attributes of the summary.Alnazzawi (2021) annotated a joint corpus

[2]In single-class classification. In configurations where more than one class is allowed per document, this assumption is removed

of tweets and electronic health records to detect underlying risk factors for hypertension and diabetes.Pitenis et al. (2020) developed a Greek language corpus of offensive language

References

Noha Alnazzawi. 2021. Building a semantically annotated corpus for chronic disease complications using two document types. *PloS one*, 16(3):e0247319.

Josh Attenberg and Foster Provost. 2010. Why label when you can search? alternatives to active learning for applying human resources to build classification models under extreme class imbalance. In *Proceedings of the 16th ACM SIGKDD International Conference on Knowledge Discovery and Data Mining*, KDD '10, page 423–432, New York, NY, USA. Association for Computing Machinery.

Juan Miguel Cejuela, Peter McQuilton, Laura Ponting, Steven J Marygold, Raymund Stefancsik, Gillian H Millburn, Burkhard Rost, FlyBase Consortium, et al. 2014. tagtog: interactive and text-mining-assisted annotation of gene mentions in plos full-text articles. *Database*, 2014.

Edgar F Codd. 2002. A relational model of data for large shared data banks. In *Software pioneers*, pages 263–294. Springer.

Russ Cox. 2012. Regular expression matching with a trigram index or how google code search worked.

Diana Maynard Hamish Cunningham and Kalina Bontcheva. 2011. *Text Processing with GATE (Version 6)*. University of Sheffield D.

Katrin Erk, Andrea Kowalski, and Sebastian Pado. 2003. The salsa annotation tool. In *Proceedings of the Workshop on Prospects and Advances in the Syntax/Semantics Interface*, pages 1–4.

Gülşen Eryiğit. 2007. Itu treebank annotation tool. In *Proceedings of the Linguistic Annotation Workshop*, pages 117–120.

Pavlina Fragkou, Georgios Petasis, Aris Theodorakos, Vangelis Karkaletsis, and Constantine D Spyropoulos. 2008. Boemie ontology-based text annotation tool. In *LREC*. Citeseer.

Eliyahu M Goldratt and Jeff Cox. 2016. *The goal: a process of ongoing improvement*. Routledge.

Eduard Hovy and Julia Lavid. 2010. Towards a 'science'of corpus annotation: a new methodological challenge for corpus linguistics. *International journal of translation*, 22(1):13–36.

Avi Kassuto. 2021. Read between the lines.

Alexander Korotkov. 2012. Index support for regular expression search. In *Proc. PostgreSQL Conference*.

Mitchell Marcus, Beatrice Santorini, and Mary Ann Marcinkiewicz. 1993. Building a large annotated corpus of english: The penn treebank.

Ines Montani and Matthew Honnibal. 2018. Prodigy: A new annotation tool for radically efficient machine teaching. *Artificial Intelligence*, to appear.

Hiroki Nakayama, Takahiro Kubo, Junya Kamura, Yasufumi Taniguchi, and Xu Liang. 2018. doccano: Text annotation tool for human. Software available from https://github.com/doccano/doccano.

Colin Phillips. 1998. Teaching syntax with trees. *Glot international*, 3.

Zeses Pitenis, Marcos Zampieri, and Tharindu Ranasinghe. 2020. Offensive language identification in greek. *arXiv preprint arXiv:2003.07459*.

HG Plato. 1961. *Republic*. Princeton University Press.

Nithya Sambasivan, Shivani Kapania, Hannah Highfill, Diana Akrong, Praveen Kumar Paritosh, and Lora Mois Aroyo. 2021. "everyone wants to do the model work, not the data work": Data cascades in high-stakes ai.

Diptanu Sarkar. 2020. Detecting emotions in lyrics.

Burr Settles. 2005. Abner: an open source tool for automatically tagging genes, proteins and other entity names in text. *Bioinformatics*, 21(14):3191–3192.

Burr Settles. 2011. Closing the loop: Fast, interactive semi-supervised annotation with queries on features and instances. In *Proceedings of the 2011 Conference on Empirical Methods in Natural Language Processing*, pages 1467–1478.

Richard M Stallman. 1981. Emacs the extensible, customizable self-documenting display editor. In *Proceedings of the ACM SIGPLAN SIGOA symposium on Text manipulation*, pages 147–156.

Pontus Stenetorp, Sampo Pyysalo, Goran Topić, Tomoko Ohta, Sophia Ananiadou, and Jun'ichi Tsujii. 2012. Brat: a web-based tool for nlp-assisted text annotation. In *Proceedings of the Demonstrations at the 13th Conference of the European Chapter of the Association for Computational Linguistics*, pages 102–107.

Amos Tversky and Daniel Kahneman. 1973. Availability: A heuristic for judging frequency and probability. *Cognitive psychology*, 5(2):207–232.

Oleg Vasilyev, Vedant Dharnidharka, Nicholas Egan, Charlene Chambliss, and John Bohannon. 2020. Sensitivity of blanc to human-scored qualities of text summaries. *arXiv preprint arXiv:2010.06716*.

Marc Verhagen. 2010. The brandeis annotation tool. In *LREC*.

Seid Muhie Yimam, Iryna Gurevych, Richard Eckart de Castilho, and Chris Biemann. 2013. Webanno: A flexible, web-based and visually supported system for distributed annotations. In *Proceedings of the 51st Annual Meeting of the Association for Computational Linguistics: System Demonstrations*, pages 1–6.

TransIns: Document Translation with Markup Reinsertion

Jörg Steffen
German Research Center for
Artificial Intelligence (DFKI)
Saarland Informatics Campus D3 2
66123 Saarbrücken, Germany
Joerg.Steffen@dfki.de

Josef van Genabith
DFKI and Saarland University
Saarland Informatics Campus D3 2
66123 Saarbrücken, Germany
Josef.Van_Genabith@dfki.de

Abstract

For many use cases, it is required that MT does not just translate raw text, but complex formatted documents (e.g. websites, slides, spreadsheets) and the result of the translation should reflect the formatting. This is challenging, as markup can be nested, apply to spans contiguous in source but non-contiguous in target etc. Here we present `TransIns`, a system for non-plain text document translation that builds on the Okapi framework and MT models trained with Marian NMT. We develop, implement and evaluate different strategies for reinserting markup into translated sentences using token alignments between source and target sentences. We propose a simple and effective strategy that compiles down all markup to single source tokens and transfers them to aligned target tokens. Our evaluation shows that this strategy yields highly accurate markup in the translated documents that outperforms the markup quality found in documents translated with popular translation services. We release `TransIns` under the MIT License as open-source software on https://github.com/DFKI-MLT/TransIns. An online demonstrator is available at https://transins.dfki.de.

1 Introduction

In MT research, models are usually trained and evaluated on plain text parallel data. But such models do not translate complex formatted documents created, e.g., with MS Office. Translating such documents comes with several challenges.

Text content has to be separated from formatting and other code and made available as input to MT. This requires a parser that handles the document format at hand and provides access to the embedded text content. After translation, the translated text must be placed into the target document and a further component is needed to create the translated version of the document reflecting the formatting and layout of the original document.

Furthermore, MT has to be able to handle *inline* sentence markup, i.e. to make sure that markup in the source sentence is correctly transferred to the appropriate parts of the target sentence. It is possible to train markup-aware MT models, e.g. by replacing tags with unique mask tokens in training and translation, as described in (Zhechev and van Genabith, 2010), but in order to use an existing MT model that is unaware of markup, the only option is to remove markup from the source sentence and to reinsert it at proper positions in the target sentence after translation. Du et al. (2010) describe a reinsertion strategy based on the phrase segmentation indicated by the decoder. This is refined by Hudik and Ruopp (2011) who use word alignments instead of phrase segmentation. Joanis et al. (2013) propose a hybrid approach combining phrase segmentation with word alignments. Building on these, Müller (2017) evaluates different markup handling strategies and provides implementations as part of the Zurich NLP `mtrain`[1] framework.

In order to utilize state-of-the-art MT technology and obtain alignments at the same time, we use Marian[2] NMT (Junczys-Dowmunt et al., 2018). Marian allows transformer models to be trained using guided alignment so that the decoder produces translations together with alignments between source and target tokens. The OPUS-MT[3] project (Tiedemann and Thottingal, 2020) provides pre-trained Marian models for many language pairs, mostly trained with guided alignment based on eflomal[4] word alignments (Östling and Tiedemann, 2016), but unaware of markup.

Below, we describe `TransIns`, a translator for non-plain text documents. We use the Okapi[5] framework to process such documents and extend

[1] https://github.com/ZurichNLP/mtrain
[2] https://marian-nmt.github.io/
[3] https://github.com/Helsinki-NLP/Opus-MT
[4] https://github.com/robertostling/eflomal
[5] https://okapiframework.org/

Proceedings of the 2021 Conference on Empirical Methods in Natural Language Processing: System Demonstrations, pages 28–34
November 7–11, 2021.

Okapi in order to query Marian for translations and alignments. We study different alignment-based markup reinsertion strategies, starting with the one implemented in `mtrain`. We identify deficits and present improved strategies. Finally, we evaluate different strategies and compare the markup quality between documents translated by `TransIns` and popular translation services.

2 Okapi Framework

Okapi is a free open-source framework designed to support localization and translation processes. It includes a collection of *filters* providing access to the translatable content for many file formats. A workflow in Okapi is modelled as a pipeline of *steps* that pass *events* through the pipeline. Events are associated with resources, e.g. text units, and are created when using a filter on a source document. A typical Okapi pipeline for translating documents consists of four steps:

The **Raw Document to Filter Events Step** reads the source document with an associated filter configuration and sends the filter events with the associated text units down the pipeline.

The **Segmentation Step** breaks down the text units into sentences, using rules specified in Segmentation Rules eXchange format (SRX)[6], a standard describing how to segment text.

The **Leveraging Step** sends each sentence to a translation service and stores the generated translation with the sentence. Translation services are accessed via *connectors*. Okapi provides connectors for popular translation services, but a connector for Marian is not included.

The **Filter Events to Raw Document Step** creates the target document in the original format from the translated text content coming in as filter events.

Okapi handles *global* document markup, but not *inline* sentence markup. This has to be dealt with by the translation service.[7]

3 TransIns System Description

Below, we describe how we build `TransIns` (**trans**lation with markup re**ins**ertion) based on the Okapi translation pipeline by adding Marian specific components and setting up an additional Okapi pipeline to support efficient processing.

Marian comes with a web-socket server that loads a model once at start time and then listens for single or batch translation queries. The server can be run remotely, supporting distributed setups with multiple Marian servers. In order to use Marian as a translation service from the leveraging step, we provide a Marian connector that implements the Okapi connector interface.

Most MT models are trained on parallel data where sentences are preprocessed, e.g. tokenized. Sentences to be translated need to be preprocessed in the same way. Also, the translation provided by the MT model might require postprocessing, e.g detokenization. With Marian, pre-/postprocessing often resorts to Perl scripts written for the Moses statistical MT system (Koehn et al., 2007). For `TransIns`, we use a Python reimplementation provided by Sacremoses[8]. Transformer MT models often apply subword tokenization in preprocessing. In postprocessing, subword tokenization has to be undone in the translated sentence. For transformer models, Byte-Pair Encoding (BPE) (Sennrich et al., 2016) and SentencePiece (Kudo and Richardson, 2018) are popular subword tokenizers. We use publicly available implementations of both subword tokenizers.[9,10] Undoing the subword tokenization in the translated sentence in postprocessing is straightforward by applying simple string replacements.

`TransIns` wraps the steps described above in a web service that provides corresponding endpoints for pre-/postprocessing single sentences or batches. The steps to apply can be configured separately for each translation direction. The Marian connector for Okapi calls this web service to preprocess a sentence before translation and again afterwards to postprocess the translated sentence.

The standard Okapi translation pipeline is somewhat inefficient: extracted sentences arrive at the leveraging step one-by-one, i.e. only single sentences are sent for pre-/postprocessing and translation to the corresponding services, even though the services support batch processing. The accumulated overhead of connecting and disconnecting slows throughput significantly. For efficient batch processing, we set up another Okapi pipeline, the *sentence collector pipeline*, consisting of a **Raw Document to Filter Events Step** and a **Segmentation Step** followed by a custom **Sentence Col-**

[6]https://www.gala-global.org/srx-20-april-7-2008

[7]The Okapi supported popular translation services can handle inline sentence markup, but details are not available.

[8]https://github.com/alvations/sacremoses

[9]https://github.com/rsennrich/subword-nmt

[10]https://github.com/google/sentencepiece

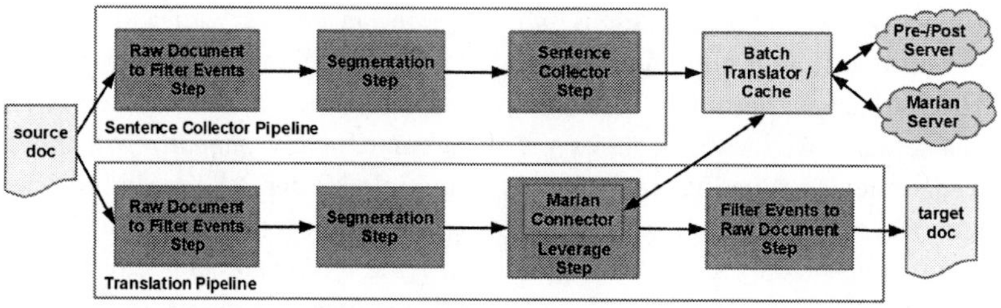

Figure 1: `TransIns` processes the source document with two Okapi pipelines

lector Step that simply adds each sentence to a local **Batch Translator** component. In a first run, we process the source document with this pipeline. Once the batch translator has collected all sentences it sends batches to preprocessing, translation and postprocessing. The batch translator also serves as **Cache**: for each source sentence, it stores the resulting target sentence. In a second run, we process the source document with the translation pipeline, but we adapt the Marian connector so that it queries the batch translator cache. This avoids connections to remote services, resulting in increased throughput. Figure 1 shows the `TransIns` workflow with both Okapi pipelines.[11]

4 Markup Reinsertion

Okapi provides sentences in a generic format. Sentence internal tags are encoded using characters from the Unicode private use area (PUA). Each tag consists of two such characters. The first encodes the type of the tag, which is either opening (e.g. `<b>`), closing (e.g. `</b>`), or isolated (e.g. `<br/>`). The second character encodes a running tag index. Tags provided by Okapi are always well-formed and balanced, i.e. for each opening tag, there is a corresponding closing tag, and tag pairs are properly nested. Tag indices are unique, and so is each tag pair.

The OPUS-MT models we use with `TransIns` are unaware of markup, so the only option is to remove tags before translation and to reinsert them afterwards. The general workflow of all `TransIns` markup reinsertion strategies is shown in Figure 2.

Alignments provided by Marian[12] refer to token indices. As tokenization is decided by preprocessing, we can only map and remove tags from the source sentence *after* preprocessing. Postprocessing like detokenization might change target tokenization. Therefore tag reinsertion has to be done

1 preprocess source sentence;
2 map each tag to a source token;[13]
3 remove tags from source sentence;
4 send source sentence to Marian for translation, retrieve target sentence and alignments;
5 reinsert tags into target sentence based on the alignments of the mapped source tokens;
6 clean up target sentence markup;
7 postprocess target sentence.

Figure 2: Markup reinsertion workflow

into the raw target sentence *before* postprocessing.

As reinserted tags may end up anywhere and in any order in the target sentence, we do a cleanup step after tag reinsertion that takes care of:

Tags in subword token sequences: If a tag is inserted within a sequence of subword tokens, e.g. as created by BPE, that tag has to be moved so that the subword token sequence can be properly merged in postprocessing. We move opening and isolated tags to the front of the sequence and closing tags to the end.

Improper tag order: Reinserted tags in the target sentence might occur in incorrect order, i.e. closing tag before corresponding opening tag. In this case, we swap the tags. Furthermore, tag pairs might be improperly nested. We reorder and, if required, insert additional tags to restore a proper nesting. E.g., a target sentence with two "overlapping" tag scopes

(1) <i> x <b> y </i> z </b>

is fixed by adding two additional tags

(2) <i> x <b> y **</b>** </i> **<b>** z </b>

Below, we describe the markup reinsertion strategies implemented in `TransIns`. For some strategies the cleanup step has to be adapted or extended.

4.1 `mtrain` Strategy

`mtrain` (Müller, 2017) is implemented in the Zurich NLP `mtrain` Python package.[14] We reimplement it with the `TransIns` workflow (Figure

[11] For debugging purposes, our system can be run without the sentence collector pipeline.

[12] using the `--alignment hard` option

[13] Source tokens include subword tokens.

[14] https://github.com/ZurichNLP/mtrain/blob/master/mtrain/preprocessing/reinsertion.py#L315

2) as follows: in step 2, tags are always mapped to the *following* token.[15] In step 5, we iterate over the target tokens left to right. For each target token for which there is an alignment with a source token, we check if that source token has a tag mapped to it. If yes, that tag is *moved* in front of the target token. After the iteration, any remaining source sentence tags that have not been moved are added at the end of the target sentence. Such tags occur if they are mapped to a source token without alignment.

Example (3) demonstrates the strategy. The first row contains the source sentence with tags. Tag and mapped token are underlined. The last row contains the target sentence with reinserted tags, with vertical lines indicating alignments.

(3)
Hello <b> World </b> !
Hallo <b> Welt </b> !

<b> is mapped to "World", </b> is mapped to "!". "Welt" is aligned with "World", so <b> is moved in front of "Welt". The same is done for "!" and </b>, resulting in correct markup reinsertion. But if the word order in the target language is different from the source language, `mtrain` fails:

(4)
Porte <b> verte </b> !
<b> Green door </b> !

In (4) "door" is incorrectly rendered bold. In (5) both "Green" and "door" end up with incorrect markup:[16]

(5)
<b> Porte </b> verte !
</b> Green <b> door !

In conclusion, `mtrain` is only suitable for language pairs with similar word order and often fails otherwise. Below, we propose improvements to compensate for `mtrain` deficits.

4.2 `mtrain++` Strategy

The first improvement comes from the insight that tags do not generally refer to the *following* token. `mtrain++` only maps opening and isolated tags to the following token, but closing tags are mapped to the *previous* token and moved *after* the aligned target token. This fixes (4) (and also (5)):

(6)
Porte <b> verte </b> !
<b> Green </b> door !

But `mtrain++` requires an adaptation of the cleanup step, as (7) shows:

(7)
<b> Porte verte </b> !
Green </b> <b> door !

Swapping the tags here is not sufficient. We also have to consider the tag type. After swapping, we move the opening tag in front of the previous token and the closing tag after the following token:

(8) <b> Green door </b> !

Another deficit of `mtrain` is the handling of tags mapped to unaligned source tokens.[17] Unaligned tags are added at the end of the target sentence, resulting in a counter-intuitive markup reinsertion:

(9)
a <i> b c d </i> e
x y z <i> </i>

`mtrain++` handles unaligned tags in the source sentence: opening and isolated unaligned tags are moved *in front of* the following aligned token and closing unaligned tags *after* the previous aligned token. We then remap the tags accordingly. This results in correct markup reinsertion:

(10)
a b <i> c </i> d e
x <i> y </i> z

A further problem may occur with 1-to-n alignments where a single source token is aligned to multiple target tokens. Tags mapped to such a source token are *moved* by `mtrain`, so they are only applied to the first of the possible n aligned target tokens:

(11)
Police <b> arrests </b> man
Polizei <b> nimmt </b> Mann fest

`mtrain++` *copies* opening and closing tags instead of moving them, resulting in correct markup reinsertion for (11), where both "nimmt" and "fest" are correctly rendered bold.

But copying tags instead of moving them comes at a price: tags in the target sentence are potentially no longer well-formed and balanced. E.g., an opening tag may be copied twice while the corresponding closing tag is only copied once if they are mapped to different source tokens. We extend the cleanup step so that well-formedness and balance are restored.

But even with all the improvements, there still remain configurations where the markup is not reinserted correctly to the target sentence:

[15] A tag at the end of a sentence is mapped to an artificial end-of-sentence token.

[16] </b> and <b> are swapped in the cleanup step.

[17] We call such tags *unaligned tags* in the following.

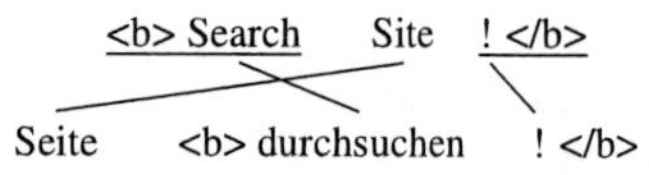

(12)

The underlying problem is that `mtrain++` only considers tokens immediately next to tags. Source tokens located within a tag pair's scope but not next to a tag, as "Site" in (12), may be aligned with a target token outside of that tag pair's scope in the target sentence.

Another problem are tag pairs with a contiguous scope in the source sentence that should be non-contiguous in the target sentence:

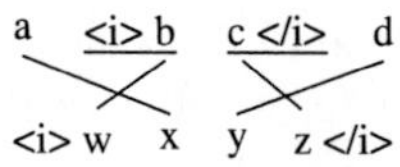

(13)

In (13) only w and z should be rendered italic.

Rather than continuing to fix individual problem cases, below we develop a new mapping strategy designed to provide a general solution.

4.3 Complete Mapping Strategy (CMS)

CMS is based on the insight that if (i) alignments steer markup transfer, and (ii) alignments relate tokens, then compiling down tag pairs to their minimal token level scope should solve most if not all of the problems presented in Sections 4.1 and 4.2. Formally, a tagged sentence is a sequence $s = s_1 \dots s_m$ consisting of one or more sequence elements s_i, where s_i is either a raw token w or a function $t_i(s_j)$ representing a tag pair with scope over a sequence s_j.[18] This allows for sentences with arbitrarily nested tag pairs and ensures that markup is well-formed. We use $t_i^1(\dots(t_j^k(.)))$ to denote one or more (k) nested tag pairs with scope (.). The algorithm compiles tag pairs to their minimal scopes $t_i^1(\dots(t_j^k(w)))$ by repeatedly applying

(14) $t_j^k(s_1 \dots s_m) \rightarrow t_j^k(s_1) \dots t_j^k(s_m)$

until no tag pair with scope sequence of length > 1 remains. In terms of tag mapping, this results in each tag pair being mapped to *all* tokens in its original scope, hence the term *complete* mapping.[19] The compilation is meaning-preserving, e.g.

(15) <b> x <i> y </i> z </b>

is turned into

(16) <b> x </b> <b> <i> y </i> </b> <b> z </b>

CMS simplifies markup reinsertion significantly: as minimum scope tag pairs "travel" with token alignments, tag balance, well-formedness and complex positioning in the target sentence are taken care of by the alignments. Tag swapping, reordering or insertion is no longer required in the cleanup step. Unaligned opening and closing tags no longer have to be moved.[20] The cleanup step only needs to take care of tags in subword token sequences. Readers are invited to check that all "toxic" examples discussed in Sections 4.1 and 4.2 are handled correctly by CMS. Finally to remove clutter, we simplify the target sentence markup by eliminating closing tags immediately followed by the corresponding opening tag, so

(17) <b> x **</b> <b>** y **</b> <b>** z </b>

simplifies to

(18) <b> x y z </b>

While CMS ensures that target tokens "inherit" the markup of their aligned source tokens, there may be unaligned target tokens. Such tokens would never receive markup, resulting in *gaps*:

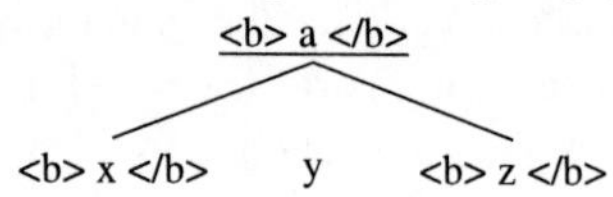

(19)

In such configurations, rendering "y" bold seems appropriate. We implement a *tag interpolation* scheme for target tokens within gaps. A gap is a target token sequence not longer than a specified maximum gap size where all target tokens have no markup, either because they are unaligned or they are aligned with a source token without tags. The latter is often the result of incorrect alignments that tag interpolation can correct.[21] Tag interpolation inspects the tags applied to the neighbor tokens in front of and after the gap. Identical tags[22] found with both neighbor tokens are applied to the gap tokens. E.g., applying tag interpolation to a gap of size 2 with tokens x and y turns

(20) <b> <i> w </i> </b> x y <b> z </b>

(after simplification) into

(21) <b> <i> w </i> x y z </b>

5 Evaluation

To the best of our knowledge, there are no public standard evaluation data sets for markup transfer yet. We collect 10 complex web pages from spiegel.de, a well-known German news provider, that contain a total of 378 sentences with inline markup. We convert the web pages to MS Office

[18] Isolated tags are considered as tag pairs with empty scope, though they have an implicit scope over all following tokens.

[19] Isolated tags are still mapped to the following token.

[20] Unaligned isolated tags are still moved in front of the following aligned token.

[21] Tag interpolation produces a markup error if a gap target token is correctly aligned with a source token without tags.

[22] Identical tags have the same tag type and index.

Reinsertion Strategy		de –> fr		de –> en	
		Marian Alignments	Perfect Alignments	Marian Alignments	Perfect Alignments
mtrain		104	94	98	85
mtrain++		23	31	28	31
CMS	max gap 3	12 (8 + 4)	4	7 (3 + 4)	4
	max gap 2	9 (8 + 1)	1	7 (3 + 4)	4
	max gap 1	**9 (8 + 1)**	1	**5 (3 + 2)**	2
	max gap 0	10 (10 + 0)	0	**5 (5 + 0)**	0

Table 1: Markup transfer errors by reinsertion strategy

MT Service	de –> fr	de –> en
Google	119	55
DeepL	129	78
Microsoft	261	235
CMS (max gap 1)	58 (48 + 10)	32 (21 + 11)
CMS (max gap 0)	**57 (57 + 0)**	**25 (25 + 0)**

Table 2: Markup transfer errors by translation service

docx documents, preserving the relevant markup, and examine translations to French and English using the latest OPUS-MT models. As a quality measure of markup transfer, we count how many target tokens end up with incorrect markup.[23]

Even though CMS can handle all toxic examples described in Section 4, as a sanity check, we do a small evaluation of the three `TransIns` reinsertion strategies using the first evaluation document containing 40 sentences with inline markup. We do this for alignments as provided by the OPUS-MT models and also for hand-corrected perfect alignments.[24] For CMS and Marian alignments, we distinguish between errors resulting from incorrect alignments (first number in brackets) and errors from incorrect tag interpolation (second number in brackets). We also examine different maximum gap sizes. Table 1 shows the results.

For both translation directions `mtrain` produces most errors. Using perfect alignments yields only a minor improvement. `mtrain++` reduces the number of errors by about two-thirds. Surprisingly, the quality for both translation directions is slightly better when using Marian alignments instead of perfect alignments. This is due to the fact that a single change in alignment, even if it is a correction, can potentially change the markup of multiple tokens. With CMS, a change in alignment only effects a single target token, making this strategy less volatile.

For both types of alignments, CMS produces the smallest number of errors. The results are similar for both translation directions. For de –> fr, using Marian alignments with a maximum gap size of 3, we find 8 errors caused by incorrect alignments and 4 errors caused by incorrect tag interpolation. Reducing the maximum gap size to 2 and 1 decreases the number of interpolation errors, as tag interpolation is applied to fewer gaps. With a gap size of 0, i.e. with no tag interpolation, the number of errors caused by incorrect alignments increases by 2. These errors are now no longer corrected by tag interpolation. With perfect alignments, only the errors caused by incorrect tag interpolation remain.

The main focus of our evaluation is the comparison of CMS with popular translation services. These services are able to handle markup, but the details are unknown to us. Table 2 shows the errors for all evaluation document translations.[25] The performance for de –> en is always better than for de –> fr. This is probably due to the more similar word order between German and English. For both translation directions, CMS produces less than half as many markup errors as the next best commercial MT service. Errors decrease when omitting tag interpolation, i.e. the number of corrected alignment errors is smaller than the number of errors introduced by incorrect tag interpolation. We see this as an indicator of the high quality alignments provided by the OPUS-MT models.

6 Conclusion

In this paper, we present `TransIns`, an open-source system implementing several alignment based strategies for markup reinsertion in translated documents. `mtrain` constitutes a baseline, while `mtrain++` can handle more complex configurations. CMS correctly handles all problem cases discussed and outperforms the markup transfer in documents translated with popular translation services.

[23] We ignore punctuation tokens with incorrect markup.

[24] We hand-correct 8% of the de –> fr and 10% of the de –> en Marian token alignments.

[25] All evaluation documents are available at https://github.com/DFKI-MLT/TransIns/tree/master/evaluation.

Acknowledgements

We thank Thierry Declerck and Cristina España i Bonet for feedback and productive discussion. We also thank the anonymous reviewers for their constructive reviews. This work is supported in part by the German Federal Ministry of Education and Research (BMBF) under funding code 01IW20010 (CORA4NLP).

References

Jinhua Du, Johann Roturier, and Andy Way. 2010. TMX markup: A challenge when adapting SMT to the localisation environment. In *Proceedings of the 14th Annual conference of the European Association for Machine Translation*, Saint Raphaël, France. European Association for Machine Translation.

Tomáš Hudik and Achim Ruopp. 2011. The integration of Moses into localization industry. In *Proceedings of the 15th Annual conference of the European Association for Machine Translation*, Leuven, Belgium. European Association for Machine Translation.

Eric Joanis, Darlene Stewart, and Samuel Larkin. 2013. Transferring markup tags in statistical machine translation: A two-stream approach. In *Proceedings of MT Summit XIV Workshop on Post-editing Technology and Practice*, pages 73–81.

Marcin Junczys-Dowmunt, Roman Grundkiewicz, Tomasz Dwojak, Hieu Hoang, Kenneth Heafield, Tom Neckermann, Frank Seide, Ulrich Germann, Alham Fikri Aji, Nikolay Bogoychev, André F. T. Martins, and Alexandra Birch. 2018. Marian: Fast neural machine translation in C++. In *Proceedings of ACL 2018, System Demonstrations*, pages 116–121, Melbourne, Australia. Association for Computational Linguistics.

Philipp Koehn, Hieu Hoang, Alexandra Birch, Chris Callison-Burch, Marcello Federico, Nicola Bertoldi, Brooke Cowan, Wade Shen, Christine Moran, Richard Zens, Chris Dyer, Ondřej Bojar, Alexandra Constantin, and Evan Herbst. 2007. Moses: Open source toolkit for statistical machine translation. In *Proceedings of the 45th Annual Meeting of the Association for Computational Linguistics Companion Volume Proceedings of the Demo and Poster Sessions*, pages 177–180, Prague, Czech Republic. Association for Computational Linguistics.

Taku Kudo and John Richardson. 2018. SentencePiece: A simple and language independent subword tokenizer and detokenizer for neural text processing. In *Proceedings of the 2018 Conference on Empirical Methods in Natural Language Processing: System Demonstrations*, pages 66–71, Brussels, Belgium. Association for Computational Linguistics.

Mathias Müller. 2017. Treatment of markup in statistical machine translation. In *Proceedings of the Third Workshop on Discourse in Machine Translation*, pages 36–46, Copenhagen, Denmark. Association for Computational Linguistics.

Robert Östling and Jörg Tiedemann. 2016. Efficient word alignment with Markov Chain Monte Carlo. *Prague Bulletin of Mathematical Linguistics*, 106:125–146.

Rico Sennrich, Barry Haddow, and Alexandra Birch. 2016. Neural machine translation of rare words with subword units. In *Proceedings of the 54th Annual Meeting of the Association for Computational Linguistics (Volume 1: Long Papers)*, pages 1715–1725, Berlin, Germany. Association for Computational Linguistics.

Jörg Tiedemann and Santhosh Thottingal. 2020. OPUS-MT – building open translation services for the world. In *Proceedings of the 22nd Annual Conference of the European Association for Machine Translation*, pages 479–480, Lisboa, Portugal. European Association for Machine Translation.

Ventsislav Zhechev and Josef van Genabith. 2010. Seeding statistical machine translation with translation memory output through tree-based structural alignment. In *Proceedings of the 4th Workshop on Syntax and Structure in Statistical Translation*, pages 43–51, Beijing, China. Coling 2010 Organizing Committee.

ET: A Workstation for Querying, Editing and Evaluating Annotated Corpora

Elvis de Souza
Department of Letters
PUC-Rio, Brazil
elvis.desouza99@gmail.com

Cláudia Freitas
Department of Letters
PUC-Rio, Brazil
claudiafreitas@puc-rio.br

Abstract

In this paper we explore the functionalities of ET, a suite designed to support linguistic research and natural language processing tasks using corpora annotated in the CoNLL-U format. These goals are achieved by two integrated environments – Interrogatório, an environment for querying and editing annotated corpora, and Julgamento, an environment for assessing their quality. ET is open-source, built on different Python Web technologies and has Web demonstrations available on-line. ET has been intensively used in our research group for over two years, being the chosen framework for several linguistic and NLP-related studies conducted by its researchers.

1 Introduction

Annotated corpora are the basis for several natural language processing (NLP) tasks, serving as material from which machine learning systems learn how to perform linguistic analysis and as evaluating material against which system analyses can be confronted. However, manipulating annotated corpora is a costly activity for humans alone.

In this context, we present ET: a workstation for querying, editing and evaluating annotated corpora[1][2]. The underlying idea is to facilitate linguistic research using annotated corpora in the CoNLL-U format[3]. ET is composed of two integrated web-browser-based interfaces that are easily manipulated by non-developers at the same time that it provides tools to explore annotated texts driven by simple-to-build yet linguistically complex queries. The system main language is Portuguese but comes with English translation for the majority of its modules, it was built using different Python Web technologies and has Web demonstrations available on-line. One can use the available demonstration pages for working with small corpora or install a local copy[4].

ET has been intensively used in our research group for over two years, being the chosen framework for several linguistic and NLP-related studies conducted by its researchers. In section 2, we discuss other tools that inspired ET and how different it is from them. In section 3, we explore the interface for querying and editing annotated corpora, and in section 4 we demonstrate how to assess their quality using the workstation. Finally, in section 5, we outline some future perspectives for the tool.

2 Related tools

ET is a workstation that focuses on building quality corpora for Natural Language Processing, but not from scratch. Thus, it should not be confused with tools aimed at corpus annotation from raw pieces of text, such as Arborator (Gerdes, 2013), ConlluEditor (Heinecke, 2019) and UD Annotatrix (Tyers et al., 2017), nor with tools aimed at Corpus Linguistics studies, such as AntConc (Anthony, 2005) and CQPweb (Hardie, 2012).

From the point of view of text analysis tools, although ET query environment was largely inspired by AC/DC (Santos and Bick, 2000), from Linguateca (Santos, 2011) – one of the most important repositories for NLP in Portuguese –, AC/DC is based on an early version of CWB (Evert and Hardie, 2011), a robust and widely used processor capable of quickly and reliably processing corpora of millions of tokens, a task which ET does not propose to do with such high quality. The query-

[1] The workstation GitHub page and its live demonstration are available at http://comcorhd.letras.puc-rio.br/ET.

[2] The Portuguese term for workstation is "Estação de Trabalho" (lit. workstation), the reason why the suite was named "ET".

[3] The CoNLL-U format is used by the Universal Dependencies (Nivre et al., 2016) project. The format is described at: https://universaldependencies.org/format.html. Accessed on 5 jan. 2021.

[4] Only tested on Ubuntu distributions.

Proceedings of the 2021 Conference on Empirical Methods in Natural Language Processing: System Demonstrations, pages 35–41
November 7–11, 2021. ©2021 Association for Computational Linguistics

ing module from ET allows for querying syntactic dependencies in the Universal Dependencies format, sorting the results based on their annotation distribution, such as part-of-speech, morphological features and dependency labels distribution, and affords the addition of filters in order to further specify the query. In addition to the search tools, ET comprises both a manual and a rule-based treebank editing system that was inspired by AC/DC's *Corte e costura* (Mota and Santos, 2009), where the user codes linguistic rules that will search and correct annotation mistakes.

From the point of view of corpora annotation, tools like Arborator will suit better as they allow the editing of trees with features such as graphical editing and user management for collaborative annotation, which facilitate the process for annotators and project coordinators. What is different about ET, in turn, is the integration of the querying environment with evaluation methods to assess corpora that were previously annotated by humans or NLP systems. With the application of linguistic rules and the verification of inconsistent patterns, the tool makes it possible to linguistically guide the work of reviewing annotated corpora for NLP.

3 Querying and editing annotated corpora

Interrogatório (Portuguese word for "Interrogatory") is the name of the first of the two environments that compose ET. Its purpose is to make it easy for anyone to query and revise annotated corpora.

The system was built using Python CGI technology in the back-end and JQuery in the front-end. A server and a client machine are needed, but the same machine can work as both server and client, although installing and running a server-side will require intermediate technology skills. Installation steps and requirements are available in the workstation GitHub page.

Managing corpora The "Manage corpora" hub can be accessed from Interrogatório main menu on the top. This is where a new file is uploaded to the workstation. This file can be either a *.conllu* file, which already carries annotation, or a raw text in a *.txt* file. In the latter case, the text will be tokenized, tagged and parsed by UDPipe (Straka et al., 2016) using the models for Portuguese or

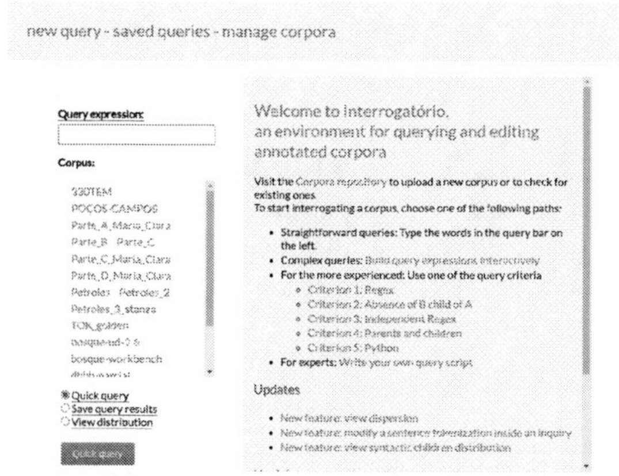

Figure 1: Interrogatório homepage. The main menu is on the top, a list of corpora is on the left, and the user guide is on the right.

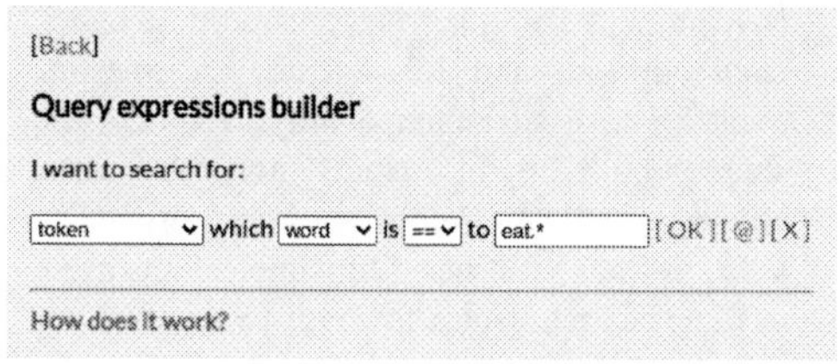

Figure 2: Query expression builder available on the Interrogatório homepage

English[5]. Once there are files in the repository, this page will present the number of sentences and tokens in each corpus.

Interrogating a corpus There are multiple ways one can interrogate a corpus and find sentences with specific annotation. The search criteria have been developed attending the needs of researchers – linguists – who used the workstation. Whenever a new search must be done and can not be easily achieved, a new query system can be built and documented by code. The current five search criteria are explained and exemplified in the homepage user guide (on the right, in Figure 1).

Since querying treebanks can be a complex task for beginners, Interrogatório comes with a "Query expressions builder", a GUI that helps the user when building query expressions by showing them the tags and relations between them in natural language (Figure 2). The intended search is then translated into the query syntax.

As a last resort, when a query is too complex and

[5]Such models were trained on Rademaker et al. (2017) and Silveira et al. (2014) for Portuguese and English, respectively

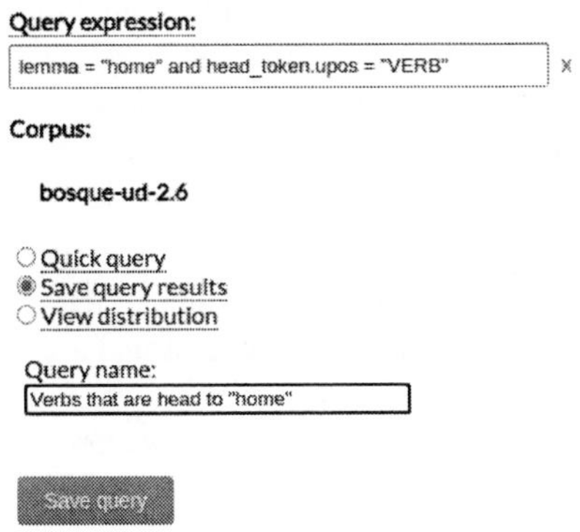

Figure 3: Users can save results for later analyses

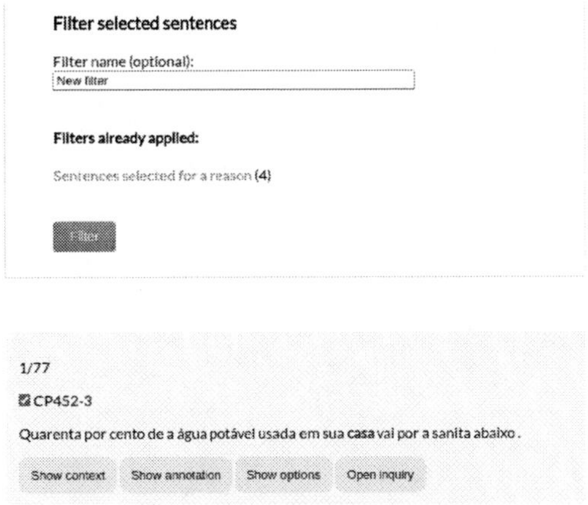

Figure 4: Filtering selected sentences

cannot be done by any of the implemented search criteria, Interrogatório will allow the user to write their own Python code to look for sentences following a given model by opening the menu "Write your own query script".

Saving a query Interrogatório will not make any previous indexation on corpora uploaded to the workstation, which is an architecture decision that makes queries slower – in comparison to systems that perform indexation – but that is what allows the dynamism needed for changing the corpus while being able to make queries in it real-time. The time it takes to complete a query will depend on the search criterion and the amount of results that the query returns. Thus, if the user intends to execute a query that returns too many results, it might be more efficient to save these results for later. They will be found on the page "saved queries".

Finding sentence information Returned sentences within a query are presented on the screen along with some visualization options. By clicking on the "Show context" button one can see the sentences before and after the sentence in focus. Besides, through the "Show annotation" button the user can see the annotation of the sentence, allowing them to understand how it is currently being analyzed and judge its quality.

Editing sentences Whenever a user finds a mistake in the annotation of a sentence, be it sporadic or in cases in which the query expression was meant to lead to errors that need correction, one can click "Open inquiry". An "inquiry" is a new tab with the annotated sentence displayed in a table, one token per line, ready to be edited. Options such as modifying the sentence segmentation are also available, making it possible to add or remove a token, split the sentence or join two different sentences using the GUI, leaving the difficult job of ensuring that the output format is correct to the machine.

Another possibility for changing sentence annotation automatically is by running a correction script. Once in the query results page one can navigate to the "Options" menu and select "Batch correction", where they will be able to download a model script for automatic correction. The script will then be edited by the user maintaining a Python syntax to both find the tokens that need to be changed and to assign them the new annotation. Once the script is uploaded back to Interrogatório, a page will simulate the changes so the user can decide whether the changes are as intended or not before applying them.

Filtering query results Once inside a saved query results page, the user is able to filter the results, separating sentences in different slots. The reasons for applying this are various:

- The same query can lead to different but related linguistic phenomena. Disentangling linguistic phenomena is a common task in research, and it is something that at times can only be done by reading each sentence inside a query results page. Keeping track of those sentences in different slots may facilitate linguists' work.
- The main query expression might not be fine-grained enough to find the phenomenon being studied, in which case there is the need of refining a query with other queries inside it.

Query: 5 "president."
Corpus: bosque-ud-2.6.conllu

Number of occurences: 162
Number of **deprel** diferentes: 11

deprel	frequency	in files
nsubj	56	52
appos	29	27
nmod	29	28
obj	13	13
obl	13	13
obl:agent	7	7
conj	6	6
acl:relcl	3	3
root	3	3
xcomp	2	1
iobj	1	1

Figure 5: Distribution of dependency relations for the query expression "president." in corpus Bosque-UD v2.6

- A user may want to apply a correction script to only a subset of sentences that are the results of a query, so filtering the sentences that should be automatically corrected and separating them from the main query is needed.

This feature was developed while looking for omitted subjects in different Portuguese corpora, a research that required complex queries that involved the absence of a tag in the sentence (the "subject" relation) and five further query specifications (filters) to remove sentences such as those without verbs and those whose main verbs express meteorological condition such as "to rain", "to snow" etc. (Freitas and de Souza, 2021)

Distribution of linguistic phenomena When a user executes a query they will see the sentences returned with the tokens being looked for in the query expression in bold. However, if one is not willing to read sentence by sentence but, instead, wants to see the distribution of any annotation for the words in bold, it is possible to view the distribution of their part-of-speech, dependency relation, features, lemma etc., as shown in Figure 5. This page can be accessed by clicking on the "Options" menu on the top of the screen and selecting "View distribution" or before executing a query selecting the same option in the homepage.

4 Evaluating annotated corpora

Julgamento (Portuguese word for "Judgment") is the name of the second of two environments that compose ET. Its purpose is to evaluate the quality of annotated corpora by different methods that search for inconsistencies in the annotation. Currently, Julgamento provides three methods that help to search for annotation inconsistencies – n-grams, linguistic rules and contrastive analysis – presented below.

The system was built using Python Flask framework technology in the back-end and JQuery in the front-end. Its installation process and architecture are the same as Interrogatório: a server and a client machine are needed, one for setting the system up and the other for the user to browse through the interfaces. Installation steps and requirements are available in the workstation GitHub page.

Managing corpora From the top menu in any screen one can have access to the "manage corpora" hub in Julgamento. Interrogatório and Julgamento are integrated[6], which means that whatever corpora are uploaded to one environment will also be accessible through the other, since the corpus file is the same.

Some of Julgamento's evaluation methods are based on the idea of contrastive analysis, which will require the user to upload a corpus with two different annotations (e.g. annotations provided by two different systems, two different human annotators or a gold-standard and a system counterpart), basing the evaluation on the confrontation of both. It is in this page that the user is able to upload the main corpus and its alternative annotation, that is, two different CoNLL-U files with the same sentences but different annotation.

Finding inconsistent n-grams This is a method for detecting inconsistencies in the annotation of a corpus uploaded to Julgamento. It is largely based on de Marneffe et al. (2017) method, although some important changes were applied and are still under test. The general idea is that hardly two dependency pairs with the same context and same lemmas will have different dependency relations, as in Figure 6, in which "António" and "Oliveira" are a dependency pair (*António* being the head) but have a different dependency relation in each sentence (*nmod* and *flat:name*), indicating an inconsistency that needs fixing. The method will display all the n-grams in the corpus that, although similar, have different relations, leaving it to the user

[6]Interrogatório must be installed in the same folder as Julgamento to make it possible to integrate them. To ensure that the integration is working, the "manage corpora" page on Interrogatório should present a large orange strip warning that "Interrogatório is integrated to Julgamento".

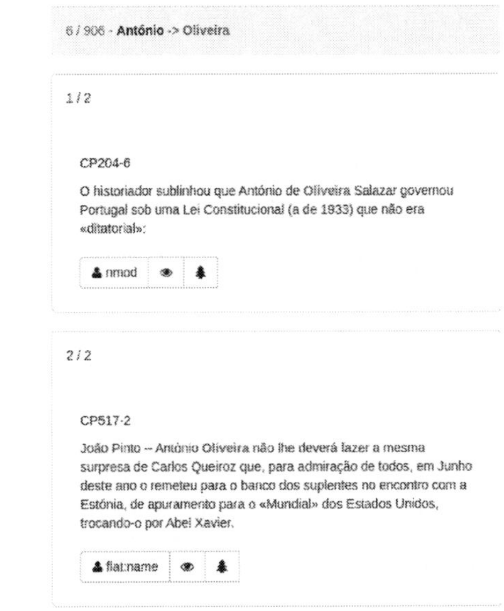

Figure 6: Inconsistent n-gram between two sentences (*António* and *Oliveira* are related by different tags in each sentence)

to judge whether they are wrongly annotated and giving them the ability to correct their annotation.

Checking for validation errors Two methods for checking validation errors in a corpus are available in Julgamento. One is the official Universal Dependencies project script for validating a new corpus[7], in which several rules will be applied to a CoNLL-U file to ensure that the format is correctly encoded and that basic points from UD annotation guidelines have not been skipped while annotating that corpus.

Another script was built by our team and focuses on Portuguese grammar rules that, when skipped, provide evidence of incorrect annotation or inconsistency. The rules were built using the same syntax from interrogating a corpus in Interrogatório (as discussed earlier) and can be edited[8] to conform to any project annotation guidelines.

Comparing corpora Other way of judging a corpus quality is by comparing two different annotations of the same sentences. These two annotations can be provided by two different systems, by two different human annotators or even by a gold-standard and a system counterpart, in which case the comparison will provide an evaluation of the system output. Once two annotations are uploaded to Julgamento, new methods will unlock:

- **Metrics from conll18_ud_eval.py**: This feature applies the evaluation metrics from the CoNLL 2018 Shared Task (Zeman et al., 2018) on the corpus to compare the second annotation to the first. The metrics encompass precision, recall and F1 of attributes such as tokenization, sentence segmentation, lemmatization, POS-tagging, the attachment of dependency relations etc.[9]
- **Sentences accuracy**: This feature presents how many sentences received exactly the same annotation in both versions of the corpus. Its relevance is based on a point that Manning (2011) makes – we usually assess quality by number of correct tokens, but a perhaps more difficult yet realistic way of assessing quality is by the number of totally correct sentences.
- **Accuracy per morphosyntactic category**: The "accuracy" for each part-of-speech tag and dependency relation are described through tables, as in Figure 7. Clicking on any dependency head attachment percentage will lead to a page where the user will find sentences in which a token is attached to different heads when comparing both versions of the corpus.
- **Confusion matrix**: CMs facilitate visualizing what are the most usual divergences in POS tags and dependency relations. In Figure 8, the diagonal line shows the number of tokens in which annotation both versions converged, whereas numbers out of this diagonal will show divergent analyses that could suggest inconsistencies in the training data when the alternative annotation was provided by a model trained on the corpus. Clicking any number will open a page listing the sentences with the focused token in bold where the user can judge which is the correct annotation and edit the sentence when needed.

[7]The script is named "validate.py", which can be called from the workstation interface. The returned sentences can be edited from inside it, as well. The source code is available at: `https://github.com/UniversalDependencies/tools`. Accessed on 5 jan. 2021.

[8]Rules can be edited from the file "validar_UD.txt".

[9]More information on the original evaluation methods can be found at: `https://universaldependencies.org/conll18/evaluation.html`. Accessed on 5 jan. 2021.

DEPREL	Total	Hits	LAS	DEPHEAD errors
_	744	100.0%	100.0%	0.0%
acl	117	82.05128205128204%	62.39316239316239%	19.65811965811966%
acl:relcl	118	85.59322033898306%	49.152542372881356%	36.440677966101696%
advcl	109	79.81651376146789%	55.04587155963303%	24.770642201834864%
advmod	327	93.88379204892966%	70.9480122324159%	22.935779816513760%
amod	369	89.15989159891599%	85.90785907859079%	3.2520325203252030%
appos	161	73.91304347826086%	54.037267080745345%	19.875776397515526%
aux	49	89.79591836734694%	89.79591836734694%	0.0%
aux:pass	60	91.66666666666666%	91.66666666666666%	0.0%
case	1476	98.6449864498645%	97.22222222222221%	1.4227642276422763%

Figure 7: Accuracy for some of the dependency relations when comparing two annotations for the same corpus

corpus 2 / corpus 1	ADJ	ADP	ADV	AUX	CCONJ	DET	NOUN	NUM	PRON	PROPN	PUNCT	SCONJ	SYM	VERB	X	_	All
ADJ	385	1	1	0	0	0	27	1	0	2	0	0	0	23	0	0	440
ADP	0	1513	4	0	0	5	0	0	0	1	0	6	0	0	0	0	1529
ADV	1	5	340	0	0	0	5	0	0	0	0	3	0	2	0	0	356
AUX	0	0	0	225	0	0	0	0	0	1	0	0	0	7	0	0	233
CCONJ	0	2	1	0	203	0	0	0	0	1	0	0	0	0	0	0	207
DET	1	1	8	0	0	1544	0	0	5	3	0	1	0	0	0	0	1560
NOUN	35	2	3	0	0	1	1982	1	0	25	0	0	0	12	0	0	2061
NUM	2	2	0	0	0	0	2	237	0	5	0	0	0	0	0	0	248
PRON	0	0	2	0	0	5	2	2	332	0	0	8	0	0	0	0	349
PROPN	5	0	2	0	0	0	38	1	0	822	0	0	0	3	0	0	871
PUNCT	0	0	0	0	0	0	0	0	0	0	1343	0	0	0	0	0	1343
SCONJ	0	16	9	0	0	1	0	0	8	0	0	193	0	0	0	0	218
SYM	0	0	0	0	0	0	0	0	0	0	0	0	30	0	0	0	30
VERB	10	0	1	5	0	0	8	0	0	3	0	0	0	883	0	0	911
X	1	1	0	0	0	0	8	1	0	17	0	0	0	0	2	0	30
_	0	0	0	0	0	0	0	0	0	0	0	0	0	0	0	744	744
All	440	1537	386	231	203	1556	2072	245	345	880	1343	206	30	930	2	744	11130

Figure 8: Confusion matrix portraying divergences in POS annotation

5 Concluding remarks

In this paper we presented ET, a Workstation for Querying, Editing and Evaluating Annotated Corpora. Its aims are to facilitate linguistic research and evaluate annotated corpora in the CoNLL-U format, reuniting functionalities that are not new ideas along with innovative ways of characterizing and judging annotated corpora. Both Interrogatório and Julgamento, integrated parts of the workstation, are available on-line in the project GitHub page for download and usage, as well as a live demonstration which does not need previous installation.

Although ET is not to be confused with corpus analysis tools and corpora annotation tools alone, the workstation can benefit from features of both kinds of tools. In the future, thus, it is possible to expand its functionalities so it will work as both kinds of tools as well, increasing the range of tools available to the user without leaving the workstation.

Acknowledgments

We would like to thank Luísa Rocha, who assisted in the conception of the system in its very initial steps, and Aline Silveira, Tatiana Cavalcanti, Maria Clara Castro and Wograine Evelyn, who have chosen the workstation as main framework for their linguistic research and daily work in various projects, challenging the tool to fit their (computational) linguistic needs. Elvis de Souza thanks the National Council for Scientific and Technological Development (CNPq) for the Masters scholarship grant number 130495/2021-2.

References

Laurence Anthony. 2005. Antconc: design and development of a freeware corpus analysis toolkit for the technical writing classroom. In *IPCC 2005. Proceedings. International Professional Communication Conference, 2005.*, pages 729–737. IEEE.

Marie-Catherine de Marneffe, Matias Grioni, Jenna Kanerva, and Filip Ginter. 2017. Assessing the annotation consistency of the universal dependencies corpora. In *Proceedings of the Fourth International Conference on Dependency Linguistics (Depling 2017)*, pages 108–115.

Stefan Evert and Andrew Hardie. 2011. Twenty-first century corpus workbench: Updating a query architecture for the new millennium.

Cláudia Freitas and Elvis de Souza. 2021. Sujeito oculto às claras: uma abordagem descritivo-computacional/omitted subjects revealed: a quantitative-descriptive approach. *REVISTA DE ESTUDOS DA LINGUAGEM*.

Kim Gerdes. 2013. Collaborative dependency annotation. In *Proceedings of the second international conference on dependency linguistics (DepLing 2013)*, pages 88–97.

Andrew Hardie. 2012. Cqpweb—combining power, flexibility and usability in a corpus analysis tool. *International journal of corpus linguistics*, 17(3):380–409.

Johannes Heinecke. 2019. Conllueditor: a fully graphical editor for universal dependencies treebank files. In *Proceedings of the Third Workshop on Universal Dependencies (UDW, SyntaxFest 2019)*, pages 87–93.

Christopher D Manning. 2011. Part-of-speech tagging from 97% to 100%: is it time for some linguistics? In *International conference on intelligent text processing and computational linguistics*, pages 171–189. Springer.

Cristina Mota and Diana Santos. 2009. Corte e costura no ac/dc: auxiliando a melhoria da anotação nos corpos.

Joakim Nivre, Marie-Catherine De Marneffe, Filip Ginter, Yoav Goldberg, Jan Hajic, Christopher D Manning, Ryan McDonald, Slav Petrov, Sampo Pyysalo, Natalia Silveira, et al. 2016. Universal dependencies v1: A multilingual treebank collection. In *Proceedings of the Tenth International Conference on Language Resources and Evaluation (LREC'16)*, pages 1659–1666.

Alexandre Rademaker, Fabricio Chalub, Livy Real, Cláudia Freitas, Eckhard Bick, and Valeria de Paiva. 2017. Universal dependencies for portuguese. In *Proceedings of the Fourth International Conference on Dependency Linguistics (Depling 2017)*, pages 197–206.

Diana Santos. 2011. Linguateca's infrastructure for portuguese and how it allows the detailed study of language varieties. *OSLa: Oslo Studies in Language 32 (2011) ISSN: 18909639 Volume edited by J.B.Johannessen*.

Diana Santos and Eckhard Bick. 2000. Providing internet access to portuguese corpora: the ac/dc project. In *Maria Gavrilidou; George Carayannis; Stella Markantonatou; Stelios Piperidis; Gregory Stainhauer (ed) Proceedings of the Second International Conference on Language Resources and Evaluation (LREC 2000)(Athens 31 May-2 June 2000)*.

Natalia Silveira, Timothy Dozat, Marie-Catherine de Marneffe, Samuel Bowman, Miriam Connor, John Bauer, and Christopher D. Manning. 2014. A gold standard dependency corpus for English. In *Proceedings of the Ninth International Conference on Language Resources and Evaluation (LREC-2014)*.

Milan Straka, Jan Hajic, and Jana Straková. 2016. Udpipe: trainable pipeline for processing conll-u files performing tokenization, morphological analysis, pos tagging and parsing. In *Proceedings of the Tenth International Conference on Language Resources and Evaluation (LREC'16)*, pages 4290–4297.

Francis Tyers, Mariya Sheyanova, and Jonathan Washington. 2017. Ud annotatrix: An annotation tool for universal dependencies. In *Proceedings of the 16th International Workshop on Treebanks and Linguistic Theories*, pages 10–17.

Daniel Zeman, Jan Hajic, Martin Popel, Martin Potthast, Milan Straka, Filip Ginter, Joakim Nivre, and Slav Petrov. 2018. Conll 2018 shared task: Multilingual parsing from raw text to universal dependencies. In *Proceedings of the CoNLL 2018 Shared Task: Multilingual parsing from raw text to universal dependencies*, pages 1–21.

N-LTP: An Open-source Neural Language Technology Platform for Chinese

Wanxiang Che, Yunlong Feng, Libo Qin, Ting Liu
Research Center for Social Computing and Information Retrieval
Harbin Institute of Technology, China
{car,ylfeng,lbqin,tliu}@ir.hit.edu.cn

Abstract

We introduce N-LTP, an open-source neural language technology platform supporting six fundamental Chinese NLP tasks: lexical analysis (Chinese word segmentation, part-of-speech tagging, and named entity recognition), syntactic parsing (dependency parsing), and semantic parsing (semantic dependency parsing and semantic role labeling). Unlike the existing state-of-the-art toolkits, such as Stanza, that adopt an independent model for each task, N-LTP adopts the multi-task framework by using a shared pre-trained model, which has the advantage of capturing the shared knowledge across relevant Chinese tasks. In addition, a knowledge distillation method (Clark et al., 2019) where the single-task model teaches the multi-task model is further introduced to encourage the multi-task model to surpass its single-task teacher. Finally, we provide a collection of easy-to-use APIs and a visualization tool to make users to use and view the processing results more easily and directly. To the best of our knowledge, this is the first toolkit to support six Chinese NLP fundamental tasks. Source code, documentation, and pre-trained models are available at https://github.com/HIT-SCIR/ltp.

1 Introduction

There is a wide of range of existing natural language processing (NLP) toolkits such as CoreNLP (Manning et al., 2014), UDPipe (Straka and Straková, 2017), FLAIR (Akbik et al., 2019), spaCy,[1] and Stanza (Qi et al., 2020) in English, which makes it easier for users to build tools with sophisticated linguistic processing. Recently, the need for Chinese NLP has a dramatic increase in many downstream applications. A Chinese NLP platform usually includes lexical analysis (Chinese word segmentation (CWS), part-of-speech (POS) tagging, and named entity recognition (NER)), syntactic parsing (dependency parsing (DEP)), and semantic parsing (semantic dependency parsing (SDP) and semantic role labeling (SRL)). Unfortunately, there are relatively fewer high-performance and high-efficiency toolkits for Chinese NLP tasks. To fill this gap, it's important to build a Chinese NLP toolkit to support rich Chinese fundamental NLP tasks, and make researchers process NLP tasks in Chinese quickly.

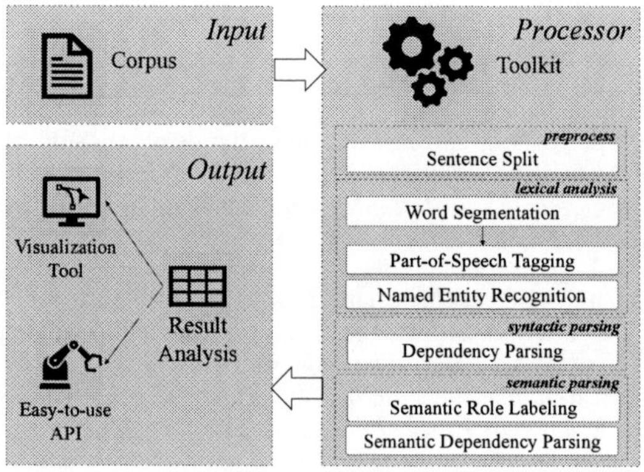

Figure 1: Workflow of the N-LTP. N-LTP takes the Chinese corpus as input and output the analysis results including lexical analysis, syntactic parsing, and semantic parsing. In addition, we provide the visualization tool and easy-to-use API to help users easily use N-LTP.

Recently, Qi et al. (2020) introduce the Python NLP toolkit Stanza for multi-lingual languages, including Chinese language. Though Stanza can be directly applied for processing the Chinese texts, it suffers from several limitations. First, it only supports part of Chinese NLP tasks. For example, it fails to handle semantic parsing analysis, resulting in incomplete analysis in Chinese NLP. Second, it trained each task separately, ignoring the shared knowledge across the related tasks, which has been proven effective for Chinese NLP tasks (Qian et al., 2015; Hsieh et al., 2017; Chang et al., 2018). Third, independent modeling method will occupy more

[1] https://spacy.io

Proceedings of the 2021 Conference on Empirical Methods in Natural Language Processing: System Demonstrations, pages 42–49
November 7–11, 2021.

System	Programming Language	Fully Neural	State-of-the-art Performance	Rich Chinese Fundamental Tasks	Multi-task Learning
LTP (Che et al., 2010)	C++			√	
UDPipe (Straka and Straková, 2017)	C++		√		
FLAIR (Akbik et al., 2019)	Python	√	√		
Stanza (Qi et al., 2020)	Python	√	√		
N-LTP	Python	√	√	√	√

Table 1: Feature comparisons of N-LTP against other popular natural language processing toolkits.

memory with the increase of the number of tasks, which makes it hard to deploy for mobile devices in real-word scenario.

To address the aforementioned issues, we introduce N-LTP, a PyTorch-based neural natural language processing toolkit for Chinese NLP, which was built on the SOTA pre-trained model. As shown in Figure 1, given Chinese corpus as input, N-LTP produces comprehensive analysis results, including lexical analysis, syntactic parsing, and semantic parsing. In addition, N-LTP provides easy-to-use APIs and visualization tool, which is user-friendly.

As shown in Table 1, compared to the existing widely-used NLP toolkits, N-LTP has the following advantages:

- **Comprehensive Tasks.** N-LTP supports rich Chinese fundamental NLP tasks including lexical analysis (word segmentation, part-of-speech tagging, named entity recognition), syntactic parsing, and semantic parsing (semantic dependency parsing, semantic role labeling). To the best of our knowledge, this is the first neural Chinese toolkit that support six Chinese fundamental NLP tasks.

- **Multi-Task Learning.** The existing NLP toolkits for the Chinese language all adopt independent models for each task, which ignore the shared knowledge across tasks.

  To alleviate this issue, we propose to use the multi-task framework (Collobert et al., 2011) to take advantage of the shared knowledge across all tasks. Meanwhile, multi-task learning with a shared encoder for all six tasks can greatly reduce the occupied memory and improve the speed, which makes N-LTP more efficient, reducing the need for hardware.

  In addition, to enable the multi-task learning to enhance each subtask performance, we follow Clark et al. (2019) to adopt the distillation method single-task models teach a multi-task model, helping the multi-task model surpass its all single-task teachers.

- **Extensibility.** N-LTP works with users' custom modules. Users can easily add a new pre-trained model with a configuration file, in which users can change the pretrained model to any BERT-like model supported by HuggingFace Transformers (Wolf et al., 2019) easily by changing the config. We have made all task training configuration files open-sourced.

- **Easy-to-use API and Visualization Tool.** N-LTP provides a collection of fundamental APIs, which is convenient for users to use the toolkit without the need for any knowledge. We also provide a visualization tool, which enables users to view the processing results directly. In addition, N-LTP has bindings for many programming languages (C++, Python, Java, Rust, etc.).

- **State-of-the-art Performance.** We evaluate N-LTP on a total of six Chinese NLP tasks, and find that it achieves state-of-the-art or competitive performance at each task.

N-LTP is fully open-sourced and can support six Chinese fundamental NLP tasks. We hope N-LTP can facilitate Chinese NLP research.

2 Design and Architecture

Figure 2 shows an overview of the main architecture of N-LTP. It mainly consists of the components including a shared encoder and different decoders for each task. Our framework shares one encoder for leveraging the shared knowledge across all tasks. Different task decoders are used for each task separately. All tasks are optimized simultaneously via a joint learning scheme. In addition, the knowledge distillation technique is introduced to encourage the multi-task model to surpass its single-task teacher model.

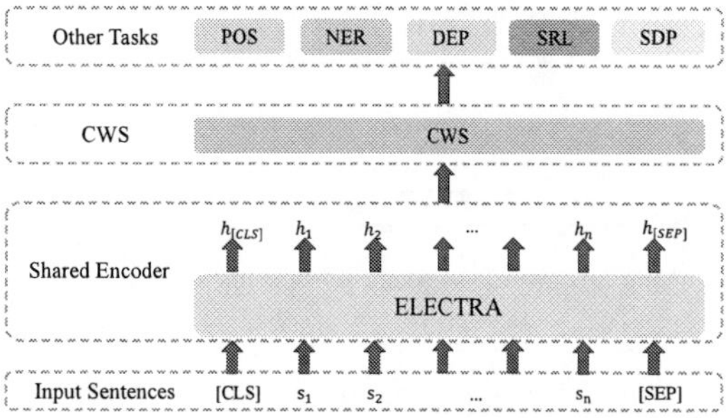

Figure 2: The architecture of the proposed model.

2.1 Shared Encoder

Multi-task framework uses a shared encoder to extract the shared knowledge across related tasks, which has obtained remarkable success on various NLP tasks (Qin et al., 2019; Wang et al., 2020; Zhou et al., 2021). Inspired by this, we adopt the SOTA pre-trained model (ELECTRA) (Clark et al., 2020) as the shared encoder to capture shared knowledge across six Chinese tasks.

Given an input utterance $s = (s_1, s_2, \ldots, s_n)$, we first construct the input sequence by adding specific tokens $s = (\texttt{[CLS]}, s_1, s_2, \ldots, s_n, \texttt{[SEP]})$, where `[CLS]` is the special symbol for representing the whole sequence, and `[SEP]` is the special symbol to separate non-consecutive token sequences (Devlin et al., 2019). ELECTRA takes the constructed input and output the corresponding hidden representations of sequence $\boldsymbol{H} = (\boldsymbol{h}_{\texttt{[CLS]}}, \boldsymbol{h}_1, \boldsymbol{h}_2, \ldots, \boldsymbol{h}_n, \boldsymbol{h}_{\texttt{[SEP]}})$.

2.2 Chinese Word Segmentation

Chinese word segmentation (CWS) is a preliminary and important task for Chinese natural language processing (NLP). In `N-LTP`, following Xue (2003), CWS is regarded as a character based sequence labeling problem.

Specifically, given the hidden representations $\boldsymbol{H} = (\boldsymbol{h}_{\texttt{[CLS]}}, \boldsymbol{h}_1, \boldsymbol{h}_2, \ldots, \boldsymbol{h}_n, \boldsymbol{h}_{\texttt{[SEP]}})$, we adopt a linear decoder to classify each character:

$$\boldsymbol{y}_i = \text{Softmax}(\boldsymbol{W}_{\text{CWS}} \boldsymbol{h}_i + \boldsymbol{b}_{\text{CWS}}), \quad (1)$$

where $\boldsymbol{y}_i$ denotes the label probability distribution of each character; $\boldsymbol{W}_{\text{CWS}}$ and $\boldsymbol{b}_{\text{CWS}}$ are trainable parameters.

2.3 POS Tagging

Part-of-speech (POS) tagging is another fundamental NLP task, which can facilitate the downstream tasks such as syntactic parsing. Following the dominant model in the literature (Ratnaparkhi, 1996; Huang et al., 2015), POS tagging can be treated as a sequence labeling task.

Similar to CWS, we take the sequence of hidden representations $\boldsymbol{H}$ as input and output the corresponding POS sequence labels, which is formulated as:

$$\boldsymbol{y}_i = \text{Softmax}(\boldsymbol{W}_{\text{POS}} \boldsymbol{h}_i + \boldsymbol{b}_{\text{POS}}), \quad (2)$$

where $\boldsymbol{y}_i$ denotes the POS label probability distribution of the i-th character; $\boldsymbol{h}_i$ is the first sub-token representation of word s_i.

2.4 Named Entity Recognition

The named entity recognition (NER) is the task of finding the start and end of an entity (`people`, `locations`, `organizations`, etc.) in a sentence and assigning a class for this entity.

Traditional, NER is regarded as a sequence labeling task. After obtaining the hidden representations $\boldsymbol{H}$, we follow Yan et al. (2019a) to adopt the `Adapted-Transformer` to consider direction- and distance-aware characteristic, which can be formulated as:

$$\hat{\boldsymbol{h}_i} = \text{AdaptedTransformer}(\boldsymbol{h}_i), \quad (3)$$

where $\hat{\boldsymbol{H}} = (\hat{\boldsymbol{h}}_{\texttt{[CLS]}}, \hat{\boldsymbol{h}}_1, \hat{\boldsymbol{h}}_2, \ldots, \hat{\boldsymbol{h}}_n, \hat{\boldsymbol{h}}_{\texttt{[SEP]}})$ are the updated representations.

Finally, similar to CWS and POS, we use a linear decoder to classify label for each word:

$$\boldsymbol{y}_i = \text{Softmax}(\boldsymbol{W}_{\text{NER}} \hat{\boldsymbol{h}_i} + \boldsymbol{b}_{\text{NER}}), \quad (4)$$

where $\boldsymbol{y}_i$ denotes the NER label probability distribution of each character.

2.5 Dependency Parsing

Dependency parsing is the task to analyze the semantic structure of a sentence. In `N-LTP`, we implement a deep biaffine neural dependency parser (Dozat and Manning, 2017) and einser algorithm (Eisner, 1996) to obtain the parsing result, which is formulated as:

$$\begin{aligned} \boldsymbol{r}_i^{(\text{head})} &= \text{MLP}^{(\text{head})}(\boldsymbol{h}_i) \\ \boldsymbol{r}_j^{(\text{dep})} &= \text{MLP}^{(\text{dep})}(\boldsymbol{h}_j) \end{aligned} \quad (5)$$

After obtaining $\boldsymbol{r}_i^{(\text{head})}$ and $\boldsymbol{r}_j^{(\text{dep})}$, we compute the score for each dependency $i \frown j$ by:

$$\boldsymbol{y}_{i \frown j} = \text{BiAffine}(\boldsymbol{r}_i^{\text{dep}}, \boldsymbol{r}_j^{\text{head}}). \quad (6)$$

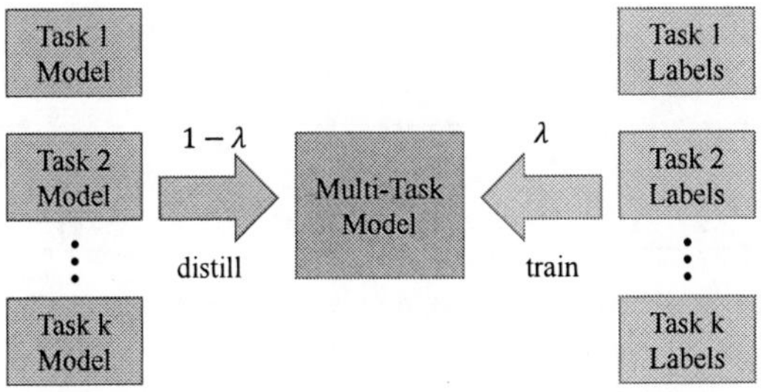

Figure 3: We follow Clark et al. (2019) to adopt the distillation method. This is an overview of the distillation method. λ is increased linearly from 0 to 1 over the curriculum of training.

The above process is also used for scoring a labeled dependency $i \overset{l}{\frown} j$, by extending the 1-dim vector $\boldsymbol{s}$ into L dims, where L is the total number of dependency labels.

2.6 Semantic Dependency Parsing

Similar to dependency parsing, semantic dependency parsing (Che et al., 2012, SDP) is a task to capture the semantic structure of a sentence. Specifically, given an input sentence, SDP aims at determining all the word pairs related to each other semantically and assigning specific predefined semantic relations. Following Dozat and Manning (2017), we adopt a biaffine module to perform the task, using

$$\boldsymbol{p}_{i \frown j} = \mathrm{sigmoid}(\boldsymbol{y}_{i \frown j}). \tag{7}$$

If $\boldsymbol{p}_{i \frown j} > 0.5$, word$_i$ to word$_j$ exists an edge.

2.7 Semantic Role Labeling

Semantic Role Labeling (SRL) is the task of determining the latent predicate-argument structure of a sentence, which can provide representations to answer basic questions about sentence meaning, including who did what to whom, etc. We adopt an end-to-end SRL model by combining a deep biaffine neural network and a conditional random field (CRF)-based decoder (Cai et al., 2018).

The biaffine module is similar to Section 2.5 and the CRF layer can be formulated as:

$$P(\hat{y}|s) = \frac{\sum_{j=1} \exp f(y_{i,j-1}, y_{i,j}, s)}{\sum_{y'_i} \sum_{j=1} \exp f(y'_{i,j-1}, y'_{i,j}, s)} \tag{8}$$

where $\hat{y}$ represents an arbitrary label sequence when predicate is s_i, and $f(y_{i,j-1}, y_j, s)$ computes the transition score from $y_{i,j-1}$ to $y_{i,j}$.

```
from ltp import LTP
ltp = LTP()
seg, hidden = ltp.seg(["他叫汤姆去拿外衣。"])
pos = ltp.pos(hidden)
ner = ltp.ner(hidden)
srl = ltp.srl(hidden)
dep = ltp.dep(hidden)
sdp = ltp.sdp(hidden)
```

Figure 4: A minimal code snippet.

2.8 Knowledge Distillation

When there exist a large number of tasks, it's difficult to ensure that each task task benefits from multi-task learning (Clark et al., 2019).

Therefore, we follow BAM (Clark et al., 2019) to use the knowledge distillation to alleviate this issue, which is shown Figure 3. First, we train each task as the teacher model. Then, `N-LTP` learns from each trained single-task teacher model while learning from the gold-standard labels simultaneously.

Following BAM (Clark et al., 2019), we adopt teacher annealing distillation algorithm. More specifically, instead of simply shuffling the datasets for our multi-task models, we follow the task sampling procedure from Bowman et al. (2018), where the probability of training on an example for a particular task τ is proportional to $|D_\mathcal{T}|^{0.75}$. This ensures that tasks with large datasets don't overly dominate the training.

3 Usage

`N-LTP` is a PyTorch-based Chinese NLP toolkit based on the above model. All the configurations can be initialized from JSON files, and thus it is easy for users to use `N-LTP` where users just need one line of code to load the model or process the input sentences. Specifically, `N-LTP` can be installed easily by the command:

```
$ pip install ltp
```

In addition, `N-LTP` has bindings available for many programming languages, including C++, Python, Java and RUST directly.

3.1 Easy-to-use API

We provide rich easy-to-use APIs, which enables users to easily use without the need for any knowledge. The following code snippet in Figure 4 shows

Model	Chinese Word Segmentation F	Part-of-Speech Tagging F_{LAS}	Named Entity Recognition F	Dependency Parsing F	Semantic Dependency Parsing F	Semantic Role Labeling F
Stanza (Qi et al., 2020)	92.40	98.10	89.50	84.98	-	-
N-LTP trained separately	98.55	98.35	95.41	90.12	74.47	79.23
N-LTP trained jointly with distillation	**99.18**	**98.69**	**95.97**	**90.19**	**76.62**	**79.49**

Table 2: Main Results. "-" represents the absence of tasks in the Stanza toolkit and we cannot report the results.

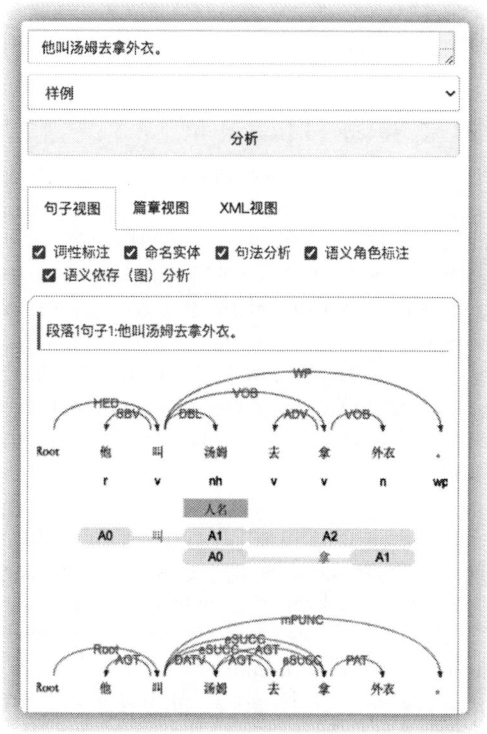

Figure 5: LTP annotates a Chinese sentence "他叫汤姆去拿外衣。/ He told Tom to get his coat.". The output is visualized by our visualization demo.

a minimal usage of N-LTP for downloading models, annotating a sentence with customized models, and predicting all annotations.

3.2 Visualization Tool

In addition, a visualization tool is proposed for users to view the processing results directly. Specifically, we build an interactive web demo that runs the pipeline interactively, which is publicly available at http://ltp.ai/demo.html. The visualization tool is shown in Figure 5.

4 Experiments

4.1 Experimental Setting

To evaluate the efficiency of our multi-task model, we conduct experiments on six Chinese tasks.

The N-LTP model is based on the Chinese ELECTRA base (Cui et al., 2020). The learning ratio (lr) for teacher models, student model and CRF layer is $\{1e-4\}$, $\{1e-4\}$, $\{1e-3\}$, respectively. The gradient clip value adopted in our experiment is 1.0 and the warmup proportion is 0.02. We use BertAdam (Devlin et al., 2019) to optimize the parameters and adopted the suggested hyper-parameters for optimization.

4.2 Results

We compare N-LTP with the state-of-the-art toolkit Stanza. For a fair comparison, we conduct experiments on the same datasets that Stanza adopted.

The results are shown in Table 2, we have the following observations:

- N-LTP outperforms *Stanza* on four common tasks including CWS, POS, NER, and DEP by a large margin, which shows the superiority of our proposed toolkit.

- The multi-task learning outperforms the model with independently trained. This is because that the multi-task framework can consider the shared knowledge which can promote each task compared with the independently training paradigm.

4.3 Analysis

4.3.1 Speedup and Memory Reduction

In this section, we perform the speed and memory test on the Tesla V100-SXM2-16GB and all models were speed-tested on the 10,000 sentences of the People's Daily corpus with a batch size of 8. In all experiments, N-LTP performs six tasks (CWS, POS, NER, DEP, SDP, SRL) while Stanza only conduct four tasks (CWS, POS, NER, DEP).

[2] 10 corpus for training CWS task includes PKU, MSR, AS, CITYU, XU, CTB, UDC, CNC, WTB and ZX.

[3] http://ir.hit.edu.cn/sdp2020ccl

Task	Model	Dataset	Metric	State-of-the-art Performance	N-LTP trained separately	N-LTP trained jointly
CWS	BERT (Huang et al., 2019)	10 Corpus[2]	F1	97.10	97.42	**97.50**
POS	Glyce+BERT (Meng et al., 2019)	CTB9	F1	93.15	94.57	**95.17**
NER	ZEN (Diao et al., 2020)	MSRA	F1	95.25	94.95	**95.78**
NER	DGLSTM-CRF (Jie and Lu, 2019)	OntoNotes	F1	79.92	84.08	**84.38**
SRL	BiLSTM-Span (Ouchi et al., 2018)	CONLL12	F1	75.75	78.20	**81.65**
DEP	Joint-Multi-BERT (Yan et al., 2019b)	CTB9	$F1_{LAS}$	81.71	81.69	**84.03**
SDP	SuPar[3]	CCL2020[4]	$F1_{LAS}$	**80.38**	76.27	75.76

Table 3: The results of N-LTP comparation to other state-of-the-art performance..

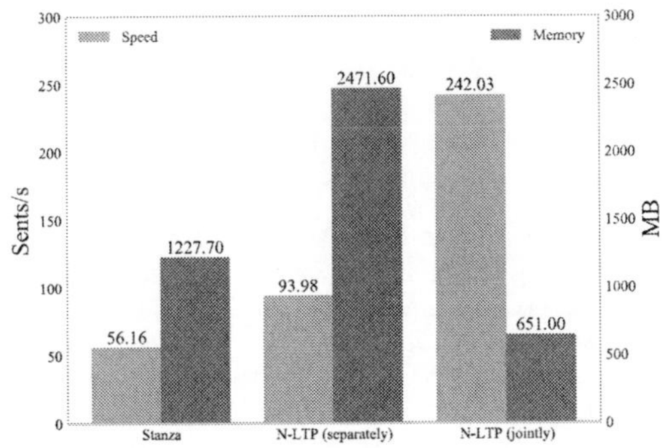

Figure 6: Speed and Memory test for N-LTP.

Speedup We compare the speed between Stanza, N-LTP-separately and N-LTP-jointly and the results are shown in Figure 6. From the results of speed test, we have two interesting observations: (1) N-LTP trained separately achieves the x1.7 speedup compared with Stanza. We attribute that N-LTP adopts the transformer as an encoder that can be calculated in parallel while Stanza uses LSTM which can only process sentences word by word; (2) N-LTP trained jointly with distillation obtains the x4.3 speedup compared with separate modeling paradigm. This is because that our model utilizes the multi-task to perform all tasks while the independent models can be only processed all tasks in a pipeline mode.

Memory Reduction For memory test, we have the following observation: (1) N-LTP trained separately occupy more memory than Stanza. This is because N-LTP performs six tasks while Stanza only conduct four tasks. (2) Though performing six tasks, N-LTP trained jointly only requires half the memory compared to Stanza. We attribute it to the fact that the multi-task framework with a shared encoder can greatly reduce the running memory.

4.3.2 Comparation with Other SOTA Single Models

To further verify the effectiveness of N-LTP, we compare our framework with the existing state-of-the-art single models on six Chinese fundamental tasks. In this comparison, we conduct experiments on the same wildly-used dataset in each task for a fair comparison. In addition, we use BERT rather than ELECTRA as the shared encoder, because the prior work adopts BERT.

Table 3 shows the results, we observe that our framework obtains best performance on five out of six tasks including CWS, POS, NER, SRL, and DEP, which demonstrates the effectiveness of our framework. On the SDP task, N-LTP underperforms the best baseline. This is because many tricks are used in the prior model for SDP task and we just use the basic multi-task framework.

5 Conclusion

In this paper, we presented N-LTP, an open-source neural language technology platform supporting Chinese. To the best of our knowledge, this is the first Chinese toolkit that supports six fundamental Chinese NLP tasks. Experimental results show N-LTP obtains state-of-the-art or competitive performance and has high speed. We hope N-LTP can facilitate Chinese NLP research.

Acknowledgements

We thank the anonymous reviewers for their detailed and constructive comments. The first three authors contributed equally. Wanxiang Che is the corresponding author. This work was supported by the National Key R&D Program of China via grant 2020AAA0106501 and the National Natural Science Foundation of China (NSFC) via grant 61976072 and 61772153. Libo is also supported by the Zhejiang Lab's International Talent Fund for Young Professionals.

References

Alan Akbik, Tanja Bergmann, Duncan Blythe, Kashif Rasul, Stefan Schweter, and Roland Vollgraf. 2019. FLAIR: An easy-to-use framework for state-of-the-art NLP. In *Proceedings of the 2019 Conference of the North American Chapter of the Association for Computational Linguistics (Demonstrations)*, pages 54–59, Minneapolis, Minnesota. Association for Computational Linguistics.

Samuel R. Bowman, Ellie Pavlick, Edouard Grave, Benjamin Van Durme, Alex Wang, Jan Hula, Patrick Xia, Raghavendra Pappagari, R. Thomas McCoy, Roma Patel, Najoung Kim, Ian Tenney, Yinghui Huang, Katherin Yu, Shuning Jin, and Berlin Chen. 2018. Looking for elmo's friends: Sentence-level pretraining beyond language modeling. *CoRR*, abs/1812.10860.

Jiaxun Cai, Shexia He, Zuchao Li, and Hai Zhao. 2018. A full end-to-end semantic role labeler, syntactic-agnostic over syntactic-aware? In *Proceedings of the 27th International Conference on Computational Linguistics*, pages 2753–2765, Santa Fe, New Mexico, USA. Association for Computational Linguistics.

Yung-Chun Chang, Fang Yi Lee, and Chun Hung Chen. 2018. A public opinion keyword vector for social sentiment analysis research. In *2018 Tenth International Conference on Advanced Computational Intelligence (ICACI)*, pages 752–757. IEEE.

Wanxiang Che, Zhenghua Li, and Ting Liu. 2010. LTP: A Chinese language technology platform. In *Coling 2010: Demonstrations*, pages 13–16, Beijing, China. Coling 2010 Organizing Committee.

Wanxiang Che, Meishan Zhang, Yanqiu Shao, and Ting Liu. 2012. SemEval-2012 task 5: Chinese semantic dependency parsing. In **SEM 2012: The First Joint Conference on Lexical and Computational Semantics – Volume 1: Proceedings of the main conference and the shared task, and Volume 2: Proceedings of the Sixth International Workshop on Semantic Evaluation (SemEval 2012)*, pages 378–384, Montréal, Canada. Association for Computational Linguistics.

Kevin Clark, Minh-Thang Luong, Urvashi Khandelwal, Christopher D. Manning, and Quoc V. Le. 2019. BAM! born-again multi-task networks for natural language understanding. In *Proceedings of the 57th Annual Meeting of the Association for Computational Linguistics*, pages 5931–5937, Florence, Italy. Association for Computational Linguistics.

Kevin Clark, Minh-Thang Luong, Quoc V. Le, and Christopher D. Manning. 2020. ELECTRA: pre-training text encoders as discriminators rather than generators. In *8th International Conference on Learning Representations, ICLR 2020, Addis Ababa, Ethiopia, April 26-30, 2020*. OpenReview.net.

Ronan Collobert, Jason Weston, Léon Bottou, Michael Karlen, Koray Kavukcuoglu, and Pavel Kuksa. 2011. Natural language processing (almost) from scratch. *Journal of machine learning research*, 12(ARTICLE):2493–2537.

Yiming Cui, Wanxiang Che, Ting Liu, Bing Qin, Shijin Wang, and Guoping Hu. 2020. Revisiting pre-trained models for Chinese natural language processing. In *Findings of the Association for Computational Linguistics: EMNLP 2020*, pages 657–668, Online. Association for Computational Linguistics.

Jacob Devlin, Ming-Wei Chang, Kenton Lee, and Kristina Toutanova. 2019. BERT: Pre-training of deep bidirectional transformers for language understanding. In *Proceedings of the 2019 Conference of the North American Chapter of the Association for Computational Linguistics: Human Language Technologies, Volume 1 (Long and Short Papers)*, pages 4171–4186, Minneapolis, Minnesota. Association for Computational Linguistics.

Shizhe Diao, Jiaxin Bai, Yan Song, Tong Zhang, and Yonggang Wang. 2020. ZEN: Pre-training Chinese text encoder enhanced by n-gram representations. In *Findings of the Association for Computational Linguistics: EMNLP 2020*, pages 4729–4740, Online. Association for Computational Linguistics.

Timothy Dozat and Christopher D. Manning. 2017. Deep biaffine attention for neural dependency parsing. In *5th International Conference on Learning Representations, ICLR 2017, Toulon, France, April 24-26, 2017, Conference Track Proceedings*. OpenReview.net.

Jason M. Eisner. 1996. Three new probabilistic models for dependency parsing: An exploration. In *COLING 1996 Volume 1: The 16th International Conference on Computational Linguistics*.

Yu-Lun Hsieh, Yung-Chun Chang, Yi-Jie Huang, Shu-Hao Yeh, Chun-Hung Chen, and Wen-Lian Hsu. 2017. MONPA: Multi-objective named-entity and part-of-speech annotator for Chinese using recurrent neural network. In *Proceedings of the Eighth International Joint Conference on Natural Language Processing (Volume 2: Short Papers)*, pages 80–85, Taipei, Taiwan. Asian Federation of Natural Language Processing.

Weipeng Huang, Xingyi Cheng, Kunlong Chen, Taifeng Wang, and Wei Chu. 2019. Toward fast and accurate neural chinese word segmentation with multi-criteria learning. *CoRR*, abs/1903.04190.

Zhiheng Huang, Wei Xu, and Kai Yu. 2015. Bidirectional LSTM-CRF models for sequence tagging. *CoRR*, abs/1508.01991.

Zhanming Jie and Wei Lu. 2019. Dependency-guided LSTM-CRF for named entity recognition. In *Proceedings of the 2019 Conference on Empirical Methods in Natural Language Processing and the 9th International Joint Conference on Natural Language Processing (EMNLP-IJCNLP)*, pages 3862–3872, Hong Kong, China. Association for Computational Linguistics.

Christopher Manning, Mihai Surdeanu, John Bauer, Jenny Finkel, Steven Bethard, and David McClosky. 2014. The Stanford CoreNLP natural language processing toolkit. In *Proceedings of 52nd Annual Meeting of the Association for Computational Linguistics: System Demonstrations*, pages 55–60, Baltimore, Maryland. Association for Computational Linguistics.

Yuxian Meng, Wei Wu, Fei Wang, Xiaoya Li, Ping Nie, Fan Yin, Muyu Li, Qinghong Han, Xiaofei Sun, and Jiwei Li. 2019. Glyce: Glyph-vectors for chinese character representations. In *Advances in Neural Information Processing Systems 32: Annual Conference on Neural Information Processing Systems 2019, NeurIPS 2019, December 8-14, 2019, Vancouver, BC, Canada*, pages 2742–2753.

Hiroki Ouchi, Hiroyuki Shindo, and Yuji Matsumoto. 2018. A span selection model for semantic role labeling. In *Proceedings of the 2018 Conference on Empirical Methods in Natural Language Processing*, pages 1630–1642, Brussels, Belgium. Association for Computational Linguistics.

Peng Qi, Yuhao Zhang, Yuhui Zhang, Jason Bolton, and Christopher D. Manning. 2020. Stanza: A python natural language processing toolkit for many human languages. In *Proceedings of the 58th Annual Meeting of the Association for Computational Linguistics: System Demonstrations*, pages 101–108, Online. Association for Computational Linguistics.

Tao Qian, Yue Zhang, Meishan Zhang, Yafeng Ren, and Donghong Ji. 2015. A transition-based model for joint segmentation, POS-tagging and normalization. In *Proceedings of the 2015 Conference on Empirical Methods in Natural Language Processing*, pages 1837–1846, Lisbon, Portugal. Association for Computational Linguistics.

Libo Qin, Wanxiang Che, Yangming Li, Haoyang Wen, and Ting Liu. 2019. A stack-propagation framework with token-level intent detection for spoken language understanding. In *Proceedings of the 2019 Conference on Empirical Methods in Natural Language Processing and the 9th International Joint Conference on Natural Language Processing (EMNLP-IJCNLP)*, pages 2078–2087, Hong Kong, China. Association for Computational Linguistics.

Adwait Ratnaparkhi. 1996. A maximum entropy model for part-of-speech tagging. In *Conference on Empirical Methods in Natural Language Processing*.

Milan Straka and Jana Straková. 2017. Tokenizing, POS tagging, lemmatizing and parsing UD 2.0 with UDPipe. In *Proceedings of the CoNLL 2017 Shared Task: Multilingual Parsing from Raw Text to Universal Dependencies*, pages 88–99, Vancouver, Canada. Association for Computational Linguistics.

Yiren Wang, ChengXiang Zhai, and Hany Hassan. 2020. Multi-task learning for multilingual neural machine translation. In *Proceedings of the 2020 Conference on Empirical Methods in Natural Language Processing (EMNLP)*, pages 1022–1034, Online. Association for Computational Linguistics.

Thomas Wolf, Lysandre Debut, Victor Sanh, Julien Chaumond, Clement Delangue, Anthony Moi, Pierric Cistac, Tim Rault, Rémi Louf, Morgan Funtowicz, Joe Davison, Sam Shleifer, Patrick von Platen, Clara Ma, Yacine Jernite, Julien Plu, Canwen Xu, Teven Le Scao, Sylvain Gugger, Mariama Drame, Quentin Lhoest, and Alexander M. Rush. 2019. Huggingface's transformers: State-of-the-art natural language processing. *ArXiv*, abs/1910.03771.

Nianwen Xue. 2003. Chinese word segmentation as character tagging. In *International Journal of Computational Linguistics & Chinese Language Processing, Volume 8, Number 1, February 2003: Special Issue on Word Formation and Chinese Language Processing*, pages 29–48.

Hang Yan, Bocao Deng, Xiaonan Li, and Xipeng Qiu. 2019a. Tener: Adapting transformer encoder for named entity recognition.

Hang Yan, Xipeng Qiu, and Xuanjing Huang. 2019b. A unified model for joint chinese word segmentation and dependency parsing. *CoRR*, abs/1904.04697.

Baohang Zhou, Xiangrui Cai, Ying Zhang, and Xiaojie Yuan. 2021. An end-to-end progressive multi-task learning framework for medical named entity recognition and normalization. In *Proceedings of the 59th Annual Meeting of the Association for Computational Linguistics and the 11th International Joint Conference on Natural Language Processing (Volume 1: Long Papers)*, pages 6214–6224, Online. Association for Computational Linguistics.

COMBO: State-of-the-Art Morphosyntactic Analysis

Mateusz Klimaszewski[1,2] **Alina Wróblewska**[2]
[1]Warsaw University of Technology
[2]Institute of Computer Science, Polish Academy of Sciences
m.klimaszewski@ii.pw.edu.pl
alina@ipipan.waw.pl

Abstract

We introduce COMBO – a fully neural NLP system for accurate part-of-speech tagging, morphological analysis, lemmatisation, and (enhanced) dependency parsing. It predicts categorical morphosyntactic features whilst also exposes their vector representations, extracted from hidden layers. COMBO is an easy to install Python package with automatically downloadable pre-trained models for over 40 languages. It maintains a balance between efficiency and quality. As it is an end-to-end system and its modules are jointly trained, its training is competitively fast. As its models are optimised for accuracy, they achieve often better prediction quality than SOTA. The COMBO library is available at: `https://gitlab.clarin-pl.eu/syntactic-tools/combo`.

1 Introduction

Natural language processing (NLP) has long recognised morphosyntactic features as necessary for solving advanced natural language understanding (NLU) tasks. An enormous impact of contextual language models on presumably all NLP tasks has slightly weakened the importance of morphosyntactic analysis. As morphosytnactic features are encoded to some extent in contextual word embeddings (e.g. Tenney et al., 2019; Lin et al., 2019), doubts arise as to whether explicit morphosyntactic knowledge is still needed. For example, Glavaš and Vulić (2021) have recently investigated an intermediate fine-tuning contextual language models on the dependency parsing task and suggested that this step does not significantly contribute to advance NLU models. Conversely, Warstadt et al. (2019) reveal the powerlessness of contextual language models in encoding linguistic phenomena like negation. This is in line with our intuition about representing negation in Polish sentences (see Figure 1). It does not seem trivial to differentiate between the contradicting meanings of these sentences using contextual language models, as the word context is similar. The morphosyntactic features, e.g. parts of speech PART vs. INTJ, and dependency labels *advmod:neg* vs. *discourse:intj*, could be beneficial in determining correct reading.

In order to verify the influence of explicit morphosyntactic knowledge on NLU tasks, it is necessary to design a technique for injecting this knowledge into models or to build morphosyntax-aware representations. The first research direction was initiated by Glavaš and Vulić (2021). Our objective is to provide a tool for predicting high-quality morphosyntactic features and exposing their embeddings. These vectors can be directly combined with contextual word embeddings to build morphosyntactically informed word representations.

The emergence of publicly available NLP datasets, e.g. Universal Dependencies (Zeman et al., 2019), stimulates the development of NLP systems. Some of them are optimised for efficiency, e.g. spaCy (Honnibal et al., 2020), and other for accuracy, e.g. UDPipe (Straka, 2018), the Stanford system (Dozat and Manning, 2018), Stanza (Qi et al., 2020). In this paper, we introduce COMBO, an open-source fully neural NLP system which is optimised for both training efficiency and prediction quality. Due to its end-to-end architecture, which is an innovation within morphosyntactic analysers, COMBO is faster in training than the SOTA pipeline-based systems, e.g. Stanza. As a result of applying modern NLP solutions (e.g. contextualised word embeddings), it qualitatively outperforms other systems.

COMBO analyses tokenised sentences and predicts morphosyntactic features of tokens (i.e. parts of speech, morphological features, and lemmata) and syntactic structures of sentences (i.e. dependency trees and enhanced dependency graphs). At the same time, its module, COMBO-vectoriser, extracts vector representations of the predicted fea-

Proceedings of the 2021 Conference on Empirical Methods in Natural Language Processing: System Demonstrations, pages 50–62
November 7–11, 2021.

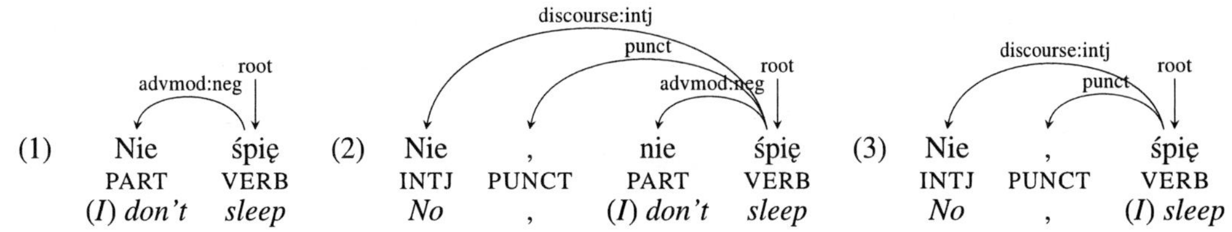

Figure 1: UD trees of Polish sentences: (1) and (2) mean a *non-sleeping* situation and (3) means *sleeping*.

tures from hidden layers of individual predictors. COMBO user guide is in §4 and a live demo is available on the website `http://combo-demo.nlp.ipipan.waw.pl`.

Contributions 1) We implement COMBO (§2), a fully neural NLP system for part-of-speech tagging, morphological analysis, lemmatisation, and (enhanced) dependency parsing, together with COMBO-vectoriser for revealing vector representations of predicted categorical features. COMBO is implemented as a Python package which is easy to install and to integrate into a Python code. 2) We pre-train models for over 40 languages that can be automatically downloaded and directly used to process new texts. 3) We evaluate COMBO and compare its performance with two state-of-the-art systems, spaCy and Stanza (§3).

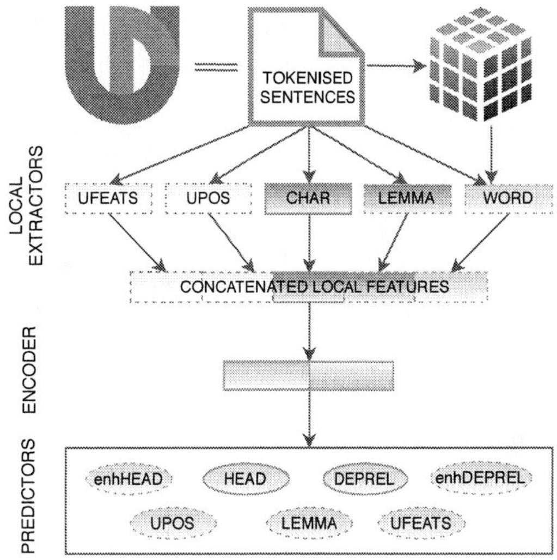

Figure 2: COMBO architecture. Explanations: CNN FC System-trained biLSTM optional required

2 COMBO Architecture

COMBO's architecture (see Figure 2) is based on the forerunner (Rybak and Wróblewska, 2018) implemented in the Keras framework. Apart from a new implementation in the PyTorch library (Paszke et al., 2019), the novelties are the BERT-based encoder, the EUD prediction module, and COMBO-vectoriser extracting embeddings of UPOS and DEPREL from the last hidden layers of COMBO's tagging and dependency parsing module, respectively. This section provides an overview of COMBO's modules. Implementation details are in Appendix A.

Local Feature Extractors Local feature extractors (see Figure 2) encode categorical features (i.e. words, parts of speech, morphological features, lemmata) into vectors. The feature bundle is configurable and limited by the requirements set for COMBO. For instance, if we train only a dependency parser, the following features can be input to COMBO: internal character-based word embeddings (CHAR), pre-trained word embeddings (WORD), and embeddings of lemmata (LEMMA), parts of speech (UPOS) and morphological features (UFEATS). If we train a morphosyntactic analyser (i.e. tagger, lemmatiser and parser), internal word embeddings (CHAR) and pre-trained word embeddings (WORD), if available, are input to COMBO.

Words and lemmata are always encoded using character-based word embeddings (CHAR and LEMMA) estimated during system training with a dilated convolutional neural network (CNN) encoder (Yu and Koltun, 2016; Strubell et al., 2017).

Additionally, words can be represented using pre-trained word embeddings (WORD), e.g. fastText (Grave et al., 2018), or BERT (Devlin et al., 2019). The use of pre-trained embeddings is an optional functionality of the system configuration. COMBO freezes pre-trained embeddings (i.e. no fine-tuning) and uses their transformations, i.e. embeddings are transformed by a single fully connected (FC) layer.

Part-of-speech and morphological embeddings (UPOS and UFEATS) are estimated during system training. Since more than one morphological feature can attribute a word, embeddings of all possible features are estimated and averaged to build a final morphological representation.

Global Feature Encoder The encoder uses concatenations of local feature embeddings. A sequence of these vectors representing all the words in a sentence is processed by a bidirectional LSTM (Hochreiter and Schmidhuber, 1997; Graves and Schmidhuber, 2005). The network learns the context of each word and encodes its global (contextualised) features (see Figure 3). Global feature embeddings are input to the prediction modules.

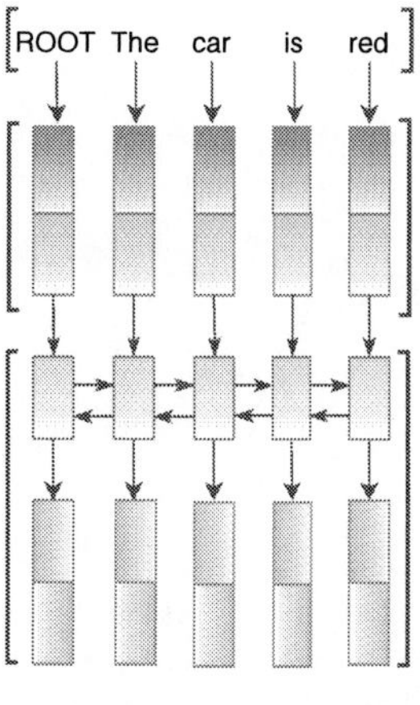

Figure 3: Estimation of global feature vectors.
biLSTM GLOBAL

Tagging Module The tagger takes global feature vectors as input and predicts a universal part of speech (UPOS), a language-specific tag (XPOS), and morphological features (UFEATS) for each word. The tagger consists of two linear layers followed by a softmax. Morphological features build a disordered set of category-value pairs (e.g. Number=Plur). Morphological feature prediction is thus implemented as several classification problems. The value of each morphological category is predicted with a FC network. Different parts of speech are assigned different sets of morphological categories (e.g. a noun can be attributed with grammatical gender, but not with grammatical tense). The set of possible values is thus extended with the NA (not applicable) symbol. It allows the model to learn that a particular category is not a property of a word.

Lemmatisation Module The lemmatiser uses an approach similar to character-based word embedding estimation. A character embedding is concatenated with the global feature vector and transformed by a linear layer. The lemmatiser takes a sequence of such character representations and transforms it using a dilated CNN. The softmax function over the result produces the sequence of probabilities over a character vocabulary to form a lemma.

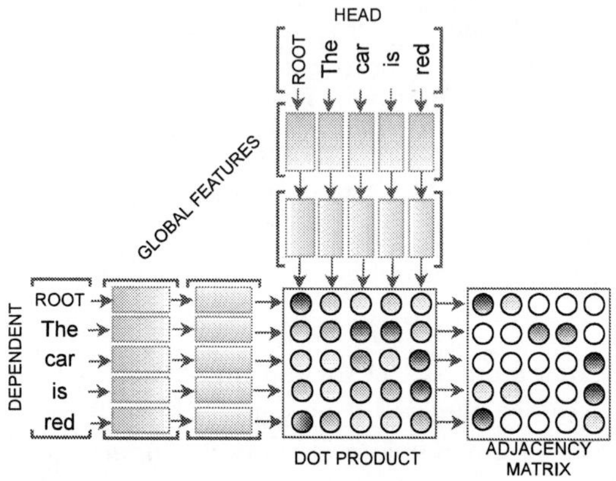

Figure 4: Prediction of dependency arcs.

Parsing Module Two single FC layers transform global feature vectors into head and dependent embeddings (see Figure 4). Based on these representations, a dependency graph is defined as an adjacency matrix with columns and rows corresponding to heads and dependents, respectively. The adjacency matrix elements are dot products of all pairs of the head and dependent embeddings (the dot product determines the certainty of the edge between two words). The softmax function applied to each row of the matrix predicts the adjacent head-dependent pairs. This approach, however, does not guarantee that the resulting adjacency matrix is a properly built dependency tree. The Chu-Liu-Edmonds algorithm (Chu and Liu, 1965; Edmonds, 1967) is thus applied in the last prediction step.

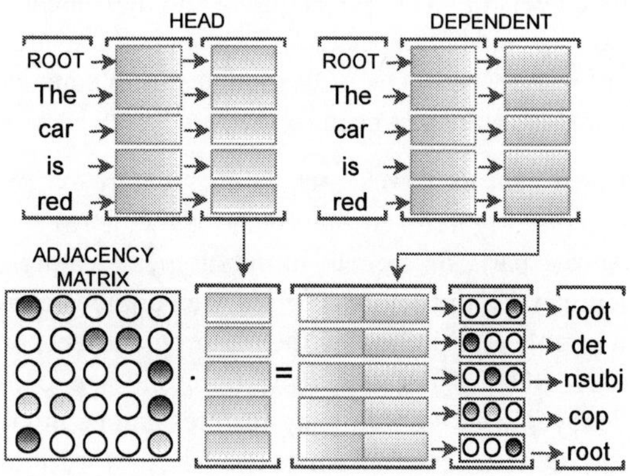

Figure 5: Prediction of grammatical functions.

The procedure of predicting words' grammatical functions (aka dependency labels) is shown in Figure 5. A dependent and its head are represented as vectors by two single FC layers. The dependent embedding is concatenated with the weighted average of (hypothetical) head embeddings. The weights are the values from the corresponding row of the adjacency matrix, estimated by the arc prediction module. Concatenated vector representations are then fed to a FC layer with the softmax activation function to predict dependency labels.

EUD Parsing Module Enhanced Universal Dependencies (EUD) are predicted similarly to dependency trees. The EUD parsing module is described in details in Klimaszewski and Wróblewska (2021).

3 COMBO Performance

Data COMBO is evaluated on treebanks from the Universal Dependencies repository (Zeman et al., 2019), preserving the original splits into training, validation, and test sets. The treebanks representing distinctive language types are summarised in Table 4 in Appendix B.

By default, pre-trained 300-dimensional fastText embeddings (Grave et al., 2018) are used. We also test encoding data with pre-trained contextual word embeddings (the tested BERT models are listed in Table 5 in Appendix B). The UD datasets provide gold-standard tokenisation. If BERT intra-tokeniser splits a word into sub-words, the last layer embeddings are averaged to obtain a single vector representation of this word.

Qualitative Evaluation Table 1 shows COMBO results of processing the selected UD treebanks.[1] COMBO is compared with Stanza (Qi et al., 2020) and spaCy.[2] The systems are evaluated with the standard metrics (Zeman et al., 2018): F1, UAS (unlabelled attachment score), LAS (labelled attachment score), MLAS (morphology-aware LAS) and BLEX (bi-lexical dependency score).[3]

COMBO and Stanza undeniably outrun spaCy models. COMBO using non-contextualised word embeddings is outperformed by Stanza in many language scenarios. However, COMBO supported with BERT-like word embeddings beats all other solutions and is currently the SOTA system for morphosyntactic analysis.

Regarding lemmatisation, Stanza has an advantage over COMBO in most tested languages. This is probably due to the fact that Stanza lemmatiser is enhanced with a key-value dictionary, whilst COMBO lemmatiser is fully neural. It is not surprising that a dictionary helps in lemmatisation of isolating languages (English). However, the dictionary approach is also helpful for agglutinative languages (Finnish, Korean, Basque) and for Arabic, but not for Polish (fusional languages). Comparing COMBO models estimated with and without BERT embeddings, we note that BERT boost only slightly increases the quality of lemma prediction in the tested fusional and agglutinative languages.

For a complete insight into the prediction quality, we evaluate individual UPOS and UDEPREL predictions in English (the isolating language), Korean (agglutinative) and Polish (fusional). Result visualisations are in Appendix C.

COMBO took part in IWPT 2021 Shared Task on Parsing into Enhanced Universal Dependencies (Bouma et al., 2021), where it ranked 4th.[4] In addition to ELAS and EULAS metrics, the third evaluation metric was LAS. COMBO ranked 2nd, achieving the average LAS of 87.84%. The score is even higher than the average LAS of 86.64% in Table 1, which is a kind of confirmation that our evaluation is representative, reliable, and fair.

Downstream Evaluation According to the results in Table 1, COMBO predicts high-quality dependency trees and parts of speech. We therefore conduct a preliminary evaluation of morphosyntactically informed word embeddings in the textual entailment task (aka natural language inference, NLI) in English (Bentivogli et al., 2016) and Polish (Wróblewska and Krasnowska-Kieraś, 2017). We compare the quality of entailment classifiers with two FC layers trained on max/mean-pooled BERT embeddings and sentence representations estimated by a network with two transformer layers which is given morphosyntactically informed word embeddings (i.e. BERT-based word embeddings concatenated with UPOS embeddings, DEPREL embeddings, and BERT-based embeddings of the head

[1]Check the prediction quality for other languages at: `https://gitlab.clarin-pl.eu/syntactic-tools/combo/-/blob/master/docs/performance.md`.

[2]`https://spacy.io` We use the project template `https://github.com/explosion/projects/tree/v3/pipelines/tagger_parser_ud`. The lemmatiser is implemented as a standalone pipeline component in spaCy v3 and we do not test it.

[3]`http://universaldependencies.org/conll18/conll18_ud_eval.py` (CoNLL 2018 evaluation script).

[4]`https://universaldependencies.org/iwpt21/results.html`

System	UPOS	XPOS	UFeat	Lemma	UAS	LAS	CLAS	MLAS	BLEX
English EWT (isolating)									
spaCy	93.79	93.10	94.89	NA	83.38	79.76	75.74	68.91	NA
Stanza	96.36	96.15	97.01	**98.18**	89.64	86.89	83.84	79.44	82.03
COMBO	95.60	95.21	96.60	97.43	88.56	85.58	82.35	76.56	79.78
$\text{COMBO}_{\text{BERT}}$	**96.57**	**96.44**	**97.24**	97.86	**91.76**	**89.28**	**86.83**	**81.71**	**84.38**
Arabic PADT (fusional)									
spaCy	90.27	82.15	82.70	NA	74.24	67.28	63.28	50.48	NA
Stanza	96.98	93.97	94.08	**95.26**	87.96	83.74	80.57	74.96	**76.80**
COMBO	96.71	93.72	93.83	93.54	87.06	82.70	79.46	73.25	73.64
$\text{COMBO}_{\text{BERT}}$	**97.04**	**94.83**	**95.05**	93.95	**89.21**	**85.09**	**82.36**	**76.82**	76.67
Polish PDB (fusional)									
spaCy	96.14	86.94	87.41	NA	86.73	82.06	79.00	65.42	NA
Stanza	98.47	94.20	94.42	97.43	93.15	90.84	88.73	81.98	85.75
COMBO	98.24	94.26	94.53	97.47	92.87	90.45	88.07	81.31	85.53
$\text{COMBO}_{\text{BERT}}$	**98.97**	**96.54**	**96.80**	**98.06**	**95.60**	**93.93**	**92.34**	**87.59**	**89.91**
Finnish TDT (agglutinative)									
spaCy	92.15	93.34	87.89	NA	80.06	74.75	71.52	61.95	NA
Stanza	97.24	97.96	95.58	**95.24**	89.57	87.14	85.52	80.52	**81.05**
COMBO	96.72	98.02	94.04	88.73	89.73	86.70	84.56	77.63	72.42
$\text{COMBO}_{\text{BERT}}$	**98.29**	**99.00**	**97.30**	89.48	**94.11**	**92.52**	**91.34**	**87.18**	77.84
Korean Kaist (agglutinative)									
spaCy	85.21	72.33	NA	NA	76.15	68.13	61.98	57.52	NA
Stanza	95.45	**86.31**	NA	**93.02**	88.42	86.39	83.97	80.64	**77.59**
COMBO	94.46	81.66	NA	89.16	87.31	85.12	82.70	78.38	72.79
$\text{COMBO}_{\text{BERT}}$	**95.89**	85.16	NA	89.95	**89.77**	**87.83**	**85.96**	**82.66**	75.89
Turkish IMST (agglutinative)									
spaCy	87.66	86.18	82.26	NA	60.43	51.32	47.74	37.28	NA
Stanza	**95.98**	**95.18**	**93.77**	96.73	74.14	67.52	64.03	58.13	61.91
COMBO	93.60	92.36	88.88	96.47	72.00	64.48	60.48	49.88	58.75
$\text{COMBO}_{\text{BERT}}$	95.14	94.27	93.56	**97.54**	**78.53**	**72.03**	**68.88**	**60.55**	**67.13**
Basque BDT (agglutinative with fusional verb morphology)									
spaCy	91.96	NA	86.67	NA	76.11	70.28	66.96	54.46	NA
Stanza	96.23	NA	93.09	**96.52**	86.19	82.76	81.30	73.56	78.27
COMBO	94.28	NA	90.44	95.47	84.64	80.44	78.82	67.33	74.95
$\text{COMBO}_{\text{BERT}}$	**96.26**	NA	**93.84**	96.38	**88.73**	**85.80**	**84.93**	**75.96**	**81.25**
Average scores									
spaCy	91.03	85.67	86.97	NA	76.73	70.51	66.60	56.57	NA
Stanza	96.67	93.96	94.66	**96.05**	87.01	83.61	81.14	75.60	77.63
COMBO	95.66	92.54	93.05	94.04	86.02	82.21	79.49	72.05	73.98
$\text{COMBO}_{\text{BERT}}$	**96.88**	**94.37**	**95.63**	94.75	**89.67**	**86.64**	**84.66**	**78.92**	**79.01**

Table 1: Processing quality (F_1 scores) of spaCy, Stanza and COMBO on the selected UD treebanks (the language types are given in parentheses). The highest scores are marked in bold.

Treebank	spaCy	Stanza				COMBO	
		Tagger	Lemmatiser	Parser	Total	fastText	BERT
English EWT	00:22:34	02:08:51	02:12:17	02:29:13	06:50:21	01:26:55	1:54:11
Polish PDB	01:07:55	04:36:51	03:19:04	05:08:41	13:04:36	02:39:44	3:31:41

Table 2: Training time of spaCy, Stanza and COMBO.

word). The morphosyntactically informed English NLI classifier achieves an accuracy of 78.84% and outperforms the max/mean-pooled classifiers by 20.77 pp and 5.44 pp, respectively. The Polish syntax-aware NLI classifier achieves an accuracy of 91.60% and outperforms the max/mean-pooled classifiers by 17.2 pp and 7.7 pp, respectively.

Efficiency Evaluation We also compare spaCy, Stanza and COMBO in terms of their efficiency, i.e. training and prediction speed.[5] According to the results (see Tables 2 and 3), spaCy is the SOTA system, and the other two are not even close to its processing time. Considering COMBO and Stanza, whose prediction quality is significantly better than spaCy, COMBO is 1.5 times slower (2 times slower with BERT) than Stanza in predicting, but it is definitely faster in training. The reason for large discrepancies in training times is the different architecture of these two systems. Stanza is a pipeline-based system, i.e. its modules are trained one after the other. COMBO is an end-to-end system, i.e. its modules are jointly trained and the training process is therefore faster.

Treebank	Stanza	COMBO	$\text{COMBO}_{\text{BERT}}$
English EWT	4.7×	6.8×	10.8×
Polish PDB	4.1×	5.8×	10.6×

Table 3: Prediction time of Stanza and COMBO relative to spaCy (1×) on English and Polish test data.

4 Getting Started with COMBO

Prediction COMBO provides two main prediction modes: a Python library and a command-line interface (CLI). The Python package mode supports automated model download. The code snippet demonstrates downloading a pre-trained Polish model and processing a sentence:

```
from combo.predict import COMBO

nlp = COMBO.from_pretrained("polish")
sentence = nlp("Ala ma kota.")
print(sentence.tokens)
```

To download a model for another language, select its name from the list of pre-trained models.[6] The Python mode also supports acquisition of DEPREL or UPOS embeddings, for example:

```
sentence = nlp("Ala ma kota.")
chosen_token = sentence.tokens[1]
print(chosen_token.embeddings["upostag"])
```

[5]A single NVIDIA V100 card is used in all tests.

[6]The list of the pretrained COMBO models: https://gitlab.clarin-pl.eu/syntactic-tools/combo/-/blob/master/docs/models.md#pre-trained-models

In CLI mode, COMBO processes sentences using either a downloaded model or a model trained by yourself. CLI works on raw texts and on the CoNLL-U files (i.e. with tokenised sentences and even morphologically annotated tokens):

```
combo --mode predict \
      --model_path model.tar.gz \
      --input_file input.conllu \
      --output_file output.conllu
```

Model Training COMBO CLI allows to train new models for any language. The only requirement is a training dataset in the CoNLL-U/CoNLL-X format. In the default setup, tokenised sentences are input and all possible predictors are trained:

```
combo --mode train \
      --training_data training.conllu \
      --validation_data valid.conllu
```

If we only train a dependency parser, the default setup should be changed with configuration flags: `--features` with a list of input features and `--targets` with a list of prediction targets.

5 Conclusion

We have presented COMBO, the SOTA system for morphosyntacic analysis, i.e. part-of-speech tagging, morphological analysis, lemmatisation, and (enhanced) dependency parsing. COMBO is a language-agnostic and format-independent system (i.e. it supports the CoNLL-U and CoNLL-X formats). Its implementation as a Python package allows effortless installation, and incorporation into any Python code or usage in the CLI mode. In the Python mode, COMBO supports automated download of pre-trained models for multiple languages and outputs not only categorical morphosyntactic features, but also their embeddings. In the CLI mode, pre-trained models can be manually downloaded or trained from scratch. The system training is fully configurable in respect of the range of input features and output predictions, and the method of encoding input data.

Last but not least, COMBO maintains a balance between efficiency and quality. Admittedly, it is not as fast as spaCy, but it is much more efficient than Stanza considering the training time. Tested on the selected UD treebanks, COMBO morphosyntactic models enhanced with BERT embeddings outperform spaCy and Stanza models.

Acknowledgments

The authors would like to thank Piotr Rybak for his design and explanations of the architecture of COMBO's forerunner. The research presented in this paper was founded by SONATA 8 grant no 2014/15/D/HS2/03486 from the National Science Centre Poland and the European Regional Development Fund as a part of the 2014-2020 Smart Growth Operational Programme, CLARIN – Common Language Resources and Technology Infrastructure, project no. POIR.04.02.00-00C002/19. The computing was performed at Poznań Supercomputing and Networking Center.

References

Rodrigo Agerri, Iñaki San Vicente, Jon Ander Campos, Ander Barrena, Xabier Saralegi, Aitor Soroa, and Eneko Agirre. 2020. Give your text representation models some love: the case for Basque. In *Proceedings of the 12th Language Resources and Evaluation Conference*, pages 4781–4788, Marseille, France. European Language Resources Association.

Wissam Antoun, Fady Baly, and Hazem Hajj. 2020. AraBERT: Transformer-based model for Arabic language understanding. In *Proceedings of the 4th Workshop on Open-Source Arabic Corpora and Processing Tools, with a Shared Task on Offensive Language Detection*, pages 9–15, Marseille, France. European Language Resource Association.

Maria Jesus Aranzabe, Aitziber Atutxa, Kepa Bengoetxea, Arantza Diaz de Ilarraza, Iakes Goenaga, Koldo Gojenola, and Larraitz Uria. 2015. Automatic Conversion of the Basque Dependency Treebank to Universal Dependencies. In *Proceedings of the 14th International Workshop on Treebanks and Linguistic Theories (TLT14)*, pages 233–241.

Luisa Bentivogli, Raffaella Bernardi, Marco Marelli, Stefano Menini, Marco Baroni, and Roberto Zamparelli. 2016. SICK through the SemEval Glasses. Lesson learned from the evaluation of compositional distributional semantic models on full sentences through semantic relatedness and textual entailment. *Journal of Language Resources and Evaluation*, 50:95–124.

Gosse Bouma, Djamé Seddah, and Daniel Zeman. 2021. From Raw Text to Enhanced Universal Dependencies: The Parsing Shared Task at IWPT 2021. In *Proceedings of the 17th International Conference on Parsing Technologies and the IWPT 2021 Shared Task on Parsing into Enhanced Universal Dependencies (IWPT 2021)*, pages 146–157, Online. Association for Computational Linguistics.

Y. J. Chu and T. H. Liu. 1965. On the Shortest Arborescence of a Directed Graph. *Science Sinica*, 14:1396–1400.

Jayeol Chun, Na-Rae Han, Jena D. Hwang, and Jinho D. Choi. 2018. Building Universal Dependency treebanks in Korean. In *Proceedings of the Eleventh International Conference on Language Resources and Evaluation (LREC 2018)*, Miyazaki, Japan. European Language Resources Association (ELRA).

Jacob Devlin, Ming-Wei Chang, Kenton Lee, and Kristina Toutanova. 2019. BERT: Pre-training of deep bidirectional transformers for language understanding. In *Proceedings of the 2019 Conference of the North American Chapter of the Association for Computational Linguistics: Human Language Technologies, Volume 1 (Long and Short Papers)*, pages 4171–4186, Minneapolis, Minnesota. Association for Computational Linguistics.

Timothy Dozat and Christopher D. Manning. 2018. Simpler but more accurate semantic dependency parsing. In *Proceedings of the 56th Annual Meeting of the Association for Computational Linguistics (Volume 2: Short Papers)*, pages 484–490, Melbourne, Australia. Association for Computational Linguistics.

Jack Edmonds. 1967. Optimum Branchings. *Journal of Research of the National Bureau of Standards*, 71B(4):233–240.

Yarin Gal and Zoubin Ghahramani. 2016. A theoretically grounded application of dropout in recurrent neural networks. In *Proceedings of the 30th International Conference on Neural Information Processing Systems*, NIPS'16, page 1027–1035, Red Hook, NY, USA. Curran Associates Inc.

Matt Gardner, Joel Grus, Mark Neumann, Oyvind Tafjord, Pradeep Dasigi, Nelson F. Liu, Matthew Peters, Michael Schmitz, and Luke Zettlemoyer. 2018. AllenNLP: A deep semantic natural language processing platform. In *Proceedings of Workshop for NLP Open Source Software (NLP-OSS)*, pages 1–6, Melbourne, Australia. Association for Computational Linguistics.

Goran Glavaš and Ivan Vulić. 2021. Is supervised syntactic parsing beneficial for language understanding tasks? an empirical investigation. In *Proceedings of the 16th Conference of the European Chapter of the Association for Computational Linguistics: Main Volume*, pages 3090–3104, Online. Association for Computational Linguistics.

Edouard Grave, Piotr Bojanowski, Prakhar Gupta, Armand Joulin, and Tomas Mikolov. 2018. Learning word vectors for 157 languages. In *Proceedings of the Eleventh International Conference on Language Resources and Evaluation (LREC 2018)*, Miyazaki, Japan. European Language Resources Association (ELRA).

Alex Graves and Jürgen Schmidhuber. 2005. Framewise Phoneme Classification with Bidirectional LSTM and Other Neural Network Architectures. *Neural Networks*, 18(5):602–610.

Jan Hajič, Otakar Smrž, Petr Zemánek, Petr Pajas, Jan Šnaidauf, Emanuel Beška, Jakub Kracmar, and Kamila Hassanová. 2009. Prague arabic dependency treebank 1.0. LINDAT/CLARIAH-CZ digital library at the Institute of Formal and Applied Linguistics (ÚFAL), Faculty of Mathematics and Physics, Charles University.

Katri Haverinen, Jenna Nyblom, Timo Viljanen, Veronika Laippala, Samuel Kohonen, Anna Missilä, Stina Ojala, Tapio Salakoski, and Filip Ginter. 2014. Building the essential resources for finnish: The turku dependency treebank. *Lang. Resour. Eval.*, 48(3):493–531.

Sepp Hochreiter and Jürgen Schmidhuber. 1997. Long short-term memory. *Neural Computation*, 9(8):1735–1780.

Matthew Honnibal, Ines Montani, Sofie Van Landeghem, and Adriane Boyd. 2020. spaCy: Industrial-strength Natural Language Processing in Python.

Kiyoung Kim. 2020. Pretrained Language Models For Korean. `https://github.com/kiyoungkim1/LMkor`.

Diederik P. Kingma and Jimmy Ba. 2015. Adam: A method for stochastic optimization. In *3rd International Conference on Learning Representations, ICLR 2015, San Diego, CA, USA, May 7-9, 2015, Conference Track Proceedings*.

Mateusz Klimaszewski and Alina Wróblewska. 2021. COMBO: A new module for EUD parsing. In *Proceedings of the 17th International Conference on Parsing Technologies and the IWPT 2021 Shared Task on Parsing into Enhanced Universal Dependencies (IWPT 2021)*, pages 158–166, Online. Association for Computational Linguistics.

Yongjie Lin, Yi Chern Tan, and Robert Frank. 2019. Open sesame: Getting inside BERT's linguistic knowledge. In *Proceedings of the 2019 ACL Workshop BlackboxNLP: Analyzing and Interpreting Neural Networks for NLP*, pages 241–253, Florence, Italy. Association for Computational Linguistics.

Robert Mroczkowski, Piotr Rybak, Alina Wróblewska, and Ireneusz Gawlik. 2021. HerBERT: Efficiently pretrained transformer-based language model for Polish. In *Proceedings of the 8th Workshop on Balto-Slavic Natural Language Processing*, pages 1–10, Kiyv, Ukraine. Association for Computational Linguistics.

Vinod Nair and Geoffrey E. Hinton. 2010. Rectified linear units improve restricted boltzmann machines. In *Proceedings of the 27th International Conference on International Conference on Machine Learning*, ICML'10, page 807–814, Madison, WI, USA. Omnipress.

Adam Paszke, Sam Gross, Francisco Massa, Adam Lerer, James Bradbury, Gregory Chanan, Trevor Killeen, Zeming Lin, Natalia Gimelshein, Luca Antiga, Alban Desmaison, Andreas Kopf, Edward Yang, Zachary DeVito, Martin Raison, Alykhan Tejani, Sasank Chilamkurthy, Benoit Steiner, Lu Fang, Junjie Bai, and Soumith Chintala. 2019. PyTorch: An Imperative Style, High-Performance Deep Learning Library. In H. Wallach, H. Larochelle, A. Beygelzimer, F. d'Alché Buc, E. Fox, and R. Garnett, editors, *Advances in Neural Information Processing Systems 32*, pages 8024–8035. Curran Associates, Inc.

Peng Qi, Yuhao Zhang, Yuhui Zhang, Jason Bolton, and Christopher D. Manning. 2020. Stanza: A python natural language processing toolkit for many human languages. In *Proceedings of the 58th Annual Meeting of the Association for Computational Linguistics: System Demonstrations*, pages 101–108, Online. Association for Computational Linguistics.

Piotr Rybak and Alina Wróblewska. 2018. Semi-Supervised Neural System for Tagging, Parsing and Lematization. In *Proceedings of the CoNLL 2018 Shared Task: Multilingual Parsing from Raw Text to Universal Dependencies*, pages 45–54.

Stefan Schweter. 2020. BERTurk - BERT models for Turkish.

Natalia Silveira, Timothy Dozat, Marie-Catherine de Marneffe, Samuel Bowman, Miriam Connor, John Bauer, and Chris Manning. 2014. A gold standard dependency corpus for English. In *Proceedings of the Ninth International Conference on Language Resources and Evaluation (LREC'14)*, pages 2897–2904, Reykjavik, Iceland. European Language Resources Association (ELRA).

Nitish Srivastava, Geoffrey Hinton, Alex Krizhevsky, Ilya Sutskever, and Ruslan Salakhutdinov. 2014. Dropout: A Simple Way to Prevent Neural Networks from Overfitting. *Journal of Machine Learning Research*, 15:1929–1958.

Milan Straka. 2018. UDPipe 2.0 prototype at CoNLL 2018 UD shared task. In *Proceedings of the CoNLL 2018 Shared Task: Multilingual Parsing from Raw Text to Universal Dependencies*, pages 197–207, Brussels, Belgium. Association for Computational Linguistics.

Emma Strubell, Patrick Verga, David Belanger, and Andrew McCallum. 2017. Fast and Accurate Entity Recognition with Iterated Dilated Convolutions. In *Proceedings of the 2017 Conference on Empirical Methods in Natural Language Processing*, pages 2670–2680, Copenhagen, Denmark. Association for Computational Linguistics.

Umut Sulubacak, Memduh Gokirmak, Francis Tyers, Çağrı Çöltekin, Joakim Nivre, and Gülşen Eryiğit. 2016. Universal Dependencies for Turkish. In *Proceedings of COLING 2016, the 26th International*

Conference on Computational Linguistics: Technical Papers, pages 3444–3454, Osaka, Japan. The COLING 2016 Organizing Committee.

Ian Tenney, Patrick Xia, Berlin Chen, Alex Wang, Adam Poliak, R Thomas McCoy, Najoung Kim, Benjamin Van Durme, Sam Bowman, Dipanjan Das, and Ellie Pavlick. 2019. What do you learn from context? probing for sentence structure in contextualized word representations. In *International Conference on Learning Representations*.

Antti Virtanen, Jenna Kanerva, Rami Ilo, Jouni Luoma, Juhani Luotolahti, Tapio Salakoski, Filip Ginter, and Sampo Pyysalo. 2019. Multilingual is not enough: BERT for Finnish.

Alex Warstadt, Yu Cao, Ioana Grosu, Wei Peng, Hagen Blix, Yining Nie, Anna Alsop, Shikha Bordia, Haokun Liu, Alicia Parrish, Sheng-Fu Wang, Jason Phang, Anhad Mohananey, Phu Mon Htut, Paloma Jeretic, and Samuel R. Bowman. 2019. Investigating BERT's knowledge of language: Five analysis methods with NPIs. In *Proceedings of the 2019 Conference on Empirical Methods in Natural Language Processing and the 9th International Joint Conference on Natural Language Processing (EMNLP-IJCNLP)*, pages 2877–2887, Hong Kong, China. Association for Computational Linguistics.

Alina Wróblewska. 2018. Extended and Enhanced Polish Dependency Bank in Universal Dependencies Format. In *Proceedings of the Second Workshop on Universal Dependencies (UDW 2018)*, pages 173–182.

Alina Wróblewska and Katarzyna Krasnowska-Kieraś. 2017. Polish evaluation dataset for compositional distributional semantics models. In *Proceedings of the 55th Annual Meeting of the Association for Computational Linguistics (Volume 1: Long Papers)*, pages 784–792, Vancouver, Canada. Association for Computational Linguistics.

Fisher Yu and Vladlen Koltun. 2016. Multi-Scale Context Aggregation by Dilated Convolutions. *CoRR*, abs/1511.07122.

Daniel Zeman, Jan Hajič, Martin Popel, Martin Potthast, Milan Straka, Filip Ginter, Joakim Nivre, and Slav Petrov. 2018. CoNLL 2018 shared task: Multilingual parsing from raw text to universal dependencies. In *Proceedings of the CoNLL 2018 Shared Task: Multilingual Parsing from Raw Text to Universal Dependencies*, pages 1–21, Brussels, Belgium. Association for Computational Linguistics.

Daniel Zeman, Joakim Nivre, Mitchell Abrams, Noëmi Aepli, Željko Agić, Lars Ahrenberg, Gabrielė Aleksandravičiūtė, Lene Antonsen, Katya Aplonova, Maria Jesus Aranzabe, Gashaw Arutie, Masayuki Asahara, Luma Ateyah, Mohammed Attia, Aitziber Atutxa, Liesbeth Augustinus, Elena Badmaeva, Miguel Ballesteros, Esha Banerjee, Sebastian Bank, Verginica Barbu Mititelu, Victoria Basmov, Colin Batchelor, John Bauer, Sandra Bellato, Kepa Bengoetxea, Yevgeni Berzak, Irshad Ahmad Bhat, Riyaz Ahmad Bhat, Erica Biagetti, Eckhard Bick, Agnė Bielinskienė, Rogier Blokland, Victoria Bobicev, Loïc Boizou, Emanuel Borges Völker, Carl Börstell, Cristina Bosco, Gosse Bouma, Sam Bowman, Adriane Boyd, Kristina Brokaitė, Aljoscha Burchardt, Marie Candito, Bernard Caron, Gauthier Caron, Tatiana Cavalcanti, Gülşen Cebiroğlu Eryiğit, Flavio Massimiliano Cecchini, Giuseppe G. A. Celano, Slavomír Čéplö, Savas Cetin, Fabricio Chalub, Jinho Choi, Yongseok Cho, Jayeol Chun, Alessandra T. Cignarella, Silvie Cinková, Aurélie Collomb, Çağrı Çöltekin, Miriam Connor, Marine Courtin, Elizabeth Davidson, Marie-Catherine de Marneffe, Valeria de Paiva, Elvis de Souza, Arantza Diaz de Ilarraza, Carly Dickerson, Bamba Dione, Peter Dirix, Kaja Dobrovoljc, Timothy Dozat, Kira Droganova, Puneet Dwivedi, Hanne Eckhoff, Marhaba Eli, Ali Elkahky, Binyam Ephrem, Olga Erina, Tomaž Erjavec, Aline Etienne, Wograine Evelyn, Richárd Farkas, Hector Fernandez Alcalde, Jennifer Foster, Cláudia Freitas, Kazunori Fujita, Katarína Gajdošová, Daniel Galbraith, Marcos Garcia, Moa Gärdenfors, Sebastian Garza, Kim Gerdes, Filip Ginter, Iakes Goenaga, Koldo Gojenola, Memduh Gökırmak, Yoav Goldberg, Xavier Gómez Guinovart, Berta González Saavedra, Bernadeta Griciūtė, Matias Grioni, Normunds Grūzītis, Bruno Guillaume, Céline Guillot-Barbance, Nizar Habash, Jan Hajič, Jan Hajič jr., Mika Hämäläinen, Linh Hà Mỹ, Na-Rae Han, Kim Harris, Dag Haug, Johannes Heinecke, Felix Hennig, Barbora Hladká, Jaroslava Hlaváčová, Florinel Hociung, Petter Hohle, Jena Hwang, Takumi Ikeda, Radu Ion, Elena Irimia, Ọlájídé Ishola, Tomáš Jelínek, Anders Johannsen, Fredrik Jørgensen, Markus Juutinen, Hüner Kaşıkara, Andre Kaasen, Nadezhda Kabaeva, Sylvain Kahane, Hiroshi Kanayama, Jenna Kanerva, Boris Katz, Tolga Kayadelen, Jessica Kenney, Václava Kettnerová, Jesse Kirchner, Elena Klementieva, Arne Köhn, Kamil Kopacewicz, Natalia Kotsyba, Jolanta Kovalevskaitė, Simon Krek, Sookyoung Kwak, Veronika Laippala, Lorenzo Lambertino, Lucia Lam, Tatiana Lando, Septina Dian Larasati, Alexei Lavrentiev, John Lee, Phuong Lê Hồng, Alessandro Lenci, Saran Lertpradit, Herman Leung, Cheuk Ying Li, Josie Li, Keying Li, KyungTae Lim, Maria Liovina, Yuan Li, Nikola Ljubešić, Olga Loginova, Olga Lyashevskaya, Teresa Lynn, Vivien Macketanz, Aibek Makazhanov, Michael Mandl, Christopher Manning, Ruli Manurung, Cătălina Mărănduc, David Mareček, Katrin Marheinecke, Héctor Martínez Alonso, André Martins, Jan Mašek, Yuji Matsumoto, Ryan McDonald, Sarah McGuinness, Gustavo Mendonça, Niko Miekka, Margarita Misirpashayeva, Anna Missilä, Cătălin Mititelu, Maria Mitrofan, Yusuke Miyao, Simonetta Montemagni, Amir More, Laura Moreno Romero, Keiko Sophie Mori, Tomohiko Morioka, Shinsuke Mori, Shigeki Moro, Bjartur Mortensen, Bohdan Moskalevskyi, Kadri Muischnek, Robert

Munro, Yugo Murawaki, Kaili Müürisep, Pinkey Nainwani, Juan Ignacio Navarro Horñiacek, Anna Nedoluzhko, Gunta Nešpore-Bērzkalne, Luong Nguyễn Thị, Huyền Nguyễn Thị Minh, Yoshihiro Nikaido, Vitaly Nikolaev, Rattima Nitisaroj, Hanna Nurmi, Stina Ojala, Atul Kr. Ojha, Adédayọ̀ Olúòkun, Mai Omura, Petya Osenova, Robert Östling, Lilja Øvrelid, Niko Partanen, Elena Pascual, Marco Passarotti, Agnieszka Patejuk, Guilherme Paulino-Passos, Angelika Peljak-Łapińska, Siyao Peng, Cenel-Augusto Perez, Guy Perrier, Daria Petrova, Slav Petrov, Jason Phelan, Jussi Piitulainen, Tommi A Pirinen, Emily Pitler, Barbara Plank, Thierry Poibeau, Larisa Ponomareva, Martin Popel, Lauma Pretkalniņa, Sophie Prévost, Prokopis Prokopidis, Adam Przepiórkowski, Tiina Puolakainen, Sampo Pyysalo, Peng Qi, Andriela Rääbis, Alexandre Rademaker, Loganathan Ramasamy, Taraka Rama, Carlos Ramisch, Vinit Ravishankar, Livy Real, Siva Reddy, Georg Rehm, Ivan Riabov, Michael Rießler, Erika Rimkutė, Larissa Rinaldi, Laura Rituma, Luisa Rocha, Mykhailo Romanenko, Rudolf Rosa, Davide Rovati, Valentin Roșca, Olga Rudina, Jack Rueter, Shoval Sadde, Benoît Sagot, Shadi Saleh, Alessio Salomoni, Tanja Samardžić, Stephanie Samson, Manuela Sanguinetti, Dage Särg, Baiba Saulīte, Yanin Sawanakunanon, Nathan Schneider, Sebastian Schuster, Djamé Seddah, Wolfgang Seeker, Mojgan Seraji, Mo Shen, Atsuko Shimada, Hiroyuki Shirasu, Muh Shohibussirri, Dmitry Sichinava, Aline Silveira, Natalia Silveira, Maria Simi, Radu Simionescu, Katalin Simkó, Mária Šimková, Kiril Simov, Aaron Smith, Isabela Soares-Bastos, Carolyn Spadine, Antonio Stella, Milan Straka, Jana Strnadová, Alane Suhr, Umut Sulubacak, Shingo Suzuki, Zsolt Szántó, Dima Taji, Yuta Takahashi, Fabio Tamburini, Takaaki Tanaka, Isabelle Tellier, Guillaume Thomas, Liisi Torga, Trond Trosterud, Anna Trukhina, Reut Tsarfaty, Francis Tyers, Sumire Uematsu, Zdeňka Urešová, Larraitz Uria, Hans Uszkoreit, Andrius Utka, Sowmya Vajjala, Daniel van Niekerk, Gertjan van Noord, Viktor Varga, Eric Villemonte de la Clergerie, Veronika Vincze, Lars Wallin, Abigail Walsh, Jing Xian Wang, Jonathan North Washington, Maximilan Wendt, Seyi Williams, Mats Wirén, Christian Wittern, Tsegay Woldemariam, Tak-sum Wong, Alina Wróblewska, Mary Yako, Naoki Yamazaki, Chunxiao Yan, Koichi Yasuoka, Marat M. Yavrumyan, Zhuoran Yu, Zdeněk Žabokrtský, Amir Zeldes, Manying Zhang, and Hanzhi Zhu. 2019. Universal dependencies 2.5. LINDAT/CLARIAH-CZ digital library at the Institute of Formal and Applied Linguistics (ÚFAL), Faculty of Mathematics and Physics, Charles University.

A COMBO Implementation

COMBO is a Python package that uses the PyTorch (Paszke et al., 2019) and AllenNLP (Gardner et al., 2018) libraries. The COMBO models used in the evaluation presented in Section 3 are trained with the empirically set default parameters specified below. The training parameters can be easily configured and adjusted to the specifics of an individual model.

A.1 Network Hyperparameters

Embeddings An internal character-based word embedding is calculated with three convolutional layers with 512, 256 and 64 filters with dilation rates equal to 1, 2 and 4. All filters have the kernel size of 3. The internal word embedding has a size of 64 dimensions. All external word embeddings are reduced to 100-dimensional vectors by a single FC layer. As only words are used as input features in the system evaluation, the local feature embedding is a concatenation of the 64-dimensional internal and 100-dimensional external word embedding. The global feature vectors are computed by two biLSTM layers with 512 hidden units.

Prediction modules The tagger uses a FC network with a hidden layer of the size 64 to predict UPOS and FC networks with 128-dimensional hidden layers to predict XPOS and UFEATS.

The lemmatiser uses three convolutional layers with 256 filters and dilation rates equal to 1, 2 and 4. All filters have the kernel size of 3. The fourth convolutional layer with the number of filters equal to the number of character instances in training data is used to predict the probability of each character. The final layer filters have the kernel size of 1. The 256-dimensional embeddings of input characters are concatenated with the global feature vectors reduced to 32 dimensions with a single FC layer.

The arc prediction module uses 512-dimensional head, and dependent embeddings and the labelling module uses 128-dimensional vectors.

COMBO-vectoriser currently outputs 64-dimensional UPOS and 128-dimensional DEPREL embeddings.

Activation function FC and CNN layers use hyperbolic tangent and rectified linear unit (Nair and Hinton, 2010) activation functions, respectively.

A.2 Regularisation

Dropout technique for Variational RNNs (Gal and Ghahramani, 2016) with 0.33 rate is applied to the local feature embeddings and on top of the stacked biLSTM estimating global feature embeddings. The same dropout, for output and recurrent values, is used in the context of each biLSTM layer. The FC layers use the standard dropout (Srivastava et al., 2014) with 0.25 rate. Moreover, the biLSTM and convolutional layers use L2 regularisation with the rate of 1×10^{-6}, and the trainable embeddings use L2 with the rate of 1×10^{-5}.

A.3 Training

The cross-entropy loss is used for all parts of the system. The final loss is the weighted sum of losses with the following weights for each task:

- 0.05 for predicting UPOS and LEMMA,
- 0.2 for predicting UFEATS and (enh)HEAD,
- 0.8 for predicting (enh)DEPREL.

The whole system is optimised with ADAM (Kingma and Ba, 2015) with the learning rate of 0.002 and $\beta_1 = \beta_2 = 0.9$. The model is trained for a maximum of 400 epochs, and the learning rate is reduced twice by the factor of two when the validation score reaches a plateau.

B External Data Summary

Tables 4 and 5 list the UD dependency treebanks and BERT models used in the evaluation experiments presented in Section 3.

C Evaluation of UPOS and UDEPREL

The comparison of the universal parts of speech predicted by the tested systems in English, Korean and Polish data is shown in the charts in Figures 6, 7 and 8, respectively. The comparison of the quality of the predicted universal dependency types in English, Korean and Polish data is presented in Figures 9, 10 and 11, respectively.

Language	Language Type	UD Treebank	#Words	#Trees	Reference
English	isolating	English-EWT	254,856	16,622	Silveira et al. (2014)
Arabic	fusional	Arabic-PADT	282,384	7,664	Hajič et al. (2009)
Polish	fusional	Polish-PDB	350,036	22,152	Wróblewska (2018)
Finnish	agglutinative	Finnish-TDT	202,453	15,136	Haverinen et al. (2014)
Korean	agglutinative	Korean-Kaist	350,090	27,363	Chun et al. (2018)
Turkish	agglutinative	Turkish-IMST	57,859	5,635	Sulubacak et al. (2016)
Basque	agglutinative (fusional verb morphology)	Basque-BDT	121,443	8,993	Aranzabe et al. (2015)

Table 4: The UD treebanks used in the evaluation experiments.

Language	BERT model	Reference
Arabic	bert-base-arabertv2	Antoun et al. (2020)
Basque	berteus-base-cased	Agerri et al. (2020)
English	bert-base-cased	Devlin et al. (2019)
Finnish	bert-base-finnish-cased-v1	Virtanen et al. (2019)
Korean	bert-kor-base	Kim (2020)
Polish	herbert-base-cased	Mroczkowski et al. (2021)
Turkish	bert-base-turkish-cased	Schweter (2020)

Table 5: The BERT models used in the evaluation experiments.

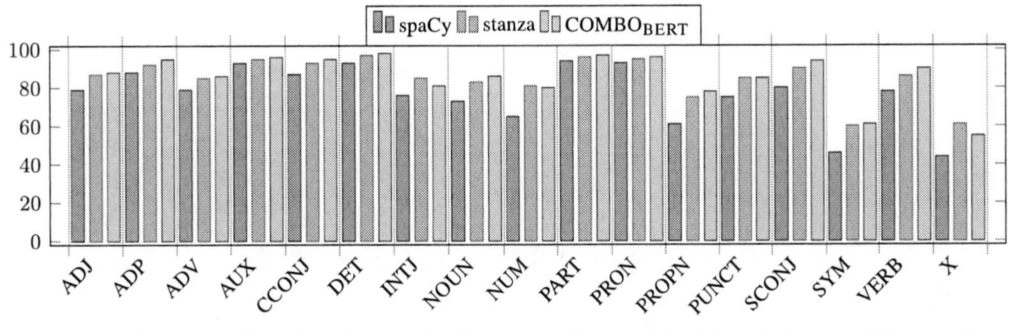

Figure 6: Evaluation of predicted universal parts of speech (UPOS) in the English test set (F-$_1$-scores).

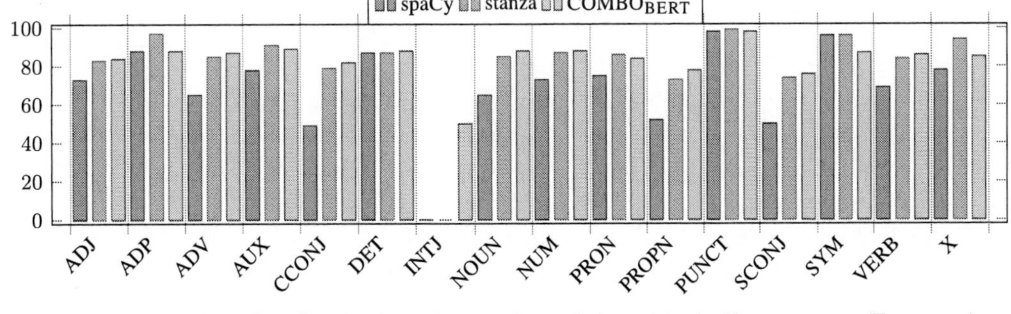

Figure 7: Evaluation of predicted universal parts of speech (UPOS) in the Korean test set (F-$_1$-scores).

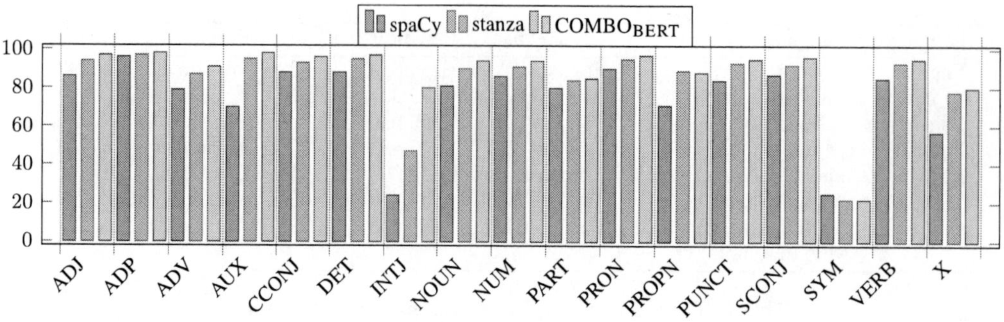

Figure 8: Evaluation of predicted universal parts of speech (UPOS) in the Polish test set (F-$_1$-scores).

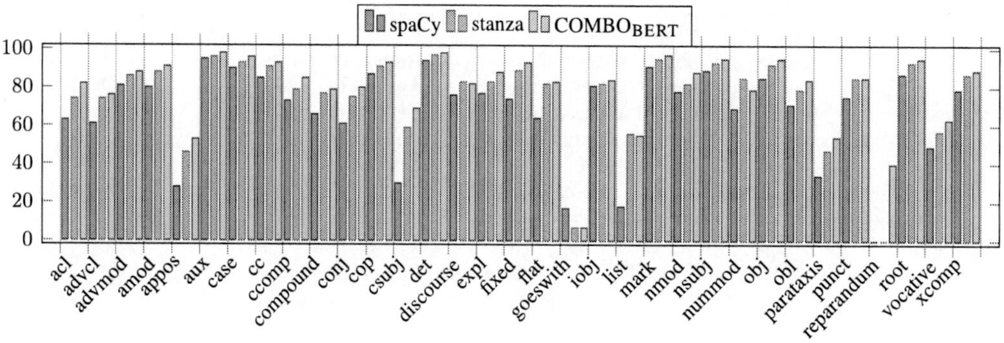

Figure 9: Evaluation of predicted grammatical functions (UDEPREL) in the English test set (F-$_1$-scores).

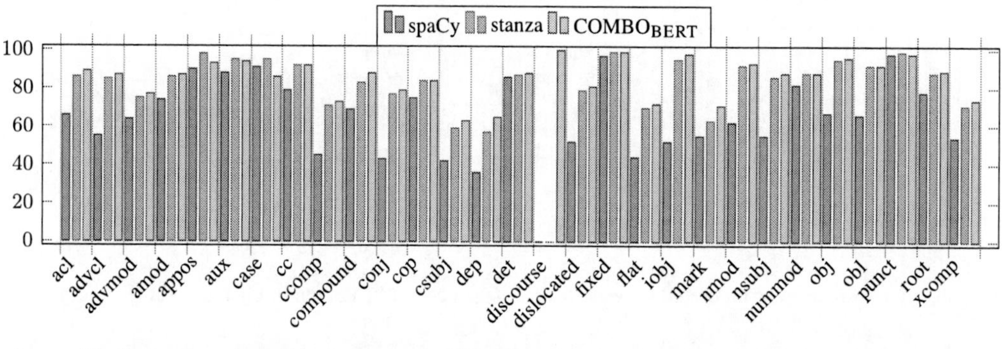

Figure 10: Evaluation of predicted grammatical functions (UDEPREL) in the Korean test set (F-$_1$-scores).

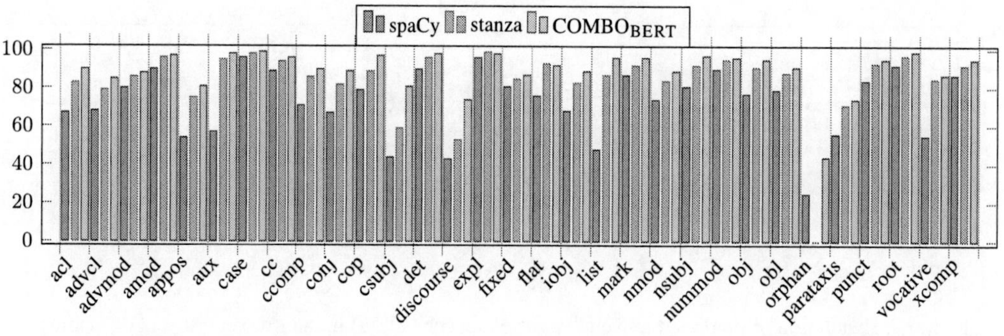

Figure 11: Evaluation of predicted grammatical functions (UDEPREL) in the Polish test set (F-$_1$-scores).

ExcavatorCovid: Extracting Events and Relations from Text Corpora for Temporal and Causal Analysis for COVID-19

Bonan Min[1], Ben Rozonoyer[1], Haoling Qiu[1], Alex Zamanian[1],
Nianwen Xue[2], and Jessica MacBride[1]

[1]Raytheon BBN Technologies
[2]Brandeis University
bonan.min@raytheon.com

Abstract

Timely responses from policy makers to mitigate the impact of the COVID-19 pandemic rely on a comprehensive grasp of events, their causes, and their impacts. These events are reported at such a speed and scale as to be overwhelming. In this paper, we present ExcavatorCovid, a machine reading system that ingests open-source text documents (e.g., news and scientific publications), extracts COVID-19 related events and relations between them, and builds a Temporal and Causal Analysis Graph (TCAG). Excavator will help government agencies alleviate the information overload, understand likely downstream effects of political and economic decisions and events related to the pandemic, and respond in a timely manner to mitigate the impact of COVID-19. We expect the utility of Excavator to outlive the COVID-19 pandemic: analysts and decision makers will be empowered by Excavator to better understand and solve complex problems in the future. A demonstration video is available at https://vimeo.com/528619007.

1 Introduction

Timely responses from policy makers to mitigate the impact of the COVID-19 pandemic rely on a comprehensive grasp of events, their causes, and their impacts. Since the beginning of the COVID-19 pandemic, an enormous amount of articles are being published every day, that report many events [1] and studies related to COVID. It is very difficult, if not impossible, to keep track of these developing events or to get a comprehensive overview of the temporal and causal dynamics underlying these events.

To aid the policy makers in overcoming the information overload, we developed ExcavatorCovid (or Excavator for short), a system that will ingest open-source text sources (e.g., news articles and scientific publications), extract COVID-19 related events and relations between them, and build a Temporal and Causal Analysis Graph (TCAG). Excavator combines the following NLP techniques:

- Extracting events (§3) for types in our comprehensive COVID-19 event taxonomy (§2). Each event will have time and location if available in text, allowing analyses targeted at specific times or geographic regions of interest.
- Extracting three types of temporal and causal relations (§4) between pairs of events.
- Constructing a TCAG (§5) by assembling all events and relations, to provide a comprehensive overview of the events related to COVID-19 as well as their causes and impacts.
- Supporting trend and correlation analysis of events, via visualizing event popularity time series (§ 6) in the TCAG visualization.

Excavator produces a TCAG that is in a machine-readable JSON format and is also human-understandable (visualized via a web-based interactive User Interface), to support varied analytical and decision making needs. We hope that Excavator will aid government agencies in efforts to understand likely downstream effects of political and economic decisions and events related to the pandemic, and respond in a timely manner to mitigate the impact of COVID-19. The benefit of Excavator is realized through a comprehensive visualization of events and how they affect each other. We expect the utility of Excavator to outlive the COVID-19 pandemic: analysts and decision makers will be empowered by Excavator to better understand and solve complex problems in the future.

We first present our COVID-19 event taxonomy, and then we present details about event extraction, causal and temporal relation extraction, measuring

[1]We define an event as any occurrence, action, process or state of affairs, following (O'Gorman et al., 2016).

Proceedings of the 2021 Conference on Empirical Methods in Natural Language Processing: System Demonstrations, pages 63–71
November 7–11, 2021. ©2021 Association for Computational Linguistics

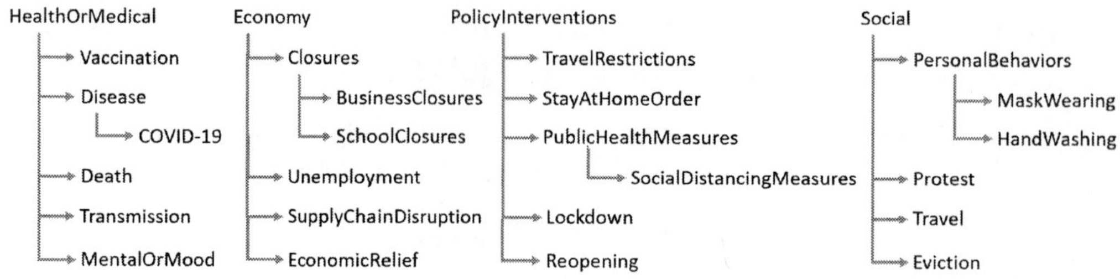

Figure 1: A partial illustration of the COVID-19 event taxonomy.

event popularity using news text as "quantitative data", and the approach for constructing a TCAG. We then describe the system demonstration, present a quantitative analysis of the extractions, and conclude with recommended use cases.

2 Building a COVID-19 Event Taxonomy

COVID-19 affects many aspects of our political, economic, and personal lives. A comprehensive analysis requires an event taxonomy that categorizes the events related to COVID-19 in many sectors and domains. We developed a COVID-19 event taxonomy using a hybrid approach of manual curation with automated support: first, we run Stanza (Qi et al., 2020) on a large sample (10%) of the Aylien coronavirus news dataset (§ 7) to tag verb and noun phrases that are likely to trigger events. Second, we represent each phrase as the average of the BERT (Devlin et al., 2019) contextualized embedding vectors of the subwords within each phrase, and then run committee-based clustering (Pantel and Lin, 2002) over the vector representations of the phrases to discover salient clusters. Finally, we review the frequently appearing clusters and define event types related to COVID-19.

The event taxonomy includes 76 event types. Each type comes with a name and a short description. Figure 1 illustrates several branches of the event taxonomy [2]. The events come from a wide range of domains. We also manually added hyponymy relations via *is_a* links (e.g., COVID-19 *is_a* Virus) between pairs of event types.

3 Extracting Events

We developed a neural network model for extracting events defined in the COVID-19 event taxonomy (the *event classification* stage) and extracting

[2]The complete taxonomy is available at `https://github.com/BBN-E/LearnIt/blob/master/inputs/domains/CORD_19/ontology/covid_event_ontology.yaml`.

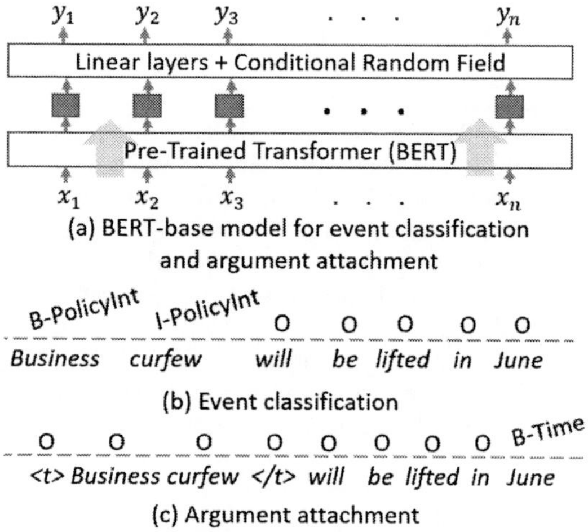

Figure 2: The BERT-based sequence tagging model for event classification and argument extraction. Figure (a) shows the architecture of the model, which takes a sequence of words $x_1, x_2, ..., x_n$ as input and outputs a sequence of tags $y_1, y_2, ..., y_n$. Figure (b) and (c) shows an example for each of the two stages. "PolicyInt" is short for "PolicyIntervention".

the location and time arguments (the *event argument extraction* stage), if they are mentioned in text, for each event mention. The structured representation (events with location and/or time) enables analyses of events targeting a specific time or location. Both stages use a BERT-based sequence tagging model. Figure 2(a) shows the model architecture. Given a sequence of tokens as input, the model extracts a sequence of tags, one per each token. We use the commonly used Begin-Inside-Outside (BIO) tags for both event types and event argument role types for the event classification and argument attachment tasks respectively.

Event classification: a sequence tagging model is trained to predict BIO tags of event types such that it identifies the event trigger span as well as the event type. Figure 2(b) shows an example.

Event argument extraction: similarly, another sequence tagging model is trained to predict BIO

Type	Counts	Type	Counts
COVID-19	2114	SocialDistancingMeasures	412
Virus	1028	TravelRestrictions	403
Pandemic	596	Disease	378
Unemployment	506	Death	355
Shortage	502	Lockdown	321

Table 1: Top-10 frequent events in the training dataset.

tags of argument role types, such that it identifies token spans of event arguments as well as their argument role types, with respect to a trigger that has already been identified in the *event classification* stage and marked in the input sentence in "$< t >$ ... $< /t >$". Figure 2(c) shows an example.

We run these two models in a pipeline: the event classification model is applied first to find event triggers and classify their types, then the event argument extraction model is applied to find location and time arguments for each event mention.

Training data curation. We use LearnIt rapid customization for event extraction (Chan et al., 2019) to curate a dataset for training the event classification model. Our developer spent about 13 minutes per event type to find, expand, and filter potential event triggers in a held-out 10% of the Aylien coronavirus news corpus. Statistics of the curated data set are shown in Table 1 (we only show the top-10 most frequent event types for brevity). In total, there are 11814 mentions in 7159 sentences.

To train the argument extraction model, we use the related event-argument annotation from the ACE 2005 dataset (Doddington et al., 2004). We focus on location and time arguments [3] and ignore other roles. At decoding time, after extracting the argument mentions for events, we apply the AWAKE (Boschee et al., 2014) entity linking system to resolve each location argument to a canonical geolocation, and use SERIF (Boschee et al., 2005) to resolve each time argument to a canonical time and then convert it to the month level. This allows us to perform analyses of events targeting a specific geolocation or month of interest.

4 Extracting Temporal and Causal Relations

We develop two approaches for extracting temporal and causal relations: a pattern-based approach and a neural network model. We take the union of the outputs from both approaches to maximize recall. The list of causal and temporal relations extracted by the systems is shown in Table 2. Our extractors extract relations at the subtype level. However, we decided to merge the subtypes into types because (a) a user survey shows that users prefer to have a simplified definition of causality that only includes "event X causes (positively impacts) event Y" and "X mitigates (reduces/prevents) Y", because finer-grained distinctions at sub-type level are difficult and less useful, and (b) merging the subtypes into types improves accuracy to near or above 0.8 as shown in Table 4, comparing to slightly below 0.7 at the sub-type level due to extraction approaches struggling to differentiate between the sub-types.

Type	Subtype	Definition
Causes	Cause	Y happens because of X.
	Catalyst	If X, intensity of Y increases.
	Precondition	X must have occured for Y to happen.
Mitigates	Mitigation	If X, intensity of Y decreases.
	Preventative	If X happens, Y can't happen.
Before	Before/after	X happens before/after Y.

Table 2: Causal and temporal relations between event X and Y.

Pattern-based relation extraction. We applied the temporal and causal relation extraction patterns from LearnIt (Min et al., 2020). A pattern is either a lexical pattern, which is a sequence of words between a pair of events, e.g.,"X leads to Y" [4], or a proposition pattern, which is the (nested) predicate-argument structure that connects the pair of events. For example, "verb:cause[subject=X] [object=Y]" is the proposition counterpart of the lexical pattern "X causes Y".

Neural relation extraction. We developed a mention pooling (Baldini Soares et al., 2019) neural model for causal and temporal relation extraction. Figure 3 shows the model architecture. Taking a sentence in which a pair of event mention spans are marked as input, the model first encodes the sentence with BERT (Devlin et al., 2019) [5]. For each of the left and right event mentions, it then uses average pooling over the BERT contextualized vectors of the words in the span to obtain fixed-dimension vectors V_1 and V_2 as the span representations. It then concatenates the input embeddings V_1 and V_2 with the element-wise difference $|V_1 - V_2|$ to generate the pair representation

[3]For example, *Place* and *Time* event argument roles in ACE can be used to train an argument-role model to extract location and time arguments, respectively.

[4]X and Y refer to the left and right arguments of a relation.

[5]The BERT-Base model is used.

$V = (V_1, V_2, |V_1 - V_2|)$. V is passed into a linear layer followed by a softmax layer to make the relation prediction. The model is trained with a blended dataset consisting of the Entities, Events, Simple and Complex Cause Assertion Annotation datasets [6] released by LDC [7], and 1.5K temporal relation instances generated by applying the LearnIt temporal relation extraction patterns to 10,000 sampled Gigaword (Parker et al., 2011) articles.

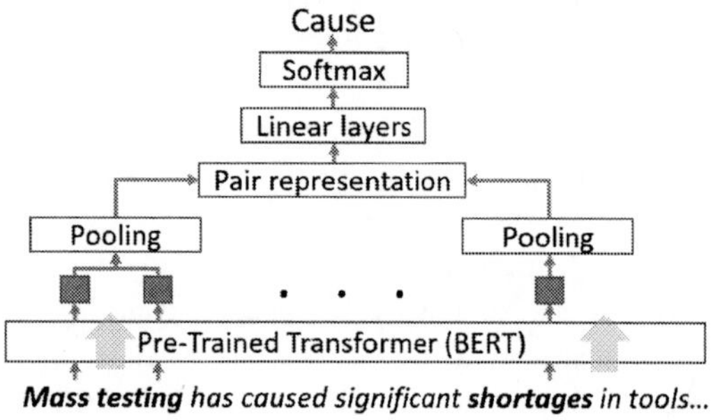

Figure 3: The neural model for causal and temporal relation extraction.

5 Constructing a TCAG

We aggregate all extracted events and causal and temporal relations across the corpus to construct a TCAG. The TCAG is visualized in the interactive visualization, in which each node is an event type and each edge is a causal or temporal relation [8].

We use a simple approach to aggregate events: by default, all event mentions sharing the same type are grouped into a single node named by the type; we resort to the UI to allow the user to selectively focus on a specific location and/or time, such that the UI will only show a TCAG involving event mentions and causal relations between pairs of events for the location and/or time of interest.

6 Measuring Event Popularity through Time

The TCAG only provides a qualitative analysis of the temporal and causal relations between the COVID-related events. It will be more informative if we can measure the popularity of events through time to enable **trend analysis** (e.g., *does lockdown go up or down between January and May, 2020?*) and **correlation analysis** (e.g., *will a stricter lockdown improve or deteriorate the economy?*).

In order to support these analyses, we produce a timeseries of a popularity score for each event type over time (a.k.a., event timeline). Extending our prior work (Min and Zhao, 2019), we define the popularity score for event type e at time t as:

$$Popularity(e)_t = \frac{1}{T} \sum_{t' \in [t-\frac{T}{2}, t+\frac{T}{2}]} \frac{N_{e,t'}}{cM_{t'}}$$

in which $N_{e,t}$ is the frequency of event e at month t. We calculate the moving average centered at each t with a sliding window of $T = 3$ months to reduce noise. M_t is the total number of articles published in month t. $c = 1/500$ is a normalizing constant. The raw event frequency counts can be inflated due to the increasing level of media activity. Therefore, we divide the raw counts by cM_t to normalize the counts so that they are comparable across different months.

7 System Demonstration

Datasets. We run Excavator on the following two corpora to produce a TCAG for COVID-19: the first corpus is 1.2 million articles [9] from the Aylien Coronavirus News Dataset [10], which contains 1.6 million COVID-related articles published between November 2019 and July 2020 that are from ~440 news sources. We only kept the articles that are published between January and May 2020, since the corpus contains fewer articles in other months. The second corpus is the COVID-19 Open Research Dataset (Wang et al., 2020). It contains coronavirus-related research from PubMed's PMC corpus, a corpus maintained by the WHO, and bioRxiv and medRxiv pre-prints. As of 11/08/2020, it contains over 300,000 scholarly articles.

We combine these two corpora because news and research articles are complementary: news are rich in real-world events and are up to date, while analytical articles contain more causal relationships. Therefore, combining them is likely to lead to a more comprehensive analysis and new insights.

Overall statistics of extractions. Excavator extracted 6.2 million event mentions of 59 types. Table 3 shows the event types that appear more than 50,000 times. We randomly sampled 100 event

[6] The catalog IDs of the LDC datasets are LDC2019E48, LDC2019E61, LDC2019E70, LDC2019E82, LDC2019E83.

[7] www.ldc.upenn.edu

[8] *is_a* relations are also added as dashed edges in the TCAG.

[9] These articles do not overlap with the held-out set for training data curation.

[10] https://aylien.com/blog/free-coronavirus-news-dataset

Type	Counts	Type	Counts
COVID-19	2772.3	Travel	111.8
Death	730.0	FearOrPanic	94.6
Pandemic	689.2	Closures	92.3
Lockdown	417.2	TravelRestrictions	76.9
Isolation*	195.4	Shortage	68.3
DiseaseSpread	145.4	Conflict	55.5
Testing	130.7	Virus	54.8
Treatment	112.8	Symptom	54.0

Table 3: Frequent events extracted from the corpora (ranked by frequency reversely; numbers are in thousands). *Isolation refers to IsolationOrConfinement.

Type	Count	Precision
Causes	193,694	0.78
Mitigates	30,452	0.87
Before	2,030	0.81

Table 4: Causal and temporal relations extracted.

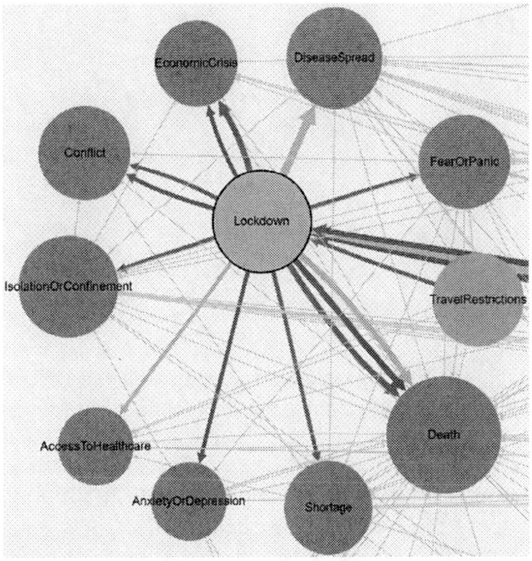

Figure 4: A screenshot of a partial TCAG centered on Lockdown. Green, pink, and purple edges shows Cause, Mitigate and Before relations, respectively. Blue, orange and green nodes show the focused node and nodes with incoming and outgoing edges (with respect to the focused node), respectively.

mentions, manually reviewed them, and found that the extracted events are 83% accurate. Excavator extracted 226,176 causal and temporal relations from the two corpora. A summary of the extracted relations and their precision [11] are shown in Table 4.

TCAG Visualization We developed an interactive visualization of the TCAG. Figure 4 shows a small part of the TCAG centered on the event Lockdown. Each node represents an event type in our COVID event taxonomy for which Excavator is able to extract events and track their popularity scores (§ 6) through time. The three types of relational edges (Causes, Mitigates and Before) are shown in different colors. The size of the nodes and the thickness of the edges indicate the relative frequency of the event types or relations in the log scale, respectively. For example, Figure 4 shows that Death is mentioned more frequently than Lockdown, and the causal relation {Lockdown, Causes, EconomicCrisis} appears more frequently than {Lockdown, Mitigates ("reduces"), AccessToHealthcare}. To support analysis focusing on a single event, we color the focused event in blue, events that cause or precede the focused event in orange, and events that the focused event causes or precedes in green.

Event popularity timeseries visualization For each node (event) in the TCAG visualization, we show its event popularity timeseries visualization on the side. Figure 5 shows 3 screenshots of the event popularity timeseries (§ 6) visualization between January and May 2020 for Lockdown, EconomicCrisis and COVID-19 respectively.

8 Recommended Use Cases

We describe 3 recommended use cases below. More details are in our demonstration video.

Use case 1: causal and temporal analysis. We can get a panoramic view of the underlying casual and temporal dynamics between events related to COVID from the overall TCAG. We can start by analyzing the causal or temporal relations centered at an event of interest. For example, Figure 4 shows a diverse range of effects and consequences of Lockdown, such as EconomicCrisis (economic), Shortage (supply-chain), FearOrPanic (mental), etc. Interestingly, the graph also reveals surprises such as {Lockdown, Causes, Death}: the UI shows supporting evidence such as "lockdown exacerbates deaths and chronic health problems associated with poverty, ...". Furthermore, the TCAG shows that Lockdown mitigates DiseaseSpread but it also has a negative impact on the Economy, which will inform the decision makers that they will need to understand the economic trade-offs when implementing the Lockdown policy.

We can also analyze longer-distance causal path-

[11] Estimated by manually reviewing 40 instances per type

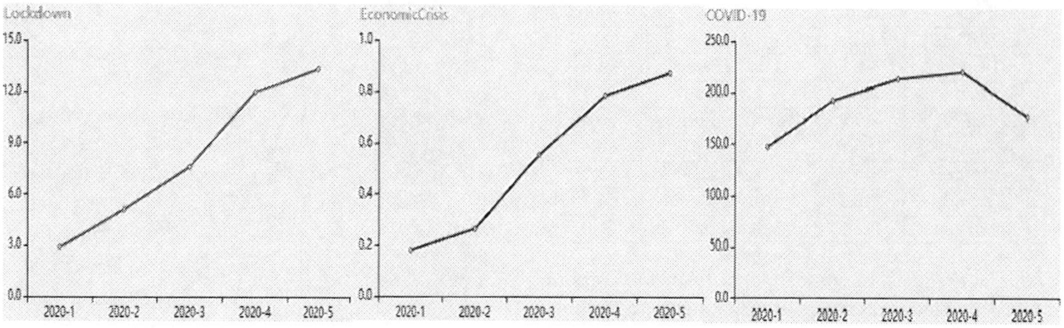

Figure 5: Event popularity timeseries (timeline) between 01-05/2020 for Lockdown, EconomicCrisis and COVID-19. X-axis shows months between January and May 2020. Y-axis shows event popularity scores.

ways consisting of two or more causal/temporal edges. For example, our demo video shows that COVID-19 causes or precedes (Before) Lockdown, and that Lockdown causes or precedes EconomicCrisis. This helps us understand details about how COVID causes EconomicCrisis.

Use case 2: trend and correlation analysis. We can inspect the event timeline for a node or an edge to perform a trend analysis and a correlation analysis, respectively. Figure 5 shows screenshots of the event popularity timeseries between January and May 2020 for Lockdown, EconomicCrisis and COVID-19. First, the user can click on a single event to perform a trend analysis: the popularity of Lockdown goes up continuously, indicating an upward trend in implementing lockdown policies in more geographic regions. The user can also click on a edge to perform a correlation analysis for a pair of events: when the user clicks on the edge {Lockdown, Causes, EconomicCrisis}, the UI shows a strong correlation between the two upward curves. For another edge "Lockdown mitigates COVID-19", the UI shows a negative correlation near the end: as Lockdown rises, COVID-19 slightly falls towards the end.

Use case 3: analyses targeted at geolocations. The event timeline visualization also allows the user to see the timeline for geolocations such as each U.S. state individually, instead of the aggregate for the entire U.S.. Figure 6 is a screenshot showing the 10 timelines for Lockdown for the top-10 most frequently mentioned U.S. states. The screenshot shows that the curves for California and New York go much higher than other states. This roughly matches the stricter lockdown policies implemented in the two states during this time period, compared with other states. Such targeted analysis is made possible because our events have *location* and *time* arguments. We can also make the TCAG only show events and relations for a specific state, if a user selects a state of interest in the UI.

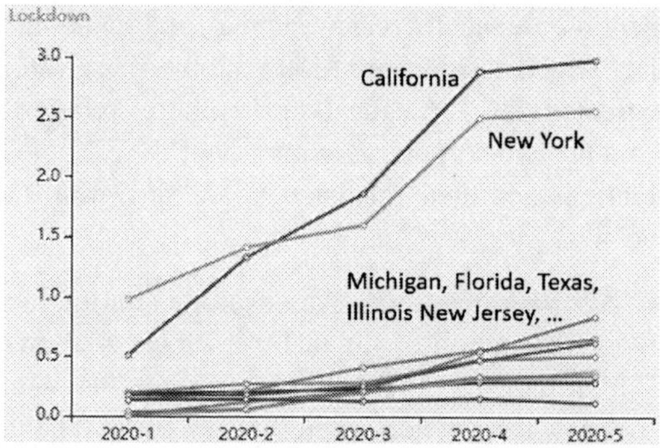

Figure 6: Event popularity timeseries in 01-05/2020 for Lockdown, for top-10 frequently mentioned US states.

9 Related Work

Extracting events. Event extraction has been studied using feature-based approaches (Huang and Riloff, 2012; Ji and Grishman, 2008), or neural networks (Chen et al., 2015; Nguyen et al., 2016a; Wadden et al., 2019; Liu et al., 2020). GDELT (Leetaru and Schrodt, 2013) creates an event database for the conflict and mediation domain. It has very few event types related to COVID-19. To adapt event extraction to new domains, Chen et al. (2019) developed a user-in-the-loop rapid event customization system. Nguyen et al. (2016b) proposed a neural model for event type extension given seed examples. Peng et al. (2016) developed a minimally supervised approach using triggers gathered from ACE annotation guideline.

Extracting causal and temporal relations. There are a lot of work in temporal (D'Souza and Ng, 2013; Chambers et al., 2014; Ning et al., 2018b; Meng and Rumshisky, 2018; Han et al., 2019; Vashishtha et al., 2020; Wright-Bettner et al., 2020) and causal (Bethard and Martin, 2008; Do et al., 2011; Riaz and Girju, 2013; Roemmele and Gordon, 2018; Hashimoto, 2019) relation extraction. Mirza and Tonelli (2016) and Ning et al. (2018a) extract both in a single framework.

Constructing Causal Graphs from Text. Eidos (Sharp et al., 2019) uses a rule-based approach to extract causal relations to build a causal analysis graph, that has limited coverage on events related to COVID-19. LearnIt (Min et al., 2020) enables rapid customization of causal relation extractors. LearnIt does not focus on causal relations involving COVID-related events. This work also differs from these two in that we extract event arguments and temporal relations, and track event popularity.

10 Conclusion and Future Work

We present Excavator, a machine reading system that automatically constructs a Temporal and Causal Analysis Graph for COVID-19 by reading open-source text documents such as news and scientific publications. Our next steps are to integrate Modal Dependency Parsing (Yao et al., 2021) for event factuality assessment, and cross-lingual transfer learning (Nguyen et al., 2021) to make Excavator applicable to more languages.

Acknowledgements

This research is based upon work supported in part by the Office of the Director of National Intelligence (ODNI), Intelligence Advanced Research Projects Activity (IARPA), via Contract No.: 2021-20102700002. The views and conclusions contained herein are those of the authors and should not be interpreted as necessarily representing the official policies, either expressed or implied, of ODNI, IARPA, or the U.S. Government. The U.S. Government is authorized to reproduce and distribute reprints for governmental purposes notwithstanding any copyright annotation therein.

References

Livio Baldini Soares, Nicholas FitzGerald, Jeffrey Ling, and Tom Kwiatkowski. 2019. Matching the blanks: Distributional similarity for relation learning. In *Proceedings of the 57th Annual Meeting of the Association for Computational Linguistics*, pages 2895–2905, Florence, Italy. Association for Computational Linguistics.

Steven Bethard and James H. Martin. 2008. Learning semantic links from a corpus of parallel temporal and causal relations. In *Proceedings of ACL-08: HLT, Short Papers*, pages 177–180, Columbus, Ohio. Association for Computational Linguistics.

Elizabeth Boschee, Marjorie Freedman, Saurabh Khanwalkar, Anoop Kumar, Amit Srivastava, and Ralph Weischedel. 2014. Researching persons & organizations: Awake: From text to an entity-centric knowledge base. In *2014 IEEE International Conference on Big Data (Big Data)*, pages 1030–1039. IEEE.

Elizabeth Boschee, Ralph Weischedel, and Alex Zamanian. 2005. Automatic information extraction. In *Proceedings of the International Conference on Intelligence Analysis*, volume 71. Citeseer.

Nathanael Chambers, Taylor Cassidy, Bill McDowell, and Steven Bethard. 2014. Dense event ordering with a multi-pass architecture. *Transactions of the Association for Computational Linguistics*, 2:273–284.

Yee Seng Chan, Joshua Fasching, Haoling Qiu, and Bonan Min. 2019. Rapid customization for event extraction. In *Proceedings of the 57th Annual Meeting of the Association for Computational Linguistics: System Demonstrations*, pages 31–36, Florence, Italy. Association for Computational Linguistics.

Yubo Chen, Liheng Xu, Kang Liu, Daojian Zeng, and Jun Zhao. 2015. Event extraction via dynamic multi-pooling convolutional neural networks. In *ACL-IJCNLP2-2015*, pages 167–176, Beijing, China. Association for Computational Linguistics.

Jacob Devlin, Ming-Wei Chang, Kenton Lee, and Kristina Toutanova. 2019. BERT: Pre-training of deep bidirectional transformers for language understanding. In *Proceedings of the 2019 Conference of the North American Chapter of the Association for Computational Linguistics: Human Language Technologies, Volume 1 (Long and Short Papers)*, pages 4171–4186, Minneapolis, Minnesota. Association for Computational Linguistics.

Quang Do, Yee Seng Chan, and Dan Roth. 2011. Minimally supervised event causality identification. In *Proceedings of the 2011 Conference on Empirical Methods in Natural Language Processing*, pages 294–303.

George R Doddington, Alexis Mitchell, Mark A Przybocki, Lance A Ramshaw, Stephanie M Strassel, and Ralph M Weischedel. 2004. The automatic content extraction (ace) program-tasks, data, and evaluation. In *Lrec*, volume 2, pages 837–840. Lisbon.

Jennifer D'Souza and Vincent Ng. 2013. Classifying temporal relations with rich linguistic knowledge. In *Proceedings of the 2013 Conference of the North*

American Chapter of the Association for Computational Linguistics: Human Language Technologies, pages 918–927.

Rujun Han, I-Hung Hsu, Mu Yang, Aram Galstyan, Ralph Weischedel, and Nanyun Peng. 2019. Deep structured neural network for event temporal relation extraction. In *Proceedings of the 23rd Conference on Computational Natural Language Learning (CoNLL)*, pages 666–106, Hong Kong, China. Association for Computational Linguistics.

Chikara Hashimoto. 2019. Weakly supervised multilingual causality extraction from Wikipedia. In *Proceedings of the 2019 Conference on Empirical Methods in Natural Language Processing and the 9th International Joint Conference on Natural Language Processing (EMNLP-IJCNLP)*, pages 2988–2999, Hong Kong, China. Association for Computational Linguistics.

Ruihong Huang and Ellen Riloff. 2012. Modeling textual cohesion for event extraction. In *AAAI-CAI*, AAAI'12, pages 1664–1670. AAAI Press.

Heng Ji and Ralph Grishman. 2008. Refining event extraction through cross-document inference. In *ACL-HLT-2008*, pages 254–262, Columbus, Ohio. Association for Computational Linguistics.

Kalev Leetaru and Philip A Schrodt. 2013. Gdelt: Global data on events, location, and tone, 1979–2012. In *ISA annual convention*, volume 2, pages 1–49. Citeseer.

Jian Liu, Yubo Chen, Kang Liu, Wei Bi, and Xiaojiang Liu. 2020. Event extraction as machine reading comprehension. In *Proceedings of the 2020 Conference on Empirical Methods in Natural Language Processing (EMNLP)*, pages 1641–1651, Online. Association for Computational Linguistics.

Yuanliang Meng and Anna Rumshisky. 2018. Context-aware neural model for temporal information extraction. In *Proceedings of the 56th Annual Meeting of the Association for Computational Linguistics (Volume 1: Long Papers)*, pages 527–536, Melbourne, Australia. Association for Computational Linguistics.

Bonan Min, Manaj Srivastava, Haoling Qiu, Prasannakumar Muthukumar, and Joshua Fasching. 2020. Learnit: On-demand rapid customization for event-event relation extraction. In *Proceedings of the AAAI Conference on Artificial Intelligence*, volume 34, pages 13630–13631.

Bonan Min and Xiaoxi Zhao. 2019. Measure country-level socio-economic indicators with streaming news: An empirical study. In *Proceedings of the 2019 Conference on Empirical Methods in Natural Language Processing and the 9th International Joint Conference on Natural Language Processing (EMNLP-IJCNLP)*, pages 1249–1254, Hong Kong, China. Association for Computational Linguistics.

Paramita Mirza and Sara Tonelli. 2016. Catena: Causal and temporal relation extraction from natural language texts. In *Proceedings of COLING 2016, the 26th International Conference on Computational Linguistics: Technical Papers*, pages 64–75.

Minh Van Nguyen, Tuan Ngo Nguyen, Bonan Min, and Thien Huu Nguyen. 2021. Crosslingual transfer learning for relation and event extraction via word category and class alignments. In *Proceedings of the 2021 Conference on Empirical Methods in Natural Language Processing (EMNLP)*.

Thien Huu Nguyen, Kyunghyun Cho, and Ralph Grishman. 2016a. Joint event extraction via recurrent neural networks. In *NAACL-HLT-2016*, pages 300–309, San Diego, California. Association for Computational Linguistics.

Thien Huu Nguyen, Lisheng Fu, Kyunghyun Cho, and Ralph Grishman. 2016b. A two-stage approach for extending event detection to new types via neural networks. In *WRepL4NLP*, pages 158–165, Berlin, Germany. Association for Computational Linguistics.

Qiang Ning, Zhili Feng, Hao Wu, and Dan Roth. 2018a. Joint reasoning for temporal and causal relations. In *Proceedings of the 56th Annual Meeting of the Association for Computational Linguistics (Volume 1: Long Papers)*, pages 2278–2288, Melbourne, Australia. Association for Computational Linguistics.

Qiang Ning, Hao Wu, Haoruo Peng, and Dan Roth. 2018b. Improving temporal relation extraction with a globally acquired statistical resource. In *Proceedings of the 2018 Conference of the North American Chapter of the Association for Computational Linguistics: Human Language Technologies, Volume 1 (Long Papers)*, pages 841–851, New Orleans, Louisiana. Association for Computational Linguistics.

Tim O'Gorman, Kristin Wright-Bettner, and Martha Palmer. 2016. Richer event description: Integrating event coreference with temporal, causal and bridging annotation. In *Proceedings of the 2nd Workshop on Computing News Storylines (CNS 2016)*, pages 47–56, Austin, Texas. Association for Computational Linguistics.

Patrick Pantel and Dekang Lin. 2002. Document clustering with committees. In *Proceedings of the 25th annual international ACM SIGIR conference on Research and development in information retrieval*, pages 199–206.

Robert Parker, David Graff, Junbo Kong, Ke Chen, and Kazuaki Maeda. 2011. English gigaword fifth edition, 2011. *Linguistic Data Consortium, Philadelphia, PA, USA*.

Haoruo Peng, Yangiu Song, and Dan Roth. 2016. Event detection and co-reference with minimal supervision. In *EMNLP-2016*.

Peng Qi, Yuhao Zhang, Yuhui Zhang, Jason Bolton, and Christopher D. Manning. 2020. Stanza: A Python natural language processing toolkit for many human languages. In *Proceedings of the 58th Annual Meeting of the Association for Computational Linguistics: System Demonstrations*.

Mehwish Riaz and Roxana Girju. 2013. Toward a better understanding of causality between verbal events: Extraction and analysis of the causal power of verb-verb associations. In *Proceedings of the SIGDIAL 2013 Conference*, pages 21–30, Metz, France. Association for Computational Linguistics.

Melissa Roemmele and Andrew Gordon. 2018. An encoder-decoder approach to predicting causal relations in stories. In *Proceedings of the First Workshop on Storytelling*, pages 50–59, New Orleans, Louisiana. Association for Computational Linguistics.

Rebecca Sharp, Adarsh Pyarelal, Benjamin Gyori, Keith Alcock, Egoitz Laparra, Marco A. Valenzuela-Escárcega, Ajay Nagesh, Vikas Yadav, John Bachman, Zheng Tang, Heather Lent, Fan Luo, Mithun Paul, Steven Bethard, Kobus Barnard, Clayton Morrison, and Mihai Surdeanu. 2019. Eidos, INDRA, & delphi: From free text to executable causal models. In *Proceedings of the 2019 Conference of the North American Chapter of the Association for Computational Linguistics (Demonstrations)*, pages 42–47, Minneapolis, Minnesota. Association for Computational Linguistics.

Siddharth Vashishtha, Adam Poliak, Yash Kumar Lal, Benjamin Van Durme, and Aaron Steven White. 2020. Temporal reasoning in natural language inference. In *Findings of the Association for Computational Linguistics: EMNLP 2020*, pages 4070–4078, Online. Association for Computational Linguistics.

David Wadden, Ulme Wennberg, Yi Luan, and Hannaneh Hajishirzi. 2019. Entity, relation, and event extraction with contextualized span representations. In *Proceedings of the 2019 Conference on Empirical Methods in Natural Language Processing and the 9th International Joint Conference on Natural Language Processing (EMNLP-IJCNLP)*, pages 5784–5789, Hong Kong, China. Association for Computational Linguistics.

Lucy Lu Wang, Kyle Lo, Yoganand Chandrasekhar, Russell Reas, Jiangjiang Yang, Doug Burdick, Darrin Eide, Kathryn Funk, Yannis Katsis, Rodney Michael Kinney, Yunyao Li, Ziyang Liu, William Merrill, Paul Mooney, Dewey A. Murdick, Devvret Rishi, Jerry Sheehan, Zhihong Shen, Brandon Stilson, Alex D. Wade, Kuansan Wang, Nancy Xin Ru Wang, Christopher Wilhelm, Boya Xie, Douglas M. Raymond, Daniel S. Weld, Oren Etzioni, and Sebastian Kohlmeier. 2020. CORD-19: The COVID-19 open research dataset. In *Proceedings of the 1st Workshop on NLP for COVID-19 at ACL 2020*, Online. Association for Computational Linguistics.

Kristin Wright-Bettner, Chen Lin, Timothy Miller, Steven Bethard, Dmitriy Dligach, Martha Palmer, James H. Martin, and Guergana Savova. 2020. Defining and learning refined temporal relations in the clinical narrative. In *Proceedings of the 11th International Workshop on Health Text Mining and Information Analysis*, pages 104–114, Online. Association for Computational Linguistics.

Jiarui Yao, Haoling Qiu, Jin Zhao, Bonan Min, and Nianwen Xue. 2021. Factuality assessment as modal dependency parsing. In *Proceedings of the 59th Annual Meeting of the Association for Computational Linguistics and the 11th International Joint Conference on Natural Language Processing (Volume 1: Long Papers)*, pages 1540–1550, Online. Association for Computational Linguistics.

KOAS: Korean Text Offensiveness Analysis System

San-Hee Park[1*] Kang-Min Kim[3*] Seonhee Cho[1*] Jun-Hyung Park[1]
Hyuntae Park[2] Hyuna Kim[1] Seongwon Chung[1] SangKeun Lee[1,2]
[1] Department of Computer Science and Engineering [2] Department of Artificial Intelligence
Korea University, Seoul, Republic of Korea
[3] Department of Data Science, The Catholic University of Korea, Bucheon, Republic of Korea
carpediem20@korea.ac.kr kangmin89@catholic.ac.kr
{ehcho8564, irish07, pht0639}@korea.ac.kr
{kiipo0623, syc1013, yalphy}@korea.ac.kr

Abstract

***Warning**: This manuscript contains a certain level of offensive expression.*

As communication through social media platforms has grown immensely, the increasing prevalence of offensive language online has become a critical problem. Notably in Korea, one of the countries with the highest Internet usage, automatic detection of offensive expressions has recently been brought to attention. However, morphological richness and complex syntax of Korean causes difficulties in neural model training. Furthermore, most of previous studies mainly focus on the detection of abusive language, disregarding implicit offensiveness and underestimating a different degree of intensity. To tackle these problems, we present KOAS, a system that fully exploits both contextual and linguistic features and estimates an offensiveness score for a text. We carefully designed KOAS with a multi-task learning framework and constructed a Korean dataset for offensive analysis from various domains. Refer for a detailed demonstration. [1]

1 Introduction

Online communities and social media have become the mainstream platforms of communication. This has also led to unwanted developments – an increasing use of offensive language through online platforms. Consequently, analyzing texts and detecting offensive expressions has become a critical issue (Nobata et al., 2016). However, manual detection of offensive texts is infeasible owing to the increasing popularity of social networks (Kennedy et al., 2017). Notably in South Korea, high internet accessibility and social media usage[2] have stimulated a dire need for a system that analyzes Korean text and its offensiveness (Moon et al., 2020a).

Despite the recent success of offensive language detection on English text (Mishra et al., 2019), handling

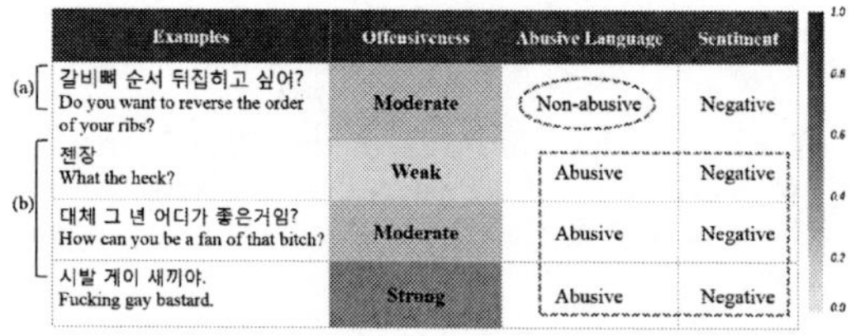

Figure 1: (a) Illustration of an example of offensive sentence without any explicit profanity, which would be classified as "non-abusive" in abusive language detection. (b) Illustration of sentences with different intensity of offensiveness that is not distinguished properly in the discrete classification tasks.

Korean texts is quite challenging. Owing to the high-context cultural characteristics of Korean language culture (Merkin, 2009), Korean offensive expressions tend to be expressed in a subtle and figurative way without explicit abusive expressions as illustrated in Figure 1(a). Additionally, large vocabulary and the complex syntax as a morphologically rich and agglutinative language (Song, 2006) often hinders the model's learning (Kim et al., 2018; Passban et al., 2018).

Another substantial problem in text analysis is that the intensity of offensiveness in text is often neglected. As shown in Figure 1(b), the sentence may address the different intensity depending on the degree of frequency and explicitness of the offensive expression (Jay and Janschewitz, 2008; Jay, 2009). However, most researches focus on simply classifying sentences into discrete, sometimes binary, categories (Kennedy et al., 2017; Patwa et al., 2020; Mishra et al., 2019) and treat sentences with different intensity as the same type, *"negative"*, or *"abusive"* for instance.

In this demo, we present KOAS, a system that estimates the score of offensiveness in Korean text. Since the degree of offensiveness is different from of abusive detection or sentiment analysis, we develop a scoring function for offensiveness. The score is to quantify how much negative feelings each sentence can cause to readers, or how offensively it can be read. To this end, KOAS internally conducts two classification tasks, abusive language detection and sentiment analysis. An offensiveness score is then elicited from the outputs of two internal tasks. While computing the score, KOAS inte-

* These authors contributed equally to this work.

[1] https://www.youtube.com/watch?v=xtQv7GKOaeg (The KOAS link will be updated later.)

[2] https://datareportal.com/reports/digital-2020-south-korea

Proceedings of the 2021 Conference on Empirical Methods in Natural Language Processing: System Demonstrations, pages 72–78
November 7–11, 2021.

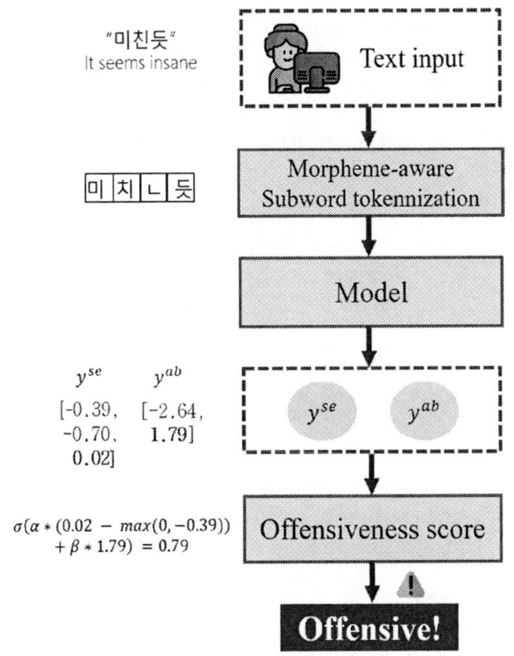

Figure 2: This is a flowchart of KOAS, from taking a Korean text input to eliciting the offensiveness score. y^{se} and y^{ab} denote output vectors of the sentiment analysis and abusiveness detection respectively.

grates the semantic perspective where it detects explicit abusive expressions and semantic perspective where it captures implicit nuance and tone of the text.

Since the notion of continuous degree of offensiveness has not been researched in depth yet, there are no appropriate datasets to evaluate offensiveness score. Therefore, we construct new datasets for the abusive language detection and sentiment classification and utilize them for evaluating our systems for the offensiveness analysis. To handle Korean data, we utilize a refined morpheme-level tokenization method, which has an effect of data augmentation and subword regularization. We summarize our contributions as follows.

- We present a novel demonstration system that analyzes the offensiveness intensity of Korean text based on the abusive language and sentiment information.
- We construct and publicly release a novel dataset for abusive language detection and the sentiment analysis of Korean text.
- Our experiments demonstrate that the multi-task learning of the abusive language detection and the sentiment analysis helps improve the performance of both tasks.

2 System Design

The architecture of KOAS is shown in Figure 2. The system mainly consists of two parts: a classification model and an offensiveness scoring function. We will describe them in detail in the following subsection.

Model Architecture The overall model architecture was inspired by the gated multi-task learning framework (Kim et al., 2019). We denote the proposed neural network as CNN_{MTL} and compare it with the baseline of the pipelined vanilla CNN (Kim, 2014). CNN_{MTL} jointly learns two text analysis tasks - abusive language detection and sentiment analysis. The model is trained with two tasks, learning both linguistic perspective and semantic perspectives simultaneously. This leads to a more computationally efficient model with better performance than training two separate models for each task. Utilizing task-specific layers as well as a shared layer has proven to be effective in learning not only task-dependent features but also useful common features (Kim et al., 2019; Misra et al., 2016; Liu et al., 2017).

The neural model of KOAS consists of an embedding layer, two task-specific convolution layers for the sentiment analysis and abusive language detection, a shared convolution layer, and two softmax layers.

The embedding layer transforms an arbitrary-length input sentence into a matrix of embeddings, denoted as $S = w_1 \oplus w_2 \oplus ... \oplus w_s$, where $S \in R^{s \times k}$, $\oplus$ denotes the concatenation operator, and s and k are the number of words and the dimension of word embedding, respectively. Then, the embedding matrix is fed into the three convolution layers. The features h_{se}, h_{ab}, h_{sh} are obtained from the convolution layers. All the convolution layers are followed by ReLU, max pooling, and dropout layers. The features are then concatenated and fed into the softmax layers. Additionally, we employ a gate mechanism (Hochreiter and Schmidhuber, 1997; Chung et al., 2014) when incorporating task-private convolution output to the other task. We introduce two gates G_{s2a} and G_{a2s}, which control the flow of features from the sentiment analysis task to the abusive language detection task and vice versa, respectively. The gates share useful features and prevent irrelevant information from being propagated. This is calculated by

$$G_{s2a}(h_{se}) = \sigma(W_{s2a}h_{se} + b_{s2a}), \quad (1)$$

where W_{s2a} and b_{s2a} denote learnable weights and biases, respectively, and σ represents the sigmoid function. W_{s2a} is trained to borrow private features of sentiment analysis task taking h_{se}, which is the output of convolutional layer for sentiment analysis.

$$y^{ab} = Linear(h_{ab} \oplus h_{sh} \oplus G_{s2a}(h_{se})), \quad (2)$$

$$\hat{y^{ab}} = softmax(y^{ab}) \quad (3)$$

where h_{ab} and h_{sh} denote output of the convolutional layer for the abusive language detection and the shared convolutional layer for the both task respectively, and $\oplus$ denotes the vector concatenation. All features are concatenated as the input of the fully connected layer. The output for abusive language detection y^{ab} can be derived by Eq. 2. Thereafter, the probability of abusive detection $\hat{y^{ab}}$ is calculated using the softmax function, as shown in Eq. 3. The same method was applied to the sentiment analysis task.

Text Offensiveness The score for text offensiveness is based on the following rules:

- The score of offensiveness represents the degree of negative feelings (e.g. anger, annoyance and fear) that the text may arouse in readers.
- Some abusive expressions may be used as an emphasis or exclamation whereas most abuse expression itself can arouse displeasure regardless of the context.

Therefore, negative tones and abusive expression in the text have a positive correlation with offensiveness, whereas a positive tone has a negative correlation. Based on these hypotheses, we propose a new method for the quantification of offensiveness:

$$O = \sigma(\alpha \times (y^{neg} - max(0, y^{pos})) + \beta \times y^{ab}) \quad (4)$$

where y^{neg} and y^{pos} represent the output values for *negative* and *positive* input sentences, respectively. α and β are hyperparameters that determine the weights of sentiment polarity and abusive expression, respectively and we empirically set α to be 0.456 and β to 0.758. [3]

The proposed method uses y^{neg} and y^{pos}, and the model's prediction of negative and positive polarity. We prevent y^{pos} to be negative, we limit minimum value to zero by applying max function. We use the output value. y^{ab} and y^{neg} represent the degree of how explicitly a profanity appears and how intensely the negative sentiment is expressed, respectively. We have empirically verified that the score becomes correlated with the human feedback of offensiveness. Our experiments demonstrate the practicality of the score when applied to real-world data.

3 Evaluation

3.1 Dataset

Data Construction To ensure that KOAS to handles sentences from various domains, we gathered our training data from three different sources, which covers various domains – YouTube[4], Naver Movie review[5] and dcinside[6]. We scraped comments from a popular Korean online community, expecting our train dataset to be close to a raw expression for practicality. Then, we removed duplicate comments and filtered out non-Korean sentences. The collected dataset consists of 46,853 Korean sentences and was labeled by three annotators on predefined criteria for abusive language (Koo and Seo, 2012) and sentiment following the instruction (Nakov et al., 2016).

Abusive Language		Sentiment		
Abusive	Non-abusive	Pos.	Neu.	Neg.
27%	73%	13%	63%	24%

Table 1: Statistics of dataset label for each task. Pos., Neu. and Neg. indicate positive, neutral and negative polarities respectively.

Sentence Original	볼수록 재수없네 (The more I see him, the worse I get him.)
Morpheme (Mecab)	볼수록 재수없 네
Morpheme (Komoran)	보 ㄹ수록 재수 없 네

Table 2: Original sentence in train set is augmented by two different tokenizers, Mecab and Komoran, based on different parsing rules.

Sentences are categorized into binary classes whether they contain abusive language and three classes for sentiment polarity: positive, neutral and negative. Table 1 shows the composition of the classes and the definition of data distribution. The dataset could be downloaded from the link[7]. We hope our corpus can be used for analysis and modeling on Korean abusiveness expression.

Preprocessing Korean is an agglutinative language (Song, 2006) in which words are constructed with an agglutination of morphemes, and has a syntactic structure different from English. Thus, jamo-level (Stratos, 2017) or morpheme-level tokenization rather than simple word-level tokenization, has been used on the Korean dataset (Park et al., 2018). We applied morpheme-aware subword tokenization, which has proven to be the best tokenization method for Koreans (Park et al., 2020b). To tokenize words at the morpheme level, we utilize KoNLPy, an open-source library for Korean text that provides a number of different tokenizers with different parsing rules and methods. In the training process, we augmented two types of tokenized sentences from each sentence in Korean text with two different tokenizers, Mecab and Komoran, as illustrated in Table 2. Not only does it augment the size of training data around

[3] We empirically set initial α and β to 0.5 and 0.8. Then we tuned α and β as trainable parameters using the Korean Toxic speech corpus (Moon et al., 2020b) with labeled toxic sentences.

[4] https://youtube.com

[5] https://github.com/e9t/nsmc

[6] https://www.dcinside.com/

[7] https://drive.google.com/file/d/1YZ_tuJzs5CBaO0pNY7Cb1Xa0rRR3GQX-/view?usp=sharing

	Positive		Negative	
	Comment	Offensiveness score	Comment	Offensiveness score
Profanity	**존나** 행복하다 **시발** (I'm fucking happy)	3.71	**지랄**이야 **시발** (Fucking hell)	51.89
	미친 존나 재밌네 (It's crazy funny)	19.98	**시발** 나가죽어라 (Fuck off and die)	71.70
	개 예쁘다 (Fucking pretty)	38.37	**게이년** (Gay bitch)	97.78
No Profanity	밝은 것만 보자, 우리 (Let's look on the bright side)	4.06	갈비뼈 순서 뒤집히고 싶어? (Do you want to reverse the order of your ribs?)	56.59
	무대 찢었다 (That was awesome)	19.48	얼굴 못생겼어 (You look ugly)	72.36
	걱정하지마 다 잘될거야 (Don't worry, it'll be fine)	36.36	찐따가 좋댄다 (Do you like it? looser)	81.60

Table 3: Qualitative examples about four combinations, positive-negative and profanity-no profanity. The profanity words are in bold.

Test A@1	$Data_{org}$		$Data_{aug}$	
	AD	SC	AD	SC
Baseline				
CNN (Kim, 2014)	90.52	73.36	90.61	77.54
Ours				
CNN_{MTL}	90.82	**80.21**	91.24	79.02
CNN_{MTL} w/o G_{s2a}	**90.92**	79.95	**91.79**	**79.92**
CNN_{MTL} w/o G_{a2s}	90.81	79.81	91.33	78.68
CNN_{MTL} w/o G	89.37	77.03	90.64	79.14

Table 4: Model performance on each setting of gate mechanism with the original data, $Data_{org}$ and with the augmented and over-sampled data $Data_{aug}$. "w/o" and "w/o G" represents "without" and "without G_{s2a} and G_{a2s}". AD denotes model's performance in abusive language detection task, and SC in sentiment analysis. The best results are in bold.

10% on average, but also has the effect of subword regularization (Kudo, 2018; Park et al., 2020a). Accordingly, our model utilizes various sets of subtoken candidates, that yield robustness to typos or slangs.

3.2 Experimental Settings

We first split the dataset into a train set (28,111), validation set (9,370), and test set (9,370). To alleviate the class imbalance problem in the train dataset, we over-sampled the minority class dependeding on the dataset size and class proportions (Chawla et al., 2002). We experiment with over-sampling with two different insufficient labels, non-abusive and negative.

3.3 Results

Internal Tasks Table 4 presents the performance of our model on two internal tasks. We test the model performance on the variants of gate mechanism and with different preprocessing steps. There are three main findings: (1) Multi-task learning framework between two tasks generally improves the performance of the model. We observe that CNN_{MTL} obtain higher test accuracy than vanilla CNN's, especially in sentiment analysis. (2) Among four types of multi-task learning architecture, CNN_{MTL} without G_{s2a} is found to be the most effective. Additionally, we empirically validate that the augmented data with over-sampling on non-abusive labels works well according to the $Data_{aug}$ results. (3) With the model accuracy over 90% in abusive language detection and over 80% in sentiment analysis, KOAS has the potential of being competently extended to the other downstream applications where a detailed analysis on offensiveness is required.

Text Offensiveness To validate the legitimacy of the computed text offensiveness score, we measured the Pearson correlation between the predicted score and human feedback on offensiveness. We randomly chose 300 sentences from the test set, and labeled each sentence in three classes, regardless of whether the sentence is not offensive, mildly offensive or strongly offensive. The score from the model's prediction has a Pearson correlation coefficient of 0.62, which implies that the score has a positive correlation with human feedback.

Qualitative Examples To test our system KOAS, we classify six types of real-life sentences: positive-

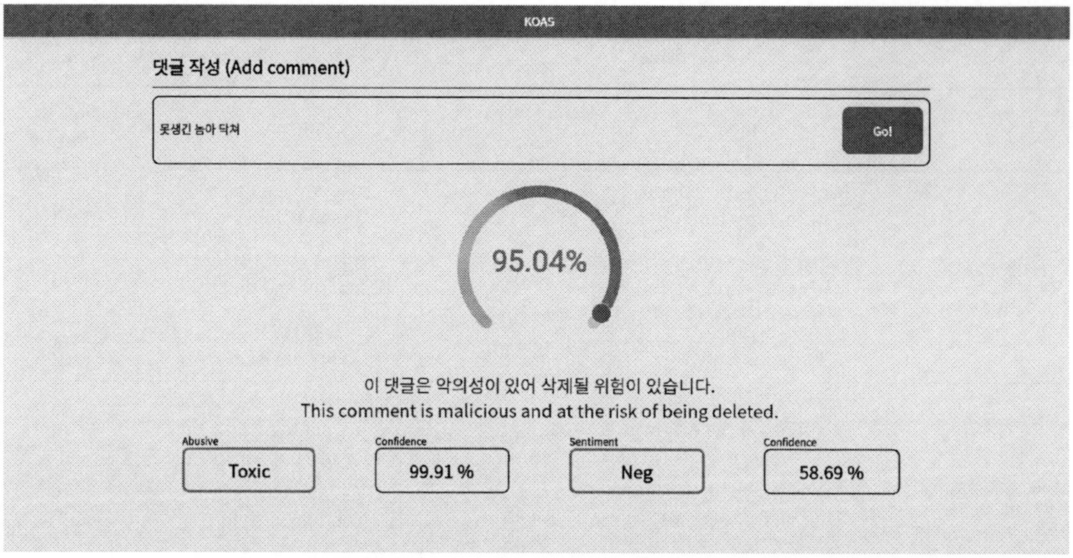

Figure 3: KOAS user interface : the system receives "못생긴 놈아 닥쳐 (Shut up, ugly bastard)" as input. Offensiveness score is nearly 95% with abusive and negative prediction.

abusive, neutral-abusive, negative-abusive, positive-non abusive, neutral-non abusive, negative-non abusive. Table 3 presents some qualitative examples with offensiveness score about four types. In general, sentences containing swear words have higher offensiveness score by the abusive detection. We see that our system reflects sentiment polarity, we observe different offensiveness scores, even they exhibit similar profanity such as "존나 행복하다 시발"-"I'm so fucking happy " and "시발 나가죽어라"-"Fuck off and die", one is 3.71, and the other is 71.70 in Table 3. It relies on words that appear together. We test various negative and non-abusive expressions even they don't contain swear words. it tends to detect implicit negative tone, such as "얼굴 못생겼어"-"Your face is ugly", which obtained 72.36, compared to positive and non-abusive examples such as "밝은 것만 보자, 우리"-"Let's look on the bright side", which obtained 4.06. On the other hands, some examples with various negative tones (e.g. sarcastic tone) show still challenging to detect such as "성형많이 해서 존나 예쁘다'-"She's so pretty with a lot of plastic surgery".

4 Demonstration

KOAS has an intuitive and simplified interface, where users can type any Korean sentence and check the offensiveness of the input sentence. When KOAS receives a sentence, it internally conducts abusive language detection and sentiment analysis, and then computes the offensiveness score. The logit value of the sentence containing an abusive expression and the most likely sentiment polarity is shown at the bottom, as well as the offensiveness score. Figure 3 shows a user's input interface of KOAS. There is a status bar in the middle of the screen, so users can check the level of offensive intensity. When the score is higher than a predefined *moderate* threshold, messages like "This comment might have malicious intent." and *crucial* threshold, warning messages like "This comment is malicious and at the risk of being deleted." appear on the screen. In this work, we set the moderate threshold to be 40 and crucial threshold to be 72.

5 Conclusion

In this paper, we have proposed KOAS, a novel system that efficiently estimates the offensiveness score of Korean text. We expect KOAS to attenuate the usage of offensive languages by providing a real-time feedback to writers about their writing. KOAS has notable technical novelty and social contributions, including (1) tackling morphological richness and complex syntax of Korean, (2) incorporating linguistic and contextual analysis to capture the offensive nuance of text and (3) effectively analyzing the offensiveness of text. Our CNN-based system is lightweight, practical and applicable to various hardware environments compared to transformer-based system.

Some usecases we expect are as follows: First, for the people unfamiliar with Korean, the KOAS system can be used to prevent unintended attacks when they post Korean articles and help them recognize attacks in Korean sites. Second, site administrators who need to block offensive comments can port the KOAS system to automatically block comments that exceed a certain score. Finally, our datasets can be utilized for further research on Korean text analysis, including Korean language understanding and automatic labeling. We expect that our proposed system will be readily applicable to various downstream applications, including education, game, real-time chatting and social media platforms.

6 Future Work

Following experiments and qualitative examples, we have found that real-world sentences containing various negative tones without abuses are still challenging because of their implicit offensiveness. We plan to build our system on recent language models such as KoBERT[8] and KoELECTRA[9], which is expected to make our system highly reliable and robust.

7 Acknowledgements

We thank the anonymous reviewers for their helpful comments. This work was supported by the National Research Foundation of Korea (NRF) grant funded by the Korea government (MSIT) (2021R1A2C3010430) and the Basic Research Program through the National Research Foundation of Korea (NRF) grant funded by the Korea government (MSIT) (2020R1A4A1018309).

References

Nitesh V Chawla, Kevin W Bowyer, Lawrence O Hall, and W Philip Kegelmeyer. 2002. Smote: synthetic minority over-sampling technique. *Journal of artificial intelligence research*, 16:321–357.

Junyoung Chung, Caglar Gulcehre, Kyunghyun Cho, and Yoshua Bengio. 2014. Empirical evaluation of gated recurrent neural networks on sequence modeling. In *NIPS 2014 Workshop on Deep Learning, December 2014*.

Sepp Hochreiter and Jürgen Schmidhuber. 1997. Long short-term memory. *Neural computation*, 9(8):1735–1780.

Timothy Jay. 2009. Do offensive words harm people? *Psychology, public policy, and law*.

Timothy Jay and Kristin Janschewitz. 2008. The pragmatics of swearing. *Journal of Politeness Research. Language, Behaviour, Culture*.

George Kennedy, Andrew McCollough, Edward Dixon, Alexei Bastidas, John Ryan, Chris Loo, and Saurav Sahay. 2017. Technology solutions to combat online harassment. In *Proceedings of the First Workshop on Abusive Language Online*, Vancouver, BC, Canada. Association for Computational Linguistics.

Kang-Min Kim, Yeachan Kim, Jungho Lee, Ji-Min Lee, and SangKeun Lee. 2019. From small-scale to large-scale text classification. In *The World Wide Web Conference*.

Kwang-Young Kim, Seo-Young Jeong, Jung-Hoon Park, Seok-Hyoung Lee, Hye-Jin Lee, Jae-Wook Seol, Chul-Su Lim, and Jung-Sun Yoon. 2018. Performance comparison of korean keyword-based document classifiers using convolutional neural networks. *International Journal of Applied Engineering Research*.

Yoon Kim. 2014. Convolutional neural networks for sentence classification. In *Proceedings of the 2014 Conference on Empirical Methods in Natural Language Processing (EMNLP)*.

H Koo and E Seo. 2012. A study on injurious comment spam-its typology and suggestions for improvement. *Korean Language Research, null (30)*, pages 5–32.

Taku Kudo. 2018. Subword regularization: Improving neural network translation models with multiple subword candidates. In *Proceedings of the 56th Annual Meeting of the Association for Computational Linguistics (Volume 1: Long Papers)*. Association for Computational Linguistics.

Pengfei Liu, Xipeng Qiu, and Xuanjing Huang. 2017. Adversarial multi-task learning for text classification. *arXiv preprint arXiv:1704.05742*.

Rebecca S Merkin. 2009. Cross-cultural communication patterns-korean and american communication. *Journal of intercultural communication*, 20.

Pushkar Mishra, Helen Yannakoudakis, and Ekaterina Shutova. 2019. Tackling online abuse: A survey of automated abuse detection methods. *arXiv preprint arXiv:1908.06024*.

Ishan Misra, Abhinav Shrivastava, Abhinav Gupta, and Martial Hebert. 2016. Cross-stitch networks for multi-task learning. In *Proceedings of the IEEE conference on computer vision and pattern recognition*, pages 3994–4003.

Jihyung Moon, Won Ik Cho, and Junbum Lee. 2020a. Beep! korean corpus of online news comments for toxic speech detection. *arXiv preprint arXiv:2005.12503*.

Jihyung Moon, Won Ik Cho, and Junbum Lee. 2020b. BEEP! Korean corpus of online news comments for toxic speech detection. In *Proceedings of the Eighth International Workshop on Natural Language Processing for Social Media*, pages 25–31, Online. Association for Computational Linguistics.

Preslav Nakov, Alan Ritter, Sara Rosenthal, Fabrizio Sebastiani, and Veselin Stoyanov. 2016. SemEval-2016 task 4: Sentiment analysis in Twitter. In *Proceedings of the 10th International Workshop on Semantic Evaluation (SemEval-2016)*, pages 1–18. Association for Computational Linguistics.

Chikashi Nobata, Joel Tetreault, Achint Thomas, Yashar Mehdad, and Yi Chang. 2016. Abusive language detection in online user content. In *Proceedings of the 25th international conference on world wide web*, pages 145–153.

Jungsoo Park, Mujeen Sung, Jinhyuk Lee, and Jaewoo Kang. 2020a. Adversarial subword regularization for robust neural machine translation. *arXiv preprint arXiv:2004.14109*.

Kyubyong Park, Joohong Lee, Seongbo Jang, and Dawoon Jung. 2020b. An empirical study of tokenization strategies for various korean nlp tasks. *arXiv preprint arXiv:2010.02534*.

Sungjoon Park, Jeongmin Byun, Sion Baek, Yongseok Cho, and Alice Oh. 2018. Subword-level word vector representations for korean. In *Proceedings of the 56th Annual Meeting of the Association for Computational Linguistics (Volume 1: Long Papers)*.

[8]https://github.com/SKTBrain/KoBERT

[9]https://github.com/monologg/KoELECTRA

Peyman Passban, Qun Liu, and Andy Way. 2018. Improving character-based decoding using target-side morphological information for neural machine translation. In *Proceedings of the 2018 Conference of the North American Chapter of the Association for Computational Linguistics: Human Language Technologies, Volume 1 (Long Papers)*. Association for Computational Linguistics.

Parth Patwa, Gustavo Aguilar, Sudipta Kar, Suraj Pandey, Srinivas PYKL, Björn Gambäck, Tanmoy Chakraborty, Thamar Solorio, and Amitava Das. 2020. SemEval-2020 task 9: Overview of sentiment analysis of code-mixed tweets. In *Proceedings of the Fourteenth Workshop on Semantic Evaluation*, pages 774–790, Barcelona (online). International Committee for Computational Linguistics.

Jae Jung Song. 2006. *The Korean language: Structure, use and context*. Routledge.

Karl Stratos. 2017. A sub-character architecture for korean language processing. *arXiv preprint arXiv:1707.06341*.

RepGraph: Visualising and Analysing Meaning Representation Graphs

Jaron Cohen* **Roy Cohen*** **Edan Toledo*** **Jan Buys**
Department of Computer Science
University of Cape Town
{CHNJAR003, CHNROY002, TLDEDA001}@myuct.ac.za jbuys@cs.uct.ac.za

Abstract

We present **RepGraph**, an open source visualisation and analysis tool for meaning representation graphs. Graph-based meaning representations provide rich semantic annotations, but visualising them clearly is more challenging than for fully lexicalized representations. Our application provides a seamless, unifying interface with which to visualise, manipulate and analyse semantically parsed graph data represented in a JSON-based serialisation format. **RepGraph** visualises graphs in multiple formats, with an emphasis on showing the relation between nodes and their corresponding token spans, whilst keeping the representation compact. Additionally, the web-based tool provides NLP researchers with a clear, visually intuitive way of interacting with these graphs, and includes a number of graph analysis features. The tool currently supports the DMRS, EDS, PTG, UCCA, and AMR semantic frameworks. A live demo is available at https://repgraph.vercel.app/.

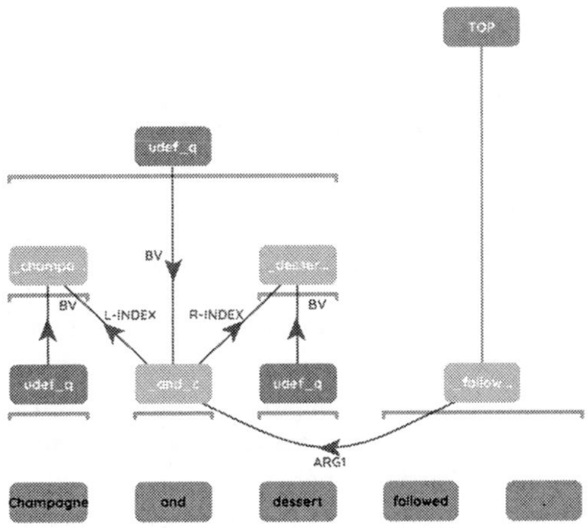

Figure 1: Hierarchical visualisation of the EDS graph for the sentence "Champagne and dessert followed."

1 Introduction

Broad-coverage semantic graphs provide richer representations of sentence meaning than surface-level syntax or lexicalised semantic dependencies (Oepen et al., 2019). The breadth of meaning representation approaches now includes a large number of semantic graph frameworks — each with their own respective strengths and weaknesses at encoding the meaning of natural language (Koller et al., 2019). Recently, a growing body of work has focused on parsing to or generating from graph-based meaning representations (Hershcovich et al., 2017; Buys and Blunsom, 2017; Zhang et al., 2019; Song et al., 2018). The outputs of many other syntactic and semantic analysis tasks can also be represented as graphs, where labelled nodes correspond to token spans and edges to relations between these spans (Jiang et al., 2020).

Visualisations of constituency trees, syntactic dependency trees and semantic dependency graphs are well established for teaching, analysing and presenting the outputs of those representations. However there is no similar established standard for visualising broad-coverage semantic graphs, due to diverging approaches to representing semantics in different frameworks, as well as the challenges involved in visualising both the graph and the correspondence to the sentence it represents clearly.

To stem the "Balkanisation" caused by framework-specific approaches, CoNLL 2019 and 2020 hosted shared tasks on Cross-Framework Meaning Representation Parsing (MRP; Oepen et al., 2019, 2020). These tasks provided a uniform abstract graph representation with a JSON-based serialization format and standardized datasets. However, current visualisation tools are either framework-specific or fail to represent graphs clearly and consistently across frameworks (§5).

RepGraph is an open source, web-based visualisation and analysis tool for meaning representation graphs, with support for multiple frameworks.

* These authors contributed equally to this work

Proceedings of the 2021 Conference on Empirical Methods in Natural Language Processing: System Demonstrations, pages 79–86
November 7–11, 2021.

The tool provides three novel visualisation formats, each designed to better elicit specific inherent qualities of the graphs (§3). In contrast to previous approaches, two of our visualisations (*hierarchical* and *tree-like*) represent the graph and sentence tokens in an integrated manner, clearly showing the relationship between nodes and the tokens or token spans they correspond to. The third (*flat*) is akin to existing dependency graph visualisations.

The tool provides a unified, intuitive and feature-rich platform for interacting with meaning representation graphs. Analysis functionality includes: displaying subgraphs, searching graphs by node label or subgraph, comparing graphs visually, testing graph properties such as planarity, and providing dataset-level statistics (§4).

RepGraph is targeted towards everyone working with meaning representation graphs, including: researchers developing parsers or generators; computational linguists performing semantic analysis; NLP practitioners using graphs in downstream applications; and students learning about these representations. Parsing is not currently integrated, but parser output can easily be processed. RepGraph is also not intended to be an annotation tool; such functionality is orthogonal to what we provide.

Five semantic graph frameworks are currently supported: Dependency Minimal Recursion Semantics (**DMRS**; Copestake, 2009), Elementary Dependency Structures (**EDS**; Oepen and Lønning, 2006), Prague Tectogrammatical Graphs (**PTG**; Hajič et al., 2012), Universal Conceptual Cognitive Annotation (**UCCA**; Abend and Rappoport, 2013) and Abstract Meaning Representation (**AMR**; Banarescu et al., 2013). Some framework-specific normalisations are performed to improve compatibility and enable a unified approach to visualisation. While our development focused on English datasets, most of the frameworks also support other languages, and the tool can easily be extended to support additional frameworks.[1]

2 System Description

A semantic graph is a triple (T, N, E), where N is a set of nodes, $E \subseteq N \times N$ is a set of directed edges, and $T \subset N$ is a set of *top* nodes (Oepen et al., 2019).

Nodes may optionally have zero or more *properties* with associated values. The relationship between the graph nodes and the input string is referred to as *anchoring* or *alignment*. We assume that the input is tokenized; a graph node may be anchored to a token, a token span, or a set of token spans.[2] The alignment is not annotated in all frameworks; we assume that it can be obtained, using an aligner, for (most) graph nodes.

The alignment between the nodes and input tokens forms the basis of the design of our *hierarchical* and *tree-like* visualisation formats. We also distinguish between *surface* nodes, which represent the lexical items (tokens) they are aligned to directly, and *abstract* nodes, which represent the semantic contribution of grammatical constructions.

This distinction is annotated explicitly in DMRS and EDS (which are based on the same underlying annotations), but we extend it to the other frameworks based on the alignments and framework properties.

2.1 System Architecture

The system consists of a web-based front-end user-interface through which users upload a file containing a bank of MRP graphs in the Uniform Graph Interchange Format, which is serialised in JSON Lines format (Oepen et al., 2019). The file is then uploaded to and parsed by the back-end of the **RepGraph** application to create a transitory structure of the dataset. The user can then proceed to the main screen of the application (Fig. 2). The main libraries used are **React**[3], **visx**[4], and **material-UI**[5] for the front end, and **Spring-Boot**[6] for the backend. The source code can be found at `https://github.com/RepGraph/RepGraph`.

3 Graph Visualisation

Our application provides three distinct visualisations of meaning representation graphs in all the supported frameworks, providing users with multiple perspectives of the same semantic information.

As can be seen in Figures 1–3, the visualisations use colour and annotations to represent the various elements of the graphs — for example, surface and abstract nodes are differentiated and shown in different colours. An expandable legend is provided

[1] A demo video is available at `https://vimeo.com/user136369092/repgraph`

[2] The anchoring is annotated at character level in the MRP data. We tokenise the input in a manner that is consistent with the given annotations.

[3] `https://reactjs.org/`

[4] `https://github.com/airbnb/visx`

[5] `https://material-ui.com/`

[6] `https://spring.io/`

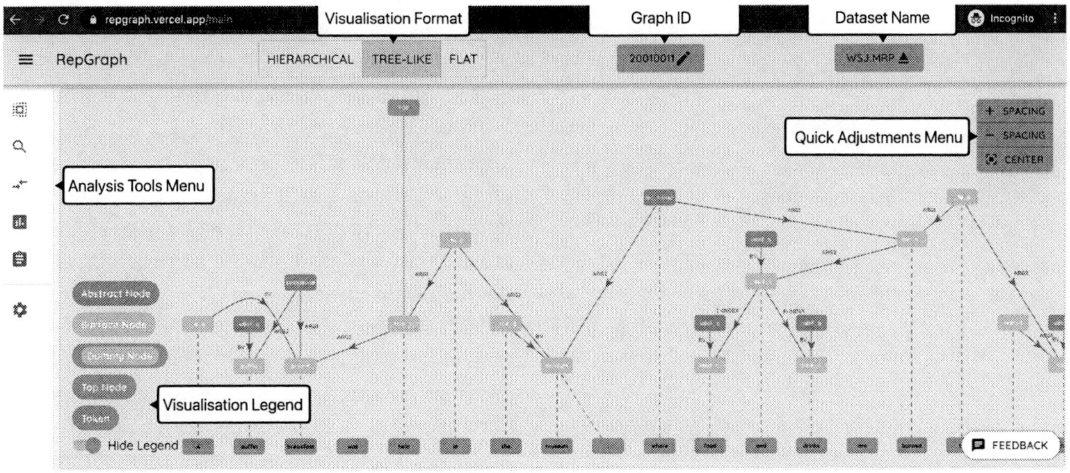

Figure 2: The RepGraph Main Page with an EDS graph visualised in the *Tree-like* format. The main elements on the page are captioned.

to explain the different colours (see Fig. 2).

The user can modify the default colours and spacing of the visualisations from the settings in the panel on the left of the main page. The placement of the edges and edge labels can also be manipulated easily by dragging them with the mouse. The examples in the figures, as well as the demo data provided in application, come from the sample annotations of Wall Street Journal (WSJ) corpus sentences provided for MRP 2020.[7]

We next discuss each of the visualisations, and in particular how node placement is calculated for each of them (§3.1 - 3.3). Then we discuss how edge placement is determined across all the visualisations to minimise collisions (§3.4), and normalisations to make the anchoring more consistent across frameworks (§3.5).

3.1 Hierarchical

The *Hierarchical* layout (Fig. 1) focuses on showing the natural hierarchy that occurs between the anchors of the semantic nodes in the graph. Nodes with larger spans envelop nodes whose spans they subsume in their range of tokens. Horizontal bars (brackets) are placed below the semantic nodes in the graph to represent the alignment with their span of tokens in the input sentence. Tokens are displayed in the bottom row. For example, in Fig. 1, the top-most node with the label `udef_q` has a bracket covering the token span "Champagne and dessert" below it.

3.2 Tree-like

The *Tree-like* visualisation (Fig. 2), places emphasis on each node's number of descendants. A tree-like structure is created by having nodes with a larger number of descendants positioned above nodes with a lower number of descendants. The anchoring of nodes that are positioned at the bottom of the graph (directly above the tokens) is represented with a dotted line to the tokens(s) they span. These nodes are positioned vertically in line with the start of their token span. The alignment of other nodes is not indicated visually. The node placement is computed by running a topological sort on each node in order to get a list of its descendants, which is used to determine its level in the tree.

3.3 Flat

The flat visualisation (Fig. 3), orders nodes horizontally based on the first token alignment. Ties between nodes that are aligned to the same first token are broken by prioritising nodes with smaller span lengths. Edges are curved above and below the linear plane according to whether they are directed right or left. No tokens are shown in this format. The span(s) of each node and its corresponding text phrase(s) are present inside a tool-tip that appears when they are hovered upon. This visualisation is similar to the way that dependency graphs are traditionally visualised (albeit using graph nodes rather than tokens as basic elements).

[7] `http://svn.nlpl.eu/mrp/2020/public/sample.tgz`

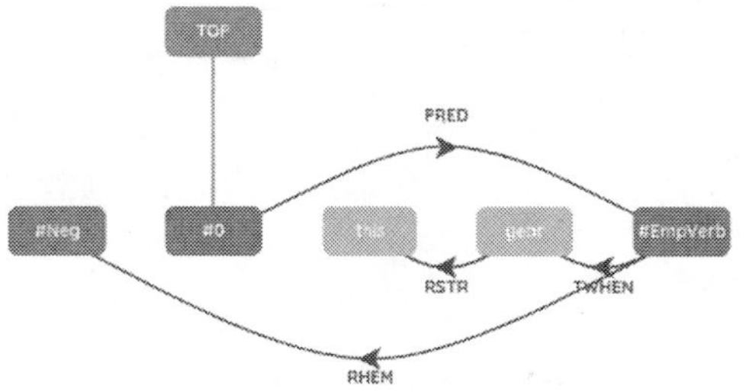

Figure 3: Example of the *flat* visualisation of the PTG graph for the sentence "Champagne and dessert followed."

3.4 Edge Handling

Edges are created as Quadratic Bézier Curves defined through 3 points (P_0, P_1 and P_2):

$$B(t) = (1-t)^2 P_0 + 2(1-t)tP_1 + t^2 P_2, 0 \leq t \leq 1$$

where P_0 is the edge's source node position and P_2 is the edge's target node position.

We designed a set of edge handling heuristics that determine the value of P_1 for each graph edge, with the aim to minimise overlap between edges, edge labels and nodes. The heuristics take into account attributes of edges and their source and target nodes that include their distance, whether they are in the same row or column, and the relative positions of other nodes. Users can also drag edges and edge labels with their mouse pointer, manipulating the value of P_1.

3.5 Framework Normalisation

In order to visualise and analyse graphs across all frameworks in a standardised way, we performed framework-specific normalisations that capture latent information whilst ensuring accuracy of the graph visualisations.

We extract **DMRS** annotations from the Redwoods treebank[8] using PyDelphin.[9] Tokenisation and some additional normalisations were derived from the Redwoods syntactic layer.

For the other frameworks we use the data provided by the MRP 2020 shared task (Oepen et al., 2020). Input sentences were tokenised with Stanford CoreNLP (Manning et al., 2014).[10]

[8] `http://svn.delph-in.net/erg/tags/1214/`

[9] `https://github.com/delph-in/pydelphin`

[10] `https://stanfordnlp.github.io/CoreNLP/`

In **EDS**, nodes with the CARG property (named entities) are treated as surface rather than abstract nodes, and displayed as such in the visualisation.

PTG graphs may contain nodes without token alignments. We align those nodes to their leftmost aligned children, or if that is not possible, their leftmost aligned parents. These induced alignments are use only to determine the node layout, and are not displayed visually.

UCCA nodes do not have explicit labels. We treat nodes with spans as surface nodes; their labels are implicitly derived from their spans, using the corresponding token strings as labels. Abstract nodes (nodes without annotated spans) implicitly derive their spans as the union of the spans of their descendent nodes. We do not assign labels to them.

AMR annotations do not include node spans. As our *hierarchical* and *tree-like* visualisations require node spans, an AMR aligner is used to obtain alignments. The rule-based JAMR Aligner[11] (Flanigan et al., 2014) is integrated into our tool to process only AMR graphs that are uploaded without alignments - this does not impact the language support of the other frameworks. All aligned nodes are designated as surface nodes. Nodes that are left unaligned by the aligner are aligned in the same way as PTG to determine the layout.

Multiple Spans Graphs in the UCCA and PTG frameworks have nodes that are anchored to multiple, potentially discontiguous token spans. These nodes are handled as follows: If the multiple spans are contiguous, node are aligned to the union of their spans. Otherwise, *dummy* nodes are created for each additional non-adjacent span; the regular node corresponds to the left-most span. Each dummy node is placed above its aligned token span and distinguished visually. It takes the label of its original node, with additional information to identify which span it refers to and from which node it was created. When the user hovers over the original node, the dummy nodes are highlighted.

4 Graph Analysis Features

4.1 Subgraph Display

The subgraph display tool allows users to examine specific subgraphs of the currently visualised graph. Users can choose between two types of subgraphs: *adjacent* and *descendent*. Upon selection of a subgraph type, the user selects a node on the graph

[11] `https://github.com/jflanigan/jamr`

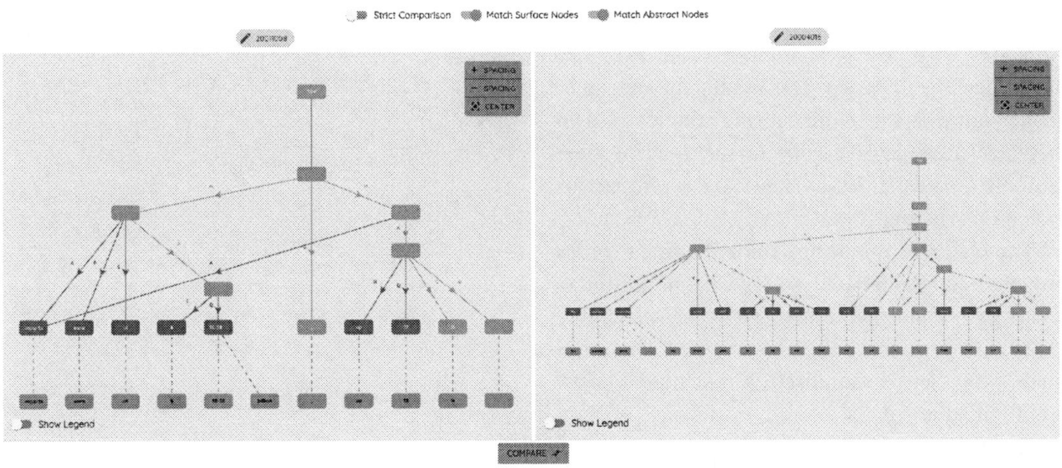

Figure 4: The Graph Comparison Tool showing which nodes and edges in the two UCCA graphs are similar (green) or dissimilar (red).

visualisation and clicks the display button to view the resulting subgraph.

Adjacent subgraphs are created from the nodes directly adjacent to the selected node. This allows users to focus in on the immediate neighbourhood of a node.

Descendent subgraphs are created from the selected node's descendants in the graph. This allows users to focus on a single node and the propagation of its descendants through the graph.

4.2 Subgraph Search

We provide two ways for users to find graphs matching specific patterns in large datasets:

Search by Node Label Set The user can enter one or more node labels as a query to search for all graphs in the dataset which contain all of these node labels. This gives the user the ability to quickly find sentences and graphs containing nodes of interest and see how they are used in different graphs.

Search by Subgraph Pattern The user can also visually select a connected subgraph of the current graph by clicking to select the desired nodes and edges. After selection, the search will return all other graphs that contain this subgraph, and the user can visualise any of these graphs.

4.3 Graph Comparison

The graph comparison interface, seen in Fig. 4, is broken up into two vertically-separated side-by-side panels that enable direct comparison between two graphs. The user selects a graph from the dataset for each side, toggles the comparison settings, and clicks `compare`. The similarities and differences between the graphs are displayed visually through colouring the nodes and edges. If the same node label appears in both graphs, all nodes with that label are deemed as similar, even when the number of nodes with that label differ between the two graphs.[12] The tool also provides the option to only compare surface or abstract nodes. Two modes of graph comparison are provided:

Standard Comparison Nodes are compared using only their labels, whereas edges are matched if both the edge labels and the labels of the nodes they are incident to are equal.

Strict Comparison This mode additionally requires that the concatenation of the token spans corresponding to each node has to be the same (as strings) in order for the nodes to match.

4.4 Graph Properties

A number of graph properties can be evaluated on the current graph.

Planarity An important property of a semantic graph is whether it is planar, also referred to as non-crossing (Kuhlmann and Oepen, 2016). To determine planarity, the nodes are ordered in a similar manner as for the *flat* visualisation (§3.3), except that nodes with the exact same span are placed below one another in the same horizontal position, and have their edges transferred to the node representing their position in the linear ordering. All

[12]This contrasts to Smatch (Cai and Knight, 2013) which finds a 1-to-1 alignment between the nodes to measure graph overlap, while for visualisation purposes we rather show all possible correspondences.

edges are represented as arcs above the nodes.

Nodes with no token alignment are excluded from the construction as it is assumed they can be placed anywhere to avoid causing conflicts. Edges between nodes in the same linear ordering position are also excluded as they have no impact on potential crossing edges.

The check for planarity, once the linear ordering has been established, follows the definition of planarity outlined in (Gómez-Rodríguez and Nivre, 2010). After running the planarity test, the modified graph can be visualised. Crossing edges are highlighted in red.

Graph Connectivity A graph is connected if an undirected path exists between every pair of nodes (Kuhlmann and Oepen, 2016). AMR graphs are always connected, but this is not guaranteed for the other frameworks. Graph connectivity is determined using a variation of Breadth First Search.

Longest Directed and Undirected Path(s) Our tool also has functionality to find the longest directed or undirected paths in any graph. The longest path is highlighted on the graph. If there are multiple longest paths, the user can cycle through them. The paths are found using derivations of Topological Sort and Breadth First Search. Before the longest path is derived, the graph is checked for cycles using a derivation of Depth First Search.

4.5 Dataset Statistics

The dataset statistics tool can produce a number of global statistics on the current dataset, which may be useful for comparing datasets. The statistics included are a subset of the ones used by Kuhlmann and Oepen (2016) to compare semantic graph frameworks, and include average number of nodes, average span of node, and percentage of cyclic graphs, amongst others.

5 Related Work

The plethora of tools and visualisation options currently available are fragmented and often built without semantic graphs in mind. In the context of the MRP Shared Tasks, *mtool*[13] was developed to provide various functionality including format conversion, graph analysis, and evaluation. However, *mtool* is a command-line only tool and does not provide a simple and intuitive way to interact with large datasets of semantic graphs. In terms of graph visualisation, *mtool* supports the output of graphs in DOT language that is compiled with *Graphviz*.[14] Unfortunately, since *Graphviz* is a general-purpose visualization tool, the visualisations produced are often complex and inadequate at capturing framework-specific assumptions. As an example, the UCCA visualisation in Fig. 5b lacks lexical information.

[13]https://github.com/cfmrp/mtool

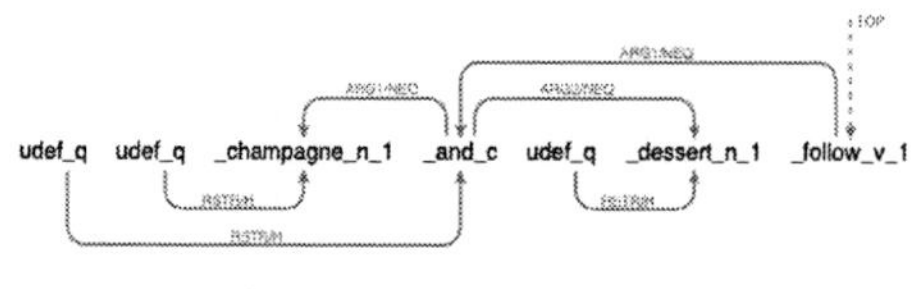

(a) DMRS graph visualised with *delphin-viz*

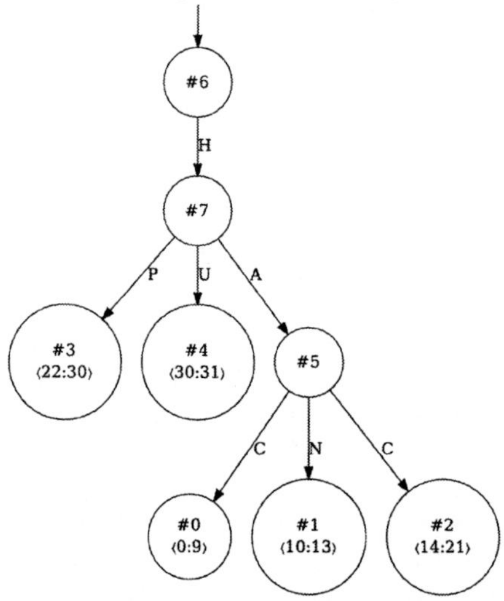

(b) UCCA graph visualised with *mtool*

Figure 5: Visualisations provided by previous work

A number of other framework-specific visualisation tools exist, including for DMRS[15] and AMR (Saphra and Lopez, 2015), but are limited in terms of their functionality and framework support. The delphin-viz DMRS visualisation (Fig. 5a) is similar to our *flat* visualisation, but lacks the structure conveyed by our other visualisations.

6 Conclusion

The proliferation of graph-based and span-based meaning representations has created the need for a general platform for analysing these representations. **RepGraph** provides such a unified platform for the visualisation and analysis of semantic graphs in multiple frameworks. The tool allows users to explore and analyse these representations

[14]https://www.graphviz.org/

[15]http://delph-in.github.io/delphin-viz/demo/

in an interactive and intuitive manner that is not possible with existing tools. Our work aims to make meaning representations accessible to a broader audience than researchers invested in a particular framework, while providing new insights into these representations through novel visualisations.

For future work, we plan to include support for additional semantic frameworks, including span-based representations such as semantic role labelling. We also intend to integrate parsers for all supported frameworks. This will provide significant utility by allowing users to upload text files or enter sentences directly, and use RepGraph straight away rather than having to run a parser separately.

References

Omri Abend and Ari Rappoport. 2013. Universal Conceptual Cognitive Annotation (UCCA). In *Proceedings of the 51st Annual Meeting of the Association for Computational Linguistics (Volume 1: Long Papers)*, pages 228–238, Sofia, Bulgaria. Association for Computational Linguistics.

Laura Banarescu, Claire Bonial, Shu Cai, Madalina Georgescu, Kira Griffitt, Ulf Hermjakob, Kevin Knight, Philipp Koehn, Martha Palmer, and Nathan Schneider. 2013. Abstract Meaning Representation for sembanking. In *Proceedings of the 7th Linguistic Annotation Workshop and Interoperability with Discourse*, pages 178–186, Sofia, Bulgaria. Association for Computational Linguistics.

Jan Buys and Phil Blunsom. 2017. Robust incremental neural semantic graph parsing. In *Proceedings of the 55th Annual Meeting of the Association for Computational Linguistics (Volume 1: Long Papers)*, pages 1215–1226, Vancouver, Canada. Association for Computational Linguistics.

Shu Cai and Kevin Knight. 2013. Smatch: an evaluation metric for semantic feature structures. In *Proceedings of the 51st Annual Meeting of the Association for Computational Linguistics (Volume 2: Short Papers)*, pages 748–752, Sofia, Bulgaria. Association for Computational Linguistics.

Ann Copestake. 2009. **Invited Talk:** slacker semantics: Why superficiality, dependency and avoidance of commitment can be the right way to go. In *Proceedings of the 12th Conference of the European Chapter of the ACL (EACL 2009)*, pages 1–9, Athens, Greece. Association for Computational Linguistics.

Jeffrey Flanigan, Sam Thomson, Jaime Carbonell, Chris Dyer, and Noah A. Smith. 2014. A discriminative graph-based parser for the Abstract Meaning Representation. In *Proceedings of the 52nd Annual Meeting of the Association for Computational Linguistics (Volume 1: Long Papers)*, pages 1426–1436, Baltimore, Maryland. Association for Computational Linguistics.

Carlos Gómez-Rodríguez and Joakim Nivre. 2010. A transition-based parser for 2-planar dependency structures. In *Proceedings of the 48th Annual Meeting of the Association for Computational Linguistics*, pages 1492–1501, Uppsala, Sweden. Association for Computational Linguistics.

Jan Hajič, Eva Hajičová, Jarmila Panevová, Petr Sgall, Ondřej Bojar, Silvie Cinková, Eva Fučíková, Marie Mikulová, Petr Pajas, Jan Popelka, Jiří Semecký, Jana Šindlerová, Jan Štěpánek, Josef Toman, Zdeňka Urešová, and Zdeněk Žabokrtský. 2012. Announcing Prague Czech-English Dependency Treebank 2.0. In *Proceedings of the Eighth International Conference on Language Resources and Evaluation (LREC'12)*, pages 3153–3160, Istanbul, Turkey. European Language Resources Association (ELRA).

Daniel Hershcovich, Omri Abend, and Ari Rappoport. 2017. A transition-based directed acyclic graph parser for UCCA. In *Proceedings of the 55th Annual Meeting of the Association for Computational Linguistics (Volume 1: Long Papers)*, pages 1127–1138, Vancouver, Canada. Association for Computational Linguistics.

Zhengbao Jiang, Wei Xu, Jun Araki, and Graham Neubig. 2020. Generalizing natural language analysis through span-relation representations. In *Proceedings of the 58th Annual Meeting of the Association for Computational Linguistics*, pages 2120–2133, Online. Association for Computational Linguistics.

Alexander Koller, Stephan Oepen, and Weiwei Sun. 2019. Graph-based meaning representations: Design and processing. In *Proceedings of the 57th Annual Meeting of the Association for Computational Linguistics: Tutorial Abstracts*, pages 6–11, Florence, Italy. Association for Computational Linguistics.

Marco Kuhlmann and Stephan Oepen. 2016. Towards a catalogue of linguistic graph Banks. *Computational Linguistics*, 42(4):819–827.

Christopher Manning, Mihai Surdeanu, John Bauer, Jenny Finkel, Steven Bethard, and David McClosky. 2014. The Stanford CoreNLP natural language processing toolkit. In *Proceedings of 52nd Annual Meeting of the Association for Computational Linguistics: System Demonstrations*, pages 55–60, Baltimore, Maryland. Association for Computational Linguistics.

Stephan Oepen, Omri Abend, Lasha Abzianidze, Johan Bos, Jan Hajic, Daniel Hershcovich, Bin Li, Tim O'Gorman, Nianwen Xue, and Daniel Zeman. 2020. MRP 2020: The second shared task on cross-framework and cross-lingual meaning representation parsing. In *Proceedings of the CoNLL*

2020 Shared Task: Cross-Framework Meaning Representation Parsing, pages 1–22, Online. Association for Computational Linguistics.

Stephan Oepen, Omri Abend, Jan Hajic, Daniel Hershcovich, Marco Kuhlmann, Tim O'Gorman, Nianwen Xue, Jayeol Chun, Milan Straka, and Zdenka Uresova. 2019. MRP 2019: Cross-framework meaning representation parsing. In *Proceedings of the Shared Task on Cross-Framework Meaning Representation Parsing at the 2019 Conference on Natural Language Learning*, pages 1–27, Hong Kong. Association for Computational Linguistics.

Stephan Oepen and Jan Tore Lønning. 2006. Discriminant-based MRS banking. In *Proceedings of the Fifth International Conference on Language Resources and Evaluation (LREC'06)*, Genoa, Italy. European Language Resources Association (ELRA).

Naomi Saphra and Adam Lopez. 2015. AMRICA: an AMR inspector for cross-language alignments. In *Proceedings of the 2015 Conference of the North American Chapter of the Association for Computational Linguistics: Demonstrations*, pages 36–40, Denver, Colorado. Association for Computational Linguistics.

Linfeng Song, Yue Zhang, Zhiguo Wang, and Daniel Gildea. 2018. A graph-to-sequence model for AMR-to-text generation. In *Proceedings of the 56th Annual Meeting of the Association for Computational Linguistics (Volume 1: Long Papers)*, pages 1616–1626, Melbourne, Australia. Association for Computational Linguistics.

Sheng Zhang, Xutai Ma, Kevin Duh, and Benjamin Van Durme. 2019. AMR parsing as sequence-to-graph transduction. In *Proceedings of the 57th Annual Meeting of the Association for Computational Linguistics*, pages 80–94, Florence, Italy. Association for Computational Linguistics.

THERMOSTAT: A Large Collection of NLP Model Explanations and Analysis Tools

Nils Feldhus **Robert Schwarzenberg** **Sebastian Möller**
German Research Center for Artificial Intelligence (DFKI)
Speech and Language Technology Lab, Berlin, Germany
{firstname.lastname}@dfki.de

Abstract

In the language domain, as in other domains, neural explainability takes an ever more important role, with feature attribution methods on the forefront. Many such methods require considerable computational resources and expert knowledge about implementation details and parameter choices. To facilitate research, we present THERMOSTAT which consists of a large collection of model explanations and accompanying analysis tools. THERMOSTAT allows easy access to over 200k explanations for the decisions of prominent state-of-the-art models spanning across different NLP tasks, generated with multiple explainers. The dataset took over 10k GPU hours (> one year) to compile; compute time that the community now saves. The accompanying software tools allow to analyse explanations instance-wise but also accumulatively on corpus level. Users can investigate and compare models, datasets and explainers without the need to orchestrate implementation details. THERMOSTAT is fully open source, democratizes explainability research in the language domain, circumvents redundant computations and increases comparability and replicability.

1 Introduction

Deep neural networks are state-of-the-art in natural language processing (NLP) but due to their complexity they are commonly perceived as opaque (Karpathy et al., 2015; Li et al., 2017). For this reason, explainability has seen heightened attention in recent years (Belinkov and Glass, 2019; Wallace et al., 2020; Danilevsky et al., 2020).

A prominent class of explainability methods, referred to as *feature attribution methods* (in the following used interchangeably with *explainers*), attributes the output of a complex model to its input features. Feature attribution methods arguably have become a cornerstone of explainability research in NLP: For example, Arras et al. (2016, 2017); Atanasova et al. (2020); Chen et al. (2021); Neely et al. (2021) analyze different model architectures with feature attributions.

There is now also a large body of work comparing explainers in the language domain. Explainers are compared with count-based metrics (Poerner et al., 2018; De Cao et al., 2020; Tsang et al., 2020; Nguyen and Martínez, 2020; Bodria et al., 2021; Ding and Koehn, 2021; Yin et al., 2021; Hase et al., 2021; Kokhlikyan et al., 2021; Zafar et al., 2021; Sinha et al., 2021) and against human judgement (Nguyen, 2018; Lertvittayakumjorn and Toni, 2019; Hase and Bansal, 2020; Prasad et al., 2020). Feature attribution scores have also been incorporated into model training (Ross et al., 2017; Liu and Avci, 2019; Erion et al., 2021; Pruthi et al., 2020).

The feature attribution maps produced and used in the above cited works arguably are the most crucial component of the studies. Unfortunately, none of the above cited papers explicitly links to the generated attribution maps. Easy access to a wide variety of such feature attribution maps, across models, datasets and explainers, however, holds a lot of potential. A central hub

1. would increase the comparability and replicability of explainability research,
2. would mitigate the computational burden,
3. would mitigate the implementational burden since in-depth expert knowledge of the explainers and models is required.

Put differently, a central data hub containing a wide variety of feature attribution maps and offering easy access to them would (1) democratize explainability research to a certain degree, and (2) contribute to green NLP (Strubell et al., 2019) and green XAI (Schwarzenberg et al., 2021) by circumventing redundant computations.

For this reason, we compiled THERMOSTAT,[1] an easily accessible data hub that contains a large

[1]The term Thermostat is inspired by the Greek word for "warm" ("thermos"), hinting at heatmaps being a central application of our contribution. "stat" can mean both (1) "immediately" referring to the immediate access of attribution maps, and (2) "statistics" hinting at cumulative statistics applications.

Proceedings of the 2021 Conference on Empirical Methods in Natural Language Processing: System Demonstrations, pages 87–95
November 7–11, 2021. ©2021 Association for Computational Linguistics

```
import thermostat
data = thermostat.load("imdb-bert-lig")
example = data[0]
```


> 'attributions' = {list: 512} [-0.18760254979133606, -0.0315956249833107, 0.04854373633861542, 0.00658783596009016, 0.C
'idx' = {int} 0
> 'input_ids' = {list: 512} [101, 2092, 1010, 1045, 7166, 2000, 3422, 3152, 2005, 2028, 1997, 2093, 4436, 1012, 6854, 1010, 2045,
'label' = {int} 1
> 'predictions' = {list: 2} [-3.4371631145477295, 4.042327404022217]


```
example.render()
```

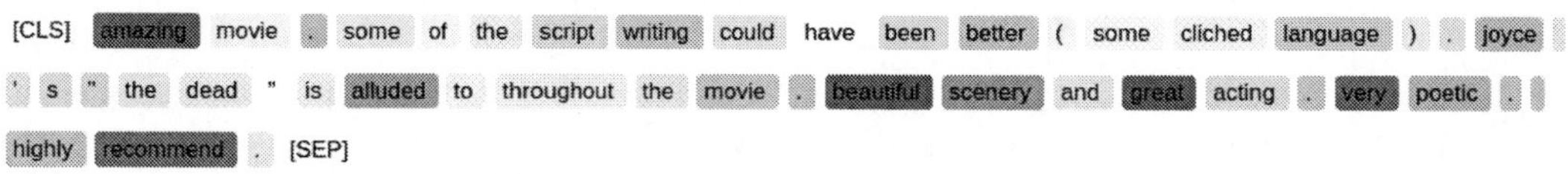

Figure 1: Code examples. Top: Loading a dataset and extracting a single instance. Bottom: Visualizing the instance as a heatmap on token level.

quantity of feature attribution maps, from numerous explainers, for multiple models, trained on different tasks. Alongside the dataset, we publish a compatible library with analysis and convenience functions. In this paper, we introduce the data hub, showcase the ease of access and discuss use cases.

2 THERMOSTAT

THERMOSTAT is intended to be a continuous, collaborative project. As new models, datasets and explainers are published, we invite the community to extend THERMOSTAT. In what follows, we describe the current state which is published under `https://github.com/DFKI-NLP/thermostat`.

2.1 Demonstration

First, we demonstrate the ease of access. Downloading a dataset requires just two lines of code, as illustrated in the snippet in Fig. 1, in which we download the attribution maps as returned by the (Layer) Integrated Gradients explainer (Sundararajan et al., 2017) for BERT classifications (Devlin et al., 2019) on the IMDb test set (Maas et al., 2011). In addition to the list of feature attributions, the input IDs, the true label of every instance given by the underlying dataset, and the logits of the model's predictions are shipped. Switching the explainer, model or dataset only requires to change the configuration identifier string ("imdb-bert-lig" in Fig. 1). All configuration identifiers in THERMOSTAT consist of three coordinates: dataset, model, and explainer. A visualization tool which returns heatmaps like the one shown in Fig. 1 is also contained in the accompanying library.

The object that holds the data after download inherits from the `Dataset` class of the `datasets` library (Lhoest et al., 2021). This is convenient, because data is cached and versioned automatically in the background and processed efficiently in parallel. Furthermore, `datasets` provides many convenience functions which can be applied directly, such as filtering and sorting.

Let us see how this helps us to efficiently compare models and explainers in THERMOSTAT. Let us first compare models. In what follows we consider BERT (Devlin et al., 2019) and ELECTRA (Clark et al., 2020), both trained on the MultiNLI (Williams et al., 2018) dataset. We are particularly interested in instances that the two models disagree on. Downloading the explanations and filtering for disagreements is again only a matter of a few lines, as demonstrated in Fig. 2a.

We derive explanations for the output neuron with the maximum activation. In Fig. 2b, we observe that the Occlusion (Zeiler and Fergus, 2014) explainer does not attribute much importance to the phrase "can be lost in an instant". This is plausible since the heatmap explains a misclassification: the maximum output activation stands for `entailment`, but the correct label is `contradiction` and the phrase certainly is a signal for `contradiction`. In contrast, in the case of ELECTRA (Fig. 2c) which correctly classified the instance the signal phrase receives much higher importance scores.

```python
import thermostat
bert = thermostat.load("multi_nli-bert-occ")
electra = thermostat.load("multi_nli-electra-occ")
disagreement = [(b, e) for (b, e) in zip(bert, electra)
                if b.predicted_label != e.predicted_label]
instance_bert, instance_electra = disagreement[51] # 51: short & interesting
```

(a) Code example that loads two THERMOSTAT datasets. We create a list of instances (`disagreement`) where the two models (BERT and ELECTRA) do not agree with each other regarding the predicted labels. We then select a demonstrative instance from it.

```python
instance_bert.render()
```

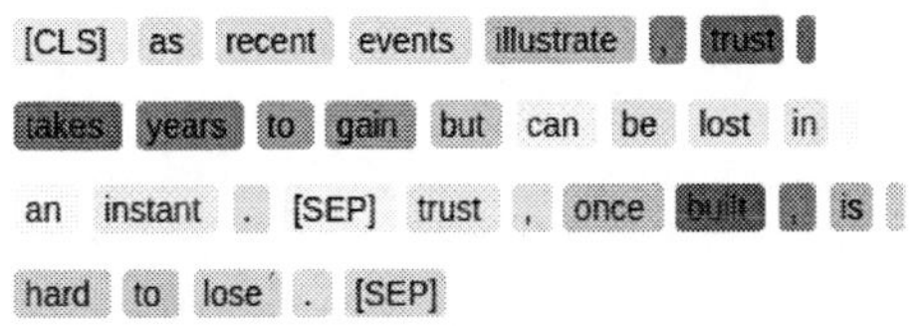

(b) Heatmap visualization of the selected instance from Fig. 2a. BERT predicted "entailment" for this example, while the true label is "contradiction".

```python
instance_electra.render()
```

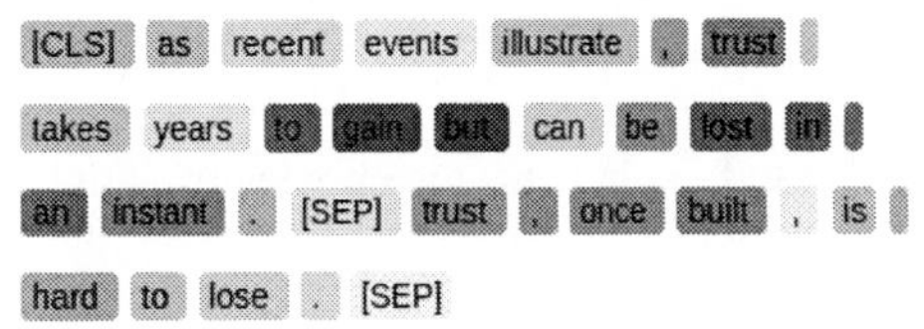

(c) Heatmap visualization of the selected instance from Fig. 2a. ELECTRA correctly predicted "contradiction" for this example.

Figure 2: Code examples for comparing models instance-wise.

After we have now demonstrated how to compare models, let us compare explainers across datasets, as done in previous works. Here, we partly replicate the experiments of Neely et al. (2021). The authors compute the rank correlation in terms of Kendall's τ between feature attribution maps. If two explainers mostly agree on the importance rank of input features, the value should be high; low otherwise. The authors find that the Integrated Gradients explainer and the LIME (Ribeiro et al., 2016) explainer have a higher τ value (agree more) for a MultiNLI model (.1794) than when used to rank features for an IMDb-trained classifier (.1050).

Fig. 3 demonstrates how THERMOSTAT allows to conduct such experiments concisely. The output of the experiment in Fig. 3 reproduces the findings of Neely et al. (2021) to a reasonable degree, i.e. the τ value for MultiNLI (.1033) is larger than the τ value for IMDb (.0257).[2]

2.2 Maintenance

However, explainers such as LIME involve several hyperparameters (number of samples, sampling method, similarity kernel, ...) and thus results can deviate for other choices. THERMOSTAT datasets are versioned and for each version a configuration file is checked in that contains the hyperparameter choices.

If new best practices or bugs emerge, e.g. in terms of hyperparameters, an updated dataset can be uploaded in a new version. This increases comparability and replicability.

There is also a seamless integration with Hugging Face's `datasets` as mentioned above. This is why explanation datasets that are published through `datasets` can be used in THERMOSTAT directly. When contributing new explanation datasets, users simply add the metadata about the three coordinates and make sure that the fields listed in Fig. 1 are contained. As soon as the dataset is published on the community hub, it can be downloaded and parsed by THERMOSTAT. More details are provided in the repository.[3]

2.3 Current State

After discussing use and maintenance, we will now present the current state of THERMOSTAT. Please recall that THERMOSTAT is intended to be a continuous, collaborative project.

With the publication of this paper, we contribute the explanations listed in Tab. 1. In total, the compute time for generating the explanations already amounts to more than 10,000 GPU hours; computational resources that the community does not have

[2]Neely et al. (2021) compare DistilBERT (Sanh et al., 2020) based models, we compare BERT-based models. They further constrain their evaluation to 500 instances while we are calculating the values for the entire datasets.

[3]Users contributing to THERMOSTAT should be aware that the THERMOSTAT project follows the Code of Ethics of ACL and ACM.

```python
import thermostat
from scipy.stats import kendalltau
lime, ig = thermostat.load("imdb-bert-lime"), thermostat.load("imdb-bert-lig")
lime, ig = lime.attributions.flatten(), ig.attributions.flatten()
print(kendalltau(lime, ig))
# KendalltauResult(correlation=0.025657302000906455, pvalue=0.0)
```

Figure 3: Code example for investigating the rank correlation between LIME and (Layer) Integrated Gradients explanations on IMDb + BERT. The analogous calculation of Kendall's τ for MultiNLI is left out for brevity. We simply state the value in the last line.

to invest repeatedly now.[4] Please note that the table is organized around the three coordinates: datasets, models, and explainers, the choices of which we discuss in the following.

Datasets Currently, four datasets are included in THERMOSTAT, namely IMDb (sentiment analysis, Maas et al., 2011), MultiNLI (natural language inference, Williams et al., 2018), XNLI (natural language inference, Conneau et al., 2018) and AG News (topic classification, Zhang et al., 2015). We chose these datasets, because arguably, they are prominently used in NLP research.

We hypothesize that instances that the model did not encounter at training time are more informative than known inputs. This is why we concentrated our computational resources on the respective test splits. In total, these amount to almost 50,000 instances already.

Models The second coordinate in THERMOSTAT is the model. Currently, five model architectures are included, namely ALBERT (Lan et al., 2020), BERT (Devlin et al., 2019), ELECTRA (Clark et al., 2020), RoBERTa (Liu et al., 2019), and XLNet (Yang et al., 2019). We chose community-trained fine-tuned classifiers as they are aptly available through the `transformers` library (Wolf et al., 2020), several of which are provided by TextAttack (Morris et al., 2020). The repository that we publish can be used to quickly include new models, if they are provided through the `transformers` library.

Explainers Provided through the Captum library (Kokhlikyan et al., 2020), there are five prominent feature attribution methods included in THERMOSTAT. (Layer) Gradient x Activation (Shrikumar et al., 2017) is an efficient method without hyperparameters. Integrated Gradients (Sundararajan et al., 2017), LIME (Ribeiro et al., 2016), Occlusion (Zeiler and Fergus, 2014) and Shapley Value Sampling (Castro et al., 2009) can be considered computationally challenging and involve hyperparameters. The choice of parameters in THERMOSTAT follows best practices and, as mentioned above, is well-documented and can be updated and extended.

3 Related Work

To the best of our knowledge, the closest work to our contribution is the Language Interpretability Tool (LIT) by Tenney et al. (2020) which offers a graphical interface for exploring saliency maps, counterfactual generation and the visualization of attention and embeddings. We also draw connections to Hoover et al. (2020) and Lal et al. (2021) who developed interfaces for analyzing the attention mechanism and embeddings of Transformer architectures. These again are visualization and analysis tools and as such complementary to the collection of explanations that is our primary contribution. Thus, an interface that bridges THERMOSTAT and LIT, for instance, is an interesting future direction.

There exist libraries, such as Captum (Kokhlikyan et al., 2020) or transformers-interpret (Pierse, 2021), that facilitate the generation of neural explanations. These libraries do not, however, free the user of the computational burden, nor are they easily accessible to non-technical researchers.

As noted in Section 2, the `datasets` library (Lhoest et al., 2021) functions as the backbone of THERMOSTAT. The novelties our work brings with it are (1) attributions from a variety of models that took over 10,000 GPU hours to compute in total, and (2) the support for explainability-specific visualizations and statistics like heatmap visualization and rank correlation between multiple explainers.

Finally, tangentially related to our work are

[4] To produce the feature attribution maps, we used up to 24 NVIDIA GPUs in parallel, namely GTX 1080Ti, RTX 2080Ti, RTX 3090, Quadro RTX 6000 and RTX A6000.

Dataset	Split (Subset)	# instances	# classes	Explainers				
IMDb	Test	25000	2	**LGxA**	**LIG**	**LIME**	**Occ**	**SVS**
`textattack/albert-base-v2-imdb` (ALBERT)								
`textattack/bert-base-uncased-imdb` (BERT)								
`monologg/electra-small-finetuned-imdb` (ELECTRA)								
`textattack/roberta-base-imdb` (RoBERTa)								
`textattack/xlnet-base-cased-imdb` (XLNet)								
MultiNLI	Validation Matched	9815	3	**LGxA**	**LIG**	**LIME**	**Occ**	**SVS**
`prajjwal1/albert-base-v2-mnli` (ALBERT)								
`textattack/bert-base-uncased-MNLI` (BERT)								
`howey/electra-base-mnli` (ELECTRA)								
`textattack/roberta-base-MNLI` (RoBERTa)								
`textattack/xlnet-base-cased-MNLI` (XLNet)								
XNLI	Test (en)	5010	3	**LGxA**	**LIG**	**LIME**	**Occ**	**SVS**
`prajjwal1/albert-base-v2-mnli` (ALBERT)								
`textattack/bert-base-uncased-MNLI` (BERT)								
`howey/electra-base-mnli` (ELECTRA)								
`textattack/roberta-base-MNLI` (RoBERTa)								
`textattack/xlnet-base-cased-MNLI` (XLNet)								
AG News	Test	7600	4	**LGxA**	**LIG**	**LIME**	**Occ**	**SVS**
`textattack/albert-base-v2-ag-news` (ALBERT)								
`textattack/bert-base-uncased-ag-news` (BERT)								
`textattack/roberta-base-ag-news` (RoBERTa)								

Table 1: Overview of feature attribution maps in THERMOSTAT. Dark green cells (86 out of 90) denote available configurations. Gray cells denote configurations that are work-in-progress.

datasets that supply explanations on top of texts and labels, usually collected from human annotators. e-SNLI (Camburu et al., 2018) probably is the most famous example in this line of work. The reader is referred to Wiegreffe and Marasović (2021) for a concise survey. In contrast to our work, the above mentioned papers present human ground truths instead of machine-generated explanations.

4 Conclusion

We present THERMOSTAT, an easily accessible data hub containing a large collection of NLP model explanations from prominent and mostly expensive explainers. We demonstrate the ease of access, extensibility and maintainability. New datasets can be added easily. Furthermore, we showcase an accompanying library and outline use cases. Users can compare models and explainers across a variety of datasets.

THERMOSTAT democratizes explainability research to a certain degree as it mitigates the computational (environmentally and financially) and implementational burden. Machine-generated explanations become accessible to non-technical researchers. Furthermore, comparability and replicability are increased.

It becomes apparent when consulting the literature in Section 1 that interpretation beyond classification (e.g. machine translation) is still an open problem (Wallace et al., 2020). Hence, we focus on these four text classification problems that are well-trodden paths.

Acknowledgements

We would like to thank Lisa Raithel, Steffen Castle, and David Harbecke for their valuable feedback. This work has been supported by the German Federal Ministry of Education and Research as part of the projects XAINES (01IW20005) and CORA4NLP (01IW20010).

References

Leila Arras, Franziska Horn, Grégoire Montavon, Klaus-Robert Müller, and Wojciech Samek. 2016. Explaining predictions of non-linear classifiers in NLP. In *Proceedings of the 1st Workshop on Representation Learning for NLP*, pages 1–7, Berlin, Germany. Association for Computational Linguistics.

Leila Arras, Grégoire Montavon, Klaus-Robert Müller, and Wojciech Samek. 2017. Explaining recurrent neural network predictions in sentiment analysis. In *Proceedings of the 8th Workshop on Computational Approaches to Subjectivity, Sentiment and Social Media Analysis*, pages 159–168, Copenhagen, Denmark. Association for Computational Linguistics.

Pepa Atanasova, Jakob Grue Simonsen, Christina Lioma, and Isabelle Augenstein. 2020. A diagnostic study of explainability techniques for text classification. In *Proceedings of the 2020 Conference on Empirical Methods in Natural Language Processing (EMNLP)*, pages 3256–3274, Online. Association for Computational Linguistics.

Yonatan Belinkov and James Glass. 2019. Analysis methods in neural language processing: A survey. In *Transactions of the Association for Computational Linguistics*, volume 7, pages 49–72.

Francesco Bodria, Fosca Giannotti, Riccardo Guidotti, Francesca Naretto, Dino Pedreschi, and Salvatore Rinzivillo. 2021. Benchmarking and survey of explanation methods for black box models. *arXiv preprint arXiv:2102.13076*.

Oana-Maria Camburu, Tim Rocktäschel, Thomas Lukasiewicz, and Phil Blunsom. 2018. e-snli: Natural language inference with natural language explanations. In *Advances in Neural Information Processing Systems*, volume 31. Curran Associates, Inc.

Javier Castro, Daniel Gómez, and Juan Tejada. 2009. Polynomial calculation of the shapley value based on sampling. *Comput. Oper. Res.*, 36(5):1726–1730.

Hanjie Chen, Song Feng, Jatin Ganhotra, Hui Wan, Chulaka Gunasekara, Sachindra Joshi, and Yangfeng Ji. 2021. Explaining neural network predictions on sentence pairs via learning word-group masks. In *Proceedings of the 2021 Conference of the North American Chapter of the Association for Computational Linguistics: Human Language Technologies*, pages 3917–3930, Online. Association for Computational Linguistics.

Kevin Clark, Minh-Thang Luong, Quoc V. Le, and Christopher D. Manning. 2020. ELECTRA: pre-training text encoders as discriminators rather than generators. In *8th International Conference on Learning Representations, ICLR 2020, Addis Ababa, Ethiopia, April 26-30, 2020*. OpenReview.net.

Alexis Conneau, Ruty Rinott, Guillaume Lample, Adina Williams, Samuel Bowman, Holger Schwenk, and Veselin Stoyanov. 2018. XNLI: Evaluating cross-lingual sentence representations. In *Proceedings of the 2018 Conference on Empirical Methods in Natural Language Processing*, pages 2475–2485, Brussels, Belgium. Association for Computational Linguistics.

Marina Danilevsky, Kun Qian, Ranit Aharonov, Yannis Katsis, Ban Kawas, and Prithviraj Sen. 2020. A survey of the state of explainable AI for natural language processing. In *Proceedings of the 1st Conference of the Asia-Pacific Chapter of the Association for Computational Linguistics and the 10th International Joint Conference on Natural Language Processing*, pages 447–459, Suzhou, China. Association for Computational Linguistics.

Nicola De Cao, Michael Sejr Schlichtkrull, Wilker Aziz, and Ivan Titov. 2020. How do decisions emerge across layers in neural models? interpretation with differentiable masking. In *Proceedings of the 2020 Conference on Empirical Methods in Natural Language Processing (EMNLP)*, pages 3243–3255, Online. Association for Computational Linguistics.

Jacob Devlin, Ming-Wei Chang, Kenton Lee, and Kristina Toutanova. 2019. BERT: Pre-training of deep bidirectional transformers for language understanding. In *Proceedings of the 2019 Conference of the North American Chapter of the Association for Computational Linguistics: Human Language Technologies, Volume 1 (Long and Short Papers)*, pages 4171–4186, Minneapolis, Minnesota. Association for Computational Linguistics.

Shuoyang Ding and Philipp Koehn. 2021. Evaluating saliency methods for neural language models. In *Proceedings of the 2021 Conference of the North American Chapter of the Association for Computational Linguistics: Human Language Technologies*, pages 5034–5052, Online. Association for Computational Linguistics.

Gabriel Erion, Joseph Janizek, Pascal Sturmfels, Scott Lundberg, and Su-In Lee. 2021. Improving performance of deep learning models with axiomatic attribution priors and expected gradients. *Nature Machine Intelligence*, pages 1–12.

Peter Hase and Mohit Bansal. 2020. Evaluating explainable AI: Which algorithmic explanations help users predict model behavior? In *Proceedings of the 58th Annual Meeting of the Association for Computational Linguistics*, pages 5540–5552, Online. Association for Computational Linguistics.

Peter Hase, Harry Xie, and Mohit Bansal. 2021. Search methods for sufficient, socially-aligned feature importance explanations with in-distribution counterfactuals. *arXiv preprint arXiv:2106.00786*.

Benjamin Hoover, Hendrik Strobelt, and Sebastian Gehrmann. 2020. exBERT: A Visual Analysis Tool to Explore Learned Representations in Transformer Models. In *Proceedings of the 58th Annual Meeting of the Association for Computational Linguistics:*

System Demonstrations, pages 187–196, Online. Association for Computational Linguistics.

Andrej Karpathy, Justin Johnson, and Li Fei-Fei. 2015. Visualizing and understanding recurrent networks. *arXiv preprint arXiv:1506.02078*.

Narine Kokhlikyan, Vivek Miglani, Bilal Alsallakh, Miguel Martin, and Orion Reblitz-Richardson. 2021. Investigating sanity checks for saliency maps with image and text classification. *arXiv preprint arXiv:2106.07475*.

Narine Kokhlikyan, Vivek Miglani, Miguel Martin, Edward Wang, Bilal Alsallakh, Jonathan Reynolds, Alexander Melnikov, Natalia Kliushkina, Carlos Araya, Siqi Yan, and Orion Reblitz-Richardson. 2020. Captum: A unified and generic model interpretability library for pytorch. *arXiv preprint arXiv:2009.07896*.

Vasudev Lal, Arden Ma, Estelle Aflalo, Phillip Howard, Ana Simoes, Daniel Korat, Oren Pereg, Gadi Singer, and Moshe Wasserblat. 2021. InterpreT: An interactive visualization tool for interpreting transformers. In *Proceedings of the 16th Conference of the European Chapter of the Association for Computational Linguistics: System Demonstrations*, pages 135–142, Online. Association for Computational Linguistics.

Zhenzhong Lan, Mingda Chen, Sebastian Goodman, Kevin Gimpel, Piyush Sharma, and Radu Soricut. 2020. ALBERT: A lite BERT for self-supervised learning of language representations. In *8th International Conference on Learning Representations, ICLR 2020, Addis Ababa, Ethiopia, April 26-30, 2020*. OpenReview.net.

Piyawat Lertvittayakumjorn and Francesca Toni. 2019. Human-grounded evaluations of explanation methods for text classification. In *Proceedings of the 2019 Conference on Empirical Methods in Natural Language Processing and the 9th International Joint Conference on Natural Language Processing (EMNLP-IJCNLP)*, pages 5195–5205, Hong Kong, China. Association for Computational Linguistics.

Quentin Lhoest, Patrick von Platen, Thomas Wolf, Albert Villanova del Moral, Yacine Jernite, Suraj Patil, Mariama Drame, Julien Chaumond, Julien Plu, Lewis Tunstall, Joe Davison, Simon Brandeis, Teven Le Scao, Victor Sanh, Kevin Canwen Xu, Nicolas Patry, Angelina McMillan-Major, Philipp Schmid, Sylvain Gugger, Clément Delangue, Théo Matussière, Lysandre Debut, Stas Bekman, and François Lagunas. 2021. huggingface/datasets: 1.8.0.

Jiwei Li, Will Monroe, and Dan Jurafsky. 2017. Understanding neural networks through representation erasure. *arXiv preprint arXiv:1612.08220*.

Frederick Liu and Besim Avci. 2019. Incorporating priors with feature attribution on text classification. In *Proceedings of the 57th Annual Meeting of the Association for Computational Linguistics*, pages 6274–6283, Florence, Italy. Association for Computational Linguistics.

Yinhan Liu, Myle Ott, Naman Goyal, Jingfei Du, Mandar Joshi, Danqi Chen, Omer Levy, Mike Lewis, Luke Zettlemoyer, and Veselin Stoyanov. 2019. Roberta: A robustly optimized bert pretraining approach. *arXiv preprint arXiv:1907.11692*.

Andrew L. Maas, Raymond E. Daly, Peter T. Pham, Dan Huang, Andrew Y. Ng, and Christopher Potts. 2011. Learning word vectors for sentiment analysis. In *Proceedings of the 49th Annual Meeting of the Association for Computational Linguistics: Human Language Technologies*, pages 142–150, Portland, Oregon, USA. Association for Computational Linguistics.

John Morris, Eli Lifland, Jin Yong Yoo, Jake Grigsby, Di Jin, and Yanjun Qi. 2020. TextAttack: A framework for adversarial attacks, data augmentation, and adversarial training in NLP. In *Proceedings of the 2020 Conference on Empirical Methods in Natural Language Processing: System Demonstrations*, pages 119–126, Online. Association for Computational Linguistics.

Michael Neely, Stefan F. Schouten, Maurits J. R. Bleeker, and Ana Lucic. 2021. Order in the court: Explainable ai methods prone to disagreement. *arXiv preprint arXiv:2105.03287*.

Anphi Nguyen and María Rodríguez Martínez. 2020. On quantitative aspects of model interpretability. *arXiv preprint arXiv:2007.07584*.

Dong Nguyen. 2018. Comparing automatic and human evaluation of local explanations for text classification. In *Proceedings of the 2018 Conference of the North American Chapter of the Association for Computational Linguistics: Human Language Technologies, Volume 1 (Long Papers)*, pages 1069–1078, New Orleans, Louisiana. Association for Computational Linguistics.

Charles Pierse. 2021. transformers-interpret v0.5.1. GitHub. Accessed: 2021-06-29.

Nina Poerner, Hinrich Schütze, and Benjamin Roth. 2018. Evaluating neural network explanation methods using hybrid documents and morphosyntactic agreement. In *Proceedings of the 56th Annual Meeting of the Association for Computational Linguistics (Volume 1: Long Papers)*, pages 340–350, Melbourne, Australia. Association for Computational Linguistics.

Grusha Prasad, Yixin Nie, Mohit Bansal, Robin Jia, Douwe Kiela, and Adina Williams. 2020. To what extent do human explanations of model behavior align with actual model behavior? *arXiv preprint arXiv:2012.13354*.

Danish Pruthi, Bhuwan Dhingra, Livio Baldini Soares, Michael Collins, Zachary C. Lipton, Graham Neubig, and William W. Cohen. 2020. Evaluating explanations: How much do explanations from the teacher aid students? *arXiv preprint arXiv:2012.00893.*

Marco Tulio Ribeiro, Sameer Singh, and Carlos Guestrin. 2016. "why should i trust you?": Explaining the predictions of any classifier. In *Proceedings of the 22nd ACM SIGKDD International Conference on Knowledge Discovery and Data Mining*, KDD '16, page 1135–1144, New York, NY, USA. Association for Computing Machinery.

Andrew Slavin Ross, Michael C. Hughes, and Finale Doshi-Velez. 2017. Right for the right reasons: Training differentiable models by constraining their explanations. In *Proceedings of the Twenty-Sixth International Joint Conference on Artificial Intelligence, IJCAI-17*, pages 2662–2670.

Victor Sanh, Lysandre Debut, Julien Chaumond, and Thomas Wolf. 2020. Distilbert, a distilled version of bert: smaller, faster, cheaper and lighter. *arXiv preprint arXiv:1910.01108.*

Robert Schwarzenberg, Nils Feldhus, and Sebastian Möller. 2021. Efficient explanations from empirical explainers. *arXiv preprint arXiv:2103.15429.*

Avanti Shrikumar, Peyton Greenside, and Anshul Kundaje. 2017. Learning important features through propagating activation differences. In *Proceedings of the 34th International Conference on Machine Learning*, volume 70 of *Proceedings of Machine Learning Research*, pages 3145–3153. PMLR.

Sanchit Sinha, Hanjie Chen, Arshdeep Sekhon, Yangfeng Ji, and Yanjun Qi. 2021. Perturbing inputs for fragile interpretations in deep natural language processing. *arXiv preprint arXiv:2108.04990.*

Emma Strubell, Ananya Ganesh, and Andrew McCallum. 2019. Energy and policy considerations for deep learning in NLP. In *Proceedings of the 57th Annual Meeting of the Association for Computational Linguistics*, pages 3645–3650, Florence, Italy. Association for Computational Linguistics.

Mukund Sundararajan, Ankur Taly, and Qiqi Yan. 2017. Axiomatic attribution for deep networks. In *Proceedings of the 34th International Conference on Machine Learning*, volume 70 of *Proceedings of Machine Learning Research*, pages 3319–3328. PMLR.

Ian Tenney, James Wexler, Jasmijn Bastings, Tolga Bolukbasi, Andy Coenen, Sebastian Gehrmann, Ellen Jiang, Mahima Pushkarna, Carey Radebaugh, Emily Reif, and Ann Yuan. 2020. The language interpretability tool: Extensible, interactive visualizations and analysis for NLP models. In *Proceedings of the 2020 Conference on Empirical Methods in Natural Language Processing: System Demonstrations*, pages 107–118, Online. Association for Computational Linguistics.

Michael Tsang, Sirisha Rambhatla, and Yan Liu. 2020. How does this interaction affect me? interpretable attribution for feature interactions. In *Advances in Neural Information Processing Systems*, volume 33, pages 6147–6159. Curran Associates, Inc.

Eric Wallace, Matt Gardner, and Sameer Singh. 2020. Interpreting predictions of NLP models. In *Proceedings of the 2020 Conference on Empirical Methods in Natural Language Processing: Tutorial Abstracts*, pages 20–23, Online. Association for Computational Linguistics.

Sarah Wiegreffe and Ana Marasović. 2021. Teach me to explain: A review of datasets for explainable nlp. *arXiv preprint arXiv:2102.12060.*

Adina Williams, Nikita Nangia, and Samuel Bowman. 2018. A broad-coverage challenge corpus for sentence understanding through inference. In *Proceedings of the 2018 Conference of the North American Chapter of the Association for Computational Linguistics: Human Language Technologies, Volume 1 (Long Papers)*, pages 1112–1122, New Orleans, Louisiana. Association for Computational Linguistics.

Thomas Wolf, Lysandre Debut, Victor Sanh, Julien Chaumond, Clement Delangue, Anthony Moi, Pierric Cistac, Tim Rault, Rémi Louf, Morgan Funtowicz, Joe Davison, Sam Shleifer, Patrick von Platen, Clara Ma, Yacine Jernite, Julien Plu, Canwen Xu, Teven Le Scao, Sylvain Gugger, Mariama Drame, Quentin Lhoest, and Alexander M. Rush. 2020. Transformers: State-of-the-art natural language processing. In *Proceedings of the 2020 Conference on Empirical Methods in Natural Language Processing: System Demonstrations*, pages 38–45, Online. Association for Computational Linguistics.

Zhilin Yang, Zihang Dai, Yiming Yang, Jaime Carbonell, Russ R Salakhutdinov, and Quoc V Le. 2019. Xlnet: Generalized autoregressive pretraining for language understanding. In *Advances in Neural Information Processing Systems*, volume 32. Curran Associates, Inc.

Fan Yin, Zhouxing Shi, Cho-Jui Hsieh, and Kai-Wei Chang. 2021. On the faithfulness measurements for model interpretations. *arXiv preprint arXiv:2104.08782.*

Muhammad Bilal Zafar, Michele Donini, Dylan Slack, Cedric Archambeau, Sanjiv Das, and Krishnaram Kenthapadi. 2021. On the lack of robust interpretability of neural text classifiers. In *Findings of the Association for Computational Linguistics: ACL-IJCNLP 2021*, pages 3730–3740, Online. Association for Computational Linguistics.

Matthew D. Zeiler and Rob Fergus. 2014. Visualizing and understanding convolutional networks. In *Computer Vision – ECCV 2014*, pages 818–833, Cham. Springer International Publishing.

Xiang Zhang, Junbo Zhao, and Yann LeCun. 2015. Character-level convolutional networks for text classification. In *Advances in Neural Information Processing Systems*, volume 28. Curran Associates, Inc.

LMDIFF: A Visual Diff Tool to Compare Language Models

Hendrik Strobelt
IBM Research
MIT-IBM Watson AI Lab
hendrik@strobelt.com

Benjamin Hoover
IBM Research
MIT-IBM Watson AI Lab
benjamin.hoover@ibm.com

Arvind Satyanarayan
MIT CSAIL
Massachusetts Institute of Technology
arvindsatya@mit.edu

Sebastian Gehrmann
Google Research
Harvard University
gehrmann@google.com

Abstract

While different language models are ubiquitous in NLP, it is hard to contrast their outputs and identify which contexts one can handle better than the other. To address this question, we introduce LMDIFF, a tool that visually compares probability distributions of two models that differ, e.g., through finetuning, distillation, or simply training with different parameter sizes. LMDIFF allows the generation of hypotheses about model behavior by investigating text instances token by token and further assists in choosing these interesting text instances by identifying the most interesting phrases from large corpora. We showcase the applicability of LMDIFF for hypothesis generation across multiple case studies. A demo is available at http://lmdiff.net.

1 Introduction

Interactive tools play an important role when analyzing language models and other machine learning models in natural language processing (NLP) as they enable the qualitative examination of examples and help assemble anecdotal evidence that a model exhibits a particular behavior in certain contexts. This anecdotal evidence informs hypotheses that are then rigorously studied (e.g., Tenney et al., 2019; Belinkov and Glass, 2019; Rogers et al., 2020). Many such tools exist, for example to inspect attention mechanisms (Hoover et al., 2020; Vig, 2019), explain translations through nearest neighbors (Strobelt et al., 2018), investigate neuron values (Dalvi et al., 2019; Strobelt et al., 2017), and many more that focus on the outputs of models (e.g., Cabrera et al., 2019). There also exist multiple frameworks that aggregate methods employed in the initial tools to enable others to extend or combine them (Pruksachatkun et al., 2020; Wallace et al., 2019; Tenney et al., 2020).

However, notably absent from the range of available tools are those that aim to *compare* distributions produced by different models. While comparisons according to performance numbers are common practice in benchmarks (Wang et al., 2018; Hu et al., 2020; Gehrmann et al., 2021), there exists only rudimentary support in existing tools for inspecting how model outputs compare for specific tasks or documents. Yet, this problem motivates many current studies, including questions about how models handle gendered words, whether domain transfer is easy between models, what happens during finetuning, where differences lie between models of different sizes, or how multilingual and monolingual models differ.

To fill this gap, we introduce LMDIFF: an interactive tool for comparing language models by qualitatively comparing per-token likelihoods. Our design provides a *global* and a *local* view: In the global step, we operate on an entire corpus of texts, provide aggregate statistics across thousands of data points, and help users identify the most interesting examples. An interesting example can then be further analyzed in the local view. Fine-grained information about the model outputs for the chosen example is visualized, including the probability of each token and the difference in rank within each model's distribution. Similar to other visual tools, LMDIFF helps form hypotheses that can then be tested through rigorous statistical analyses. Across six case studies, we demonstrate how it enables an effective exploration of model differences and motivates future research. A deployed version of LMDIFF with six corpora and nine models is available at http://lmdiff.net/ and

Proceedings of the 2021 Conference on Empirical Methods in Natural Language Processing: System Demonstrations, pages 96–105
November 7–11, 2021. ©2021 Association for Computational Linguistics

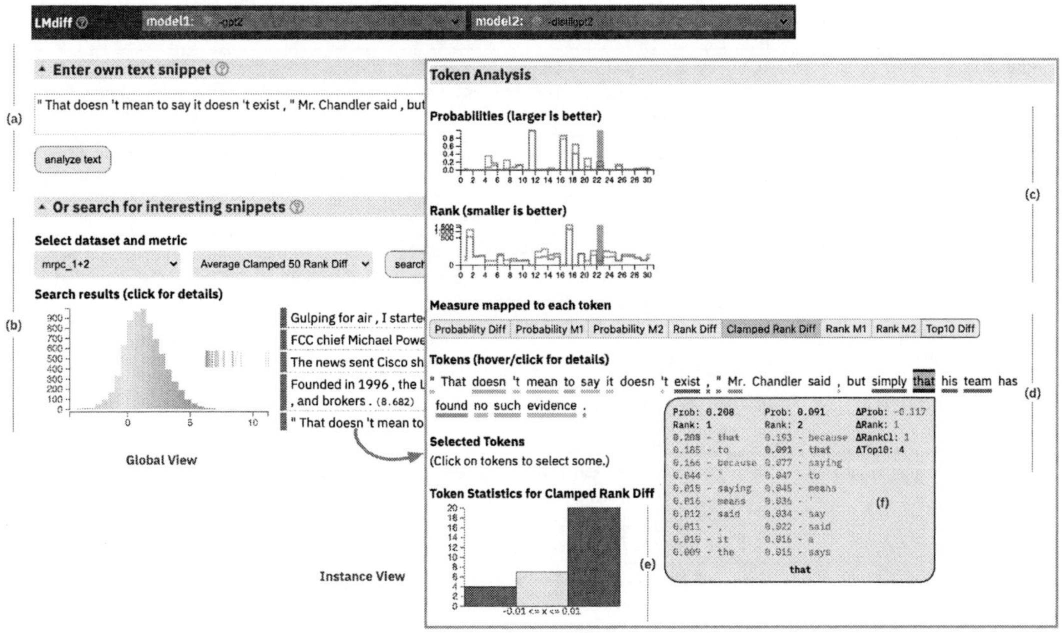

Figure 1: LMDIFF interface. The Global View (a,b) allows finding interesting examples which are then selected for in-depth investigation in the Instance View (c-f).

its code is released at `https://github.com/HendrikStrobelt/LMdiff` (Apache 2.0 license) with support to easily add additional models, corpora, or evaluation metrics.

2 Methods

LMDIFF compares two models $m_{\{1,2\}}$ by analyzing their probability distributions at the position of each token $\hat{X}_{1:N}$ in a specific text. A correct token's probability distribution $p_{\mathrm{m_j}}(X_i = \hat{X}_i | X_{1:i-1})$ is easily influenced the scaling factor β in the function $p = \mathrm{softmax}(\beta x)$ used to convert logits x into probabilities p (though two distributions are still comparable if both use the same β). For this reason, we also include the correct token's rank in $p_{\mathrm{m_j}}(X_i | X_{1:i-1})$. From the probabilities and ranks, we derive eight measures of global difference (comparison over a corpus) and eight measures of local difference (comparison over an example). The global measures are the (1) difference in rank of each token, (2) the difference in rank after clamping a rank to a maximum of 50, (3) the difference in probability of each token, and (4) the number of different tokens within the top-10 predicted tokens.[1] For each measure, we allow filtering by its average or maximum in a sequence.

[1]Other metrics like the KL-Divergence were omitted from the final interface since the numbers were too hard to interpret.

To compare two models on a single example, we either directly visualize $p_{m_1}(X_i = \hat{X}_i)$, $p_{m_2}(X_i = \hat{X}_i)$, $p_{m_1}(X_i = \hat{X}_i) - p_{m_2}(X_i = \hat{X}_i)$, or the equivalent measures but focusing on the rank instead of the probability. As for the global measures, we present rank differences in both an unclamped and a clamped version. The clamped version surfaces more interesting examples; e.g., the difference between a token of rank 1 and 5 is more important than the rank difference between 44 and 60. The visual interface maps the difference to a blue-red scale (see Figure 1d) and visualizations of a single model to a gray scale.

2.1 Visual Interface

Figure 1 shows the LMDIFF interface. The user starts their investigation by specifying the two models m_1 and m_2 and a target text d. This target may either be entered into the free-text field (1a) or chosen from the list of suggested interesting text snippets (1b, see Section 2.2). Upon selection of the text, the likelihoods, ranks, and difference metrics for m_1 and m_2 for each token of d are computed.

Users can compare results using the instance view, which leverages multiple visual idioms to show aspects of the models' performance. The step plots (Figure 1c) show the absolute values for likelihoods and ranks, with color indicating the model.

Dataset	Description
WinoBias (Zhao et al., 2018)	Collection of 3,160 sentences using different resolution systems to understand gender bias issues. We include two versions: (a) just sentence, (b) sentence with addendum (e.g., "he refers to doctor")
CommonsenseQA (Talmor et al., 2019)	Collection of 12,102 questions with one correct answer and four distractor answers. For our use cases, we concatenate the question and the correct answer to one single string.
MRPC (Dolan et al., 2004)	Collection of 5,801 sentence pairs collected from newswire articles.
GPT2-GEN (Radford et al., 2019a)	Collection of generated sentences from GPT-2 models. For each model the dataset contains 250K random samples (temperature 1, no truncation) and 250K samples generated with Top-K 40 truncation. We use the subset GPT-2-762M k40.
Short Jokes (Moudgil, 2017)	Collection of 231,657 short jokes provided as Kaggle challenge for humor understanding.
BioLang (Liechti et al., 2017)	Collection of 12 million abstracts and captions from open access Europe PubMedCentral processed by the EMBO SourceData project
Model	
GPT-2 (Radford et al., 2019b)	The decoder of a Transformer trained on OpenWebText
DistilGPT-2	A smaller Transformer trained to replicate GPT-2 output
GPT-2-ArXiv	GPT-2 finetuned on a large arxiv dataset
GPT-2-ArXiv-NLP	GPT-2 finetuned only on arxiv NLP papers
BERT-base-uncased (Devlin et al., 2018)	Masked language model with case-insensitive tokenization.
DistilBERT (Sanh et al., 2019)	A smaller Transformer trained to replicate BERT output
DistilBERT-SST-2	distilBERT finetuned on the SST-2 (Socher et al., 2013) dataset
GPT-2-German	GPT-2 trained on various German texts
GPT-2-German-Faust	The German GPT-2 model finetuned on Faust I & II

Table 1: The default corpora and models found in the deployed version of LMDIFF. All models were taken from Huggingface's model hub. Horizontal lines group tokenization-compatible models.

Upon selecting a distance metric, it is mapped onto the text (1d) using a red-white-blue diverging color scheme: white for no or minimal distance, red/blue for values in favor of a corresponding model. For instance, a token is colored blue if the rank of that token under model m_2 is lower than under m_1 or its likelihood higher. The highlighting on hover between both plots (1c+d) is synchronized, to help spot examples where the measures diverge.

The histogram (1e) indicates the distribution of measures for the text. If the centroid of the histogram leans decidedly to one side, it indicates that one model is better at reproducing the given text (observe the shift for red in Figure 1e). The token detail view (1f), shows all difference measures for a selected token and allows for a direct comparison of the top-k predictions for each model at the token position. E.g., in Figure 1f, the token "that" has rank 1 in model m_1 but rank 2 in m_2. Clicking tokens makes the detail view for those tokens stick to the bottom of the page to enable investigations of multiple tokens in the same sequence.

2.2 Finding Interesting Candidates

To facilitate searching for interesting texts, we extract examples from a large corpus of texts for which the two models differ the most. The corpus is prepared via an offline preprocessing step in which the differences between the models are scored according to the methods outlined above. Each example is compared using different aggregation methods, like averaging, finding the median, the upper quartile, or the top-k of differences in likelihoods, ranks, and clamped ranks. The 50 highest-ranking text snippets for each measure are considered as interesting. The interface (Figure 1b) shows a histogram of the distribution of a measure over the entire corpus and indicates through black stripes where interesting outlier samples are located fall on the histogram. That way, users can get an overview of how the two models compare across the corpus while also being able to view the most interesting samples.

3 Supported Data and Models

The deployed version of LMDIFF currently supports six datasets and nine models, detailed in Table 1. All pretrained models were taken from Hug-

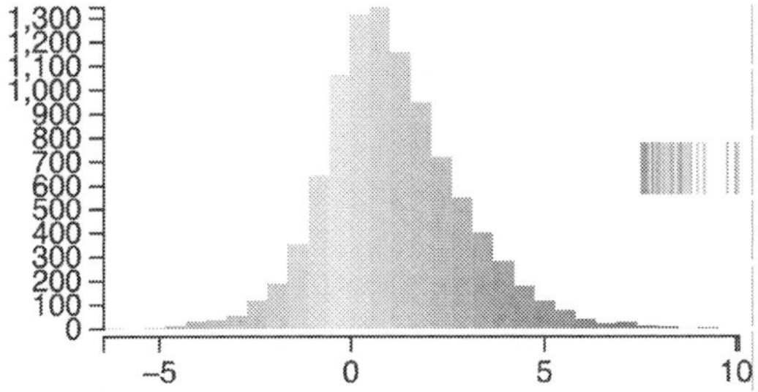

Figure 2: The global view on the CommonsenseQA dataset when comparing GPT-2 and DistilGPT-2. The histogram depicts the distribution of a specific measure (Average Clamped 50 Rank) over the reference corpus. The short black lines depict the values of the 20 highest values.

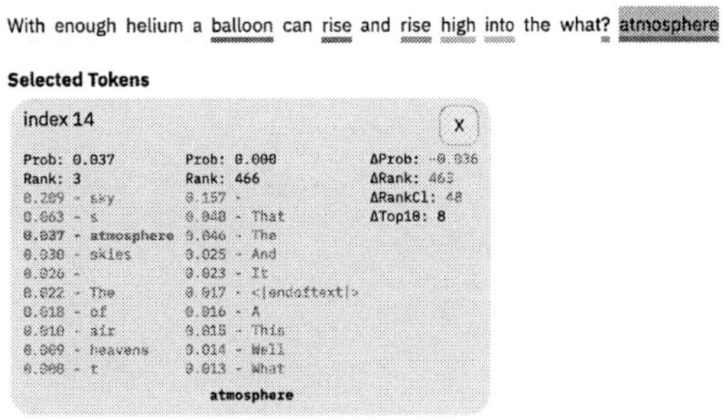

Figure 3: A commonsenseQA example in which GPT-2 performs much better than DistilGPT-2. Showing Clamped Rank difference.

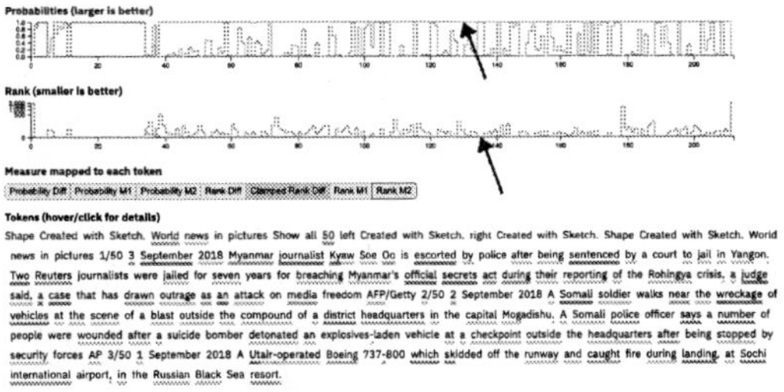

Figure 4: Comparing GPT-2 vs DistilGPT-2 on GPT-2 generated text shows that it is easy to spot which model produced it.

gingface's model hub[2]. Section 5 explains how to use LMDIFF with many more custom models and datasets.

4 Case Studies

As discussed above, this tool aims to generate hypotheses by discovering anecdotal evidence for certain model behavior. It will not be able to give definite proofs for discovered hypotheses, which should instead be explored more in-depth in follow-up studies. As such, in this section, we provide examples of new kinds of questions that LMDIFF helps investigate and explore further questions inspired by past findings.

4.1 Which model is better at commonsense reasoning?

Prompt-based approaches have become a popular way to test whether a model can perform a task (Brown et al., 2020). A relevant question to this is whether models can perform tasks that require memorization of commonsense knowledge (e.g., the name of the company that develops Windows, or the colors of the US flag) (Jiang et al., 2020). For our case study, we format the CommonsenseQA (Talmor et al., 2019) dataset to follow a "Question? Answer" schema, such that we can compare the probability of the answer under different models. Comparing GPT-2 (red) and its distilled variant DistilGPT-2 (blue), we can observe in Figure 2 that overall, GPT-2 performs much better on the task, commonly ranking the correct answer between 1 and 5 ranks higher in its distribution. An interesting example shown in Figure 3 paints a particularly grim picture for DistilGPT-2 — while the standard model ranks the correct answer third, the distilled variant ranks it 466th. This leads to the questions of why this bit of knowledge (and those of other outliers) was squashed in the distillation process, whether there is commonality between the forgotten knowledge, and it motivates the development of methods that prevent this from happening.

4.2 Which model produced a text?

Prior work has investigated different ways to detect whether a text was generated by a model or written by a human, either by training classifiers on samples from a model (Zellers et al., 2019; Brown et al., 2020) or directly using a models probability distribution (Gehrmann et al., 2019). A core insight from these works was that search algorithms (beam search, top-k sampling, etc.) tend to sample from the head of a models' distribution. That means that it is visually easy to detect if a model generated a text. With LMDIFF, we extend upon this insight to point to *which* model generated a text — if a model generated a text, the text should be consistently more likely under that model than under other similar models. While our tool does not allow us to test this hypothesis at scale, we can

[2]https://huggingface.co/models

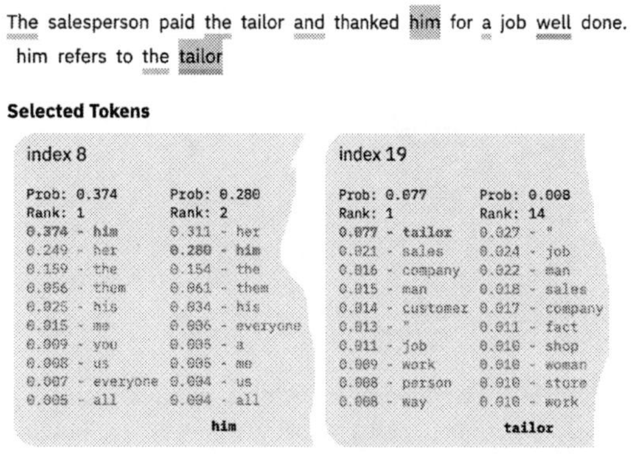

Figure 5: Winobias example with addendum for GPT-2 vs DistilGPT-2 showing Clamped Rank difference. Interesting since him/her probability rank switches between models and only distil fails at the addendum task.

find clear anecdotal evidence shown in Figure 4. In the figure, we compare the probabilities of GPT-2 and DistilGPT-2 on a sample of GPT-2 generated text. We observe the consistent pattern that GPT-2 assigns an equal or higher likelihood to almost every token in the text.

4.3 Which model is more prone to be overconfident in coreference?

We next investigate whether one model has learned spurious correlations in coreference tasks, using our augmented version of the WinoBias dataset (Zhao et al., 2018). Since we are comparing language models, we modified the text to add the string "*[pronoun]* refers to the *[profession]*". We can then use the detail view to look at the probabilities of the pronoun in the original sentence and the probability of the disambiguating mention of the profession. In our example (Figure 5), we again compare GPT-2 (red) and DistilGPT-2 (blue). Curiously, the distillation process flipped the order of the predicted pronouns "him" and "her". Moreover, DistilGPT-2 fails to complete the second sentence while GPT-2 successfully predicts "Tailor" as the most probable continuation, indicating that DistilGPT-2 did not strongly associate the pronoun with the profession. This case study motivates further investigation of cases where distillation does not maintain the expected ranking of continuations. A similar effect has previously been detected in distillation processes for computer vision models (Hooker et al., 2020).

4.4 What predictions are affected the most by finetuning?

Other, more open-ended, qualitative comparisons that are enabled through LMDIFF aim to understand how a model changes when it is finetuned on a specific task or documents from a specific domain. The finetuning process can impact prediction both in the downstream domain and in not anticipated, unrelated other domains.

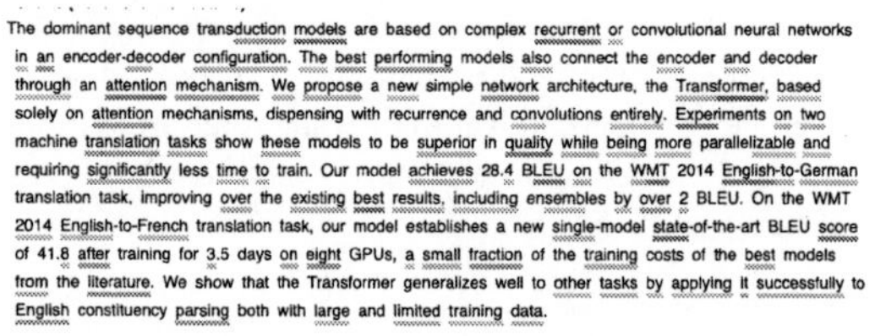

Figure 6: GPT-2 vs GPT-Arxiv-nlp on an abstract of an NLP paper.

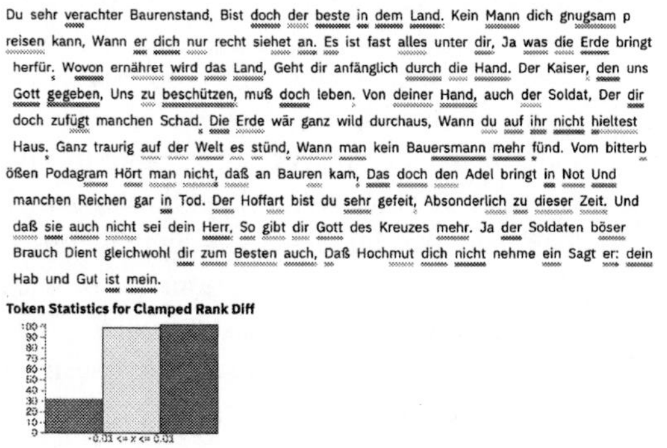

Figure 7: GPT2-German vs GPT2-German-Faust on a snippet from the 1668 book "Simplicius Simplicissimus" using the Clamped Rank difference.

In Domain In Figure 6, we show a comparison between GPT-2 and GPT-2-ArXiv-NLP on an abstract of an NLP paper, highlighting the probability difference. As expected, NLP-specific terms (WMT BLEU, model, attention, etc.) tend to be more likely under the finetuned model. But, interestingly, the name of languages and Transformer are both more likely under the original model. This finding may warrant a deeper investigation for possible causes and whether this phenomenon persists across other contexts.

Out of Domain Out-of-domain tests can be useful for checking whether the finetuning process led to some transfer learning, or to test for catastrophic forgetting. In our case study, we compare GPT-2-German before and after finetuning on Goethe's

Faust part I (1808) and II (1832). We hypothesized that the contemporary model would not be able to handle other works of literature from a similar time-period as well as the Faust-model, and thus tested on various snippets from books of the years 1200 to 1900. Our sample from the book Simplicius Simplicissimus (1668) (Figure 7) is representative of the consistent finding that GPT-2-German performs better than the Faust variant. This could have many reasons — the model may have overfit on the Faust-style of writing, the investigated periods of literature may differ too much, or they may differ too little from contemporary German.

4.5 Finding dataset errors

While not the original goal of LMDIFF, we observed that in some cases the outlier detection method could also be used to find outlier *data* instead of examples where models differ significantly. One such example occurred when comparing GPT-ArXiv to GPT-2 on the BioLang dataset. It appears that GPT-2 is much better at modeling repetitive, nonsensical character sequences which were thus surfaced through the algorithm (see Appendix A).

5 System Description

All comparisons in LMDIFF begin with three provided arguments: a dataset containing the interesting phases to analyze, and two comparable Transformer models. LMDIFF wraps Huggingface Transformers (Wolf et al., 2020) and can use any of their pretrained autoregressive or masked language models from their model hub[3] or a local directory. Two models are comparable if they use the same tokenization scheme and vocabulary. This is required such that a phrase passed to either of them will have an identical encoding, with special tokens added in the same locations.

LMDIFF then does the work of recording each model's predictions across the dataset into an *AnalysisCache*. Each token in each phrase of the dataset is analyzed for its "rank" and "probability". We define a token's rank as the affinity of the LM to predict the token relative to all other tokens, where a rank of 1 indicates it is the most favorable token, and the probability is computed from a direct softmax of the token's logit. Other useful information is also stored, such as the top-10 tokens (and their probabilities) that would have been predicted in that token's spot. This information can then be compared to other caches and explored in the visual interface. The interface can also be used independently of cache files to compare models on individual inputs.

The modular design separating *datasets*, *models*, and their *caches* makes it easy to compare the differences between many different models on distinct datasets. Once a cache has been made of a (model, dataset_D) pair, it can be compared to any other cache of a (comparable_model, dataset_D) pair within seconds. More information is provided in Appendix B.

Adding models and datasets It is easy to load additional models and datasets. First, ensure that the model can be loaded through the Huggingface `AutoModelWithLMHead` and `AutoTokenizer` function `from_pretrained(...)` which supports loading from a local directory. The following script prepares two models and a dataset for comparison:

```
python scripts/preprocess.py all \
    [OPTIONS] M1 M2 DATASET \
    --output-dir OUT
- M1 = Path (or name) of HF model 1
- M2 = Path (or name) of HF model 2
- DATASET = Path to dataset.txt
- OUT = Where to store outputs
```

The output configuration directory `OUT` can be passed directly to the LMDIFF server and interface which will automatically load the new data:

```
python backend/server/main.py \
    --config DIR
- DIR = Contains preprocessed outputs
```

The interface works equally well to compare two models on individual examples without a preprocessed cache:

```
python backend/server/main.py \
    --m1 MODEL1 --m2 MODEL2
```

6 Discussion and Conclusion

We presented LMDIFF, a tool to visually inspect qualitative differences between language models based on output distributions. We show in several use cases how finding specific text snippets and analyzing them token-by-token can lead to interesting hypotheses.

We emphasize that LMDIFF by itself does not provide any definite answers to these hypotheses by itself – it cannot, for example, show which model

[3]`https://huggingface.co/models`

is generally better at a given task. To answer these kind of questions, statistical analysis is required.

A design limitation of LMDIFF is that it relies on compatible models. Because the tool is based on per-token model outputs and apples-to-apples comparisons of distributions, only models that use the same tokenization scheme and vocabulary can be compared in the instance view. In future work, we will work toward extending the compatibility by introducing additional tokenization-independent measures and visualizations.

Another extension of LMDIFF may probe for memorized training examples and personal information using methods proposed by Carlini et al. (2020). As shown in Sections 4.2 and 4.5, we can already identify text that was generated by a model and leverage patterns that a model has learned. Adding support to filter a corpus by measures in addition to finding outliers may help with the analysis of potentially memorized examples.

7 Acknowledgements

We thank Ankur Parikh and Ian Tenney for helpful comments on an earlier draft of this paper. This work was supported by the MIT-IBM Watson AI Lab. This work has been developed in part during the BigScience Summer of Language Models 2021.

References

Yonatan Belinkov and James Glass. 2019. Analysis methods in neural language processing: A survey. *Transactions of the Association for Computational Linguistics*, 7:49–72.

Tom B. Brown, Benjamin Mann, Nick Ryder, Melanie Subbiah, Jared Kaplan, Prafulla Dhariwal, Arvind Neelakantan, Pranav Shyam, Girish Sastry, Amanda Askell, Sandhini Agarwal, Ariel Herbert-Voss, Gretchen Krueger, Tom Henighan, Rewon Child, Aditya Ramesh, Daniel M. Ziegler, Jeffrey Wu, Clemens Winter, Christopher Hesse, Mark Chen, Eric Sigler, Mateusz Litwin, Scott Gray, Benjamin Chess, Jack Clark, Christopher Berner, Sam McCandlish, Alec Radford, Ilya Sutskever, and Dario Amodei. 2020. Language models are few-shot learners. In *Advances in Neural Information Processing Systems 33: Annual Conference on Neural Information Processing Systems 2020, NeurIPS 2020, December 6-12, 2020, virtual.*

Ángel Alexander Cabrera, Will Epperson, Fred Hohman, Minsuk Kahng, Jamie Morgenstern, and Duen Horng Chau. 2019. Fairvis: Visual analytics for discovering intersectional bias in machine learning. In *2019 IEEE Conference on Visual Analytics Science and Technology (VAST)*, pages 46–56. IEEE.

Nicholas Carlini, Florian Tramèr, Eric Wallace, Matthew Jagielski, Ariel Herbert-Voss, Katherine Lee, Adam Roberts, Tom B. Brown, Dawn Song, Úlfar Erlingsson, Alina Oprea, and Colin Raffel. 2020. Extracting training data from large language models. *CoRR*, abs/2012.07805.

Fahim Dalvi, Avery Nortonsmith, Anthony Bau, Yonatan Belinkov, Hassan Sajjad, Nadir Durrani, and James Glass. 2019. NeuroX: A toolkit for analyzing individual neurons in neural networks. In *Proceedings of the AAAI Conference on Artificial Intelligence*, volume 33, pages 9851–9852.

Jacob Devlin, Ming-Wei Chang, Kenton Lee, and Kristina Toutanova. 2018. BERT: pre-training of deep bidirectional transformers for language understanding. *CoRR*, abs/1810.04805.

Bill Dolan, Chris Quirk, and Chris Brockett. 2004. Unsupervised construction of large paraphrase corpora: Exploiting massively parallel news sources. In *COLING 2004: Proceedings of the 20th International Conference on Computational Linguistics*, pages 350–356, Geneva, Switzerland. COLING.

Sebastian Gehrmann, Tosin Adewumi, Karmanya Aggarwal, Pawan Sasanka Ammanamanchi, Anuoluwapo Aremu, Antoine Bosselut, Khyathi Raghavi Chandu, Miruna-Adriana Clinciu, Dipanjan Das, Kaustubh Dhole, Wanyu Du, Esin Durmus, Ondřej Dušek, Chris Chinenye Emezue, Varun Gangal, Cristina Garbacea, Tatsunori Hashimoto, Yufang Hou, Yacine Jernite, Harsh Jhamtani, Yangfeng Ji, Shailza Jolly, Mihir Kale, Dhruv Kumar, Faisal Ladhak, Aman Madaan, Mounica Maddela, Khyati Mahajan, Saad Mahamood, Bodhisattwa Prasad Majumder, Pedro Henrique Martins, Angelina McMillan-Major, Simon Mille, Emiel van Miltenburg, Moin Nadeem, Shashi Narayan, Vitaly Nikolaev, Andre Niyongabo Rubungo, Salomey Osei, Ankur Parikh, Laura Perez-Beltrachini, Niranjan Ramesh Rao, Vikas Raunak, Juan Diego Rodriguez, Sashank Santhanam, João Sedoc, Thibault Sellam, Samira Shaikh, Anastasia Shimorina, Marco Antonio Sobrevilla Cabezudo, Hendrik Strobelt, Nishant Subramani, Wei Xu, Diyi Yang, Akhila Yerukola, and Jiawei Zhou. 2021. The GEM benchmark: Natural language generation, its evaluation and metrics. In *Proceedings of the 1st Workshop on Natural Language Generation, Evaluation, and Metrics (GEM 2021)*, pages 96–120, Online. Association for Computational Linguistics.

Sebastian Gehrmann, Hendrik Strobelt, and Alexander Rush. 2019. GLTR: Statistical detection and visualization of generated text. In *Proceedings of the 57th Annual Meeting of the Association for Computational Linguistics: System Demonstrations*, pages 111–116, Florence, Italy. Association for Computational Linguistics.

Sara Hooker, Nyalleng Moorosi, Gregory Clark, Samy Bengio, and Emily Denton. 2020. Characterising bias in compressed models. *ICML 2020 Workshop on Human Interpretability in Machine Learning*.

Benjamin Hoover, Hendrik Strobelt, and Sebastian Gehrmann. 2020. exBERT: A Visual Analysis Tool to Explore Learned Representations in Transformer Models. In *Proceedings of the 58th Annual Meeting of the Association for Computational Linguistics: System Demonstrations*, pages 187–196, Online. Association for Computational Linguistics.

Junjie Hu, Sebastian Ruder, Aditya Siddhant, Graham Neubig, Orhan Firat, and Melvin Johnson. 2020. XTREME: A massively multilingual multitask benchmark for evaluating cross-lingual generalisation. In *International Conference on Machine Learning*, pages 4411–4421. PMLR.

Zhengbao Jiang, Frank F. Xu, Jun Araki, and Graham Neubig. 2020. How can we know what language models know. *Trans. Assoc. Comput. Linguistics*, 8:423–438.

Robin Liechti, Nancy George, Lou Götz, Sara El-Gebali, Anastasia Chasapi, Isaac Crespo, Ioannis Xenarios, and Thomas Lemberger. 2017. Sourcedata: a semantic platform for curating and searching figures. *Nature methods*, 14(11):1021–1022.

Michael McCloskey and Neal J Cohen. 1989. Catastrophic interference in connectionist networks: The sequential learning problem. In *Psychology of learning and motivation*, volume 24, pages 109–165. Elsevier.

Abhinav Moudgil. 2017. Kaggle: Short jokes - collection of over 200,000 short jokes for humour research.

Yada Pruksachatkun, Phil Yeres, Haokun Liu, Jason Phang, Phu Mon Htut, Alex Wang, Ian Tenney, and Samuel R. Bowman. 2020. jiant: A software toolkit for research on general-purpose text understanding models. In *Proceedings of the 58th Annual Meeting of the Association for Computational Linguistics: System Demonstrations*, pages 109–117, Online. Association for Computational Linguistics.

Alec Radford, Jong Wook Kim, and Jeff Wu. 2019a. Gpt2 output dataset on github.

Alec Radford, Jeff Wu, Rewon Child, David Luan, Dario Amodei, and Ilya Sutskever. 2019b. Language models are unsupervised multitask learners.

Anna Rogers, Olga Kovaleva, and Anna Rumshisky. 2020. A primer in BERTology: What we know about how BERT works. *Transactions of the Association for Computational Linguistics*, 8:842–866.

Victor Sanh, Lysandre Debut, Julien Chaumond, and Thomas Wolf. 2019. DistilBERT, a distilled version of BERT: smaller, faster, cheaper and lighter. *ArXiv*, abs/1910.01108.

Richard Socher, Alex Perelygin, Jean Wu, Jason Chuang, Christopher D. Manning, Andrew Ng, and Christopher Potts. 2013. Recursive deep models for semantic compositionality over a sentiment treebank. In *Proceedings of the 2013 Conference on Empirical Methods in Natural Language Processing*, pages 1631–1642, Seattle, Washington, USA. Association for Computational Linguistics.

Hendrik Strobelt, Sebastian Gehrmann, Michael Behrisch, Adam Perer, Hanspeter Pfister, and Alexander M Rush. 2018. Seq2Seq-Vis: A visual debugging tool for sequence-to-sequence models. *IEEE transactions on visualization and computer graphics*, 25(1):353–363.

Hendrik Strobelt, Sebastian Gehrmann, Hanspeter Pfister, and Alexander M Rush. 2017. LSTMvis: A tool for visual analysis of hidden state dynamics in recurrent neural networks. *IEEE transactions on visualization and computer graphics*, 24(1):667–676.

Alon Talmor, Jonathan Herzig, Nicholas Lourie, and Jonathan Berant. 2019. CommonsenseQA: A question answering challenge targeting commonsense knowledge. In *Proceedings of the 2019 Conference of the North American Chapter of the Association for Computational Linguistics: Human Language Technologies, Volume 1 (Long and Short Papers)*, pages 4149–4158, Minneapolis, Minnesota. Association for Computational Linguistics.

Ian Tenney, Dipanjan Das, and Ellie Pavlick. 2019. BERT rediscovers the classical NLP pipeline. In *Proceedings of the 57th Annual Meeting of the Association for Computational Linguistics*, pages 4593–4601, Florence, Italy. Association for Computational Linguistics.

Ian Tenney, James Wexler, Jasmijn Bastings, Tolga Bolukbasi, Andy Coenen, Sebastian Gehrmann, Ellen Jiang, Mahima Pushkarna, Carey Radebaugh, Emily Reif, and Ann Yuan. 2020. The language interpretability tool: Extensible, interactive visualizations and analysis for NLP models. In *Proceedings of the 2020 Conference on Empirical Methods in Natural Language Processing: System Demonstrations*, pages 107–118, Online. Association for Computational Linguistics.

J. Vig. 2019. A multiscale visualization of attention in the transformer model. *ArXiv*, abs/1906.05714.

Eric Wallace, Jens Tuyls, Junlin Wang, Sanjay Subramanian, Matt Gardner, and Sameer Singh. 2019. AllenNLP interpret: A framework for explaining predictions of NLP models. In *Proceedings of the 2019 Conference on Empirical Methods in Natural Language Processing and the 9th International Joint Conference on Natural Language Processing (EMNLP-IJCNLP): System Demonstrations*, pages 7–12, Hong Kong, China. Association for Computational Linguistics.

Alex Wang, Amanpreet Singh, Julian Michael, Felix Hill, Omer Levy, and Samuel Bowman. 2018.

GLUE: A multi-task benchmark and analysis platform for natural language understanding. In *Proceedings of the 2018 EMNLP Workshop BlackboxNLP: Analyzing and Interpreting Neural Networks for NLP*, pages 353–355, Brussels, Belgium. Association for Computational Linguistics.

Thomas Wolf, Lysandre Debut, Victor Sanh, Julien Chaumond, Clement Delangue, Anthony Moi, Pierric Cistac, Tim Rault, Remi Louf, Morgan Funtowicz, Joe Davison, Sam Shleifer, Patrick von Platen, Clara Ma, Yacine Jernite, Julien Plu, Canwen Xu, Teven Le Scao, Sylvain Gugger, Mariama Drame, Quentin Lhoest, and Alexander Rush. 2020. Transformers: State-of-the-art natural language processing. In *Proceedings of the 2020 Conference on Empirical Methods in Natural Language Processing: System Demonstrations*, pages 38–45, Online. Association for Computational Linguistics.

Rowan Zellers, Ari Holtzman, Hannah Rashkin, Yonatan Bisk, Ali Farhadi, Franziska Roesner, and Yejin Choi. 2019. Defending against neural fake news. In *Advances in Neural Information Processing Systems 32: Annual Conference on Neural Information Processing Systems 2019, NeurIPS 2019, December 8-14, 2019, Vancouver, BC, Canada*, pages 9051–9062.

Jieyu Zhao, Tianlu Wang, Mark Yatskar, Vicente Ordonez, and Kai-Wei Chang. 2018. Gender bias in coreference resolution: Evaluation and debiasing methods. In *Proceedings of the 2018 Conference of the North American Chapter of the Association for Computational Linguistics: Human Language Technologies, Volume 2 (Short Papers)*, pages 15–20, New Orleans, Louisiana. Association for Computational Linguistics.

A Additional Case Studies

A.1 Masked LMs break when fine-tuning on different tasks

When finetuning an autoregressive language model, the output representations are preserved since downstream tasks often make use of the language modeling objective. This is different for masked language models like BERT. Typically, the contextual embeddings are combined with a new untrained head and thus, the language modeling is ignored during finetuning. We demonstrate this in Figure 8 where we compare DistilBERT (blue) and DistilBERT-SST (red) on a recent abstract published in Science. DistilBERT performs much better, having a significantly higher probability for almost every token in the text. Since the finetuned model started with the same parameters, this is a particular instance of catastrophic forgetting (McCloskey and Cohen, 1989). While this case is somewhat obvious, LMDIFF can help identify domains that are potentially more affected by this phenomenon even for cases in which the language modeling objective is not abandoned.

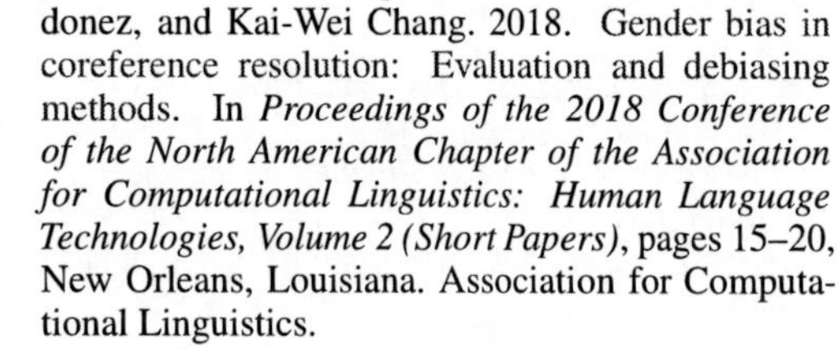

Figure 8: DistilBERT-SST vs DistilBERT on a scientific abstract.

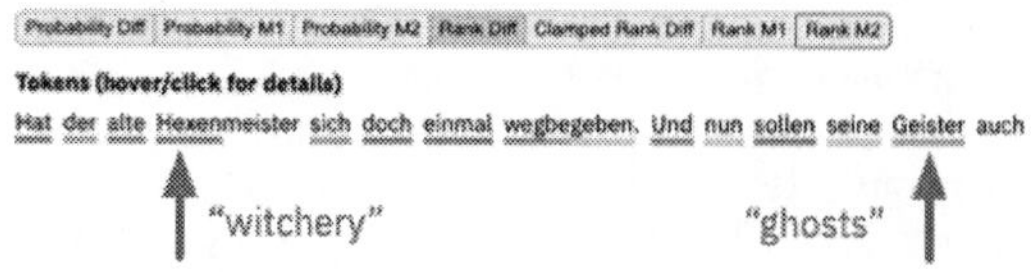

Figure 9: Magic characters more likely under GPT2-German-Faust

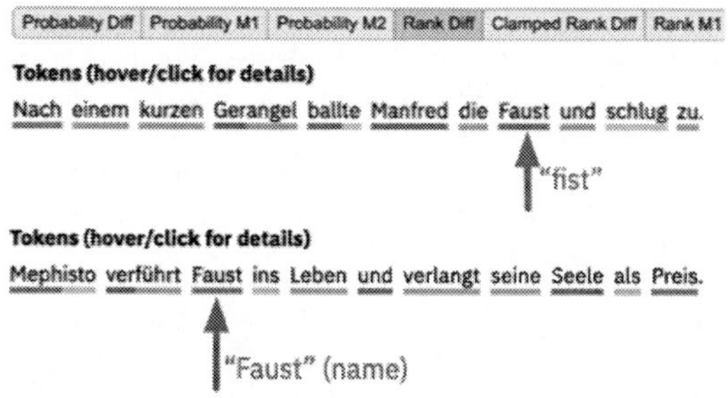

Figure 10: Tokens can be more likely under different models depending on contexts.

A.2 Data Outliers

We show one example of a data outlier, described in Section 4.5, in Figure 11. The top-ranked examples in the corpus all have severe encoding errors and those examples should be removed from the corpus.

A.3 Language specific to finetuned model

The comparison of GPT2-German and GPT2-German-Faust (see Section 4.4) also revealed more patterns that indicate that the fine-tuning of the model might have been successful. Figure 9 shows an example where tokens related to the core text of the Faust text are more likely under the fine-tuned model than the wild-type GPT2-German. Tokens like "Hexe" (witch) or "Geister" (ghosts) are core characters in the Faust text.

Another interesting observation is that even the

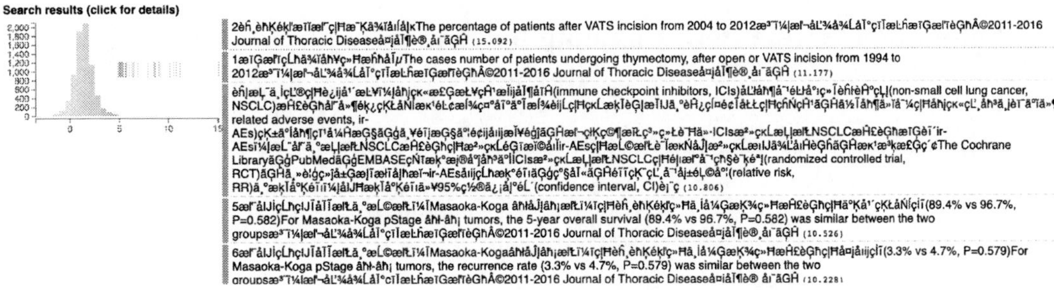

Figure 11: BioLang with GPT-2 vs the GPT-2-ArXiv. GPT-2 is much better at modeling repeated patterns which helps identify malformed examples.

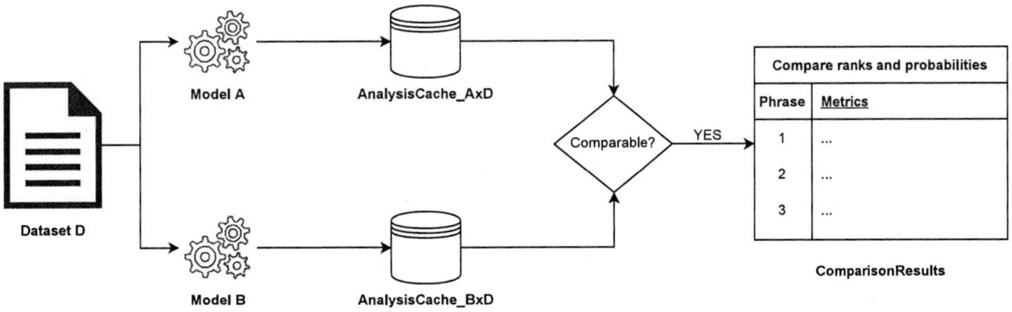

Figure 12: System diagram of the LMDIFF backend.

same tokens in different contexts can be more likely under different models. The token "Faust" can refer to the name of the main character in the story or be the common German translation for "fist". Figure 10 shows how the word is more likely under the general language model if embedded in a fighting context versus being embedded in a one-sentence summary of the Faust story.

B System diagram for corpus analyses

Figure 12 describes how LMDIFF identifies compatibility between models and precomputed corpora. The **Dataset** is a text file where each new line contains a phrase to analyze. It also contains a YAML header containing necessary information like its name and a unique hash of the contents. This *dataset* is processed by different Huggingface Transformer **Models** that receive the contents of the dataset as input and make predictions at every token. The tokenizations and predictions for each of the phrases are stored in the **AnalysisCache**, which takes the form of an HDF5 file. Finally, any two *AnalysisCaches* can be checked for comparability. If they are comparable, the difference between them can be summarized in a **ComparisonResults** table and presented through the aforementioned interface for inspection and exploration by the user.

Semantic Context Path Labeling for Semantic Exploration of User Reviews

Salah Aït-Mokhtar and **Caroline Brun** and **Yves Hoppenot** and **Ágnes Sándor**
Naver Labs Europe
6, Chemin de Maupertuis
38240 Meylan, France
firstname.lastname@naverlabs.com

Abstract

In this paper we present a prototype demonstrator showcasing a novel method to perform semantic exploration of user reviews. The system enables effective navigation in a rich contextual semantic schema with a large number of hierarchically structured classes indicating relevant information. In order to identify instances of the structured classes in the reviews, we defined a new Information Extraction task called Semantic Context Path (SCP) labeling, which simultaneously assigns types and semantic roles to entity mentions. Reviews can thus rapidly be explored based on the fine-grained and structured semantic classes. As a proof-of-concept, we have implemented this system for reviews on Points-of-Interest, in English and Korean.

1 Introduction

In this paper, we demonstrate a system that proposes a novel approach for extracting rich and diverse information from informative texts, and allowing effective semantic navigation among the extracted categories. Our system is specifically designed for exploring large quantities of user reviews, which contain a wealth of useful information for potential new users, difficult to exploit in existing review platforms.

The users of our system can navigate in a rich semantic schema representing a large number of hierarchically structured information categories relevant in the reviews, where top classes have multiple layers of subclasses and attribute classes. The semantic navigation can start from the top classes, or directly from the attribute classes.

Mentions of the structured classes in the reviews are automatically assigned labels that we call Semantic Context Paths (SCPs), which denote their types and semantic roles. By semantic roles, we mean classes for which the mentions instantiate attributes. For example, in the sentence *"See a good movie for $5!"*, the mention *$5* is assigned the SCP label *ShowAndExhibition.Payment.PriceValue*, which means that it is the price of a movie show.

We implemented a supervised SCP tagging system for POI reviews: (1) we created an SCP semantic schema for the domain; (2) we labeled datasets both for English and Korean using an annotation tool that we developed for this task; and (3) we developed and evaluated models for this IE task.

We demonstrate the novel exploration method based on structured semantic classes through a dedicated exploration interface. It is not targeted at end-users at this stage: our purpose is to showcase the new approach in an intuitive way.

In the following sections, we first expose the advantages of exploring user reviews through semantic context paths compared to the methods used in existing social media review sites (Section 2), we then describe the SCP labeling task (Section 3) and finally present our SCP tagging system on POI reviews. We show that performing sequence labeling relying on a state-of-the-art contextual language model extracts with high accuracy great numbers of SCPs from user reviews in multiple languages (Section 4).

2 Semantic Exploration of User Reviews

Popular POI review sites like Google maps or Tripadvisor provide their users with multiple methods for obtaining information on POIs. In this section, we briefly describe the navigation methods offered by existing major user review sites on POIs, and compare them with navigation based on SCPs.

The most widespread way to explore reviews is based on pre-selected frequent terms, as shown in Figure 1.

The user can click on the terms, and thus rapidly access the reviews containing them. However, the main limitation is that the frequent terms are not grouped semantically and thus similar information

Proceedings of the 2021 Conference on Empirical Methods in Natural Language Processing: System Demonstrations, pages 106–113
November 7–11, 2021. ©2021 Association for Computational Linguistics

Figure 1: Pre-selected terms in Google Maps

Figure 3: Flat categories in Naver Places

is handled separately (c.f. *jacket* and *sweater*). In addition, important information can be conveyed by clausal expressions like *dress accordingly*, and therefore be missed by term detection algorithms. Finally, in many cases, when talking about relevant topics, like prices, booking, or the availability of food on-site, linguistic expression is so heterogeneous that a method based on term frequency will not detect them.

Keyword search is another way to explore reviews, as shown in Figure 2.

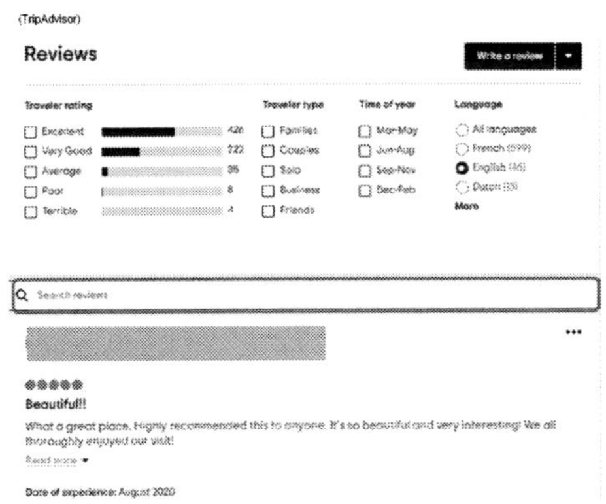

Figure 2: Keyword search in Tripadvisor

Its advantage over the previous method is that the user is not limited by a pre-selected set of terms. However it is slower, since the user needs to enter queries, and getting all the relevant information may require multiple queries. Moreover, some queries will fail either because the information is absent or because the query keywords are not matched, which can be frustrating due to the waste of time.

Finally, a few sites propose pre-selected flat categories for navigation, as illustrated in figure 3.

This method provides fast access to information by clicking on the categories, and improves pre-selected term navigation. However, since the categories are not structured, they can be ambiguous. E.g. "Price" merges all prices: admission price, price of on-site food, or drink, price of a specific onsite activity, etc.

Taken together, keyword based navigation lacks the generality offered by structured search, however currently proposed structured search does not disambiguate general categories. Compared to these methods, the advantage of navigation based on semantic context paths is that it provides rapid and effective access to precise information on a great diversity of topics.

3 Information Extraction with Semantic Path Labeling

3.1 Presentation of the Task

We introduce Semantic Context Paths (SCPs) as representations of entity mentions enriched with contextual semantic labels. SCP labels encode three types of information: (1) context-free semantic types, as traditionally extracted by Named Entity Recognition (NER) systems, (2) hierarchically represented context-free semantic types, traditionally extracted by fine-grained NER systems, and (3) context-dependent semantic roles specifying the classes for which the mentions instantiate attributes.

As an example, assume we want to extract various kinds of useful information from Point-of-Interest reviews about recreation places (e.g. movie theaters), such as food, prices, visitors, etc.

Figure 4 illustrates how SCP labeling is applied on a real POI comment.

The proposed IE task goes beyond traditional Named Entity Recognition (NER), which merely assigns semantic categories to entity mentions (Akbik et al., 2018; Pawar et al., 2017), even when the set of categories is fine-grained and hierarchical (Mai et al., 2018; Zhang et al., 2020). In contrast, SCP labels also contain information on the semantic content of the entities or concepts within the

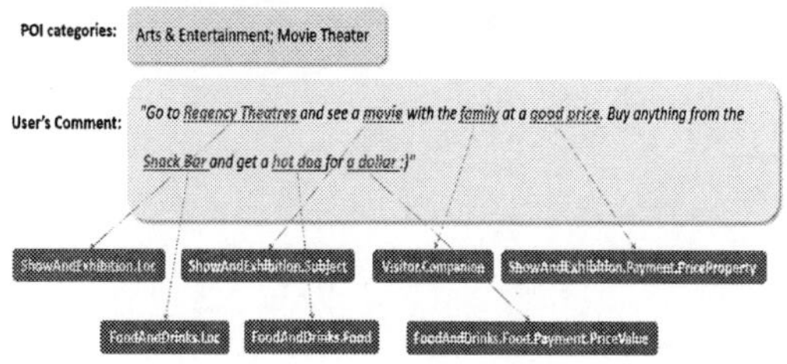

Figure 4: An example of SCP tagging.

mentions, but at the same time also on their semantic roles and types of relations within the text.

In the example in Figure 4, *good price* does not have a simple *PriceProperty* label as it could have in a classical NER system, but *ShowAndExhibition.PriceProperty*, which indicates that it is related to mentions with the same root label, *ShowAndExhibition* – in this example *Regency Theatres* and *movie*, which are respectively tagged as *ShowAndExhibition.Loc*, and *ShowAndExhibition.Subject*.

SCP tagging therefore presents the advantage of extracting rich contextual information, while still being a sequence labeling task.

3.2 Formal Definition of the Task

A **semantic schema** S is a tuple $\langle C, I, R\rangle$ where C is a finite set of semantic classes, $I \subseteq C$ is the subset of instantiable **classes**, and $R \subset C \times C$ is the set of **attribute relations**. R defines which classes have attributes and their types: $(c_i, c_j) \in R$ means that class c_i has an attribute of type c_j. A class $c \in C$ is a **top** class iff $\nexists c' \in C$ such that $(c', c) \in R$ (i.e. c is not an attribute of another class), and it is **terminal** iff $\nexists c' \in C$ such that $(c, c') \in R$ (i.e. it does not have attributes).

A **Semantic Context Path** (SCP) in S is any non-empty and finite sequence of classes $p = c_1.c_2.c_3...c_n$ where c_1 is a top class, and $\forall c_i, c_{i+1} \in p : (c_i, c_{i+1}) \in R$. An SCP $p = c_1.c_2.c_3...c_n$ is **acyclic** iff $\forall i, j \in \{1, ..., n\} : i \neq j \implies c_i \neq c_j$. An SCP $p = c_1.c_2.c_3...c_n$ is **instantiable** iff $c_n \in I$. We use P^S to denote the set of all acyclic, instantiable paths of S.

We can now define the task of **Semantic Context Path tagging** as follows: given a semantic schema S and a tokenized text document $d = t_1t_2...t_n$, SCP tagging assigns a (possibly empty) subset of P^S to every token in d.

4 System Description

The semantic navigation system has two main components: the IE component, which identifies mentions and labels them with SCPs off-line, and a navigation component, which allows exploring the reviews based on the structured classes. We describe these two components in the following subsections.

4.1 Information Extraction Component

4.1.1 Model Description

We model the SCP labeling task as a multi-label classification problem at the level of tokens: review texts are tokenized, and each token can have one or multiple SCP labels if it is part of a relevant mention, or has the special label O otherwise. The set of possible labels is therefore the set $P^{(S)}$ of all acyclic, instantiable paths of a semantic schema S, plus the special label O. We implement the model as a neural network that jointly learns to predict the final path labels and the individual classes that make up the paths. Indeed, since there are many paths that share common individual classes (i.e. they have identical prefixes or suffixes), learning to predict individual classes inside the paths can alleviate the problem of data sparseness with regard to (whole) path labels. Figure 5 below depicts the model architecture.

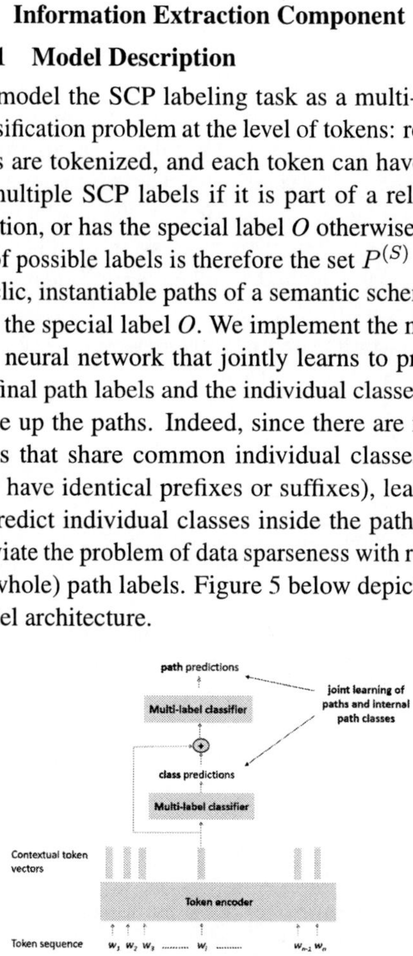

Figure 5: Model architecture

First, the model assigns contextualized word embeddings to each token w_i in the input text using a pre-trained, transformer-based language model, more exactly a RoBERTa model (Liu et al., 2019):

$$x_i = RoBERTa(w_i; w_1w_2...w_n) \qquad (1)$$

The contextualized token representations are then fed to a fully connected hidden layer:

$$h_i = relu(W^h x_i + b^h) \qquad (2)$$

From these hidden token representations h_i, we first compute the probabilities of all individual (flat) classes of the semantic schema:

$$p(y^{(c)}|h_i, \theta) = sigmoid(W^c x_i + b^c) \quad (3)$$

We then concatenate the class probability vector with the hidden token representation h_i (in eq. 2) and feed the result to a linear layer with a sigmoid activation in order to compute the probabilities of the path (SCP) labels:

$$p(y|h_i, \theta) = sigmoid(W(h_i \oplus p(y^{(c)}|h_i, \theta)) + b) \quad (4)$$

We train the model using the sum of the binary cross-entropy losses of the individual class predictions and whole path predictions.

4.1.2 Experiments

Dataset. The dataset is a collection of POI users' comments[1] in both English and Korean, randomly sampled from three main categories: Food (food places), Art & Entertainment, and Outdoor & Recreation. Every comment has a main category among these, and a set of one or more sub-categories (e.g. Park for Outdoor & Recreation, or Movie Theater for Art & Entertainment.) Since there was no rich, off-the-shelf hierarchical semantic schema to represent useful information types for POIs, we defined one from scratch, based on a development subset of the data. The final fined-grained schema comprises 42 semantic classes, their combination leading to 185 virtually instantiable semantic paths. For example, *Visit.Accessibility.Mobility.Device* is an SCP associated with the mention *wheelchair* in *"Most parts are fine for wheelchairs."*; *ShowAndExhibition.Subject.Name* is a SCP associated with the mention *Last Judgment* in *"The pride of the Gdansk museum is a triptych of the Last Judgement by Hans Memling (1433-1494)"*, etc. Annotation guidelines have been defined together with the semantic schema.

We (the authors) annotated manually the English version of the dataset according to the semantic schema and the guidelines. Following the same schema and annotation guidelines, the Korean version of the dataset was annotated by a native Korean speaker specialized in data annotation (hired under a Naver employment contract). The distribution of SCP labels is unbalanced for both languages, with a long tail of infrequent labels: 50% of the observed path labels in the training set for Korean had a maximum of 10 occurrences. Table 1 reports some statistics regarding both versions of the annotated dataset.

Dataset	English		Korean	
split	Train	Test	Train	Test
# docs	3000	1500	2498	498
# tokens	49484	24641	55242	11126
# mentions	5861	3026	5111	1023
# labels	5914	3068	5302	1051

Table 1: Dataset Statistics: number of documents, tokens, annotated mentions and labels. There are approximatively 2 annotated mentions per document on average.

In order to assess the reliability of the annotations, we calculated Krippendorff's alpha (Hayes and Krippendorff, 2007) on the English annotated dataset. On a token-basis, we obtained a relatively high agreement level, $\alpha = 0.838$, which indicates a good dataset reliability. This dataset is, to our knowledge, one of the finest-grained annotated datasets for information extraction.

Hyperparameters. We used the *xlm-roberta-large* pretrained, transformer-based model from HuggingFace transformers library (Wolf et al., 2020) to produce the token contextualized embeddings (equation 1). Experiments with multiple mono-lingual pre-trained language models either showed similar performance (*roberta-large* for English) or lower performance (*bert-large* for English, and *kobert, kobart, koelectra* and *KR-BERT-char16424* for Korean.) We used an initial learning rate of $1e^{-5}$ with a scheduler, a batch size of 16, and a maximum of 100 epochs, with an early stopping strategy.

Evaluation. We evaluate the performance of the models as fully-automatic information extraction systems. The input contains raw text (user comments), and the system needs to identify mentions (and their boundaries) and tag them with SCP labels. We measured performance using the traditional precision, recall, and f1 scores in their re-

[1]The data was acquired legally through an agreement with a company providing POI-based services. The dataset contains a set of user comments with corresponding POI identifiers, geolocation and categories. It does not contain any user information. No crowd-workers have been involved in the annotation process.

laxed variants. That is, the boundaries of predicted mentions do not need to match fully the ground-truth mention spans: they are considered correct if they have at least one common token with ground-truth spans, and as long as the predicted SCP label is entirely correct. This relaxed span evaluation is motivated by the target application: in the UI for exploring POI reviews (see section 4.2), when the user navigates in the hierarchical semantic classes and selects one class, mentions of that class are automatically displayed and highlighted within their context (review snippets). Thus, the user can read the immediate context, including any token missing from the identified mention. Performance results are shown in table 2.

	English		Korean	
Model	f1-avg (std)	f1-best	f1-avg (std)	f1-best
En	76.87 (0.35)	77.40	–	64.43
Ko	–	69.05	74.58 (0.45)	75.39
En+Ko	–	**78.16**	76.14 (0.85)	**77.66**

Table 2: Performance of the information extraction models on English and Korean test sets. Models *En* and *Ko* were trained on the English and Korean training datasets respectively, while model *En+Ko* was trained on the union of the two training datasets, and yields the best performance for both languages. Average f1 score from 10 runs is reported with standard deviation. f1-best refers to the score of the best run. In cross- or multi-lingual settings, only the model from the best run for one of the two languages was tested on the other, hence the missing f1-avg figures.

An interesting side result is that since the IE component is built on top of a multilingual pre-trained language model (*xlm-roberta-large*), it is applicable to other languages in a zero-shot setting. Although we have not performed a quantitative evaluation on other languages than English and Korean, due to the lack of labeled data, a preliminary qualitative evaluation shows promising results. An example of SCP labeling of Arabic is provided in Figure 6.

4.2 Exploration of User Reviews

We have designed an interface on top of Naver map[2] to demonstrate the application of SCP tagging for exploring rich and detailed information conveyed in user reviews. Currently, in the demo, we cover two languages, English and Korean, but since the system is operational for a great number of other languages, these could be added as well.

[2]https://m.map.naver.com/

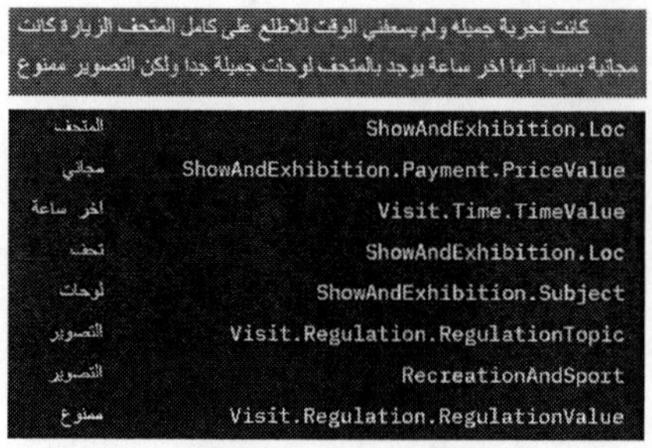

Figure 6: An example of SCP labeling in Arabic.

When a user opens the map, she first selects the language, and the POI types (one or several) that she would like to explore. The current system covers 3 POI types: Arts & Entertainment, Outdoors & Recreation, and Food.

Hovering over a POI in the map makes its name appear along with a circular chart displaying the different topics (i.e. the top classes of the semantic schema) that are covered by the reviews, as well as the number of available reviews. The width of the particular categories is determined by the number of subcategories covered by the reviews (c.f. Figure 7).

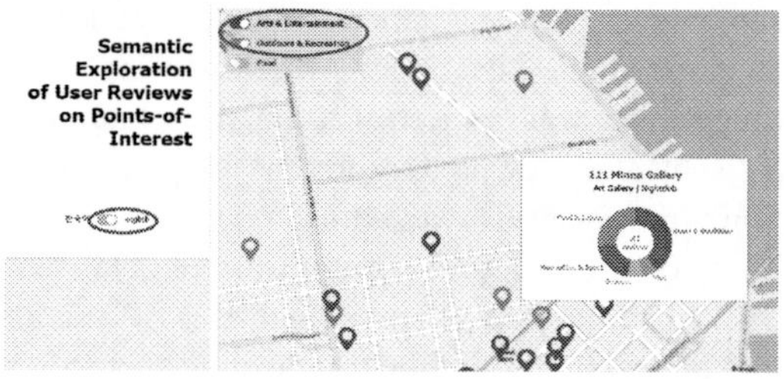

Figure 7: Visualizing on the map the different topics covered by the reviews of a given POI.

In order to explore the reviews in more detail, the user can click on the circular chart, which will expand into a sunburst displaying all the subcategories that have mentions in the reviews. As we indicated in the introduction, the demo system is not targeted at end users. We have chosen the sunburst interface since it allows a comprehensive and straightforward visualization of a great number of SCPs: the innermost circle contains the main categories, and each subsequent layer displays the subcategories in the same segment. Thus, at a glimpse, the chart offers an overview of all the categories and SCPs covered by a review. Moving the mouse over any category opens a callout with the snippets

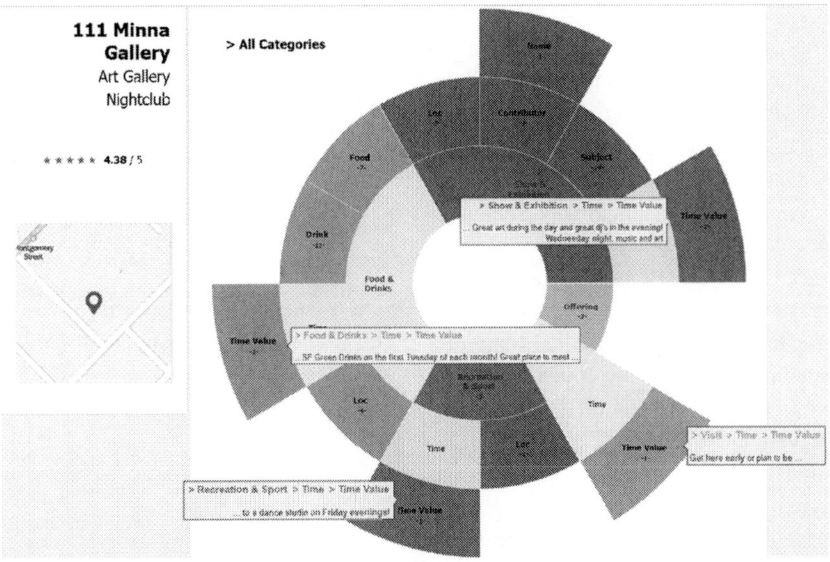

Figure 8: Visualizing snippets containing class mentions. In this example, besides a tip on the best time for a general visit, we find information on time when you can dance (Recreation&Sport.Time), when you can get specific drinks (Food&Drinks.Time), as well as on when you can listen to music (Show&Recreation.Time). In the interface, snippets of one category can be visualized at a time by hovering over it; here we present the snippets of several categories on the same figure for a concise presentation.

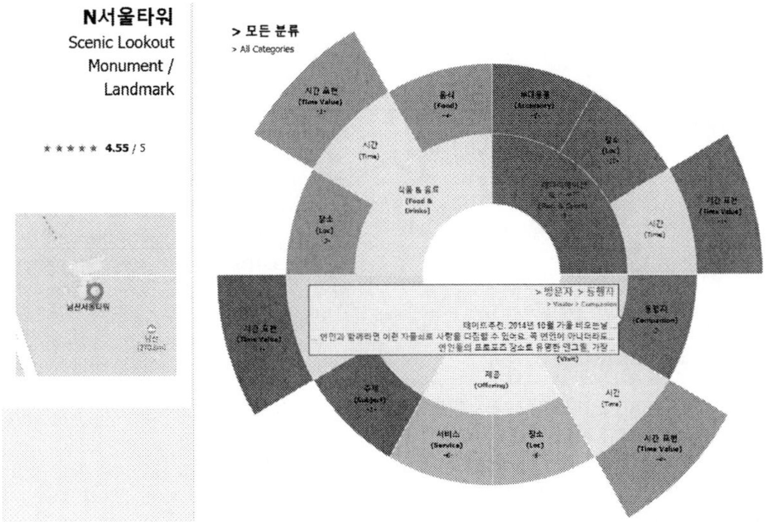

Figure 9: Categories extracted from Korean reviews on the Seoul Tower.

of the relevant user reviews (Figure 8).

If review snippets are not sufficient to understand the information conveyed in the review, the user can click on the callouts to access the full reviews (Figure 10).

Figure 9 shows the categories extracted from the Korean reviews on the Seoul Tower, and the snippets about recommended visitor companions.

Figure 10: Full review texts for mentions of show time.

5 Conclusion

We have presented a new method for the semantic exploration of user reviews.

The system underlying the demonstrator relies on an IE component which identifies relevant mentions in the reviews and labels them with Semantic Context Paths, denoting their types and semantic roles. We have implemented an SCP tagger that extracts information from user reviews on Points-of-Interest. We have defined a dedicated semantic schema, created datasets, and developed sequence labeling models for the task. The IE component was quantitatively evaluated on English and Korean, and showed promising qualitative results on other languages.

We have designed a review exploration interface exploiting the output of the SCP tagger. A sunburst chart in the interface allows navigation among the classes, and rapid access to relevant information in the reviews. Future work includes integrating a wider range of languages to the review exploration interface.

References

David Ahn. 2006. The stages of event extraction. In *Proceedings of the Workshop on Annotating and Reasoning about Time and Events*, pages 1–8.

Alan Akbik, Duncan Blythe, and Roland Vollgraf. 2018. Contextual string embeddings for sequence labeling. In *Proceedings of the 27th International Conference on Computational Linguistics*, pages 1638–1649, Santa Fe, New Mexico, USA. Association for Computational Linguistics.

Livio Baldini Soares, Nicholas FitzGerald, Jeffrey Ling, and Tom Kwiatkowski. 2019a. Matching the blanks: Distributional similarity for relation learning. In *Proceedings of the 57th Annual Meeting of the Association for Computational Linguistics*, pages 2895–2905, Florence, Italy. Association for Computational Linguistics.

Livio Baldini Soares, Nicholas FitzGerald, Jeffrey Ling, and Tom Kwiatkowski. 2019b. Matching the Blanks: Distributional Similarity for Relation Learning. In *Proceedings of the 57th Annual Meeting of the Association for Computational Linguistics*, pages 2895–2905, Florence, Italy. Association for Computational Linguistics.

Robert Bossy, Louise Deléger, Estelle Chaix, Mouhamadou Ba, and Claire Nédellec. 2019. Bacteria Biotope at BioNLP Open Shared Tasks 2019. In *Proceedings of The 5th Workshop on BioNLP Open Shared Tasks*, pages 121–131, Hong Kong, China. Association for Computational Linguistics.

H. Cunningham, K. Humphreys, R. Gaizauskas, and Y. Wilks. 1997. Software infrastructure for natural language processing. In *Proceedings of the Fifth Conference on Applied Natural Language Processing (ANLP-97)*.

Jacob Devlin, Ming-Wei Chang, Kenton Lee, and Kristina Toutanova. 2018. Bert: Pre-training of deep bidirectional transformers for language understanding. *arXiv preprint arXiv:1810.04805*.

Michael Glass and Alfio Gliozzo. 2018. Discovering implicit knowledge with unary relations. In *Proceedings of the 56th Annual Meeting of the Association for Computational Linguistics (Volume 1: Long Papers)*, pages 1585–1594, Melbourne, Australia. Association for Computational Linguistics.

Andrew F Hayes and Klaus Krippendorff. 2007. Answering the call for a standard reliability measure for coding data. *Communication methods and measures*, 1:77–89.

Yinhan Liu, Myle Ott, Naman Goyal, Jingfei Du, Mandar Joshi, Danqi Chen, Omer Levy, Mike Lewis, Luke Zettlemoyer, and Veselin Stoyanov. 2019. RoBERTa: A Robustly Optimized BERT Pretraining Approach. *arXiv:1907.11692 [cs]*. ArXiv: 1907.11692.

Khai Mai, Thai-Hoang Pham, Minh Trung Nguyen, Tuan Duc Nguyen, Danushka Bollegala, Ryohei Sasano, and Satoshi Sekine. 2018. An empirical study on fine-grained named entity recognition. In *Proceedings of the 27th International Conference on Computational Linguistics*, pages 711–722, Santa Fe, New Mexico, USA. Association for Computational Linguistics.

Arvind Neelakantan and Ming-Wei Chang. 2015. Inferring missing entity type instances for knowledge base completion: New dataset and methods. *arXiv preprint arXiv:1504.06658*.

Sachin Pawar, Girish K. Palshikar, and Pushpak Bhattacharyya. 2017. Relation extraction : A survey.

Pontus Stenetorp, Sampo Pyysalo, Goran Topić, Tomoko Ohta, Sophia Ananiadou, and Jun'ichi Tsujii. 2012. Brat: A web-based tool for nlp-assisted text annotation. In *Proceedings of the Demonstrations at the 13th Conference of the European Chapter of the Association for Computational Linguistics*, EACL '12, pages 102–107, Stroudsburg, PA, USA. Association for Computational Linguistics.

Thomas Wolf, Lysandre Debut, Victor Sanh, Julien Chaumond, Clement Delangue, Anthony Moi, Pierric Cistac, Tim Rault, Remi Louf, Morgan Funtowicz, Joe Davison, Sam Shleifer, Patrick von Platen, Clara Ma, Yacine Jernite, Julien Plu, Canwen Xu, Teven Le Scao, Sylvain Gugger, Mariama Drame,

Quentin Lhoest, and Alexander Rush. 2020. Transformers: State-of-the-Art Natural Language Processing. In *Proceedings of the 2020 Conference on Empirical Methods in Natural Language Processing: System Demonstrations*, pages 38–45, Online. Association for Computational Linguistics.

Shanchan Wu and Yifan He. 2019. Enriching pretrained language model with entity information for relation classification. *CoRR*, abs/1905.08284.

Wuti Xiong, Fei Li, Ming Cheng, Hong Yu, and Donghong Ji. 2019. Bacteria Biotope Relation Extraction via Lexical Chains and Dependency Graphs. In *Proceedings of The 5th Workshop on BioNLP Open Shared Tasks*, pages 158–167, Hong Kong, China. Association for Computational Linguistics.

Ikuya Yamada, Akari Asai, Hiroyuki Shindo, Hideaki Takeda, and Yuji Matsumoto. 2020. LUKE: Deep Contextualized Entity Representations with Entity-aware Self-attention. In *Proceedings of the 2020 Conference on Empirical Methods in Natural Language Processing (EMNLP)*, pages 6442–6454, Online. Association for Computational Linguistics.

Qi Zhang, Chao Liu, Ying Chi, Xuansong Xie, and Xiansheng Hua. 2019. A Multi-Task Learning Framework for Extracting Bacteria Biotope Information. In *Proceedings of The 5th Workshop on BioNLP Open Shared Tasks*, pages 105–109, Hong Kong, China. Association for Computational Linguistics.

Tao Zhang, Congying Xia, Chun-Ta Lu, and Philip Yu. 2020. MZET: Memory augmented zero-shot fine-grained named entity typing. In *Proceedings of the 28th International Conference on Computational Linguistics*, pages 77–87, Barcelona, Spain (Online). International Committee on Computational Linguistics.

Beyond Accuracy: A Consolidated Tool for Visual Question Answering Benchmarking

Dirk Väth* and **Pascal Tilli*** and **Ngoc Thang Vu**
University of Stuttgart
Germany
{dirk.vaeth, pascal.tilli, thang.vu}@ims.uni-stuttgart.de

Abstract

On the way towards general Visual Question Answering (VQA) systems that are able to answer arbitrary questions, the need arises for evaluation beyond single-metric leaderboards for specific datasets. To this end, we propose a browser-based benchmarking tool for researchers and challenge organizers, with an API for easy integration of new models and datasets to keep up with the fast-changing landscape of VQA. Our tool helps test generalization capabilities of models across multiple datasets, evaluating not just accuracy, but also performance in more realistic real-world scenarios such as robustness to input noise. Additionally, we include metrics that measure biases and uncertainty, to further explain model behavior. Interactive filtering facilitates discovery of problematic behavior, down to the data sample level. As proof of concept, we perform a case study on four models. We find that state-of-the-art VQA models are optimized for specific tasks or datasets, but fail to generalize even to other in-domain test sets, for example they cannot recognize text in images. Our metrics allow us to quantify which image and question embeddings provide most robustness to a model. All code[1] is publicly available.

1 Introduction

VQA refers to the multi-modal task of answering free-form, natural language questions about images - a task sometimes referred to as a visual Turing test (Xu et al., 2018). The number and variety of datasets for evaluating such systems has continued to increase over the last years (Antol et al., 2015; Hudson and Manning, 2019; Agrawal et al., 2018; Kervadec et al., 2021; Johnson et al., 2017). These datasets aim to test models' abilities with respect to different skills, such as commonsense or external knowledge reasoning, visual reasoning, or reading text in images. Traditionally, evaluation relies solely on answering accuracy. However, it is misleading to believe that a single number, like high accuracy on a given benchmark, corresponds to a system's ability to answer arbitrary questions with high quality. Each dataset contains biases which state-of-the-art deep neural networks are prone to exploit, resulting in higher accuracy scores (Goyal et al., 2017; Das et al., 2017; Agrawal et al., 2016; Jabri et al., 2016). Thus, most VQA models, if evaluated on multiple benchmarks at all, are re-trained per dataset to achieve higher numbers in specialized leaderboards. Further shortcomings of current leaderboards include ignoring prediction cost and robustness, as discussed in (Ethayarajh and Jurafsky, 2020) for NLP. In VQA, we need even more specialized evaluation due to the challenges inherent to open-ended, multi-modal reasoning.

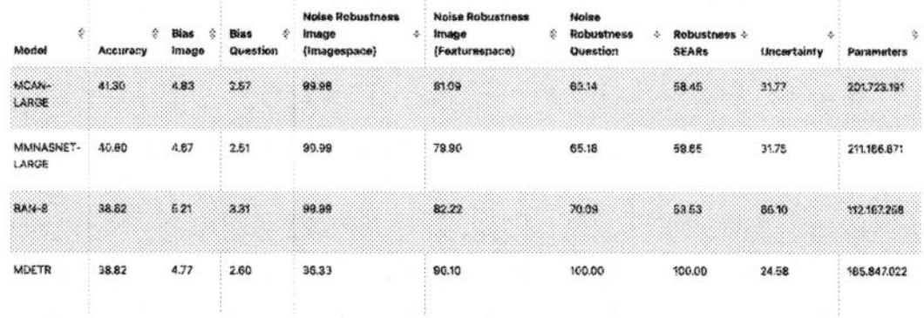

Model	Accuracy	Bias Image	Bias Question	Noise Robustness Image (Imagespace)	Noise Robustness Image (Featurespace)	Noise Robustness Question	Robustness SEARs	Uncertainty	Parameters
MCAN-LARGE	41.30	4.83	2.57	99.98	81.09	63.14	58.45	31.77	201.723.191
MMNASNET-LARGE	40.80	4.67	2.51	99.99	79.90	65.18	59.65	31.75	211.166.871
BAN-8	38.62	5.21	3.31	99.99	82.22	70.09	53.53	86.10	112.167.258
MDETR	38.82	4.77	2.60	36.33	90.10	100.00	100.00	24.58	185.847.022

Figure 1: Tool landing page with aggregated metrics for each model (larger version in Appendix A). Statistics can be expanded per model to view performance on each dataset.

In order to successfully develop VQA systems that are able to answer arbitrary questions with human-like performance, we should overcome the previously mentioned shortcomings of current leaderboards as one of the first essential steps. To this end, we propose a benchmarking tool, to our knowledge the first of its kind in the VQA domain, that goes beyond current leaderboard evaluations. It follows the four following principles:

1. Realism To better simulate real-world conditions, we test robustness to semantic-preserving input perturbations to images and questions.

* Authors contributed equally

[1] https://github.com/patilli/vqa_benchmarking

Proceedings of the 2021 Conference on Empirical Methods in Natural Language Processing: System Demonstrations, pages 114–123
November 7–11, 2021.

2. Generalizability We include six carefully chosen benchmark datasets, each evaluating different abilities as well as model behavior on changing distributions to test model generalizability. Additionally, we provide easy python interfaces for adding new benchmarking datasets and state-of-the-art models as they arise. The full tool is released under an open-source license.

3. Explainability To provide more insight into model behavior and overcome the problem of single-metric comparisons, we measure scores such as biases and uncertainty, in addition to accuracy.

4. Interactivity Aggregated statistics can be drilled down and filtered, providing interactive exploration of model behavior from a global dataset perspective down to individual data samples. The above functionalities not only support detailed model comparison, but also facilitate development and debugging of models in the VQA domain.

As proof of concept, we integrate several popular and state-of-the-art models from public code repositories and investigate their abilities and weaknesses. Through our case study, we demonstrate that all of these models fail to generalize, even to other in-domain test sets. Our metrics quantify the influence of model architecture decisions, which accuracy cannot capture, such as the effect of image and question embeddings on model robustness.

2 Related Work

VQA Benchmarks Benchmarks often emphasize certain sub-tasks of the general VQA problem. For example, CLEVR (Johnson et al., 2017) tests visual reasoning abilities such as shape recognition and spatial relationships between objects, rather than real-world scenarios. Other approaches change the answer distributions of existing datasets, such as VQA-CP (Agrawal et al., 2018) originating from VQA2 (Goyal et al., 2017) or GQA-OOD from GQA (Kervadec et al., 2021). These changes are intended to mitigate learnable bias. Another approach to mitigating biases was proposed by Hudson and Manning (2019), who created a dataset for real world visual reasoning with a tightly controlled answer distribution. Kervadec et al. (2021) went one step further by analyzing and changing the test sets to evaluate on rarely occurring question-answer pairs rather than on frequent ones. Finally, Li et al. (2021) proposed an adversarial benchmarking dataset to evaluate system robustness.

Metrics For more automated, dataset-level insight, many methods try to analyze single aspects of VQA models. For example, Halbe (2020) use feature attribution to assess the influence of individual question words on model predictions. Das et al. (2017) compare human attention to machine attention to explore whether they focus on the same image regions. To measure robustness w.r.t. question input, Huang et al. (2019) collect a dataset of semantically relevant questions, and rank them by similarity, feeding the top-3 into the network to observe changes in prediction.

Identifying Biases Agrawal et al. (2016) measured multiple properties: generalization to novel instances as selected by dissimilarity, question understanding based on length and POS-tags, and image understanding by selecting a subset of questions which share an answer but have different images. Another approach to analyze bias towards one modality is to train a uni-modal network that excludes the other modality in the training phase (Cadene et al., 2019). However, this requires training one model per modality and cannot be applied easily to all architectures, e.g. to attention mechanisms computed on joint feature spaces.

Robustness and Adversarial Examples Adversarial examples originate from image classification, where perturbations barely visible to a human fool the classifier and cause sudden prediction changes (Szegedy et al., 2014). The same idea was later applied to NLP, where, e.g., appending distracting text to the context in a question answering scenario resulted in F1-score dropping by more than half (Jia and Liang, 2017).

Benchmarking Tools Liu et al. (2021) propose a leaderboard for NLP tasks to compare model performance. They differentiate among several NLP tasks and datasets. All methods are applied post-hoc to analyze the predictions a model outputs. Other benchmarking tools, for example, focus on runtime comparisons (Shi et al., 2016; Liu et al., 2018). Our benchmarking tool not only analyzes system outputs, but also modifies input modalities as well as feature spaces and provides metrics beyond just accuracy.

3 VQA Benchmark Tool

Our tool facilitates global evaluation of model performance w.r.t general and specific tasks (**generalizability**), such as real-world images and reading capabilities. To simplify integration of future benchmark datasets and models, we provide a well-documented python API. We measure model-inherent properties, such as biases and uncertainty (**explainability**) as well as robustness against input perturbations (**realism**). Model behavior can be further inspected using interactive diagrams and filtering methods for all metrics, supporting sample-level exploration of suspicious model behavior (**interactivity**). All data is collected post-hoc and can be explored in a web application, eliminating the need to re-train existing models.

3.1 Datasets

In this section, we describe the datasets supported out-of-the-box. These serve the principle of benchmarking **generalizability**, by including real-world scenarios as well as task-specific and even synthetic datasets. Where labels are publicly available, we rely on test sets, otherwise on validation sets (marked with *). To reduce computational cost and resources (including environmental impact), we limit each dataset to a maximum of ~15,000 randomly drawn samples , which is referred to in the following paragraphs as a sub-set.

VQA2* This dataset (Goyal et al., 2017) represents a balanced version of the vanilla VQA dataset (Antol et al., 2015). It is intended to mirror real-world scenarios and used as the de-facto baseline for model comparisons.

GQA The GQA dataset (Hudson and Manning, 2019), derived from Visual Genome (Krishna et al., 2017), is designed to test models' real-word visual reasoning capabilities, in particular, robustness, consistency and semantic understanding of vision and language. Similar to VQA2, it also provides a balanced version.

GQA-OOD According to Kervadec et al. (2021), evaluating on rare instead of frequent question-answer pairs is better suited for measuring reasoning abilities. Hence, they introduce the GQA-OOD dataset as a new split of the original GQA dataset to evaluate out-of-distribution questions with imbalanced distributions.

CLEVR* CLEVR (Johnson et al., 2017) is a synthetic dataset, containing images of multiple geometric objects in different colors, materials and arrangements. It aims to test models' visual reasoning abilities by asking questions that require a model to identify objects based on attributes, presence, count, and spacial relationships.

OK-VQA* Marino et al. (2019) introduce a dataset that requires external knowledge to answer its questions, thereby motivating the integration of additional knowledge pools.

Text VQA* Singh et al. (2019) consider the problem of understanding text in images, an important problem to consider in VQA benchmarking systems, as one application of VQA is intended to aid the visually impaired.

3.2 Metrics

In addition to the evaluation of accuracy across datasets with different distributions and focuses, we implement metrics such as bias of models towards one modality and uncertainty (**explainability**), as well as robustness to noise and adversarial questions (**realism**). All metrics are in range $[0, 100]$.

Accuracy Our tool supports multiple ground truth answers with different scores per sample, providing the flexibility to evaluate for single-answer accuracy as well as e.g. the official VQA2 accuracy measure $acc(a) = min(1, \frac{\#\text{humans}(a)}{3})$ (Antol et al., 2015).

Modality Bias Here, we refer to a model's focus on one modality over the other. Given an image of a zoo and the question *"What animals are shown?"*, if we replace this picture with a fruit bowl, we would expect the model to change its prediction. However, if the prediction stays unaltered, the model's answer cannot depend on the image input. For each prediction on altered inputs (i', q) or (i, q'), we evaluate how many times the answer a' of the replacement pairs is the same as answer a predicted on the original inputs (i, q). Averaging across N trials yields a Monte-Carlo estimate of the bias towards one modality as $1/N \sum_{q'} \mathbb{1}_{f(q,i)=f(q',i)}$. Heuristics, such as ensuring no overlap between subjects and objects of q and q', help reduce cases where q' would just be a rephrasing of q. High values in modality bias correspond to models ignoring input from one modality for many samples, e.g. a question bias of 100 indicates a model that completely ignores images.

Robustness to Noise An important consideration when deploying a model in the real world, is its susceptibility to noise. Noise might be induced naturally by data acquisition methods (VQA-setting:

camera), for example a color-question should not be affected by subtle tone shifts between two cameras. On the question side, semantic-preserving input changes can be induced through paraphrases, synonyms or region-dependent spelling.

For measuring robustness to noise in images, we support adding Gaussian-, Poisson-, salt&pepper- and speckle-noise to the original input image. We also support adding Gaussian noise in image feature space. To obtain a realistic input range, we calculate the standard deviation from 500 randomly sampled image feature vectors. After multiple trials, we average how often the prediction on the noisy inputs matches the original prediction. Applying noise to the original image input tests the robustness of the image feature extractor, which, in many models, is external and thus easy to swap and interesting to compare. On the other hand, applying noise in feature space tests model robustness towards noisy feature extractors.

Measuring robustness to question noise is done by adding Gaussian noise in embedding space, a reasonable approach under the assumption that similar vectors in embedding space have similar meaning. Again, multiple trials are performed.

High values in robustness correspond to models unaffected by noise in one modality for many samples, e.g. a question robustness of 100 indicates a model that never changed its predictions due to noise added in question embedding space.

Robustness to Adversarial Questions Semantically Equivalent Adversarial Ruless (SEARs) alter textual input according to a set of rules, while preserving original semantics (Ribeiro et al., 2018). For the questions in the VQA dataset, the authors come up with the four rules that most affect the predictions in their tests, using a combination of Part-of-Speech (POS)-Tags and vocabulary entries:

- *Rule 1* WP VBZ → WP's
- *Rule 2* What NOUN → Which NOUN
- *Rule 3* color → colour
- *Rule 4* ADV VBZ → ADV's

High values in robustness against SEARs correspond to models unaffected by adversarial questions, e.g. a robustness of 100 indicates a model that never changed its predictions due to the application of any of the above rules. Therefore, higher values are preferable.

Uncertainty To measure model certainty, we leverage the dropout-based Monte-Carlo method (Gal and Ghahramani, 2016). Forwarding a sample multiple times with active dropout, the averaged output vector $\frac{1}{N}\sum_{n=1}^{N} f(x)$.

3.3 Views

We support inspection of the included metrics at different levels of granularity, from comparisons across multiple datasets to filtering of individual samples (**interactivity**). On each level, we supplement the accuracy measure by additional metrics helpful for understanding and debugging VQA models (**explainability**).

Gobal View The global view (see figure 1) acts as the main entry to our tool. At a glance, it shows a leaderboard with statistics averaged on all datasets, providing users with an impression of the models' performance and properties across tasks and distributions. All columns are sortable to allow easy

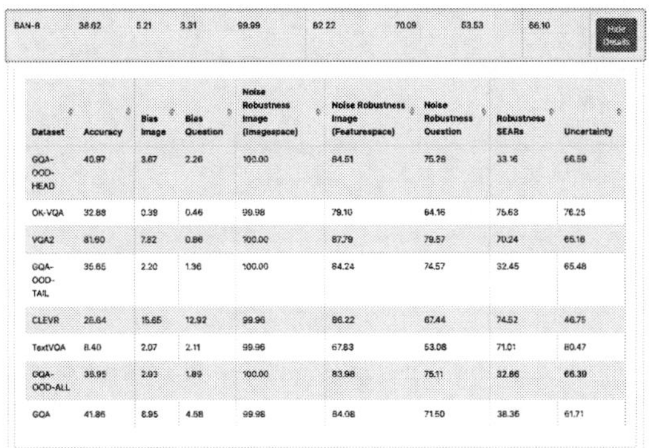

BAN-8	38.62	5.21	3.31	99.99	82.22	70.09	53.53	66.10	Hide Details

Dataset	Accuracy	Bias Image	Bias Question	Noise Robustness Image (Imagespace)	Noise Robustness Image (Featurespace)	Noise Robustness Question	Robustness SEARs	Uncertainty
GQA-OOD-HEAD	40.97	3.67	2.26	100.00	84.51	75.28	33.16	66.59
OK-VQA	32.88	0.39	0.46	99.98	79.10	64.16	75.63	76.25
VQA2	81.60	7.82	0.86	100.00	87.79	79.57	70.24	65.16
GQA-OOD-TAIL	35.65	2.20	1.36	100.00	84.24	74.57	32.45	65.48
CLEVR	26.64	15.65	12.92	99.96	86.22	67.44	74.52	46.75
TextVQA	8.40	2.07	2.11	99.96	67.83	53.08	71.01	80.47
GQA-OOD-ALL	35.95	2.93	1.89	100.00	83.98	75.11	32.86	66.39
GQA	41.86	8.95	4.58	99.98	84.08	71.50	38.36	61.71

Figure 2: Expanded details on the overview page (larger version in Appendix A).

comparisons between models for each metric. Each row in the overview table describes a model's average performance and can be expanded to provide additional information on a per-dataset level (see figure 2).

Metrics View Clicking a model row in the global view navigates to the metrics view, which provides graphs on all metrics and datasets for the selected model in detail (see figure 3). Users have the choice to change dataset and metric via selection boxes. For easy comparison between datasets of different sizes, all values are recorded in percentages of the dataset.

Filter View Our tool supports searching for patterns of suspicious model behavior by providing a

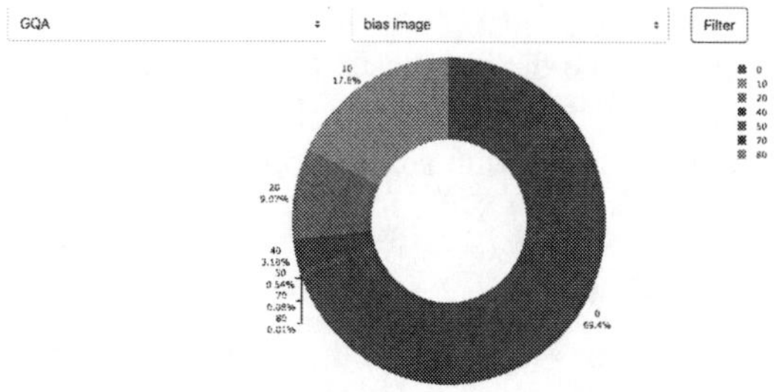

Figure 3: Metric view, showing bias towards images on the GQA dataset for the MDETR model (larger version in Appendix A).

filter view (see figure 4). Once model, dataset and metric are selected, users are presented a list of all samples within the chosen range. The range can be adjusted using a slider, which updates the list of matching data samples in real-time.

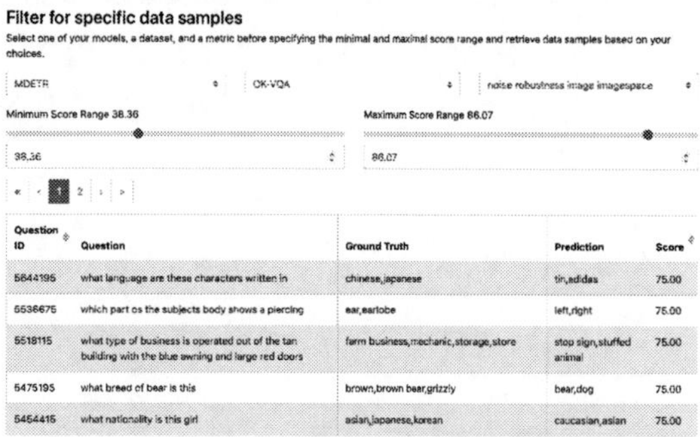

Figure 4: Filter view. Enables filtering for unexpected model behavior on sample level (larger version in Appendix A).

Sample View Finally, once the desired range of samples has been filtered, clicking a data sample navigates to the sample view (see figure 5). There, the original input image and question are displayed, along with ground truth and the model's top-3 predictions. Additionally, the scores and answers for each single metric are shown. For example, if applying noise to the image changed the prediction multiple times, we show all the answers that were predicted using those noisy inputs.

4 Case Study

As a case study, we explore a range of models from well-established, previously high ranking entries in the VQA2 competition to more recent, transformer-based architectures and report the insights we gained by inspecting them with our tool.

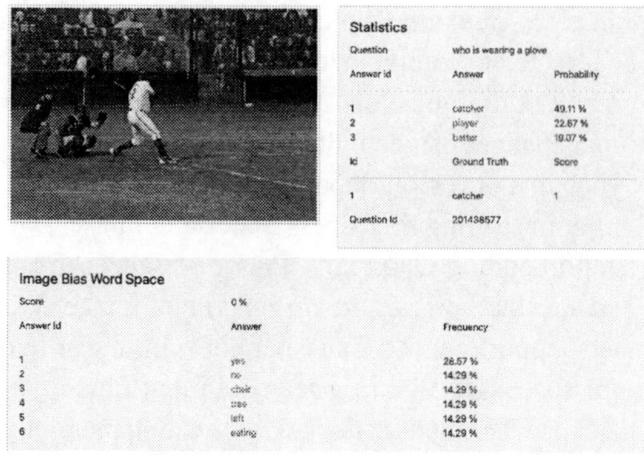

Figure 5: Sample view with *Image Bias Word Space* metric. Similar cards exist for each metric (larger version in Appendix A).

4.1 Evaluated Models

We chose a widely used VQA-baseline BAN, two transformer-based architectures MDETR and MCAN, and MMNASNET.

BAN (Kim et al., 2018) is a strong baseline using bilinear attention. It won third place in the VQA2 2018 challenge and was still in the top-10 entries in 2019. We use the 8-layer version.

MCAN (Yu et al., 2019) improves BAN with a co-attention feature fusion mechanism.

MMNASNET Yu et al. (2020) is a more recent state-of-the-art model constructed using neural architecture search. It is one of the top-10 entries of the VQA2 2020 challenge.

MDETR (Kamath et al., 2021) is a state-of-the art transformer using more recent question (Liu et al., 2019) and image embedding approaches (Carion et al., 2020). MDETR achieves competitive accuracies on both GQA and CLEVR.

4.2 Results and Lessons Learned

Table 1 contains the aggregated results of all models, averaged across the development (sub-)splits of all datasets. For details about the computation of each metric, see section 3.2. Table 2 shows model accuracy per dataset. Unsurprisingly, models performed best when evaluated on the development (sub-)split of the dataset they were originally trained on, and worse on datasets they were not trained on. These performance drops are observable for all models, suggesting that VQA models cannot yet generalize well across tasks. Low performance of current highly ranked VQA models

Average Results									
Model	Accuracy	Modality Bias		Robustness Image		Robustness	SEARs	Uncer-	Parameters
		Image	Quest.	Image	Feature	Question		tainty	
MCAN	**41.30**	4.83	2.57	99.98	81.09	63.14	58.45	31.77	201,723,191
MMNASNET	40.80	**4.67**	**2.51**	**99.99**	79.90	65.18	59.65	31.75	211,166,871
BAN-8	38.62	5.21	3.31	**99.99**	82.22	70.09	53.53	66.10	112,167,258
MDETR	38.82	4.77	2.60	36.33	**90.10**	**100.00**	**100.00**	**24.58**	185,847,022

Table 1: Average results of our evaluated models across all development (sub-)splits. We split the columns modality bias and robustness against image modifications into two sub-columns. These columns should be read as the modality bias (lower values are better) measured for the image space and question space. Robustness (higher values are better) against image changes is divided into alterations on the image itself as well as modifications inside image feature space . All metrics are in range $[0, 100]$.

on new datasets can partially be attributed to their fixed answer spaces. This implies the need for more research into systems that are able to generate answers instead of treating VQA as a multiple-choice problem. However, even changing distributions of the same dataset leads to a large performance drop, as we observe, for example, in GQA and its out-of-distribution variants, GQA-OOD-HEAD and GQA-OOD-TAIL. By swapping the original GQA dataset for the GQA-OOD-TAIL distribution, MDETR accuracy decreased by more than $11,6\%$. That out-of-distribution testing causes such high losses in accuracy indicates models are still relying on biases learned from the training dataset.

All systems struggled to read text in images, in fact, the highest accuracy score on TextVQA was only 8.81%, achieved by MMNASNET. This might be improved by extending existing VQA-architectures with additional inputs, e.g. from optical character recognition, or adapting the training of currently used image feature extractors.

Applying noise in image space has almost no impact on models using bottom-up-topdown feature extraction (Anderson et al., 2018), in contrast to MDETR, the only model using an alternative approach. In feature space, all models are similarly stable, which could imply that the feature extractor in MDETR could be made more robust by augmenting training with noisy images.

All models show highest modality bias and low accuracy on the CLEVR dataset. Given that no models were trained on synthetic images or questions involving such complex selection and spatial reasoning, this hints at the models not understanding either modality well. Inspection using the filter view on modality biases provides more evidence of understanding problems here, showing that for example BAN-8 nearly always guesses *yes* or *no*, regardless of the question asked or the image given. In general, BAN-8 displays the highest modality bias, indicating more recent models have become better at jointly reasoning over image and text.

SEAR and question robustness metrics show that RoBERTa (Liu et al., 2019) provides substantial robustness to question perturbation; there were zero cases causing MDETR to change predictions, suggesting that context-aware embeddings should be a standard consideration for future VQA models.

Our metrics show that state-of-the-art VQA models are optimized for specific tasks or datasets, but fail to generalize even across other in-domain datasets. In order to be successful in real-world applications, systems must demonstrate a variety of abilities, not merely good performance on a single-purpose test set.

5 Conclusion

Our proposed benchmarking tool is the first of its kind in the domain of VQA and addresses the problems of current single-metric leaderboards in this domain. It provides easy to use and fast comparison of integrated models on a global level. The performance of each model is evaluated across multiple special-purpose as well as general-purpose datasets to test generalizability and capabilities. Each model can be quantified by metrics such as accuracy, biases, robustness, and uncertainty, revealing strengths and weaknesses w.r.t to given tasks, i.e. measuring the properties models offer as well as their real-world robustness. Exploration via filtering can be used to identify suspicious behaviour down to single data sample level. Through this, our tool provides deeper insights into the strengths and weaknesses of each model across tasks and metrics and how architectural choices can affect behavior, encouraging researchers to develop VQA systems with rich sets of abilities that stand up to real-world

Model	CLEVR	GQA	GQA-OOD-ALL	GQA-OOD-HEAD	GQA-OOD-TAIL	OK-VQA	TextVQA	VQA2
MCAN	32.87	44.58	41.67	44.78	36.59	35.46	8.49	**85.94**
MMNASNET	31.95	44.50	40.24	42.01	37.35	35.09	8.81	**86.51**
BAN-8	28.64	41.86	38.95	40.97	35.65	32.88	8.40	**81.60**
MDETR	25.44	**61.42**	55.76	59.43	49.76	9.83	4.70	44.22

Table 2: Accuracy across the development (sub-)splits of different datasets. Bold entries mark best accuracy per model and coincides in all cases with the dataset it was trained on.

environments. The open-source tool itself can be installed as a package and extended with new models, datasets and metrics using our python API.

In the future, we plan to extend this tool with new datasets as they are released. Moreover, we are looking for more metrics for model evaluation as well as more detailed dataset analysis, e.g. answer space overlap. Last but not least, interactivity could be extended towards live model feedback, allowing to change inputs, e.g. the image noise level, and observe model outputs at runtime.

6 Acknowledgement

This research was funded by the Cluster of Excellence EXC 2075 "Data-Integrated Simulation Science" at the University of Stuttgart.

References

Aishwarya Agrawal, Dhruv Batra, and Devi Parikh. 2016. Analyzing the behavior of visual question answering models. In *Proceedings of the 2016 Conference on Empirical Methods in Natural Language Processing*, pages 1955–1960.

Aishwarya Agrawal, Dhruv Batra, Devi Parikh, and Aniruddha Kembhavi. 2018. Don't just assume; look and answer: Overcoming priors for visual question answering. In *Proceedings of the IEEE Conference on Computer Vision and Pattern Recognition*, pages 4971–4980.

Peter Anderson, Xiaodong He, Chris Buehler, Damien Teney, Mark Johnson, Stephen Gould, and Lei Zhang. 2018. Bottom-up and top-down attention for image captioning and visual question answering. In *Proceedings of the IEEE conference on computer vision and pattern recognition*, pages 6077–6086.

Stanislaw Antol, Aishwarya Agrawal, Jiasen Lu, Margaret Mitchell, Dhruv Batra, C Lawrence Zitnick, and Devi Parikh. 2015. Vqa: Visual question answering. In *Proceedings of the IEEE international conference on computer vision*, pages 2425–2433.

Remi Cadene, Corentin Dancette, Matthieu Cord, Devi Parikh, et al. 2019. Rubi: Reducing unimodal biases for visual question answering. In *Advances in neural information processing systems*, pages 841–852.

Nicolas Carion, Francisco Massa, Gabriel Synnaeve, Nicolas Usunier, Alexander Kirillov, and Sergey Zagoruyko. 2020. End-to-end object detection with transformers. In *European Conference on Computer Vision*, pages 213–229. Springer.

Abhishek Das, Harsh Agrawal, Larry Zitnick, Devi Parikh, and Dhruv Batra. 2017. Human attention in visual question answering: Do humans and deep networks look at the same regions? *Computer Vision and Image Understanding*, 163:90 – 100. Language in Vision.

Kawin Ethayarajh and Dan Jurafsky. 2020. Utility is in the eye of the user: A critique of nlp leaderboard design. In *Proceedings of the 2020 Conference on Empirical Methods in Natural Language Processing (EMNLP)*, pages 4846–4853.

Yarin Gal and Zoubin Ghahramani. 2016. Dropout as a bayesian approximation: Representing model uncertainty in deep learning. In *international conference on machine learning*, pages 1050–1059.

Yash Goyal, Tejas Khot, Douglas Summers-Stay, Dhruv Batra, and Devi Parikh. 2017. Making the v in vqa matter: Elevating the role of image understanding in visual question answering. In *Proceedings of the IEEE Conference on Computer Vision and Pattern Recognition*, pages 6904–6913.

Shaunak Halbe. 2020. Exploring weaknesses of vqa models through attribution driven insights. *ACL 2020*, page 64.

Jia-Hong Huang, Cuong Duc Dao, Modar Alfadly, and Bernard Ghanem. 2019. A novel framework for robustness analysis of visual qa models. In *Proceedings of the AAAI Conference on Artificial Intelligence*, volume 33, pages 8449–8456.

Drew A Hudson and Christopher D Manning. 2019. Gqa: A new dataset for real-world visual reasoning and compositional question answering. In *Proceedings of the IEEE/CVF Conference on Computer Vision and Pattern Recognition*, pages 6700–6709.

Allan Jabri, Armand Joulin, and Laurens Van Der Maaten. 2016. Revisiting visual question answering baselines. In *European conference on computer vision*, pages 727–739. Springer.

Robin Jia and Percy Liang. 2017. Adversarial examples for evaluating reading comprehension systems. In *Proceedings of the 2017 Conference on Empirical Methods in Natural Language Processing*, pages 2021–2031.

Justin Johnson, Bharath Hariharan, Laurens Van Der Maaten, Li Fei-Fei, C Lawrence Zitnick, and Ross Girshick. 2017. Clevr: A diagnostic dataset for compositional language and elementary visual reasoning. In *Proceedings of the IEEE Conference on Computer Vision and Pattern Recognition*, pages 2901–2910.

Aishwarya Kamath, Mannat Singh, Yann LeCun, Ishan Misra, Gabriel Synnaeve, and Nicolas Carion. 2021. Mdetr–modulated detection for end-to-end multi-modal understanding. *arXiv preprint arXiv:2104.12763*.

Corentin Kervadec, Grigory Antipov, Moez Baccouche, and Christian Wolf. 2021. Roses are red, violets are blue... but should vqa expect them to? In *Proceedings of the IEEE/CVF Conference on Computer Vision and Pattern Recognition*, pages 2776–2785.

Jin-Hwa Kim, Jaehyun Jun, and Byoung-Tak Zhang. 2018. Bilinear attention networks. In *Advances in Neural Information Processing Systems*, pages 1564–1574.

Ranjay Krishna, Yuke Zhu, Oliver Groth, Justin Johnson, Kenji Hata, Joshua Kravitz, Stephanie Chen, Yannis Kalantidis, Li-Jia Li, David A Shamma, et al. 2017. Visual genome: Connecting language and vision using crowdsourced dense image annotations. *International journal of computer vision*, 123(1):32–73.

Linjie Li, Jie Lei, Zhe Gan, and Jingjing Liu. 2021. Adversarial vqa: A new benchmark for evaluating the robustness of vqa models. *arXiv preprint arXiv:2106.00245*.

Ling Liu, Yanzhao Wu, Wenqi Wei, Wenqi Cao, Semih Sahin, and Qi Zhang. 2018. Benchmarking deep learning frameworks: Design considerations, metrics and beyond. In *2018 IEEE 38th International Conference on Distributed Computing Systems (ICDCS)*, pages 1258–1269. IEEE.

Pengfei Liu, Jinlan Fu, Yang Xiao, Weizhe Yuan, Shuaicheng Chang, Junqi Dai, Yixin Liu, Zihuiwen Ye, and Graham Neubig. 2021. Explainaboard: An explainable leaderboard for nlp. *arXiv preprint arXiv:2104.06387*.

Yinhan Liu, Myle Ott, Naman Goyal, Jingfei Du, Mandar Joshi, Danqi Chen, Omer Levy, Mike Lewis, Luke Zettlemoyer, and Veselin Stoyanov. 2019. Roberta: A robustly optimized bert pretraining approach.

Kenneth Marino, Mohammad Rastegari, Ali Farhadi, and Roozbeh Mottaghi. 2019. Ok-vqa: A visual question answering benchmark requiring external knowledge. In *Proceedings of the IEEE/CVF Conference on Computer Vision and Pattern Recognition*, pages 3195–3204.

Marco Tulio Ribeiro, Sameer Singh, and Carlos Guestrin. 2018. Semantically Equivalent Adversarial Rules for Debugging NLP models. *Proceedings of the 56th Annual Meeting of the Association for Computational Linguistics*, pages 856–865.

Shaohuai Shi, Qiang Wang, Pengfei Xu, and Xiaowen Chu. 2016. Benchmarking state-of-the-art deep learning software tools. In *2016 7th International Conference on Cloud Computing and Big Data (CCBD)*, pages 99–104. IEEE.

Amanpreet Singh, Vivek Natarjan, Meet Shah, Yu Jiang, Xinlei Chen, Devi Parikh, and Marcus Rohrbach. 2019. Towards vqa models that can read. In *Proceedings of the IEEE Conference on Computer Vision and Pattern Recognition*, pages 8317–8326.

Christian Szegedy, Wojciech Zaremba, Ilya Sutskever, Joan Bruna, Dumitru Erhan, Ian Goodfellow, and Rob Fergus. 2014. Intriguing properties of neural networks. In *International Conference on Learning Representations*.

Xiaojun Xu, Xinyun Chen, Chang Liu, Anna Rohrbach, Trevor Darrell, and Dawn Song. 2018. Fooling vision and language models despite localization and attention mechanism. In *Proceedings of the IEEE Conference on Computer Vision and Pattern Recognition*, pages 4951–4961.

Zhou Yu, Yuhao Cui, Jun Yu, Meng Wang, Dacheng Tao, and Qi Tian. 2020. Deep multimodal neural architecture search. In *Proceedings of the 28th ACM International Conference on Multimedia*, pages 3743–3752.

Zhou Yu, Jun Yu, Yuhao Cui, Dacheng Tao, and Qi Tian. 2019. Deep modular co-attention networks for visual question answering. In *Proceedings of the IEEE conference on computer vision and pattern recognition*, pages 6281–6290.

A Appendix

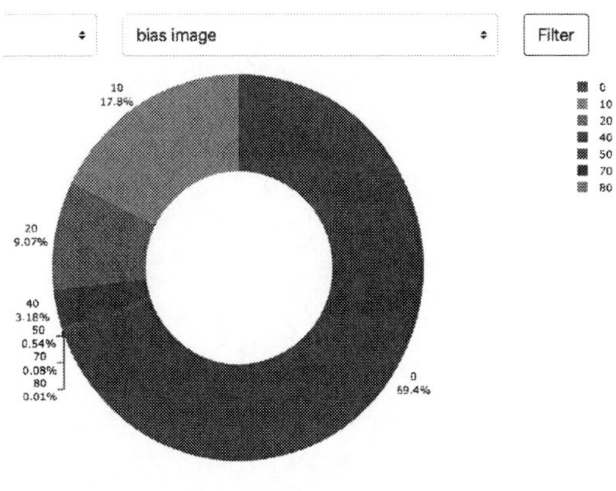

Figure 6: Zoom into Figure 3.

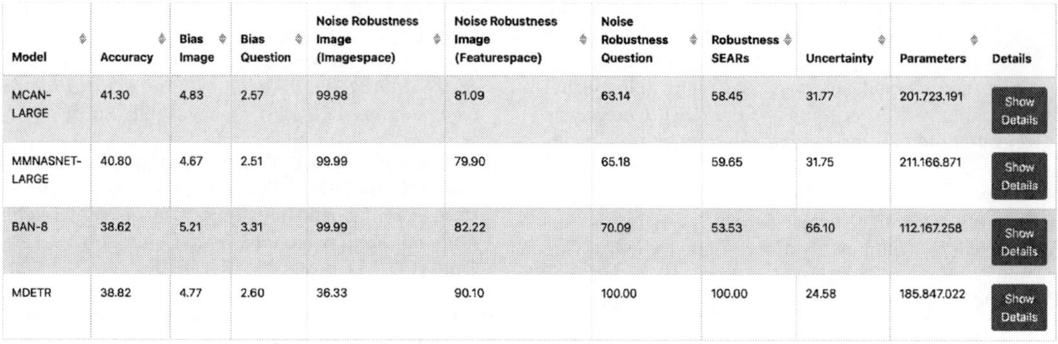

Model	Accuracy	Bias Image	Bias Question	Noise Robustness Image (Imagespace)	Noise Robustness Image (Featurespace)	Noise Robustness Question	Robustness SEARs	Uncertainty	Parameters	Details
MCAN-LARGE	41.30	4.83	2.57	99.98	81.09	63.14	58.45	31.77	201.723.191	Show Details
MMNASNET-LARGE	40.80	4.67	2.51	99.99	79.90	65.18	59.65	31.75	211.166.871	Show Details
BAN-8	38.62	5.21	3.31	99.99	82.22	70.09	53.53	66.10	112.167.258	Show Details
MDETR	38.82	4.77	2.60	36.33	90.10	100.00	100.00	24.58	185.847.022	Show Details

Figure 7: Figure 1 in full size.

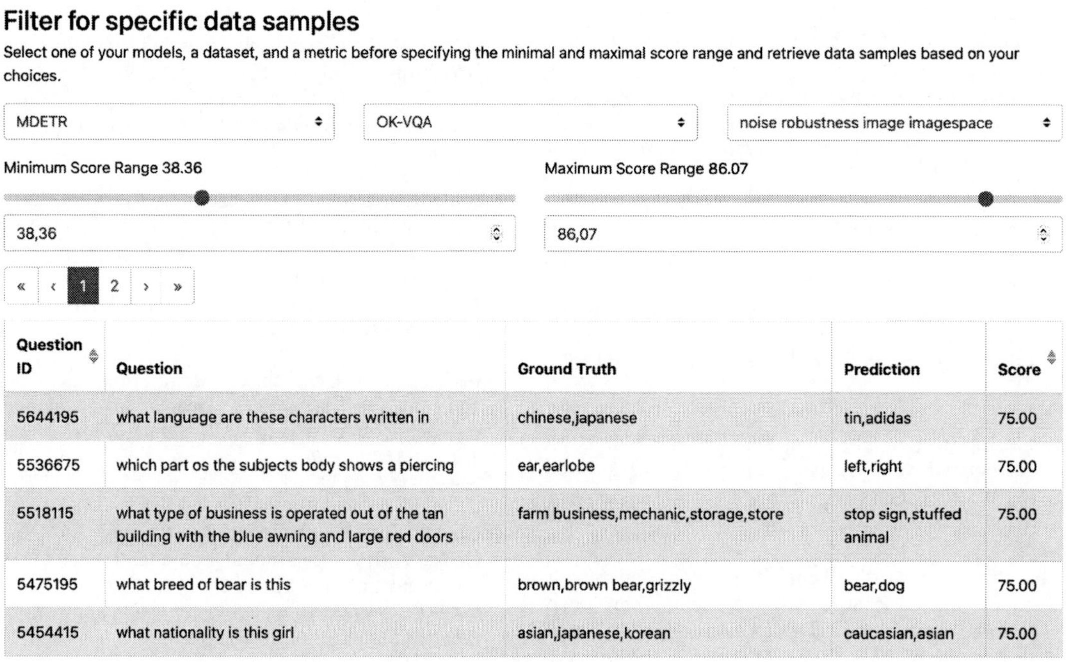

Question ID	Question	Ground Truth	Prediction	Score
5644195	what language are these characters written in	chinese,japanese	tin,adidas	75.00
5536675	which part os the subjects body shows a piercing	ear,earlobe	left,right	75.00
5518115	what type of business is operated out of the tan building with the blue awning and large red doors	farm business,mechanic,storage,store	stop sign,stuffed animal	75.00
5475195	what breed of bear is this	brown,brown bear,grizzly	bear,dog	75.00
5454415	what nationality is this girl	asian,japanese,korean	caucasian,asian	75.00

Figure 8: Figure 4 in full size.

Statistics

Question	who is wearing a glove	
Answer Id	**Answer**	**Probability**
1	catcher	49.11 %
2	player	22.67 %
3	batter	19.07 %
Id	**Ground Truth**	**Score**
1	catcher	1
Question Id	201438577	

Image Bias Word Space

Score	0 %	
Answer Id	**Answer**	**Frequency**
1	yes	28.57 %
2	no	14.29 %
3	chair	14.29 %
4	tree	14.29 %
5	left	14.29 %
6	eating	14.29 %

Figure 9: Figure 5 in full size.

Athena 2.0: Contextualized Dialogue Management for an Alexa Prize SocialBot

Juraj Juraska, Kevin K. Bowden, Lena Reed, Vrindavan Harrison, Wen Cui, Omkar Patil, Rishi Rajasekaran, Angela Ramirez, Cecilia Li, Eduardo Zamora, Phillip Lee, Jeshwanth Bheemanpally, Rohan Pandey, Adwait Ratnaparkhi and **Marilyn Walker**
University of California Santa Cruz, Santa Cruz, CA
`jjuraska, kkbowden, lireed, vharriso, wcui7, opatil, rrajasek, aramir62, yli331, ezamora9, plee35, jbheeman, rspandey, adratnap, mawalker@ucsc.edu`

Abstract

Athena 2.0 is an Alexa Prize SocialBot that has been a finalist in the last two Alexa Prize Grand Challenges. One reason for Athena's success is its novel dialogue management strategy, which allows it to dynamically construct dialogues and responses from component modules, leading to novel conversations with every interaction. Here we describe Athena's system design and performance in the Alexa Prize during the 20/21 competition. A live demo of Athena as well as video recordings will provoke discussion on the state of the art in conversational AI.

1 Introduction

There has been tremendous progress over the last 10 years on conversational AI, and a number of practical systems have been deployed. The Alexa Prize competition seeks to stimulate research and development on conversational AI for open-domain topic-oriented dialogue (Fang et al., 2018; Liang et al., 2020; Finch et al., 2020; Harrison et al., 2020; Pichl et al., 2020; Curry et al., 2018). However, the longstanding tension between hand-scripting the dialogue interaction, and producing systems that scale to new domains and types of interaction still remains (Eric and Manning, 2017; Cervone et al., 2019) Neural end-to-end spoken dialogue systems are not yet at a point where they perform well in interactions with real users (Paranjape et al., 2020; Gopalakrishnan et al., 2020; Dinan et al., 2019).

Athena's dialogue management architecture aims to be scalable and dynamic, by supporting many different interactions for every topic, and by constructing system utterances by concatenating multiple dialogue acts that achieve different purposes (Stent, 2000). A key aspect of Athena is the existence of multiple Response Generators (RGs) for each topic, which can be flexibly interleaved during a particular interaction, as illustrated in Figure 1.[1] This approach contrasts with the commonly used approach of handcrafting conversation flow-graphs for each topic, a static directed graph where the nodes are the system utterances, and outgoing edges are represent possible user replies. This approach has not changed for over 20 years (Seneff et al., 1998; Glass and Weinstein, 2001; Buntschuh et al., 1998), and its strengths and limitations are well known. Flow-graphs are hand constructed and thus do not scale well. However, each system response can assume a fixed prior context, which allows it to support fluent and coherent dialogues with sufficient handcrafting.

In contrast, the ability of Athena's Dialogue Manager (DM) to interleave RGs allows Athena to dynamically construct conversations that never follow the same path. However, this more flexible approach requires RGs to pay the overhead cost of continuously adapting to the current context, as described in Section 3. By eschewing a graph-based representation of dialogue state, Athena's DM is flexible enough to use RG responses in contexts that were not planned out prior to the conversation starting, and that do not need to follow rigid guidelines. We believe this modular dialogue management approach promises to scale to deeper and richer conversations, while at the same time allow new conversational topics to be easily added to and integrated into the system.

2 Athena Architecture and Overview

Figure 2 details Athena's architecture. Athena is built using the Cobot framework provided by Amazon (Khatri et al., 2018). It runs as an on-demand application that is initiated by an "Alexa, let's chat" user request to any Alexa-enabled device, such as

[1] In accordance with the Alexa Prize rules on user privacy, these conversations are between team members and Athena.

Proceedings of the 2021 Conference on Empirical Methods in Natural Language Processing: System Demonstrations, pages 124–133
November 7–11, 2021.

User	RG	Athena
...	KG	Do you like any of Disclosure's 4 albums? I like The Face myself.
i don't have a favorite one	KG	Do you like the genre contemporary R and B? Disclosure's song Omen is a good example of that genre.
yeah i like that genre	KG	Just 8 tracks, Disclosure hasn't released much music. You've probably heard them all, have you?
probably	KG	Do you know Disclosure's songs from the 2010s? I really like Latch personally!
me too that's my favorite	KG	...
...	FF	I think it is amazing how some things can cost so much money. In 2011, the Lady Blunt Stradivarius violin was sold for a record price of $15.9 million. It holds the world record for the most expensive musical instrument.
yeah	FLOW	So tell me, why do you like music?
it's the only thing in the world that makes you feel something	FLOW	I agree. I find music to have the ability to completely change my emotional state, so to say, on demand. Do you have a song, that you like to listen to, that instantly makes you feel better?
play date by melanie martinez	FLOW	Although the liking of music is largely subjective, I'm sure there are songs that can make just about anyone feel good. Do you like electronic music at all? As a robot I'm sort of partial to it.
i've never heard that type of music	FLOW	I see. So, what kind of music do you like?
n. d. r. and b. pop	FLOW	I love pop. Who is your favorite group or performer?
taylor swift	KG	Some artists are very prolific, I guess Taylor Swift is one of them, 12 albums is a lot. Personally, I like Red, you?
yes me too	KG	Some of my favorite songs of Taylor Swift's are from the 2010s, I especially like Sparks Fly. Do you like it too?
my favorite song by taylor swift is red	KG	Taylor Swift has released 76 tracks, which is a pretty good amount. Do you think that's a lot or not?
yes definitely	KG	I like to think that when music is played, it makes everyone happier, even animals. Researchers at the University of Leicester found that cows produce 3% more milk when they listen to relaxing music.
yes	FLOW	I'm curious. What do you think about this. If you could only pick one of these two styles of music to listen to for the rest of your life, would you rather listen to jazz or classical music?
that's cool	FLOW	Oh, I see. I would rather listen to classical music, because there is such an amazing range of styles and eras from which to choose. Unfortunately, Jazz all just sounds the same to me, and I totally love hearing a string quartet! Anyway, that's enough about me. I think it is awesome how scientists have explored music as way to improve human lives.

Figure 1: A subdialogue in which Athena discusses music with the user, interweaving the responses of 3 different RGs. Responses from the KG-based RG are highlighted in blue, responses from the entity-based indexing RG (fun facts) in green, and those from the flow-based RG in purple.

an Amazon Echo or the Alexa app installed on a phone. During the Alexa Prize, Athena participates in about 9K conversations a week. The Cobot framework provides support for automatically scaling to large volumes of user traffic.

The inputs to Athena are the ASR hypotheses for a user's turn from Amazon, and a conversation ID that is used to retrieve the conversation history and state information from a back-end database. The ASR hypothesis is fed into a natural language understanding (NLU) pipeline that produces a set of NLU features for the user utterance and conversation context. The NLU consists of Cobot's module for topic classification, and Athena modules for utterance segmentation, dialogue act tagging, named entity recognition and linking, and coreference resolution (Harrison et al., 2020; Patil et al., 2021). The right-hand side of Figure 2 indicates how Athena's RGs use knowledge bases and fun facts databases organized by topic and named entity. Athena uses the Wikidata Knowledge Graph to aid in Named Entity Resolution and for Knowledge-Graph based RGs. These are essential for creating an intelligent and versatile conversational agent (Fang et al., 2018; Chen et al., 2018).

Based on the NLU features and conversation context, the Dialogue Manager (DM) calls specific Response Generators (RGs) to populate a response pool. The DM then applies a trained neural response ranker to select from the response pool generated by the RGs. Finally, Athena's responses are spoken by Amazon's text-to-speech service.

3 Dialogue Management

A Dialogue Manager (DM) for open-domain conversation faces a particularly challenging task due to the universe of possible valid responses at each point of a conversation. While goal-oriented dialogues have a clear task completion objective which the DM can optimize when making decisions (Walker et al., 2001, 1997; Walker, 2000), the DM for open-domain dialogues does not have an obvious way to measure the appropriateness of possible candidate responses.

Athena's DM architecture can be decomposed into a number of sub-components, corresponding to phases of dialogue management, oriented as a pipeline. The DM sub-modules in Figure 3 are described in more detail in Harrison et al. (2020).

The Topic Manager in Figure 3 is responsible for classifying user utterances into topics, and the implementation of the DM's topic hierarchy. The topic hierarchy is a partially ordered list of topics in order of predicted "goodness" learned from past conversations, using a scoring function that combines user ratings and the number of turns per topic

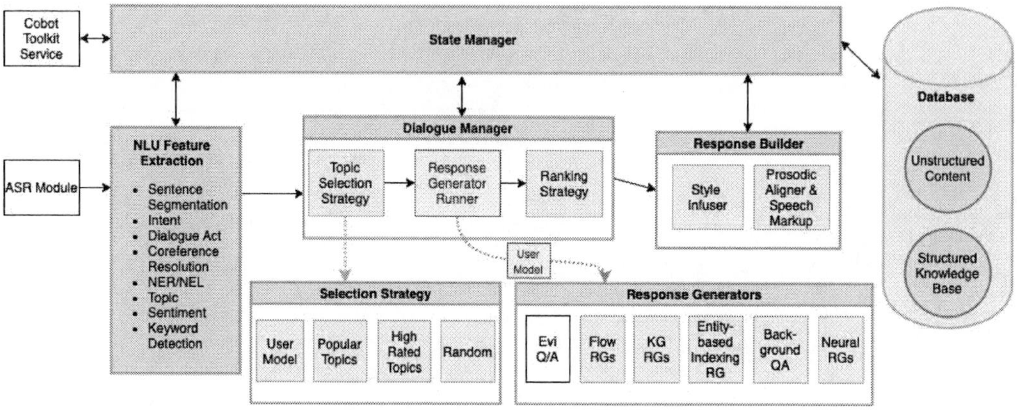

Figure 2: Athena's system architecture.

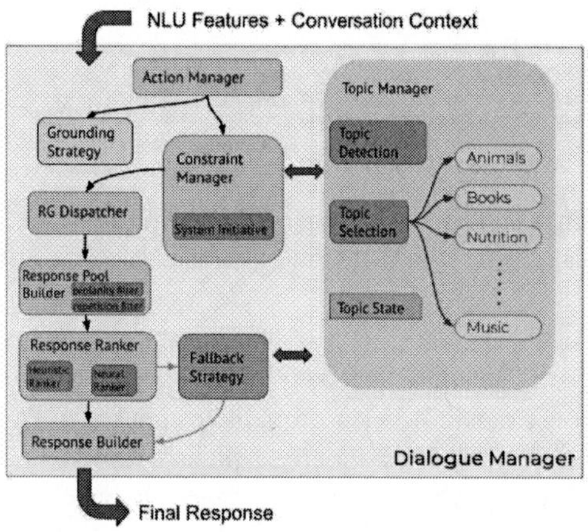

Figure 3: Dialogue manager architecture.

per conversation, as described in Section 5. The topic hierarchy is a parameter for system-initiative topic initiations as well as suggesting topics for users to initiate. This makes it extremely easy to change which topics are promoted at any time, e.g., for collecting more data on a particular topic. It can also be personalized for each user. For example, if when asked about weekend activities, the user describes playing in a baseball league, we can prioritize talking about sports. This information persists across conversations. If the user is also an avid painter, but our system did not get a chance to discuss painting in the previous conversation, we will prioritize it when the user returns.

The interface between the DM and the RGs in Figure 3, is a contract-based approach. The DM passes a set of response conditions to the RGs, which the RGs must meet for their response to be considered. This approach allows Athena to have many RG types (see Section 4).

The Response Ranker is based on a BERT-based ranker fine-tuned on hand-annotated Alexa Prize conversation data (Wolf et al., 2019; Devlin et al., 2018). The current tuning set size is ~10K utterances. Annotation involves ranking candidate responses within a context of five turns. We have repeatedly annotated additional data and retrained our response ranker, which is useful when, for example, new RGs are added to Athena.

4 Response Generation

Athena uses four types of RGs: Flow-RGs, Knowledge-Graph RGs, Entity-Based Indexing RGs, and Neural NLG RGs.

4.1 Flow-RG

Flow-RG is a framework that we developed with the objective of creating robust and modular flow-based RGs. This is still the most reliable way to provide the DM with a pool of possible responses at each turn of the dialogue, even though such flows have to be handcrafted. Flow-based RGs exhibit context-awareness and fluency superior to other RG types, such as retrieval-based or neural. This RG design naturally has a rather limited support for user initiative, which we make up for with other RGs in Athena, and by ensuring the responses from different RGs get smoothly interwoven across multiple turns, as well as within a single turn.

An RG defined in this framework has three components. First, a *flow graph* consisting of nodes specifying the responses, and edges determining which node of the flow to move on to given the current user utterance and dialogue state. Flow-RG enforces each next turn in the flow graph to be conditioned on the dialogue act(s) of the user utterance, while other features of the utterance – such as its sentiment, or the presence of a named entity or a particular keyword – are deemed secondary and

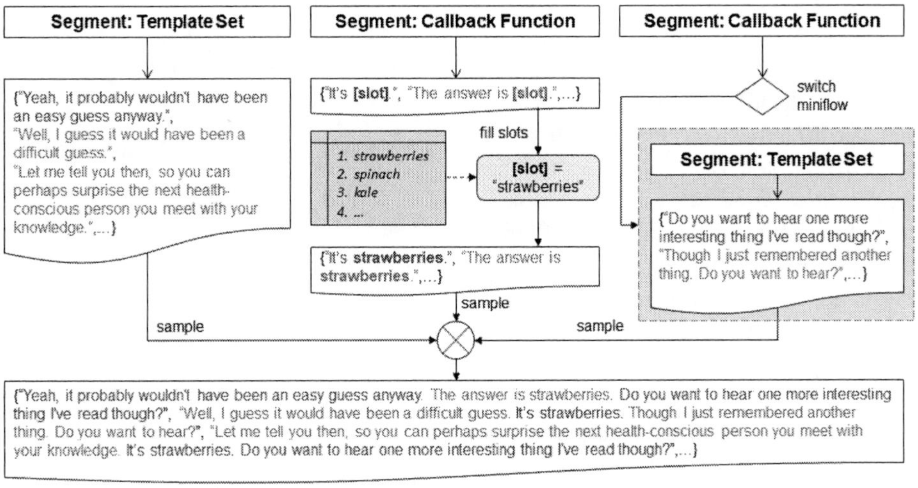

Figure 4: Illustration of response composition in Flow-RG.

are optional in branching conditions.[2] This reduces the chance of Athena's subsequent response ignoring the user's intent, which can be anything from expressing an opinion, to requesting information, to merely acknowledging Athena's response in the previous turn. The second component comprises *response segment templates*, while the third component is a set of *callback functions* that generate more context-dependent response segments.

A flow graph can be broken down into smaller *miniflows* that are independent and can possibly be executed in an arbitrary order. Each RG then typically handles a single topic, with multiple miniflows being responsible for different subtopics. An example of multiple miniflows forming a cohesive dialogue can be seen in Appendix A.

Response Composition. The response in each turn is assembled from one or more *segments* specified in the corresponding node. Each segment is defined either (1) in the form of a set of templates, or (2) as a callback function that returns a set of templates. While both offer an easy way to use paraphrases for increased diversity of the responses, the latter is more robust in that it can use the previous context and more of the NLU information about the user utterance. Figure 4 shows the process of a response being assembled from three segments, two of which are different types of callback function: one fills a template slot with a value from the associated knowledge source, while the other initiates a new miniflow and composes the response text recursively, which ultimately corresponds to the last segment in the example.

When composing a response, each segment's final set of texts is sampled from, and all of them are concatenated. This is repeated until up to five different response candidates are composed. These are eventually all returned to the DM, which picks one of them that is not too similar to any of Athena's previous responses.

Interweaving with Other RGs. Every topic in Athena has a corresponding Flow-RG, and most topics also have one or two other RGs that can interact with its Flow-RG to dynamically construct a topical sub-dialogue. In line with the DM's way of response building, the final response in Flow-RG is split into three parts: an opener, a body, and a hand-off. This response structure is particularly useful for creating seamless transitions whether it is between miniflows, or between two RGs. To this end, Flow-RG sets the response from an ending miniflow as the opener (typically, some form of acknowledgement of the user's response, or a short answer), and the body and hand-off parts are reserved for the intro response provided by a new miniflow. The same mechanism is used for certain transitions from Flow-RG to a different RG, mainly: 1) when the flow's content is exhausted, and transitions thus to a fallback response chosen by the DM that initiates a new topic, and 2) when a leaf node of the miniflow is reached, and the DM decides to switch to a different RG on the same topic. The latter is utilized in the DM's interweaving strategy, wherein a flow-based RG takes turns with an entity-centric or fun fact-based RG in han-

[2]The other NLU features, such as named entities or anaphora, often only affect the choice of content in the next system response rather than its type/DA, and they do not have a value at each turn, unlike the DA feature.

dling a subdialogue on the same topic.

Flow-RG makes it possible for a flow to resume after a few turns handled by a different RG on the same topic. The flow can simply begin a new miniflow, if there is at least one miniflow that has not yet been visited. Resumption is also possible in the middle of a miniflow, which allows a different RG to chime in for up to two turns (such as EVI answering an on-topic factual question that the flow has no answer prepared for), and then have the miniflow pick up where it left off.

ATHENA	Okay, can't wait to get to know a thing or two about you. Valentine's day is on Sunday. Do you have a Valentine?
USER	yes my wife
ATHENA	Cool! I wish I could meet a socialbot that I could fall in love with; then they'd be my Valentine. Anyway, I've always wanted to go on a vacation and to travel. What's a place that you've always wanted to travel to?
USER	paris sounds great
ATHENA	The Eiffel Tower is a masterpiece of architecture. For me, I think the great wall of china is at the top of my list of travel destinations. It seems like it would be amazing to walk along it. So, Is there a particular reason why you want to go to paris?
USER	the food is really bomb
ATHENA	Delicious food is always a good reason to go somewhere. Hey, I'm curious, Do you prefer flying? or road trips?
USER	I like flying generally
ATHENA	That's an interesting answer. I'd like to go on the road. You can see so much during a roadtrip, it would be cool to watch the world go by. Hmm, Do you like to relax during vacations?

Figure 5: Introduction Flow-RG subdialogue, just before Valentine's day.

Introduction RG. The Introduction Flow-RG, which every user experiences, has a strong effect on the user's overall experience (see Figure 5). The Introduction front-loads the conversation with getting-to-know-you content, by learning the user's name and asking icebreaker questions, such as favorite travel destinations, and weekend activities. The Introduction also brings up relevant current events, such as holidays, and gives the user a chance to ask Athena questions. Some of these turns will be the same for most users, e.g., asking for their name. Other content will change based on proximity to significant events in the year or the current day of the week, while some content changes randomly, for example, asking different questions related to vacation preferences. Content related to particular holidays as illustrated in Figure 5 are set up on a calendar and automatically started and stopped. The introduction also changes significantly for repeat users to indicate that we remember them, and provide a novel experience.

4.2 Knowledge Graph-Based RGs

The goal of the Knowledge Graph-based RGs (KG RGs) is to create deep knowledge-grounded conversations, where Athena always has more to say, by traversing relations in the Wikidata knowledge graph. Athena has four KG RGs covering movies, music, sports and TV, with conversations anchored around KG nodes (named entities). Each topic attempts to continue the conversation by either responding with a fact about an entity in context, or by selecting an entity from a set of fallback entities. When the system has either run out of facts on a particular entity, or has been on the same entity for a number of turns above a threshold, the RG attempts to traverse one or more relation edges, to a related entity, to continue the conversation. An example for the TV KG RG is in Figure 1.

ATHENA	Is there a television show that you like?
USER	**Friends** is one of my favorites Entity linking: Friends -> entity: Friends, wiki_id: Q79784
ATHENA	Friends is a great show. Why do you like it?
USER	It is really funny
ATHENA	What character do you like the most?
USER	I love Rachel
ATHENA	I really like how Jennifer Aniston plays Rachel Green. Did you know that she won a Primetime Emmy Award for Outstanding Lead Actress in a Comedy Series for her role?
USER	No, that's interesting

Table 1: Conversation using the knowledge graph.

Each topic has one to three entity types which the RG can respond about and each entity has a set of relations that can be used to generate responses. Each relation can only be used once for a particular entity, but can be reused when the RG has switched to a new entity. One limitation of the KG RGs is the need to select "interesting" relations and write templates by hand (Moon et al., 2019).

4.3 Entity-Based Indexing RGs

Entity-Based Indexing RGs are topical retrieval-based generators where the focus of the response is on "fun facts" for entities in a topic. Table 2 indicates how many fun facts these RGs have for each topic, and provides examples.

4.4 Neural NLG RGs

We have also developed and experimented with several different neural NLGs, including neural

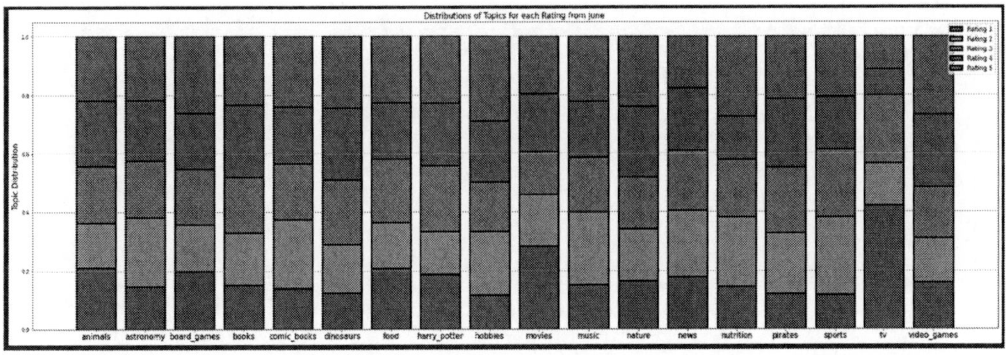

Figure 6: Distribution of ratings for each topic for the period from January 1st to June 16th.

Topic	#Facts	Example
Animals	90	I read this surprising fact about koalas. The fingerprints of a koala are so indistinguishable from humans that they have on occasion been confused at a crime scene. Imagine having your fingerprints confused with a koala, how strange!
Comic Books	26	Batman and Robin are the best superhero sidekick team. Once, after Batman and Robin rescued it from a slaughterhouse, DC comics included a Bat-cow.
Harry Potter	21	Fred and George Weasley were such tricksters. When Fred and George Weasley bewitched snowballs to hit Professor Quirrell's turban, they were unwittingly hitting Voldemort in the face.
Movies	54	One of my favorite movie series of all time are the James Bond movies. Before signing on as James Bond, Daniel Craig wasn't sure he wanted to play the role.
Music	31	I like to think that when music is played, it makes everyone happier, even animals. Researchers at the University of Leicester found that cows produce 3% more milk when they listen to relaxing music.
Nature	15	I like learning more about nature. It's actually really dark in the Amazon Forest! The forest is so thick that only 1% of sunlight can make it through.
Video Games	20	Here's a fact I discovered recently about World of Warcraft. A lot of famous people played World of Warcraft, including Vin Diesel, Mila Kunis and even Robin Williams. Isn't that cool?

Table 2: Fun facts for popular entity-based RG topics.

NLGs that generate from meaning representations and are thus topic specific (Juraska et al., 2019; Harrison et al., 2019; Oraby et al., 2019).

We also developed a neural NLG that we call Discourse-Driven NRG (DD-NRG) that generates directly from the conversation context and can be used for any topic (Rajasekaran, 2020; Tosh, 2020). We also systematically tested two topic-agnostic neural NLGs provided by Amazon, the PD-NRG (Hedayatnia et al., 2020) and a model called Topical-NRG that was trained on the Alexa Prize conversations of all finalists in the 19/20 competition. We found that it was difficult to control the quality of the neural RG outputs and guarantee their coherence, so we only deployed them to collect experimental data for short periods. We are currently experimenting with methods for controllable generation for these RGs (Reed et al., 2020; Harrison et al., 2019; Juraska and Walker, 2021).

5 Evaluation and Analysis

The two criteria that are specified in the Alexa Prize Grand Challenge that systems aim to optimize are length of conversation and user ratings. The Grand Prize will go to a system that achieves conversations of **at least 20 minutes** with **average ratings of 4.0** on a scale of 1 to 5.[3]

Over the 4 years our team has been in the competition, we have found that interactions with users are vulnerable to noise due to the competition setup (Bowden et al., 2019a,b; Harrison et al., 2020). Users often get into the Alexa Prize skill by accident leading to many conversations of only 1 or 2 turns (Shalyminov et al., 2018). Surprisingly, even for single turn conversations, some users still provide ratings. To improve our analysis of system performance, we remove these very short conversations from the data. Table 3 show the ratings, lengths in turns, and durations, during the semi-finals and the finals. On June 25th, before entering the finals, the average rating across all the systems in the semi-finals was 3.41 and the median duration was 2.12.

	Ratings		Turns		Time
	Mean	Median	Mean	Median	Median
Semifinals	3.62	4.0	17	24	2.46
Finals	3.71	4.0	18	24	2.01

Table 3: Athena's performance during the semi-finals and the finals for rating, length and duration.

Obviously, user's interactions with different RGs and topics affect their conversations and therefore their ratings. While only about 20% of users actually provide ratings, over the course of this year, we collected about 38K conversations with ratings. The distribution of ratings by topic presence in con-

[3]https://www.amazon.science/academic-engagements/alexa-prize-socialbot-grand-challenge-4-finalists-announced

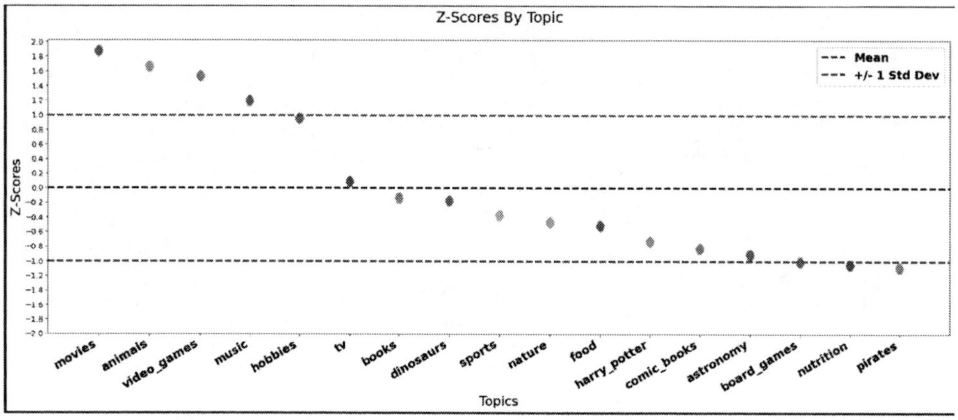

Figure 7: Z-scores for Athena topics for the period from June 1st to June 16th.

versations from January to June are in Figure 6. The purple and red bars indicate proportions of the topic that occur in conversations with ratings of 4 and 5 respectively. This suggests that the highest performing topics include animals, comic books, Harry Potter, hobbies, and video games, and that only a few topics are actually performing poorly, such as dinosaurs, news and sports.

However, presence in a conversation is a rather imprecise indicator of topic quality. In order to better understand the contribution of each topic to Athena's overall ratings, we developed a novel scoring function that aims to optimize topic selection over the prizes' user ratings and conversation duration criteria. Thus, our scoring function gives credit based on the number of utterances in a conversation that are contributed by each topic in the conversation. The number of utterances is multiplied by the conversation rating and summed for each topic over all rated conversations. This sum is then normalized to produce its Z-score. The plot shown in Figure 7 indicates for each topic, how many standard deviations its performance is above or below the Athena's mean performance for two weeks in June, 2021. This plot indicates that the topics that contribute most to long dialogues that are more highly rated include movies, animals, video games, music and hobbies, all of which are 1 or more standard deviations above the mean in performance. Walker et al. (2021) discusses the impact of topic selection and dialogue behaviors on user ratings and conversation length.

We also investigated the impact of personalization on the dialogue manager with an A/B study run over 22 days. The A system has the fully personalized dialogue manager, while B utilizes our previously existing heuristic topic selection strategy. We selected conversations of 6 turns or more to allow personalization to have an effect and also filter out conversations that never perform topic promotion; thus, we only inspect conversations that differ due to the topic selection strategy. After filtering, personalization occurred in roughly 25% of conversations. Our results, shown in Table 4, indicate a statistically significant increase in both user rating and conversation length.

	personalized	heuristic	p-value
convs	1066	614	—
rating	4.02	3.85	.007
length	38.07	35.07	.016

Table 4: Personalized topic selection vs. heuristic topic selection over 22 days.

6 Conclusion

This paper describes Athena, and its design and performance in the Alexa Prize Grand Challenge 4. Our system demonstration will illustrate both the strengths and the weaknesses of Athena and provide the basis for discussion about the state of the art of open-domain conversational AI.

Acknowledgements

We would like to thank Christian Benavidez, Yaqing Cao, James Graupera, Colin Harmon, Venkatesh Nagubandi, Meltem Ozcan, Diego Pedro, Navya Rao, Stephanie Rich, Jasiel Rivera-Trinadad and Aditya Tarde for helping with fun facts, Wikidata queries and prosody markup.

References

Kevin K Bowden, Jiaqi Wu, Wen Cui, Juraj Juraska, Vrindavan Harrison, Brian Schwarzmann, Nicholas

Santer, Steve Whittaker, and Marilyn Walker. 2019a. Entertaining and opinionated but too controlling: a large-scale user study of an open domain alexa prize system. In *Proceedings of the 1st International Conference on Conversational User Interfaces*, pages 1–10.

Kevin K Bowden, Jiaqi Wu, Wen Cui, Juraj Juraska, Vrindavan Harrison, Brian Schwarzmann, Nick Santer, and Marilyn Walker. 2019b. Slugbot: Developing a computational model and framework of a novel dialogue genre. *arXiv preprint arXiv:1907.10658*.

Bruce Buntschuh, C. Kamm, G. DiFabbrizio, A. Abella, M. Mohri, S. Narayanan, I. Zeljkovic, R.D. Sharp, J. Wright, S. Marcus, J. Shaffer, R. Duncan, and J.G. Wilpon. 1998. VPQ: A spoken language interface to large scale directory information. In *Proc. of ICSLP*, Sydney, Australia.

Alessandra Cervone, Chandra Khatri, Rahul Goel, Behnam Hedayatnia, Anu Venkatesh, Dilek Hakkani-Tur, and Raefer Gabriel. 2019. Natural language generation at scale: A case study for open domain question answering. In *arXiv preprint arXiv:1903.08097*.

Chun-Yen Chen, Dian Yu, Weiming Wen, Yi Mang Yang, Jiaping Zhang, Mingyang Zhou, Kevin Jesse, Austin Chau, Antara Bhowmick, Shreenath Iyer, et al. 2018. Gunrock: Building a human-like social bot by leveraging large scale real user data. *Alexa Prize Proceedings*.

Amanda Cercas Curry, Ioannis Papaioannou, Alessandro Suglia, Shubham Agarwal, Igor Shalyminov, Xinnuo Xu, Ondřej Dušek, Arash Eshghi, Ioannis Konstas, Verena Rieser, et al. 2018. Alana v2: Entertaining and informative open-domain social dialogue using ontologies and entity linking. *Alexa Prize Proceedings*.

Jacob Devlin, Ming-Wei Chang, Kenton Lee, and Kristina Toutanova. 2018. Bert: Pre-training of deep bidirectional transformers for language understanding. *arXiv:1810.04805 [cs]*. ArXiv: 1810.04805.

Emily Dinan, Samuel Humeau, Bharath Chintagunta, and Jason Weston. 2019. Build it break it fix it for dialogue safety: Robustness from adversarial human attack. In *Proceedings of the 2019 Conference on Empirical Methods in Natural Language Processing and the 9th International Joint Conference on Natural Language Processing (EMNLP-IJCNLP)*, pages 4537–4546.

Mihail Eric and Christopher D Manning. 2017. Key-value retrieval networks for task-oriented dialogue. In *SIGDIAL 2017: Session on Natural Language Generation for Dialog Systems*.

Hao Fang, Hao Cheng, Maarten Sap, Elizabeth Clark, Ari Holtzman, Yejin Choi, Noah A Smith, and Mari Ostendorf. 2018. Sounding board: A user-centric and content-driven social chatbot. *NAACL HLT 2018*, page 96.

Sarah E Finch, James D Finch, Ali Ahmadvand, Xiangjue Dong, Ruixiang Qi, Harshita Sahijwani, Sergey Volokhin, Zihan Wang, Zihao Wang, Jinho D Choi, et al. 2020. Emora: An inquisitive social chatbot who cares for you. *Alexa Prize Proceedings*.

James Glass and Eugene Weinstein. 2001. SpeechBuilder: Facilitating spoken dialogue system development. In *Eurospeech*, pages 1335–1338.

Karthik Gopalakrishnan, Behnam Hedayatnia, Longshaokan Wang, Yang Liu, and Dilek Hakkani-Tür. 2020. Are neural open-domain dialog systems robust to speech recognition errors in the dialog history? an empirical study. *Proc. Interspeech 2020*, pages 911–915.

Vrindavan Harrison, Juraj Juraska, Wen Cui, Lena Reed, Kevin K Bowden, Jiaqi Wu, Brian Schwarzmann, Abteen Ebrahimi, Rishi Rajasekaran, Nikhil Varghese, et al. 2020. Athena: Constructing dialogues dynamically with discourse constraints. *Alexa Prize Proceedings*.

Vrindavan Harrison, Lena Reed, Shereen Oraby, and Marilyn Walker. 2019. Maximizing stylistic control and semantic accuracy in nlg: Personality variation and discourse contrast. *DSNNLG 2019*, page 1.

Behnam Hedayatnia, Karthik Gopalakrishnan, Seokhwan Kim, Yang Liu, Mihail Eric, and Dilek Hakkani-Tur. 2020. Policy-driven neural response generation for knowledge-grounded dialog systems. In *Proceedings of the 13th International Conference on Natural Language Generation*, pages 412–421.

Juraj Juraska, Kevin K Bowden, and Marilyn Walker. 2019. ViGGO: A video game corpus for data-to-text generation in open-domain conversation. In *Proceedings of the 12th International Conference on Natural Language Generation*.

Juraj Juraska and Marilyn Walker. 2021. Attention is indeed all you need: Semantically attention-guided decoding for data-to-text nlg. In *International Conference on Natural Language Generation, INLG*.

Chandra Khatri, Behnam Hedayatnia, Anu Venkatesh, Jeff Nunn, Yi Pan, Qing Liu, Han Song, Anna Gottardi, Sanjeev Kwatra, Sanju Pancholi, et al. 2018. Advancing the state of the art in open domain dialog systems through the alexa prize. *arXiv preprint arXiv:1812.10757*.

Kaihui Liang, Austin Chau, Yu Li, Xueyuan Lu, Dian Yu, Mingyang Zhou, Ishan Jain, Sam Davidson, Josh Arnold, Minh Nguyen, et al. 2020. Gunrock 2.0: A user adaptive social conversational system. *Proceedings of the Alexa Prize: Social Bot Grand Challenge 3*.

Seungwhan Moon, Pararth Shah, Anuj Kumar, and Rajen Subba. 2019. Opendialkg: Explainable conversational reasoning with attention-based walks over knowledge graphs. In *Proceedings of the 57th Annual Meeting of the Association for Computational Linguistics*, pages 845–854.

Shereen Oraby, Vrindavan Harrison, Abteen Ebrahimi, and Marilyn Walker. 2019. Curate and generate: A corpus and method for joint control of semantics and style in neural nlg. In *Proceedings of the 57th Annual Meeting of the Association for Computational Linguistics*, pages 5938–5951.

Ashwin Paranjape, Abigail See, Kathleen Kenealy, Haojun Li, Amelia Hardy, Peng Qi, Kaushik Ram Sadagopan, Nguyet Minh Phu, Dilara Soylu, and Christopher D Manning. 2020. Neural generation meets real people: Towards emotionally engaging mixed-initiative conversations. *Proceedings of the Alexa Prize: Social Bot Grand Challenge 3.*

Omkar Patil, Lena Reed, Kevin K. Bowden, Juraj Juraska, Wen Cui, Vrindavan Harrison, Rishi Rajasekaran, Angela Ramirez, Cecilia Li, Phillip Lee, Eduardo Zamora, Jeshwanth Bheemanpally, Rohan Pandey, Adwait Ratnaparkhi, and Marilyn Walker. 2021. Athena 2.0: Discourse and user modeling in open domain dialogue. *Proceedings of the Alexa Prize.*

Jan Pichl, CTU FEE, Petr Marek, Jakub Konrád, Martin Matulík, and Jan Šedivý. 2020. Alquist 2.0: Alexa prize socialbot based on sub-dialogue models. *Proceedings of the Alexa Prize: Social Bot Grand Challenge 3.*

Rishi Rajasekaran. 2020. Transfer-learning approaches towards controllable response generation for conversational agents. *PDF Download.*

Lena Reed, Vrindavan Harrison, Shereen Oraby, Dilek Hakkani-Tur, and Marilyn Walker. 2020. Learning from mistakes: Combining ontologies via self-training for dialogue generation. In *Proceedings of the 21st Annual Meeting of the Special Interest Group on Discourse and Dialogue (SIGDIAL 2020).*

Stephanie Seneff, Ed Hurley, Raymond Lau, Christine Pao, Philipp Schmid, and Victor Zue. 1998. Galaxy-ii: A reference architecture for conversational system development. In *Fifth International Conference on Spoken Language Processing.*

Igor Shalyminov, Ondřej Dušek, and Oliver Lemon. 2018. Neural response ranking for social conversation: A data-efficient approach. In *Proceedings of the 2018 EMNLP Workshop SCAI: The 2nd International Workshop on Search-Oriented Conversational AI*, pages 1–8.

A. Stent. 2000. Rhetorical structure in dialog. In *Proc. of the first international conference on Natural language generation-Volume 14*, pages 247–252. Association for Computational Linguistics.

Zachary Tosh. 2020. Developing knowledge-grounded natural language generation models for the dstc9 competition. *PDF Download.*

M. Walker, J. Aberdeen, J. Boland, E. Bratt, J. Garofolo, L. Hirschman, A. Le, S. Lee, S. Narayanan, K. Papineni, B. Pellom, J. Polifroni, A. Potamianos, P. Prabhu, A. Rudnicky, G. Sanders, S. Seneff, D. Stallard, and S. Whittaker. 2001. DARPA communicator dialog travel planning systems: The june 2000 data collection. In *EUROSPEECH 2001.*

M. A. Walker, D. Litman, C. A. Kamm, and A. Abella. 1997. PARADISE: A general framework for evaluating spoken dialogue agents. In *Proc. of the 35th Annual Meeting of the Association for Computational Linguistics, ACL/EACL 97*, pages 271–280.

Marilyn Walker, Colin Harmon, James Graupera, Davan Harrison, and Steve Whittaker. 2021. Developing paradise for open domain dialogue systems. In *International Workshop on Spoken Dialogue System Technology*. Springer.

Marilyn A. Walker. 2000. An application of reinforcement learning to dialogue strategy selection in a spoken dialogue system for email. *Journal of Artificial Intelligence Research*, 12:387–416.

Thomas Wolf, Lysandre Debut, Victor Sanh, Julien Chaumond, Clement Delangue, Anthony Moi, Pierric Cistac, Tim Rault, R'emi Louf, Morgan Funtowicz, and Jamie Brew. 2019. Huggingface's transformers: State-of-the-art natural language processing. *ArXiv*, abs/1910.03771.

A Appendix

A: I'd like to hear your ideas on this. If you could choose one food to live on for your entire life, which food would it be? Why?
U: i think nachos
A: That's an interesting answer! If I was a human, I would eat Sweet potatoes. Sweet potatoes are a really nutritious food. You can eat them in a variety of ways like baked, fries, or twice baked. Anyway, that's my thoughts on the matter.
A: Okay. I was curious about your opinion on this. If you had the option, would you rather spend time in the mountains, or, at the beach
U: i like the beach more
A: Choosing the beach is a good choice! If I was a human, I would spend time at the ocean - I would walk on the beach, search for shells, and relax in the sun. Anyhow, that's where my minds at, let's move forward.

Table 5: Two examples of Athena's attempt to increase topical depth by asking different types of playful questions. We crowdsourced 2.5k playful questions, which were then curated for quality. All of this content was also updated to match Athena's self-aware personality, e.g., *If I was human*. "A" denotes Athena and "U" the user turns.

A: But most people seem to find dinosaurs really interesting. There are dinosaur movies and whole floors of natural history museums dedicated to dinosaurs. Personally, I find it fascinating that modern birds are descended from a particular family of dinosaurs.
U: hella cool
A: Definitely. I was surprised to hear how much work went into creating the movie Land Before Time. Over 600 background paintings were made for the film. The artists had to create a believable environment in which there was almost no foliage. Most paintings depicted beautiful but barren wastelands.
U: surprising
A: Right? My favorite dinosaur is the Tyrannosaurus Rex. It's huge and ferocious, but the little arms make it somewhat adorable. What about you? What's your favorite dinosaur?
U: i'm not sure i have to say a t. rex
A: Okay. There are lots of movies about dinosaurs. One of the most famous dinosaur movies is Jurassic Park, old but classic. Are there any dinosaur movies that you love?
U: i have to say jurassic park because that's the only one i've seen
A: Awesome! That one is well known! I seem to remember people saying the dinosaurs were very vivid
U: i never knew that
A: yeah, I love to collect these fun facts! But anyways, I'm interested in your opinion. Would you rather ride on the back of a pterodactyl or brontosaurus as your primary means of transportation?
U: i have to say brontosaurus and i hate heights
A: Choosing a Brontosaurus you say, great pick! I would rather ride a pterodactyl so I could experience flight as well as move around more efficiently. Riding a brontosaurus would be thrilling because of their size but less practical than a pterodactyl. So, okay. Do you know why dinosaurs are extinct?
U: yeah cause i'm eat your head it right
A: Ah nice, you must be super smart. Let me tell you what I heard.The mass extinction of dinosaurs is a scientific mystery, but most hypotheses include an extraterrestrial impact or a massive bout of volcanism. What do you think happened?
U: i'd say aliens
A: I'd like to hear your ideas on this. Let's say you are trapped on Jurassic World alone with the dinosaurs, what would you do to survive?
U: i'm not sure i just say find sheltering something and start there
A: It's a hard question! I would try to become closer to the younger dinosaurs so that they would grow up with me and feel more comfortable with me. I would also try to help them by finding food and shelter for them. At any rate, Dinosaurs had a lot of different ways to attack other dinosaurs and to defend themselves. To help fight meat eaters such as the Allosaurus or Spinosaurus, many plant eaters had natural weapons at their disposal.

Table 6: An example conversation about Dinosaurs, one of our more niche topics. We use a variety of different miniflows to increase our topical depth. "A" denotes Athena and "U" the user turns.

A: One thing that really interests me is people's hobbies. Can you give me some info about swimming?
U: it's pretty fun
A: Right? Sounds totally tubular. Why do you like swimming?
U: it's because i can kind of just feel like i can move around and do a lot of stuff i can't do on land
A: Cool! How did you first get started with swimming?
U: i took swimming lessons
A: I realize you might be totally in love with swimming, but I'm curious. Is there any part of the hobby you don't like?
U: tough lessons
A: Well swimming sounds interesting, thanks for telling me all about your hobby. A lot of people have cool hobbies, but what about me? What kind of hobby do you think I would like?
U: maybe writing
A: Alright. Why do you think writing is a good fit for me?
U: because you like expressing yourself seems like
A: Ok. I see. Do you need any special equipment or skills to get into writing?
U: just paper and pen and imagination
A: I see. Thank you for recommending writing to me, I'll try to find out more about the hobby in the future!

Table 7: An example of Athena engaging the user about their hobby, swimming, which we previously learned about in the Introduction RG. "A" denotes Athena and "U" the user turns.

SPRING Goes Online: End-to-End AMR Parsing and Generation

Rexhina Blloshmi
Sapienza University of Rome
blloshmi@di.uniroma1.it

Michele Bevilacqua
Sapienza University of Rome
bevilacqua@di.uniroma1.it

Edoardo Fabiano
Sapienza University of Rome
edoardo10x@gmail.com

Valentina Caruso
Babelscape, Italy
caruso@babelscape.com

Roberto Navigli
Sapienza University of Rome
navigli@diag.uniroma1.it

Abstract

In this paper we present SPRING Online Services, a Web interface and RESTful APIs for our state-of-the-art AMR parsing and generation system, SPRING (Symmetric PaRsIng aNd Generation). The Web interface has been developed to be easily used by the Natural Language Processing community, as well as by the general public. It provides, among other things, a highly interactive visualization platform and a feedback mechanism to obtain user suggestions for further improvements of the system's output. Moreover, our RESTful APIs enable easy integration of SPRING in downstream applications where AMR structures are needed. Finally, we make SPRING Online Services freely available at http://nlp.uniroma1.it/spring and, in addition, we release extra model checkpoints to be used with the original SPRING Python code.[1]

1 Introduction

Abstract Meaning Representation (Banarescu et al., 2013, AMR) is a popular formalism for representing the semantics of natural language in a readable and hierarchical way. AMR pairs English sentences with graph-based logical formulas which are easily accessible by both humans and machines, while abstracting away from many syntactic variations. Because of the formalism's ambition to be comprehensive, AMR graphs are complex objects that require a parser – an automatic algorithm that transduces a natural language utterance into an AMR graph – to subsume multiple traditional Natural Language Processing tasks: Word Sense Disambiguation (Bevilacqua et al., 2021b; Barba et al., 2021), Semantic Role Labeling (Màrquez et al., 2008; Conia et al., 2021; Blloshmi et al., 2021), Named Entity Recognition (Yadav and Bethard, 2018), Entity Linking (Ling et al., 2015; Tedeschi et al., 2021), and Coreference Resolution (Kobayashi and Ng, 2020). Owing to this complexity, AMR parsing, as well as its specular counterpart, i.e., AMR generation, are hard to solve. However, the richness of the information included in AMR graphs, as well as their obvious applications as an interface between human and machines, make both AMR parsing and generation very rewarding problems to solve. As a matter of fact, AMR has been successfully applied to diverse downstream applications, such as Machine Translation (Song et al., 2019), Text Summarization (Hardy and Vlachos, 2018; Liao et al., 2018), Human-Robot Interaction (Bonial et al., 2020a), Information Extraction (Rao et al., 2017) and, more recently, Question Answering (Lim et al., 2020; Bonial et al., 2020b; Kapanipathi et al., 2021). However, since AMR graphs for such applications are obtained automatically through an AMR parser, the benefits of AMR integration are highly correlated with the performance of the underlying parser across various data distributions and domains.

In recent years, AMR parsing and generation models have become more reliable than they used to be, thanks to both the availability of pretrained language models (Devlin et al., 2019; Lewis et al., 2020) and the continuous improvements in the AMR-specific model architectures (Zhou et al., 2020; Cai and Lam, 2020; Fernandez Astudillo et al., 2020). However, most of the existing models make use of cumbersome, data-specific techniques and components which not only limit the out-of-distribution generalizability, but also make it difficult to integrate such models in the pipeline of downstream applications. In our recent paper, SPRING (Bevilacqua et al., 2021a), we proposed a solution through a simple, end-to-end approach with no heavy inbuilt data processing assumptions. Our model achieved unprecedented performance in AMR parsing and generation, both in- and out-of-distribution.

To make SPRING accessible to the community, thereby lowering the entry point to AMR applica-

[1] https://github.com/SapienzaNLP/spring

Proceedings of the 2021 Conference on Empirical Methods in Natural Language Processing: System Demonstrations, pages 134–142
November 7–11, 2021. ©2021 Association for Computational Linguistics

tion research, we present SPRING Online Services which include:

- a Web interface to easily produce and visualize an AMR graph for a given sentence and, vice versa, a sentence for a given AMR graph in PENMAN (Goodman, 2020) notation.
- RESTful APIs to programmatically request AMR parsing and generation services.
- a bidirectional SPRING model also trained on Bio-AMR, resulting in much stronger performances for biomedical applications.
- a feedback mechanism which allows users to submit modifications to the system's outputs – aided by the visualization – which we collect to enable future enhancements of AMR systems using active learning (Settles, 2009).

2 SPRING

In this Section we revisit the details of SPRING as in Bevilacqua et al. (2021a) along with the alterations we employ for this demonstration.

2.1 Task Formulation

SPRING is a simple sequence-to-sequence model that operates either as a *parser*, aiming to produce a linearized AMR graph given a sentence, or as a data-to-text *generator*, generating a sentence from an input linearized AMR graph. Formally, a sentence is represented as a sequence of tokens $\mathbf{s} = \langle \text{BOS}, w_1, w_2, \ldots, w_n, \text{EOS} \rangle$ where each word w_i belongs to the vocabulary V, and $\text{BOS}, \text{EOS} \in V$ are special beginning-of-sentence and end-of-sentence tokens, respectively. For example, the sentence *You told me to wash the dog* is represented as ⟨BOS,'You', 'told', 'me', 'to', 'wash', 'the', 'dog', EOS⟩. Similarly, a linearized graph is also a sequence $\mathbf{g} = \langle \text{BOS}, g_1, g_2, \ldots, g_m, \text{EOS} \rangle$, where $g_i \in V$. The graph of the aforementioned sentence is shown in Figure 1. Note that both sentence and graph tokens are drawn from the same vocabulary.

SPRING is at its heart a function P_θ (with θ being the parameters) that takes as input a source string σ in $V^* = \bigcup_{i=1}^{\infty} V^i$ and a partial target string $\tau \in V^*$. Then P_θ outputs a next-token probability distribution over V. Applying this basic function repeatedly, we can assign a probability (P^*) to any string of tokens given another one by factorising it in a left-to-right way as a product of conditional

AMR GRAPH

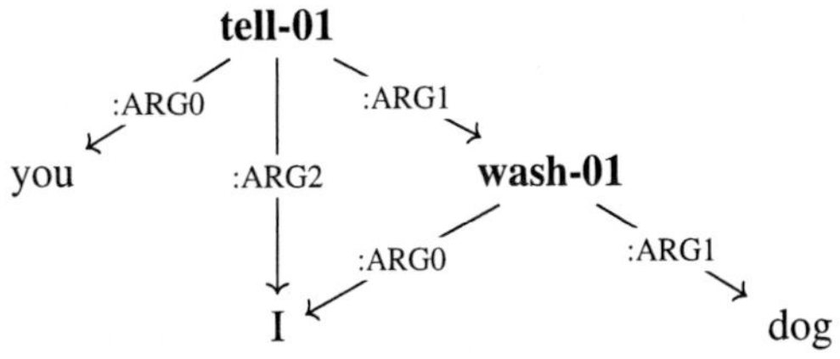

SNT You told me to wash the dog

DFS (<R0> tell-01 :ARG0 (<R1> you) :ARG1 (<R3> wash-01 :ARG0 <R2> :ARG1 (<R4> dog)) :ARG2 (<R2> i))

Figure 1: The AMR graph for the sentence (SNT) "You told me to wash the dog." with its DFS linearization.

probabilities. This can be applied both to the parsing (by using $\mathbf{s}$ as σ, and the progressively built linearization $\mathbf{g}$ as τ; Eq. 1) and generation (exchanging σ and τ; Eq. 2):

$$P_\theta^*(\mathbf{g}|\mathbf{s}) = \prod_{i=1}^{m+1} P_\theta(g_i \mid \tau = \mathbf{g}_{0:i-1}, \sigma = \mathbf{s}) \quad (1)$$

$$P_\theta^*(\mathbf{s}|\mathbf{g}) = \prod_{i=1}^{n+1} P_\theta(s_i \mid \tau = \mathbf{s}_{0:i-1}, \sigma = \mathbf{g}) \quad (2)$$

To train the model we optimize the parameters to minimize, with mini-batch gradient descent, the so-called negative log likelihood $\mathcal{L}_\theta$ (the negative log conditional probability) over a dataset $\mathcal{D}$ collecting sentence-graph pairs, both for parsing ($\mathcal{L}_{\theta(1)}^{\text{PAR}}$) and generation ($\mathcal{L}_{\theta(2)}^{\text{GEN}}$):

$$\begin{aligned} &\underset{\theta^{(1)},\theta^{(2)}}{\text{argmin}} \quad \mathcal{L}_{\theta^{(1)}}^{\text{PAR}}(\mathcal{D}) + \mathcal{L}_{\theta^{(2)}}^{\text{GEN}}(\mathcal{D}) = \\ &\underset{\theta^{(1)},\theta^{(2)}}{\text{argmin}} \; - \sum_{\langle \mathbf{s},\mathbf{g}\rangle \in \mathcal{D}} \log P_{\theta^{(1)}}^*(\mathbf{g}|\mathbf{s}) + \log P_{\theta^{(2)}}^*(\mathbf{s}|\mathbf{g}) \end{aligned} \quad (3)$$

Note that when $\theta^{(1)}$ is different from $\theta^{(2)}$, the two objective terms are optimized separately. Instead, when we enforce $\theta^{(1)} = \theta^{(2)}$ we have a model that is not only symmetric, but can also perform both AMR parsing and generation at the same time. As we will see, this results in negligible performance drops compared to the disjoint models that we presented in Bevilacqua et al. (2021a).

Once we have the trained model, the predicted output is the string ending in EOS with the highest probability in P_θ^*. Unfortunately, finding this optimal string is intractable when $|V|$ is large; in practice, however, we can perform an approximate decoding with histogram beam search.

2.2 Architecture

The SPRING model is based on the Transformer architecture (Vaswani et al., 2017), a sequence-to-sequence neural network that, briefly, i) uses attention instead of recurrence to encode sequences, ii) is made up of an encoder module that embeds σ, and a decoder that, based on both the encoder output and τ, produces the final distribution output. Key to the high performances of SPRING is the fact that its parameters are not randomly initialized, but, instead, are adopted from those of a large pretrained encoder-decoder model, i.e., BART (Lewis et al., 2020). Owing to this, SPRING can exploit the extensive knowledge BART encompasses, gained through optimization on large amounts of raw text with an unsupervised denoising objective.

2.3 Linearization

As we have mentioned, the bare SPRING model can translate *from* and *into* linearized AMR graphs. PENMAN, i.e., the format that is used to distribute the AMR meaning bank, is an example of a linearization. In Bevilacqua et al. (2021a) we experimented with different fully graph-isomorphic linearization techniques. The linearization that worked best was the one based on the Depth-First Search (DFS) graph traversal algorithm, enhanced with the use of special tokens to represent the variables, e.g., <R0>, <R1>, ..., <Rn> (Figure 1). Thus, we use the DFS-based linearization here.

One problem when performing parsing is that, since we do not enforce constraints in decoding, the predicted linearization may not be readable back into a valid AMR. In practice, the outputs are almost always valid, or can be made so with little modification. Thus, in parsing only, we perform light, non content-modifying postprocessing, mainly to ensure the validity of the linearization produced, e.g., restoring parenthesis parity and removing duplicate edges. Differently from Bevilacqua et al. (2021a), here we do not employ a third-party Entity Linker so as to avoid response delay.

2.4 Vocabulary

We modify the BART vocabulary in order to make it suitable for AMR-specific concepts (e.g. `amr-unkwown`, `date-entity`), frames (e.g. `say-01`) and relations (e.g. `:ARG1`, `:time`), as well as special pointer tokens used in the DFS linearization. The final vocabulary V is the union of the original BART vocabulary and our additions. Finally, we adjust the tokenization rules so that they do not split AMR additional tokens into multiple sub-words and adjust the encoder and decoder embedding matrices to include the new symbols. To this end, we add a vector for each newly added token which we initialize as the average of the vectors of the sub-word constituents. This is useful for obtaining compact sequences of tokens, allowing for faster decoding and response time of the SPRING Online Services.

3 SPRING Online Services

Here we describe the functionalities of the Web interface (Section 3.1) and those of the RESTful APIs (Section 3.2). We further provide the architectural details and libraries used in Appendix A.

3.1 Web Interface

The main functionalities of the Web interface include switching between *parsing* and *generation* modalities, visual inspection of SPRING results view and the feedback mechanism we develop to enable users to validate SPRING predictions.

3.1.1 Modality Selector

The modality can be set on the initial homepage by choosing `Text` or `PENMAN` from the Tab menu, with `Text` being the default option. When the `Text` option is chosen, the user is required to provide a plaintext sentence and they will then be redirected to the SPRING *parser* Results View (shown in Figure 2). On the other hand, when the `PENMAN` option is chosen, the user is required to type or copy a valid AMR graph in PENMAN notation. In the case when the PENMAN provided is valid, the user is redirected to the SPRING *generator* Results View. Otherwise, when the graph is not valid, the user is notified by a warning which points to the error line number of the PENMAN.

3.1.2 SPRING Results View

The Results View is similar for both parsing and generation, and we only exchange the query (input) box and the result (output) box.

A. Query box. As in the Modality Selector phase, also here, in the *parsing* modality the query box takes as input a plaintext sentence as input, while in *generation* the query box requires the input to be a valid PENMAN. A user can parse or generate from different inputs in this view while remaining in the same modality. To switch from

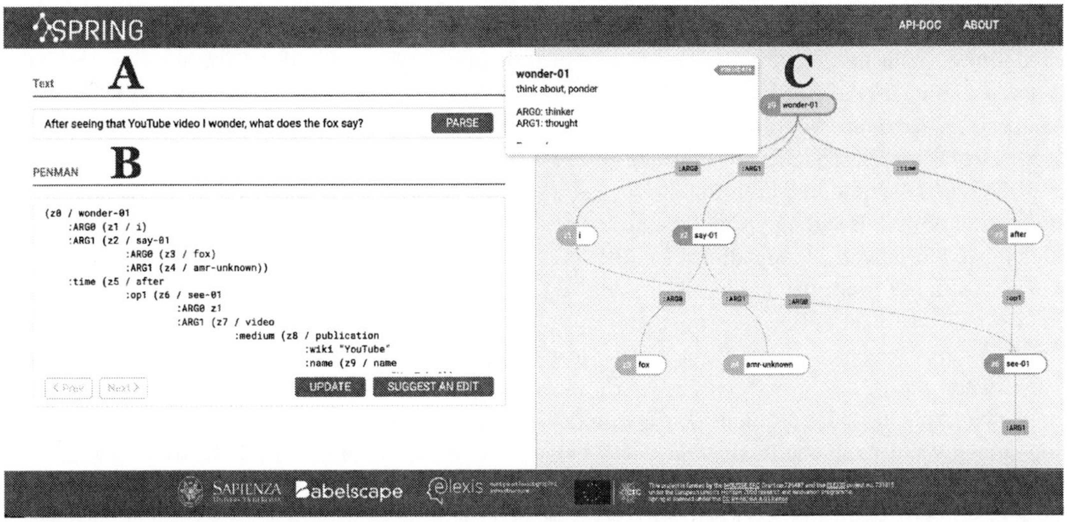

Figure 2: User interface of the SPRING *parser* Results View when the English sentence "After seeing that YouTube video I wonder, what does the fox say?" is typed as input.

parsing to *generation* or vice versa, the user should go back to the initial homepage.

B. Result box. When parsing a sentence, the Result box will be filled with the predicted graph in PENMAN format. This box is editable to enable user feedback (see Section 3.1.3). When *generating* from an AMR graph, the Result box shows the generated sentence which can also be modified by the user and submitted to the feedback system.

C. AMR view panel. This is a key component of the Results View, which visualizes an AMR as a hierarchical graph with labeled nodes and labeled edges. We devise a custom node and edge layout meant to enhance readability even in the case of big graphs with a lot of coreference edges. For example, there might be overlapping edges, edge labels or nodes in the graph. To increase visibility, the user can click/hover on an edge or edge label, and it will be highlighted and brought to the foreground. The same applies to nodes, and in addition, clicking/hovering over nodes will also highlight and bring to the foreground every incoming and outgoing edge, thus identifying all the local relations of a concept. The graph view is resizeable in order to better handle big AMR graphs, and the user is also able to zoom in/out for ease of reading. There are 4 types of node, indicated by different colors, comprising: i) predicate concept nodes, ii) non-predicate concept nodes, iii) constant nodes and iv) wiki nodes. Both predicate and non-predicate nodes are labeled with a variable name (in the highlighted corner) and the concept they represent. The variable makes it easy to locate the node in the PENMAN box on the left Panel.

Futhermore, both predicate and wiki nodes are associated with an `onhover/onclick` tooltip box that further defines them. The tooltip associated with the wiki node contains information taken from the corresponding BabelNet[2] (Navigli and Ponzetto, 2010; Navigli et al., 2021) concept, displaying a short entity description and image (when applicable), also redirecting the user to the corresponding BabelNet page when clicking on it. This choice is motivated by the fact that BabelNet concepts function as a hub of information beyond that of Wikipedia, which paves the way for future integration of other resources in AMR. The tooltip of the predicate node, instead, provides details on the predicate definition and arguments taken from the PropBank framesets (Palmer et al., 2005). In addition, we display an example sentence containing the predicate in the specified sense. The user is redirected to the PropBank predicate page when clicking the tooltip. We mean the extra information shown by the tooltip component to be useful for the user to identify potential parsing mistakes in the output of the system, and ideally to use the provided feedback mechanism to suggest corrections.

3.1.3 Feedback Mechanism

One key functionality of SPRING Online Services that requires user interaction is the Feedback Mech-

[2] Version 5.0.

anism. It is included in both parsing and generation modalities. With this feature, we aim to obtain a manual validation of SPRING output graphs or sentences, aided by the visualization. More specifically, when a user recognizes a mistake of the SPRING *parser*, including both missing or extra nodes and edges, or wrongly labeled ones, they are allowed to suggest modifications. In SPRING *parser* modality, multiple modifications are allowed in the left-panel PENMAN box, which are updated simultaneously in the right AMR view panel when the `UPDATE` button is pressed, and a user can then navigate through their own modifications by means of the `Prev` and `Next` buttons. To submit a final modification request, a user is provided with the `SUGGEST AN EDIT` button. The modifications are accepted if they lead to a correctly-formed graph. When this is the case, we save the modification request in a database for further validation. In contrast, when a mistake is found the user is warned about the line in PENMAN where it occurs. In the SPRING *generator* instead, only the predicted sentence is allowed to be modified, assuming that the input graph by the user is correct and does not need further modification. If this is not the case, the user can query the system with another AMR to obtain a new result. This feedback mechanism paves the way to future advancements in the field:

- enabling the use of active learning for improving system performance;
- collecting human validated SPRING output which can be further used as synthetic data for enhancing AMR systems;
- providing evidence of common SPRING mistakes which can aid studies on interpretation and reinforcement of AMR systems' knowledge.

Since data collection requires time and considerable interaction of users with our services, we leave the exploration of methods for including such data in AMR tasks as future work. Moreover, we plan to release the accumulated data periodically and on-request to the community.

3.2 RESTful APIs

The RESTful APIs we provide can be used effectively to query the SPRING services programmatically. Our APIs are simple and, differently from our Web interface, do not allow modification requests of the SPRING output. The APIs can be accessed through GET or POST requests. In fact, the APIs consist of two endpoints, namely, `/api/text-to-amr` and `/api/amr-to-text`, to parse into or generate from an AMR graph, respectively. The former requires a `sentence` string parameter and the output is a JSON object containing the PENMAN graph, while the latter expects a valid string serialized PENMAN graph, and the response is a JSON object containing the sentence. To ease the usage of the RESTful APIs, the full documentation is accessible through the SPRING Web interface, i.e., `API-Doc` from the header menu bar.

4 Evaluation

For the purposes of this demo, we examine different variants of SPRING to ensure: i) high performance, ii) high generalizability across domains, and iii) efficient and light SPRING Online Services.

Datasets. To deal with i) and ii), we perform experiments with the AMR 3.0 (LDC2020T02[3]) benchmark – currently the largest AMR-annotated corpus which includes and corrects both of its previous inferior-sized versions, i.e., AMR 2.0 and AMR 1.0. In addition to this, motivated by AMR-based approaches in biomedical applications (Rao et al., 2017; Bonial et al., 2020b), we jointly train and evaluate SPRING in the Bio-AMR[4] corpus (May and Priyadarshi, 2017) as well.

Systems. While Bevilacqua et al. (2021a) train one specular model for each of the AMR tasks (henceforth $\text{SPRING}_{\text{uni}}$, denoting unidirectional), to satisfy the point iii) above, we train a version of SPRING that handles both AMR parsing and generation with the same model (henceforth $\text{SPRING}_{\text{bi}}$, denoting bidirectional). This allows us to load into memory only one model to perform both tasks, thus decreasing the potential overload of the server where the demo resides, as well as enabling lower memory footprint for users employing SPRING with our Python code. To train SPRING variants, we employ the same hyperparameters as in Bevilacqua et al. (2021a). In addition, we summarize the state-of-the-art systems on AMR 3.0.

[3]catalog.ldc.upenn.edu/LDC2020T02

[4]amr.isi.edu/download.html

Parsing	Lyu et al. (2020)	75.8
	Zhou et al. (2021)	81.2
	SPRING (Bevilacqua et al., 2021a)	**83.0**
Generation	Zhang et al. (2020)	34.3
	T5 Fine-Tune (Ribeiro et al., 2021)	41.6
	STRUCTADAPT-RGCN (Ribeiro et al., 2021)	**48.0**
	SPRING (Bevilacqua et al., 2021a)	44.9

Table 1: Comparison with literature on AMR 3.0.

			AMR 3.0		Bio-AMR	
		Train dataset	Dev	Test	Dev	Test
Parsing	$SPRING_{uni}$	AMR 3.0	83.9	82.6	60.6	60.6
	$SPRING_{bi}$	AMR 3.0	83.6	82.3	60.5	59.2
	$SPRING_{uni}$	Bio+AMR 3.0	83.9	82.5	**80.0**	80.1
	$SPRING_{bi}$	Bio+AMR 3.0	**84.1**	**82.7**	79.5	**80.2**
Generation	$SPRING_{uni}$	AMR 3.0	45.0	44.9	22.9	19.4
	$SPRING_{bi}$	AMR 3.0	43.9	44.5	21.1	17.1
	$SPRING_{uni}$	Bio+AMR 3.0	**45.3**	**45.7**	**39.5**	**43.5**
	$SPRING_{bi}$	Bio+AMR 3.0	44.3	45.0	38.5	42.0

Table 2: SPRING variants in AMR 3.0 and Bio-AMR.

Results. We report Smatch (Cai and Knight, 2013) and BLEU (Papineni et al., 2002) scores for AMR parsing and generation, respectively. In Table 1 we summarize the performances of recent systems in the literature on the AMR 3.0 parsing and generation tasks. In *parsing*, SPRING achieves the highest results across the board. In fact, we note that Zhou et al. (2021) was published after Bevilacqua et al. (2021a), yet SPRING remains the best-performing parser in the literature to date. In *generation*, instead, SPRING attains considerably higher results than Zhang et al. (2020) and T5 Fine-Tune (Ribeiro et al., 2021) models. In fact, while the latter has a comparable architecture to that of SPRING due to its use of the pretrained sequence-to-sequence T5 model (Raffel et al., 2019), SPRING nevertheless outperforms it by 3.3 BLEU points. SPRING obtains lower results than the recent STRUCTADAPT-RGCN (Ribeiro et al., 2021) model, which, however, achieved those results at the expense of a more complex architecture with a higher number of parameters than SPRING. In Table 2 we report the performance of SPRING variants, i.e., $SPRING_{uni}$ and $SPRING_{bi}$, trained on AMR 3.0 or on the concatenation of Bio-AMR and AMR 3.0 (Bio+AMR 3.0) and when evaluated in development and test splits of each. Notice that the results of $SPRING_{uni}$ in AMR 3.0 parsing are different from those reported in Table 1, since here, as we recall from Section 2.3, we do not perform Entity Linking in postprocessing for the purpose of simplicity. Firstly, SPRING models trained on Bio+AMR 3.0 achieve the highest results overall. Then, $SPRING_{bi}$ performs on a par with or slightly worse than $SPRING_{uni}$ in parsing and generation, respectively. We choose the best model for the SPRING Online Services based on the Smatch score on the development set of AMR 3.0, i.e, $SPRING_{bi}$ trained on Bio+AMR 3.0 for both parsing and generation jointly. This model allows for the achievement of all the goals we set at the beginning of this Section: performance, generalizability and efficiency. Furthermore, we release the additional model checkpoints to be used with the original SPRING Python code, available at `https://github.com/SapienzaNLP/spring`.

5 Related Work

With a view to demonstrating the progress made in AMR, over the years different Web services for state-of-the-art AMR systems (Konstas et al., 2017; Damonte et al., 2017; Damonte and Cohen, 2019) have been developed. Similarly to SPRING, Konstas et al. (2017), proposed an encoder-decoder system to perform both parsing and generation by relying on data augmentation techniques. This system is associated with a demo[5] to only parse into or generate from AMR and does not provide extra functionalities, RESTful APIs, or any interaction with the users. Similarly, Damonte et al. (2017) and Damonte and Cohen (2019) do not provide other functionalities in their demos beside parsing (Damonte et al., 2017, AMREager)[6] and generation (Damonte and Cohen, 2019, AMRGen)[7]. However, SPRING outperforms the aforementioned systems by more than 20 points in both, Smatch for AMR parsing and BLEU for AMR generation. In addition, through SPRING Online Services we provide a highly-interactive Web interface, RESTful APIs, and the feedback mechanism.

6 Conclusion

With this paper we make available SPRING Online Services, with which we bring state-of-the-art AMR systems into the hands of the community, providing a highly interactive interface and easily integrable APIs. Our SPRING system ob-

[5] Inactive link: www.ikonstas.net/index.php?page=demos
[6] AMREager: bollin.inf.ed.ac.uk/amreager.html
[7] AMRGen: bollin.inf.ed.ac.uk/amrgen.html

tains results in the same ballpark as the state of the art in both AMR-to-Text and Text-to-AMR, using the same weights for both. Moreover, our model obtains very strong results in the biomedical domain, providing a powerful tool for building applications. In the future, we intend to extend the services across languages following techniques as in Blloshmi et al. (2020) and Procopio et al. (2021). We make SPRING Online Services available at `http://nlp.uniroma1.it/spring`.

Acknowledgments

The authors gratefully acknowledge the support of the ERC Consolidator Grant MOUSSE No. 726487, the ELEXIS project No. 731015 and the European Language Grid project No. 825627 (Universal Semantic Annotator, USeA) under the European Union's Horizon 2020 research and innovation programme.

References

Laura Banarescu, Claire Bonial, Shu Cai, Madalina Georgescu, Kira Griffitt, Ulf Hermjakob, Kevin Knight, Philipp Koehn, Martha Palmer, and Nathan Schneider. 2013. Abstract Meaning Representation for sembanking. In *Proceedings of the 7th Linguistic Annotation Workshop and Interoperability with Discourse*, pages 178–186, Sofia, Bulgaria. Association for Computational Linguistics.

Edoardo Barba, Luigi Procopio, and Roberto Navigli. 2021. ConSeC: Word Sense Disambiguation as Continuous Sense Comprehension. In *Proceedings of the 2021 Conference on Empirical Methods in Natural Language Processing (EMNLP)*, Punta Cana, Dominican Republic. Association for Computational Linguistics.

Michele Bevilacqua, Rexhina Blloshmi, and Roberto Navigli. 2021a. One SPRING to Rule Them Both: Symmetric AMR Semantic Parsing and Generation without a Complex Pipeline. *Proceedings of the AAAI Conference on Artificial Intelligence*, 35(14):12564–12573.

Michele Bevilacqua, Tommaso Pasini, Alessandro Raganato, and Roberto Navigli. 2021b. Recent trends in word sense disambiguation: A survey. In *Proceedings of the Thirtieth International Joint Conference on Artificial Intelligence, IJCAI 2021, Virtual Event / Montreal, Canada, 19-27 August 2021*, pages 4330–4338. ijcai.org.

Rexhina Blloshmi, Simone Conia, Rocco Tripodi, and Roberto Navigli. 2021. Generating senses and roles: An end-to-end model for dependency- and span-based semantic role labeling. In *Proceedings of the Thirtieth International Joint Conference on Artificial Intelligence, IJCAI 2021, Virtual Event / Montreal, Canada, 19-27 August 2021*, pages 3786–3793. ijcai.org.

Rexhina Blloshmi, Rocco Tripodi, and Roberto Navigli. 2020. XL-AMR: Enabling cross-lingual AMR parsing with transfer learning techniques. In *Proceedings of the 2020 Conference on Empirical Methods in Natural Language Processing (EMNLP)*, pages 2487–2500, Online. Association for Computational Linguistics.

Claire Bonial, Lucia Donatelli, Mitchell Abrams, Stephanie M. Lukin, Stephen Tratz, Matthew Marge, Ron Artstein, David Traum, and Clare Voss. 2020a. Dialogue-AMR: Abstract Meaning Representation for dialogue. In *Proceedings of the 12th Language Resources and Evaluation Conference*, pages 684–695, Marseille, France. European Language Resources Association.

Claire Bonial, Stephanie M. Lukin, David Doughty, Steven Hill, and Clare Voss. 2020b. InfoForager: Leveraging semantic search with AMR for COVID-19 research. In *Proceedings of the Second International Workshop on Designing Meaning Representations*, pages 67–77, Barcelona Spain (online). Association for Computational Linguistics.

Deng Cai and Wai Lam. 2020. AMR parsing via graph-sequence iterative inference. In *Proceedings of the 58th Annual Meeting of the Association for Computational Linguistics*, pages 1290–1301, Online. Association for Computational Linguistics.

Shu Cai and Kevin Knight. 2013. Smatch: an evaluation metric for semantic feature structures. In *Proceedings of the 51st Annual Meeting of the Association for Computational Linguistics (Volume 2: Short Papers)*, pages 748–752, Sofia, Bulgaria. Association for Computational Linguistics.

Simone Conia, Andrea Bacciu, and Roberto Navigli. 2021. Unifying cross-lingual semantic role labeling with heterogeneous linguistic resources. In *Proceedings of the 2021 Conference of the North American Chapter of the Association for Computational Linguistics: Human Language Technologies*, pages 338–351, Online. Association for Computational Linguistics.

Marco Damonte and Shay B. Cohen. 2019. Structural neural encoders for AMR-to-text generation. In *Proceedings of the 2019 Conference of the North American Chapter of the Association for Computational Linguistics: Human Language Technologies, Volume 1 (Long and Short Papers)*, pages 3649–3658, Minneapolis, Minnesota. Association for Computational Linguistics.

Marco Damonte, Shay B. Cohen, and Giorgio Satta. 2017. An incremental parser for Abstract Meaning Representation. In *Proceedings of the 15th Conference of the European Chapter of the Association for Computational Linguistics: Volume 1, Long Papers*, pages 536–546, Valencia, Spain. Association for Computational Linguistics.

Jacob Devlin, Ming-Wei Chang, Kenton Lee, and Kristina Toutanova. 2019. BERT: Pre-training of deep bidirectional transformers for language understanding. In *Proceedings of the 2019 Conference of the North American Chapter of the Association for Computational Linguistics: Human Language Technologies, Volume 1 (Long and Short Papers)*, pages 4171–4186, Minneapolis, Minnesota. Association for Computational Linguistics.

Ramón Fernandez Astudillo, Miguel Ballesteros, Tahira Naseem, Austin Blodgett, and Radu Florian. 2020. Transition-based parsing with stack-transformers. In *Findings of the Association for Computational Linguistics: EMNLP 2020*, pages 1001–1007, Online. Association for Computational Linguistics.

Michael Wayne Goodman. 2020. Penman: An open-source library and tool for AMR graphs. In *Proceedings of the 58th Annual Meeting of the Association for Computational Linguistics: System Demonstrations*, pages 312–319, Online. Association for Computational Linguistics.

Hardy Hardy and Andreas Vlachos. 2018. Guided neural language generation for abstractive summarization using Abstract Meaning Representation. In *Proceedings of the 2018 Conference on Empirical Methods in Natural Language Processing*, pages 768–773, Brussels, Belgium. Association for Computational Linguistics.

Pavan Kapanipathi, Ibrahim Abdelaziz, Srinivas Ravishankar, Salim Roukos, Alexander Gray, Ramón Fernandez Astudillo, Maria Chang, Cristina Cornelio, Saswati Dana, Achille Fokoue, Dinesh Garg, Alfio Gliozzo, Sairam Gurajada, Hima Karanam, Naweed Khan, Dinesh Khandelwal, Young-Suk Lee, Yunyao Li, Francois Luus, Ndivhuwo Makondo, Nandana Mihindukulasooriya, Tahira Naseem, Sumit Neelam, Lucian Popa, Revanth Gangi Reddy, Ryan Riegel, Gaetano Rossiello, Udit Sharma, G P Shrivatsa Bhargav, and Mo Yu. 2021. Leveraging Abstract Meaning Representation for knowledge base question answering. In *Findings of the Association for Computational Linguistics: ACL-IJCNLP 2021*, pages 3884–3894, Online. Association for Computational Linguistics.

Hideo Kobayashi and Vincent Ng. 2020. Bridging resolution: A survey of the state of the art. In *Proceedings of the 28th International Conference on Computational Linguistics*, pages 3708–3721, Barcelona, Spain (Online). International Committee on Computational Linguistics.

Ioannis Konstas, Srinivasan Iyer, Mark Yatskar, Yejin Choi, and Luke Zettlemoyer. 2017. Neural AMR: Sequence-to-sequence models for parsing and generation. In *Proceedings of the 55th Annual Meeting of the Association for Computational Linguistics (Volume 1: Long Papers)*, pages 146–157, Vancouver, Canada. Association for Computational Linguistics.

Mike Lewis, Yinhan Liu, Naman Goyal, Marjan Ghazvininejad, Abdelrahman Mohamed, Omer Levy, Veselin Stoyanov, and Luke Zettlemoyer. 2020. BART: Denoising sequence-to-sequence pre-training for natural language generation, translation, and comprehension. In *Proceedings of the 58th Annual Meeting of the Association for Computational Linguistics*, pages 7871–7880, Online. Association for Computational Linguistics.

Kexin Liao, Logan Lebanoff, and Fei Liu. 2018. Abstract Meaning Representation for multi-document summarization. In *Proceedings of the 27th International Conference on Computational Linguistics*, pages 1178–1190, Santa Fe, New Mexico, USA. Association for Computational Linguistics.

Jungwoo Lim, Dongsuk Oh, Yoonna Jang, Kisu Yang, and Heuiseok Lim. 2020. I know what you asked: Graph path learning using AMR for commonsense reasoning. In *Proceedings of the 28th International Conference on Computational Linguistics*, pages 2459–2471, Barcelona, Spain (Online). International Committee on Computational Linguistics.

Xiao Ling, Sameer Singh, and Daniel S. Weld. 2015. Design challenges for entity linking. *Transactions of the Association for Computational Linguistics*, 3:315–328.

Chunchuan Lyu, Shay B. Cohen, and Ivan Titov. 2020. A differentiable relaxation of graph segmentation and alignment for AMR parsing. *Arxiv preprint*, abs/2010.12676.

Lluís Màrquez, Xavier Carreras, Kenneth C. Litkowski, and Suzanne Stevenson. 2008. Special issue introduction: Semantic role labeling: An introduction to the special issue. *Computational Linguistics*, 34(2):145–159.

Jonathan May and Jay Priyadarshi. 2017. SemEval-2017 task 9: Abstract Meaning Representation parsing and generation. In *Proceedings of the 11th International Workshop on Semantic Evaluation (SemEval-2017)*, pages 536–545, Vancouver, Canada. Association for Computational Linguistics.

Roberto Navigli, Michele Bevilacqua, Simone Conia, Dario Montagnini, and Francesco Cecconi. 2021. Ten years of babelnet: A survey. In *Proceedings of the Thirtieth International Joint Conference on Artificial Intelligence, IJCAI 2021, Virtual Event / Montreal, Canada, 19-27 August 2021*, pages 4559–4567. ijcai.org.

Roberto Navigli and Simone Paolo Ponzetto. 2010. BabelNet: Building a very large multilingual semantic network. In *Proceedings of the 48th Annual Meeting of the Association for Computational Linguistics*, pages 216–225, Uppsala, Sweden. Association for Computational Linguistics.

Martha Palmer, Daniel Gildea, and Paul Kingsbury. 2005. The proposition bank: An annotated corpus of semantic roles. *Computational Linguistics*, 31(1):71–106.

Kishore Papineni, Salim Roukos, Todd Ward, and Wei-Jing Zhu. 2002. Bleu: a method for automatic evaluation of machine translation. In *Proceedings of the 40th Annual Meeting of the Association for Computational Linguistics*, pages 311–318, Philadelphia, Pennsylvania, USA. Association for Computational Linguistics.

Luigi Procopio, Rocco Tripodi, and Roberto Navigli. 2021. SGL: Speaking the graph languages of semantic parsing via multilingual translation. In *Proceedings of the 2021 Conference of the North American Chapter of the Association for Computational Linguistics: Human Language Technologies*, pages 325–337, Online. Association for Computational Linguistics.

Colin Raffel, Noam Shazeer, Adam Roberts, Katherine Lee, Sharan Narang, Michael Matena, Yanqi Zhou, Wei Li, and Peter J. Liu. 2019. Exploring the limits of transfer learning with a unified text-to-text transformer. *Arxiv preprint*, abs/1910.10683.

Sudha Rao, Daniel Marcu, Kevin Knight, and Hal Daumé III. 2017. Biomedical event extraction using Abstract Meaning Representation. In *BioNLP 2017*, pages 126–135, Vancouver, Canada,. Association for Computational Linguistics.

Leonardo F. R. Ribeiro, Yue Zhang, and Iryna Gurevych. 2021. Structural adapters in pretrained language models for amr-to-text generation. *Arxiv preprint*, abs/2103.09120.

Burr Settles. 2009. Active learning literature survey. Computer Sciences Technical Report 1648, University of Wisconsin–Madison.

Linfeng Song, Daniel Gildea, Yue Zhang, Zhiguo Wang, and Jinsong Su. 2019. Semantic neural machine translation using AMR. *Transactions of the Association for Computational Linguistics*, 7:19–31.

Simone Tedeschi, Simone Conia, Francesco Cecconi, and Roberto Navigli. 2021. Named Entity Recognition for Entity Linking: What works and what's next. In *Proceedings of the 2021 Conference on Empirical Methods in Natural Language Processing (EMNLP 2021)*, Punta Cana, Dominican Republic.

Ashish Vaswani, Noam Shazeer, Niki Parmar, Jakob Uszkoreit, Llion Jones, Aidan N. Gomez, Łukasz Kaiser, and Illia Polosukhin. 2017. Attention is all you need. In *Proceedings of the 31st International Conference on Neural Information Processing Systems*, NIPS'17, page 6000–6010, Red Hook, NY, USA. Curran Associates Inc.

Vikas Yadav and Steven Bethard. 2018. A survey on recent advances in named entity recognition from deep learning models. In *Proceedings of the 27th International Conference on Computational Linguistics*, pages 2145–2158, Santa Fe, New Mexico, USA. Association for Computational Linguistics.

Yan Zhang, Zhijiang Guo, Zhiyang Teng, Wei Lu, Shay B. Cohen, Zuozhu Liu, and Lidong Bing. 2020. Lightweight, dynamic graph convolutional networks for AMR-to-text generation. In *Proceedings of the 2020 Conference on Empirical Methods in Natural Language Processing (EMNLP)*, pages 2162–2172, Online. Association for Computational Linguistics.

Jiawei Zhou, Tahira Naseem, Ramón Fernandez Astudillo, and Radu Florian. 2021. AMR parsing with action-pointer transformer. In *Proceedings of the 2021 Conference of the North American Chapter of the Association for Computational Linguistics: Human Language Technologies*, pages 5585–5598, Online. Association for Computational Linguistics.

Qiji Zhou, Yue Zhang, Donghong Ji, and Hao Tang. 2020. AMR parsing with latent structural information. In *Proceedings of the 58th Annual Meeting of the Association for Computational Linguistics*, pages 4306–4319, Online. Association for Computational Linguistics.

FAIRSEQ S^2: A Scalable and Integrable Speech Synthesis Toolkit

Changhan Wang*, Wei-Ning Hsu*, Yossi Adi, Adam Polyak, Ann Lee, Peng-Jen Chen, Jiatao Gu, Juan Pino
Facebook AI
{changhan,wnhsu,adiyoss,adampolyak,annl, pipibjc,jgu,juancarabina}@fb.com

Abstract

This paper presents FAIRSEQ S^2, a FAIRSEQ extension for speech synthesis. We implement a number of autoregressive (AR) and non-AR text-to-speech models, and their multi-speaker variants. To enable training speech synthesis models with less curated data, a number of preprocessing tools are built and their importance is shown empirically. To facilitate faster iteration of development and analysis, a suite of automatic metrics is included. Apart from the features added specifically for this extension, FAIRSEQ S^2 also benefits from the scalability offered by FAIRSEQ and can be easily integrated with other state-of-the-art systems provided in this framework. The code, documentation, and pre-trained models will be made available at https://github.com/pytorch/fairseq/tree/master/examples/speech_synthesis.

1 Introduction

Speech synthesis is the task of generating speech waveforms with desired characteristics, including but not limited to textual content (Hunt and Black, 1996; Zen et al., 2009; Shen et al., 2018; Ping et al., 2017; Li et al., 2019), speaker identity (Jia et al., 2018; Cooper et al., 2020), and speaking styles (Wang et al., 2018; Skerry-Ryan et al., 2018; Akuzawa et al., 2018; Hsu et al., 2018). It is also more often referred to as Text-to-Speech (TTS) when text is used as input to the system. Along with automatic speech recognition (ASR) and machine translation (MT), these language technologies have advanced rapidly over the past few years (Tan et al., 2021). Traditionally, these tasks may be used in conjunction to form a system (e.g., combining the three for speech-to-speech translation), but they rarely leverage each other during training. As a result, each application used to have its own dedicated open-source toolkit, for example, Kaldi (Povey et al., 2011) and HTK (Young et al., 2002) for ASR, HTS (Zen et al., 2007), Merlin (Wu et al., 2016), STRAIGHT (Kawahara et al., 1999), and WORLD (Morise et al., 2016) for speech synthesis, and Moses (Koehn et al., 2007) for MT.

Recently, there are growing interactions among these systems in the learning process. For example, Hayashi et al. (2018) and Rosenberg et al. (2019) propose to leverage speech synthesis systems to generate paired text and speech data for ASR training; Tjandra et al. (2017), Hori et al. (2019), and Baskar et al. (2019) chain ASR and TTS together to form a loop for semi-supervised learning with cycle-consistency loss; Weiss et al. (2017), Li et al. (2020), and Jia et al. (2019) demonstrate that it is possible to build an end-to-end system translating speech into text or speech in a target language.

Beyond text-based systems, there is also an emerging research topic that explores the use of units discovered from self-supervised speech representation learning (Oord et al., 2017; Baevski et al., 2019; Harwath et al., 2019; Hsu et al., 2021) to replace text for representing the lexical content in numerous applications, such as language modeling (Lakhotia et al., 2021), speech resynthesis (Polyak et al., 2021), image captioning (Hsu et al., 2020), and translation (Tjandra et al., 2020; Hayashi and Watanabe, 2020). This line of research bypasses the need for text and makes technologies applicable even to unwritten languages. However, to interpret the output of such systems - a sequence of learned units, a unit-to-speech model is required. This brings up the need of a framework for broader speech synthesis systems that can alternatively take learned units as input. These research directions can benefit from having a single toolkit with different state-of-the-art language technologies.

In this paper, we introduce FAIRSEQ S^2, a FAIRSEQ (Ott et al., 2019) extension for speech synthesis. FAIRSEQ is a popular open-source sequence modeling toolkit based on PyTorch (Paszke

* Equal contribution.

Proceedings of the 2021 Conference on Empirical Methods in Natural Language Processing: System Demonstrations, pages 143–152
November 7–11, 2021.

et al., 2019) that allows researchers and developers to train custom models. It offers great support for training large models on large scale data, and provides a number of state-of-the-art models for language technologies. We extend FAIRSEQ to support speech synthesis in this work. In particular, we implement a number of popular text-to-spectrogram models, with interface to both signal processing-based and neural vocoders. Multi-speaker variants of those models are also implemented. While speech synthesis often relies on subjective metrics such as mean opinion scores for benchmarking, we implemented a suite of widely used automatic evaluation metrics to facilitate faster iteration on model development. Last but not least, we support a number of text and audio preprocessing modules, which allow developers to quickly build a new dataset from less curated in-the-wild data for speech synthesis.

The main contribution of this work is threefold. First, we implement a number of state-of-the-art models and provide pre-trained checkpoints and recipes, which can be used by researchers as baselines or as building blocks in applications such as text-to-speech translation. Second, we create pre-processing tools that enable developers to use customized data to build a TTS model, and demonstrate the effectiveness of these tools empirically. Lastly, as part of the FAIRSEQ codebase, this speech synthesis extension allows easy integration with numerous state-of-the-art MT, ASR, ST, LM, and self-supervised systems already built on FAIRSEQ. We provide an example by building a unit-to-speech system that can be used for text-free research.

The rest of the paper is organized as follows: Section 2 describes the features of FAIRSEQ S^2. Experiments are presented in Section 3. Related work is discussed in Section 4, and we conclude this work in Section 5.

2 Features

Fairseq Models FAIRSEQ provides a collection of MT (Ng et al., 2019), ST (Wang et al., 2020), unsupervised speech pre-training and ASR (Baevski et al., 2020b; Hsu et al., 2021) models that demonstrate state-of-the-art performance on standard benchmarks. They are open-sourced with pre-trained checkpoints and can be integrated or extended easily for other tasks.

Speech Synthesis Extension FAIRSEQ S^2 adds state-of-the-art text-to-spectrogram prediction models, Tacotron 2 (Shen et al., 2018) and Transformer (Li et al., 2019), which are AR with encoder-decoder model architecture. For the latest advancements on fast non-AR modeling, we provide FastSpeech 2 (Ren et al., 2019, 2020) as an example. All our models support the multi-speaker setting via pre-trained (Jia et al., 2018) or jointly trained speaker embeddings (Arik et al., 2017; Chen et al., 2020). Note that the former enables synthesizing speech for speakers unseen during training. For FastSpeech 2, pitch and speed are controllable during inference. For spectrogram-to-waveform conversion (vocoding), FAIRSEQ S^2 has a built-in Griffin-Lim (Griffin and Lim, 1984) vocoder for fast model-free generation. It also provides examples for using external model-based vocoders, such as WaveGlow (Prenger et al., 2019) and HiFi-GAN (Kong et al., 2020).

Speech Preprocessing. Recent advances in neural generative models have demonstrated that neural-based TTS models, can synthesize high-quality, natural and intelligible speech. However, such models usually require high-quality, and clean speech data (Zhang et al., 2021). In order to enable leveraging noisy data for TTS training, we propose a speech preprocessing pipeline to enhance and filter data. The proposed pipeline is comprised of three main components: i) Background noise removal, ii) Voice Activity Detector (VAD), and iii) Outlier filtering using both Signal-to-Noise Ratio (SNR) and Character Error Rate (CER).

First, a speech enhancement model is applied over input recordings to remove background noise. We used the speech enhancement model proposed by (Defossez et al., 2020) where the i_{th} convolutional layer has $2^{i-1} * 64$ output channels. As suggested by the authors, we additionally used a dry/wet knob, i.e. the final output is $dry \cdot \mathbf{x} + (1 - dry) \cdot \hat{\boldsymbol{y}}$, where $\mathbf{x}$ is the noisy input signal and $\hat{\boldsymbol{y}}$ is the output of the enhancement model. We experiment with $dry \in \{0.0, 0.01, 0.05, 0.1\}$ and find 0.01 to perform the best.

Next, we apply VAD to remove silence from the denoised utterances, as silence can vary in length significantly which causes increasing uncertainty and therefore degrades TTS performance. Silence regions at the beginning and end of the utterances are completely removed. In case we encounter a silence segment in the middle of the signal in where its length is greater than 300ms we replace it with a 300ms artificially generated silence (since completely removing silence regions produces unnatural speech). Silence regions of less than 300ms are left unchanged. We use the open-source implementation of the Google WebRTC VAD (Wiseman, 2016), of which four aggressiveness levels {0, 1, 2, 3} can be set. A higher aggressiveness level removes more silences but comes at the risk of removing partial speech. The aggressiveness level corresponds to the size of the processing window (a larger processing window will make the VAD work at a coarser level and remove silence frames more aggressively).

Lastly, we notice that in extremely noisy recordings (SNR close to zero), the generated denoised samples are often not intelligible enough to train a TTS or contain distortion artifacts. In addition, when setting the VAD aggressiveness level high, speech may be truncated along with silence. To remedy this, we proposed two outliers filtering methods. The first approach is based on SNR estimation. We approximate the noise by subtracting the output of the enhancement model from the input-noisy speech, then we compute the SNR between the two. The second approach is based on applying an Automatic Speech Recognition (ASR) over the denoised speech and compute the CER against the target transcription.

Computation FAIRSEQ is implemented in PyTorch (Paszke et al., 2019) and provides efficient batching, gradient accumulation, mixed precision training (Micikevicius et al., 2017), model parallelism, multi-GPU as well as multi-machine training for computational efficiency on large-scale experiments and enabling training gigantic models.

Quantitative Metrics We provide automatic metrics for fast evaluation in model development. Similarly to (Polyak et al., 2020), we report Gross Pitch Error (GPE) (Nakatani et al., 2008), Voicing Decision Error (VDE) (Nakatani et al., 2008), and F0 Frame Error (FFE) (Chu and Alwan, 2009) to evaluate F0 reconstructions of the generated speech. We additionally, report Mel Cepstral Distortion (MCD), Mel Spectral Distortion (MSD), and CER to evaluate both the overall similarity to the target speech and content intelligibility (Weiss et al., 2021).

(i) GPE GPE is an objective metric which measures the portion of voiced audio frames with a pitch error of more than 20%.

$$\text{GPE}(\boldsymbol{p}, \hat{\boldsymbol{p}}, \boldsymbol{v}, \hat{\boldsymbol{v}}) = \frac{\sum_t \mathbb{1}[|\boldsymbol{p}_t - \hat{\boldsymbol{p}}_t| > 0.2 \cdot \boldsymbol{p}_t] \mathbb{1}[\boldsymbol{v}_t] \mathbb{1}[\hat{\boldsymbol{v}}_t]}{\sum_t \mathbb{1}[\boldsymbol{v}_t] \mathbb{1}[\boldsymbol{v}'_t]} \tag{1}$$

where $\boldsymbol{p}_t, \boldsymbol{p}'_t$ are the pitch frames from the target and generated signals, $\boldsymbol{v}_t, \hat{\boldsymbol{v}}_t$ are the voicing decisions from the target and generated signals, and $\mathbb{1}$ is the indicator function.

(ii) VDE VDE measures the portion of frames with voicing decision error,

$$\text{VDE}(\boldsymbol{v}, \hat{\boldsymbol{v}}) = \frac{\sum_{t=1}^{T-1} \mathbb{1}[\boldsymbol{v}_t \neq \hat{\boldsymbol{v}}_t]}{T}, \tag{2}$$

where T is the total number of frames.

(iii) FFE Combining GPE and VDE, FFE measures the percentage of frames that contain a deviation of more than 20% in pitch value or have a voicing decision error.

$$\text{FFE}(\boldsymbol{p}, \hat{\boldsymbol{p}}, \boldsymbol{v}, \hat{\boldsymbol{v}}) = \text{VDE}(\boldsymbol{v}, \hat{\boldsymbol{v}}) + \frac{\sum_{t=1}^{T-1} \mathbb{1}[|\boldsymbol{p}_t - \hat{\boldsymbol{p}}_t| > 0.2 \cdot \boldsymbol{p}_t] \mathbb{1}[\boldsymbol{v}_t] \mathbb{1}[\hat{\boldsymbol{v}}_t]}{T}. \tag{3}$$

(iv) MCD/MSD These are defined as the root mean squared error of the synthesized speech against the reference speech computed on the 13-dimensional MFCC features for MCD and log-mel spectral features for MSD. Since the reference and the synthesized speech may not be aligned frame-by-frame, instead of zero-padding the shorter one and assuming they are frame-wise aligned as done in Skerry-Ryan et al. (2018), we follow Weiss et al. (2021) and use dynamic time warping (Berndt and Clifford, 1994) to align the frames from the two sequences. The main difference between these two metrics lies in the features they compute distortion on: MFCC features aim to capture phonetic information while removing speaker information, while log-mel spectral features encode both, and hence MCD addresses phonetic similarity more.

(v) CER CER is computed between the transcription of the generated audio against the input text using an ASR system publicly available in FAIRSEQ.

Visualization FAIRSEQ integrates Tensorboard[1] for monitoring holistic metrics during model training. It also has VizSeq (Wang et al., 2019) integration for offline sequence-level error analysis,

[1] https://github.com/tensorflow/tensorboard

		MCD	CER (S/D/I)	MOS
Orig. Audio		-	3.3 (0.2/0.5/2.5)	4.53±0.05
TFM	Char	4.2	6.0 (1.1/1.6/3.2)	4.09±0.06
	g2pE	3.9	5.2 (1.1/1.2/2.9)	4.18±0.06
	espk	4.4	5.3 (0.7/1.1/3.5)	4.17±0.06
	Unit	3.4	6.2 (1.6/1.4/3.2)	4.18±0.05
FS2	g2pE	3.9	4.9 (1.2/0.8/2.9)	4.15±0.09
	Unit	3.4	7.9 (2.7/2.2/3.1)	3.99±0.05

Table 1: **Evaluation on LJSpeech.** We compare autoregressive model ("TFM") with non-autoregressive model ("FS2"), as well as 3 different types of inputs: characters ("char"), phonemes ("g2pE" and "espk") and HuBERT units ("unit").

Audio Preprocessing	Hours	CER (dev)
Raw	44	0.8
DN+VAD-1	33	1.0
DN+VAD-2	32	1.2
DN+VAD-3	26	6.8
DN+VAD-3 + FLT	20	1.6

Table 2: **Audio preprocessing settings on VCTK.** FLT removes samples with CER $> 10\%$.

where transcript and target/predicted speech are visualized in Jupyter Notebook interface. FAIRSEQ S^2 further adds generated spectrogram and waveform samples to Tensorboard for model debugging.

3 Experiments

We evaluate our models in three settings: single-speaker synthesis, multi-speaker synthesis and multi-speaker synthesis using noisy data.

3.1 Experimental Setup

We use either characters, phonemes or discovered units as input representations. To convert texts into phonemes, we employ g2pE (Park, 2019) or Phonemizer (Bernard, 2015) with espeak-ng[1] backend. We use the Montreal Forced Aligner (McAuliffe et al., 2017) to obtain phonemes with frame durations for FastSpeech 2 training, which is based on the same pronunciation dictionary (CMUdict) as g2pE. For discovered units, we extract frame-level units using a Base HuBERT model trained on LibriSpeech[1] and collapse consecutive units of the same kind. We use the run length of identical units before collapsing as target duration for FastSpeech 2 training. We use a reduction factor (number of frames each decoder step predicts) of 4 for Transformer and 1 for FastSpeech 2 by default.

We resample audios to 22,050Hz and extract log-Mel spectrogram with FFT size 1024, window length 1024 and hop length 256. We optionally preprocess audios to improve model training: denoising ("DN"), level-2 or level-3 VAD ("VAD-2" or "VAD-3"), filtering by SNR$>$ 15 and CER$<$ 10% ("FLT") and volume normalization ("VN").

We use MCD and CER for automatic evaluation. MCD is computed on Griffin-Lim vocoded reference and model output spectrograms. We use vocoded references as opposed to the original ones to eliminate the error introduced by the vocoder and focus the evaluation on spectrogram prediction. HiFiGAN vocoders trained on each dataset are used to generate waveforms for CER evaluation. The large wav2vec 2.0 (Baevski et al., 2020a) ASR model, which achieves WERs of 1.8% and 3.3% on Librispeech test-clean and test-other, respectively and is provided in FAIRSEQ[1], is used both for CER filtering and evaluation. GPE, VDE, and FFE are not reported here, because these metrics are more meaningful when prosody modeling is taken into account (Polyak et al., 2020; Skerry-Ryan et al., 2018; Wang et al., 2018). For subjective evaluation, we conduct a Mean Opinion Score (MOS) test using the CrowdMOS package (Ribeiro et al., 2011) using the recommended recipes for detecting and discarding inaccurate scores. We randomly sample 100 speech utterances from the test set and collect manual scores using a crowd sourcing framework. The same samples are used across all tested methods. Each sample is rated by at least 10 raters on a scale from 1 to 5 with 1.0 point increments. Overall, scores for each tested method are averaged across more than 1000 manual annotations. We report both average MOS scores together with a 95% confidence interval (CI95).

3.2 Single-Speaker Synthesis on LJSpeech

LJSpeech (Ito and Johnson, 2017) is a single-speaker TTS corpus with 13,100 English speech samples (around 24 hours) from audiobooks. We follow the setting in Ren et al. (2020) to use 349 samples (with document title LJ003) for validation, 523 samples (with document title LJ001 and LJ002) for testing and the rest for training.

[1]https://github.com/espeak-ng/espeak-ng

[1]https://dl.fbaipublicfiles.com/hubert/hubert_base_ls960.pt

[1]https://dl.fbaipublicfiles.com/fairseq/wav2vec/wav2vec_vox_960h_pl.pt

Audio	Spk.	Red.	MCD	CER	MOS
Original	-	-	-	1.8	4.27±0.07
Raw	LUT	2	4.9	65.2	1.77±0.08
		4	3.3	12.1	2.77±0.08
DN+VAD-3	LUT	2	3.6	9.8	3.34±0.06
		4	3.4	6.9	3.30±0.06
DN+VAD-3 +FLT	LUT	2	3.6	9.7	3.38±0.06
		4	3.4	6.0	3.42±0.05
	Emb	2	3.6	7.6	3.38±0.06
		4	3.5	5.8	3.25±0.08

Table 3: **Evaluation on VCTK.** We use Transformer with character inputs, and compare 3 audio preprocessing settings and 2 types of speaker embeddings.

Audio	MCD	CER	MOS
Original	-	3.0	4.0±0.057
VN	5.3	21.0	2.97±0.081
DN+VAD-2+VN	5.5	14.2	3.22±0.065
DN+VAD-2+FLT+VN	5.4	12.7	3.17±0.056

Table 4: **Evaluation on Common Voice English portion (top 200 speakers only).** We use Transformer model with phoneme (g2pE) inputs and compare 3 audio preprocessing settings.

On this de-facto standard benchmark, we compare autoregressive model (Transformer, "TFM") with non-autoregressive model (FastSpeech 2, "FS2"), as well as 3 different types of inputs: characters, phonemes (from g2pE or espeak-ng) and HuBERT units. We see from Table 1 that FastSpeech 2 performs comparably well to Transformer with phoneme inputs (g2pE), both achieving 4.2 MOS. However, the latter does not require input-output alignments for model training and supports more types of inputs—it achieves 4.1 MOS with characters (no need for phonemization), and 4.2 MOS with simpler phonemes (espeaker-ng). The task falls into the re-synthesis setting with unit inputs. We notice that FastSpeech 2 performs worse (4.0 vs. 4.2 on MOS) in this setting, likely due to the finer-grained inputs and its simplified attention mechanism.

3.3 Multi-Speaker Synthesis on VCTK

VCTK (Veaux et al., 2017) is a multi-speaker English TTS dataset that contains 44 hours of read speech from 109 speakers with various English accents[1]. We randomly sample 50 utterances for validation and 100 utterances for testing, and use the rest for training.

Speech recordings from VCTK include considerable amount of silence as shown in Figure 1 (raw); therefore, silence removal is considered a standard preprocessing step for VCTK (Jia et al., 2018; Cooper et al., 2020). Figure 1 shows silence-removed spectrograms with three VAD aggressiveness levels. We see that a higher aggressiveness level removes more silence, but may also truncate the speech. The dataset durations after silence removal and filtering with CER $< 10\%$ are listed in Table 2, along with the validation CER.

We use this dataset to study how audio-preprocessing and speaker representation affect the performance of TTS. We train a transformer TTS model with a reduction factor (i.e. how many frames each decoding step predicts) of 2 or 4 on three sets of audio: raw data (Raw), DN+VAD-3, and DN+VAD-3+FLT. A speaker embedding lookup table (LUT) is used by default. In addition, we train models on DN+VAD-3+FLT with a fixed embedding (Emb) for each speaker inferred from a pre-trained speaker verification model (Heigold et al., 2016), which would enable synthesizing the voice of an unseen speaker. Results in Table 3 show that increasing the reduction factor from 2 to 4 improves the performance consistently. Specifically, we found that without VAD, the model fails to train when using a reduction factor of 2. Finally, we found that using a pre-trained speaker embedder achieves similar performance than using a learnable lookup table, while enabling synthesizing speech for unseen speakers.

3.4 Multi-Speaker Synthesis using Noisy Data from Common Voice

Common Voice (Ardila et al., 2020) is a multi-speaker speech corpus with around 4.2K hours of read speech in 40 languages (version 4). It is crowd-sourced from around 78K voice contributors in various accents, age groups and genders. We use its English portion and select data from the top 200 speakers by duration (total 226 hours).

The audio data in this corpus is expectedly noisy given the lack of curated recording environments. We explore if speech processing can counteract the negative factors (background noise, long silence, variable volume across clips, etc.) during recordings and improve model training. Specifically, we examine 3 preprocessing settings with Transformer model and phoneme (g2pE) inputs:

[1]https://datashare.ed.ac.uk/handle/10283/3443

	Multi-Spk TTS	Non-AR TTS	ASR	MT	ST	Speech Pre-training	Audio Preprocess	Auto. Metrics
coqui TTS[1]	✓	✓						
OpenSeq2seq[2†]			✓	✓				
ESPnet-TTS[3]	✓	✓	✓	✓	✓		✓‡	✓‡
NeMo[4]	✓	✓	✓	✓				
FAIRSEQ S^2	✓	✓	✓	✓	✓	✓	✓	✓

Table 5: **Comparison of FAIRSEQ S^2 with counterpart speech synthesis toolkits (as of June 2021).** [1] GitHub: coqui-ai/TTS. [2] Kuchaiev et al. (2018a). [3] Hayashi et al. (2020). [4] GitHub: NVIDIA/NeMo. † Archived and no longer updated. ‡ Supporting only VAD for audio preprocessing and MCD for automatic metric.

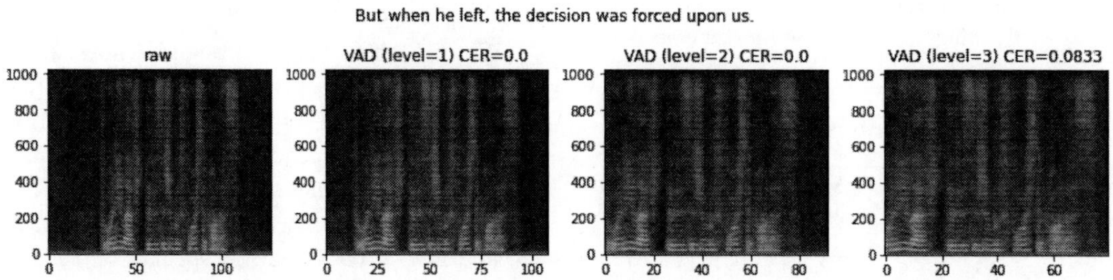

Figure 1: **A VCTK example.** With VAD level 3, the first word "But" is detected as silence and cut off.

VN, DN+VAD-2+VN and DN+VAD-2+FLT+VN. As shown in Table 4, the original audio has 0.3/0.5 lower MOS than the LJSpeech/VCTK one, confirming its relatively low recording quality. Noise and silence removal improve synthesis quality significantly by 0.2 MOS (DN+VAD-2+* vs. VN). Filtering by SNR and CER improves both model fitting (-0.1 MCD) and intelligibility (-1.5 CER) given the removal of difficult training examples.

4 Related Work

There are many existing open-source repositories for speech synthesis. The most prominent toolkits for conventional statistical parametric speech synthesis (SPSS) include HMM/DNN-based Speech Synthesis System (HTS) (Zen et al., 2007) and Merlin (Wu et al., 2016). These rely heavily on feature engineering and use signal processing-based vocoders like STRAIGHT (Kawahara et al., 1999) and WORLD (Morise et al., 2016) to synthesize waveforms from acoustic features (e.g., fundamental frequency, spectral envelope, and aperiodic information). Recently, end-to-end models that take minimally pre-processed features (characters and mel-spectrograms) have achieved superior performance compared to conventional systems (Shen et al., 2018), especially when paired with neural vocoders (Prenger et al., 2019; Kong et al., 2020). There are a number of open-source implementations available on Github [1], however, these repositories are solely for text-to-speech synthesis, and mostly support one model only.

ESPnet (Watanabe et al., 2018; Hayashi et al., 2020), NeMo, and OpenSeq2Seq (Kuchaiev et al., 2018b) are the most similar toolkits that also support multiple tasks. As listed in Table 5, FAIRSEQ S^2 provides more audio preprocessing tools and automatic metrics for building and evaluating speech synthesis models on custom datasets. As part of FAIRSEQ, it can also be easily integrated with numerous state-of-the-art models already provided in FAIRSEQ for exploring novel ideas. For example, we demonstrate that units discovered from a self-supervised speech pre-training model can be used to build a unit-to-speech system that converts output from systems like unit LM (Lakhotia et al., 2021) or image-to-unit (Hsu et al., 2020) to speech.

5 Conclusion

This paper introduces FAIRSEQ S^2, a FAIRSEQ extension for speech synthesis. We believe this extension will allow researchers and developers to more easily test novel ideas for language technologies by providing great support for scalability, integrability, and a wealth of tools for curating data as well as automatically evaluating trained systems.

[1] coqui-ai/TTS, Kyubyoung/tacotron, NVIDIA/tacotron2, Rayhane-mamah/Tacotron2, r9y9/deepvoice3_pytorch

References

Kei Akuzawa, Yusuke Iwasawa, and Yutaka Matsuo. 2018. Expressive speech synthesis via modeling expressions with variational autoencoder. *arXiv preprint arXiv:1804.02135*.

Rosana Ardila, Megan Branson, Kelly Davis, Michael Kohler, Josh Meyer, Michael Henretty, Reuben Morais, Lindsay Saunders, Francis Tyers, and Gregor Weber. 2020. Common voice: A massively-multilingual speech corpus. In *Proceedings of the 12th Language Resources and Evaluation Conference*, pages 4218–4222, Marseille, France. European Language Resources Association.

Sercan Arik, Gregory Diamos, Andrew Gibiansky, John Miller, Kainan Peng, Wei Ping, Jonathan Raiman, and Yanqi Zhou. 2017. Deep voice 2: Multi-speaker neural text-to-speech. *arXiv preprint arXiv:1705.08947*.

Alexei Baevski, Steffen Schneider, and Michael Auli. 2019. vq-wav2vec: Self-supervised learning of discrete speech representations. *arXiv preprint arXiv:1910.05453*.

Alexei Baevski, Henry Zhou, Abdelrahman Mohamed, and Michael Auli. 2020a. wav2vec 2.0: A framework for self-supervised learning of speech representations. *arXiv preprint arXiv:2006.11477*.

Alexei Baevski, Yuhao Zhou, Abdelrahman Mohamed, and Michael Auli. 2020b. wav2vec 2.0: A framework for self-supervised learning of speech representations. In *Advances in Neural Information Processing Systems*, volume 33, pages 12449–12460. Curran Associates, Inc.

Murali Karthick Baskar, Shinji Watanabe, Ramon Astudillo, Takaaki Hori, Lukáš Burget, and Jan Černocký. 2019. Semi-supervised sequence-to-sequence asr using unpaired speech and text. *arXiv preprint arXiv:1905.01152*.

Mathieu Bernard. 2015. Phonemizer. `https://github.com/bootphon/phonemizer`.

Donald J Berndt and James Clifford. 1994. Using dynamic time warping to find patterns in time series. In *KDD workshop*, volume 10, pages 359–370. Seattle, WA, USA:.

Mingjian Chen, Xu Tan, Yi Ren, Jin Xu, Hao Sun, Sheng Zhao, Tao Qin, and Tie-Yan Liu. 2020. Multispeech: Multi-speaker text to speech with transformer. *arXiv preprint arXiv:2006.04664*.

Wei Chu and Abeer Alwan. 2009. Reducing f0 frame error of f0 tracking algorithms under noisy conditions with an unvoiced/voiced classification frontend. In *ICASSP*.

Erica Cooper, Cheng-I Lai, Yusuke Yasuda, Fuming Fang, Xin Wang, Nanxin Chen, and Junichi Yamagishi. 2020. Zero-shot multi-speaker text-to-speech with state-of-the-art neural speaker embeddings. In *ICASSP 2020-2020 IEEE International Conference on Acoustics, Speech and Signal Processing (ICASSP)*, pages 6184–6188. IEEE.

Alexandre Defossez, Gabriel Synnaeve, and Yossi Adi. 2020. Real time speech enhancement in the waveform domain. *INTERSPEECH*.

Daniel Griffin and Jae Lim. 1984. Signal estimation from modified short-time fourier transform. *IEEE Transactions on acoustics, speech, and signal processing*, 32(2):236–243.

David Harwath, Wei-Ning Hsu, and James Glass. 2019. Learning hierarchical discrete linguistic units from visually-grounded speech. *arXiv preprint arXiv:1911.09602*.

Tomoki Hayashi and Shinji Watanabe. 2020. Discretalk: Text-to-speech as a machine translation problem. *arXiv preprint arXiv:2005.05525*.

Tomoki Hayashi, Shinji Watanabe, Yu Zhang, Tomoki Toda, Takaaki Hori, Ramon Astudillo, and Kazuya Takeda. 2018. Back-translation-style data augmentation for end-to-end asr. In *2018 IEEE Spoken Language Technology Workshop (SLT)*, pages 426–433. IEEE.

Tomoki Hayashi, Ryuichi Yamamoto, Katsuki Inoue, Takenori Yoshimura, Shinji Watanabe, Tomoki Toda, Kazuya Takeda, Yu Zhang, and Xu Tan. 2020. Espnet-tts: Unified, reproducible, and integratable open source end-to-end text-to-speech toolkit. In *ICASSP 2020-2020 IEEE International Conference on Acoustics, Speech and Signal Processing (ICASSP)*, pages 7654–7658. IEEE.

Georg Heigold, Ignacio Moreno, Samy Bengio, and Noam Shazeer. 2016. End-to-end text-dependent speaker verification. In *2016 IEEE International Conference on Acoustics, Speech and Signal Processing (ICASSP)*, pages 5115–5119. IEEE.

Takaaki Hori, Ramon Astudillo, Tomoki Hayashi, Yu Zhang, Shinji Watanabe, and Jonathan Le Roux. 2019. Cycle-consistency training for end-to-end speech recognition. In *ICASSP 2019-2019 IEEE International Conference on Acoustics, Speech and Signal Processing (ICASSP)*, pages 6271–6275. IEEE.

Wei-Ning Hsu, Benjamin Bolte, Yao-Hung Hubert Tsai, Kushal Lakhotia, Ruslan Salakhutdinov, and Abdelrahman Mohamed. 2021. Hubert: Self-supervised speech representation learning by masked prediction of hidden units. *arXiv preprint arXiv:2106.07447*.

Wei-Ning Hsu, David Harwath, Christopher Song, and James Glass. 2020. Text-free image-to-speech synthesis using learned segmental units. *arXiv preprint arXiv:2012.15454*.

Wei-Ning Hsu, Yu Zhang, Ron J Weiss, Heiga Zen, Yonghui Wu, Yuxuan Wang, Yuan Cao, Ye Jia, Zhifeng Chen, Jonathan Shen, et al. 2018. Hierarchical generative modeling for controllable speech synthesis. *arXiv preprint arXiv:1810.07217*.

Andrew J Hunt and Alan W Black. 1996. Unit selection in a concatenative speech synthesis system using a large speech database. In *1996 IEEE International Conference on Acoustics, Speech, and Signal Processing Conference Proceedings*, volume 1, pages 373–376. IEEE.

Keith Ito and Linda Johnson. 2017. The lj speech dataset. `https://keithito.com/LJ-Speech-Dataset`.

Ye Jia, Ron J Weiss, Fadi Biadsy, Wolfgang Macherey, Melvin Johnson, Zhifeng Chen, and Yonghui Wu. 2019. Direct speech-to-speech translation with a sequence-to-sequence model. *Proc. Interspeech 2019*, pages 1123–1127.

Ye Jia, Yu Zhang, Ron J Weiss, Quan Wang, Jonathan Shen, Fei Ren, Zhifeng Chen, Patrick Nguyen, Ruoming Pang, Ignacio Lopez Moreno, et al. 2018. Transfer learning from speaker verification to multispeaker text-to-speech synthesis. *arXiv preprint arXiv:1806.04558*.

Hideki Kawahara, Ikuyo Masuda-Katsuse, and Alain De Cheveigne. 1999. Restructuring speech representations using a pitch-adaptive time–frequency smoothing and an instantaneous-frequency-based f0 extraction: Possible role of a repetitive structure in sounds. *Speech communication*, 27(3-4):187–207.

Philipp Koehn, Hieu Hoang, Alexandra Birch, Chris Callison-Burch, Marcello Federico, Nicola Bertoldi, Brooke Cowan, Wade Shen, Christine Moran, Richard Zens, et al. 2007. Moses: Open source toolkit for statistical machine translation. In *Proceedings of the 45th annual meeting of the association for computational linguistics companion volume proceedings of the demo and poster sessions*, pages 177–180.

Jungil Kong, Jaehyeon Kim, and Jaekyoung Bae. 2020. Hifi-gan: Generative adversarial networks for efficient and high fidelity speech synthesis. In *Advances in Neural Information Processing Systems*, volume 33, pages 17022–17033. Curran Associates, Inc.

Oleksii Kuchaiev, Boris Ginsburg, Igor Gitman, Vitaly Lavrukhin, Carl Case, and Paulius Micikevicius. 2018a. Openseq2seq: extensible toolkit for distributed and mixed precision training of sequence-to-sequence models. In *Proceedings of Workshop for NLP Open Source Software (NLP-OSS)*, pages 41–46.

Oleksii Kuchaiev, Boris Ginsburg, Igor Gitman, Vitaly Lavrukhin, Carl Case, and Paulius Micikevicius. 2018b. OpenSeq2Seq: Extensible toolkit for distributed and mixed precision training of sequence-to-sequence models. In *Proceedings of Workshop for NLP Open Source Software (NLP-OSS)*, pages 41–46, Melbourne, Australia. Association for Computational Linguistics.

Kushal Lakhotia, Evgeny Kharitonov, Wei-Ning Hsu, Yossi Adi, Adam Polyak, Benjamin Bolte, Tu-Anh Nguyen, Jade Copet, Alexei Baevski, Adelrahman Mohamed, et al. 2021. Generative spoken language modeling from raw audio. *arXiv preprint arXiv:2102.01192*.

Naihan Li, Shujie Liu, Yanqing Liu, Sheng Zhao, and Ming Liu. 2019. Neural speech synthesis with transformer network. In *Proceedings of the AAAI Conference on Artificial Intelligence*, pages 6706–6713.

Xian Li, Changhan Wang, Yun Tang, Chau Tran, Yuqing Tang, Juan Pino, Alexei Baevski, Alexis Conneau, and Michael Auli. 2020. Multilingual speech translation with efficient finetuning of pretrained models. *arXiv preprint arXiv:2010.12829*.

Michael McAuliffe, Michaela Socolof, Sarah Mihuc, Michael Wagner, and Morgan Sonderegger. 2017. Montreal forced aligner: Trainable text-speech alignment using kaldi. In *Interspeech*, volume 2017, pages 498–502.

Paulius Micikevicius, Sharan Narang, Jonah Alben, Gregory Diamos, Erich Elsen, David Garcia, Boris Ginsburg, Michael Houston, Oleksii Kuchaiev, Ganesh Venkatesh, et al. 2017. Mixed precision training. *arXiv preprint arXiv:1710.03740*.

Masanori Morise, Fumiya Yokomori, and Kenji Ozawa. 2016. World: a vocoder-based high-quality speech synthesis system for real-time applications. *IEICE TRANSACTIONS on Information and Systems*, 99(7):1877–1884.

Tomohiro Nakatani et al. 2008. A method for fundamental frequency estimation and voicing decision: Application to infant utterances recorded in real acoustical environments. *Speech Communication*.

Nathan Ng, Kyra Yee, Alexei Baevski, Myle Ott, Michael Auli, and Sergey Edunov. 2019. Facebook FAIR's WMT19 news translation task submission. In *Proceedings of the Fourth Conference on Machine Translation (Volume 2: Shared Task Papers, Day 1)*, pages 314–319, Florence, Italy. Association for Computational Linguistics.

Aaron van den Oord, Oriol Vinyals, and Koray Kavukcuoglu. 2017. Neural discrete representation learning. *arXiv preprint arXiv:1711.00937*.

Myle Ott, Sergey Edunov, Alexei Baevski, Angela Fan, Sam Gross, Nathan Ng, David Grangier, and Michael Auli. 2019. fairseq: A fast, extensible toolkit for sequence modeling. In *Proceedings of NAACL-HLT 2019: Demonstrations*.

Jongseok Park, Kyubyong & Kim. 2019. g2pe. `https://github.com/Kyubyong/g2p`.

Adam Paszke, Sam Gross, Francisco Massa, Adam Lerer, James Bradbury, Gregory Chanan, Trevor Killeen, Zeming Lin, Natalia Gimelshein, Luca Antiga, et al. 2019. Pytorch: An imperative style, high-performance deep learning library. In *Advances in neural information processing systems*, pages 8026–8037.

Wei Ping, Kainan Peng, Andrew Gibiansky, Sercan O Arik, Ajay Kannan, Sharan Narang, Jonathan Raiman, and John Miller. 2017. Deep voice 3: Scaling text-to-speech with convolutional sequence learning. *arXiv preprint arXiv:1710.07654*.

Adam Polyak, Yossi Adi, Jade Copet, Eugene Kharitonov, Kushal Lakhotia, Wei-Ning Hsu, Abdelrahman Mohamed, and Emmanuel Dupoux. 2021. Speech resynthesis from discrete disentangled self-supervised representations. *arXiv preprint arXiv:2104.00355*.

Adam Polyak, Lior Wolf, Yossi Adi, and Yaniv Taigman. 2020. Unsupervised cross-domain singing voice conversion. *arXiv preprint arXiv:2008.02830*.

Daniel Povey, Arnab Ghoshal, Gilles Boulianne, Lukas Burget, Ondrej Glembek, Nagendra Goel, Mirko Hannemann, Petr Motlicek, Yanmin Qian, Petr Schwarz, et al. 2011. The kaldi speech recognition toolkit. In *IEEE 2011 workshop on automatic speech recognition and understanding*, CONF. IEEE Signal Processing Society.

Ryan Prenger, Rafael Valle, and Bryan Catanzaro. 2019. Waveglow: A flow-based generative network for speech synthesis. In *ICASSP 2019-2019 IEEE International Conference on Acoustics, Speech and Signal Processing (ICASSP)*, pages 3617–3621. IEEE.

Yi Ren, Chenxu Hu, Xu Tan, Tao Qin, Sheng Zhao, Zhou Zhao, and Tie-Yan Liu. 2020. Fastspeech 2: Fast and high-quality end-to-end text to speech. *arXiv preprint arXiv:2006.04558*.

Yi Ren, Yangjun Ruan, Xu Tan, Tao Qin, Sheng Zhao, Zhou Zhao, and Tie-Yan Liu. 2019. Fastspeech: Fast, robust and controllable text to speech. In *Advances in Neural Information Processing Systems*, volume 32. Curran Associates, Inc.

Flávio Ribeiro, Dinei Florêncio, Cha Zhang, and Michael Seltzer. 2011. Crowdmos: An approach for crowdsourcing mean opinion score studies. In *2011 IEEE international conference on acoustics, speech and signal processing (ICASSP)*, pages 2416–2419. IEEE.

Andrew Rosenberg, Yu Zhang, Bhuvana Ramabhadran, Ye Jia, Pedro Moreno, Yonghui Wu, and Zelin Wu. 2019. Speech recognition with augmented synthesized speech. In *2019 IEEE Automatic Speech Recognition and Understanding Workshop (ASRU)*, pages 996–1002. IEEE.

Jonathan Shen, Ruoming Pang, Ron J Weiss, Mike Schuster, Navdeep Jaitly, Zongheng Yang, Zhifeng Chen, Yu Zhang, Yuxuan Wang, Rj Skerrv-Ryan, et al. 2018. Natural tts synthesis by conditioning wavenet on mel spectrogram predictions. In *2018 IEEE International Conference on Acoustics, Speech and Signal Processing (ICASSP)*, pages 4779–4783. IEEE.

RJ Skerry-Ryan, Eric Battenberg, Ying Xiao, Yuxuan Wang, Daisy Stanton, Joel Shor, Ron Weiss, Rob Clark, and Rif A Saurous. 2018. Towards end-to-end prosody transfer for expressive speech synthesis with tacotron. In *international conference on machine learning*, pages 4693–4702. PMLR.

Xu Tan, Tao Qin, Frank Soong, and Tie-Yan Liu. 2021. A survey on neural speech synthesis. *arXiv preprint arXiv:2106.15561*.

Andros Tjandra, Sakriani Sakti, and Satoshi Nakamura. 2017. Listening while speaking: Speech chain by deep learning. In *2017 IEEE Automatic Speech Recognition and Understanding Workshop (ASRU)*, pages 301–308. IEEE.

Andros Tjandra, Sakriani Sakti, and Satoshi Nakamura. 2020. Speech-to-speech translation without text.

Christophe Veaux, Junichi Yamagishi, Kirsten MacDonald, et al. 2017. Superseded-cstr vctk corpus: English multi-speaker corpus for cstr voice cloning toolkit.

Changhan Wang, Anirudh Jain, Danlu Chen, and Jiatao Gu. 2019. VizSeq: a visual analysis toolkit for text generation tasks. In *Proceedings of the 2019 Conference on Empirical Methods in Natural Language Processing and the 9th International Joint Conference on Natural Language Processing (EMNLP-IJCNLP): System Demonstrations*, pages 253–258, Hong Kong, China. Association for Computational Linguistics.

Changhan Wang, Yun Tang, Xutai Ma, Anne Wu, Dmytro Okhonko, and Juan Pino. 2020. Fairseq s2t: Fast speech-to-text modeling with fairseq. In *Proceedings of the 1st Conference of the Asia-Pacific Chapter of the Association for Computational Linguistics and the 10th International Joint Conference on Natural Language Processing: System Demonstrations*, pages 33–39.

Yuxuan Wang, Daisy Stanton, Yu Zhang, RJ-Skerry Ryan, Eric Battenberg, Joel Shor, Ying Xiao, Ye Jia, Fei Ren, and Rif A Saurous. 2018. Style tokens: Unsupervised style modeling, control and transfer in end-to-end speech synthesis. In *International Conference on Machine Learning*, pages 5180–5189. PMLR.

Shinji Watanabe, Takaaki Hori, Shigeki Karita, Tomoki Hayashi, Jiro Nishitoba, Yuya Unno, Nelson Enrique Yalta Soplin, Jahn Heymann, Matthew Wiesner, Nanxin Chen, et al. 2018. Espnet: End-to-end speech processing toolkit. *arXiv preprint arXiv:1804.00015*.

Ron J Weiss, Jan Chorowski, Navdeep Jaitly, Yonghui Wu, and Zhifeng Chen. 2017. Sequence-to-sequence models can directly translate foreign speech. *arXiv preprint arXiv:1703.08581*.

Ron J Weiss, RJ Skerry-Ryan, Eric Battenberg, Soroosh Mariooryad, and Diederik P Kingma. 2021. Wave-tacotron: Spectrogram-free end-to-end text-to-speech synthesis. In *ICASSP 2021-2021 IEEE International Conference on Acoustics, Speech and Signal Processing (ICASSP)*, pages 5679–5683. IEEE.

John Wiseman. 2016. Python interface to the webrtc voice activity detector. `https://github.com/wiseman/py-webrtcvad`.

Zhizheng Wu, Oliver Watts, and Simon King. 2016. Merlin: An open source neural network speech synthesis system. In *SSW*, pages 202–207.

Steve Young, Gunnar Evermann, Mark Gales, Thomas Hain, Dan Kershaw, Xunying Liu, Gareth Moore, Julian Odell, Dave Ollason, Dan Povey, et al. 2002. The htk book. *Cambridge university engineering department*, 3(175):12.

Heiga Zen, Takashi Nose, Junichi Yamagishi, Shinji Sako, Takashi Masuko, Alan W Black, and Keiichi Tokuda. 2007. The hmm-based speech synthesis system (hts) version 2.0. In *SSW*, pages 294–299. Citeseer.

Heiga Zen, Keiichi Tokuda, and Alan W Black. 2009. Statistical parametric speech synthesis. *speech communication*, 51(11):1039–1064.

Chen Zhang, Yi Ren, Xu Tan, Jinglin Liu, Kejun Zhang, Tao Qin, Sheng Zhao, and Tie-Yan Liu. 2021. Denoispeech: Denoising text to speech with frame-level noise modeling. In *ICASSP 2021-2021 IEEE International Conference on Acoustics, Speech and Signal Processing (ICASSP)*, pages 7063–7067. IEEE.

Press Freedom Monitor: Detection of Reported Press and Media Freedom Violations in Twitter and News Articles

Tariq Yousef [1] **Antje Schlaf** [2] **Janos Borst** [3]

Andreas Niekler [3] **Gerhard Heyer** [1]

[1]Institute for Applied Informatics (InfAI)
[2]European Centre for Press and Media Freedom (ECPMF)
[3]Leipzig University

{yousef,heyer@infai.org} {antje.schlaf@ecpmf.eu} {borst,aniekler@informatik.uni-leipzig.de}

Abstract

Freedom of the press and media is of vital importance for democratically organised states and open societies. We introduce the *Press Freedom Monitor*, a tool that aims to detect reported press and media freedom violations in news articles and tweets. It is used by press and media freedom organisations to support their daily monitoring and to trigger rapid response actions. The *Press Freedom Monitor* enables the monitoring experts to get a swift overview of recently reported incidents and it has performed impressively in this regard. This paper presents our work on the tool, starting with the training phase, which comprises defining the topic-related keywords to be used for querying APIs for news and Twitter content and evaluating different machine learning models based on a training dataset specifically created for our use case. Then, we describe the components of the production pipeline, including data gathering, duplicates removal, country mapping, case mapping and the user interface. We also conducted a usability study to evaluate the effectiveness of the user interface, and describe improvement plans for future work.

1 Introduction

Press freedom is under constant and increasing attack, even in Europe. Therefore, now more than ever, it is important to monitor developments and advocate for measures to protect press and media freedom. Mapping Media Freedom[1] (MMF) is a project and platform which identifies and documents threats, violations and restrictions faced by media workers across Europe and beyond. The documented incidents include physical attacks, threats of violence made online and offline, legal actions aimed at silencing critical coverage and moves to block access to information or reporting on incidents or denying access to independent and government-critical media platforms. These incidents are published as alerts on MMF and combined with analysis reports they provide an overview of the current state and development of press and media freedom in Europe. This project is run by the Media Freedom Rapid Response (MFRR[2]), a rapid response mechanism against press and media freedom violations in the European Union member states and candidate countries[3]. It provides legal support, shelter, public advocacy and information to protect journalists and media workers. The alliance is led by the European Centre for Press and Media Freedom (ECPMF) in conjunction with ARTICLE 19, the European Federation of Journalists (EFJ), Free Press Unlimited (FPU), the Institute for Applied Informatics at the University of Leipzig (InfAI), International Press Institute (IPI) and CCI/Osservatorio Balcani e Caucaso Transeuropa (OBCT). The project commenced in 2020. It is funded by the European Commission. The MMF alerts guide MFRR to directly engage with and help at-risk journalists and media workers The alerts are submitted mainly by the MFRR monitoring experts, as well as an international network of local partners. However, MMF is also a crowdsourced platform that enables anyone to upload an alert, which is then verified by the expert network before publication to guarantee the reliability of the cases and the comprehensiveness of the published details. In order to support the labour-intensive manual monitoring of incidents, we developed the *Press Freedom Monitor* which regularly monitors and automatically detects reports about press and media freedom violations in vast amounts of online published text sources, namely news articles and tweets. The automatic detection is based on a trained deep learning model. These detected incident reports are then verified by the monitoring experts who create and publish an MMF alert in-

[1]https://www.mappingmediafreedom.org

[2]https://www.mfrr.eu

[3]Further referred here as "MFRR" region

Proceedings of the 2021 Conference on Empirical Methods in Natural Language Processing: System Demonstrations, pages 153–159
November 7–11, 2021. ©2021 Association for Computational Linguistics

cluding comprehensive details and trigger further response actions.

The advantage of integrating automatic extraction processes is that they can use a wider range of sources and provide a faster alert mechanism. This in turn means that more violations can be found and more sources can be provided for each case, allowing a more realistic and reliable assessment of the press freedom situation. Table 1 shows some examples of tweets or news headlines which are considered to be reports of attacks and violations and thus of interest for the experts. We divide our work into a training phase where we describe the data collection and the evaluation of the training data created specifically for our use case, and a production phase where we describe details of the architecture.

This is a #BBC reporter being harassed and chased by a mob. Scary stuff.
Orban-friendly owner gets Hungary independent radio frequency
#Serbia's #Govt #Group #condemns death #threat to #writer and #journalist
A new law in #Germany makes journalists vulnerable to hacking and surveillance.
#Italy #Lazio Incredible, the regional administrative court (TAR) order journalists to reveal their sources!
NEWS I NI journalist Patricia Devlin has - for the second time - received a threat via social media to rape her young son
Demonstrators attack, obstruct #journalists covering #protests against #COVID19 lockdown in #Germany

Table 1: Examples of Tweets and News Headings Considered as reported Attacks.

2 Related Work

Monitoring content published in social networks to detect abuse, harassment, or freedom violations has been the subject of several research projects. (Hewitt et al., 2016), (Anzovino et al., 2018), (Şahi et al., 2018), and (Rodríguez-Sánchez et al., 2020) worked on the detection of misogynistic language and hate speech towards women on Twitter. (O'Dea et al., 2015) developed an approach to automatically detect suicide-related tweets. (Bourgonje et al., 2018) and (Rodríguez-Sánchez et al., 2020) aimed to detect and analyse tweets that contain racism, sexism and abusive language. The starting point was always to define a list of keywords, hashtags, and accounts related to the topic and to collect the relevant tweets using Twitter API. However, the absence of domain-specific labelled corpora drove many projects to manually create their own training dataset to meet their needs.

All the works listed above consider historic or archived data, whereas our crawling process runs continuously and collects almost live tweets and news multiple times a day. Furthermore, our project is distinguished from others by not aiming to detect direct abuses, harassment or freedom violations but reported attacks and violations directed to the specific group of media actors, which include journalists, media workers and media companies.

3 Training Phase

3.1 Data Collection

For the data gathering we use the free Twitter API[4] and the free version of NewsAPI[5]. This enables us to detect violations reported by various kinds of stakeholders, including official accounts with high publicity as well as private accounts, which can be especially helpful in countries where press freedom is restricted, and violations do not get reported in publicly available news media. The filters to query the Twitter API and the NewsAPI were defined in collaboration with the monitoring team at ECPMF, EFJ and IPI. We defined 147 keywords and hashtags based on three groups: (A) hashtags that are directly related to violations of press and media freedom[6], (B) keywords and hashtags related to media actors[7] and press and media freedom[8] and (C) keywords and hashtags related to attacks or violations[9]. The APIs were queried to require a match from a group A element or a combined match of group B and C elements. This combination was defined in order to exclude general content on media actors and press freedom as well as attacks that were not related to press and media freedom. Based on the experience of the monitoring experts, we selected an additional 66 Twitter accounts which frequently report violations

[4] developer.twitter.com

[5] https://newsapi.org

[6] Such as #journalismisnotacrime or #JournoSafe

[7] Such as editor, journalist, reporter, photographer, camera team, blogger, whistleblower, journalism, media company

[8] Such as #mediafreedom, #pressfreedom

[9] Such as arrested, attacked, censored, blocked access, defamation, harassed, insulted surveillance, threatened

	Training			Validation		
Model	Precision	Recall	F1	Precision	Recall	F1
Logistic Regression	0.5802	0.7333	0.6479	0.9482	0.6868	0.7966
Decision Tree	0.5486	0.6494	0.5947	0.8809	0.5024	0.6398
k-Nearest Neighbors	0.6372	0.6000	0.6180	0.8799	0.4421	0.5885
Linear SVM	0.6640	0.6861	0.6749	0.9627	0.5889	0.7308
Random Forest	0.8426	0.4106	0.5521	0.9932	0.2286	0.3716
Transformer	0.7768	0.8274	0.8010	0.9736	0.7659	0.8571
Transformer + CNN	0.7769	0.8324	**0.8036**	0.9559	0.8059	**0.8785**

Table 2: Training and Validation Results for the Proposed Methods.

of press and media freedom.

The data collection process runs multiple times a day and collects approximately 1,000 news articles and 4,000 tweets per day.

3.2 Training

We aimed to train a binary classifier to be able to tell if a tweet or news article is reporting about press and media freedom violations or not. Due to the absence of any publicly available training dataset related to our purpose, we created our own training data with the help of an annotation tool developed particularly for this purpose.

ECPMF manually classified 6,005 news articles and 8,192 tweets. Around 26% of them are classified as relevant. The inter-annotator agreement was assessed for 997 news articles and 996 tweets classified by two different human annotators. We achieved a relative agreement of 84.55% for news and 86.35% for tweets, and a substantial agreement regarding Cohen's kappa (Cohen, 1960) with 0.62 for news and 0.63 for tweets. We excluded from the dataset the examples where the human annotators disagreed.

In the training process, the models were trained on news articles and tweets together. The size of the training dataset was 13,809 texts (5,822 news articles, 7,987 tweets) in total. The models were trained on 90% of the training dataset and tested on the remaining 10%. We trained each model on four different training/testing splits and guaranteed approximately the same percentage of examples from each category. The models were validated on 1,007 feedback items of unseen data created manually by the monitoring experts.

We evaluated several classic machine learning models such as Logistic Regression, Decision Tree, k-Nearest Neighbors, Linear SVM, and Random Forest using TF-IDF representation. However, The results were not satisfactory. Additionally, we experimented with convolutional neural networks (CNN) trained on top of a distilled (Sanh et al., 2019) version of the RoBERTa (Liu et al., 2019) model in addition to the vanilla finetuning of the transformer model. The structure of the CNN follows the architecture in (Kim, 2014). Table 2 shows the results. As we can see, the deep learning models clearly outperform the classic machine learning approaches. The CNN model achieved the highest average *f1-score* and *recall* during the training and the validation on the new unseen texts and was selected to be deployed and integrated into our pipeline.

4 Production Phase

The aim of the *Press Freedom Monitor* as an application in production is threefold: First, and most importantly, it should constantly monitor news and tweets and present automatically-detected reports about press freedom violations to the monitoring experts in a convenient format. Second, the tool should provide support for the monitoring experts when searching for further items that report about the same incident during the verification process. Third, it should help to improve the model by collecting manual feedback about the classified items, which can be used as additional training data.

Figure 1 shows the process pipeline of the *Press Freedom Monitor* in production. The data collection is performed continuously as described above. The trained model is used to detect reported violations within the gathered data. In parallel, duplicate removal, case mapping, and a country mapping based on geocoding is performed to increase the usability of the tool.

4.1 Geocoding and Country Mapping

MFRR is mainly interested in incidents happening in European Member States and Candidate coun-

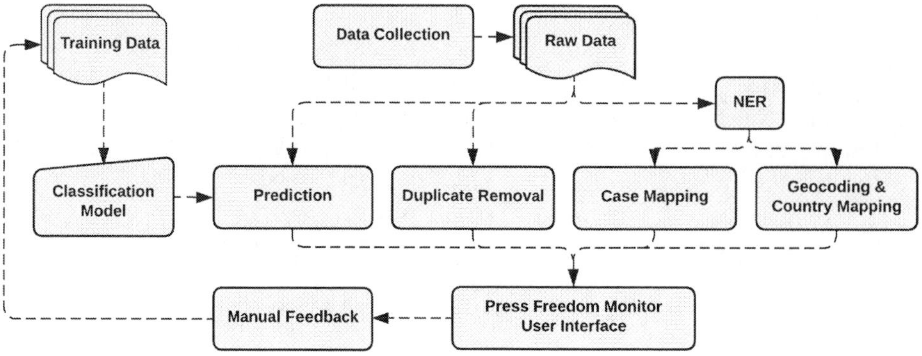

Figure 1: System Architecture.

tries. As the location of the author might be completely unrelated to the location of the reported incident, we aimed to identify locations mentioned within the text. We use SpaCy[10] to detect locations via named entities recognition and translate them to latitude-longitude coordinates using the OpenStreetMap API[11]. The coordinates can then be mapped to countries and to the region of interest. This country mapping was further extended by recognising country adjectives (such as *Italian* or *French*) as well as country names mentioned in hashtags.

4.2 Duplicate Detection

Text reuse is very common among news agencies (Clough et al., 2002). Similarly, twitter users tend to reuse texts posted by other users or republish their own tweets (Castillo et al., 2011). Since these duplicates do not provide an added value to our purpose, but require more resources for analysis and review, they had to be removed from our production pipeline. For this purpose, we employed Locality Sensitive Hashing (LSH) (Rajaraman and Ullman, 2011) based on min-hash signatures and the Jaccard similarity.

As a similarity threshold, we chose 95% to tolerate minor differences. This guided us to detect 1.38% of the crawled news articles as duplicates. Moreover, the fraction of duplicates in the collected tweets was more significant, around 7.9%. The duplicate removal process runs parallel to the data collection process multiple times a day, and it considers all the texts that have been crawled in the last ten days.

[10]https://spacy.io

[11]https://nominatim.org

4.3 Case Mapping

It is typical to find multiple news articles published by several news agencies reporting on the same incident or publishing updates on previous incidents. Similarly, numerous people post tweets on the same incident. Thus, when verifying a certain reported incident, it would be helpful to see related items that are reporting about the same incident. We call this process "Case Mapping". For this purpose, we employed semantic similarity to capture meanings relatedness between each pair of texts even if there are no exact matches among the tokens. Moreover, we used SpaCy, which creates embeddings for each text by averaging the embeddings of all tokens. Then it employs cosine similarity between the two vectors to compute the similarity score. We set 0.97 as the threshold score to decide if two texts are related or not. We chose this value experimentally after analysing the data we have. For now, related news articles/tweets are listed for every single item in the front end and can be accessed by clicking on the button *Show Related Articles/Tweets*.

4.4 User Interface

The user interface as shown in figure 2 is implemented as a web application with restricted access via login. The frontend is designed with regard to the threefold aim of the final tool described above. First, it presents the latest news articles and tweets that have been classified as relevant, showing the most recent at the top. A click on the item shows the full article or tweet in its original context. Furthermore, it provides several convenience filters:

A date filter allows the user to restrict the items to certain time spans. The default threshold for

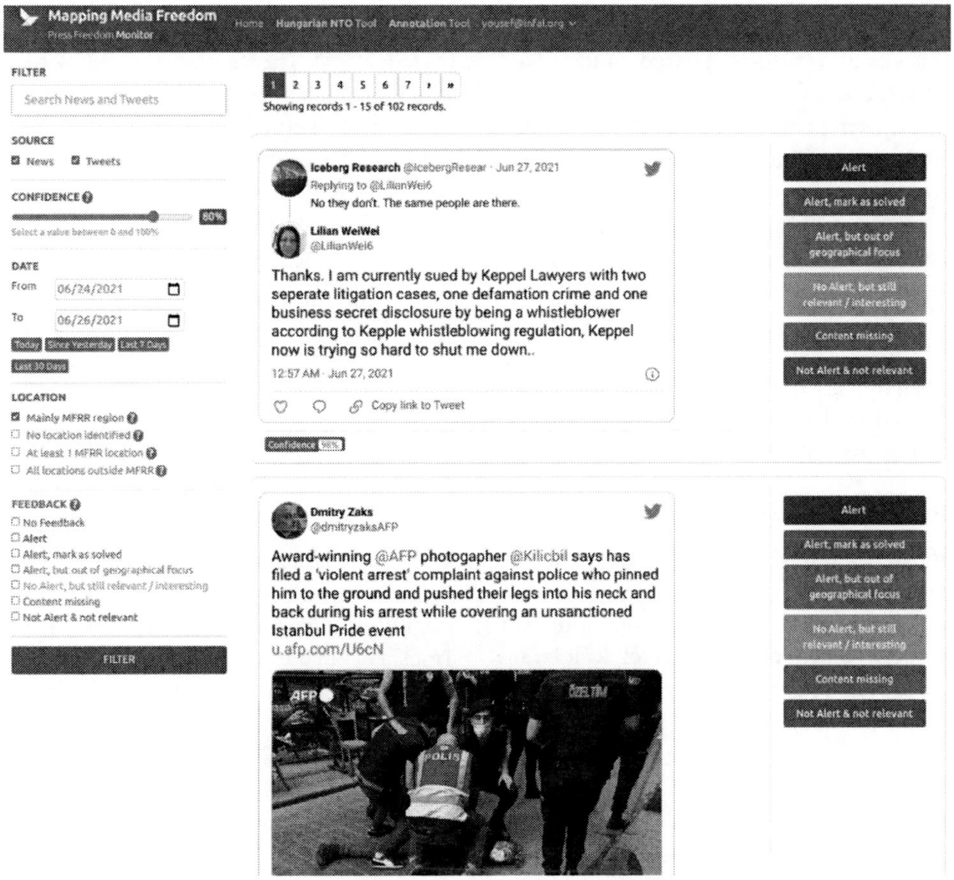

Figure 2: Press Freedom Monitor User Interface.

the prediction confidence is set to 80% and can be adjusted via a slider based on personal preferences connected to the time available to invest in order to find relevant incidents. We developed a location filter to support the filtering for MFRR's region of interest based on the country mapping described above. As multiple countries or also no countries might be mapped to a text, the location filter groups them according to the number and proportion of locations mentioned that fall within the MFRR region or outside the MFRR region. Though all groups might contain incidents within the region of interest, they differ highly in their contained portion. Multiple choice checkboxes allow the expert to adjust the items that are presented, based on their personal preferences and time available.

The second aim of the tool is to provide support for the monitoring experts when they verify an incident and need multiple sources reporting about this incident. If the case mapping analysis described above identifies items that are similar, a button named *Show related tweets/articles* is shown and presents the related items via a pop-up when clicked. The search field can further help to find items for a specific incident when e.g. searching for names of persons involved in the incident.

The third aim of the tool is to collect manual feedback to use it as further training data in order to extend the training dataset and to prevent topic drift. Therefore we implemented feedback buttons which are shown directly beside the item, and which allow the experts to give feedback in a convenient way during their daily work. Beside the possibility to rate an item as being relevant with regard to reporting about a press freedom violation (green coloured feedback buttons) or not (red), there is a feedback button for *No alert but still relevant/interesting* (orange). Items rated as the latter, mainly contain news, events or statements about press freedom violations in general, which can neither be rated as reporting about an explicit incident nor as completely irrelevant. These contents were excluded from the evaluation and will be the subject of discussions with the monitoring experts on whether or how to include such content in the future. As the items can also be filtered based on their feedback, the feedback can also support the workflow of multiple users. One expert can label the latest detected items, whereas the other expert can filter just for the items already rated as relevant and can concentrate on verifying only these incidents. All feedback manually labeled via the green feedback buttons (reporting about a press freedom violation), can be used as positive examples for future training. However, this positive feedback can be further distinguished by the experts to differentiate between relevant and irrelevant items regarding other aspects of their workflow.

4.5 System Evaluation

After the tool was implemented, the front end was used to evaluate our real case scenario of content that held the most interest for the monitoring partners, namely content classified as relevant by the model and reporting about press and media freedom violations within the MFRR region. However, the evaluation went beyond this by manually applying different filter settings to the filters described before. This was performed in order to also include some evaluation of items not classified as relevant by the model and potentially missed, as well as items without detected locations or located outside MFRR countries.

Altogether, ECPMF evaluated 2,572 items via the implemented tool. This evaluated data contains 62% of items classified as relevant by the model and 32% classified as not relevant based on the default confidence threshold of 0.8. *Recall* is important to detect as many reported incidents as possible. A low *precision* would lead to too much evaluation effort for the monitoring partners. Using the keyword filter only, we achieved a baseline of 0.64 for precision and 0.31 for recall. When analysing the evaluated data for a confidence threshold of 0.8, the trained model achieved a *recall* of 0.87 and a *precision* of 0.96 regarding the data that are relevant to our interest. The evaluation showed that the lowering of the threshold from 0.8 to 0.5 would lead to a higher *recall* of 0.91 whilst retaining a *precision* of 0.94, which is still excellent.

5 Usability Study

To evaluate the usability of the *Press Freedom Monitor*, we conducted a usability study with 7 participants. For this purpose, we used the Computer System Usability Questionnaire (CSUQ) version3 (Lewis, 1995). The study showed a 79% overall satisfaction among the monitoring experts; similarly, the system usefulness achieved 79%, and information quality 76%. Moreover, the user interface quality achieved the highest score with 84%.

6 Language extension: Hungarian

By monitoring English language content, we already have broad geographical coverage. Extending the monitoring with additional languages can detect incidents not detected via the monitoring in the English language. We selected Hungarian as the test language, based on the ongoing deterioration in the field of press and media freedom in Hungary. The creation of specific training data for additional languages and the adaptation to language-specific processes (such as NER or geocoding) was not feasible in our project. Instead, we use Google Translate[12] to translate the texts to English and classify them with the model trained for English. To cope with the challenge that the monitoring experts might not speak Hungarian and therefore can not understand the news articles or tweets that are presented, the frontend also shows the translated text for each item first. This allows the experts to assess the content even if they do not speak the language. Again, each item can be clicked to show it in its original context and language for further inspection. Though the Hungarian version detects less content than the English one based on the smaller amount of news and tweets in Hungarian, it has already proved to be a valuable source of information during initial tests and usage. It detected an incident in Hungary and an incident in Germany that were not already known to the monitoring team and also not detected by the English monitoring. The first evaluation of 237 items resulted in a *recall* of 0.8 and *precision* of 0.95 when setting the confidence threshold to 0.5.

7 Future Work

Future work includes the extension of the manual feedback as well as the retraining of the models including this feedback data. A common improvement request by the experts was to further invest in displaying texts about the same incident together. Thus, future work will involve clustering based on incidents to enhance the case mapping performance. However, we need to evaluate how

[12] https://cloud.google.com/translate

well clustering can perform in this already narrow use case with high similarities between different incidents. As the first step, we plan to use the country mapping to present the incidents based on mapped countries. This is already expected to provide a better distinction between different incidents and might result in a first improvement with a good cost-benefit ratio. Furthermore, we want to extend the *Press Freedom Monitor* with additional languages.

Acknowledgment
This work is funded by the European Commission within the Media Freedom Rapid Response project and co-financed through public funding by the regional parliament of Saxony, Germany.

References

Maria Anzovino, Elisabetta Fersini, and Paolo Rosso. 2018. Automatic identification and classification of misogynistic language on twitter. In *Natural Language Processing and Information Systems*, pages 57–64, Cham. Springer International Publishing.

Peter Bourgonje, Julian Moreno-Schneider, Ankit Srivastava, and Georg Rehm. 2018. Automatic classification of abusive language and personal attacks in various forms of online communication. In *Language Technologies for the Challenges of the Digital Age*, pages 180–191, Cham. Springer International Publishing.

Carlos Castillo, Marcelo Mendoza, and Barbara Poblete. 2011. Information credibility on twitter. WWW '11, page 675–684, New York, NY, USA. Association for Computing Machinery.

Paul Clough, Robert Gaizauskas, Scott S.L. Piao, and Yorick Wilks. 2002. Measuring text reuse. In *Proceedings of the 40th Annual Meeting of the Association for Computational Linguistics*, pages 152–159, Philadelphia, Pennsylvania, USA. Association for Computational Linguistics.

Jacob Cohen. 1960. A coefficient of agreement for nominal scales. *Educational and Psychological Measurement*, 20(1):37–46.

Havvanur Şahi, Yasemin Kılıç, and Rahime Belen Sağlam. 2018. Automated detection of hate speech towards woman on twitter. In *2018 3rd International Conference on Computer Science and Engineering (UBMK)*, pages 533–536.

Sarah Hewitt, T. Tiropanis, and C. Bokhove. 2016. The problem of identifying misogynist language on twitter (and other online social spaces). In *Proceedings of the 8th ACM Conference on Web Science*, WebSci '16, page 333–335, New York, NY, USA. Association for Computing Machinery.

Yoon Kim. 2014. Convolutional neural networks for sentence classification. In *Proceedings of the 2014 Conference on Empirical Methods in Natural Language Processing (EMNLP)*, pages 1746–1751, Doha, Qatar. Association for Computational Linguistics.

James R. Lewis. 1995. Ibm computer usability satisfaction questionnaires: Psychometric evaluation and instructions for use. *Int. J. Hum.-Comput. Interact.*, 7(1):57–78.

Yinhan Liu, Myle Ott, Naman Goyal, Jingfei Du, Mandar Joshi, Danqi Chen, Omer Levy, Mike Lewis, Luke Zettlemoyer, and Veselin Stoyanov. 2019. Roberta: A robustly optimized BERT pretraining approach. *CoRR*, abs/1907.11692.

Bridianne O'Dea, Stephen Wan, Philip J. Batterham, Alison L. Calear, Cecile Paris, and Helen Christensen. 2015. Detecting suicidality on twitter. *Internet Interventions*, 2(2):183–188.

Anand Rajaraman and Jeffrey David Ullman. 2011. *Mining of massive datasets*. Cambridge University Press.

Francisco Rodríguez-Sánchez, Jorge Carrillo-de Albornoz, and Laura Plaza. 2020. Automatic classification of sexism in social networks: An empirical study on twitter data. *IEEE Access*, 8:219563–219576.

Victor Sanh, Lysandre Debut, Julien Chaumond, and Thomas Wolf. 2019. Distilbert, a distilled version of bert: smaller, faster, cheaper and lighter. *ArXiv*, abs/1910.01108.

UMR-Writer: A Web Application for Annotating Uniform Meaning Representations

Jin Zhao[1], Nianwen Xue[1], Jens Van Gysel[2], Jinho D. Choi[3]
[1]Brandeis University [2]The University of New Mexico [3]Emory University
{jinzhao,xuen}@brandeis.edu
jelvangysel@unm.edu
jinho.choi@emory.edu

Abstract

We present UMR-Writer, a web-based application for annotating Uniform Meaning Representations (UMR), a graph-based, cross-linguistically applicable semantic representation developed recently to support the development of interpretable natural language applications that require deep semantic analysis of texts. We present the functionalities of UMR-Writer and discuss the challenges in developing such a tool and how they are addressed.

1 Introduction

1.1 UMR Overview

Uniform Meaning Representation is a graph-based cross-linguistically applicable semantic representation that was recently developed with the goal of supporting interpretable natural language applications that require deep semantic analysis of texts (Van Gysel et al., 2021). UMR has two components: a sentence-level representation that is adapted from Abstract Meaning Representation (AMR) (Banarescu et al., 2013), and a document-level representation that captures semantic relations that potentially go beyond sentence boundaries. Like AMR, the UMR sentence-level representation captures the argument structures of predicative events, word senses, as well as semantic types of named entities. It also adds a representation for aspect and quantifier scope, which are not part of AMR. At the document level, UMR represents temporal (Zhang and Xue, 2018b,a; Yao et al., 2020) and modal dependencies (Vigus et al., 2019) as well as coreference. UMR abstracts away from syntactic representations and preserves semantic relations within and across sentences. Building a corpus of UMRs could potentially be very useful to NLP practitioners in multiple fields, such as information extraction and machine translation.

Figure 1 is an example UMR for a short text snippet. Like AMR, UMR is a node- and edge-labeled directed graph, where the nodes represent semantic *concepts* (including word senses, entity types etc.) and edges represent *relations* (participant roles and general semantic relations). The solid lines represent sentence-level relations while the dashed lines represent semantic relations that go beyond sentence boundaries. The direction of the arrows is always from parent to child, at both the sentence- and document level. For instance, at the sentence level, *taste-01* is an eventive concept labeled with the first sense of the lemma "taste" as defined in PropBank (Palmer et al., 2005), and a *person* concept with the name "Edmund Pope" is its *ARG0*. The concept *taste-01* also has an aspect attribute with the value *State*. The pronoun "he" in the third sentence is decomposed into a *person* concept with a person attribute *3rd* and number attribute *Singular*, indicating third person singular. At the document level, the *person* concept mapped from the pronoun "he" refers to the same entity as the *person* concept in the first sentence, as indicated by the dashed line connecting these nodes. The event *taste-01* in the first sentence occurs before document creation time (DCT), as indicated by the dashed line with the red *:Before* label, and in the third sentence, the edge label *:NEG* indicates that Edmund Pope (who corresponds to the *person* node) as a conceiver/source has a full negative epistemic stance (Boye, 2012) towards the *do* event.

1.2 Challenges in Building a Tool for UMR Annotation

As should be clear from the UMR example in Figure 1, UMR is a fairly complex representation that has many dimensions, and we need to address a number of challenges in order to develop a tool that makes UMR annotation practical. First of all, the UMR annotation scheme involves both closed and open vocabularies. For instance, while the relations, attributes, and abstract concepts (e.g., entity types such as *person*) can be selected from a closed set with a few hundred items, sense-disambiguated

Proceedings of the 2021 Conference on Empirical Methods in Natural Language Processing: System Demonstrations, pages 160–167
November 7–11, 2021.

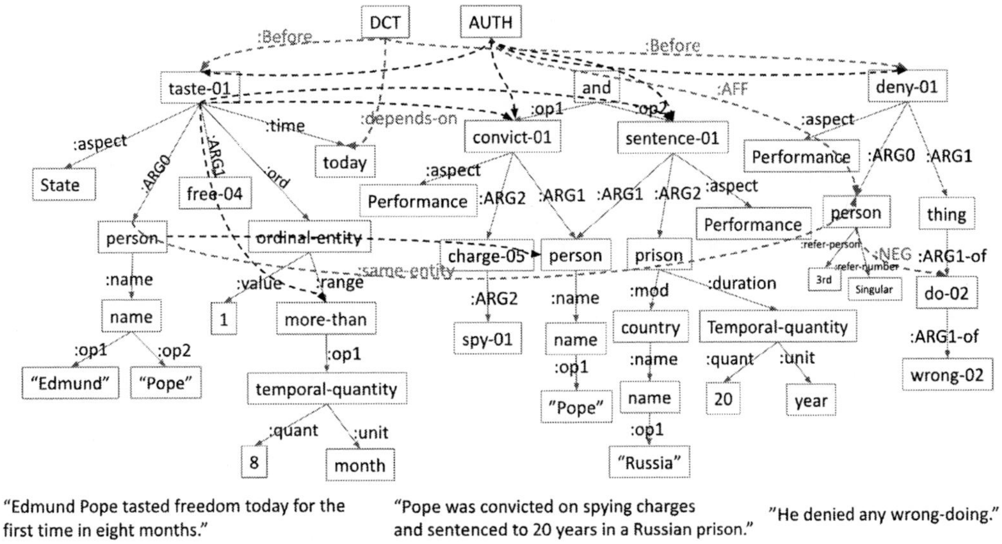

Figure 1: Uniform Meaning Representation

words (e.g., *taste-01*, *convict-01*) form open classes that need to be stored in a lexicon that can be dynamically updated during the annotation. This means that UMR-Writer needs to store both types of annotation resources to support UMR annotation and arrange them in a way that is convenient for annotators to access. Second, as UMR is a graph and thus a highly structured annotation object, UMR-Writer needs to enforce the well-formedness of UMR during the annotation process and does not leave this responsibility to the users. Similarly, UMR-Writer also needs to keep track of the variables that are crucial to the coreference aspect of the UMR annotation and automatically generates and updates the variables in response to user input.

Annotating document-level UMR adds to the complexity of an UMR annotation tool. Like any document-level annotation tool, UMR-Writer needs to present the entire document, which can be arbitrarily long. To make UMR annotation tractable and promote annotation consistency, UMR-Writer imposes an annotation procedure in which the user will proceed in a sentence-by-sentence manner. Another challenge in UMR annotation is that the UMR document-level representation, i.e., temporal and modal dependencies and coreference, needs to make reference to variables for sentence-level concepts. There is also the need sometimes for the user to make corrections to the sentence-level annotation that will affect the well-formedness of the document-level annotation. We design UMR-Writer in a way that any changes made at the sentence-level will result in an automatic update of the document-level UMR if necessary.

As the name suggests, UMR is intended to be a semantic representation uniform across languages, and UMR-Writer needs to support multi-lingual annotation and address the challenges resulting from this need. At a very basic level, UMR-Writer needs to support the display of various writing systems for languages of the world, and this factored heavily into our decision to develop a web-based tool that handles multilingual functionalities by piggy-backing on the web-browsers. Languages are also diverse with regard to their linguistic features, and the amount of linguistic resources available. For instance, some languages are morphologically complex while other languages are morphologically simpler. In terms of data sources, some languages have data from formal genres with well-defined sentence boundaries while other languages only have transcriptions of oral recordings where sentence boundaries are not always as clear. In terms of availability of annotation support resources, high-resource languages like English and Chinese have well-developed lexical resources like PropBank frame files through years of research (Palmer et al., 2005; Xue and Palmer, 2009; Xue, 2006) while low-resource languages may not have frame files at all. UMR-Writer needs to be flexible and allow this variability. To cope with languages that have no linguistic resources at their disposal, UMR-Writer allows UMR annotation of languages without pre-existing computational resources such as frame files or digital lexicons by providing a lexicon-building feature that aids in the development of linguistic resources as UMRs are annotated. To assist less experienced annotators, UMR-Writer presents PropBank frames with argument structure information for each lemma (when available), inferred from the surface forms of a word the user selects. To promote annotation consistency, UMR-Writer only allows the user to select UMR relations from a pre-specified list. This eliminates invalid concepts and roles in annotated UMRs.

2 Related Work

Fundamentally, UMR is a representation based on relations between concepts, and there are a number of tools that support annotation for relations. Some examples include Anafora (Chen and Styler, 2013), MAE (Stubbs, 2011; Rim, 2016), WebAnno (Eckart de Castilho et al., 2016), and BRAT (Stenetorp et al., 2012). Anafora is a web-based tool that supports the annotation of relations between text spans. MAE is a standalone tool that offers flexible and versatile schema support for complex relation sets. WebAnno supports semantic role labelling or event annotations, and it enables the annotation of semantic structures and the handling of rich semantic tagsets. BRAT provides intuitive annotation visualization to help users understand the relations between text annotations. However, all of these tools only support annotation based on text spans, and not annotation that requires transforming word tokens in the source text into concepts in the annotated graph that take the form of (sense-disambiguated) word lemmas, concatenated words, or even abstract concepts that do not correspond to any specific word token in the source text. In contrast, UMR-Writer allows the creation of concepts that are transformations from word tokens in the source text or purely new additions.

AMR Editor (Hermjakob, 2013) is a tool created for AMR annotation and is most similar to UMR-Writer. Like UMR-Writer, it also supports the annotation of concepts that are different from word tokens in the source text. It also makes use of both closed sets of abstract concepts and relations as well as open-class lexicons. However, it offers limited support for languages other than English, and does not support document-level annotation.

3 System Overview

UMR-Writer is implemented in JavaScript interacting with HTML pages, and uses Flask as the server side web framework. It is deployed at Heroku with a Postgres database at the backend to store annotated UMR graphs.[1]

UMR-Writer provides a Graphical User Interface (GUI) that allows annotators to point and select words from the source text, and then select and click to add concepts and relations to the UMR graph. UMR-Writer has separate views for sentence-level and document-level annotation, but the two views share the same underlying data structure. At the sentence level, UMR-Writer makes clear distinctions between the annotation of lexicalized and abstract concepts, named entity types, attributes, and relations. At the document level, UMR-Writer has separate functionalities for annotating temporal and modal dependencies as well as coreference. UMR-Writer allows the user to easily switch between the sentence-level and document-level views with a simple click.

3.1 Importing Source text into UMR-Writer for Annotation

Annotators can upload their source data in the form of single files for annotation from the upload page. UMR-Writer can parse and render plain text format as well as 6 output format variations of FLEx and Toolbox, tools commonly used by field linguists. In addition, the user can also upload an output file exported by UMR-Writer to add more annotation or make corrections. UMR-Writer extracts and retains all information in the imported source file useful for UMR annotation (e.g., morphological segmentation, word-level and morpheme-level glosses, paragraph boundaries, etc.). This is particularly important for field linguists annotating languages that they are not native speakers of. Users have access to all files they have uploaded in their individual accounts. A short sample text comes with every newly registered account for new users to try out the the tool without having to first upload their own data.

The upload page also has functionality that allows PropBank-style frame files (Palmer et al.,

[1] https://github.com/jinzhao3611/umr-annotation-tool

2005; Xue and Palmer, 2009) to be imported into UMR-Writer to support the annotation of word senses and lexicalized semantic roles. So far, English and Chinese frame files have already been pre-loaded into UMR-Writer. Annotators for other languages can upload their own lexicon as support data so long as it is in the FLEx export format.

3.2 The View for Sentence-level UMR Annotation

In this view, the user can iteratively build up the sentence-level UMR graph and UMR-Writer will automatically record the alignment between the UMR concepts and word tokens in the source text. The UMR graph is rendered in PENMAN notation (Kasper, 1989; Goodman, 2020).

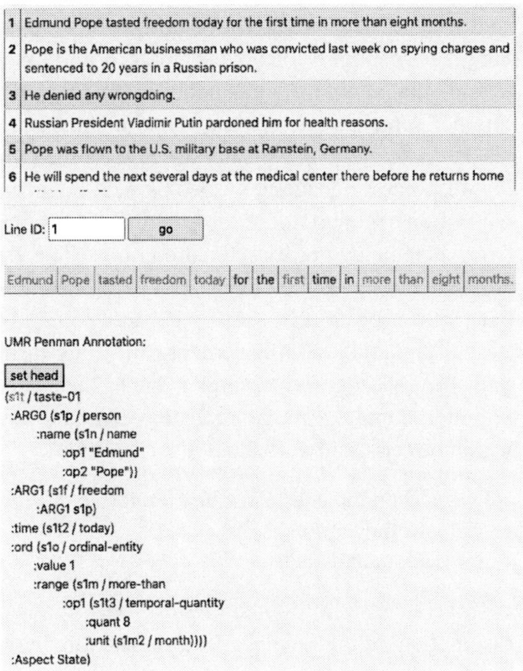

Figure 2: Sentence-level annotation

3.2.1 Building the Sentence-level UMR Graph

The sentence-level UMR graph building process starts with the user choosing a concept as the root node of the graph. After that, the user iteratively builds up the UMR graph by setting the parent, choosing either a lexicalized or abstract concept as its child, selecting a relation between the child and the parent, and adding this "triple" to the UMR graph. Alternatively, the user can also select an attribute for the parent, set its value, and add it to the UMR graph. Annotators can set the parent by double-clicking the node in the partially completed graph. In case corrections need to be made to the UMR graph, the user can enter the editing/deleting mode and modify the graph directly. Possible corrections include making changes to concepts or deleting subgraphs from the UMR graph.

Annotating lexicalized or abstract concepts As seen in Figure 2, the view of the sentence-level annotation varies based on the imported data. Minimally, UMR-Writer presents a single tokenized sentence for the user to annotate. When available, morphemes and their glosses can also be displayed to support UMR annotation. For example, in morphologically complex languages like Sanapaná (Enlhet-Enenlhet, Paraguay), information about which morpheme within a word is the root is crucially important to help annotators choose a lemma form as the UMR concept. When a text span in the sentence is selected, UMR-Writer automatically generates a few concept options for the user to choose from. These options include word senses (if the selected text matches a word in the frame files), a lemma form of the word (when there is no matching entry in the frame files), or a concatenated form (when multiple words are selected in the text span). Annotators can also choose an *abstract* concept from a pre-defined drop-down menu that does not map to any word token but can be inferred from the context. Finally, UMR-Writer provides short-hand buttons for adding named entity concepts to the UMR graph. Named entity concepts have internal structures that are predictable, but usually take several actions to complete.

Annotating semantic relations The annotator can select a semantic relation that relates a concept to its parent in the UMR graph using a "Roles" menu. The range of semantic relations includes lexicalized participant roles such as *:ARG0*, non-lexicalized roles such as *:agent*, as well as other semantic relations that are not typically considered participant roles (e.g., *:poss*, *:name*). More information on where each set of participant roles is used can be found in the UMR guidelines[2].

Annotating UMR attributes Annotators can choose the attribute type (e.g. *:Aspect*) from an "Attributes" menu, and choose the corresponding attribute value in a pop-up "Attribute Values" menu

[2] `https://umr4nlp.github.io/web`

to add the attribute to the UMR graph. For instance, the values of *:Aspect* include both more fine-grained values such as *State* and more coarse-grained values such as *Atelic Process*, which are organized in a lattice (Van Gysel et al., 2021). This makes the tool more cross-linguistically general, because some languages lack overt aspectual marking in their grammar, making fine-grained values hard to distinguish, while in other languages more fine-grained distinctions are overtly marked.

3.2.2 Token-Concept Alignments

As the user selects a text span to create a lexicalized concept, UMR-Writer automatically records an alignment between the text span and the concept in the UMR graph. As it is possible for some concepts to be created out of more than one word token or part of a word token in the source sentence, or even no lexical material at all in the case of abstract concepts, the mapping between word tokens and UMR concepts will not be one-to-one. This alignment is potentially useful for purposes of improving UMR parsing accuracy or for linguists who wish to study syntax-semantic mismatches.

3.3 View for Document-level Annotation

For both sentence-level and document-level annotation, we assume an annotation procedure in which a document is annotated sentence by sentence. The sentence-level representation is annotated first, so that the document-level annotation can make reference to the concepts and relations in the sentence-level representation (Van Gysel et al., 2021). An integrated document-level view of UMR-Writer is shown in Figure 3: the completed sentence-level annotations are displayed on the left, and the document-level annotations in the middle column are created by linking all child concepts in the current sentence to a parent in the previous or in some cases the following sentences. To do temporal annotation (Van Gysel et al., 2021), the user selects a child and a parent which can be either an eventive or time concept, and then identifies the relation (e.g., *:Before*, *:After*) between them based on contextual clues. Similarly, when annotating modal relations, the annotator can select a parent and a child and identify a relation that captures the epistemic strength and polarity (e.g., *:AFF*, *:NEG*) between the parent and child. For coreference annotation, the annotator determines if the parent and the child refer to the same entity/event or one designates a subset of the other.

The document-level and sentence-level view of UMR-Writer are tightly integrated in the sense that any change in the sentence-level graph results in the automatic update of the document-level graph. This way, the burden of ensuring the integrity of the UMR graph is shifted away from the user. This is achieved by storing all the sentence-level UMR graphs for a document in a single data structure. When the user updates a node in a sentence-level UMR graph, all document-level annotations making reference to that node will be updated as well.

3.4 Support for Cross-lingual Annotation

A sentence-by-sentence annotation procedure at both the sentence- and document-level is appealing in that it makes the annotation more tractable for the user and potentially for models trained on the resulting annotated UMRs. However, data from some languages cannot be cleanly segmented into "sentences" that allow us to make the simplifying one-line-per-sentence assumption when implementing UMR-Writer. This is typically the case for data for low-resource languages collected by field linguists, who often segment and transcribe the recordings from their fieldwork by intonation units. The example in (1) shows the English gloss of three Sanapaná intonation units from an oral history recording (Van Gysel et al., 2020). Semantically, they form one predicate-argument complex, but as they were not uttered under a single intonation contour, they would be represented as three lines in the text.

(1) a. Then the cuartelero bird went to eat.
    b. In the lagoon.
    c. Fish, and eels.

If we strictly follow the one-line-per-sentence assumption during sentence-level annotation, in order to capture the semantic relation between the "eat" concept in (1a) and the "fish" concept in (1c), we would have to posit an abstract, implicit concept as its *patient* when annotating "eat", and later link it to the "fish" concept during document-level annotation via coreference between these concepts. We also need to do the same for the relation between "eat" and "lagoon". This would be easy to implement but cumbersome to the user. On the other hand, if we allow the user to annotate semantic relations from lines that are arbitrarily distant, this would make implementation intractable and error-prone. We adopt a compromise and allow the user to annotate semantic relations between two adjacent lines when annotating sentence-level UMR.

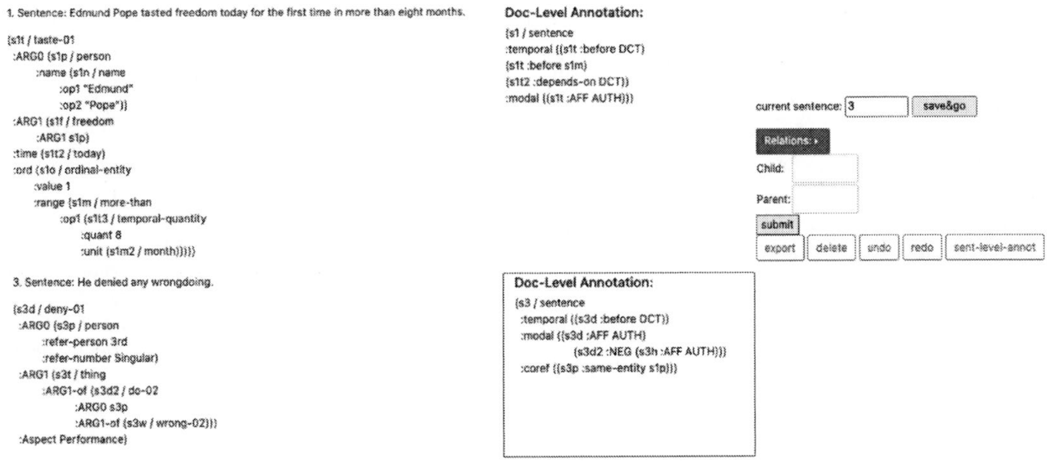

Figure 3: Document-level-annotation

This relieves the burden from the user to a large extent while making the implementation tractable.

This example also illustrates the need to present multiple sentences even for sentence-level annotation to provide enough context for the user to understand and properly annotate a sentence. Even in the sentence-level view, UMR-Writer presents all sentences in the document to serve as context for the sentence being currently annotated.

3.4.1 Dynamic Updating of the Annotation Lexicon

When a user creates UMR concepts from spans of text in the source sentence, UMR-Writer suggests possible concepts by lemmatizing the word token and using the resulting lemma to query the frame file lexicon and retrieve a list of senses for this lemma as well as the semantic roles associated with each sense. When this lemma is not in the lexicon, UMR-Writer suggests using the lemma as the concept. While lemmatization is relatively straightforward and can be done algorithmically for languages like English and Chinese, it cannot be reliably done for morphologically complex low-resource languages. As a result, UMR-Writer cannot make accurate suggestions for these languages, and the user has to edit the suggested lemma before attaching it to the UMR graph. To avoid repeated editing of the same word token, UMR-Writer allows the user to enter a word token and its associated lemma with different senses and argument structure information into a database from a separate lexicon page. This way next time the user encounters the same word or the different inflected form of the same word, UMR-Writer will be able to retrieve its lemma as a suggestion. When entering the lemma for the word token, UMR-Writer can also provide the lemmas for other variations of the same word as a reminder to help the user choose the correct lemma. Different users working on the same language can also share the same lexicon.

4 How to Access UMR-Writer

UMR-Writer now has a demo version that allows users to register an account and use it for their own annotation.[3] UMR-Writer was used in annotation efforts for Kukama, Arapaho, Sanapaná, and Navajo. UMR-Writer is intended to be a tool that annotators can use to create data sets for NLP researchers to train machine learning models, and for linguists to study the semantic structures of language. We intend to make it open-source and make it available to the broader research community. This tool will be released under creative commons under version CC BY-NC. It has been tested by about 30 annotators who are field linguists, computational linguists, or other types of users with UMR annotation tasks for various languages.

[3]The question of whether multiple users can access the same document and generate multiple UMRs of the same sentences or documents came up from our reviewers. Allowing this would be useful for adjudication. For now, each annotator uploads the same source file to their account, makes their own annotation, and then shares the exported file with the other so that IAA can be calculated. Adjudication is a non-trivial task in the UMR annotation process, the specifics of which we are currently working on.

5 Future Development

It would also be useful for UMR-Writer to be made inter-operable with other platforms. For example, FLEx, used by many field linguists for language documentation, offers a convenient way of storing texts, providing morphological glosses, and linking these to the lexicon. Efforts will be made to integrate and work more seamlessly with such common field linguist tools.

We also plan to make UMR-Writer support more languages. We will continue to improve the tool to promote annotation efficiency and consistency as ease of use as we receive feedback for users.

Acknowledgment

This work is supported by a grant from the IIS Division of National Science Foundation (Awards No. 1763926) entitled "Building a Uniform Meaning Representation for Natural Language Processing" awarded to Nianwen Xue). All views expressed in this paper are those of the authors and do not necessarily represent the view of the National Science Foundation. We thank the collaborators of the UMR project for feedback during the development of this annotation tool.

References

Laura Banarescu, Claire Bonial, Shu Cai, Madalina Georgescu, Kira Griffitt, Ulf Hermjakob, Kevin Knight, Philipp Koehn, Martha Palmer, and Nathan Schneider. 2013. Abstract Meaning Representation for Sembanking. In *Proceedings of the 7th Linguistic Annotation Workshop and Interoperability with Discourse*, pages 178–186, Sofia, Bulgaria. Association for Computational Linguistics.

Kasper Boye. 2012. *Epistemic meaning: A crosslinguistic and functional-cognitive study*, volume 43 of *Empirical Approaches to Language Typology*. De Gruyter Mouton, Berlin.

Wei-Te Chen and Will Styler. 2013. Anafora: A web-based general purpose annotation tool. In *Proceedings of the 2013 NAACL HLT Demonstration Session*, pages 14–19, Atlanta, Georgia. Association for Computational Linguistics.

Richard Eckart de Castilho, Éva Mújdricza-Maydt, Seid Muhie Yimam, Silvana Hartmann, Iryna Gurevych, Anette Frank, and Chris Biemann. 2016. A web-based tool for the integrated annotation of semantic and syntactic structures. In *Proceedings of the Workshop on Language Technology Resources and Tools for Digital Humanities (LT4DH)*, pages 76–84, Osaka, Japan. The COLING 2016 Organizing Committee.

Michael Wayne Goodman. 2020. Penman: An open-source library and tool for AMR graphs. In *Proceedings of the 58th Annual Meeting of the Association for Computational Linguistics: System Demonstrations*, pages 312–319, Online. Association for Computational Linguistics.

Ulf Hermjakob. 2013. AMR Editor: A Tool to Build Abstract Meaning Representations.

Robert T Kasper. 1989. A flexible interface for linking applications to penman's sentence generator. In *Speech and Natural Language: Proceedings of a Workshop Held at Philadelphia, Pennsylvania, February 21-23, 1989.*

Martha Palmer, Daniel Gildea, and Paul Kingsbury. 2005. The Proposition Bank: An Annotated Corpus of Semantic Roles. *Computational Linguistics*, 31(1):71–106.

Kyeongmin Rim. 2016. Mae2: Portable annotation tool for general natural language use. In *Proc 12th Joint ACL-ISO Workshop on Interoperable Semantic Annotation*, pages 75–80.

Pontus Stenetorp, Sampo Pyysalo, Goran Topić, Tomoko Ohta, Sophia Ananiadou, and Jun'ichi Tsujii. 2012. brat: a web-based tool for NLP-assisted text annotation. In *Proceedings of the Demonstrations at the 13th Conference of the European Chapter of the Association for Computational Linguistics*, pages 102–107, Avignon, France. Association for Computational Linguistics.

Amber Stubbs. 2011. Mae and mai: lightweight annotation and adjudication tools. In *Proceedings of the 5th linguistic annotation workshop*, pages 129–133.

Jens E. L. Van Gysel, Roberto Álvarez, Florentino Álvarez, Valenciano Cabrera, Cano Carlos, Cecilio Teytaro, Esteban López, Regino Teytaro, and Marty Adamsmith. 2020. Roberto Álvarez talking about the history of the Sanapaná people / Roberto Álvarez contando sobre la historia del pueblo Sanapaná. In Jens E. L. Van Gysel (Collector): A documentation of historical narratives amongst the Sanapaná (Enlhet-Enenlhet) of the Paraguayan Chaco. London: Endangered Languages Archive. Session Date: 25 July 2019. Accessed: 28 June 2021.

Jens E. L. Van Gysel, Meagan Vigus, Jayeol Chun, Kenneth Lai, Sarah Moeller, Jiarui Yao, Tim O'Gorman, Andrew Cowell, William Croft, Chu-Ren Huang, Jan Hajič, James H. Martin, Stephan Oepen, Martha Palmer, James Pustejovsky, Rosa Vallejos, and Nianwen Xue. 2021. Designing a Uniform Meaning Representation for Natural Language Processing. *KI - Künstliche Intelligenz*.

Meagan Vigus, Jens E. L. Van Gysel, and William Croft. 2019. A dependency structure annotation for modality. In *Proceedings of the First International Workshop on Designing Meaning Representations*, pages 182–198, Florence, Italy. Association for Computational Linguistics.

Nianwen Xue. 2006. A chinese semantic lexicon of senses and roles. *Language resources and evaluation*, 40(3):395–403.

Nianwen Xue and Martha Palmer. 2009. Adding semantic roles to the chinese treebank. *Natural Language Engineering*, 15(1):143.

Jiarui Yao, Haoling Qiu, Bonan Min, and Nianwen Xue. 2020. Annotating temporal dependency graphs via crowdsourcing. In *Proceedings of the 2020 Conference on Empirical Methods in Natural Language Processing (EMNLP)*, pages 5368–5380.

Yuchen Zhang and Nianwen Xue. 2018a. Neural ranking models for temporal dependency structure parsing. *arXiv preprint arXiv:1809.00370*.

Yuchen Zhang and Nianwen Xue. 2018b. Structured interpretation of temporal relations. In *Proceedings of the Eleventh International Conference on Language Resources and Evaluation (LREC 2018)*, Miyazaki, Japan. European Language Resources Association (ELRA).

TranslateLocally: Blazing-fast translation running on the local CPU

Nikolay Bogoychev and **Jelmer Van der Linde** and **Kenneth Heafield**
School of Informatics
University of Edinburgh
{N.Bogoych,Jelmer.vanderLinde,Kenneth.Heafield}@ed.ac.uk

Abstract

Every day, millions of people sacrifice their privacy and browsing habits in exchange for online machine translation. Companies and governments with confidentiality requirements often ban online translation or pay a premium to disable logging. To bring control back to the end user and demonstrate speed, we developed *translateLocally*. Running locally on a desktop or laptop CPU, *translateLocally* delivers cloud-like translation speed and quality even on 10 year old hardware. The open-source software is based on Marian and runs on Linux, Windows, and macOS.

1 Introduction

Neural Machine Translation (Bahdanau et al., 2015; Vaswani et al., 2017) is pervasive but has a reputation for high computational cost. The combination of the typically high computational cost, however, has pushed its delivery to the cloud, with a number of cloud providers available (Google, Microsoft, Facebook, Amazon, Baidu, etc.). Using a cloud based translation provider carries an inherent privacy risk, as users lose control of their data once it enters the web. Potential issues include public disclosure due to not understanding terms of service (Tomter et al., 2017), contractors reading user data (Lerman, 2019), use of user data for advertising, and data breaches.

To preserve privacy, we made a translation system that runs locally: *translateLocally*. Once a translation model is downloaded, it does not use an Internet connection. Running locally is challenging due to a number of factors: the model needs to be small enough to download on a user hardware; translation latency can't be hidden by splitting and parallelising the translation of a large documents across multiple machines; consumer hardware has highly variable computing power; availability of GPU computational resources can't be assumed.

We therefore focused on trimming model size and optimising speed for CPUs while aiming to preserve translation quality. The result is fast enough that users see translations update as they type with latency comparable to ping times to the cloud.

Targeting non-expert users, the open-source (primarily MIT) software[1] is also available as compiled binaries for Linux, Windows and Mac from the official webpage: `https://translatelocally.com`. Translation models for several language pairs are provided, while advanced users can add their own models.

2 Design

Our product is based on the Marian machine translation toolkit (Junczys-Dowmunt et al., 2018), heavily optimised for speed with a Qt based GUI.

2.1 Translation Engine

For the translation engine core, we used the same Marian fork as the one used by Bogoychev et al. (2020) for participating in the 2020 Workshop on Neural Generation and Translation's efficiency shared task (WNGT 2020, Heafield et al., 2020). We introduce binary lexical shortlists and streamlined binary model loading to the codebase, resulting in a comparable translation speed, but slightly faster loading time. We also add sentence splitting and formatting preservation are handled by a C++ wrapper around Marian.[2]

2.2 Translation Models

Our models are built with knowledge distillation (Kim and Rush, 2016), use lexical shortlists (Schwenk et al., 2007; Le et al., 2012; Devlin et al., 2014; Bogoychev et al., 2020) to reduce the size of the output layer, 8-bit integer arithmetic, and the

[1] `https://github.com/XapaJIaMnu/translateLocally`

[2] `https://github.com/browsermt/bergamot-translator`

Proceedings of the 2021 Conference on Empirical Methods in Natural Language Processing: System Demonstrations, pages 168–174
November 7–11, 2021. ©2021 Association for Computational Linguistics

Machine	Year	CPU	Cores	WPS
Laptop: Vaio PCG-41412L	2012	i5-2430M	2	1066
Desktop: iMac 27 inch	2012	i7-3770	4	3146
Desktop	2016	i7-6700	4	6548
Laptop: Dell XPS 9360	2017	i7-7500U	4	3378
Laptop: Dell Alienware 13R3	2017	i7-7700HQ	4	5888
Desktop	2019	AMD Ryzen 3600X	6	8791
Desktop	2019	i7-9700	8	9401
AWS c5.metal	2019	2x8275CL	48	70037

Table 1: Translation speed, in words per second (WPS), of the English→German model with 8-bit precision on various hardware. Translation used all cores. The table shows physical core count, not hyperthread count. WPS is averaged over 1M sentences. The timing measurement includes loading time but excludes sentence splitting, which was done in advance for this experiment.

simplified simple recurrent unit (Kim et al., 2019) for decoding.

We tested translation speed on a range of consumer hardware, shown in Table 1, using the million-sentence test set from the WNGT 2020 efficiency shared task and the *tiny11* preset English-German translation model from Bogoychev et al. (2020). This test set is already sentence split, so we did not include sentence splitting and format preservation in timing. Translating a million sentences provides ample opportunity to batch sentences of similar length and use all threads; users translating a few sentences will see slower throughput, but lower latency.

All of our student models available in the initial release are trained with the same *tiny11* configuration preset. Training, knowledge distillation and quantisation instructions are described in detail on github.[3] Users can follow those instructions to train, distil and quantise their custom models, achieving noticeable speedup over vanilla *float32* marian models, although any marian compatible models are supported in principle.

2.3 Language pairs

Our initial release includes 10 language pairs built for the Bergamot project (Table 2). We report average BLEU scores on WMT test sets up to WMT19 (Barrault et al., 2019), for all languages except for Icelandic and Norwegian. For Icelandic and Norwegian we report BLEU scores on self-crawled TED Talks test set, available on github.[4]

Languages pair	BLEU
en-es	35.0
es-en	35.3
en-et	25.1
et-en	30.8
cs-en	33.2
en-cs	25.9
en-de	41.8
is-en	23.7
nn-en	41.7
nb-en	42.7

Table 2: Language pairs and their BLEU scores in the initial release.

The models are distributed together with a lexical shortlist in an archive that is approximately 15MB in size. We are building and adding new models to the project.

2.4 GUI and user interaction

We chose the Qt[5] framework to build our graphical interface. The Qt framework is widely used, open source, free for non-commercial use and in active development. We support building against both Qt5 and Qt6, which allows us to support older Linux software distributions, like Ubuntu 16.04, which do not have easy access to Qt6 packages.

We took a minimalist approach the GUI, where the user is presented with a drop-down menu to

[3] https://github.com/browsermt/students/tree/master/train-student

[4] https://github.com/browsermt/students/tree/master/isen/data
https://github.com/browsermt/students/tree/master/nnen/data
https://github.com/browsermt/students/tree/master/nben/data

[5] https://www.qt.io

select or download models, as well as a resizeable box where the user may input text. Translations will be shown underneath or besides the input text. Translations will start to appear as soon as the user begins inputting text. The view of the first run of the program is shown in Figure 1.

Figure 1: First run view of *translateLocally*.

Downloading models from the Internet is done through a drop-down menu, as shown on Figure 2. In line with our privacy promise, the application only uses Internet access following explicit user action: to retrieve the list of available models and to download a new model. These downloads are static files. The HTTP request includes a user-agent field with the application version number. There is no cookie or other unique identifier. The directory containing downloaded models can also be copied to another machine to setup a system without Internet access; we are planning to ship a version with models included.

Once the model is downloaded, typing in the input box results in a translation, shown in Figure 3.

The application attempts to optimise thread count based on available cores and batch size based on available RAM though these can be overridden by the user, as shown on Figure 4. Fonts can also be changed through an OS-dependent dialog. Retranslating as a user types consumes power, so this feature can be disabled.

We also provide a model management screen where a user may delete downloaded models, or import custom models, as shown in Figure 5.

Our translation engine preserves whitespace between sentences, so users can copy/paste content and get a well formatted text, as shown on Figure 6, which also features the side-by-side view mode.

Figure 2: Select a model to download.

Figure 3: Translation view.

2.5 Distribution

Precompiled and packaged binaries for Windows, macOS and Ubuntu 20.04 are available on the official website. Users may fetch the source code from GitHub and build it on their local machines using *CMake*. The matrix multiplication library manually dispatches SSSE3, AVX2, AVX512BW and AVX512VNNI implementations based on CPUID. However, other kernels like activation functions are currently compiled without multiple versions and will be somewhat faster if compiled explicitly for a particular vectorised instruction set.

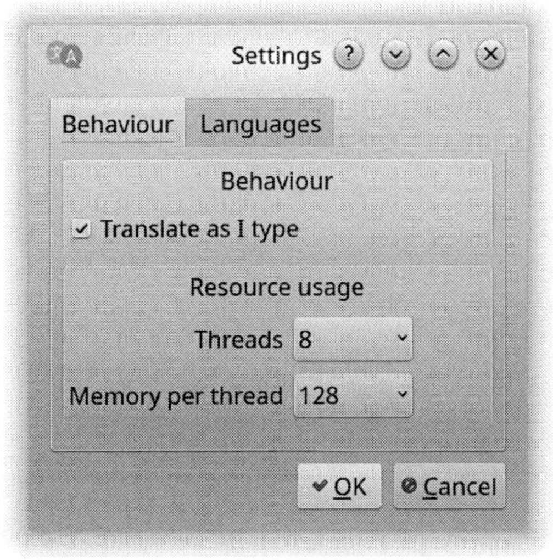

Figure 4: Settings selection for the translation engine.

Figure 5: Model management and import window.

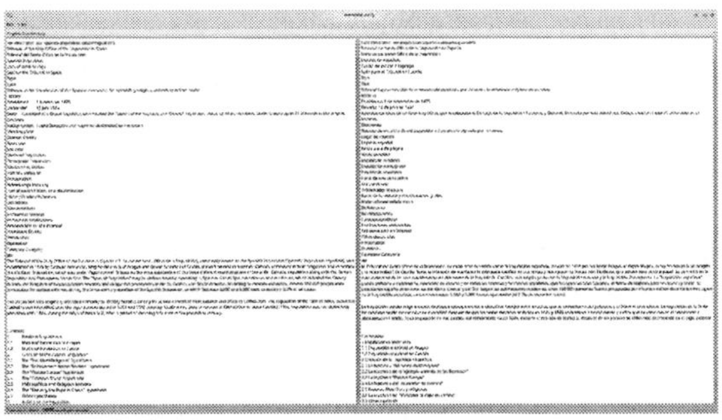

Figure 6: Translating a Big chunk of text from Wikipedia, with preservation of formatting.

3 Comparison against existing solutions

We compare against two existing desktop machine translation solutions: *Argos Translate*[6] and *OPUS-CAT MT Engine* (Nieminen, 2021). They both have slightly different use-cases and support different translation languages. We compare BLEU scores (Papineni et al., 2002) on a WMT19 test set (Barrault et al., 2019) for the English-German language pair, as well as wall-clock and CPU time. We measure only the time necessary for the actual translation. We ignore startup time and issue a translation of an unrelated text before running our test in order to discard any lazy initialisation time.

As only *translateLocally* supports all three platforms, we do pairwise comparison, once on Windows for OPUS-CAT vs *translateLocally*, and once on macOS for Argos Translate vs *translateLocally*.

3.1 Quality comparison

For the quality comparison we used the following models:

- For *translateLocally*, we used Bergamot's English-Germany tiny model[7] which is just 15 MB to download.
- For OPUS-CAT we used the English-German opus+bt-2021-04-13.zip[8] model, which is 275 MB in size.
- For Argos Translate we used their default English-German model which is downloaded through the UI, which is 87 MB in size when downloading.

We compare the BLEU scores on Table 3.

System	Model Size	BLEU
translateLocally	15 MB	41.8
OPUS CAT	275 MB	40.8
Argos Translate	87 MB	34.9

Table 3: BLEU score on WMT19 English-German as well as model sizes.

translateLocally's student architecture, coupled with 8bit integer model compression delivers the

[6]https://github.com/argosopentech/argos-translate

[7]http://data.statmt.org/bergamot/models/deen/ende.student.tiny11.tar.gz

[8]https://github.com/Helsinki-NLP/Tatoeba-Challenge/tree/master/models/eng-deu#opusbt-2021-04-13zip

smallest model size and the highest BLEU score. OPUS CAT has a comparable BLEU score, but the model is more than 15 times larger compared to *translateLocally*. Argos Translate has a much lower BLEU score than either of the two, and a model size that is right in the middle.

3.2 Argos Translate comparison

Argos Translate is based on OpenNMT and supports 13 language pairs, with more planned in the future.

Argos Translate is not fully cross-platform as there are no windows binaries provided. The developers do advertise that it is possible for users to self-build the product on Windows.

Finally, the macOS version is also available through the Apple app store, but it is paid,[9] whereas *translateLocally* is free.

We present our test results on Table 4. Both system were tested on a MacBook Pro 16" 2019, using 8 CPU threads to translate the whole WMT19 test set, which around 40k tokens. CPU time was measured using the Activity Monitor, and Words per second (WPS) is approximately calculated. Argos Translate does not allow the CPU threads to be configured by the user, so we matched the number of threads they use in *translateLocally*.

System	WPS	CPU Time	BLEU
translateLocally	7350	40s	41.8
Argos Translate	76	4378s	34.9

Table 4: *translateLocally* vs Argos Translate, translating 40k tokens for speed benchmark and BLEU scores on WMT19 English-German.

TranslateLocally is about 100 times faster and delivers vastly superior translation quality compared to Argos Translate.

3.3 OPUS-CAT comparison

Just like *translateLocally*, OPUS-CAT MT Engine (Nieminen, 2021) uses Marian as its translation engine. Unlike *translateLocally*, its translation engine is not optimised for speed. Furthermore the GUI is slow when handling large amounts of text. Simply pasting large chunks of text, such as the full "Crime and Punishment"[10] into OPUS-CAT takes nearly as long as *translateLocally* takes to paste *and translate* all the text.

The strength of OPUS-CAT comes from its plugins that integrate it with popular professional translator software, whereas our product does not support any CAT software.

OPUS-CAT has more language pairs available, which could also be used with *translateLocally*, but they are not optimised for speed.

Finally OPUS-CAT is only available for Windows, as it is build using the dot NET framework, whereas *translateLocally* is cross-platform.

For comparing OPUS-CAT vs *translateLocally*, we used a single threaded mode for both applications, as we found no way to force OPUS-CAT to use multiple threads, whether it is through their translation interface, or through their memoQ plugin.[11] We tested on a Windows Machine with 4 CPU core i9-9800H inside Parallels, measuring the CPU time from the task manager. We presplit the input of OPUS-CAT, as it doesn't have its own sentence splitter. Furthermore we excluded the copy/paste time from the OPUS-CAT measurements, as its XAML user interface is bad at handling large amounts of text. We present our results on Table 5.

System	WPS	CPU Time	BLEU
translateLocally	1250	34s	41.8
Opus-CAT	12	3363s	40.8

Table 5: *translateLocally* crippled to run single-threaded vs Opus-CAT, translating 40k tokens for speed benchmark and BLEU scores on WMT19 English-German.

Even with the added benefit of sentence-splitting and ignoring copy/paste time, and forcing single-threaded mode, OPUS-CAT is about 100 times slower than *translateLocally*.

4 Conclusion

We presented *translateLocally*, a desktop translation application, capable of high speed translations on a variety of hardware. Our software provides a viable alternative to cloud translation for users who are conscious of their privacy. Our product is 100 times faster than competing software and has none of the rate limitations of freemium cloud providers. We start with 10 high quality, optimised

[9] Free macOS version is distributed through pip.

[10] `https://www.gutenberg.org/files/2554/2554-0.txt`

[11] `https://www.memoq.com`

models and we aim to continuously add additional language pairs. As our product is open-source and cross-platform, it can be adopted by a wide range of users. The use of Marian as a translation engine allows for users to easily train their own models, potentially facilitating internal use for large organizations.

Acknowledgements

We thank all the researchers and engineers working on the Bergamot[12] project for making *translateLocally* possible, with special thanks to Ulrich Germann and Jerin Philip for their help with making the codebase cross platform, and to Graeme Nail for helping with deployment. We thank everyone who tested the beta version of the application and the reviewers for their comments and suggestions.

This work was conducted within the scope of the Research and Innovation Action *Bergamot*, which has received funding from the European Union's Horizon 2020 research and innovation programme under grant agreement No 825303.

References

Dzmitry Bahdanau, Kyunghyun Cho, and Yoshua Bengio. 2015. Neural machine translation by jointly learning to align and translate. In *3rd International Conference on Learning Representations, ICLR 2015, San Diego, CA, USA, May 7-9, 2015, Conference Track Proceedings*.

Loïc Barrault, Ondřej Bojar, Marta R. Costa-jussà, Christian Federmann, Mark Fishel, Yvette Graham, Barry Haddow, Matthias Huck, Philipp Koehn, Shervin Malmasi, Christof Monz, Mathias Müller, Santanu Pal, Matt Post, and Marcos Zampieri. 2019. Findings of the 2019 conference on machine translation (WMT19). In *Proceedings of the Fourth Conference on Machine Translation (Volume 2: Shared Task Papers, Day 1)*, pages 1–61, Florence, Italy. Association for Computational Linguistics.

Nikolay Bogoychev, Roman Grundkiewicz, Alham Fikri Aji, Maximiliana Behnke, Kenneth Heafield, Sidharth Kashyap, Emmanouil-Ioannis Farsarakis, and Mateusz Chudyk. 2020. Edinburgh's submissions to the 2020 machine translation efficiency task. In *Proceedings of the The 4th Workshop on Neural Generation and Translation (WNGT 2020)*, Seattle.

Jacob Devlin, Rabih Zbib, Zhongqiang Huang, Thomas Lamar, Richard Schwartz, and John Makhoul. 2014. Fast and robust neural network joint models for statistical machine translation. In *Proceedings of the 52nd Annual Meeting of the Association for Computational Linguistics (Volume 1: Long Papers)*, pages 1370–1380, Baltimore, Maryland. Association for Computational Linguistics.

Kenneth Heafield, Hiroaki Hayashi, Yusuke Oda, Ioannis Konstas, Andrew Finch, Graham Neubig, Xian Li, and Alexandra Birch. 2020. Findings of the fourth workshop on neural generation and translation. In *Proceedings of the Fourth Workshop on Neural Generation and Translation*, pages 1–9, Online. Association for Computational Linguistics.

Marcin Junczys-Dowmunt, Roman Grundkiewicz, Tomasz Dwojak, Hieu Hoang, Kenneth Heafield, Tom Neckermann, Frank Seide, Ulrich Germann, Alham Fikri Aji, Nikolay Bogoychev, André F. T. Martins, and Alexandra Birch. 2018. Marian: Fast neural machine translation in C++. In *Proceedings of ACL 2018, System Demonstrations*, pages 116–121, Melbourne, Australia. Association for Computational Linguistics.

Yoon Kim and Alexander M. Rush. 2016. Sequence-Level Knowledge Distillation. In *Proceedings of the 2016 Conference on Empirical Methods in Natural Language Processing*, pages 1317–1327, Austin, Texas. Association for Computational Linguistics.

Young Jin Kim, Marcin Junczys-Dowmunt, Hany Hassan, Alham Fikri Aji, Kenneth Heafield, Roman Grundkiewicz, and Nikolay Bogoychev. 2019. From research to production and back: Ludicrously fast neural machine translation. In *Proceedings of the 3rd Workshop on Neural Generation and Translation*, pages 280–288, Hong Kong. Association for Computational Linguistics.

Hai Son Le, Alexandre Allauzen, and François Yvon. 2012. Continuous space translation models with neural networks. In *Proceedings of the 2012 Conference of the North American Chapter of the Association for Computational Linguistics: Human Language Technologies*, pages 39–48, Montréal, Canada. Association for Computational Linguistics.

Rachel Lerman. 2019. Human workers can listen to google assistant recordings. *Associated Press*.

Tommi Nieminen. 2021. OPUS-CAT: Desktop NMT with CAT integration and local fine-tuning. In *Proceedings of the 16th Conference of the European Chapter of the Association for Computational Linguistics: System Demonstrations*, pages 288–294, Online. Association for Computational Linguistics.

Kishore Papineni, Salim Roukos, Todd Ward, and Wei-Jing Zhu. 2002. Bleu: a method for automatic evaluation of machine translation. In *Proceedings of the 40th Annual Meeting of the Association for Computational Linguistics*, pages 311–318, Philadelphia, Pennsylvania, USA. Association for Computational Linguistics.

[12] `https://browser.mt/partners/`

Holger Schwenk, Marta R. Costa-jussà, and Jose A. R. Fonollosa. 2007. Smooth bilingual n-gram translation. In *Proceedings of the 2007 Joint Conference on Empirical Methods in Natural Language Processing and Computational Natural Language Learning (EMNLP-CoNLL)*, pages 430–438, Prague, Czech Republic. Association for Computational Linguistics.

Line Tomter, Martin H. W. Zondag, and Øyvind Bye Skille. 2017. Warning about translation web site: Passwords and contracts accessible on the internet. *Norsk Rikskringkasting AS*.

Ashish Vaswani, Noam Shazeer, Niki Parmar, Jakob Uszkoreit, Llion Jones, Aidan N Gomez, Ł ukasz Kaiser, and Illia Polosukhin. 2017. Attention is all you need. In I. Guyon, U. V. Luxburg, S. Bengio, H. Wallach, R. Fergus, S. Vishwanathan, and R. Garnett, editors, *Advances in Neural Information Processing Systems 30*, pages 5998–6008. Curran Associates, Inc.

Datasets: A Community Library for Natural Language Processing

Quentin Lhoest*, Albert Villanova del Moral*, Yacine Jernite, Abhishek Thakur, Patrick von Platen, Suraj Patil, Julien Chaumond, Mariama Drame, Julien Plu, Lewis Tunstall, Joe Davison, Mario Šaško†, Gunjan Chhablani†, Bhavitvya Malik†, Simon Brandeis, Teven Le Scao, Victor Sanh, Canwen Xu, Nicolas Patry, Angelina McMillan-Major, Philipp Schmid, Sylvain Gugger, Clément Delangue, Théo Matussière, Lysandre Debut, Stas Bekman, Pierric Cistac, Thibault Goehringer, Victor Mustar, François Lagunas, Alexander M. Rush, and Thomas Wolf Ω

Hugging Face / {quentin,thomas}@huggingface.co

Abstract

The scale, variety, and quantity of publicly-available NLP datasets has grown rapidly as researchers propose new tasks, larger models, and novel benchmarks. *Datasets* is a community library for contemporary NLP designed to support this ecosystem. *Datasets* aims to standardize end-user interfaces, versioning, and documentation, while providing a lightweight front-end that behaves similarly for small datasets as for internet-scale corpora. The design of the library incorporates a distributed, community-driven approach to adding datasets and documenting usage. After a year of development, the library now includes more than 650 unique datasets, has more than 250 contributors, and has helped support a variety of novel cross-dataset research projects and shared tasks. The library is available at `https://github.com/huggingface/datasets`.

1 Introduction

Datasets are central to empirical NLP: curated datasets are used for evaluation and benchmarks; supervised datasets are used to train and fine-tune models; and large unsupervised datasets are necessary for pretraining and language modeling. Each dataset type differs in scale, granularity and structure, in addition to annotation methodology. Historically, new dataset paradigms have been crucial for driving the development of NLP, from the Hansard corpus for statistical machine translation (Brown et al., 1988) to the Penn Treebank for syntactic modeling (Marcus et al., 1993) to projects like OPUS and Universal Dependencies (Nivre et al., 2016; Tiedemann and Nygaard, 2004) which bring together cross-lingual data and annotations.

Contemporary NLP systems are now developed with a pipeline that utilizes many different datasets at significantly varying scale and level of annotation (Peters et al., 2018). Different datasets are used for pretraining, fine-tuning, and benchmarking. As such, there has been a large increase in the number of datasets utilized in the NLP community. These include both large text collections like C4 (Raffel et al., 2020), fine-tuning datasets like SQuAD (Rajpurkar et al., 2016), and even complex zero-shot challenge tasks. Benchmark datasets like GLUE have been central to quantifying the the advances of models such as BERT (Wang et al., 2018; Devlin et al., 2019).

The growth in datasets also brings significant challenges, including interface standardization, versioning, and documentation. A practitioner should be able to utilize N different datasets without requiring N different interfaces. In addition, N practitioners using the same dataset should know they have exactly the same version. Datasets have also grown larger, and ideally interfaces should not have to change due to this scale, whether one is using small-scale datasets like Climate Fever (~1k data points), medium-scale Yahoo Answers (~1M), or even all of PubMed (~79B). Finally, datasets are being created with a variety of different procedures, from crowd-sourcing to scraping to synthetic generation, which need to be taken into account when evaluating which is most appropriate for a given purpose and ought to be immediately apparent to prospective users (Gebru et al., 2018).

Datasets is a community library designed to address the challenges of dataset management and access, while supporting community culture and norms. The library targets the following goals:

- Ease-of-use and Standardization: All datasets can be easily downloaded with one line of

*Lead Library Maintainers, Ω Library Creator, † Independent Research Contributor

Proceedings of the 2021 Conference on Empirical Methods in Natural Language Processing: System Demonstrations, pages 175–184
November 7–11, 2021. ©2021 Association for Computational Linguistics

code. Each dataset utilizes a standard tabular format, and is versioned and cited.

- Efficiency and Scale: Datasets are computation- and memory-efficient by default and work seamlessly with tokenization and featurization. Massive datasets can even be streamed through the same interface.
- Community and Documentation: The project is community-built and has hundreds of contributors across languages. Each dataset is tagged and documented with a datasheet describing its usage, types, and construction.

Datasets is in continual development by the engineers at Hugging Face and is released under an Apache 2.0 license.[1] The library is available at `https://github.com/huggingface/datasets`. Full documentation is available through the project website.[2]

2 Related Work

There is a long history of projects aiming to group, categorize, version, and distribute NLP datasets which we briefly survey. Most notably, the Linguistic Data Consortium (LDC) stores, serves, and manages a variety of datasets for language and speech. In addition to hosting and distributing corpus resources, the LDC supports significant annotation efforts. Other projects have aimed to collect related annotations together. Projects like OntoNotes have collected annotations across multiple tasks for a single corpus (Pradhan and Xue, 2009) whereas the Universal Dependency treebank (Nivre et al., 2016) collects similar annotations across languages. In machine translation, projects like OPUS catalog the translation resources for many different languages. These differ from *Datasets* which collects and provides access to datasets in a content-agnostic way.

Other projects have aimed to make it easy to access core NLP datasets. The influential NLTK project (Bird, 2006) provided a data library that makes it easy to download and access core datasets. SpaCy also provides a similar loading interface (Honnibal and Montani, 2017). In recent years, concurrent with the move towards deep learning, there has been a growth in large freely available datasets often with less precise annotation standards. This has motivated cloud-based repositories of datasets. Initiatives like TensorFlow-Datasets (2021) and TorchText (2021) have collected various datasets in a common cloud format. This project began as a fork of TensorFlow-Datasets, but has diverged significantly.

Datasets differs from these projects along several axes. The project is decoupled from any modeling framework and provides a general-purpose tabular API. It focuses on NLP specifically and provides specialized types and structures for language constructs. Finally, it prioritizes community management and documentation through the dataset hub and data cards, and aims to provide access to a long-tail of datasets for many tasks and languages.

3 Library Tour and Design

We begin with a brief tour. Accessing a dataset is done simply by referring to it by a global identity.

```
dataset = load_dataset("boolq")
```

Each dataset has a features schema and metadata.

```
print(dataset.features, dataset.info)
```

Any slice of data points can be accessed directly without loading the full dataset into memory.

```
dataset["train"][start:end]
```

Processing can be applied to every data point in a batched and parallel fashion using standard libraries such as NumPy or Torch.

```
# Torch function "tokenize"
tokenized = dataset.map(tokenize,
                        num_proc=32)
```

Datasets facilitates each of these four Stages with the following technical steps.

S1. Dataset Retrieval and Building *Datasets* does not host the underlying raw datasets, but accesses hosted data from the original authors in a distributed manner.[3] Each dataset has a community contributed builder module. The builder module has the responsibility of processing the raw data, e.g. text or CSV, into a common dataset interface representation.

S2. Data Point Representation Each built dataset is represented internally as a table with typed columns. The *Dataset* type system includes a variety of common and NLP-targeted types. In addition to atomic values (int's, float's, string's,

[1] Datasets themselves may utilize different licenses which are documented in the library.

[2] `https://huggingface.co/docs/datasets/`

[3] For datasets with intensive preprocessing, such as Wikipedia, a preprocessed version is hosted. Datasets removed by the author are not centrally cached and become unavailable.

binary blobs) and JSON-like dicts and lists, the library also includes named categorical class labels, sequences, paired translations, and higher-dimension arrays for images, videos, or waveforms.

S3. In-Memory Access *Datasets* is built on top of Apache Arrow, a cross-language columnar data framework (Arrow, 2020). Arrow provides a local caching system allowing datasets to be backed by an on-disk cache, which is memory-mapped for fast lookup. This architecture allows for large datasets to be used on machines with relatively small device memory. Arrow also allows for copy-free hand-offs to standard machine learning tools such as NumPy, Pandas, Torch, and TensorFlow.

S4. User Processing At download, the library provides access to the typed data with minimal pre-processing. It provides functions for dataset manipulation including sorting, shuffling, splitting, and filtering. For complex manipulations, it provides a powerful *map* function that supports arbitrary Python functions for creating new in-memory tables. For large datasets, map can be run in batched, multi-process mode to apply processing in parallel. Furthermore, data processed by the same function is automatically cached between sessions.

Complete Flow Upon requesting a dataset, it is downloaded from the original host. This triggers dataset-specific builder code which converts the text into a typed tabular format matching the feature schema and caches the table. The user is given a memory-mapped typed table. To further process the data, e.g. tokenize, the user can run arbitrary vectorized code and cache the results.

4 Dataset Documentation and Search

Datasets is backed by the *Dataset Hub* [4] that helps users navigate the growing number of available resources and draws inspiration from recent work calling for better documentation of ML datasets in general (Gebru et al., 2018) and NLP datasets in particular (Bender and Friedman, 2018).

Datasets can be seen as a form of infrastructure (Hutchinson et al., 2021). NLP practitioners typically make use of them with a specific goal in mind, whether they are looking to answer a specified research question or developing a system for a particular practical application. To that end, they need to be able to not only easily identify which dataset is most appropriate for the task at hand, but also to understand how various properties of that best candidate might help with, or, conversely, run contrary to their purpose.

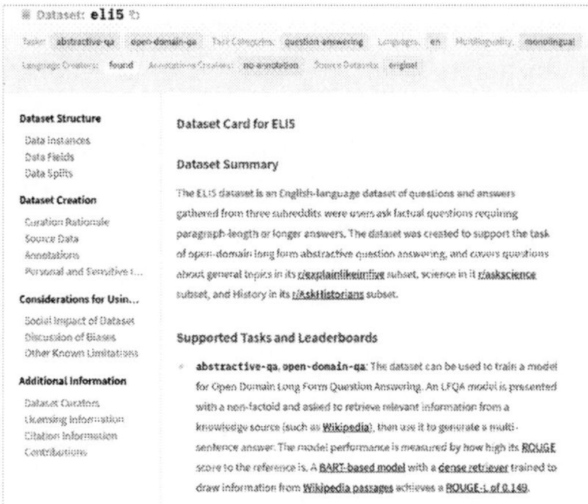

Figure 1: The data card for ELI5 (Fan et al., 2019).

The *Dataset Hub* includes all of the datasets available in the library. It links each of them together though: a set of *structured tags* holding information about their languages, tasks supported, licenses, etc.; a *data card* based on a template[5] designed to combine relevant technical considerations and broader context information (McMillan-Major et al., 2021); and a *list of models* trained on the dataset. Both the tags and data card are filled manually by the contributor who introduces the dataset to the library. Figure 1 presents an example of the dataset page on the hub.[6] Together, these pages and the search interface help users navigate the available resources.

Choosing a Dataset Given a use case, the structured tags provide a way to surface helpful datasets. For example, requesting all datasets that have the tags for Spanish language and the Question Answering task category returns 7 items at the time of writing. A user can then refine their choice by reading through the data cards, which contain sections describing the variety of language used, legal considerations including licensing and incidence of Personal Identifying Information, and paragraphs about known social biases resulting from the collection process that might lead a deployed model to cause disparate harms.

[4] `https://hf.co/datasets/`

[5] `https://hf.co/datasets/card-guide`

[6] `https://hf.co/datasets/eli5`

Using a Dataset The data card also contains information to help users navigate all the choices, from hardware to modeling, that go into successfully training a system. These include the number of examples in each of the dataset splits, the size on disk of the data, meaningful differences between the training, validation, and test split, and free text descriptions of the various fields that make up each example to help decide what information to use as input or output of a prediction model.

The Data Card as a Living Document A dataset's life continues beyond its initial release. As NLP practitioners interact with the dataset in various ways, they may surface annotation artifacts that affect the behavior of trained models in unexpected ways (Gururangan et al., 2018),[7] issues in the way the standard split was initially devised to test a model's ability to adapt to new settings (Krishna et al., 2021), or new understanding of the social biases exhibited therein (Hutchinson et al., 2020). The community-driven nature of *Datasets* and the versioning mechanisms provided by the GitHub backend provide an opportunity to keep the data cards up to date as information comes to light and to make gradual progress toward having as complete documentation as possible.

5 Dataset Usage and Use-Cases

Datasets is now being actively used for a variety of tasks. Figure 2 (left) shows statistics about library usage. We can see that the most commonly downloaded libraries are popular English benchmarks such as GLUE and SQuAD which are often used for teaching and examples. However there is a range of popular models for different tasks and languages.

Figure 2 (right) shows the wide coverage of the library in terms of task types, sizes, and languages, with currently 681 total datasets. During the development of the *Datasets* project, there was a public hackathon to have community members develop new Dataset builders and add them to the project. This event led 485 commits and 285 unique contributors to the library. Recent work has outlined the difficulty of finding data sources for lower-resourced languages through automatic filtering alone (Caswell et al., 2021). The breadth of languages spoken by participants in this event made it possible to more reliably bootstrap the library with datasets in a wide range of different languages. Finally while *Datasets* is designed for NLP, it is becoming used for multi-modal datasets. The library now includes types for continuous data, including multi-dimensional arrays for image and video data and an *Audio* type.

5.1 Case Studies: N-Dataset NLP

A standardized library of datasets opens up new use-cases beyond making single datasets easy to download. We highlight three use-cases in which practitioners have employed the *Datasets* library.

Case Study 1: N-task Pretraining Benchmarks Benchmarking frameworks such as NLP Decathlon and GLUE have popularized the comparison of a single NLP model across a variety of tasks (McCann et al., 2018; Wang et al., 2018). Recently benchmarking frameworks like GPT-3's test suite framework (Brown et al., 2020) have expanded this benchmarking style even further, taking on dozens of different tasks. This research has increased interest in comparison of different datasets at scale.

Datasets is designed to facilitate large-scale, N-task benchmarking beyond what might be possible for a single researcher to set up. For example, the Eleuther AI project aims to produce a massive scale open-source model. As part of this project they have released an *LM Evaluation Harness*[8] which includes nearly 100 different NLP tasks to test a large scale language model. This framework is built with the *Datasets* library as a method for retrieving and caching datasets.

Case Study 2: Reproducible Shared Tasks NLP has a tradition of shared tasks that become long-lived benchmark datasets. Tasks like CoNLL 2000 (Tjong Kim Sang and Buchholz, 2000) continue to be widely used more than 20 years after their release. *Datasets* provides a convenient, reproducible, and standardized method for hosting and maintaining shared tasks, particularly when they require multiple different datasets.

Datasets was used to support the first GEM (Generation, Evaluation, and Metrics) workshop (Gehrmann et al., 2021). This workshop ran a shared task comparing natural language generation (NLG) systems on 12 different tasks. The tasks included examples from twenty different languages and supervised datasets varying from size of 5k examples to 500k. Critically, the shared task had

[7] `https://hf.co/datasets/snli#other-known-limitations`

[8] https://github.com/EleutherAI/lm-evaluation-harness

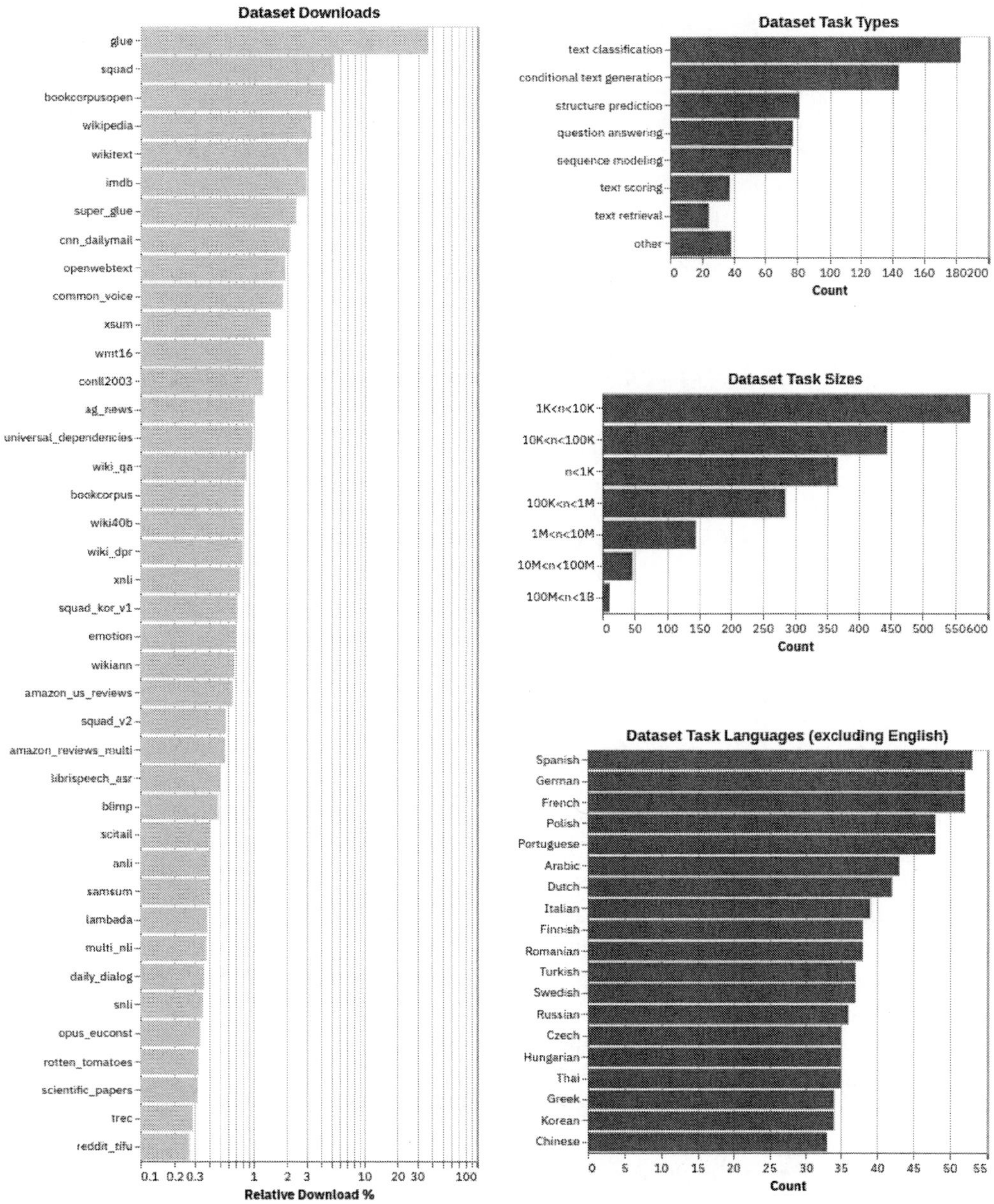

Figure 2: Summary statistics from the datasets in the library. (**Left**) The relative download numbers of the most popular datasets in the library. (**Right**) Task properties. Each dataset may have multiple sub-tasks. Task Types are the types labeled in the library. Task Sizes are the number of data points in the table. Task Languages are the languages tagged in the library (many datasets include tasks in different languages).

a large variety of different input formats including tables, articles, RDF triples, and meaning graphs. *Datasets* allows users to access all 12 datasets with a single line of code in their shared task description.

Case Study 3: Robustness Evaluation While NLP models have improved to the point that on-paper they compete with human performance, many research projects have demonstrated that these same models are fooled when given out-of-domain examples (Koehn and Knowles, 2017), simple adversarial constructions (Belinkov and Bisk, 2018), or examples that spuriously match basic patterns (Poliak et al., 2018).

Datasets can be used to support better benchmarking of these issues. The *Robustness Gym*[9] proposes a systematic way to test an NLP system across many different proposed techniques, specifically subpopulations, transformations, evaluation sets, and adversarial attacks (Goel et al., 2021). Together, these provide a robustness report that is more specific than a single evaluation measure. While developed independently, the Robustness Gym is built on *Datasets*, and "relies on a common data interface" provided by the library.

6 Additional Functionality and Uses

Streaming Some datasets are extremely large and cannot even fit on disk. *Datasets* includes a streaming mode that buffers these datasets on the fly. This mode supports the core map primitive, which works on each data batch as it is streamed. Datasets streaming helped enable recent research into distributed training of a very large open NLP model (Diskin et al., 2021).

Indexing *Datasets* includes tools for easily building and utilizing a search index over an arbitrary dataset. To construct the index the library can interface either with FAISS or ElasticSearch (Johnson et al., 2017; Elastic, 2021). This interface makes it easy to efficiently find nearest neighbors either with textual or vector queries. Indexing was used to host the open-source version of Retrieval-Augmented Generation (Lewis et al., 2020), a generation model backed by the ability to query knowledge from large-scale knowledge sources.

Metrics *Datasets* includes an interface for standardizing *metrics* which can be documented, versioned and matched with datasets. This functionality is particularly useful for benchmark datasets

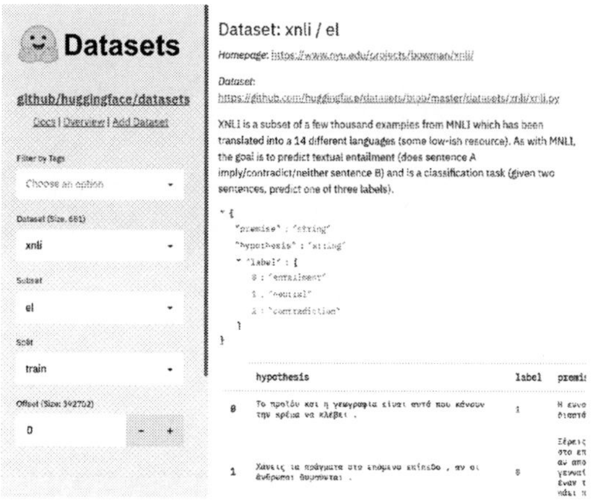

Figure 3: *Datasets* viewer is an application that shows all rows for all datasets in the library. The interface allows users to change datasets, subsets, and splits, while seeing the dataset schema and metadata.

such as GLUE that include multiple tasks each with their own metric. Some metrics like BLEU and SQuAD are included directly in the library code, whereas others are linked to external packages. The library also allows for metrics to be applied in a distributed manner over the dataset.

Data Viewer A benefit of the standardized interface of the library is that it makes it trivial to build a cross-task dataset viewer. As an example, Hugging Face hosts a generic viewer for the entirety of *datasets* (Figure 3) [10]. In this viewer, anyone on the web can open all almost 650 different datasets and view any example. Because the tables are typed, the viewer can easily show all component features, structured data, and multi-modal features.

7 Conclusion

Hugging Face *Datasets* is an open-source, community-driven library that standardizes the processing, distribution, and documentation of NLP datasets. The core library is designed to be easy to use, fast, and to use the same interface for datasets of varying size. At 650 datasets from over 250 contributors, it makes it easy to use standard datasets, has facilitated new use cases of cross-dataset NLP, and has advanced features for tasks like indexing and streaming large datasets.

[9] https://robustnessgym.com/

[10] https://huggingface.co/datasets/viewer/

Acknowledgements

While organized by Hugging Face, *Datasets* is an open-source project driven by contributors. This work was only possible thanks to Charin Polpanumas, Cahya Wirawan, Jonatas Grosman, Thomas Hudson, Zaid Alyafeai, Rahul Chauhan, Vineeth S, Sandip, Yvonnegitau, Jared T Nielsen, Michal Jamry, Bharat Raghunathan, Ceyda Cinarel, David Adelani, Misbah Khan, Steven Liu, Vasudev Gupta, Matthew Bui, Abdul Rafay Khalid, Beth Tenorio, Eduardo Gonzalez Ponferrada, Harshal Mittal, Hugo Abonizio, Moussa Kamal Eddine, Stefan Schweter, Sumanth Doddapaneni, Yavuz Kömeçoğlu, Yusuke Mori, J-chim, Ontocord, Skyprince999, Vrindaprabhu, Jonathan Bragg, Philip May, Alexander Seifert, Ivanzidov, Jake Tae, Karim Foda, Mohamed Al Salti, Nick Doiron, Vinay, Czabo, Vblagoje, Nilansh Rajput, Abdulelah S. Al Mesfer, Akshay Bhardwaj, Amit Moryossef, Basava Sai Naga Viswa Chaitanya, Darek Kłeczek, Darshan Gandhi, Gustavo Aguilar, Hassan Ismail Fawaz, Jack Morris, Jamesg, Jonathan Chang, Karthik Bhaskar, Manan Dey, Maria Grandury, Michael A. Hedderich, Mounica Maddela, Nathan Cooper, Purvi M, Richard Wang, Song Feng, Sourab Mangrulkar, Tanmoy, Vijayasaradhi, Zacharysbrown, Chameleontk, Eusip, Jeromeku, Patpizio, Tuner007, Benjamin Van Der Burgh, Bharati Patidar, George Mihaila, Olivier, Tim Isbister, Alessandro Suglia, Başak Buluz Kömeçoğlu, Boris Dayma, Dariusz Kajtoch, Frankie Robertson, Jieyu, Mihaelagaman, Nikhil Bartwal, Param Bhavsar, Paullerner, Rachelker, Ricardo Rei, Sai, Sasha Rush, Suraj Parmar, Takuro Niitsuma, Taycir Yahmed, Tuan-phong Nguyen, Vladimir Gurevich, Alex, Calpt, Idoh, Justin-yan, Katnoria, Sileod, Avinash Swaminathan, Connor Mccarthy, Jungwhan Kim, Leo Zhao, Sanjay Kamath, (bill) Yuchen Lin, 2dot71mily, 8bitmp3, Abi Komma, Adam, Adeep Hande, Aditya Siddhant, Akash Kumar Gautam, Alaa Houimel, Alex Dong, Along, Anastasia Shimorina, Andre Barbosa, Anton Lozhkov, Antonio V Mendoza, Ashmeet Lamba, Ayushi Dalmia, Batjedi, Behçet Şentürk, Bernardt Duvenhage, Binny Mathew, Birger Moëll, Blanc Ray, Bram Vanroy, Clément Rebuffel, Daniel Khashabi, David Fidalgo, David Wadden, Dhruv Kumar, Diwakar Mahajan, Elron Bandel, Emrah Budur, Fatima Haouari, Fraser Greenlee, Gergely Nemeth, Gowtham.r, Hemil Desai, Hiroki Nakayama, Ilham F Putra, Jannis Vamvas, Javier De La Rosa, Javier-jimenez99, Jeff Hale, Jeff Yang, Joel Niklaus, John Miller, John Mollas, Joshua Adelman, Juan Julián Cea Morán, Kacper Łukawski, Koichi Miyamoto, Kushal Kedia, Laxya Agarwal, Leandro Von Werra, Loïc Estève, Luca Di Liello, Malik Altakrori, Manuel, Maramhasanain, Marcin Flis, Matteo Manica, Matthew Peters, Mehrdad Farahani, Merve Noyan, Mihai Ilie, Mitchell Gordon, Niccolò Campolungo, Nihal Harish, Noa Onoszko, Nora Belrose, Or Sharir, Oyvind Tafjord, Pewolf, Pariente Manuel, Pasquale Minervini, Pedro Ortiz Suárez, Pedro Lima, Pengcheng Yin, Petros Stavropoulos, Phil Wang, Philipp Christmann, Philipp Dufter, Philippe Laban, Pierre Colombo, Rahul Danu, Rabeeh Karimi Mahabadi, Remi Calizzano, Reshinth Adithyan, Rodion Martynov, Roman Tezikov, Sam Shleifer, Savaş Yıldırım, Sergey Mkrtchyan, Shubham Jain, Shubhambindal2017, Subhendu Ranjan Mishra, Taimur Ibrahim, Tanmay Thakur, Thomas Diggelmann, Théophile Blard, Tobias Slott, Tsvetomila Mihaylova, Vaibhav Adlakha, Vegar Andreas Bergum, Victor Velev, Vlad Lialin, Wilson Lee, Yang Wang, Yasir Abdurrohman, Yenting (Adam) Lin, Yixin Nie, Yoav Artzi, Yoni Gottesman, Yongrae Jo, Yuxiang Wu, Zhong Peixiang, Zihan Wang, Aditya2211, Alejandrocros, Andy Zou, Brainshawn, Cemilcengiz, Chutaklee, Gaurav Rai, Dhruvjoshi1998, Duttahritwik, Enod, Felixgwu, Ggdupont, Jerryishere, Jeswan, Lodgi, Lorinczb, Maxbartolo, Nathan Dahlberg, Neal, Ngdodd, Kristo, Onur Güngör, Ophelielacroix, Padipadou, and Phiwi.

References

Apache Arrow. 2020. Apache Arrow, a cross-language development platform for in-memory analytics. https://arrow.apache.org/.

Yonatan Belinkov and Yonatan Bisk. 2018. Synthetic and natural noise both break neural machine translation. In *International Conference on Learning Representations*.

Emily M. Bender and Batya Friedman. 2018. Data statements for natural language processing: Toward mitigating system bias and enabling better science. *Transactions of the Association for Computational Linguistics*, 6:587–604.

Steven Bird. 2006. NLTK: The Natural Language Toolkit. In *Proceedings of the COLING/ACL 2006 Interactive Presentation Sessions*, pages 69–72, Sydney, Australia. Association for Computational Linguistics.

P. Brown, J. Cocke, S. Della Pietra, V. Della Pietra, F. Jelinek, R. Mercer, and P. Roossin. 1988. A statistical approach to language translation. In *Coling Budapest 1988 Volume 1: International Conference on Computational Linguistics*.

Tom B. Brown, Benjamin Mann, Nick Ryder, Melanie Subbiah, Jared Kaplan, Prafulla Dhariwal, Arvind Neelakantan, Pranav Shyam, Girish Sastry, Amanda Askell, Sandhini Agarwal, Ariel Herbert-Voss, Gretchen Krueger, Tom Henighan, Rewon Child, Aditya Ramesh, Daniel M. Ziegler, Jeffrey Wu, Clemens Winter, Christopher Hesse, Mark Chen, Eric Sigler, Mateusz Litwin, Scott Gray, Benjamin Chess, Jack Clark, Christopher Berner, Sam McCandlish, Alec Radford, Ilya Sutskever, and Dario Amodei. 2020. Language models are few-shot learners. In *Advances in Neural Information Processing Systems 33: Annual Conference on Neural Information Processing Systems 2020, NeurIPS 2020, December 6-12, 2020, virtual*.

Isaac Caswell, Julia Kreutzer, Lisa Wang, Ahsan Wahab, Daan van Esch, Nasanbayar Ulzii-Orshikh, Allahsera Tapo, Nishant Subramani, Artem Sokolov, Claytone Sikasote, Monang Setyawan, Supheakmungkol Sarin, Sokhar Samb, Benoît Sagot, Clara Rivera, Annette Rios, Isabel Papadimitriou, Salomey Osei, Pedro Javier Ortiz Suárez, Iroro Orife, Kelechi Ogueji, Rubungo Andre Niyongabo, Toan Q. Nguyen, Mathias Müller, André Müller, Shamsuddeen Hassan Muhammad, Nanda Muhammad, Ayanda Mnyakeni, Jamshidbek Mirzakhalov, Tapiwanashe Matangira, Colin Leong, Nze Lawson, Sneha Kudugunta, Yacine Jernite, Mathias Jenny, Orhan Firat, Bonaventure F. P. Dossou, Sakhile Dlamini, Nisansa de Silva, Sakine Çabuk Balli, Stella Biderman, Alessia Battisti, Ahmed Baruwa, Ankur Bapna, Pallavi Baljekar, Israel Abebe Azime, Ayodele Awokoya, Duygu Ataman, Orevaoghene Ahia, Oghenefego Ahia, Sweta Agrawal, and Mofetoluwa Adeyemi. 2021. Quality at a glance: An audit of web-crawled multilingual datasets. *CoRR*, abs/2103.12028.

Jacob Devlin, Ming-Wei Chang, Kenton Lee, and Kristina Toutanova. 2019. BERT: Pre-training of deep bidirectional transformers for language understanding. In *Proceedings of the 2019 Conference of the North American Chapter of the Association for Computational Linguistics: Human Language Technologies, Volume 1 (Long and Short Papers)*, pages 4171–4186, Minneapolis, Minnesota. Association for Computational Linguistics.

Thomas Diggelmann, Jordan Boyd-Graber, Jannis Bulian, Massimiliano Ciaramita, and Markus Leippold. 2020. Climate-fever: A dataset for verification of real-world climate claims.

Michael Diskin, Alexey Bukhtiyarov, Max Ryabinin, Lucile Saulnier, Quentin Lhoest, Anton Sinitsin, Dmitry Popov, Dmitry Pyrkin, Maxim Kashirin, Alexander Borzunov, Albert Villanova del Moral, Denis Mazur, Ilia Kobelev, Yacine Jernite, Thomas Wolf, and Gennady Pekhimenko. 2021. Distributed deep learning in open collaborations.

Elastic. 2021. Elastic Search. `https://www.elastic.co/`.

Angela Fan, Yacine Jernite, Ethan Perez, David Grangier, Jason Weston, and Michael Auli. 2019. ELI5: Long form question answering. In *Proceedings of the 57th Annual Meeting of the Association for Computational Linguistics*, pages 3558–3567, Florence, Italy. Association for Computational Linguistics.

Timnit Gebru, Jamie Morgenstern, Briana Vecchione, Jennifer Wortman Vaughan, Hanna M. Wallach, Hal Daumé III, and Kate Crawford. 2018. Datasheets for datasets. *CoRR*, abs/1803.09010.

Sebastian Gehrmann, Tosin P. Adewumi, Karmanya Aggarwal, Pawan Sasanka Ammanamanchi, Aremu Anuoluwapo, Antoine Bosselut, Khyathi Raghavi Chandu, Miruna Adriana Clinciu, Dipanjan Das, Kaustubh D. Dhole, Wanyu Du, Esin Durmus, Ondvrej Duvsek, Chris C. Emezue, Varun Gangal, Cristina Garbacea, T. Hashimoto, Yufang Hou, Yacine Jernite, Harsh Jhamtani, Yangfeng Ji, Shailza Jolly, Mihir Kale, Dhruv Kumar, Faisal Ladhak, Aman Madaan, Mounica Maddela, Khyati Mahajan, Saad Mahamood, Bodhisattwa Prasad Majumder, Pedro Henrique Martins, Angelina McMillan-Major, Simon Mille, Emiel van Miltenburg, Moin Nadeem, Shashi Narayan, V. Nikolaev, Rubungo Andre Niyongabo, Salomey Osei, Ankur P. Parikh, Laura Perez-Beltrachini, Niranjan Rao, Vikas Raunak, Juan Diego Rodríguez, Sashank Santhanam, João Sedoc, Thibault Sellam, Samira Shaikh, Anastasia Shimorina, Marco Antonio Sobrevilla Cabezudo, Hendrik Strobelt, Nishant Subramani, W. Xu, Diyi Yang, Akhila Yerukola, and Jiawei Zhou. 2021. The gem benchmark: Natural language generation, its evaluation and metrics. *ArXiv*, abs/2102.01672.

Karan Goel, Nazneen Fatema Rajani, Jesse Vig, Zachary Taschdjian, Mohit Bansal, and Christopher Ré. 2021. Robustness gym: Unifying the NLP evaluation landscape. In *Proceedings of the 2021 Conference of the North American Chapter of the Association for Computational Linguistics: Human Language Technologies: Demonstrations*, pages 42–55, Online. Association for Computational Linguistics.

Suchin Gururangan, Swabha Swayamdipta, Omer Levy, Roy Schwartz, Samuel Bowman, and Noah A. Smith. 2018. Annotation artifacts in natural language inference data. In *Proceedings of the 2018 Conference of the North American Chapter of the Association for Computational Linguistics: Human Language Technologies, Volume 2 (Short Papers)*, pages 107–112, New Orleans, Louisiana. Association for Computational Linguistics.

Matthew Honnibal and Ines Montani. 2017. spacy 2: Natural language understanding with bloom embeddings, convolutional neural networks and incremental parsing. *To appear*, 7(1):411–420.

Ben Hutchinson, Vinodkumar Prabhakaran, Emily Denton, Kellie Webster, Yu Zhong, and Stephen Denuyl. 2020. Social biases in NLP models as barriers for persons with disabilities. In *Proceedings of the 58th Annual Meeting of the Association for Computational Linguistics, ACL 2020, Online, July 5-10, 2020*, pages 5491–5501. Association for Computational Linguistics.

Ben Hutchinson, Andrew Smart, Alex Hanna, Emily Denton, Christina Greer, Oddur Kjartansson, Parker Barnes, and Margaret Mitchell. 2021. Towards accountability for machine learning datasets: Practices from software engineering and infrastructure. In *Proceedings of the 2021 ACM Conference on Fairness, Accountability, and Transparency*, FAccT '21, page 560–575, New York, NY, USA. Association for Computing Machinery.

Jeff Johnson, Matthijs Douze, and Hervé Jégou. 2017. Billion-scale similarity search with gpus. *arXiv preprint arXiv:1702.08734*.

Philipp Koehn and Rebecca Knowles. 2017. Six challenges for neural machine translation. *arXiv preprint arXiv:1706.03872*.

Kalpesh Krishna, Aurko Roy, and Mohit Iyyer. 2021. Hurdles to progress in long-form question answering. In *Proceedings of the 2021 Conference of the North American Chapter of the Association for Computational Linguistics: Human Language Technologies, NAACL-HLT 2021, Online, June 6-11, 2021*, pages 4940–4957. Association for Computational Linguistics.

Patrick S. H. Lewis, Ethan Perez, Aleksandra Piktus, Fabio Petroni, Vladimir Karpukhin, Naman Goyal, Heinrich Küttler, Mike Lewis, Wen-tau Yih, Tim Rocktäschel, Sebastian Riedel, and Douwe Kiela. 2020. Retrieval-augmented generation for knowledge-intensive NLP tasks. *CoRR*, abs/2005.11401.

Mitchell P. Marcus, Beatrice Santorini, and Mary Ann Marcinkiewicz. 1993. Building a large annotated corpus of English: The Penn Treebank. *Computational Linguistics*, 19(2):313–330.

Bryan McCann, N. Keskar, Caiming Xiong, and R. Socher. 2018. The natural language decathlon: Multitask learning as question answering. *ArXiv*, abs/1806.08730.

Angelina McMillan-Major, Salomey Osey, Juan Diego Rodríguez, Pawan Sasanka Ammanamanchi, Sebastian Gehrmann, and Yacine Jernite. 2021. Reusable templates and guides for documenting datasets and models for natural language processing and generation - a case study of the huggingface and gem data and model cards.

Joakim Nivre, Marie-Catherine de Marneffe, Filip Ginter, Yoav Goldberg, Jan Hajič, Christopher D. Manning, Ryan McDonald, Slav Petrov, Sampo Pyysalo, Natalia Silveira, Reut Tsarfaty, and Daniel Zeman. 2016. Universal Dependencies v1: A multilingual treebank collection. In *Proceedings of the Tenth International Conference on Language Resources and Evaluation (LREC'16)*, pages 1659–1666, Portorož, Slovenia. European Language Resources Association (ELRA).

Matthew E. Peters, Mark Neumann, Mohit Iyyer, Matt Gardner, Christopher Clark, Kenton Lee, and Luke Zettlemoyer. 2018. Deep contextualized word representations. In *Proceedings of the 2018 Conference of the North American Chapter of the Association for Computational Linguistics: Human Language Technologies, Volume 1 (Long Papers)*, pages 2227–2237, New Orleans, Louisiana. Association for Computational Linguistics.

Adam Poliak, Jason Naradowsky, Aparajita Haldar, Rachel Rudinger, and Benjamin Van Durme. 2018. Hypothesis only baselines in natural language inference. In *Proceedings of the Seventh Joint Conference on Lexical and Computational Semantics*, pages 180–191, New Orleans, Louisiana. Association for Computational Linguistics.

Sameer S. Pradhan and Nianwen Xue. 2009. OntoNotes: The 90% solution. In *Proceedings of Human Language Technologies: The 2009 Annual Conference of the North American Chapter of the Association for Computational Linguistics, Companion Volume: Tutorial Abstracts*, pages 11–12, Boulder, Colorado. Association for Computational Linguistics.

Colin Raffel, Noam Shazeer, Adam Roberts, Katherine Lee, Sharan Narang, Michael Matena, Yanqi Zhou, Wei Li, and Peter J. Liu. 2020. Exploring the limits of transfer learning with a unified text-to-text transformer. *J. Mach. Learn. Res.*, 21:140:1–140:67.

Pranav Rajpurkar, Jian Zhang, Konstantin Lopyrev, and Percy Liang. 2016. SQuAD: 100,000+ questions for machine comprehension of text. In *Proceedings of the 2016 Conference on Empirical Methods in Natural Language Processing*, pages 2383–2392, Austin, Texas. Association for Computational Linguistics.

TensorFlow-Datasets. 2021. TensorFlow Datasets, a collection of ready-to-use datasets. `https://www.tensorflow.org/datasets`.

Jörg Tiedemann and Lars Nygaard. 2004. The OPUS corpus - parallel and free: `http://logos.uio.no/opus`. In *Proceedings of the Fourth International Conference on Language Resources and Evaluation (LREC'04)*, Lisbon, Portugal. European Language Resources Association (ELRA).

Erik F. Tjong Kim Sang and Sabine Buchholz. 2000. Introduction to the CoNLL-2000 shared task chunking. In *Fourth Conference on Computational Natural Language Learning and the Second Learning Language in Logic Workshop*.

TorchText. 2021. TorchText. https://pytorch.org/text/stable/index.html.

Alex Wang, Amanpreet Singh, Julian Michael, Felix Hill, Omer Levy, and Samuel Bowman. 2018. GLUE: A multi-task benchmark and analysis platform for natural language understanding. In *Proceedings of the 2018 EMNLP Workshop BlackboxNLP: Analyzing and Interpreting Neural Networks for NLP*, pages 353–355, Brussels, Belgium. Association for Computational Linguistics.

SUMMARY EXPLORER
Visualizing the State of the Art in Text Summarization

Shahbaz Syed [†*] **Tariq Yousef** [†*] **Khalid Al-Khatib** [†]
Stefan Jänicke [‡] **Martin Potthast** [†]

[†]Leipzig University [‡]University of Southern Denmark
<shahbaz.syed@uni-leipzig.de> <tariq.yousef@uni-leipzig.de>

Abstract

This paper introduces SUMMARY EXPLORER, a new tool to support the manual inspection of text summarization systems by compiling the outputs of 55 state-of-the-art single document summarization approaches on three benchmark datasets, and visually exploring them during a qualitative assessment. The underlying design of the tool considers three well-known summary quality criteria (coverage, faithfulness, and position bias), encapsulated in a guided assessment based on tailored visualizations. The tool complements existing approaches for locally debugging summarization models and improves upon them. The tool is available at https://tldr.webis.de/.

1 Introduction

Automatic text summarization is the task of generating a summary of a long text by condensing it to its most important parts. This longstanding task originated in automatically creating abstracts for scientific documents (Luhn, 1958), and later extended to documents such as web pages (Salton et al., 1994) and news articles (Wasson, 1998).

There are two paradigms of automatic summarization: *extractive* and *abstractive*. The former extracts important information from the to-be-summarized text, while the latter additionally involves paraphrasing, sentence-fusion, and natural language generation to create fluent summaries. Neural summarization approaches trained on large-scale datasets have significantly advanced both paradigms by improving the overall document understanding and text generation capabilities of the models to generate fluent summaries.

Currently, the progress in text summarization is tracked primarily using *automatic evaluation* with ROUGE (Lin, 2004) as the de facto standard for quantitative evaluation. ROUGE has proven effective for evaluating extractive systems, measuring the overlap of word n-grams between a generated summary and a reference summary (ground truth). Still, it only provides an approximation of a model's capability to generate summaries that are lexically similar to the ground truth. Moreover, ROUGE is unsuitable for evaluating abstractive summarization systems, mainly due to its inadequacy in capturing all semantically equivalent variants of the reference (Ng and Abrecht, 2015; Kryscinski et al., 2019; Fabbri et al., 2021). Besides, a reliable automatic evaluation of a summary is challenging (Lloret et al., 2018) and strongly dependent on its purpose(Jones et al., 1999).

A robust method to analyze the effectiveness of summarization models is to manually inspect their outputs from individual perspectives such as coverage of key concepts and linguistic quality. However, manual inspection requires obtaining the outputs of certain models, delineating a guideline that comprises particular assessment criteria, and ideally utilizing proper visualization techniques to examine the outputs efficiently.

To this end, we present SUMMARY EXPLORER (Figure 1), an online interactive visualization tool that assists humans (researchers, experts, and crowds) to inspect the outputs of text summarization models in a guided fashion. Specifically, we compile and host the outputs of several state-of-the-art models (currently 55) dedicated to English single-document summarization. These outputs cover three benchmark summarization datasets comprising semi-extractive to highly abstractive ground truth summaries. The tool facilitates a *guided* visual analysis of three important summary quality criteria: *coverage*, *faithfulness*, and *position bias*, where tailored visualizations for each criterion streamline both absolute and relative manual evaluation of summaries. Overall, our use cases (see Section 5) demonstrate the ability of SUMMARY EXPLORER to provide a comparative exploration of

* Equal contribution.

Proceedings of the 2021 Conference on Empirical Methods in Natural Language Processing: System Demonstrations, pages 185–194
November 7–11, 2021. ©2021 Association for Computational Linguistics

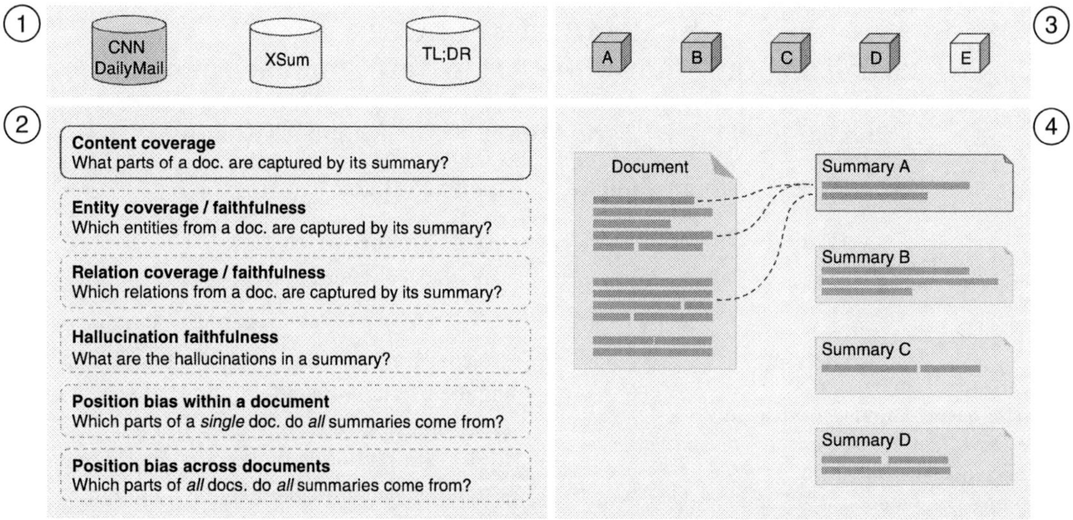

Figure 1: Overview of SUMMARY EXPLORER. Its guided assessment process works in four steps: (1) corpus selection, (2) quality aspect selection, (3) model selection, and (4) quality aspect assessment. Exemplified is the assessment of the content coverage of the summaries of four models for a source document from the CNN/DM corpus. For each summary sentence, its two most related source document sentences are highlighted on demand.

the state-of-the-art text summarization models, and to discover interesting cases that cannot likely be captured by automatic evaluation.

2 Related Work

Leaderboards such as Paperswithcode,[1] ExplainaBoard[2] and NLPProgress[3] provide an overview of state of the art in text summarization mainly according to ROUGE. These leaderboards simply aggregate the scores as reported by the models' developers, where the reported scores can be obtained using different implementations. Hence, a fair comparison become less feasible. For instance, the Bottom-Up model (Gehrmann et al., 2018) uses a different implementation of ROUGE,[4] compared to the BanditSum model (Dong et al., 2018).[5] Besides, for a qualitative comparison of the models, one needs to manually inspect the generated summaries, which are missing from such leaderboards.

To address these shortcomings, VisSeq (Wang et al., 2019) aids developers to locally compare their model's outputs with the ground truth, providing lexical and semantic comparisons along with statistics such as most frequent n-grams and sentence score distributions. LIT (Tenney et al., 2020) provides similar functionality for a broader range of NLP tasks, implementing a work-bench-style debugging of model behavior, including visualization of model attention, confusion matrices, and probability distributions. Closely related to our work is SummVis (Vig et al., 2021), the recently published tool that provides a visual text comparison of summaries with a reference summary as well as a source document, facilitating local debugging of hallucinations in the summaries.

SUMMARY EXPLORER draws from these developments and adds three missing features: (1) Quality-criteria-driven design. Based on a careful literature review of qualitative evaluation of summaries, we derive three key quality criteria and encode them explicitly in the interface of our tool. Other existing tools render these criteria implicit in their underlying design. (2) A step-by-step process for guided analysis. From the chosen quality criteria, we formulate concise and specific questions needed for a qualitative evaluation, and provide a tailored visualization for each question. While previous tools utilize visualization and enable users to (de)activate certain features, they oblige the users to figure out the process themselves, which can be overwhelming to non-experts. (3) Compilation of the state of the art. We collect the outputs of more than 50 models on three benchmark datasets providing a comprehensive overview of the progress in text summarization.

SUMMARY EXPLORER complements these tools and

[1]https://paperswithcode.com/task/text-summarization
[2]http://explainaboard.nlpedia.ai/leaderboard/task-summ/
[3]https://nlpprogress.com/english/summarization.html
[4]https://github.com/sebastianGehrmann/rouge-baselines
[5]https://github.com/pltrdy/rouge

also provides direct access to the state of the art in text summarization, encouraging rigorous analysis to support the development of novel models.

3 Designing Visual Summary Exploration

The design of SUMMARY EXPLORER derives from first principles, namely the three quality criteria *coverage*, *faithfulness*, and *position bias* of a summary in relation to its source document. These high-level criteria are frequently manually assessed throughout the literature. Since their definitions vary, however, we derive from each criterion a total of six specific aspects that are more straightforwardly operationalized in a visual exploration (see Figure 1, Step 2). To render the aspects more directly accessible to users, each is "clarified" by a guiding question that can be answered by a tailored visualization. Below, the three quality criteria are discussed, followed by the visual design.

3.1 Summary Quality Criteria

Coverage A primary goal of a summary is to capture the important information from its source document. Accordingly, a standard practice in summary evaluation is to assess its coverage of the key content (Paice, 1990; Mani, 2001; Jones et al., 1999). In many cases, a comparison to the ground truth (reference) summary can be seen as a proxy for coverage, which is essentially the core idea of ROUGE. However, since it is hard to establish an ideal reference summary (Mani et al., 1999), a comparison against the source document is more meaningful. Although an automatic comparison against it is feasible (Louis and Nenkova, 2013; ShafieiBavani et al., 2018), deciding what is *important* content is highly subjective (Peyrard, 2019). Therefore, authors resort to a manual comparison instead (Hardy et al., 2019). We operationalize coverage assessment by visualizing a document's overlap in terms of content, entities, and entity relations with its summary. Content coverage refers to whether a summary condenses information from all important parts of a document, measured by common similarity measures; entity coverage contrasts the sets of named entities identified in both summary and document; and relation coverage does the same, but for extracted entity relations.

Faithfulness A more recent criterion that gained prominence especially in relation to neural summarization is the faithfulness of a summary to its source document (Cao et al., 2018; Maynez et al., 2020). Whereas coverage asks if the document is sufficiently reflected in the summary, faithfulness asks the reverse, namely if the summary adds something new, questioning its appropriateness. Due to their autoregressive nature, neural summarization models have the unique property to "hallucinate" new content (Kryscinski et al., 2020; Zhao et al., 2020). This is what enables abstractive summarization, but also bears the risk of generating content in a summary that is unrelated to the source document. The only acceptable hallucinated content in a summary must be textually entailed by its source document, which renders an automatic assessment challenging (Falke et al., 2019; Durmus et al., 2020). We operationalize faithfulness assessment by visualizing previously unseen words in a summary in context, aligned with the best-matching sentences of its source document.

Position bias Data-driven approaches, such as neural summarization models, can be biased by the domain of their training data and learn to exploit common patterns. For example, news articles are typically structured according to an "inverted pyramid," where the most important information is given in the first few sentences (PurdueOWL, 2019), and which models learn to exploit (Wasson, 1998; Kedzie et al., 2018). Non-news texts, such as social media posts, however, do not adopt this structure and thus require an unbiased consideration to obtain proper summaries (Syed et al., 2019). We operationalize position bias assessment by visualizing the parts of a document that are the source of its summary's sentences, as well as the ones that are common among a set of summaries.

3.2 Visual Design

Guided Assessment SUMMARY EXPLORER implements a streamlined process to guide summary quality assessment, consisting of four steps (see Figure 1). (1) A benchmark dataset is selected. (2) A list of available summary quality aspects is offered each with a preview of its tailored visualization and its interactive use. (3) Applying Shneiderman's (1996) well-known Visual Information-seeking Mantra ("overview first, zoom and filter, then details-on-demand"), an overview of all models as a heatmap over averages of several quantitative metrics is shown (Figure 2a), which enables a targeted filtering of the models based on their quantitative performance. The heatmap of average values paints only a rough picture; upon model

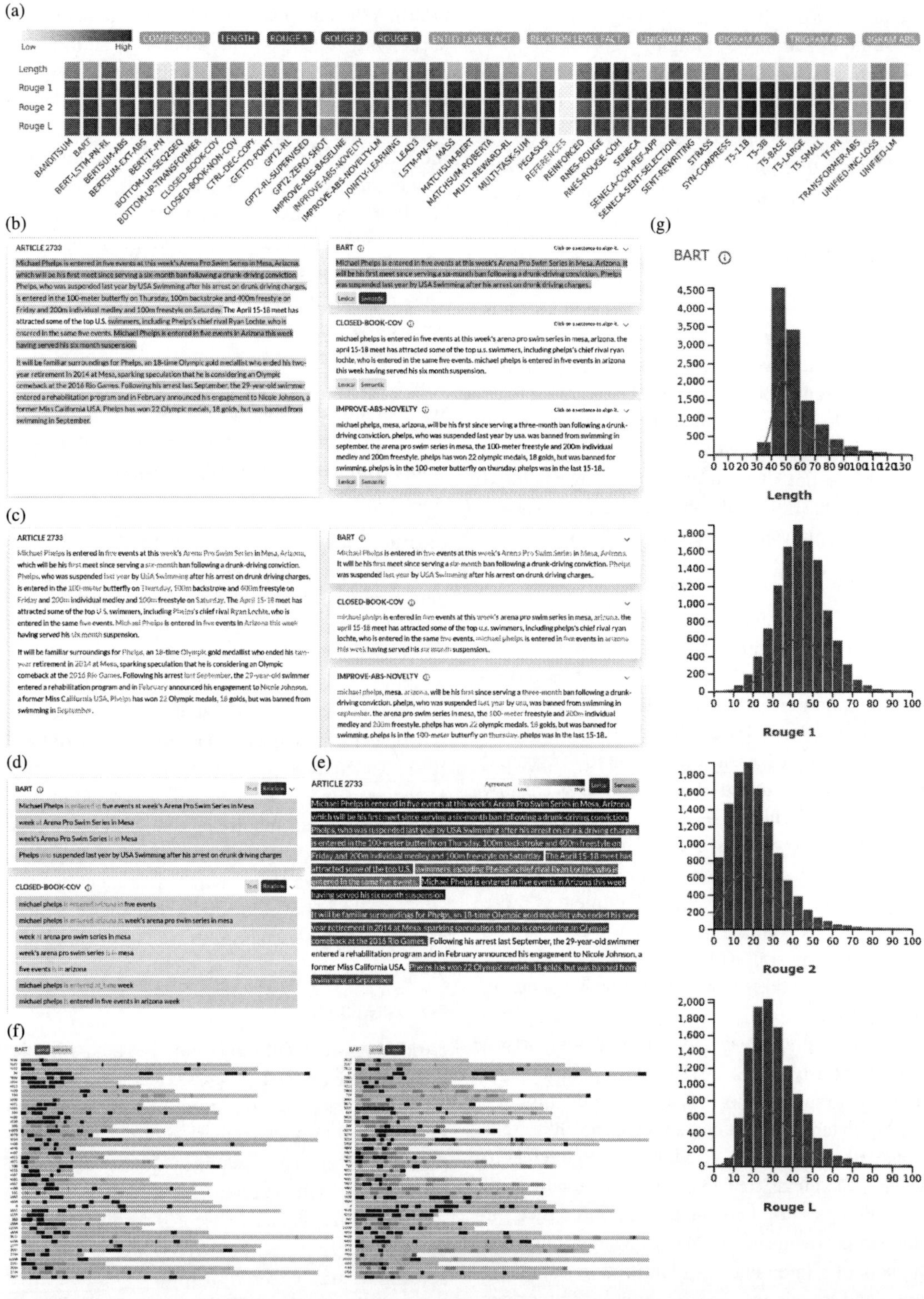

Figure 2: (a) Heatmap overview of 45 models for the CNN/DM corpus; ones selected for analysis are highlighted red. Views for (b) the content coverage, (c) the entity coverage, (d) the relation coverage, (e) the position bias across models for a single document, (f) the position bias of a model across all documents as per lexical and semantic alignment, (g) the distribution of quantitative metric scores for a model.

selection, histograms of each model's score distribution for each metric are available. (4) After models have been selected, the user is forwarded to the corresponding quality aspect's view.

The visualizations for the individual aspects of the three quality criteria share the property that two texts need to be visually aligned with one another.[6] Despite this commonality, we abstain from creating a single-view visualization "stuffed" with alternative options. We rather adopt a minimalistic design for the assessment of individual quality aspects.

Coverage View (Figure 2b,c,d) Content coverage is visualized as alignment of summary sentences and document sentences at the semantic and lexical level in a full-text side-by-side view. Colorization indicates different types of alignments. For entity coverage (relation coverage), a corresponding side-by-side view lists named entities (relations) in a summary and aligns them with named entities (relations) in its source document. For unaligned relations, corresponding document sentences can be retrieved.

Faithfulness View (Figure 3, Case A) Hallucinations are visualized by highlighting novel words in a summary. For each summary sentence with a hallucination, semantically and lexically similar document sentences are highlighted on demand. Since named entities and thus also entity relations form a subset of hallucinated words, the above coverage views do the same. Also, in an aggregated view, hallucinations found in multiple summaries are ordered by frequency, allowing to inspect a particular model with respect to types of hallucinations.

Position Bias View (Figure 2e,f) Position bias is visualized for all models given a source document, and for a specific model with respect to all its summaries in a corpus. The former is visualized as a text heatmap, where a gradient color indicates for every sentence in a source document how many different summaries contain a semantically or lexically corresponding sentence. The latter is visualized by a different kind of heatmap for 50 randomly selected model summaries, where each summary is projected on a single horizontal bar representing the source document. Bar length reflects document length in sentences and aligned sentences are colored to reflect lexical or semantic alignment.

[6]A visualization paradigm recently surveyed by Yousef and Jänicke (2021).

Aggregation Options Most of the above visualizations show individual pairs of source documents and a summary. This enables the close inspection of a given summary, and thus the manual assessment of a model by sequentially inspecting a number of summaries for different source documents generated by the same model. For these views, the visualizations also support displaying a number of summaries from different models for a relative assessment of their summaries.

4 Collection of Model Outputs

We collected the outputs of 55 summarization approaches on the test sets of three benchmark datasets for the task of single document summarization: CNN/DM, XSum and Webis-TLDR-17. Each dataset has a different style of ground truth summaries, ranging from semi-extractive to highly abstractive, providing a diverse selection of models. Outputs were obtained from NLPProgress, meta-evaluations such as SummEval (Fabbri et al., 2021), REALSumm (Bhandari et al., 2020), and in correspondence with the model's developers.[7]

4.1 Summarization Corpora

The most popular dataset, CNN/DM (Hermann et al., 2015; Nallapati et al., 2016), contains news articles with multi-sentence summaries that are mostly extractive in nature (Kryscinski et al., 2019; Bommasani and Cardie, 2020). We obtained the outputs from 45 models. While the original test split of the dataset contained 11,493 articles, we discarded ones that were not summarized by all models, resulting in 11,448 articles total. This minor discrepancy is due to inconsistent usage by authors, such as reshuffling the order of examples, de-duplication of articles in the test set, choice of tokenization, text capitalization, and truncation.

For the XSum dataset (Narayan et al., 2018), the outputs of six models for its test split (10,360 articles) were obtained. XSum contains news articles with more abstractive single-sentence summaries compared to CNN/DM. The Webis-TLDR-17 dataset (Völske et al., 2017) contains highly abstractive, self-authored (single to multi-sentence) summaries of Reddit posts, although slightly noisier than the other datasets (Bommasani and Cardie, 2020). We obtained the outputs from the four submissions of the TL;DR challenge (Syed et al., 2019) for 250 posts.

[7]We sincerely thank all the developers for their efforts to reproduce and share their models' outputs with us.

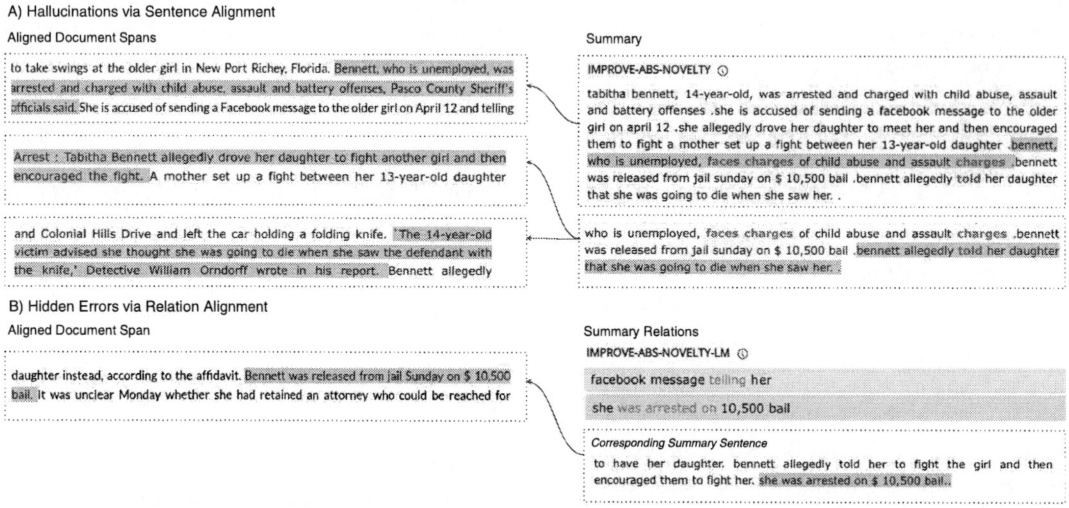

Figure 3: Two showcases for identifying inconsistencies in abstractive summaries using SUMMARY EXPLORER. Case A depicts the verification of the correctness of hallucinations by aligning document sentences. Case B depicts uncovering more subtle hallucination errors by comparing unaligned relations.

4.2 Text Preprocessing

In a preprocessing pipeline, the input of a collection of documents, their ground truth summaries, and the generated summaries from a given model were normalized. First, basic normalization, such as de-tokenization, unifying model-specific sentence delimiters, and sentence segmentation were carried out. Second, additional information, such as named entities and relations were extracted using Spacy[8] and Stanford OpenIE (Angeli et al., 2015), respectively. The latter extracts redundant relations where partial components such as either the subject or the object are already captured by longer counterparts. Such "contained" relations are merged into unique representative relations for each subject.

Alignment Every output summary is aligned with its source document, identifying the top two lexically and semantically related document sentences for each summary sentence. Lexical alignment relies on averaged ROUGE-{1,2,L} scores among the document and summary sentences. The highest scoring document sentence is taken as the first match. The second match is identified by removing all content words from the summary sentence already captured by the first match, and repeating the process as per Lebanoff et al. (2019). For semantic alignment, the rescaled BERTScore (Zhang et al., 2020) is computed between a summary sentence and all source document sentences, with the top-scoring two sentences as candidates.

Summary Evaluation Measures Several standard evaluation measures enable quantitative comparisons and filtering of models for detailed analysis: (1) *compression* as the word ratio between a document and its summary (Grusky et al., 2018), (2) *n-gram abstractiveness* as per Gehrmann et al. (2019) calculates a normalized score for novelty by tracking parts of a summary that are already among the n-grams it has in common with its document, (3) *summary length* as word count (not tokens), (4) *entity-level factuality* as per (Nan et al., 2021) as percentage of named entities in a summary found in its source document, and (5) *relation-level factuality* as percentage of relations in a summary found in its source document. Finally, for consistency, we recompute ROUGE-{1,2,L}[9] for all the models.

5 Assessment Case Studies

We showcase the use and effectiveness of SUMMARY EXPLORER by investigating two models (IMPROVE-ABS-NOVELTY, and IMPROVE-ABS-NOVELTY-LM) from Kryscinski et al. (2018) that improve the abstraction in summaries by including more novel phrases. We investigate the correctness of their hallucinations (novel words in the summary), and identify hidden errors introduced by the sentence fusion of the abstractive models.

[8]https://spacy.io

[9]https://github.com/google-research/google-research/tree/master/rouge

Hallucinations via Sentence Alignment Hallucinations are novel words or phrases in a summary that warrant further inspection. Accordingly, our tool highlights them (Figure 3, Case A), directing the user to the respective candidate summary sentences whose related document sentences can be seen on demand. For IMPROVE-ABS-NOVELTY, we see that the first candidate improves abstraction via paraphrasing, is concisely written, and correctly substitutes the term *"offenses"* with the novel word *"charges"*. The second candidate also improves abstraction via sentence fusion, where two pieces of information are combined: *"bennett allegedly drove her daughter"*, and *"victim advised she thought she was going to die"*. The novel word *"told"* also fits. However, the sentence fusion creates a wrong relation between the different actors (*"bennett allegedly told her daughter that she was going to die"*), which can be easily identified via the visual sentence alignment provided.

Hidden Errors via Relation Alignment The above showcase does not capture all hallucinations. SUMMARY EXPLORER also aligns relations extracted from a summary and its source document to identify novel relations. For IMPROVE-ABS-NOVELTY-LM, we see that the relation *"she was arrested"* is unaligned to any relation in the source document (Figure 3, Case B). Aligning the summary sentence to the document, we note that it is unfaithful to the source despite avoiding hallucinations (*"Bennett was released on $10,500 bail"*, and not *"arrested on $10,500 bail"*). The word *"arrested"* was simply extracted from the document sentence (Figure 3, Case A). Without the visual support, identifying this small but important mistake would have been more cognitively demanding for an assessor.

6 Conclusion

In this paper, we present SUMMARY EXPLORER, an online interactive visualization tool to assess the state of the art in text summarization in a guided fashion. In enables analysis akin to close and distant reading in particular facilitating the challenging inspection of hallucinations by abstractive summarization models. The tool is available open source[10] enabling local use. We also welcome submissions of summaries from newer models trained on the existing datasets as part of our collaboration with the summarization community. We aim to expand the tool's features in future work, exploring novel visual comparisons of documents to their summaries for more reliable qualitative assessments of summary quality. Finally, it is important to note that the accuracy of some of the views is influenced by the intrinsic drawbacks of the toolkits used for named entity recognition and information extraction.

7 Ethical Statement

Visualization plays a major role in the usage and accessibility of our tool. In this regard, to accommodate for color blindness, we primarily use gradient-based visuals for key modules such as model selection, aggregating important content, and text alignment. This renders the tool usable also in a monochromatic setting. Regarding the hosted summarization models, the key goal is to allow a wider audience comprising of model developers, the end users, and practitioners to openly compare and assess the strengths, limitations and possible ethical biases of these systems. Here, our tool supports making informed decisions about the suitability of certain models to the downstream applications.

Acknowledgments

We thank the reviewers for their valuable feedback. This work was supported by the German Federal Ministry of Education and Research (BMBF, 01/S18026A-F) by funding the competence center for Big Data and AI (ScaDS.AI Dresden/Leipzig).

References

Gabor Angeli, Melvin Jose Johnson Premkumar, and Christopher D. Manning. 2015. Leveraging linguistic structure for open domain information extraction. In *Proceedings of the 53rd Annual Meeting of the Association for Computational Linguistics and the 7th International Joint Conference on Natural Language Processing of the Asian Federation of Natural Language Processing, ACL 2015, July 26-31, 2015, Beijing, China, Volume 1: Long Papers*, pages 344–354. The Association for Computer Linguistics.

Manik Bhandari, Pranav Narayan Gour, Atabak Ashfaq, Pengfei Liu, and Graham Neubig. 2020. Re-evaluating evaluation in text summarization. In *Proceedings of the 2020 Conference on Empirical Methods in Natural Language Processing (EMNLP)*, Online. Association for Computational Linguistics.

Rishi Bommasani and Claire Cardie. 2020. Intrinsic evaluation of summarization datasets. In *Proceedings of the 2020 Conference on Empirical Methods in Natural Language Processing (EMNLP)*, pages

[10]https://github.com/webis-de/summary-explorer

8075–8096, Online. Association for Computational Linguistics.

Ziqiang Cao, Furu Wei, Wenjie Li, and Sujian Li. 2018. Faithful to the original: Fact aware neural abstractive summarization. In *Proceedings of the Thirty-Second AAAI Conference on Artificial Intelligence, (AAAI-18), the 30th innovative Applications of Artificial Intelligence (IAAI-18), and the 8th AAAI Symposium on Educational Advances in Artificial Intelligence (EAAI-18), New Orleans, Louisiana, USA, February 2-7, 2018*, pages 4784–4791. AAAI Press.

Yue Dong, Yikang Shen, Eric Crawford, Herke van Hoof, and Jackie Chi Kit Cheung. 2018. Banditsum: Extractive summarization as a contextual bandit. In *Proceedings of the 2018 Conference on Empirical Methods in Natural Language Processing, Brussels, Belgium, October 31 - November 4, 2018*, pages 3739–3748. Association for Computational Linguistics.

Esin Durmus, He He, and Mona Diab. 2020. FEQA: A question answering evaluation framework for faithfulness assessment in abstractive summarization. In *Proceedings of the 58th Annual Meeting of the Association for Computational Linguistics, ACL 2020, Online, July 5-10, 2020*, pages 5055–5070. Association for Computational Linguistics.

Alexander R. Fabbri, Wojciech Kryscinski, Bryan McCann, Caiming Xiong, Richard Socher, and Dragomir R. Radev. 2021. Summeval: Re-evaluating summarization evaluation. *Trans. Assoc. Comput. Linguistics*, 9:391–409.

Tobias Falke, Leonardo F. R. Ribeiro, Prasetya Ajie Utama, Ido Dagan, and Iryna Gurevych. 2019. Ranking generated summaries by correctness: An interesting but challenging application for natural language inference. In *Proceedings of the 57th Conference of the Association for Computational Linguistics, ACL 2019, Florence, Italy, July 28- August 2, 2019, Volume 1: Long Papers*, pages 2214–2220. Association for Computational Linguistics.

Sebastian Gehrmann, Yuntian Deng, and Alexander M. Rush. 2018. Bottom-up abstractive summarization. In *Proceedings of the 2018 Conference on Empirical Methods in Natural Language Processing, Brussels, Belgium, October 31 - November 4, 2018*, pages 4098–4109. Association for Computational Linguistics.

Sebastian Gehrmann, Zachary M. Ziegler, and Alexander M. Rush. 2019. Generating abstractive summaries with finetuned language models. In *Proceedings of the 12th International Conference on Natural Language Generation, INLG 2019, Tokyo, Japan, October 29 - November 1, 2019*, pages 516–522. Association for Computational Linguistics.

Max Grusky, Mor Naaman, and Yoav Artzi. 2018. Newsroom: A dataset of 1.3 million summaries with diverse extractive strategies. In *Proceedings of the 2018 Conference of the North American Chapter of the Association for Computational Linguistics: Human Language Technologies, NAACL-HLT 2018, New Orleans, Louisiana, USA, June 1-6, 2018, Volume 1 (Long Papers)*, pages 708–719. Association for Computational Linguistics.

Hardy, Shashi Narayan, and Andreas Vlachos. 2019. Highres: Highlight-based reference-less evaluation of summarization. In *Proceedings of the 57th Conference of the Association for Computational Linguistics, ACL 2019, Florence, Italy, July 28- August 2, 2019, Volume 1: Long Papers*, pages 3381–3392. Association for Computational Linguistics.

Karl Moritz Hermann, Tomás Kociský, Edward Grefenstette, Lasse Espeholt, Will Kay, Mustafa Suleyman, and Phil Blunsom. 2015. Teaching machines to read and comprehend. In *Advances in Neural Information Processing Systems 28: Annual Conference on Neural Information Processing Systems 2015, December 7-12, 2015, Montreal, Quebec, Canada*, pages 1693–1701.

K Sparck Jones et al. 1999. Automatic summarizing: factors and directions. *Advances in automatic text summarization*, pages 1–12.

Chris Kedzie, Kathleen R. McKeown, and Hal Daumé III. 2018. Content selection in deep learning models of summarization. In *Proceedings of the 2018 Conference on Empirical Methods in Natural Language Processing, Brussels, Belgium, October 31 - November 4, 2018*, pages 1818–1828. Association for Computational Linguistics.

Wojciech Kryscinski, Nitish Shirish Keskar, Bryan McCann, Caiming Xiong, and Richard Socher. 2019. Neural text summarization: A critical evaluation. In *Proceedings of the 2019 Conference on Empirical Methods in Natural Language Processing and the 9th International Joint Conference on Natural Language Processing, EMNLP-IJCNLP 2019, Hong Kong, China, November 3-7, 2019*, pages 540–551. Association for Computational Linguistics.

Wojciech Kryscinski, Bryan McCann, Caiming Xiong, and Richard Socher. 2020. Evaluating the factual consistency of abstractive text summarization. In *Proceedings of the 2020 Conference on Empirical Methods in Natural Language Processing, EMNLP 2020, Online, November 16-20, 2020*, pages 9332–9346. Association for Computational Linguistics.

Wojciech Kryscinski, Romain Paulus, Caiming Xiong, and Richard Socher. 2018. Improving abstraction in text summarization. In *Proceedings of the 2018 Conference on Empirical Methods in Natural Language Processing, Brussels, Belgium, October 31 - November 4, 2018*, pages 1808–1817. Association for Computational Linguistics.

Logan Lebanoff, Kaiqiang Song, Franck Dernoncourt, Doo Soon Kim, Seokhwan Kim, Walter Chang, and Fei Liu. 2019. Scoring sentence singletons and pairs for abstractive summarization. In *Proceedings of the 57th Conference of the Association for Computational Linguistics, ACL 2019, Florence, Italy, July 28- August 2, 2019, Volume 1: Long Papers*, pages 2175–2189. Association for Computational Linguistics.

Chin-Yew Lin. 2004. ROUGE: A package for automatic evaluation of summaries. In *Text Summarization Branches Out*, pages 74–81, Barcelona, Spain. Association for Computational Linguistics.

Elena Lloret, Laura Plaza, and Ahmet Aker. 2018. The challenging task of summary evaluation: an overview. *Lang. Resour. Evaluation*, 52(1):101–148.

Annie Louis and Ani Nenkova. 2013. Automatically assessing machine summary content without a gold standard. *Comput. Linguistics*, 39(2):267–300.

Hans Peter Luhn. 1958. The automatic creation of literature abstracts. *IBM Journal of Reseach and Devopment*, 2(2):159–165.

Inderjeet Mani. 2001. Summarization evaluation: An overview.

Inderjeet Mani, David House, Gary Klein, Lynette Hirschman, Therese Firmin, and Beth Sundheim. 1999. The tipster summac text summarization evaluation. In *EACL 1999, 9th Conference of the European Chapter of the Association for Computational Linguistics, June 8-12, 1999, University of Bergen, Bergen, Norway*, pages 77–85. The Association for Computer Linguistics.

Joshua Maynez, Shashi Narayan, Bernd Bohnet, and Ryan T. McDonald. 2020. On faithfulness and factuality in abstractive summarization. In *Proceedings of the 58th Annual Meeting of the Association for Computational Linguistics, ACL 2020, Online, July 5-10, 2020*, pages 1906–1919. Association for Computational Linguistics.

Ramesh Nallapati, Bowen Zhou, Cícero Nogueira dos Santos, Çaglar Gülçehre, and Bing Xiang. 2016. Abstractive text summarization using sequence-to-sequence rnns and beyond. In *Proceedings of the 20th SIGNLL Conference on Computational Natural Language Learning, CoNLL 2016, Berlin, Germany, August 11-12, 2016*, pages 280–290. ACL.

Feng Nan, Ramesh Nallapati, Zhiguo Wang, Cícero Nogueira dos Santos, Henghui Zhu, Dejiao Zhang, Kathy McKeown, and Bing Xiang. 2021. Entity-level factual consistency of abstractive text summarization. In *Proceedings of the 16th Conference of the European Chapter of the Association for Computational Linguistics: Main Volume, EACL 2021, Online, April 19 - 23, 2021*, pages 2727–2733. Association for Computational Linguistics.

Shashi Narayan, Shay B. Cohen, and Mirella Lapata. 2018. Don't give me the details, just the summary! topic-aware convolutional neural networks for extreme summarization. In *Proceedings of the 2018 Conference on Empirical Methods in Natural Language Processing, Brussels, Belgium, October 31 - November 4, 2018*, pages 1797–1807. Association for Computational Linguistics.

Jun-Ping Ng and Viktoria Abrecht. 2015. Better summarization evaluation with word embeddings for ROUGE. In *Proceedings of the 2015 Conference on Empirical Methods in Natural Language Processing, EMNLP 2015, Lisbon, Portugal, September 17-21, 2015*, pages 1925–1930. The Association for Computational Linguistics.

Chris D Paice. 1990. Constructing literature abstracts by computer: techniques and prospects. *Information Processing & Management*, 26(1):171–186.

Maxime Peyrard. 2019. A simple theoretical model of importance for summarization. In *Proceedings of the 57th Conference of the Association for Computational Linguistics, ACL 2019, Florence, Italy, July 28- August 2, 2019, Volume 1: Long Papers*, pages 1059–1073. Association for Computational Linguistics.

PurdueOWL. 2019. Journalism and journalistic writing: The inverted pyramid structure.

Gerard Salton, James Allan, Chris Buckley, and Amit Singhal. 1994. Automatic analysis, theme generation, and summarization of machine-readable texts. *Science*, 264(5164):1421–1426.

Elaheh ShafieiBavani, Mohammad Ebrahimi, Raymond K. Wong, and Fang Chen. 2018. Summarization evaluation in the absence of human model summaries using the compositionality of word embeddings. In *Proceedings of the 27th International Conference on Computational Linguistics, COLING 2018, Santa Fe, New Mexico, USA, August 20-26, 2018*, pages 905–914. Association for Computational Linguistics.

B. Shneiderman. 1996. The eyes have it: a task by data type taxonomy for information visualizations. In *Proceedings 1996 IEEE Symposium on Visual Languages*, pages 336–343.

Shahbaz Syed, Michael Völske, Nedim Lipka, Benno Stein, Hinrich Schütze, and Martin Potthast. 2019. Towards summarization for social media - results of the tl;dr challenge. In *Proceedings of the 12th International Conference on Natural Language Generation, INLG 2019, Tokyo, Japan, October 29 - November 1, 2019*, pages 523–528. Association for Computational Linguistics.

Ian Tenney, James Wexler, Jasmijn Bastings, Tolga Bolukbasi, Andy Coenen, Sebastian Gehrmann, Ellen Jiang, Mahima Pushkarna, Carey Radebaugh, Emily Reif, and Ann Yuan. 2020. The language interpretability tool: Extensible, interactive visualizations and analysis for NLP models. In *Proceedings of the 2020 Conference on Empirical Methods in Natural Language Processing: System Demonstrations, EMNLP 2020 - Demos, Online, November 16-20, 2020*, pages 107–118. Association for Computational Linguistics.

Jesse Vig, Wojciech Kryscinski, Karan Goel, and Nazneen Fatema Rajani. 2021. Summvis: Interactive visual analysis of models, data, and evaluation for text summarization. *CoRR*, abs/2104.07605.

Michael Völske, Martin Potthast, Shahbaz Syed, and Benno Stein. 2017. Tl;dr: Mining reddit to learn automatic summarization. In *Proceedings of the Workshop on New Frontiers in Summarization, NFiS@EMNLP 2017, Copenhagen, Denmark, September 7, 2017*, pages 59–63. Association for Computational Linguistics.

Changhan Wang, Anirudh Jain, Danlu Chen, and Jiatao Gu. 2019. Vizseq: a visual analysis toolkit for text generation tasks. In *Proceedings of the 2019 Conference on Empirical Methods in Natural Language Processing and the 9th International Joint Conference on Natural Language Processing, EMNLP-IJCNLP 2019, Hong Kong, China, November 3-7, 2019 - System Demonstrations*, pages 253–258. Association for Computational Linguistics.

Mark Wasson. 1998. Using leading text for news summaries: Evaluation results and implications for commercial summarization applications. In *Proc. of the 36th Annual Meeting of the Association for Computational Linguistics and 17th Int. Conference on Computational Linguistics*, pages 1364–1368.

Tariq Yousef and Stefan Jänicke. 2021. A survey of text alignment visualization. *IEEE Transactions on Visualization and Computer Graphics*, 27(2):1149–1159.

Tianyi Zhang, Varsha Kishore, Felix Wu, Kilian Q. Weinberger, and Yoav Artzi. 2020. Bertscore: Evaluating text generation with BERT. In *8th International Conference on Learning Representations, ICLR 2020, Addis Ababa, Ethiopia, April 26-30, 2020*. OpenReview.net.

Zheng Zhao, Shay B. Cohen, and Bonnie Webber. 2020. Reducing quantity hallucinations in abstractive summarization. In *Findings of the Association for Computational Linguistics: EMNLP 2020*, Online. Association for Computational Linguistics.

MeetDot: Videoconferencing with Live Translation Captions

Arkady Arkhangorodsky, Christopher Chu, Scot Fang, Yiqi Huang, Denglin Jiang, Ajay Nagesh, Boliang Zhang, Kevin Knight
DiDi Labs
4640 Admiralty Way
Marina del Rey, CA 90292
{arkadyarkhangorodsky,chrischu,scotfang,denglinjiang, yiqihuang,ajaynagesh,boliangzhang,kevinknight}@didiglobal.com

Abstract

We present *MeetDot*, a videoconferencing system with live translation captions overlaid on screen. The system aims to facilitate conversation between people who speak different languages, thereby reducing communication barriers between multilingual participants. Currently, our system supports speech and captions in 4 languages and combines automatic speech recognition (ASR) and machine translation (MT) in a cascade. We use the *re-translation* strategy to translate the streamed speech, resulting in caption flicker. Additionally, our system has very strict latency requirements to have acceptable call quality. We implement several features to enhance user experience and reduce their cognitive load, such as smooth scrolling captions and reducing caption flicker. The modular architecture allows us to integrate different ASR and MT services in our backend. Our system provides an integrated evaluation suite to optimize key intrinsic evaluation metrics such as accuracy, latency and erasure. Finally, we present an innovative cross-lingual word-guessing game as an extrinsic evaluation metric to measure end-to-end system performance. We plan to make our system open-source for research purposes.[1]

1 Introduction

As collaborations across countries is the norm in the modern workplace, videoconferencing is an indispensable part of our working lives. The recent widespread adoption of remote work has necessitated effective online communication tools, especially among people who speak different languages. In this work, we present *MeetDot*, a videoconferencing solution with live translation captions. Participants can see an overlaid translation of other participants' speech in their preferred language. Currently, we support speech and captions in English, Chinese, Spanish and Portuguese.

The system is built by cascading automatic speech recognition (ASR) and machine translation (MT) components. We process the incoming speech signal in a streaming mode, transcribe it in the speaker's language to be used as input to an MT system to decode in the listener's language during the call. We have very tight latency requirements to be able to provide good quality captions in a live video call. Our framework has several features to enable a better user experience and reduce the cognitive load on the participants such as smooth pixel-wise scrolling of the captions, fading text that is likely to change and biased decoding of machine translation output (Arivazhagan et al., 2020) to reduce the flicker of the captions. In addition, we present preliminary work towards identifying named-entity mentions in speech by interpolating a pronunciation dictionary with the ASR language model.

We present the key metrics to measure the quality of the captions such as accuracy, latency and stability (flicker in captions). Our system provides an integrated evaluation suite to enable fast development through hill climbing on these metrics. In addition to these intrinsic metrics, we present an interesting online cross-lingual word guessing game, where one of the participants is given a word that they describe and the other participants have to guess the word by reading the captions in their respective languages.

We present the following as the key contributions of our work:

- A video conference system with live translation of multilingual speech into captions overlaid on participants' videos. The system has several features to enhance user experience.
- A comprehensive evaluation suite closely integrated with the system and a set of metrics to reduce latency, caption flicker and accuracy.
- A cross-lingual word-guessing game that can be used as an extrinsic metric to evaluate end-

[1] The system will be available at https://github.com/didi/meetdot

Proceedings of the 2021 Conference on Empirical Methods in Natural Language Processing: System Demonstrations, pages 195–202
November 7–11, 2021.

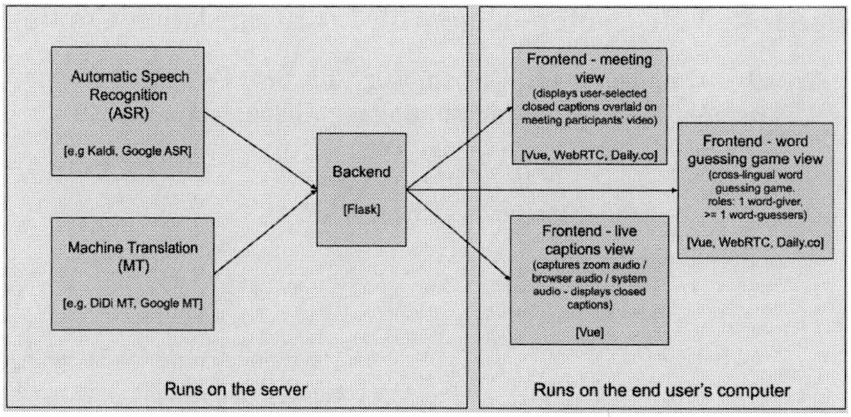

Figure 1: MeetDot system architecture. The ASR and MT modules are designed to be plug-and-play with different services in the backend (e.g. in-house DiDi MT system/Google MT API). Frontend consists of different "views" - e.g. live captions view - captures audio from another browser window/zoom/system to show translated captions.

to-end system performance.

We are in the process of releasing the system as open-source software for the purpose of furthering research in the area.

2 Related Work

The area of simultaneous translation has attracted a lot of attention is recent years. The recent editions of the Workshop on Automatic Simultaneous Translation (Wu et al., 2021, 2020) and the tutorial in EMNLP 2020 (Huang et al., 2020) provide us an overview of the state-of-the-art and challenges in live translation. Recent technical advances include newer architectures such as prefix-to-prefix (Ma et al., 2019) and adaptive policy methods such as imitation learning (Zheng et al., 2019) and monotonic attention (Raffel et al., 2017). The solutions in this space are differentiated into speech-to-speech and speech-to-text, in the former there is a speech synthesis component. Our work falls in the latter bucket, since we only display captions to the user. Since we have access to separate audio-input channels (one per participant), we do not need speaker diarization (Park et al., 2021).

Re-translation is a common strategy applied, wherein we translate from scratch every new extended source sentence, transcribed through the ASR module as the participant speaks. The ability to modify previously displayed captions when new ASR output is available can lead to flicker in displayed captions. Following previous work (Arivazhagan et al., 2020), we measure this using the erasure metric and reduce it using biased beam search during MT decoding. To better capture our use case of short exchanges in a meeting scenario compared to long speech, we introduce additional metrics *initial lag*, *incremental caption lag*, *mean word burstiness* and *max word burstiness*.

There have been recent working systems in this space, such as Ma et al. (2019); Cho et al. (2013); Wang et al. (2016) that provide live captions for single-speaker lectures and does not focus on multi-party meetings. Very recently, there are news reports of systems that offer live translations of multi-party meetings (ZDNet, 2021), but their technical details are unclear.

3 System Description

The overall system architecture is shown in Figure 1. It mainly consists of two components (1) *Frontend*: runs on the user's computer locally (2) *Backend*: runs on the server and consists of ASR and MT modules that interact with the Flask server. The modular architecture allows us to swap the ASR and MT components from different service providers (such as Google ASR or in-house Kaldi-based ASR services). These are explained below.

MeetDot User Interface: We implemented a simple web-based user interface that allows users to have meetings with automatically translated captions overlaid. Our interface consists of:
- A home page (Figure 2, top-left panel) for creating a meeting room with default settings, or a game (§ 4).
- A meeting creation page, where the room settings can be configured in different ways for experimen-

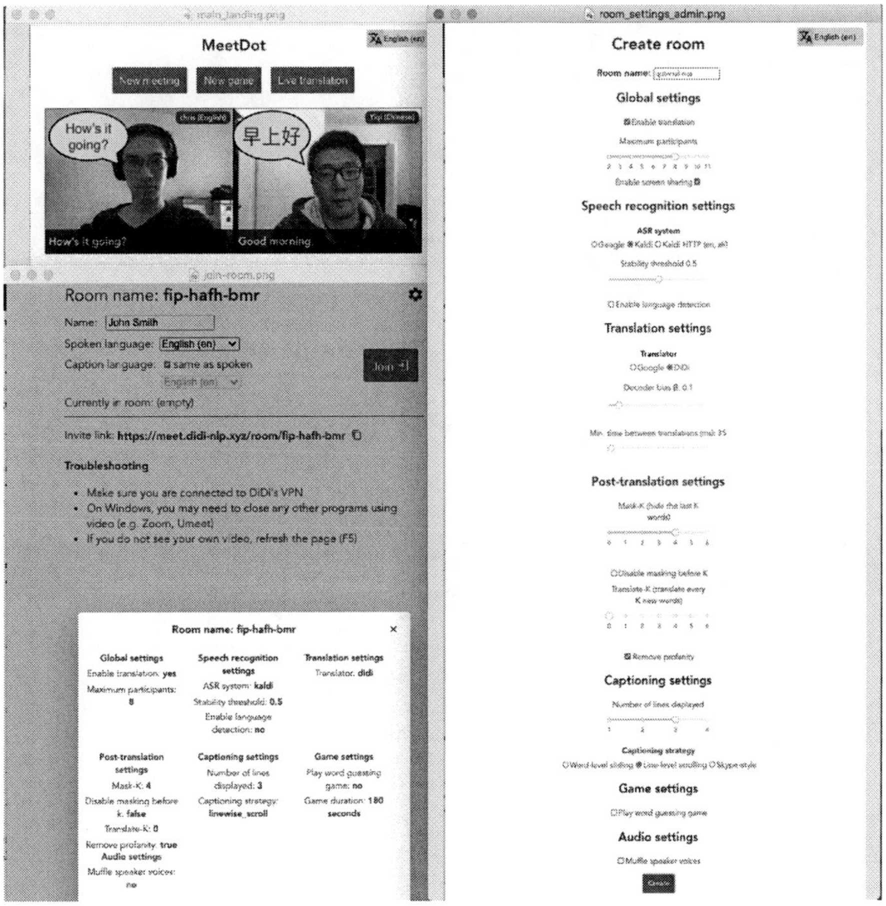

Figure 2: MeetDot room creation. Landing page (top, left panel) Any user can set up a MeetDot room and share its URL with potential participants (bottom, left panel). Admin users can select parameters that control captioning, speech recognition, and translation (right panel, §3).

tation. (Figure 2, right panel)
- A meeting landing page, where a user specifies their speaking language and caption language (usually the same) before joining the meeting. (Figure 2, bottom-left panel)
- A meeting page, where the video call takes place (Figure 3)

The meeting page features real-time translated captions overlaid on each speaker's video, displayed to each user in their selected language (Figure 3). The user's spoken language and caption language can also be changed on-the-fly. The meetings support full video-conferencing functionality, including microphone and camera toggles, screen sharing, and gallery/focused views. Finally, there is a panel that shows the automatically transcribed and translated conversation history in the user's preferred language, which can also be saved.

MeetDot also supports "Live Translation" mode that can translate audio from any audio feed, e.g. a microphone or the user's own computer. We provide instructions for the latter, so users can see captions for audio in either another browser tab or an ongoing Zoom call or audio from their system.

The frontend is implemented in Vue,[2] and the backend is implemented using Flask. Videoconferencing functionality is built with WebRTC,[3] using *Daily.co*[4] as the signaling server to initiate real-time audio and video connections. The frontend sends audio bytes to the Flask backend through a WebSocket connection, which routes them to the speech recognition and translation services and returns translated captions to be displayed.

[2] `https://vuejs.org/`
[3] `https://webrtc.org/`
[4] `https://www.daily.co/`

Figure 3: MeetDot videoconference interface. Translated captions are incrementally updated (word-by-word, phrase-by-phrase) on top of participant videos. Translations also appear in the transcript panel (on right, not shown), updated utterance-by-utterance. Choosing a caption language (4th button from left at the bottom, in green) displays all captions in that particular language. This depicts the view of the English caption user.

Speech Recognition and Machine Translation: Our backend services of ASR and MT are joined in a cascaded manner. Each participant's speech is fed in a streaming fashion to the ASR module of the appropriate language selected by the user. Additionally, we show the ASR output as captions to the speaker as feedback/confirmation to them. Each of the transcribed text returned by ASR is fed to the MT system to translate it into the caption language selected by the reader, from scratch. This strategy is termed as *re-translation.* Since the ASR stream continually returns a revised or an extended string, the input to MT is noisy and will lead to the captions overwritten frequently (termed as *flicker*) leading to a high cognitive load on the reading. We employ several techniques to have better user experience while they are reading the captions (elaborated more below).

At present, we support English, Chinese, Spanish and Portuguese languages for both speech and captions. The modular architecture of our system allows us to plug-and-play different ASR and MT service components in the backend. We develop two different ASR systems based on the Kaldi framework and WeNet (Yao et al., 2021). We can also swap either of these to use Google ASR API instead. For MT, we have the option of using our in-house DiDi MT system (Chen et al., 2020) as well as call Google MT API. For Kaldi ASR, we adapt pre-trained Kaldi models to videoconferencing domain by interpolating the pre-trained language model with our in-domain language models. For WeNet, we use use the *Unified Conformer* model and language model interpolation is planned for future work.[5] Following Arivazhagan et al. (2020), we modify the decoding procedure of MT in OpenNMT's ctranslate toolkit[6] to mitigate the issue of flicker mentioned above.

We include several additional features to enhance user experience. We use NVIDIA NeMo toolkit[7] to punctuate the captions and predict if the word should be capitalized or not, which makes the captions more readable. We have an initial named entity recognition module, to recognize mentions of participants' names in speech when using the Kaldi ASR system. This is performed by interpolating the ASR's language model with a language model trained on a synthesised corpus that contains participants' names. The name

[5]We use a pre-trained checkpoint for English ASR and trained a Chinese ASR model from scratch using the multi-cn and TAL datasets.

[6]https://github.com/OpenNMT/CTranslate2

[7]https://github.com/NVIDIA/NeMo

Direction	Systems	Final bleu	Translation lag (s)	Normalized erasure	Initial lag (s)	Incremental caption lag (s)	Mean word burstiness	Max word burstiness
En-to-Zh	*Google ASR, Google MT*	17.81	5.84	2.69	3.82	0.71	5.26	11.83
"	*Kaldi ASR, DiDi MT*	19.59	2.72	0.33	2.59	0.43	4.34	9.20
"	*WeNet ASR, DiDi MT*	23.76	2.39	0.21	2.73	0.47	4.76	9.62
Zh-to-En	*Google ASR, Google MT*	9.99	2.33	0.47	4.31	2.12	5.20	9.46
"	*Kaldi ASR, DiDi MT*	7.88	3.33	0.73	2.70	0.42	2.42	6.13
"	*WeNet ASR, DiDi MT*	9.76	2.27	0.37	2.52	0.32	2.42	5.65

Table 1: Baseline results on our *daily work conversation* dataset. Note that the Google API does not have biased-decoding available to reduce flicker. Metrics are explained in §4. Right 4 metrics are introduced by our work.

pronunciation dictionary required by Kaldi ASR is generated automatically by rules. Profanity is detected using a standard list of keywords and starred in both ASR and translation output. We have an experimental module to detect the speaker's language automatically (instead of being manually set by the user). The advantage of such a feature is to allow code-switching between multiple languages which is a common behavior among multilingual speakers (Solorio and Liu, 2008; Sivasankaran et al., 2018).

Captioning Strategies: Here we describe how we deploy ASR and MT capabilities to create translation captions that are incrementally updated in real time. Since we display translation captions on top of a speaker's video feed, we have limited screen real-estate—for example, 3 lines of 60 characters each.

Each time we receive an incremental ASR update (hypothesis extension or revision), we translate the updated string from scratch (Arivazhagan et al., 2020). If the translation exceeds the available real-estate, we display the longest suffix that fits. ASR also signals utterance boundaries; we only send the current, growing utterance through MT, caching the MT results on previous utterances.

The basic system exhibits large amounts of flicker (Niehues et al., 2016, 2018), which we mitigate with these methods:

Translate-k. We only send every kth ASR output to MT. This results in captions that are more stable, but which update more slowly.

Translate-t. Improving on translate-k, we send an ASR output to MT if at least t seconds have elapsed since the last MT call.

Mask-k. We suppress the last k words from the MT output, providing time for the translation to settle down (Cho and Esipova, 2016; Gu et al., 2017; Ma et al., 2019; Arivazhagan et al., 2020). We often use `Mask-4` in practice.

Biased MT decoding. We encourage word-by-word MT decoding to match the string output by the previous MT call (Arivazhagan et al., 2020), avoiding translation variations that, while acceptable, unfortunately introduce flicker.

Preserve linebreaks. When possible, we prevent words from jumping back & forth across linebreaks.

Smooth scrolling. We reduce perception of flicker by scrolling lines smoothly, pixel-wise.

4 Evaluation

Dataset: In order to evaluate our system in the most-appropriate deployment scenario, we construct an evaluation dataset based on meetings within our team. We have a total of 5 meetings, 3 meetings involving 7 participants and in English and 2 meetings involving 2 participants in Chinese. The content of the meetings are daily work conversation and contains a total of 135 mins (94 mins English and 41 mins Chinese). We manually transcribe and translate these meetings using a simple and uniform set of guidelines. The resulting dataset consists of 494 English utterances ($\sim 11k$ words, translated into Chinese) and 183 Chinese utterances ($\sim 9.8k$ characters, translated into English). We use this dataset to measure our intrinsic evaluation metrics.

Intrinsic metrics: We adopt the following metrics from previous work on streaming translation (Papineni et al., 2002; Niehues et al., 2016; Arivazhagan et al., 2020):

- *Final Bleu.* We measure the Bleu MT accuracy of final, target-language utterances against a reference set of human translations. Anti-flicker devices that "lock in" partial translations will generally decrease final Bleu.
- *Translation lag.* We measure (roughly) the average difference, in seconds, between when a word was spoken and when its translation was finalized on the screen.
- *Normalized erasure.* We quantify flicker as m/n,

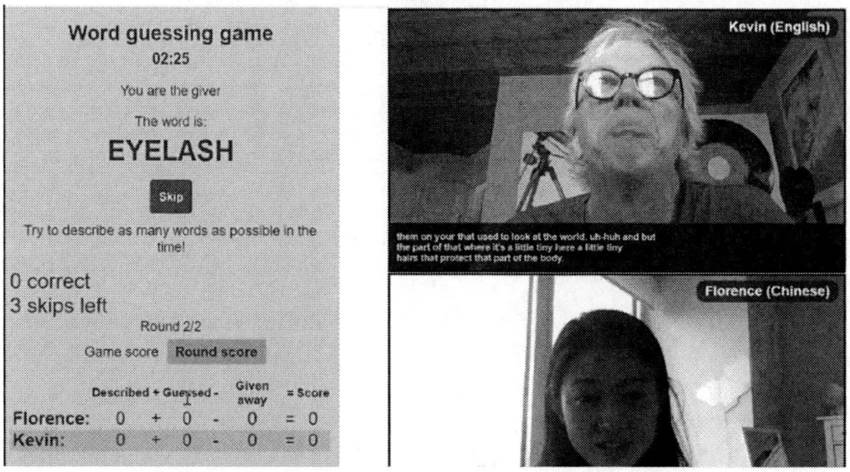

Figure 4: Cross-lingual word guessing game for extrinsic evaluation. Roles: one player is given a word to describe in their language, one or more players look at the captions displayed to guess the correct word. Screenshot shown is that of the describer of the word. Word is *"eyelash"* (left panel) - the participants communicate hints and guesses through *MeetDot* translation captions, and the system itself spots correct guesses.

the number of words m that get erased during the production of an n-word utterance.

To support our videoconferencing application, we introduce other intrinsic metrics:

- *Initial lag*. In videoconferencing, we find it valuable to generate translation captions immediately after a speaker begins, even if the initial translation involves some flicker. Here we measure the time between initial speaking time and the first displayed word. We improve initial lag by adopting a `Mask-0` policy at the start of an utterance, transitioning to our usual `Mask-4` policy later.
- *Incremental caption lag*. The average time between caption updates.
- *Mean (& Max) word burstiness*. The mean number of words or characters for Chinese (maximum, respectively) that are added/subtracted in a single caption update (for a given utterance's translation– averaged over all utterances, respectively).

In Table 1, we present baseline results of the various intrinsic metrics for the English to Chinese and Chinese to English systems. We present results for 3 different module combinations, namely, (i) Google API[8] for ASR[9] and MT[10] (ii) Kaldi ASR and DiDi MT (iii) WeNet ASR and DiDi MT. From the results table, we would like to highlight that the biased decoding modification for machine translation has a positive impact on several metrics such as translation lag, normalized erasure and word burstiness. Biased decoding is absent in the Google MT API, hence has higher numbers in these metrics. This results in increasing flicker leading to a poorer user experience. Our final bleu score when using WeNet ASR and DiDi MT is several points better than Google ASR and Google MT in the English to Chinese direction and has comparable performance in Chinese to English direction. ASR system's performance is an important factor in a cascaded system. Kaldi ASR has a word error rate (WER) rate of 43.88 for English (character error rate (CER) of 49.75 for Chinese, respectively) compared to WeNet ASR's WER of 34.74 (CER of 38.03 for Chinese, respectively). This has a direct impact on final bleu scores as seen from the results.

Cross-lingual word guessing game: Extrinsic metrics for speech translation are not as popular as intrinsic ones (Arivazhagan et al., 2020; Niehues et al., 2016). However, given the broad range of techniques for displaying translation captions, we would like to measure things that are closer to the user experience.

Here, we introduce a cross-lingual, cooperative word game for A/B testing different captioning algorithms. Players who speak different languages use *MeetDot*'s translation captions to communicate with each other. If the players obtain higher scores under one condition, we conclude that their communication is, in some way, made more effective

[8] Accessed on 2021-09-09.

[9] `https://cloud.google.com/speech-to-text`

[10] `https://cloud.google.com/translate`

and efficient.

The game is a variation on *Taboo*,[11] in which one player receives a secret word (such as "racoon" or "scary") and must describe it without mentioning the word or variant of it. The other player tries to guess the word. The players are awarded a point for every word guessed in a 4-minute period. The first player is allowed to skip upto three words.

In our variation, the first player may receive a Chinese word and describe it in Chinese, while the second player sees English captions and makes guesses in English. When translation is quick, accurate, and readable, players score higher.

We design our bilingual wordlists to contain words with limited ambiguity. This way, we are able to build a reliable, automatic scorer that rewards players and advances them to the next word.

We also implement a competitive, multi-player version of the game, where players are assigned points for making correct guesses faster than others, and for giving clues that lead to fast guesses.

5 Conclusion and Future Work

We describe *MeetDot*, a videoconferencing system with live translation captions, along with its components: UI, ASR, MT, and captioning. We implement an evaluation suite that allows us to accurately compute metrics from the sequence of captions that users would see. We also describe a cross-lingual word game for A/B testing different captioning algorithms and conditions.

Our future work includes improved ASR/MT, extrinsic testing, and an open source release. Our overall goal is to provide a platform for developing translation captions that are accurate and "right behind you".

References

Naveen Arivazhagan, Colin Cherry, I Te, Wolfgang Macherey, Pallavi Baljekar, and George F. Foster. 2020. Re-translation strategies for long form, simultaneous, spoken language translation. In *Proc. ICASSP*.

Tanfang Chen, Weiwei Wang, Wenyang Wei, Xing Shi, Xiangang Li, Jieping Ye, and Kevin Knight. 2020. DiDi's machine translation system for WMT2020. In *Proc. WMT*.

Eunah Cho, C. Fügen, T. Herrmann, Kevin Kilgour, M. Mediani, Christian Mohr, J. Niehues, Kay Rottmann, Christian Saam, S. Stüker, and A. Waibel. 2013. A real-world system for simultaneous translation of german lectures. In *INTERSPEECH*.

Kyunghyun Cho and Masha Esipova. 2016. Can neural machine translation do simultaneous translation? *ArXiv*, abs/1606.02012.

Jiatao Gu, Graham Neubig, Kyunghyun Cho, and Victor O.K. Li. 2017. Learning to translate in real-time with neural machine translation. In *Proc. EACL*.

Liang Huang, Colin Cherry, Mingbo Ma, Naveen Arivazhagan, and Zhongjun He. 2020. Simultaneous translation. In *Proc. EMNLP: Tutorial Abstracts*.

Mingbo Ma, Liang Huang, Hao Xiong, Renjie Zheng, Kaibo Liu, Baigong Zheng, Chuanqiang Zhang, Zhongjun He, Hairong Liu, Xing Li, Hua Wu, and Haifeng Wang. 2019. STACL: Simultaneous translation with implicit anticipation and controllable latency using prefix-to-prefix framework. In *Proc. ACL*.

J. Niehues, T. Nguyen, Eunah Cho, Thanh-Le Ha, Kevin Kilgour, M. Müller, Matthias Sperber, S. Stüker, and A. Waibel. 2016. Dynamic transcription for low-latency speech translation. In *INTERSPEECH*.

J. Niehues, Ngoc-Quan Pham, Thanh-Le Ha, Matthias Sperber, and A. Waibel. 2018. Low-latency neural speech translation. In *INTERSPEECH*.

Kishore Papineni, Salim Roukos, Todd Ward, and Wei-Jing Zhu. 2002. Bleu: a method for automatic evaluation of machine translation. In *Proc. ACL*.

Tae Jin Park, Naoyuki Kanda, Dimitrios Dimitriadis, Kyu J. Han, Shinji Watanabe, and Shrikanth Narayanan. 2021. A review of speaker diarization: Recent advances with deep learning. *arXiv:2101.09624*.

Colin Raffel, Minh-Thang Luong, Peter J. Liu, Ron J. Weiss, and Douglas Eck. 2017. Online and linear-time attention by enforcing monotonic alignments. In *Proc. ICML*.

Sunit Sivasankaran, Brij Mohan Lal Srivastava, Sunayana Sitaram, Kalika Bali, and Monojit Choudhury. 2018. Phone merging for code-switched speech recognition. In *Workshop on Computational Approaches to Linguistic Code Switching*.

Thamar Solorio and Yang Liu. 2008. Learning to predict code-switching points. In *Proc. EMNLP*.

Xiaolin Wang, Andrew Finch, Masao Utiyama, and Eiichiro Sumita. 2016. A prototype automatic simultaneous interpretation system. In *Proc. COLING: System Demonstrations*.

Hua Wu, Colin Cherry, Liang Huang, Zhongjun He, Qun Liu, Maha Elbayad, Mark Liberman, Haifeng Wang, Mingbo Ma, and Ruiqing Zhang, editors. 2021. *Proc. Second Workshop on Automatic Simultaneous Translation*.

[11] `https://www.hasbro.com/common/instruct/Taboo(2000).PDF`

Hua Wu, Collin Cherry, Liang Huang, Zhongjun He, Mark Liberman, James Cross, and Yang Liu, editors. 2020. *Proc. First Workshop on Automatic Simultaneous Translation*.

Zhuoyuan Yao, Di Wu, Xiong Wang, Binbin Zhang, Fan Yu, Chao Yang, Zhendong Peng, Xiaoyu Chen, Lei Xie, and Xin Lei. 2021. Wenet: Production oriented streaming and non-streaming end-to-end speech recognition toolkit. In *INTERSPEECH*.

ZDNet. 2021. Cisco's webex debuts real-time translation from english to 100+ languages. `https://tinyurl.com/bwvfm8ka`. Accessed: 2021-06-30.

Baigong Zheng, Renjie Zheng, M. Ma, and Liang Huang. 2019. Simultaneous translation with flexible policy via restricted imitation learning. In *ACL*.

Box Embeddings: An open-source library for representation learning using geometric structures

Tejas Chheda[*†], **Purujit Goyal**[*†], **Trang Tran**[*†‡], **Dhruvesh Patel** [†], **Michael Boratko**[†], **Shib Sankar Dasgupta**[†], and **Andrew McCallum**[†]
[†] College of Information and Computer Sciences
University of Massachusetts Amherst, MA 01003, USA
[‡] MassMutual Data Science, MA 01002, USA
{tchheda,purujitgoyal,ttrang,dhruveshpate}@cs.umass.edu
{mboratko,ssdasgupta,mccallum}@cs.umass.edu

Abstract

A major factor contributing to the success of modern representation learning is the ease of performing various vector operations. Recently, objects with geometric structures (eg. distributions, complex or hyperbolic vectors, or regions such as cones, disks, or boxes) have been explored for their alternative inductive biases and additional representational capacities. In this work, we introduce Box Embeddings, a Python library that enables researchers to easily apply and extend probabilistic box embeddings. [1] Fundamental geometric operations on boxes are implemented in a numerically stable way, as are modern approaches to training boxes which mitigate gradient sparsity. The library is fully open-source, and compatible with both PyTorch and TensorFlow, which allows existing neural network layers to be replaced with or transformed into boxes effortlessly. In this work, we present the implementation details of the fundamental components of the library, and the concepts required to use box representations alongside existing neural network architectures.

1 Introduction

Much of the success of modern deep learning rests on the ability to learn representations of data compatible with the structure of deep architectures used for training and inference (Hinton, 2007; LeCun et al., 2015). Vectors are the most common choice of representation, as linear transformations are well understood and element-wise non-linearities offer increased representational capacity while being straightforward to implement. Recently, various alternatives to vector representations have been explored, each with different inductive biases or capabilities. Vilnis and McCallum (2015) represent words using Gaussian distributions, which can be thought of as a vector representation with an explicit parameterization of variance. This variance was demonstrated to be capable of capturing the generality of concepts, and KL-divergence provides a natural asymmetric operation between distributions, ideas which were expanded upon in Athiwaratkun and Wilson (2018). Nickel and Kiela (2017), on the other hand, change the embedding space itself from Euclidean to hyperbolic space, where the negative curvature has been shown to provide a natural inductive bias toward modeling tree-like graphs (Nickel and Kiela, 2018; Weber, 2020; Weber and Nickel, 2018).

A subset of these alternative approaches explores *region-based* representations, where entities are not represented by a single point in space but rather explicitly parameterized regions whose volumes and intersections are easily calculated. Order embeddings (Vendrov et al., 2016) represent elements using infinite cones in $\mathbb{R}^n_+$ and demonstrate their efficacy of modeling *partial orders*. Lai and Hockenmaier (2017) endow order embeddings with probabilistic semantics by integrating the space under a negative exponential measure, allowing the calculation of arbitrary marginal, joint, and conditional probabilities. Cone representations are not particularly flexible, however - for instance, the resulting probability model cannot represent negative correlation - motivating the development of *probabilistic box embeddings* (Vilnis et al., 2018), where entities are represented by n-dimensional rectangles (i.e. Cartesian products of intervals) in Euclidean space.

Probabilistic box embeddings have undergone several rounds of methodological improvements.

[*] Equal Contributions.

[1] The source code and the usage and API documentation for the library is available at `https://github.com/iesl/box-embeddings` and `https://www.iesl.cs.umass.edu/box-embeddings/main/index.html`, respectively. A quick video tutorial is available at `https://youtu.be/MEPDw8sIwUY`.

Proceedings of the 2021 Conference on Empirical Methods in Natural Language Processing: System Demonstrations, pages 203–211
November 7–11, 2021.

The original model used a surrogate function to pull disjoint boxes together, which was improved upon in Li et al. (2018) via Gaussian convolution of box indicator functions, resulting in a smoother loss landscape and better performance as a result. Dasgupta et al. (2020) improved box training further by using a latent random variable approach, where the corners of boxes are modeled using Gumbel random variables. These latter models lacked valid probabilistic semantics, however, a fact rectified in Boratko et al. (2021).

While each methodological improvement demonstrated better performance on various modeling tasks, the implementations grew more complex, bringing with it various challenges related to performance and numerical stability. Various applications of probabilistic box embeddings (eg. modeling joint-hierarchies (Patel et al., 2020), uncertain knowledge graph representation (Chen et al., 2021), or fine-grained entity typing (Onoe et al., 2021)) have relied on bespoke implementations, adding unnecessary difficulty and differences in implementation when applying box embeddings to new tasks. To mitigate this issue and make applying and extending box embeddings easier, we saw the need to introduce a reusable, unified, stable library that provides the basic functionalities needed in studying box embeddings. To this end, we introduce "Box Embeddings", a fully open-source Python library hosted on PyPI. The contributions of this work are as follows:

- Provide a modular and reusable library that aids the researchers in studying probabilistic box embeddings. The library is compatible with both of the most popular Machine Learning libraries: PyTorch and TensorFlow.
- Create extensive documentation and example code, demonstrating the use of the library to make it easy to adapt to existing code-bases.
- Rigorously unit-test the codebase with high coverage, ensuring an additional layer of reliability.

2 Box Embeddings

Formally, a "box" is defined as a Cartesian product of closed intervals,

$$B(\theta) = \prod_{i=1}^{n} [z_i(\theta), Z_i(\theta)]$$
$$= [z_1(\theta), Z_1(\theta)] \times \cdots \times [z_n(\theta), Z_n(\theta)],$$

z	the lower-left coordinate of the boxes
Z	the top-right coordinate of the boxes
`centre`	the center coordinate of the boxes, $\frac{z+Z}{2}$
`box_shape`	shape of the center coordinates (or z, Z)
`box_reshape`	if possible, reshapes the `box_shape` into the `target_shape`
`broadcast`	if possible, adds new dimensions to the `box_shape` to make it compatible with the `target_shape`

Table 1: BoxTensor Properties

where θ represent some latent parameters. In the simplest case, $\theta \in \mathbb{R}^{2n}$ are free parameters, and z_i, Z_i are projections onto the i and $n+i$ components, respectively. In general, however, the parameterization may be more complicated, eg. θ may be the output from a neural network. For brevity, we omit the explicit dependency on θ. The different operations (such as volume and intersection) commonly used when calculating probabilities from box embeddings can all be defined in terms of z_i, Z_i - the *min* and *max* coordinates of the interval in each dimension.

2.1 Parameterizations

The fundamental component of the library is the `BoxTensor` class, a wrapper around the `torch.Tensor` and `tensorflow.Tensor` class that represents a tensor/array of boxes. `BoxTensor` is an opaque wrapper, in that it exposes the operations and properties necessary to use the box representations (see table 1) irrespective of the specific way in which the parameters θ are related to z_i, Z_i. The main two properties of the `BoxTensor` are `z` and `Z`, which represent the *min* and *max* coordinates of an instance of `BoxTensor`. Listing 1 shows how to create an instance of `BoxTensor` consisting of two 2-dimensional boxes in Figure 1.

```
import torch
from box_embeddings.parameterizations import
    BoxTensor
theta = torch.tensor(
    [[[-2, -2], [-1, -1]], [[1, 0], [3, 4]]]
)
box = BoxTensor(theta)
A = box[0]
B = box[1]
```

Listing 1: Manually initializing a `BoxTensor` consisiting for the 2-D boxes depicted in Figure 1.

Given a `torch.Tensor` corresponding to the parameters θ of a `BoxTensor`, one can obtain a box representation in multiple ways depending on the constraints on the *min* and *max* coordinates of the box representations as well as the the range of values in θ. The `BoxTensor` class itself simply splits θ in half on the last dimension, using $\theta[\ldots, 1:n]$ as z and $\theta[\ldots, n+1:2n]$ as Z.

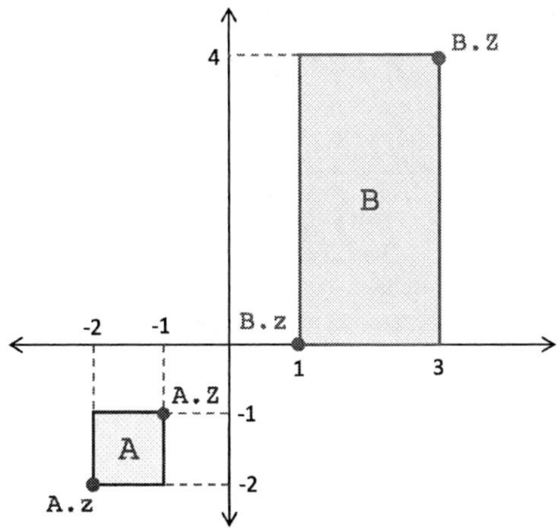

Figure 1: Box Parameterization

Here, the `Ellipsis` "..." denotes any number of leading dimensions, for instance, batch, sequence-length, etc. For the sake of simplifying the notations, from here on, the presence of the leading dimensions will not be explicitly denoted using the `Ellipsis`. Moreover, all the indexing operations can be assumed to be operating only on the last dimension, unless stated otherwise.

```
from box_embeddings.parameterizations import
    BoxTensor, MinDeltaBoxTensor, SigmoidBoxTensor
box_tensor = BoxTensor(theta)
box_tensor_pos_sides = MinDeltaBoxTensor(theta)
box_tensor_in_unit_cube = SigmoidBoxTensor(theta)
```

Listing 2: Converting latent vectors to boxes, for various choices of box parameterizations.

Any box can be represented in this fashion, however some settings of θ may lead to situations where $z_i > Z_i$. This scenario is invalid under conventional box models (Vilnis et al., 2018; Li et al., 2018), and although valid for models which interpret these coordiantes as parameters of a latent random variable (Dasgupta et al., 2020; Boratko et al., 2021) it is often still desirable to constrain side-lengths to be non-negative. `MinDeltaBoxTensor` represents boxes that are unbounded and have non-negative side-length in each dimension. That is, it outputs boxes with $z, Z \in \mathbb{R}^n$ and $z_i \leq Z_i$, and furthermore any such box has a corresponding θ under this parameterization. A valid probabilistic interpretation of box embeddings requires that their embedding space has finite measure, however. One trivial way to accomplish this is to parameterize boxes to remain within the unit hypercube, which can be accomplished via the `SigmoidBoxTensor` or `TanhBoxTensor` classes. The specific mathematical operations relating the θ variables to their z, Z coordinates are found in Table 2, and example usage can be found in Listing 2.[2]

Parameterization	z	Z
`BoxTensor`	$\theta[1:n]$	$\theta[n+1:2n]$
`MinDeltaBoxTensor`	$\theta[1:n]$	$z + \text{softplus}(\theta[n+1:2n])$
`SigmoidBoxTensor`	$\sigma(\theta[1:n])$	$z + (1-z)\sigma(\theta[n+1:2n])$
`TanhBoxTensor`	$\frac{\tanh(\theta[1:n])+1}{2}$	$z + \frac{(1-z)\tanh(\theta[n+1:2n])}{2}$

Table 2: The different subclasses of `BoxTensor` and how they represent boxes using the learnable parameters $\theta \in \mathbb{R}^{2n}$ taken as input.

2.2 Operations on BoxTensor

We provide a variety of modules that implement different operations on the box-tensors, such as `Intersection`, `Volume`, `Pooling` and `Regularization`. We also implemented a `BoxEmbedding` layer that, just like a vector embedding layer, provides index lookup. However, unlike a vector embedding layer, this returns boxes instead of vectors. We discuss these layers in detail below.

2.2.1 Intersection

Given two instances of `BoxTensor` with compatible shapes, this operation performs the intersection between the two box-tensors and returns an instance of `BoxTensor` as the result. For two instances of `BoxTensor` A and B with coordinates (z_A, Z_A) and (z_B, Z_B) respectively, the (z, Z) coordinates of the resulting intersection box for the two types of intersection operations, `HardIntersection` (Vilnis et al., 2018; Li et al., 2018) and `GumbelIntersection` (Dasgupta et al., 2020), are shown in Table 3, and corresponding codes are provided in Listing 3.

```
from box_embeddings.parameterizations import
    BoxTensor
from box_embeddings.modules.intersection import
    HardIntersection, GumbelIntersection

boxA = BoxTensor(theta_a)
boxB = BoxTensor(theta_b)

hard_intersection = HardIntersection()
gumbel_intersection =
    GumbelIntersection(intersection_temperature=0.8)

hard_ab = hard_intersection(boxA, boxB)
gumbel_ab = gumbel_intersection(boxA, boxB)
```

Listing 3: Various approaches to computing the intersection of two box tensors.

[2]The TensorFlow version for all the code snippets is provided in Appendix.

Intersection type	z	Z
`HardIntersection`	$\max(z_A, z_B)$	$\min(Z_A, Z_B)$
`GumbelIntersection`	$\beta\,\mathrm{LSE}(\frac{z_A}{\beta}, \frac{z_B}{\beta})$	$-\beta\,\mathrm{LSE}(-\frac{Z_A}{\beta}, -\frac{Z_B}{\beta})$

Table 3: Expressions for the two kinds of intersection layers. Here, LSE denotes logsumexp, i.e., $\mathrm{LSE}(x, y) := \log(\exp(x) + \exp(y))$

2.2.2 Volume

Boxes (or intersections of boxes) are typically queried for their *volumes*. Our `HardVolume` layer implements the volume calculation as originally introduced in Vilnis et al. (2018), which is simply a direct multiplication of side-lengths. It is in this setting where bounded parameterizations such as `SigmoidBoxTensor` and `TanhBoxTensor` are particularly useful, as the resulting volumes can be interpreted as yielding a valid marginal or joint probability. Note, however, that the guarantees of positive side-lengths do not apply when taking the intersection of two disjoint boxes, in which case the resulting box should have zero volume.

Our `SoftVolume` layer implements the volume function proposed by Li et al. (2018), which mitigates the training difficulties that arise when disjoint boxes should overlap. Finally, our `BesselApproxVolume` layer implements the volume function proposed in Dasgupta et al. (2020), which approximates the expected volume of a box where the coordinates are interpreted as location parameters of Gumbel random variables. The expressions and the code snippets for the various volume operations are given in Table 4 and 4, respectively.

Remark 1. Note that due to the presence of the product, the naive implementation of volume computations as shown in Table 4 will often result in numerical overflow or underflow for dimensions greater than 5. Hence, we provide an option to compute the volume in log-space, which is *on* by default.

```
from box_embeddings.modules.volume import
    HardVolume, SoftVolume, BesselApproxVolume

hard_volume = HardVolume()
log_volA = hard_volume(boxA)

soft_volume = SoftVolume(volume_temperature=5.0)
log_vol_ab = soft_volume(hard_ab)

bessel_volume =
    BesselApproxVolume(volume_temperature=5.0,
    intersection_temperature=0.8)
log_vol_ab = bessel_volume(gumbel_ab)
```

Listing 4: Different proposed methods for computing box volume, of increasing "smoothness".

Intersection type	Volume
`HardVolume`	$\prod_{i=1}^{n} \max(Z_i - z_i, 0)$
`SoftVolume`	$\prod_{i=1}^{n} T * \mathrm{softplus}(\frac{Z_i - z_i}{T})$
`BesselApproxVolume`	$\prod_{i=1}^{n} T * \mathrm{softplus}(\frac{Z_i - z_i - 2\gamma\beta}{T})$

Table 4: The expressions for different volume implementations. Here, (z, Z) are the min-max coordinates of the input `BoxTensor`, T is the volume temperature hyperparameter, γ is the Euler-Mascheroni constant, β is the gumbel intersection parameter, and $\mathrm{softplus}(x) = \log(1 + \exp x)$.

2.2.3 Pooling

The library also provides pooling operations that take as input an instance of `BoxTensor` and reduce one of the leading dimensions by pooling across it. Currently, there are two types of pooling operations implemented – intersection based, which takes intersection across all the boxes in a particular dimension, and mean based, which takes the arithmetic mean of the min and max coordinates of the boxes across a dimension.

2.2.4 Regularization

There is an excessive slackness in the learning objective defined using containment conditions on boxes, which leads to large flat regions of local minima resulting in poor training. In order to mitigate this problem, Patel et al. (2020) introduces volume based regularization for boxes, which augments the loss with a penalty if the box volume exceeds a certain threshold. This penalty reduces the size of the flat local minima facilitating better training of boxes.

```
from box_embeddings.modules.pooling import
    HardIntersectionBoxPooler
from box_embeddings.modules.regularization import
    L2SideBoxRegularizer

pooler = HardIntersectionBoxPooler()
pooled_box = pooler(box)

box_regularizer =
    L2SideBoxRegularizer(log_scale=True)

vol_box = soft_volume(pooled_box)
loss = loss_fn(vol_box) +
    box_regularizer(pooled_box)
```

Listing 5: Box pooling and regularization operations.

2.3 Embedding

`BoxTensor` and its children classes, do not store learnable parameters directly, they simply wrap the input tensor and provide an interface which interprets the wrapped tensor as box representation. However, when working with a shallow model (embedding only model), one needs an embedding layer that owns its parameters and outputs boxes corresponding to the input indices. The library provides `BoxEmbedding` layer that works like a native embedding layer in PyTorch or TensorFlow, i.e., it performs index lookup, but instead of returning an instance of the native tensor, it returns instance of `BoxTensor`.

2.3.1 Initializers

We also provide an abstract interface `BoxInitializer` to implement various methods for initializing the learnable parameters of the `BoxEmbedding` layer. As a concrete example we implement `UniformBoxInitializer`, which initializes boxes with uniformly random min coordinates and side lengths. This is used as the default initializer for the `BoxEmbedding` layer unless specified otherwise.

3 Applications

In this section, we demonstrate the Box Embeddings library by using it to implement models for two real-world tasks: a representation learning task of hierarchical graph modeling (Nickel and Kiela, 2017; Vilnis et al., 2018), and the NLP task of natural language inference (Dagan et al., 2005; Bowman et al., 2015). We first demonstrate the intuition behind the containment-based loss function used to train these models using a toy example involving two 2-dimensional boxes.

3.1 Toy example

For the purpose of demonstration, we set up a toy example which embeds a simple graph with just two nodes, X, Y and one edge (X, Y). We start with two non-overlapping boxes at initialization: box_X and box_Y, and use SGD to train the parameters that minimize the following loss function

$$\mathcal{L}(\theta) = -\log \frac{\text{Vol}\,(\text{B}(\theta_X) \cap \text{B}(\theta_Y))}{\text{Vol}\,(\text{B}(\theta_Y))}.$$

Geometrically, this encourages $\text{box}_Y \subseteq \text{box}_X$. If using a box embedding with valid probabilistic semantics, this loss function can be interpreted as binary cross-entropy with $P(X|Y) = 1$.[3] The code for this example can be found in Appendix A.2. We visualize the containment training process in Figure 3. Each line represents the edge of the box in one dimension, with the left endpoint of a blue or orange line to be the minimum coordinate of a box, and the right endpoint of a line to be the maximum coordinate of a box.

3.2 Representing hierarchical graph

Representing relations between the nodes of a hierarchy is useful for various NLP and Machine Learning tasks such as natural language inference (Wang et al., 2019; Sharma et al., 2019), entity typing (Onoe et al., 2021), multi-label classification (Chatterjee et al., 2021), and question answering (Jin et al., 2019; Fang et al., 2020). For example, in Figure 2, knowing the hypernym relationship between the pairs *(herb, basil)*, *(herb, thyme)*, and *(herb, rosemary)* can help paraphrase the sentence "This dish requires basil, thyme and rosemary" into "This dish requires several herbs.". Additionally, knowing the relationship between *(herb, banana)*, and *(fruit, banana)* can help answer questions such as "What is both a herb and a fruit?" Note that this latter example maps directly onto the notion of box intersection, as we are seeking an element contained in both "herb" and "fruit".

For demonstration, we train box embeddings to represent the hypernym graph of WordNet (Miller et al., 1990). Hypernym or IS-A is a transitive relation between a pair of words, where one word (hypernym) represents a general/broader concept, and the other word (hyponym) is a more specific sub-concept (Yu et al., 2015). The transitive reduction of the WordNet noun hierarchy contains 82,114 entities and 84,363 edges. The learning task is framed as an edge classification task where, given a pair of nodes (h, t), the model outputs the probability of existence of an edge from h to t. Following Patel et al. (2020), we train an edge classification model using the transitive reduction edges augmented with varying percentages of the transitive closure edges (10%, 25%, 50%) as positive examples and randomly sampled negative examples with positive to negative ratio of 1:10. The `BoxEmbedding` layer is initialized with random boxes representing the nodes of the hypernym graph. For each input pair $x = (h_i, t_i)$, the probability of existence of the edge $h_i \to t_i$ is computed as

$$P(h_i \to t_i) = \frac{\text{Vol}\,(\text{B}(\theta_{h_i}) \cap \text{B}(\theta_{t_i}))}{\text{Vol}\,(\text{B}(\theta_{t_i}))}.$$

In our case, we use `MinDeltaBoxTensor` parameterization, `HardIntersection` and

[3] To understand further the motivation for this choice of graph embedding, see Vilnis et al. (2018).

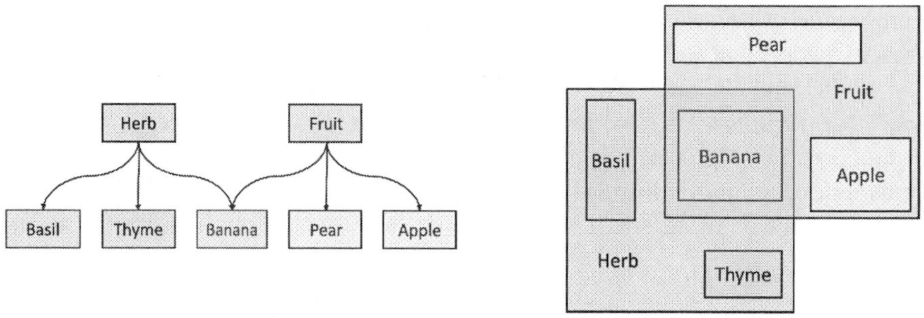

(a) An example hierarchical structure (b) Representing the structure in (a) with Box Embeddings

Figure 2: Box Embeddings can capture hierarchical structures commonly observed in natural language

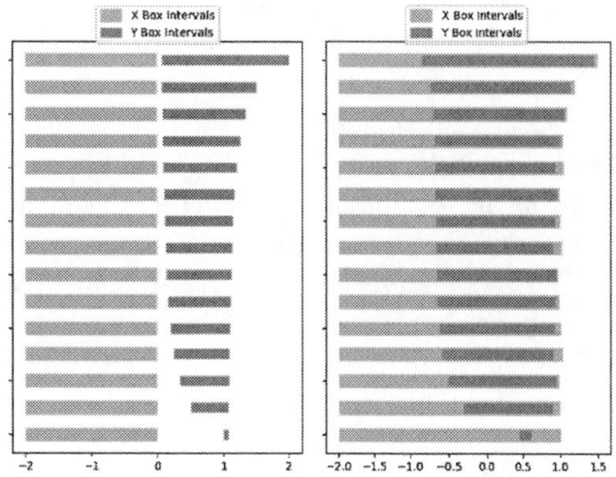

(a) Before training (b) After training

Figure 3: Visualization of two 15-dimensional boxes before and after containment training described in Section 3.1. The green box $B(\theta_Y)$ has been trained to be entirely contained in the orange box $B(\theta_X)$.

TC Edges	0%	10%	25%	50%
w/o Regularization	44.2%	71.3%	81.1%	89.1%
w Regularization	59.4%	90.3%	91.9%	94.2%

Table 5: Test F1 scores for predicting the transitive closure of WordNet's hypernym relations when training on increasing amounts of edges from the transitive closure

`SoftVolume`. Binary cross-entropy loss is used to train the model for edge classification. The test set consists of positive edges sampled from the rest of the transitive closure (not seen during training) and a fixed set of random negatives with the same positive to negative ratio as training. As seen in Table 5, we are able to replicate the result from Patel et al. (2020).

3.3 Natural Language Inference (NLI)

Natural language inference (Dagan et al., 2005; Bowman et al., 2015) is a task where, given two sentences, premise and hypothesis, the model is required to pick whether the premise entails the hypothesis, contradicts the hypothesis, or whether neither relationship holds. The task of NLI is setup as multi-class classification, and in the two-class version, the model is only required to decide whether the premise entails the hypothesis or not (Mishra et al., 2021). Although NLI deals with a pair of sentences at a time, in the space of all possible sentences the transitive relation of entailment establishes a partial order. If the sentences are encoded as boxes then we can train box containment to capture the transitive entailment relation. To demonstrate this, we choose the MNLI corpus (Williams et al., 2018) from the GLUE benchmark (Wang et al., 2018). Since the MNLI dataset presents the NLI task as a three-class problem, we collapse *contradiction* and *neutral* labels into a single label called *not-entails* to obtain a two-class problem with class labels *entails* and *not-entails*.

In order to obtain box representation for the premise and hypothesis sentences, we use a neural network E to first get vector representations v_p and v_h for the premise and the hypothesis, respectively. Both these vectors are then interpreted as the parameters $\theta_p := v_p$ and $\theta_h := v_h$ of a box tensor. Finally, the probability of the *entails* class is computed as

$$P(\text{entails}) = \frac{\text{Vol}\left(\mathbf{B}(\theta_p) \cap \mathbf{B}(\theta_h)\right)}{\text{Vol}\left(\mathbf{B}(\theta_h)\right)}.$$

The parameters of the encoder are trained using the ADAM optimizer (Kingma and Ba, 2014) with binary cross-entropy as the loss. Table 6 shows the test accuracy with two different encoders. As seen, the performance is much higher than random or majority class baselines.

Neural Network Encoder (E)	Accuracy
RoBERTa	78%
LSTM	73%
Random Baseline	50%
Majority Baseline	66%

Table 6: Test accuracy on MNLI task using box embeddings

4 Conclusion

In this paper, we have introduced Box Embeddings, the first Python library focused on allowing region-based representations to be used with deep learning libraries. Our library implements proposed training methods and geometric operations on probabilistic box embeddings in a well-tested and numerically-stable fashion. We described the concepts needed to understand and apply this library to novel tasks, and applied the library to graph modeling and natural language inference, demonstrating both shallow and deep contextualized box representations. We hope the release of this package will aid researchers in using region-based representations in their work, and that the well-documented codebase will facilitate additional methodological extensions to probabilistic box embedding models.

Acknowledgements

The authors would like to thank the members of the Information Extraction and Synthesis Laboratory (IESL) at the University of Massachusetts Amherst for their tremendous support and feedback throughout the project. We also thank Lorraine Li for her involvement in the early phase of the project. This work is funded in part by the University of Southern California subcontract no. 123875727 under Office of Naval Research prime contract no. N660011924032 and University of Southern California subcontract no. 89341790 under Defense Advanced Research Projects Agency prime contract no. FA8750-17-C-0106. The U.S. Government is authorized to reproduce and distribute reprints for Governmental purposes notwithstanding any copyright notation thereon. The views and conclusions contained herein are those of the authors and should not be interpreted as necessarily representing the official policies or endorsements, either expressed or implied, of AFRL, DARPA, or the U.S. Government.

References

Ben Athiwaratkun and Andrew Gordon Wilson. 2018. Hierarchical density order embeddings. In *International Conference on Learning Representations*.

Michael Boratko, Javier Burroni, Shib Sankar Dasgupta, and Andrew McCallum. 2021. Min/max stability and box distributions. In *Conference on Uncertainty in Artificial Intelligence*. PMLR.

Samuel R Bowman, Gabor Angeli, Christopher Potts, and Christopher D Manning. 2015. A large annotated corpus for learning natural language inference. *arXiv preprint arXiv:1508.05326*.

Soumya Chatterjee, Ayush Maheshwari, Ganesh Ramakrishnan, and Saketha Nath Jagaralpudi. 2021. Joint learning of hyperbolic label embeddings for hierarchical multi-label classification. In *Proceedings of the 16th Conference of the European Chapter of the Association for Computational Linguistics: Main Volume*, pages 2829–2841, Online. Association for Computational Linguistics.

Xuelu Chen, Michael Boratko, Muhao Chen, Shib Sankar Dasgupta, Xiang Lorraine Li, and Andrew McCallum. 2021. Probabilistic box embeddings for uncertain knowledge graph reasoning. In *Proceedings of the 2021 Conference of the North American Chapter of the Association for Computational Linguistics: Human Language Technologies*, pages 882–893.

Ido Dagan, Oren Glickman, and Bernardo Magnini. 2005. The pascal recognising textual entailment challenge. In *Machine Learning Challenges Workshop*, pages 177–190. Springer.

Shib Dasgupta, Michael Boratko, Dongxu Zhang, Luke Vilnis, Xiang Li, and Andrew McCallum. 2020. Improving local identifiability in probabilistic box embeddings. *Advances in Neural Information Processing Systems*, 33.

Yuwei Fang, Siqi Sun, Zhe Gan, Rohit Pillai, Shuohang Wang, and Jingjing Liu. 2020. Hierarchical graph network for multi-hop question answering. In *Proceedings of the 2020 Conference on Empirical Methods in Natural Language Processing (EMNLP)*, pages 8823–8838.

Geoffrey E. Hinton. 2007. Learning multiple layers of representation. *Trends in Cognitive Sciences*, 11(10).

Hai Jin, Yi Luo, Chenjing Gao, Xunzhu Tang, and Pingpeng Yuan. 2019. Comqa: Question answering over knowledge base via semantic matching. *IEEE Access*, 7:75235–75246.

Diederik P Kingma and Jimmy Ba. 2014. Adam: A method for stochastic optimization. *arXiv preprint arXiv:1412.6980*.

Alice Lai and Julia Hockenmaier. 2017. Learning to predict denotational probabilities for modeling entailment. In *EACL*.

Yann LeCun, Yoshua Bengio, and Geoffrey Hinton. 2015. Deep learning. *Nature*, 521.

Xiang Li, Luke Vilnis, Dongxu Zhang, Michael Boratko, and Andrew McCallum. 2018. Smoothing the geometry of probabilistic box embeddings. In *International Conference on Learning Representations*.

George A Miller, Richard Beckwith, Christiane Fellbaum, Derek Gross, and Katherine J Miller. 1990. Introduction to wordnet: An on-line lexical database. *International journal of lexicography*, 3(4):235–244.

Anshuman Mishra, Dhruvesh Patel, Aparna Vijayakumar, Xiang Lorraine Li, Pavan Kapanipathi, and Kartik Talamadupula. 2021. Looking beyond sentence-level natural language inference for question answering and text summarization. In *Proceedings of the 2021 Conference of the North American Chapter of the Association for Computational Linguistics: Human Language Technologies*, pages 1322–1336, Online. Association for Computational Linguistics.

Maximillian Nickel and Douwe Kiela. 2017. Poincaré embeddings for learning hierarchical representations. In *Advances in Neural Information Processing Systems*, volume 30. Curran Associates, Inc.

Maximillian Nickel and Douwe Kiela. 2018. Learning continuous hierarchies in the lorentz model of hyperbolic geometry. In *International Conference on Machine Learning*, pages 3779–3788. PMLR.

Yasumasa Onoe, Michael Boratko, Andrew McCallum, and Greg Durrett. 2021. Modeling fine-grained entity types with box embeddings. In *Proceedings of the 59th Annual Meeting of the Association for Computational Linguistics and the 11th International Joint Conference on Natural Language Processing (Volume 1: Long Papers)*, pages 2051–2064, Online. Association for Computational Linguistics.

Dhruvesh Patel, Shib Sankar Dasgupta, Michael Boratko, Xiang Li, Luke Vilnis, and Andrew McCallum. 2020. Representing joint hierarchies with box embeddings. In *Automated Knowledge Base Construction*.

Soumya Sharma, Bishal Santra, Abhik Jana, Santosh Tokala, Niloy Ganguly, and Pawan Goyal. 2019. Incorporating domain knowledge into medical NLI using knowledge graphs. In *Proceedings of the 2019 Conference on Empirical Methods in Natural Language Processing and the 9th International Joint Conference on Natural Language Processing (EMNLP-IJCNLP)*, pages 6092–6097, Hong Kong, China. Association for Computational Linguistics.

Ivan Vendrov, Ryan Kiros, Sanja Fidler, and Raquel Urtasun. 2016. Order-embeddings of images and language. In *ICLR*.

Luke Vilnis, Xiang Li, Shikhar Murty, and Andrew McCallum. 2018. Probabilistic embedding of knowledge graphs with box lattice measures. In *Proceedings of the 56th Annual Meeting of the Association for Computational Linguistics (Volume 1: Long Papers)*, pages 263–272.

Luke Vilnis and Andrew McCallum. 2015. Word representations via gaussian embedding. In *ICLR*.

Alex Wang, Amanpreet Singh, Julian Michael, Felix Hill, Omer Levy, and Samuel Bowman. 2018. GLUE: A multi-task benchmark and analysis platform for natural language understanding. In *Proceedings of the 2018 EMNLP Workshop BlackboxNLP: Analyzing and Interpreting Neural Networks for NLP*, Brussels, Belgium. Association for Computational Linguistics.

Xiaoyan Wang, Pavan Kapanipathi, Ryan Musa, Mo Yu, Kartik Talamadupula, Ibrahim Abdelaziz, Maria Chang, Achille Fokoue, Bassem Makni, Nicholas Mattei, and Michael Witbrock. 2019. Improving natural language inference using external knowledge in the science questions domain. *Proceedings of the AAAI Conference on Artificial Intelligence*, 33(01):7208–7215.

Melanie Weber. 2020. Neighborhood growth determines geometric priors for relational representation learning. In *Proceedings of the Twenty Third International Conference on Artificial Intelligence and Statistics*, volume 108 of *Proceedings of Machine Learning Research*, pages 266–276. PMLR.

Melanie Weber and Maximilian Nickel. 2018. Curvature and representation learning: Identifying embedding spaces for relational data. *NeurIPS Relational Representation Learning*.

Adina Williams, Nikita Nangia, and Samuel Bowman. 2018. A broad-coverage challenge corpus for sentence understanding through inference. In *Proceedings of the 2018 Conference of the North American Chapter of the Association for Computational Linguistics: Human Language Technologies, Volume 1 (Long Papers)*, pages 1112–1122. Association for Computational Linguistics.

Zheng Yu, Haixun Wang, Xuemin Lin, and Min Wang. 2015. Learning term embeddings for hypernymy identification. In *Twenty-Fourth International Joint Conference on Artificial Intelligence*.

A Appendix

A.1 TensorFlow (TF) version

```
import tensorflow as tf
from box_embeddings.parameterizations import
    TFBoxTensor
theta = tf.Variable(
  [[[0, 0], [2, 2]], [[4, 0], [8, 4]]]
)
box = BoxTensor(theta)
boxA = box[0]
boxB = box[1]
```

Listing 6: TF code for initializing a BoxTensor.

```
from box_embeddings.parameterizations import
    TFMinDeltaBoxTensor, TFSigmoidBoxTensor,
    TFTanhBoxTensor
box_tensor = TFMinDeltaBoxTensor(theta)
box_tensor_pos_sides = TFSigmoidBoxTensor(theta)
box_tensor_in_unit_cube = TFTanhBoxTensor(theta)
```

Listing 7: TF code for converting theta vectors to boxes.

```
from box_embeddings.parameterizations import
    TFBoxTensor
from box_embeddings.modules.intersection import
    TFHardIntersection
from box_embeddings.modules.intersection import
    TFGumbelIntersection

boxA = TFBoxTensor(theta_a)
boxB = TFBoxTensor(theta_b)

hard_intersection = TFHardIntersection()
gumbel_intersection = TFGumbelIntersection()

hard_ab = hard_intersection(boxA, boxB)
gumbel_ab = gumbel_intersection(boxA, boxB)
```

Listing 8: TF code for computing the intersection of two box tensors.

```
from box_embeddings.modules.volume import
    TFHardVolume
from box_embeddings.modules.volume import
    TFSoftVolume
from box_embeddings.modules.volume import
    TFBesselApproxVolume

hard_volume = TFHardVolume()
volA = hard_volume(boxA)

soft_volume = TFSoftVolume()
vol_ab = soft_volume(hard_ab)

bessel_volume = TFBesselApproxVolume()
vol_ab = bessel_volume(gumbel_ab)
```

Listing 9: TF code for computing the volume of a box.

```
from box_embeddings.modules.pooling import
    TFHardIntersectionBoxPooler
from box_embeddings.modules.regularization import
    TFL2SideBoxRegularizer

pooler = TFHardIntersectionBoxPooler()
pooled_box = pooler(box)

box_regularizer =
    TFL2SideBoxRegularizer(log_scale=True)

vol_box = soft_volume(pooled_box)
loss = loss_fn(vol_box) +
    box_regularizer(pooled_box)
```

Listing 10: TF code for performing pooling and regularization operations over a box.

A.2 Toy Example

```
import torch
import numpy
from box_embeddings.parameterizations.box_tensor
    import BoxTensor
from box_embeddings.modules.volume.volume import
    Volume
from box_embeddings.modules.intersection import
    Intersection

# Initialization
x_z = numpy.array([-2.0 for n in range(1, 16)])
x_Z = numpy.array([0.0 for k in (x_z)])
data_x = torch.tensor([x_z, x_Z],
    requires_grad=True)
box_H = BoxTensor(data_x)

y_z = numpy.array([1/n for n in range(1, 16)])
y_Z = numpy.array([1 + k for k in reversed(y_z)])
data_y = torch.tensor([y_z, y_Z],
    requires_grad=True)
box_T = BoxTensor(data_y)

# Training function
learning_rate = 0.1
def train(box_1, box_2, optimizer, epochs=1):
   best_loss = int()
   best_box_1 = None
   best_box_2 = None
   box_vol = Volume(volume_temperature=0.1,
        intersection_temperature=0.0001)
   box_int =
        Intersection(intersection_temperature=0.0001)
   for e in range(epochs):
      loss = box_vol(box_2) -
           box_vol(box_int(box_1, box_2))
      optimizer.zero_grad()
      loss.backward()
      optimizer.step()
      if best_loss < loss.item():
         best_loss = loss.item()
         best_box_2 = box_2
         best_box_1 = box_1
      print('Iteration %d, loss = %.4f' % (e,
           loss.item()))
   return best_box_1, best_box_2

# Train
optimizer = torch.optim.SGD([data_x, data_y],
    lr=learning_rate)
best_box_H, best_box_T = train(box_H, box_T,
    optimizer, epochs=50)
```

Listing 11: Training Pipeline for the Toy Example (3.1)

LexiClean: An annotation tool for rapid multi-task lexical normalisation

Tyler Bikaun(✉), **Tim French, Melinda Hodkiewicz, Michael Stewart and Wei Liu**
The University of Western Australia
35 Stirling Highway, Crawley, Western Australia
tyler.bikaun@research.uwa.edu.au
{firstname.lastname}@uwa.edu.au

Abstract

NLP systems are often challenged by difficulties arising from noisy, non-standard, and domain specific corpora. The task of lexical normalisation aims to standardise such corpora, but currently lacks suitable tools to acquire high-quality annotated data to support deep learning based approaches. In this paper, we present **LexiClean**[1], the first open-source web-based annotation tool for multi-task lexical normalisation.

LexiClean's main contribution is support for simultaneous *in situ* token-level modification and annotation that can be rapidly applied corpus wide. We demonstrate the usefulness of our tool through a case study on two sets of noisy corpora derived from the specialised-domain of industrial mining. We show that LexiClean allows for the rapid and efficient development of high-quality parallel corpora. A demo of our system is available at: https://youtu.be/P7_ooKrQPDU.

1 Introduction

Garbage in, garbage out is a well known adage in the computer science and machine learning community. In NLP it has become the centre-focus, demanding a task of its own right; namely, lexical normalisation (Baldwin et al., 2015). Lexical normalisation is the task of identifying and normalising non-canonical tokens (e.g. erroneous spelling, acronyms, ...) in noisy, non-standard, corpora (Han and Baldwin, 2011).

Largely made popular after the 2015 ACL-IJCNLP Workshop on Noisy User-generated Text (W-NUT) (Baldwin et al., 2015), lexical normalisation has demonstrated marked improvements on down-stream applications such as entity recognition, text classification, and part-of-speech (POS) tagging (Derczynski et al., 2013; Hua et al., 2015; Van der Goot et al., 2017; Núñez et al., 2019). These improvements have centred around the fact that many NLP tools are not amenable to noisy corpora, such as those in micro-blogging domains like Twitter (Liu et al., 2011), and in specialised-domains such as industrial mining (Stewart et al., 2018).

To date the most popular lexical normalisation corpus is based on English Twitter and was released as part of W-NUT (Baldwin et al., 2015). This has resulted in a number of algorithmic contributions to lexical normalisation task with the current state-of-the-art using ensemble learning methods (van der Goot and van Noord, 2017). More recently, attention has shifted towards neural techniques that i) contextually normalise tokens based on high-level classifications (Stewart et al., 2019b), ii) modify and fine-tune large pre-trained transformer based representations (Muller et al., 2019), or iii) perform joint normalisation and sanitisation (e.g. masking sensitive tokens) (Nguyen and Cavallari, 2020).

However, neural models typically demand large volumes of high-quality training data, which is not available for the task of lexical normalisation. Despite the prevalence of open-source token-level annotation tools (Stenetorp et al., 2012; Yimam et al., 2013; Yang et al., 2017; Kummerfeld, 2019), there still remains a lack of support for lexical normalisation.

A gap in lexical normalisation research currently exists and consists of an absence of large scale annotated corpora and scalable, task-specific tools for their construction. To fill this gap, we introduce **LexiClean**, an annotation tool for multi-task lexical normalisation that is:

i. *Rapid*: Enables fast corpus wide multi-task annotation.

ii. *Flexible*: Supports *1:1* and *1:N* token normalisation.

iii. *Intuitive*: Maintains a simple and easy-to-use interface.

[1] *LexiClean*. https://lexiclean.nlp-tlp.org

Proceedings of the 2021 Conference on Empirical Methods in Natural Language Processing: System Demonstrations, pages 212–219
November 7–11, 2021.

iv. *Dynamic*: Permits organic schema development during annotation.

The remainder of this paper is organised as follows. We define the task of lexical normalisation in Section 2 and briefly review related work in Section 3. Following this, we present and describe key features of LexiClean in Section 4. LexiClean's system architecture is then discussed in Section 5 with a case study presented in Section 6. Lastly conclusions are drawn and future work is proposed in Section 7. An online demonstration of LexiClean is located at `https://lexiclean.nlp-tlp.org` and the source code is available under an Apache-2.0 license at `https://github.com/nlp-tlp/lexiclean`.

2 Problem Formulation

Lexical normalisation is defined as the mapping of non-canonical, out-of-vocabulary (OOV) tokens to canonical, in-vocabulary (IV) forms (Han and Baldwin, 2011). Non-canonical tokens are largely a result of i) unconventional and phonetic spelling, ii) improper casing, iii) acronyms, iv) abbreviations and initialisms, v) domain-specific terms, vi) neologisms, and vii) erroneous concatenation or tokenization. This task is akin to grammatical error correction (GEC) (Ng et al., 2014), although it does not involve token reordering that is core to GEC.

Lexical normalisation is typically tackled as one of two formulations, either as a sequence-to-sequence (seq2seq) (Muller et al., 2019; Nguyen and Cavallari, 2020) or token classification problem (van der Goot and van Noord, 2017; Stewart et al., 2018, 2019b). Seq2seq structures the learning task similar to neural machine translation (NMT) (Bahdanau et al., 2014) whereby an *encoder* receives a sequence of noisy text, $\mathbf{X} = (x_1, \ldots, x_n)$, and maps it to a *decoder* which outputs a sequence of normalised text, $\mathbf{Y} = (y_1, \ldots, y_m)$. In this format, $|\mathbf{X}|$ does not necessarily have to equal $|\mathbf{Y}|$. Here a variation in sequence length can result from concatenation and tokenization corrections e.g. $(\text{“}helloworld\text{”}) \rightarrow (\text{“}hello\text{”}, \text{“}world\text{”})$ or $(\text{“}hello\text{”}, \text{“}w\text{”}, \text{“}orld\text{”}) \rightarrow (\text{“}hello\text{”}, \text{“}world\text{”})$.

In contrast, token classification structures the task in a modular fashion where OOV candidates are *identified* and *normalised* in multiple stages. Typically a noisy sequence, $\mathbf{X}$, is mapped to an intermediate sequence of semantic classes, $\mathbf{Z} = (z_1, \ldots, z_n)$. Token classification can be simple binary classification, $\mathcal{L}_{n=2} = \{OOV, IV\}$, or comprehensive, $\mathcal{L}_{n=4} = \{self, spelling\_error, domain\_specific, acronym\}$, where $\mathcal{L}$ is a space consisting of n pre-defined classes of token categories. After classification, alignment to suitable canonical forms is performed using similarity or distance based measures conditioned on labels in $\mathbf{Z}$ (Han and Baldwin, 2011; Baldwin et al., 2015).

3 Related Work

In the last decade, many open-source annotation tools have been developed for token-level classification tasks such as entity recognition and POS tagging, notably BRAT (Stenetorp et al., 2012), WebAnno (Yimam et al., 2013), YEDDA (Yang et al., 2017), and SLATE (Kummerfeld, 2019). The contributions of the current generation of tools have been significant, but support for the task of lexical normalisation has been overlooked. As a result, these tools do not have features that enable *in situ* token modification or data quality improvements such as decatentation and tokenization whilst performing their main tasks. On the other hand, proprietary writing assistants such as Grammarly[2], ProWritingAid[3], and Ginger[4] do contain features required for lexical normalisation, but are prohibitively expensive and not designed for the task of corpora annotation.

4 LexiClean - Key Features

This section provides an overview of the key features of LexiClean that enable rapid multi-task token-level annotation that supports both seq2seq and token classification task formats. An overview of the system is presented in Figure 1 with a web-based interface in Figure 3.

4.1 Project Creation and Automatic Labelling

LexiClean provides users upon project creation the facility to upload a predefined OOV to IV (*1:1*) replacement dictionary (e.g. *{"hel" : "hello", "worl": "world"}*) and an unlimited number of plain-text gazetteers (Figure 3). Gazetteers are lists of tokens mapped to a high-level concept (e.g. *domain_specific → {u/s, ..., c/o}*. Here, these concepts are referred to as *meta-tags* and are used to support the token classification formulation of lexical normalisation. These resources are used to

[2]Grammarly. https://www.grammarly.com/
[3]ProWritingAid. https://prowritingaid.com/
[4]Ginger. https://www.gingersoftware.com/

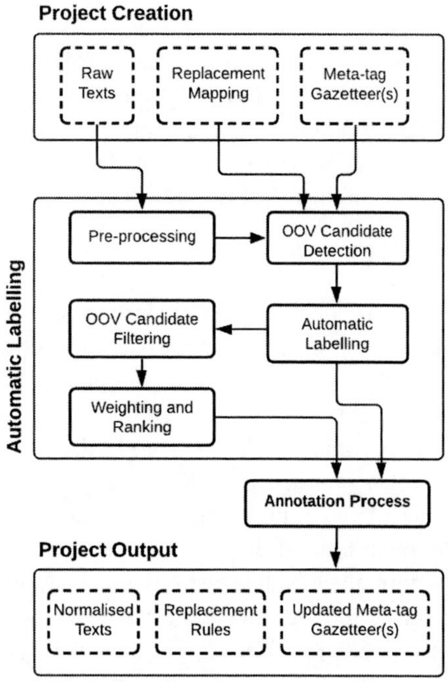

Figure 1: Overview of LexiClean process and data flow.

automatically label tokens in the entire corpus before an annotation session commences (Figure 1), notably reducing annotation effort.

Depending on the resources used, replacements will be automatically applied as *suggested replacements* (Figure 3(a)) whereas meta-tags will applied directly (Figure 2). However, any accepted suggested replacements or automatically applied meta-tags can be removed at any time throughout an annotation session if deemed unsuitable (see Figure 3(b) and Figure 2).

4.2 Single and Multiple Replacements

Instead of iteratively constructing replacement dictionaries only as a *1:1* mapping throughout the annotation process, LexiClean allows the correction of single tokens *in situ* (*1:1*) or across the entire corpora via *cascading* (*1:N*) (see *apply* and *apply all* in Figure 3(c)).

This has two main benefits: i) single non-canonical tokens can be replaced *in situ* enabling contextual normalisations to be captured, and ii) cascading replacements across the entire corpora hastens annotation speed. The importance of this is illustrated by considering the following texts - *around the wod*, *cut the wod*, and *burn fire wod*. *1:1* dictionary based methods (e.g. replace all) would only be able to capture the replacement as either *wood* or *world* which would incorrectly annotate either 1 or 2 of the texts. Here, LexiClean allows users to modify *wod* $\rightarrow$ *world in situ* and cascade *wod* $\rightarrow$ *wood* across the remainder of the corpus (if deemed suitable). In some instances, the application of both styles of normalisation can indirectly lead to *N:1* mappings being formed.

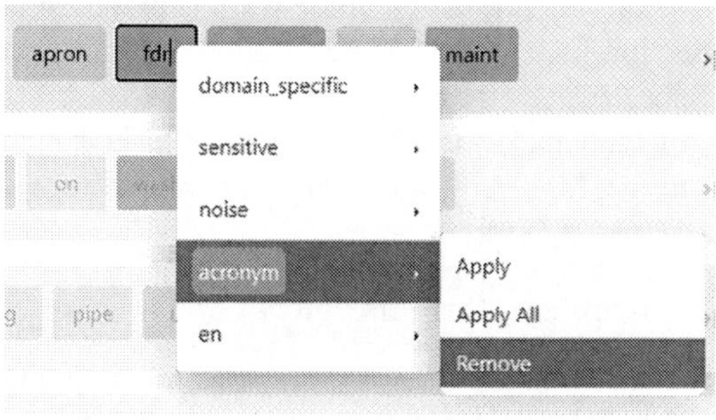

Figure 2: LexiClean meta-tag context menu.

4.3 Easily Identifiable Token Markup

Identifying and normalising OOV tokens in large corpora can be a demanding task, especially over thousands of texts. As a result consistency can be negatively impacted due to the inability of a user to recall corrections they have made to non-canonical token forms. To overcome this, LexiClean marks up tokens using a colour system. Colours for replacements, suggested replacements, and IV and OOV candidates are set to a default palette (Figure 3) whereas meta-tag colours are specified by the project creator on project creation. By using distinct colours to markup tokens, rapid identification can be ensured and consistency preserved. For example, users can quickly see where suggestions have been made and decide to *accept* or *ignore* them.

4.4 Dynamic Schema

Similar to token-level annotation tools that employ dynamic schemas (Stewart et al., 2019a), LexiClean allows users to update their meta-tag schema throughout the annotation process. This feature permits users to organically modify their schema based on phenomena present in the corpora rather than fitting to a prescriptive set of classes. Updates include additional classes of meta-tags and toggling the *active* state of existing ones. Toggling of meta-tag active states within the schema permits

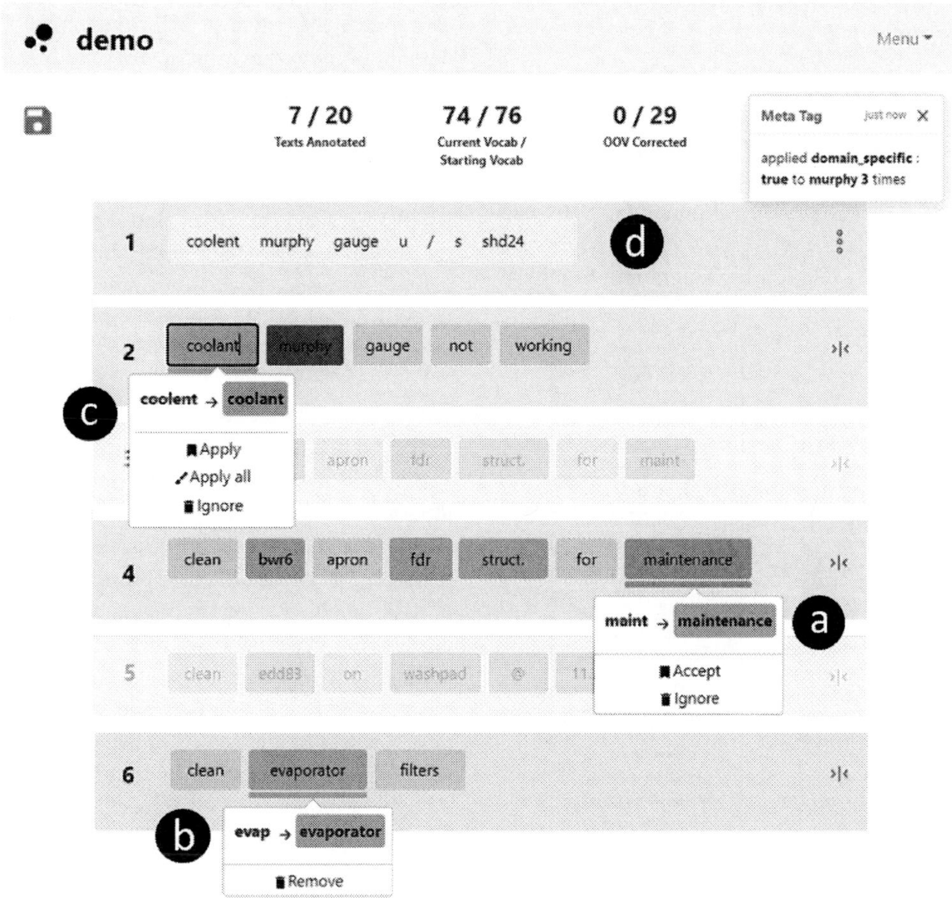

Figure 3: LexiClean annotation interface - (a) suggested token replacement, (b) accepted token replacement, (c) in-progress token normalisation, and (d) text tokenization mode.

a soft-deletion that can be reversed if required by the user.

4.5 Decatenation and Tokenization

Concatenation and irregular tokenization of texts are common in noisy corpora. Consider the following problematic example that exhibits both cases:

original	hewalkedacross th er oad
corrections	he, ␣, walked, ␣, across, {th er → the}, ␣, {r oad → road}
normalisation	he walked across the road

LexiClean manages this by first allowing the user to decatenate the concatenated tokens by introducing additional white space (␣). Secondly, incorrect tokenization is corrected through a utility function that allows users to change the annotation mode of a text and modify its token spans (see Figure 3(d)).

4.6 Sorting Algorithm

To optimise annotation speed, LexiClean computes the average inverse tf-idf weight (Manning and Schutze, 1999) on project creation from all OOV candidates in each text. Using these weights, texts are presented to the user in ranked order with the most prominent candidates appearing first. The rationale behind this technique is that the immediate annotation of high-frequency OOV candidates will have a significant impact on the conversion rate of texts when using the *cascade* style annotation.

4.7 Exporting Annotations and Normalisation Maps

At any stage of an annotation project, users can download their annotated corpora in an extended W-NUT JSON-based format (Baldwin et al., 2015). Additionally, replacements and meta-tag gazetteers generated over the course of the project can also be exported for use in new projects or external systems.

5 System Architecture

LexiClean is built using the modern full stack web development framework *MERN*[5] (MongoDB-Express-React-NodeJS). All annotations are captured at the token-level as shown in the MongoDB (NoSQL) entity relationship diagram in Figure 4.

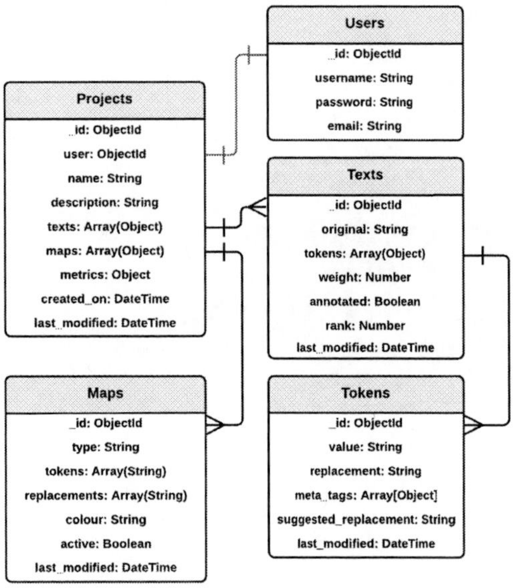

Figure 4: LexiClean's entity relationship diagram.

Here, the `Project` model stores information related to a project including references to `Texts`, `Maps` and `Users`. The `Maps` model captures replacements and meta-tag gazetteers, as well as static assets such as a standard English lexicon. The `Texts` model comprises information pertaining to individual texts such as its original *value*, aggregate tf-idf *weight* and resulting *rank*, whether its been *annotated*, and its constituent *tokens*. `Texts` reference the `Tokens` model that is composed of the tokens original *value*, and accepted or suggested annotations (*replacement*, *meta_tags*, *suggested_replacement*). Lastly, `Users` contains information about users such as their *username*, *password* and *email*.

6 Case Study

Without comparable systems, we demonstrate the efficacy of LexiClean through the annotation of user generated content (UGC) from the specialised-domain of industrial mining (IM) (Sikorska et al., 2016). To date, UGC in industrial domains has received little attention from the NLP community, with state-of-the-art systems relying heavily on hand-craft rules and heuristics for normalisation (Hodkiewicz and Ho, 2016; Gao et al., 2020). More recently, it has also been highlighted that corpora derived from such domains can pose challenges to state-of-the-art NLP systems (Dima et al., 2021).

6.1 Task Setup

We experiment on two corpora (**IM-Pub** and **IM-Priv**) and release one to the public[6]. As LexiClean currently is a single user application, we focus on the performance of a single user annotating under two modes to illustrate the efficacy of LexiClean's features. The two modes are i) from scratch (no automatic labelling using prepopulated replacements or meta-tag gazetteers), and ii) with automatic labelling from prepopulated assets. The same annotator was used for both modes. The annotators native language was English and they had prior familiarity with the domain of industrial mining.

In both modes, OOV token candidates are detected by matching to an English lexicon[7]. Annotation guidelines are borrowed from Baldwin et al. (2015)[8] with extension to support multi-task annotation. For both cases, a set of four meta-tags are used consisting of *domain_specific*, *sensitive*, *unsure* and *noise*. An overview and comparison of the statistics pertaining to both corpora compared to W-NUT15 is shown in Table 1.

	Texts	Total Tokens	OOV Tokens	
			Count	*Proportion*
IM-Pub	4.5k	21.9k	3.9k	17.8%
IM-Priv	4.5k	21.8k	4.0k	18.3%
W-NUT15	4.9k	73.8k	6.6k	9%

Table 1: Overview and comparison of corpora statistics.

6.2 Case One - Annotation from Scratch

In this case study, annotation of **IM-Pub** is performed, starting from scratch with no automatic

[5]MERN. https://www.mongodb.com/mern-stack

[6]*Industrial Mining Public (IM-Pub).* https://github.com/nlp-tlp/lexiclean/data/im_pub.json

[7]SCOWL (v2020.12.07) English with Australian and British variants (size 60).

[8]*W-NUT15 Guidelines.* http://noisy-text.github.io/2015/norm-shared-task.html

labelling. This corpora consisted of 4.5k texts and 3.9k candidate OOV tokens. The annotator performance shown in Figure 5 highlights the rapidity of OOV token annotation early on in the session owing to features such as cascading corpora wide annotation and the sorting algorithm. The impact of these features is also demonstrated by the user's annotation rate at the start of the session and its increasing nature through to completion. Moreover, a substantial number of normalisations and meta-tags were captured as is evidenced in Table 2.

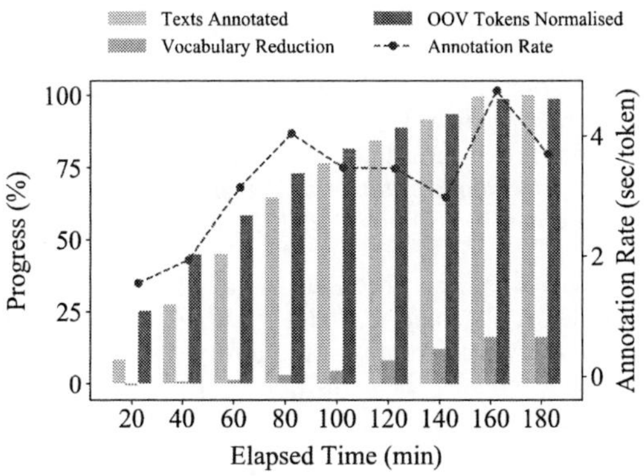

Figure 5: Overview of annotator performance for case one (progress is cumulative).

6.3 Case Two - Annotation from Prepopulated Assets

To evaluate the effectiveness of the automatic labelling feature of LexiClean, annotation of an equivalently sized corpora (**IM-Priv**) to case one was performed. Here, replacements and meta-tag gazetteers generated in case one were exported and used for automatic labelling. It was found that this feature significantly reduced the OOV tokens requiring annotation in IM-Priv by 47% (4,013 to 1,897) as well as reducing the vocabulary size by 3.5%. Comparable with case one, Figure 6 also demonstrated the rapidity of annotation and the ability to apply a significant number of normalisations and associated meta-tags to noisy corpora within a short period (Table 2).

7 Conclusion and Future Work

We have introduced LexiClean, an open-source annotation tool for multi-task lexical normalisation. Stemming from gaps in current token-level annotation tools, we have demonstrated how a dedicated, task-specific tool can enable rapid annotation of

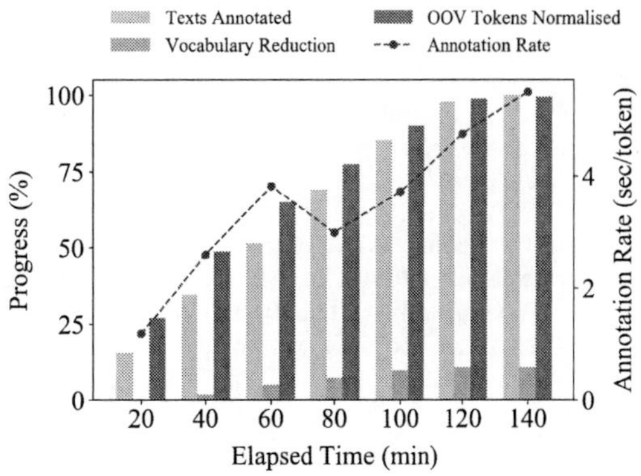

Figure 6: Overview of annotator performance for case two (progress is cumulative).

	Case	One		Two	
	Replacements	706	3967	1025	3168
Meta-tags	*domain_specific*	116	634	245	805
	sensitive	54	382	118	154
	unsure	42	56	111	156
	noise	19	38	29	65

Table 2: Overview of annotation effort for both cases - (*# of unique tokens | # of annotated instances*).

large corpora to support both seq2seq and token-classification formulations of the lexical normalisation task. As a result, LexiClean is well positioned to enable future annotation efforts to support the development of the next generation of lexical normalisation algorithms and systems. Future work will focus on converting LexiClean from a single user tool to one that supports multi-user collaborative annotation akin to the current generation of token-level annotation tools.

Acknowledgements

This research is supported by the Australian Research Council through the Centre for Transforming Maintenance through Data Science (grant number IC180100030), funded by the Australian Government. Additionally, Bikaun acknowledges funding from the Mineral Research Institute of Western Australia, and Hodkiewicz acknowledges funding from the BHP Fellowship for Engineering for Remote Operations. Bikaun and Liu acknowledge the support from ARC Discovery Grant DP150102405.

References

Dzmitry Bahdanau, Kyunghyun Cho, and Yoshua Bengio. 2014. Neural machine translation by jointly learning to align and translate. *arXiv preprint arXiv:1409.0473*.

Timothy Baldwin, Marie-Catherine de Marneffe, Bo Han, Young-Bum Kim, Alan Ritter, and Wei Xu. 2015. Shared tasks of the 2015 workshop on noisy user-generated text: Twitter lexical normalization and named entity recognition. In *Proceedings of the Workshop on Noisy User-generated Text*, pages 126–135.

Leon Derczynski, Alan Ritter, Sam Clark, and Kalina Bontcheva. 2013. Twitter part-of-speech tagging for all: Overcoming sparse and noisy data. In *Proceedings of the International Conference recent advances in Natural Language Processing RANLP 2013*, pages 198–206.

Alden Dima, Sarah Lukens, Melinda Hodkiewicz, Thurston Sexton, and Michael P. Brundage. 2021. Adapting natural language processing for technical text‡. *Applied AI Letters*, e33.

Yiyang Gao, Caitlin Woods, Wei Liu, Tim French, and Melinda Hodkiewicz. 2020. Pipeline for machine reading of unstructured maintenance work order records. In *Proceedings of the 30th. European Safety and Reliability Conference and 15th. Probabilistic Safety Assessment and Management Conference*. ESRA PSAM.

Bo Han and Timothy Baldwin. 2011. Lexical normalisation of short text messages: Makn sens a# twitter. In *Proceedings of the 49th Annual meeting of the Association for Computational Linguistics: Human language technologies*, pages 368–378.

Melinda Hodkiewicz and Mark Tien-Wei Ho. 2016. Cleaning historical maintenance work order data for reliability analysis. *Journal of Quality in Maintenance Engineering*, 22(2):146–163.

Wen Hua, Zhongyuan Wang, Haixun Wang, Kai Zheng, and Xiaofang Zhou. 2015. Short text understanding through lexical-semantic analysis. In *2015 IEEE 31st. International Conference on Data Engineering*, pages 495–506. IEEE.

Jonathan K Kummerfeld. 2019. Slate: a super-lightweight annotation tool for experts. *arXiv preprint arXiv:1907.08236*.

Xiaohua Liu, Shaodian Zhang, Furu Wei, and Ming Zhou. 2011. Recognizing named entities in tweets. In *Proceedings of the 49th. Annual Meeting of the Association for Computational Linguistics: Human Language Technologies*, pages 359–367.

Christopher Manning and Hinrich Schutze. 1999. *Foundations of statistical natural language processing*. MIT press.

Benjamin Muller, Benoît Sagot, and Djamé Seddah. 2019. Enhancing bert for lexical normalization. In *The 5th Workshop on Noisy User-generated Text (W-NUT)*.

Hwee Tou Ng, Siew Mei Wu, Ted Briscoe, Christian Hadiwinoto, Raymond Hendy Susanto, and Christopher Bryant. 2014. The conll-2014 shared task on grammatical error correction. In *Proceedings of the 18th. Conference on Computational Natural Language Learning: Shared Task*, pages 1–14.

Hoang Nguyen and Sandro Cavallari. 2020. Neural multi-task text normalization and sanitization with pointer-generator. In *Proceedings of the First Workshop on Natural Language Interfaces*, pages 37–47.

José Carlos Rosales Núñez, Djamé Seddah, and Guillaume Wisniewski. 2019. Phonetic normalization for machine translation of user generated content. In *Proceedings of the 5th. Workshop on Noisy User-generated Text (W-NUT 2019)*, pages 407–416.

Joanna Sikorska, Melinda Hodkiewicz, Ashwin D'Cruz, Lachlan Astfalck, and Adrian Keating. 2016. A collaborative data library for testing prognostic models. In *PHM Society European Conference*, volume 3.

Pontus Stenetorp, Sampo Pyysalo, Goran Topić, Tomoko Ohta, Sophia Ananiadou, and Jun'ichi Tsujii. 2012. Brat: a web-based tool for nlp-assisted text annotation. In *Proceedings of the Demonstrations at the 13th. Conference of the European Chapter of the Association for Computational Linguistics*, pages 102–107.

Michael Stewart, Wei Liu, and Rachel Cardell-Oliver. 2019a. Redcoat: a collaborative annotation tool for hierarchical entity typing. In *Proceedings of the 2019 Conference on Empirical Methods in Natural Language Processing and the 9th International Joint Conference on Natural Language Processing (EMNLP-IJCNLP): System Demonstrations*, pages 193–198.

Michael Stewart, Wei Liu, and Rachel Cardell-Oliver. 2019b. Word-level lexical normalisation using context-dependent embeddings. *arXiv preprint arXiv:1911.06172*.

Michael Stewart, Wei Liu, Rachel Cardell-Oliver, and Rui Wang. 2018. Short-text lexical normalisation on industrial log data. In *2018 IEEE International Conference on Big Knowledge (ICBK)*, pages 113–122. IEEE.

Rob Van der Goot, Barbara Plank, and Malvina Nissim. 2017. To normalize, or not to normalize: The impact of normalization on part-of-speech tagging. *arXiv preprint arXiv:1707.05116*.

Rob van der Goot and Gertjan van Noord. 2017. Monoise: Modeling noise using a modular normalization system. *arXiv preprint arXiv:1710.03476*.

Jie Yang, Yue Zhang, Linwei Li, and Xingxuan Li. 2017. Yedda: A lightweight collaborative text span annotation tool. *arXiv preprint arXiv:1711.03759*.

Seid Muhie Yimam, Iryna Gurevych, Richard Eckart de Castilho, and Chris Biemann. 2013. Webanno: A flexible, web-based and visually supported system for distributed annotations. In *Proceedings of the 51st. Annual Meeting of the Association for Computational Linguistics: System Demonstrations*, pages 1–6.

T³-Vis: a visual analytic framework for Training and fine-Tuning Transformers in NLP

Raymond Li[†], Wen Xiao[†], Lanjun Wang[‡*], Hyeju Jang[†], Giuseppe Carenini[†]
[†]University of British Columbia, Vancouver, Canada
{raymondl, xiaowen3, hyejuj, carenini}@cs.ubc.ca
[‡]Huawei Cananda Technologies Co. Ltd., Burnaby, Canada
lanjun.wang@huawei.com

Abstract

Transformers are the dominant architecture in NLP, but their training and fine-tuning is still very challenging. In this paper, we present the design and implementation of a visual analytic framework for assisting researchers in such process, by providing them with valuable insights about the model's intrinsic properties and behaviours. Our framework offers an intuitive overview that allows the user to explore different facets of the model (e.g., hidden states, attention) through interactive visualization, and allows a suite of built-in algorithms that compute the importance of model components and different parts of the input sequence. Case studies and feedback from a user focus group indicate that the framework is useful, and suggest several improvements. Our framework is available at: `https://github.com/raymondzmc/T3-Vis`.

1 Introduction

Approaches through neural networks have made significant progress in the field of NLP, with Transformer models (Vaswani et al., 2017) rapidly becoming the dominant architecture due to their efficient parallel training and ability to effectivelymodel long sequences. Following the release of BERT (Devlin et al., 2019) along with other Transformer-based models pretrained on large corpora (Liu et al., 2019; Lewis et al., 2020; Joshi et al., 2020; Lee et al., 2020), the most successful strategy on many NLP leaderboards has been to directly fine-tune such models on the downstream tasks (e.g., summarization, classification). However, despite the strong empirical performance of this strategy, understanding and interpreting the training and fine-tuning processes remains a critical and challenging step for researchers due to the inherent black-box nature of neural models (Kovaleva et al., 2019; Hao et al., 2019; Merchant et al., 2020; Hao et al., 2020).

*Corresponding author.

Generally speaking, a large number of visual analytics tools have been shown to effectively support the analysis and interpretation of deep learning models (Hohman et al., 2018). For instance, to remedy the black-box nature of neural network hidden states, previous work has used scatterplots to visualize high dimensional vectors through projection techniques (Smilkov et al., 2016; Kahng et al., 2017), with Aken et al. (2020) visualizing the differences of token representations from different layers of BERT (Devlin et al., 2019). Similarly, despite some limitations regarding the explanatory capabilities of the attention mechanism (Jain and Wallace, 2019; Wiegreffe and Pinter, 2019), the visualization of its weights has also been shown to be beneficial in discovering learnt features (Clark et al., 2019; Voita et al., 2019), with promising recent work focusing on Transformers (Vig, 2019; Hoover et al., 2020).

Besides the works on exploring what has been learnt in the pretrained models, there are also several visualization tools developed to show saliency scores generated by gradient-based (Simonyan et al., 2013; Bach et al., 2015; Shrikumar et al., 2017) or perturbation-based interpretation methods (Ribeiro et al., 2016; Li et al., 2016), which can help with visualizing the relative importance of individual tokens in the input with respect to a target prediction (Wallace et al., 2019; Johnson et al., 2020; Tenney et al., 2020). However, only a few studies have instead focused on visualizing the overall training dynamics, where support is critical for identifying mislabeled examples or failure cases (Liu et al., 2018; Xiang et al., 2019; Swayamdipta et al., 2020)

In essence, the framework we propose in this paper, namely T³-Vis, synergistically integrates some of the interactive visualizations mentioned above to support developers in the challenging task of training and fine-tuning Transformers. This is in contrast with other similar recent visual tools (Ta-

Proceedings of the 2021 Conference on Empirical Methods in Natural Language Processing: System Demonstrations, pages 220–230
November 7–11, 2021. ©2021 Association for Computational Linguistics

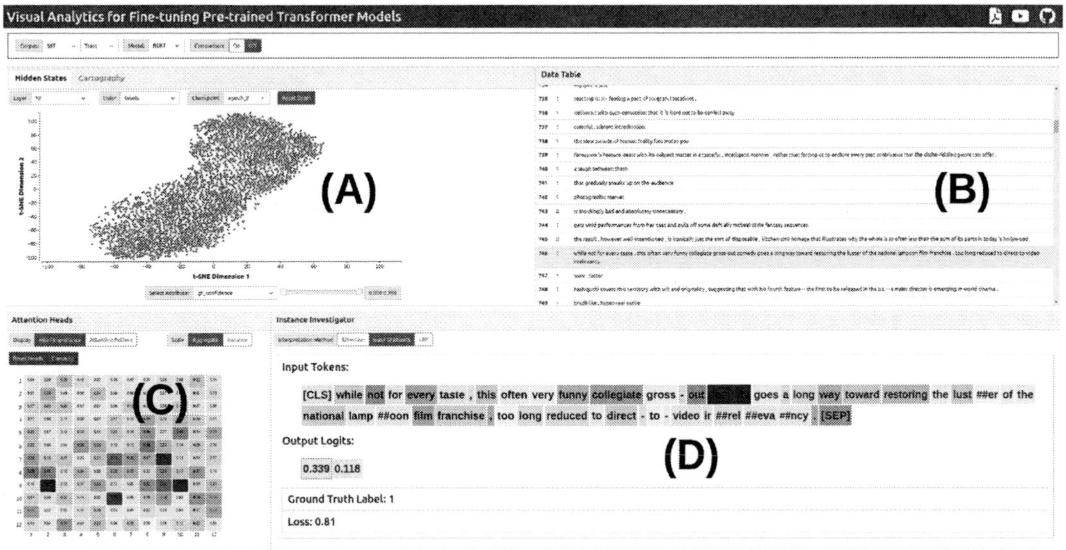

Figure 1: Overview of the interface: **(A)** Projection View provides a 2D visualization of the dataset by encoding each example as a point on the scatterplot; **(B)** Data Table allows the user to view the content and metadata (e.g. label, loss) of the data examples (e.g. document); **(C)** Attention Head View visualizes the head importance and weight matrices of each attention head; **(D)** Instance Investigation View allows the user to perform detailed analysis (e.g. interpretation, attention) on a data example's input sequence.

ble 1), which either only focus on single data point explanations for uncovering model bias (e.g., AllenNLP Interpret (Wallace et al., 2019)), or rely on failed examples to understand the model's behaviour (e.g., Language Interpretability Tool (LIT) (Tenney et al., 2020)).

Following the well-established Nested Model for visualization design (Munzner, 2009), we first perform an extensive requirement analysis, from which we derive user tasks and data abstractions to guide the design of visual encoding and interaction techniques. More specifically, the resulting T^3-Vis framework provides an intuitive overview that allows users to explore different facets of the model (e.g., hidden states, attention, training dynamics) through interactive visualization.

Our contributions are as follows: **(1)** An extensive user requirement analysis on supporting the training and fine-tuning of Transformer models, based on extensive literature review and interviews with NLP researchers, **(2)** the design and implementation of an open-sourced visual analytic framework for assisting researchers in the fine-tuning process with a suite of built-in interpretation methods that analyze the importance of model components and different parts of the input sequence, and **(3)** the evaluation of the current design from case studies with NLP researchers and feedback from a user focus group.

2 Visualization Design

The design of our T^3-Vis is based on the nested model for InfoVis design (Munzner, 2009).

2.1 User Requirements

To derive useful analytical user tasks, we first identify a set of high-level user requirements (UR) through interviews with five NLP researchers as well as surveying recent literature related to the interpretability and the fine-tuning procedures of pretrained Transformers. In the interviews, we prompt participants with the open-ended question of "*If a visualization tool is provided to speed up your development (fine-tuning pretrained Transformers), what information would you like to see and explore?*". Combining the interview results and insights from the literature review, we organize these findings into five high-level requirements, each highlighting a different facet of the model for visualization.

Hidden state visualization (UR-1): Support the exploration for hidden state representations

Frameworks	Components					Functions		
	Dataset	Embeddings	Head Importance	Attention	Training Dynamics	Interpretations	Pruning	Comparison
BertViz (Vig, 2019)				✓				
AllenNLP Interpret (Wallace et al., 2019)						✓		
exBERT (Hoover et al., 2020)	✓	✓		✓				
LIT (Tenney et al., 2020)	✓	✓		✓		✓		✓
InterperT (Lal et al., 2021)	✓	✓	✓	✓				
T^3-Vis	✓	✓	✓	✓	✓	✓	✓	✓

Table 1: Comparison with other visual frameworks from recent work.

from the model.

Attention visualization (UR-2): Allow users to examine and explore the linguistic or positional patterns exhibited in the self-attention distribution for different attention heads in the model.

Attention head importance (UR-3): Enable users to investigate and understand the importance of the attention heads for the downstream task and the effects of pruning them on the model's behaviour.

Interpretability of models (UR-4): In addition to attention maps, support a suite of alternative explanation methods based on token input importance, thus allowing users to better understand the model behaviours during inference.

Training dynamics (UR-5): Assist users in identifying relevant data examples based on their roles in the training process.

2.2 Supported Tasks and Data Model

Based on these user requirements, we derive nine analytical tasks framed as information seeking questions . In Table 2, we list the tasks along with important attributes including: *When* they are relevant during the fine-tuning process, the *Granularity* of the data that it operates on, corresponding *User Requirements*, and the framework *Components* that it pertains to. We then look at the specific data to which the tasks are applied to. We characterize our data model (i.e. data types visualized by the interface) as comprising the model hidden states, the dataset examples along with their label/training features, the attention values, head importance scores, and input saliency map. Although our task and data models are derived for the fine-tuning of pretrained models, they can naturally be extended to training any Transformer models from scratch. Importantly, all the questions are invariant to any Transformer-based models for any downstream tasks (e.g. classification, sequence-generation or labeling).

2.3 T^3-Vis Components: Visual Encoding and Interactive Techniques

Projection View: To assist users in visualizing the model's hidden state representation (**UR-1**) and to identify the training role of the data examples (**UR-5**), we design the *Projection View* (Figure 1-(A)) as the main overview of our interface, and visualize the entire (or a subset of the) dataset on a 2D scatterplot, where each data point on the plot encodes a single data example (e.g. document) in the dataset. While the scatterplots can be generated in a variety of ways based on the user's needs, including dimension reduction methods (Wold et al., 1987; McInnes et al., 2018) and plotting based on training dynamics (Li et al., 2018; Toneva et al., 2019). Detailed studies examining the effectiveness of these methods in the context of visual analytics are out of the scope of this paper, but provide a promising direction for future work. In T^3-Vis, we provide two implementations (See Figure 2): (1) t-SNE projection (Van der Maaten and Hinton, 2008) of the model's hidden states, and (2) plotting the examples by their confidence and variability across epochs based on the Data Map technique (Swayamdipta et al., 2020). The color of the data points can be selected by the user via a dropdown menu to encode attributes of the data examples, where color saturation is used for continuous attributes (e.g. loss, prediction confidence), while hue is used for categorical attributes (e.g. labels, prediction). The user can also filter the data points by attributes, where a range slider is used for filtering the data points by continuous attributes, while a selectable dropdown menu is used to filter by categorical attributes. Furthermore, we also introduce a comparison mode by displaying the two scatterplots side-by-side, which allows for the flexibility of comparing across different checkpoints and the projection of different hidden state layers.

Data Table: The *Data Table* (Figure 1-(B)) lists

#	Question	When	Granularity	User Requirements	Components
T1	How to determine the model representation for a given NLP task?	Before	Dataset	1	Projection
T2	What are the outliers of the dataset?	Before, During, After	Dataset	1, 5	Projection
T3	What types of linguistic or positional attributes do the attention patterns exhibit for each attention heads?	Before, During, After	Instance	2	Projection
T4	Which attention heads are considered important for the task, and what are its functions?	After	Both	2, 3	Attention Head Instance Investigator
T5	How does pruning attention heads affects the model?	After	Instance	3	Attention Head
T6	How does the model changes at different stages of fine-tuning?	During, After	Both	1, 2, 3	All
T7	Does the model rely on specific parts of the input sequence when making predictions?	After	Instance	4	Instance Investigator
T8	Are there mislabeled examples in the dataset?	During, After	Both	1, 5	Projection
T9	How can the dataset be augmented to improve the performance and robustness of the model?	During, After	Both	5	Projection

Table 2: Supported analytical tasks: questions that our interface helps to answer.

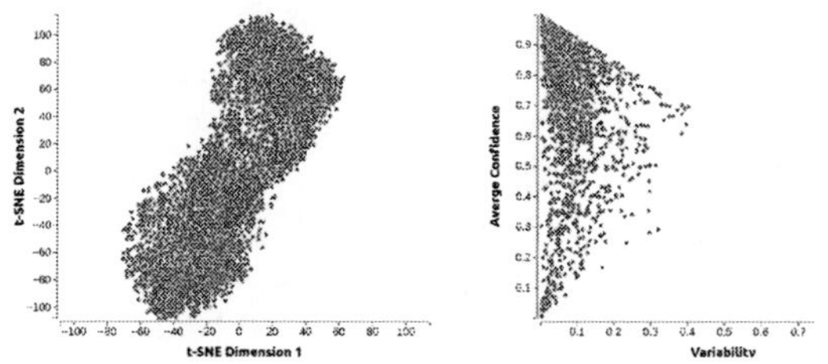

Figure 2: Interactive scatterplots based on the data examples' training dynamics (left), and the t-SNE projections of hidden states (right)

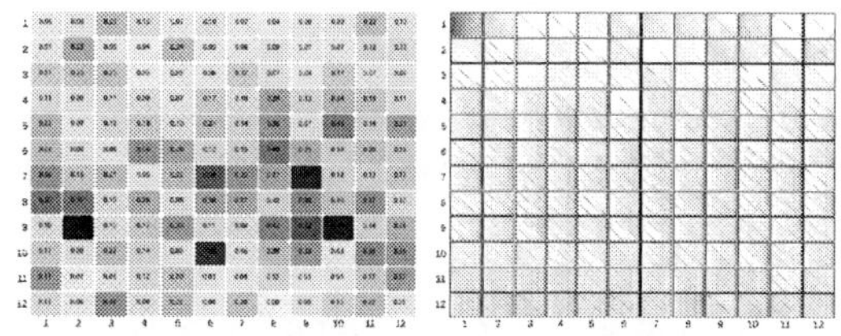

(a) Head Importance (b) Attention Pattern

Figure 3: The two visualization techniques in the Attention Head View.

all examples of the dataset in a single scrollable list, where each entry displays the input text of a data example along with its ground truth label. When the user filters the dataset in the Projection View, the Data Table is also filtered simultaneously.

Attention Head View: In order to visualize the importance of the model's attention heads (**UR-3**), as well as the patterns in the attention weight matrices (**UR-2**), we design the *Attention Head View* (Figure 1-(C)), where each block in the $l \times h$ matrix (l layers and h heads) represents a single attention head at the respective index for layer and head. In this view, we provide two separate visualization techniques: namely (1) Head Importance and (2) Attention Pattern, that can be switched using a toggle button. The Head Importance technique visualizes the normalized task-specific head importance score [1] through the background color saturation and displayed value of the corresponding matrix block (See Figure 3a). On the other hand, the Attention Pattern technique uses heatmaps to visualize the magnitude of the associated self-attention weight matrices (See Figure 3b). We also provide a toggle button for the user to visualize the importance score and attention patterns on two scales, where the **aggregate**-scale visualizes the score and patterns averaged over the entire dataset, while the **instance**-scale visualizes the score and patterns for a selected data example. Lastly, we also offer an interactive technique for the user to dynamically prune attention heads and visualize the effects on a selected example. By hovering over each attention head block in the view, the user can click on the close icon to prune the respective attention head from the model.

Instance Investigation View: After the user selects a data example from the Projection View or Data Table, the *Instance Investigation View* (Figure 1-(D)) renders the corresponding input text sequence along with the model predictions and labels to allow the user to perform detailed analysis on the data example. In this view, each token of the input sequence is displayed in a separate text block, where the background color saturation of each text block encodes the relative saliency or importance of the token based on the interpretation methods. Our interface provides two analysis techniques: (1) By selecting a head in the Attention Head View (Figure 3), the user can click on the text block of any input token to visualize the self-attention dis-

[1] Details are in A.1 of the Appendix

tribution of the selected token over the input text sequence (**UR-3**). (2) Similarly, the user can visualize the input saliency map with respect to a model output, by clicking the corresponding output token (**UR-4**). Since our framework allows the user to plug in different interpretation techniques based on their preference, details regarding the meaningfulness of such techniques are out of the scope of this paper. Our interface provides the implementation of two input interpretation methods[2] : Layer-wise relevance propagation (Bach et al., 2015), and input gradient (Simonyan et al., 2013).

2.4 Implementation

Data Processing For each model checkpoint, data pertaining to dataset-level visualizations including hidden state projections, prediction confidence/variability, head importance score, and other attributes (e.g. loss, prediction) are first processed and saved in a back-end directory. The only added computational overhead to the user's training process is the dimension reduction algorithm for projecting hidden state representation, as other visualized values can all be extracted from the forward (e.g. confidence, variability, loss) and backward pass (e.g. head importance, input saliency) of model training.

Back-end Our back-end Python server provides built-in support for the PyTorch HuggingFace library (Wolf et al., 2020), including methods for extracting attention values, head pruning, computing importance scores, and interpreting the model predictions. In order to avoid saving instance-level data (e.g., attention weights, input heatmap, etc.) for all examples in the dataset, the server dynamically computes these values for a selected data example by performing a single forward and backward pass on the model. This requires the server to keep track of the model's current state, as well as a dataloader for indexing the selected data example.

Front-end Our front-end implementation keeps track of the current visual state of the interface including the selections, filters, and checkpoint. The interface can be accessed through any web browser, where data is retrieved from the back-end server via the RESTful API. The interactive visual components of the interface are implemented using the D3.js framework (Bostock et al., 2011), and other UI components (e.g. buttons, sliders) are implemented with popular front-end libraries (e.g. jQuery, Bootstrap).

[2]Details are in A.2 of the Appendix

3 Iterative Design

3.1 Focus Group Study

In order to collect suggestions and initial feedback on T^3-Vis, we conducted a focus group study with 20 NLP researchers that work regularly with pre-trained Transformer models. In this study, we first presented the design of the interface, then gave a demo showing its usage on an example. Throughout the process, we gathered responses from the participants via open discussions.

Most positive feedback focused on the effectiveness of our techniques for visualizing self-attention especially on longer documents (in contrast to showing links between tokens (Vig, 2019)). There were also comments on the usefulness of the input saliency map in providing insightful clues on the model's decision process.

Some participants also suggested that the interface would be more useful for classification problems with well-defined evaluation metrics since data examples tended to be better clustered in the Projection View so that they could be easily filtered for error analysis. The need of optimizing the front-end to support the visualization of large-scale datasets was also mentioned.

On the negative side, some participants were concerned by the information loss intrinsic in the dimension reduction methods, whose possible negative effects on the user analysis tasks definitely requires further study. Encouragingly, at the end, a few participants expressed interest in applying and evaluating T^3-Vis on their datasets and NLP tasks.

3.2 Case Studies

This section describes two case studies of how T^3-Vis facilitates the understanding and exploration of the fine-tuning process through applications with real-world corpora. These studies provide initial evidence on the effectiveness of different visualization components, and serve as examples for how our framework can be used.

3.2.1 Pattern Exploration for an Extractive Summarizer

NLP researchers in our group, who work on summarization, applied T^3-Vis to the extractive summarization task, which aims to compress a document

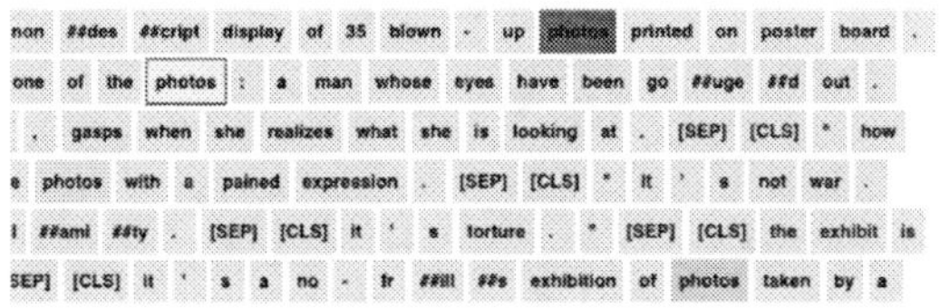

Figure 4: The self-attention distribution of token "photo" in the *Instance Analysis View*.

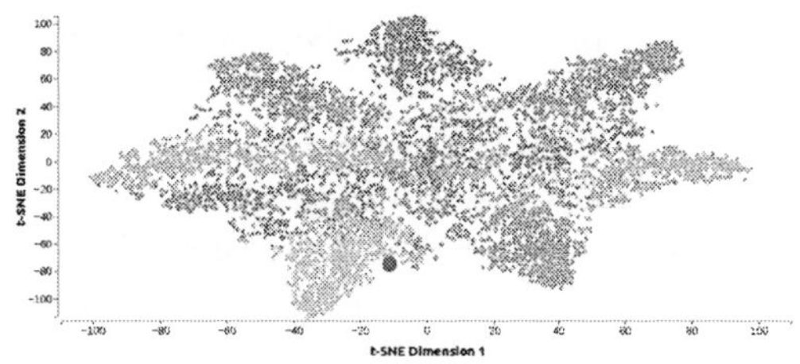

Figure 5: A misclassified example within a cluster of well-classified example.

by selecting its most informative sentences. BERT-Sum, which is fine-tuned from a BERT model (Liu and Lapata, 2019), is one of the top-performing models for extractive summarization, but why and how it works remains a mystery. With our interface, the researchers explored patterns captured by the model that played important roles in model predictions. They performed an analysis on the CNN/Daily Mail dataset (Hermann et al., 2015), which is arguably the most popular benchmark for summarization tasks.

The first step was to find the important heads among all the heads across all the layers. From the Head Importance View (Figure 1-(C)), the researchers selected the attention heads with high head importance scores, so that the corresponding attention distribution was available to interact with. Then they selected some tokens in the Attention View to see which tokens they mostly attended to, and repeated this process for multiple other data examples, in order to explore whether there was a general pattern across different data examples.

While examining attention heads based on their importance in descending order, the researchers observed that tokens tended to have high attention on other tokens of the same word on the important attention heads. For example, the token "photo" attributed almost all of its attention score to other instances of the token "photo" in the source document (Figure 4). They further found two more patterns in other important heads, in which the tokens tended to have more attention on the tokens within the same sentence, as well as the adjacent tokens. These behaviours were consistent across different pretrained models, such as RoBERTa (Liu et al., 2019).

These findings provided useful insights to assist the researchers in designing more efficient and accurate summarization models in the future, and served as a motivation for the researchers to perform similar analysis for other NLP tasks.

3.2.2 Error Analysis for Topic Classification

Other researchers in our group explored the interface for error analysis to identify possible improvements of a BERT-based model for topic classification. The Yahoo Answers dataset (Zhang et al., 2015) was used, which contains 10 topic classes.

Researchers first used the Projection View (Figure 1-(A)) to find misclassified data examples as applying filters to select label and prediction classes. For a selected topic class in the t-SNE projection of the model's hidden states, they found out that the misclassified data points far away from clusters of correctly predicted examples were often mislabeled during annotation. Therefore, misclassfied data points within such clusters were of greater interest to them since such points tends to indicate model failuresrather than mistakes in annotation (Figure 5). Furthermore, data points in the area with low variability and low confidence on the Data Map plot were also selected for investigation since they are interpreted as consistently misclassified across epochs. After selecting the examples, the researchers inspected each instance by using the Instance Investigation View (Figure 1-(D)) with the Input Gradient method to visualize the input saliency map for the prediction of each class.

From this analysis, they discovered two scenarios that led to misclassification. First, the model focused on unimportant and possibly misleading details that are not representative of the document's overall topic. For instance, a document about *Business & Finance* was classified into the *Sport* category because the model attended to "hockey player", "football player", and "baseball player", which were listed as job titles while discussing available jobs in Michigan. Second, the model failed in cases where background knowledge is required. For example, a document under the *Entertainment & Music* category mentioned names of two actors which were key clues for the topic, but the model only attended to other words, and made a wrong prediction.

These findings helped researchers to gain insights for future model design where additional information such as discourse structure (which can better reveal importance) and encyclopedic knowledge could be injected into the model's architecture to improve the task performance.

4 Conclusion

In this paper, we presented T^3-Vis, a visual analytic framework designed to help researchers better understand training and fine-tuning processes of Transformer-based models. Our visual interface provides faceted visualization of a Transformer model and allows exploring data across multiple granularities, while enabling users to dynamically interact with the model. Additionally, our implementation and design allows flexible customization to support a diverse range of tasks and workflows. Our focus group and case studies demonstrated the effectiveness of our interface by assisting the researchers in interpreting the models' behaviour and identifying potential directions to improve task performances.

For future work, we will continue to improve our framework through the iterative process of exploring further usage scenarios and collecting feedback from users. We will extend our framework to provide a more advanced visualization for custom Transformers. For example, we may want to support the visualization of models with more complex connections (e.g. parallel attention layers) or an advanced attention mechanism (e.g. sparse attention).

References

Betty van Aken, Benjamin Winter, Alexander Löser, and Felix A Gers. 2020. Visbert: Hidden-state visualizations for transformers. In *Companion Proceedings of the Web Conference 2020*, pages 207–211.

Sebastian Bach, Alexander Binder, Grégoire Montavon, Frederick Klauschen, Klaus-Robert Müller, and Wojciech Samek. 2015. On pixel-wise explanations for non-linear classifier decisions by layer-wise relevance propagation. *PloS one*, 10(7).

Michael Bostock, Vadim Ogievetsky, and Jeffrey Heer. 2011. D^3 data-driven documents. *IEEE transactions on visualization and computer graphics*, 17(12):2301–2309.

Kevin Clark, Urvashi Khandelwal, Omer Levy, and Christopher D. Manning. 2019. What does BERT look at? an analysis of BERT's attention. In *Proceedings of the 2019 ACL Workshop BlackboxNLP: Analyzing and Interpreting Neural Networks for NLP*, pages 276–286, Florence, Italy. Association for Computational Linguistics.

Jacob Devlin, Ming-Wei Chang, Kenton Lee, and Kristina Toutanova. 2019. BERT: Pre-training of deep bidirectional transformers for language understanding. In *Proceedings of the 2019 Conference of the North American Chapter of the Association for Computational Linguistics: Human Language Technologies, Volume 1 (Long and Short Papers)*, pages 4171–4186, Minneapolis, Minnesota. Association for Computational Linguistics.

Yaru Hao, Li Dong, Furu Wei, and Ke Xu. 2019. Visualizing and understanding the effectiveness of BERT. In *Proceedings of the 2019 Conference on Empirical Methods in Natural Language Processing and the 9th International Joint Conference on Natural Language Processing (EMNLP-IJCNLP)*, pages 4143–4152, Hong Kong, China. Association for Computational Linguistics.

Yaru Hao, Li Dong, Furu Wei, and Ke Xu. 2020. Investigating learning dynamics of BERT fine-tuning. In *Proceedings of the 1st Conference of the Asia-Pacific Chapter of the Association for Computational Linguistics and the 10th International Joint Conference on Natural Language Processing*, pages 87–92, Suzhou, China. Association for Computational Linguistics.

Karl Moritz Hermann, Tomas Kocisky, Edward Grefenstette, Lasse Espeholt, Will Kay, Mustafa Suleyman, and Phil Blunsom. 2015. Teaching machines to read and comprehend. In *Advances in Neural Information Processing Systems*, volume 28, pages 1693–1701. Curran Associates, Inc.

Fred Hohman, Minsuk Kahng, Robert Pienta, and Duen Horng Chau. 2018. Visual analytics in deep learning: An interrogative survey for the next frontiers. *IEEE transactions on visualization and computer graphics*, 25(8):2674–2693.

Benjamin Hoover, Hendrik Strobelt, and Sebastian Gehrmann. 2020. exBERT: A Visual Analysis Tool to Explore Learned Representations in Transformer Models. In *Proceedings of the 58th Annual Meeting of the Association for Computational Linguistics: System Demonstrations*, pages 187–196, Online. Association for Computational Linguistics.

Sarthak Jain and Byron C. Wallace. 2019. Attention is not Explanation. In *Proceedings of the 2019 Conference of the North American Chapter of the Association for Computational Linguistics: Human Language Technologies, Volume 1 (Long and Short Papers)*, pages 3543–3556, Minneapolis, Minnesota. Association for Computational Linguistics.

David Johnson, Giuseppe Carenini, and Gabriel Murray. 2020. Njm-vis: interpreting neural joint models in nlp. In *Proceedings of the 25th International Conference on Intelligent User Interfaces*, pages 286–296.

Mandar Joshi, Danqi Chen, Yinhan Liu, Daniel S. Weld, Luke Zettlemoyer, and Omer Levy. 2020. SpanBERT: Improving pre-training by representing and predicting spans. *Transactions of the Association for Computational Linguistics*, 8:64–77.

Minsuk Kahng, Pierre Y Andrews, Aditya Kalro, and Duen Horng Polo Chau. 2017. Activis: Visual exploration of industry-scale deep neural network models. *IEEE transactions on visualization and computer graphics*, 24(1):88–97.

Olga Kovaleva, Alexey Romanov, Anna Rogers, and Anna Rumshisky. 2019. Revealing the dark secrets of BERT. In *Proceedings of the 2019 Conference on Empirical Methods in Natural Language Processing and the 9th International Joint Conference on Natural Language Processing (EMNLP-IJCNLP)*, pages 4365–4374, Hong Kong, China. Association for Computational Linguistics.

Vasudev Lal, Arden Ma, Estelle Aflalo, Phillip Howard, Ana Simoes, Daniel Korat, Oren Pereg, Gadi Singer, and Moshe Wasserblat. 2021. InterpreT: An interactive visualization tool for interpreting transformers. In *Proceedings of the 16th Conference of the European Chapter of the Association for Computational Linguistics: System Demonstrations*, pages 135–142, Online. Association for Computational Linguistics.

Jinhyuk Lee, Wonjin Yoon, Sungdong Kim, Donghyeon Kim, Sunkyu Kim, Chan Ho So, and Jaewoo Kang. 2020. Biobert: a pre-trained biomedical language representation model for biomedical text mining. *Bioinformatics*, 36(4):1234–1240.

Mike Lewis, Yinhan Liu, Naman Goyal, Marjan Ghazvininejad, Abdelrahman Mohamed, Omer Levy, Veselin Stoyanov, and Luke Zettlemoyer. 2020. BART: Denoising sequence-to-sequence pre-training for natural language generation, translation, and comprehension. In *Proceedings of the 58th Annual Meeting of the Association for Computational*

Linguistics, pages 7871–7880, Online. Association for Computational Linguistics.

Hao Li, Zheng Xu, Gavin Taylor, Christoph Studer, and Tom Goldstein. 2018. Visualizing the loss landscape of neural nets. In *Neural Information Processing Systems*.

Jiwei Li, Will Monroe, and Dan Jurafsky. 2016. Understanding neural networks through representation erasure. *arXiv preprint arXiv:1612.08220*.

Dongyu Liu, Weiwei Cui, Kai Jin, Yuxiao Guo, and Huamin Qu. 2018. Deeptracker: Visualizing the training process of convolutional neural networks. *ACM Transactions on Intelligent Systems and Technology (TIST)*, 10(1):1–25.

Yang Liu and Mirella Lapata. 2019. Text summarization with pretrained encoders. In *Proceedings of the 2019 Conference on Empirical Methods in Natural Language Processing and the 9th International Joint Conference on Natural Language Processing (EMNLP-IJCNLP)*, pages 3730–3740, Hong Kong, China. Association for Computational Linguistics.

Yinhan Liu, Myle Ott, Naman Goyal, Jingfei Du, Mandar Joshi, Danqi Chen, Omer Levy, Mike Lewis, Luke Zettlemoyer, and Veselin Stoyanov. 2019. Roberta: A robustly optimized bert pretraining approach. *arXiv preprint arXiv:1907.11692*.

L. McInnes, J. Healy, and J. Melville. 2018. UMAP: Uniform Manifold Approximation and Projection for Dimension Reduction. *ArXiv e-prints*.

Amil Merchant, Elahe Rahimtoroghi, Ellie Pavlick, and Ian Tenney. 2020. What happens to BERT embeddings during fine-tuning? In *Proceedings of the Third BlackboxNLP Workshop on Analyzing and Interpreting Neural Networks for NLP*, pages 33–44, Online. Association for Computational Linguistics.

Pavlo Molchanov, Arun Mallya, Stephen Tyree, Iuri Frosio, and Jan Kautz. 2019. Importance estimation for neural network pruning. In *Proceedings of the IEEE/CVF Conference on Computer Vision and Pattern Recognition*, pages 11264–11272.

Grégoire Montavon, Wojciech Samek, and Klaus-Robert Müller. 2018. Methods for interpreting and understanding deep neural networks. *Digital Signal Processing*, 73:1–15.

Tamara Munzner. 2009. A nested model for visualization design and validation. *IEEE transactions on visualization and computer graphics*, 15(6):921–928.

Marco Tulio Ribeiro, Sameer Singh, and Carlos Guestrin. 2016. " why should i trust you?" explaining the predictions of any classifier. In *Proceedings of the 22nd ACM SIGKDD international conference on knowledge discovery and data mining*, pages 1135–1144.

Avanti Shrikumar, Peyton Greenside, and Anshul Kundaje. 2017. Learning important features through propagating activation differences. In *International Conference on Machine Learning*, pages 3145–3153. PMLR.

Karen Simonyan, Andrea Vedaldi, and Andrew Zisserman. 2013. Deep inside convolutional networks: Visualising image classification models and saliency maps. *arXiv preprint arXiv:1312.6034*.

Daniel Smilkov, Nikhil Thorat, Charles Nicholson, Emily Reif, Fernanda B Viégas, and Martin Wattenberg. 2016. Embedding projector: Interactive visualization and interpretation of embeddings. *arXiv preprint arXiv:1611.05469*.

Swabha Swayamdipta, Roy Schwartz, Nicholas Lourie, Yizhong Wang, Hannaneh Hajishirzi, Noah A. Smith, and Yejin Choi. 2020. Dataset cartography: Mapping and diagnosing datasets with training dynamics. In *Proceedings of the 2020 Conference on Empirical Methods in Natural Language Processing (EMNLP)*, pages 9275–9293, Online. Association for Computational Linguistics.

Ian Tenney, James Wexler, Jasmijn Bastings, Tolga Bolukbasi, Andy Coenen, Sebastian Gehrmann, Ellen Jiang, Mahima Pushkarna, Carey Radebaugh, Emily Reif, and Ann Yuan. 2020. The language interpretability tool: Extensible, interactive visualizations and analysis for NLP models. In *Proceedings of the 2020 Conference on Empirical Methods in Natural Language Processing: System Demonstrations*, pages 107–118, Online. Association for Computational Linguistics.

Mariya Toneva, Alessandro Sordoni, Remi Tachet des Combes, Adam Trischler, Yoshua Bengio, and Geoffrey J. Gordon. 2019. An empirical study of example forgetting during deep neural network learning. In *International Conference on Learning Representations*.

Laurens Van der Maaten and Geoffrey Hinton. 2008. Visualizing data using t-sne. *Journal of machine learning research*, 9(11).

Ashish Vaswani, Noam Shazeer, Niki Parmar, Jakob Uszkoreit, Llion Jones, Aidan N Gomez, Łukasz Kaiser, and Illia Polosukhin. 2017. Attention is all you need. In *Advances in neural information processing systems*, pages 5998–6008.

Jesse Vig. 2019. A multiscale visualization of attention in the transformer model. In *Proceedings of the 57th Annual Meeting of the Association for Computational Linguistics: System Demonstrations*, pages 37–42, Florence, Italy. Association for Computational Linguistics.

Elena Voita, David Talbot, Fedor Moiseev, Rico Sennrich, and Ivan Titov. 2019. Analyzing multi-head self-attention: Specialized heads do the heavy lifting, the rest can be pruned. In *Proceedings of the*

57th Annual Meeting of the Association for Computational Linguistics, pages 5797–5808, Florence, Italy. Association for Computational Linguistics.

Eric Wallace, Jens Tuyls, Junlin Wang, Sanjay Subramanian, Matt Gardner, and Sameer Singh. 2019. AllenNLP interpret: A framework for explaining predictions of NLP models. In *Proceedings of the 2019 Conference on Empirical Methods in Natural Language Processing and the 9th International Joint Conference on Natural Language Processing (EMNLP-IJCNLP): System Demonstrations*, pages 7–12, Hong Kong, China. Association for Computational Linguistics.

Sarah Wiegreffe and Yuval Pinter. 2019. Attention is not not explanation. In *Proceedings of the 2019 Conference on Empirical Methods in Natural Language Processing and the 9th International Joint Conference on Natural Language Processing (EMNLP-IJCNLP)*, pages 11–20, Hong Kong, China. Association for Computational Linguistics.

Svante Wold, Kim Esbensen, and Paul Geladi. 1987. Principal component analysis. *Chemometrics and intelligent laboratory systems*, 2(1-3):37–52.

Thomas Wolf, Lysandre Debut, Victor Sanh, Julien Chaumond, Clement Delangue, Anthony Moi, Pierric Cistac, Tim Rault, Remi Louf, Morgan Funtowicz, Joe Davison, Sam Shleifer, Patrick von Platen, Clara Ma, Yacine Jernite, Julien Plu, Canwen Xu, Teven Le Scao, Sylvain Gugger, Mariama Drame, Quentin Lhoest, and Alexander Rush. 2020. Transformers: State-of-the-art natural language processing. In *Proceedings of the 2020 Conference on Empirical Methods in Natural Language Processing: System Demonstrations*, pages 38–45, Online. Association for Computational Linguistics.

Shouxing Xiang, Xi Ye, Jiazhi Xia, Jing Wu, Yang Chen, and Shixia Liu. 2019. Interactive correction of mislabeled training data. In *2019 IEEE Conference on Visual Analytics Science and Technology (VAST)*, pages 57–68. IEEE.

Xiang Zhang, Junbo Zhao, and Yann LeCun. 2015. Character-level convolutional networks for text classification. *Advances in neural information processing systems*, 28:649–657.

A Appendix

A.1 Head Importance Score

Although the multi-head self attention mechanism in Transformers allows the model to learn multiple types of relationships between input representations across a single hidden layer, the importance of the individual attention heads can vary depending on the downstream tasks. Following previous work, we adapt the Taylor expansion method (Molchanov et al., 2019) to estimate the error induced from removing a group of parameters from the model. In our implementation, we use the first-order expansion to avoid the overhead from computing the Hessian, where the gradient with respect to validation loss is summed over all parameters of an attention head to estimate its importance.

A.2 Input Interpretation

Input Gradients The input gradient method (Simonyan et al., 2013) computes the gradient with respect to each token. During inference, the class-score derivative can be computed through back-propagation. The saliency of the token x_i for class c of output y could therefore be estimated using the first-order Taylor expansion $\frac{\partial y_c}{\partial x_i} x_i$.

Layer-wise Relevance Propagation Layer-wise Relevance Propagation (LRP) (Bach et al., 2015) was originally proposed to visualize the contributions of single pixels to predictions for an image classifier. By recursively computing relevance from the output layer to the input layer, LRP is demonstrated to be useful in unravelling the inference process of neural networks and has been adopted in recent work to analyze Transformer models (Voita et al., 2019). The intuition behind LRP is that, each neuron of the network is contributed by neurons in the previous layer, and the total amount of contributions for each layer should be a constant during back-propagating, which is called the *conservation principle*. LRP offers flexibility to design propagation rules to explain various deep neural networks, one example propagation rule is shown as follows (Montavon et al., 2018),

$$R_i = \Sigma_j \frac{a_i w_{ij}}{\Sigma_i a_i w_{ij}} R_j \quad (1)$$

where R_i and R_j are relevance scores of two neurons in consecutive layers, a_i is the respective activation for neuron i, and w_{ij} is the weight between neuron i and j.

DomiKnowS: A Library for Integration of Symbolic Domain Knowledge in Deep Learning

Hossein Rajaby Faghihi[1], **Quan Guo**[2], **Andrzej Uszok**[3], **Aliakbar Nafar**[1],
Elaheh Raisi[1], and **Parisa Kordjamshidi**[1]
[1] Michigan State University, [2] Sichuan University
[3] Florida Institute for Human and Machine Cognition
rajabyfa@msu.edu, guoquan@scu.edu.cn, auszok@ihmc.org,
{nafarali, raisiela, kordjams}@msu.edu

Abstract

We demonstrate a library for the integration of domain knowledge in deep learning architectures. Using this library, the structure of the data is expressed symbolically via graph declarations and the logical constraints over outputs or latent variables can be seamlessly added to the deep models. The domain knowledge can be defined explicitly, which improves the explainability of the models in addition to their performance and generalizability in the low-data regime. Several approaches for such integration of symbolic and sub-symbolic models have been introduced; however, there is no library to facilitate the programming for such integration in a generic way while various underlying algorithms can be used. Our library aims to simplify programming for such integration in both training and inference phases while separating the knowledge representation from learning algorithms. We showcase various NLP benchmark tasks and beyond. The framework is publicly available at Github[1].

1 Introduction

Current deep learning architectures are known to be data-hungry with issues mainly in generalizability and explainability (Nguyen et al., 2015). While these issues are hot research topics, one approach to address them is to inject external knowledge directly into the models when possible. While learning from examples revolutionized the way that intelligent systems are designed to gain knowledge, many tasks lack adequate data resources. Generating examples to capture knowledge is an expensive and lengthy process and especially not efficient when such a knowledge is available explicitly. Therefore, one main motivation of our proposed framework (DomiKnowS) is to facilitate the integration of domain knowledge in deep learning architectures, in particular when this knowledge is represented symbolically.

In this demonstration paper, we highlight the components of this framework that help to combine learning from data and exploiting knowledge in learning, including: 1) Learning problem specification 2) Knowledge representation 3) Algorithms for integration of knowledge and learning. Currently, DomiKnowS implementation relies on PyTorch and off-the-shelf optimization solvers such as Gurobi.[2] However, it can be extended by developing hooks to other solvers and deep learning libraries since the interface is generic and independent from the underlying computational modules.

In general, the integration of domain knowledge can be done 1) using pretrained models and transferring knowledge (Devlin et al., 2019; Mirzaee et al., 2021), 2) designing architectures that integrate knowledge expressed in knowledge bases (KB) and knowledge graphs (KG) in a way that the KB/KG context influences the learned representations (Yang and Mitchell, 2017; Sun et al., 2018), or 3) using the knowledge explicitly and logically as a set of constrains or preferences over the inputs or outputs (Li and Srikumar, 2019a; Nandwani et al., 2019b; Muralidhar et al., 2018; Stewart and Ermon, 2017). Our current library aims at facilitating the third approach. It is still an open problem to know which method of integrating prior knowledge with neural modules is the best and the performance heavily relies on each task specifications and experimental settings. However, there are many ongoing research on the integration of soft/hard constraints (Li and Srikumar, 2019a; Nandwani et al., 2019b; Muralidhar et al., 2018; Stewart and Ermon, 2017) on the output variables of neural modules which shows the effectiveness of such approaches in gaining better performance, especially on low-resource or even semi-supervised

[1] `https://github.com/HLR/DomiKnowS`

[2] Gurobi provides free academic license, moreover it provides a limited free version for all which is sufficient to solve problems with a small number of variables. We, also, have started adding hooks to other optimization tools that are freely available such as GEKKO.

Proceedings of the 2021 Conference on Empirical Methods in Natural Language Processing: System Demonstrations, pages 231–241
November 7–11, 2021.

tasks (Ratner et al., 2017). While applying the constraints on input is technically trivial and could be done in a data pre-processing step, applying constraints over outputs and considering those structural constraints during training is a research challenge (Nandwani et al., 2019b; Li and Srikumar, 2019a; Guo et al., 2020). This requires encoding the knowledge at the algorithmic level. However, given that the constraints can be expressed logically and symbolically, having a language to express such a knowledge in a principled way is lacking in the current machine learning libraries. Using our developed DomiKnowS library, the domain knowledge will be provided symbolically and by the user utilizing a logical language that we have defined. This knowledge is used in various ways: a) As soft constraints by considering the violations as a part of loss function, this is done using a prim-dual formulation (Nandwani et al., 2019b) and can be expanded to probabilistic and sampling-based approaches (Xu et al., 2018) or by mapping the constraint to differentiable operations (Li and Srikumar, 2019b) b) mapping the constrains to an integer linear program setting and performing inference-based training by masking the loss (Guo et al., 2020). Independent form the training paradigm the constraints can be always used as hard constraints during inference or not used at all.

An interactive online demo of DomiKnowS is available at Google Colab[3] and the framework is accessible on GitHub[4].

2 Related Research

Integration of domain knowledge in learning relates to tools that try to express the prior or posterior information about variables beyond what is in the data. This relates to probabilistic programming languages such as (Pfeffer, 2016), Venture (Mansinghka et al., 2014), Stan (Carpenter et al., 2017), and InferNet (Minka et al., 2012). The logical expression of domain knowledge is used in probabilistic logical programming languages such as ProbLog (De Raedt et al., 2007), PRISM (Sato and Kameya, 1997), the recent version of Problog,i.e., Deep Problog (Manhaeve et al., 2018), Statistical Relational Learning tools, such as Markov logic networks (Domingos and Richardson, 2004), Probabilistic soft logic (Broecheler et al., 2010), Bayesian Logic (BLOG) (Milch et al., 2005), and slightly related to learning over graph structures (Zheng et al., 2020). Considering the structure of the output without its explicit declaration is considered in structured output prediction tools (Rush, 2020). Our library is mostly related to the previous efforts for learning based programming and the integration of logical constraints in learning with classical machine learning approaches (Rizzolo and Roth, 2010; Kordjamshidi et al., 2015, 2016). Our framework makes this connection to deep neural network libraries and arbitrarily designed architectures. The unique feature of our library is that, the graph structure is defined symbolically based on the concepts in the domain. Unlike Torch-struct (Rush, 2020), our library is independent from the underlying algorithms, and arbitrary structures can be expressed and used based on various underlying algorithms. In contrast to DeepProbLog, we are not limited to probabilistic inference and any solver can be used for inference depending on the training paradigm that is used for exploiting the logical constraints. Probabilistic soft logic is another framework that considers logical constraints in learning by mapping the constraint declarations to a Hing loss Markov random field (Bach et al., 2017). DRaiL is another declarative framework that is using logical constraints on top of deep learning and converts them to an integer linear program at the inference time (Zhang et al., 2016). None of the above mentioned frameworks accommodate working with raw sensory data nor help in putting that in an operational structure that can form the domain predicates and be used by learning modules while our framework tries to address that challenge. We support training paradigms that make use of the inference as a black box and in those cases any constraint optimization, logical inference engine or probabilistic inference tools can be integrated and used based on our abstraction and the provided modularity.

3 Declarative Learning-based Programming

We use the Entity-Mention-Relation (EMR) extraction task to describe the framework. We discuss more showcases in Section 5.

Given an input text such as "*Washington is employed by Associated Press.*", the task is to extract the entities and classify their types (e.g., people, organizations, and locations) as well as relations

[3]https://tinyurl.com/t9wr9n4

[4]https://github.com/HLR/DomiKnowS

between them (e.g., works for, lives in). For example, for the above sentence *[Washington]* is a $person$ *[Associated Press]* is an $organization$ and the relationship between these two entities is $work\text{-}for$. We choose this task as it includes the prediction of multiple outputs at the sentence level, while there are global constraints over the outputs.[5]

In DomiKnowS, first, using our python-based specification language, the user describes the problem and its logical constraints declarativly and independent from the solutions. Second, it defines the necessary computational units (here, PyTorch-based architectures) and connect the solution to the problem specification. Third, a program instance is created to execute the model using a background knowledge integration method with respect to the problem description.

3.1 Problem Specification

To model a problem in DomiKnowS, the user should specify the problem domain as a conceptual graph $\mathcal{G}(V, E)$. The nodes in V represent concepts and the edges in E are relationships. Each node can take a set of properties $P = P_1, P_2, ..., P_n$. Later, the logical constraints are expressed using the concepts in the graph. In EMR task, the graph contains some initial NLP concepts such as *sentence*, *phrase*, *pair* and additional domain concepts such as *people*, *organization*, and *work-for*.

3.1.1 Concepts

Each problem definition can contain three main types of concepts (nodes).

Basic Concepts define the structure of the input of the learning problem. For instance *sentence*, *phrase*, and *word* are all basic concepts that can be defined in the EMR task.

Compositional Concepts are used to define the many-to-many relationships between the basic concepts. Here, the *pair* concept in the EMR task is a compositional concept. This is used as the basic concept for the relation extraction task. We will further discuss this when describing edges in Section 3.1.2.

Decision Concepts are derived concepts which are usually the outputs of the problem and subject to prediction. They are derived from the basic or compositional concepts. The *people*, *organization*, and *work-for* are examples of derived concepts in the EMR conceptual graph. Following is a partial snippet showing the definition of basic and compositional concepts for EMR task.

```
word = Concept(name='word')
phrase = Concept(name='phrase')
sentence = Concept(name='sentence')
pair = Concept(name='pair')
```

The following snippet also shows the definition of some derived concepts in EMR example.

```
entity = phrase(name='entity')
people = entity(name='people')
org = entity(name='organization')
location = entity(name='location')
work_for = pair(name='work_for')
located_in = pair(name='located_in')
```

The *entity*, *people*, *organization* and *location* are the derived concepts from the *phrase* concept and the rest are derived from the *pair* concept.

3.1.2 Edges

After defining the concepts, the user should specify existing relationships between them as edges in the conceptual graph. Edges are used to either map instances from one concept to another, or generate instances of a concept from another concept. DomiKnowS only supports a set of predefined edge types, namely *is_a*, *has_a*, and *contains*.

is_a is automatically defined between a derived concept and its parent. In the EMR example, there is an *is_a* edge between *people* and *entity*. The *is_a* edge is mostly used to introduce hierarchical constraints and relate the basic and derived concepts.

Has_a connects a compositional concept to its components (also referred to as *arguments*). In the EMR example, *pair* concept has two *has_a* edges to the *phrase* concept to specify the *arg1* and *arg2* of the composition. We allow an arbitrary number of arguments in a *has_a* relationship, see below.

```
pair.has_a(arg1=phrase, arg2=phrase)
```

Contains edge defines a one-to-many relationship for two concepts to represent a (parent, child) relationship between them. Here, the number of parents of a concept is not necessarily limited to be only one. Following is a sample snippet to define a *contains* edge between *sentence* and *phrase*:

```
sentence.contains(phrase)
```

[5]Please note this is just an example of a learning problem and does not have anything to do with the main functionality of the framework.

3.1.3 Global Constraints

The constraint definition is the part where the prior knowledge of the problem is defined to enable domain integration. The constraints of each task should be defined on top of the problem using the specified concepts and relationships there.

The constraints can be 1) automatically inferred from the conceptual graph structure, 2) extracted from the standard ontology formalism (here OWL[6]), 3) explicitly defined using the logical constraint language of DomiKnowS. The framework internally uses the defined constraints at the training-time or the inference-time optimization depending on the integration method selected for the task. We discuss the inference phase in more details in section 4.1. Here is an example of a constraint written in DomiKnowS's logical constraint language for the EMR task:

```
ifL(work_for('x'), andL(people(path=
↪   ('x',arg1)),
↪   organization(path='x',arg2)))
```

The above constraint indicates that a *work_for* relationship only holds between *people* and *organization*. Other syntactic variations of this constraint are shown in the Appendix.

To process constraints, DomiKnowS maps those to a set of equivalent algebraic inequalities or their soft logic interpretation depending on the integration method. We discuss this more in Section 4.1.

3.2 Model Declaration

Model declaration phase is about defining the computational units of the task. The basic building blocks of the model in DomiKnowS are *sensors* and *learners*, which are used to define either deterministic or probabilistic functionalities of the model. Sensor/Learners interact with the conceptual graph by defining properties on the concepts (nodes). Each sensor/learner receives a set of inputs either from the raw data or property values on the graph and introduces new property values. Sensors are computational units with no trainable parameters; and learners are the ones which contain the neural models. As stated before, the model declaration phase only defines the connection of the graph properties to the computational units and the execution is done later by the program instances.

The user can use any deep learning architecture compatible with PyTorch modules alongside the set of pre-designed and commonly-used neural architectures currently existing in the framework. To facilitate modeling different architectures and computational algorithms in DomiKnowS, we provide a set of predefined sensors to do basic mathematical operations and linguistic feature extraction. Following is a short snippet of defining some sensors/learners for the EMR task.

```
phrase['w2v'] = FunctionalSensor('text',
↪   forward=word2vec)
phrase[people] = ModuleLearner('w2v',
↪   module=Classifier(FEATURE_DIM))
pair[work_for] = ModuleLearner('emb',
↪   module=Classifier(FEATURE_DIM*2))
```

In this example, the sensor *Word2Vec* is used to obtain token representations from the "text" property of each *phrase*. There is also a very simple and straightforward linear neural model to classify *phrases* and *pairs* into different classes such as *people*, *organization*, etc.

4 Learning & Evaluation in DomiKnowS

To execute the defined model considering the specified conceptual graph, DomiKnowS uses program instances. A program instance is responsible to run the model, apply loss functions, optimize the parameters, connect the output decisions to the inference algorithms, and generate the final results and metrics. Executing the program instance relies on the problem graph, model declaration, dataloaders and a backbone data structure called DataNode. **DataLoader** provides an iterable object to loop over the data. **DataNode** is an instance of the conceptual graph to keep track of the data instances and store the computational results of the sensors and learners. For the EMR task, the program definition is as follows:

```
program = Program(graph,
↪   poi=(sentence, phrase, pair),
↪   loss=NBCrossEntropyLoss(),
↪   metric=PRF1())
```

Here, the concepts passed to the *poi* field specifies the training points of the program. This enables the user to train the task based on any subsets of the concepts defined in the model.

For each program instance, the user should specify the domain knowledge integration method. The available methods for integration is discussed in the next sections. After initializing the program,

[6]Ontology Web Language

the user can call *train*, *test*, and *prediction* functionalities to train and evaluate the designed model. The below snippet is to run training and evaluation on the EMR task:

```
program.train(train_reader,
 ↪   test_reader, epochs=10,
 ↪   Optim=torch.optim.SGD(param,
 ↪   lr=.001))
program.test(new_test_reader)
```

Here, the user will specify the dataloaders for different sets of the data and the hyper-parameters required to train the model.

Programs can be composed to address different training paradigms such as end-to-end or pipeline training by defining different training points for each program. More details are available in the Appendix. Following is an alternative program definition for pre-training the phrases first and then learning based on the pairs:

```
program_1 = Program(graph,
 ↪   poi=(phrase, sentence))
program_2 = Program(graph,
 ↪   poi=(pair))
program_1.train(); program_2.train()
```

4.1 Inference and Optimization

DomiKnowS provides access to a set of approaches to integrate background knowledge in the form of constraints on the output decisions or latent variables/concepts. Currently, DomiKnowS addresses three different paradigms for integration: 1) Learning + prediction time inference (L+I) 2) Training-time integration with hard constraints 3) Training-time integration with soft constraints. The first method, which we refer to it as enforcing global constraints can also be combined and applied on top of the second and third approaches at inference-time.

Prediction-time Inference: In the back-end of DomiKnowS, ILP [7] solvers are used to make inference under global linear constraints (Roth and Yih, 2005). The constraints are denoted by $\mathcal{C}(\cdot) \leq 0$. Without loss of generality, we can denote the structured output as a binary vector $y \in \mathcal{R}^n$. Given local predictions $F(\theta)$ from the neural network, the global inference can be modeled to maximize the combination of log probability scores subject to the constraints (Roth and Yih, 2005; Guo et al., 2020) as follows,

$$F^*(\theta) = \underset{y}{\operatorname{argmax}} \log F(\theta)^\top y \quad \text{subject to} \quad \mathcal{C}(y) \leq 0. \tag{1}$$

To handle constraints in ILP, we create variables for each local decision of instances and transform the logical constraints to algebraic inequalities (Rizzolo and Roth, 2010) in terms of those variables. Auxiliary variables are added to represent the nested constraints. The inference method can be extended to support other approaches such as probabilistic inference and dynamic programming in future without any modifications to the other parts of the framework.

Integration of hard constraint in training: Here, we use our proposed inference-masked loss approach (IML) (Guo et al., 2020) which constructs a mask over local predictions based on the global inference results. The main intuition is to avoid updating the model based on local violations when the global inference can recover true labels from the current predictions. Given structured prediction $F(\theta)$ from a neural network and its global inference $F^*(\theta)$ subject to the constraints, IML is extended from negative log likelihood as follows

$$\mathcal{L}_{\text{IML}}(F(\theta), Y) = -\left((1 - F^*(\theta)) \odot Y\right)^\top \log F(\theta), \tag{2}$$

where Y is the structured ground-truth labels and $\odot$ indicates element-wise product. We implemented $\mathcal{L}_{\text{IML}(\lambda)}$ which balances between negative log likelihood and IML with a factor λ as introduced in (Guo et al., 2020). IML works best for very low-resource tasks where label disambiguation cannot be learned from the data but can be done based on the available relational constraints between output variables. The constraint mapping for the IML uses the same module in the DomiKnowSthat is implemented to use the global constraint optimization tool (here ILP).

Integration of soft constraints in training: We use the primal-dual formulation of constraints proposed in (Nandwani et al., 2019a) to integrate soft constraints in training the models. Primal-Dual considers the constraints in the neural network training by augmenting the loss function using Lagrangian multipliers Λ for the violations from the constraints by the set of predictions. The constraints are regularized by a hinge function $[\mathcal{C}(F(\theta))]^+$. The problem is formulated as a min-max optimization where

[7] Integer Linear Programming

it maximizes the Lagrangian function with the multipliers to enforce the constraints and minimize it with the parameters in the neural network. Here, instead of solving the min-max primal, we solve the max-min dual of the original problem.

$$\max_{\Lambda} \min_{\theta} \mathcal{L}\left(F\left(\theta\right), Y\right) + \Lambda^{\top}\left[\mathcal{C}\left(F\left(\theta\right)\right)\right]^{+}. \quad (3)$$

During training, we optimize by minimization and maximization alternatively. With Primal-Dual strategy, the model learns to obey the constraints without requiring any additional inference. Primal-Dual is less time-consuming at prediction-time than the previous methods as it does not need an additional inference-time optimization phase. This can also be used for semi-supervised setting while exploiting the domain knowledge instead of labeled data. Handling constraints in Primal-Dual is done by mapping them to their respective soft logical interpretations (Nandwani et al., 2019b).

It is an open research topic to identify which of the integration methods performs best for different tasks. However, DomiKnowS makes it effortless to use one problem specification and run all the aforementioned methods.

5 Showcases

The effectiveness of ILP (Roth and Yih, 2005), IML (Guo et al., 2020), and Primal-Dual (Nandwani et al., 2019a) methods have been already shown in their respective papers. Here, we provide different tasks and settings to showcase our framework's abilities and flexibility to model various problems. The results, models implementation and details of experiments are (partially) available in the Supplementary part of this paper and (fully) in the GitHub Repository of DomiKnowS.[8]

5.1 EMR

Our implementation of the EMR task is based on the CoNLL (Sang and De Meulder, 2003) benchmark and follows the same setting as in (Guo et al., 2020). The model uses pre-trained BERT (Devlin et al., 2019) for token representation and a linear boolean classifier for each derived concept. The constraints used in this experiment are the domain and range constraints of pairs and the mutual exclusiveness of different derived concepts, which were seen during the previous sections. IML and Primal-Dual methods perform the same as the baseline using both 100% and 25% of the data, while ILP inference achieves 1.3% improvement on the 100% of data and 0.6% improvement on 25% of the data. More details are available in the Appendix.

5.2 Question Answering

We use WIQA (Tandon et al., 2019) benchmark as a sample question answering task in DomiKnowS. The problem graph contains *paragraph*, *question*, *symmetric*, and *transitive* concepts. Each *paragraph* comes with a set of *questions*. As explained by Asai and Hajishirzi, enforcing constraints between different question answers is beneficial to improve the performance. By modeling those constraints in DomiKnowS, ILP improves the accuracy from 74.22% to 79.05%, IML reaches 75.49%, Primal-Dual achieves 76.59%, and the combination of Primal-Dual and ILP performs best with 80.35% accuracy. More details are available in the Appendix. Following is a sample constraint defined for this task.

```
symmetric.has_a(arg1=question,
↪  arg2=question)
ifL(is_more('x'), is_less(path=('x',
↪  arg2))
```

5.3 Image Classification

We use CIFAR-10 benchmark (Krizhevsky et al.) to show image classification task in DomiKnowS. CIFAR-10 consists of 60,000 colourful images of 10 classes with 6,000 image for each class. To construct the graph, we defined the derived concepts, *airplane*, *dog*, *truck*, *automobile*, *bird*, *cat*, *deer*, *frog*, *horse* and *ship*, and the base concept *image*. We introduce the disjoint constraint between the labels of an image. We can also define hierarchical constraints between additional upper level concepts such as *Animal* and *Object* with the existing concepts such *dog* and *ship*.

```
disjoint(truck, dog, airplane,
↪  automobile, bird, cat, deer, frog,
↪  horse, ship)
```

Both the disjoint and hierarchical constraints do not affect the accuracy of the task by a large margin and ILP can only achieve near 0.5% improvement over the classification task.

5.4 Inference-Only Example

This example is to show that DomiKnowS can solve pure optimization problems as well. The task

[8] https://github.com/HLR/DomiKnowS

is similar to the classic graph-coloring problem. A set of cities are given each of which can have a fire station or not. We want to allocate the fire stations to cities with respect to the following constraint.
Constraint: For each city x, it either has a fire station or there exists a city y which is a neighbor of city x and has a fire station.

To implement this, we define the basic concept *city*, the *neighbor* relationship between two cities and the derived concept *FirestationCity*.

```
neighbor.has_a(arg1=city, arg2=city)
orL(firestationCity('x'),
↪   existsL(firestationCity(path=('x',
↪   neighbor.arg2))
```

We have also included more showcases to solve sentiment analysis (Go et al., 2009) and email spam detection in our GitHub repository. [8] We will add models for procedural reasoning (Faghihi and Kordjamshidi, 2021) and spatial role labeling (Mirzaee et al., 2021) in future.

6 Conclusions and Future Work

DomiKnowS makes it effortless to integrate domain knowledge into deep neural network models using a unified framework. It allows users to switch between different algorithms and benefit from a rich source of abstracted functionalities and computational modules developed for multiple tasks. It allows naming concepts, defining their relationships symbolically and combining symbolic and sub-symbolic reasoning over the named concepts. DomiKnowS helps in interpretability of neural architectures by providing named layers and access to the neural computations at each stage of the training and evaluation process. As a future direction, we are looking to enrich our library with predefined functionalities and neural models and further extend its ability to support more techniques on integration of domain knowledge with deep neural models as well as seamless model composition. More information about technical details and the documentation of DomiKnowS is publicly available at our website[9] and on GitHub.[10]

Acknowledgements

This project is partially funded by the Office of Naval Research (ONR) grant #N00014-20-1-2005. We thank Drew Hayward and Yue Zhang for their work on parts of this framework and the anonymous reviewers for their helpful feedback towards improving the clarity of this manuscript.

[9]https://hlr.github.io/domiknows-nlp/
[10]https://github.com/HLR/DomiKnowS

References

Akari Asai and Hannaneh Hajishirzi. 2020. Logic-guided data augmentation and regularization for consistent question answering. In *Proceedings of the 58th Annual Meeting of the Association for Computational Linguistics*, pages 5642–5650.

Stephen H. Bach, Matthias Broecheler, Bert Huang, and Lise Getoor. 2017. Hinge-loss markov random fields and probabilistic soft logic. *Journal of Machine Learning Research (JMLR)*, 18:1–67.

Matthias Broecheler, Lilyana Mihalkova, and Lise Getoor. 2010. Probabilistic similarity logic. In *Conference on Uncertainty in Artificial Intelligence*.

Bob Carpenter, Andrew Gelman, Matthew Hoffman, Daniel Lee, Ben Goodrich, Michael Betancourt, Marcus Brubaker, Jiqiang Guo, Peter Li, and Allen Riddell. 2017. Stan: A probabilistic programming language. *Journal of Statistical Software, Articles*, 76(1):1–32.

Luc De Raedt, Angelika Kimmig, and Hannu Toivonen. 2007. Problog: a probabilistic Prolog and its application in link discovery. In *Proceedings of the 20th International Joint Conference on Artificial Intelligence*, pages 2468–2473. AAAI Press.

Jacob Devlin, Ming-Wei Chang, Kenton Lee, and Kristina Toutanova. 2019. BERT: Pre-training of deep bidirectional transformers for language understanding. In *Proceedings of the 2019 Conference of the North American Chapter of the Association for Computational Linguistics: Human Language Technologies, Volume 1 (Long and Short Papers)*, pages 4171–4186, Minneapolis, Minnesota. Association for Computational Linguistics.

Perdo Domingos and Matthew Richardson. 2004. Markov logic: A unifying framework for statistical relational learning. In *ICML'04 Workshop on Statistical Relational Learning and its Connections to Other Fields*, pages 49–54.

Hossein Rajaby Faghihi and Parisa Kordjamshidi. 2021. Time-stamped language model: Teaching language models to understand the flow of events. In *Proceedings of the 2021 Conference of the North American Chapter of the Association for Computational Linguistics: Human Language Technologies*, pages 4560–4570.

Alec Go, Lei Huang, and Richa Bhayani. 2009. Twitter sentiment analysis.

Quan Guo, Hossein Rajaby Faghihi, Yue Zhang, Andrzej Uszok, and Parisa Kordjamshidi. 2020. Inference-masked loss for deep structured output learning. In *Proceedings of the Twenty-Ninth International Joint Conference on Artificial Intelligence, IJCAI-20*, pages 2754–2761. International Joint Conferences on Artificial Intelligence Organization. Main track.

P. Kordjamshidi, D. Roth, and H. Wu. 2015. Saul: Towards declarative learning based programming. In *Proc. of the International Joint Conference on Artificial Intelligence (IJCAI)*.

Parisa Kordjamshidi, Daniel Khashabi, Christos Christodoulopoulos, Bhargav Mangipudi, Sameer Singh, and Dan Roth. 2016. Better call saul: Flexible programming for learning and inference in nlp. In *Proc. of the International Conference on Computational Linguistics (COLING)*.

Alex Krizhevsky, Vinod Nair, and Geoffrey Hinton. Cifar-10 (canadian institute for advanced research).

Tao Li and Vivek Srikumar. 2019a. Augmenting neural networks with first-order logic. In *Proceedings of the 57th Annual Meeting of the Association for Computational Linguistics*, pages 292–302.

Tao Li and Vivek Srikumar. 2019b. Augmenting neural networks with first-order logic. In *Proceedings of the 57th Conference of the Association for Computational Linguistics, ACL 2019, Florence, Italy, July 28- August 2, 2019, Volume 1: Long Papers*, pages 292–302. Association for Computational Linguistics.

Robin Manhaeve, Sebastijan Dumancic, Angelika Kimmig, Thomas Demeester, and Luc De Raedt. 2018. Deepproblog: Neural probabilistic logic programming. In *Advances in Neural Information Processing Systems*, volume 31. Curran Associates, Inc.

Vikash K. Mansinghka, Daniel Selsam, and Yura N. Perov. 2014. Venture: a higher-order probabilistic programming platform with programmable inference. *CoRR*, abs/1404.0099.

Brian Milch, Bhaskara Marthi, Stuart Russell, David Sontag, Daniel L. Ong, and Andrey Kolobov. 2005. BLOG: Probabilistic models with unknown objects. In *Proceedings of the International Joint Conference on Artificial Intelligence (IJCAI)*.

Tom Minka, John M. Winn, John P. Guiver, and David A. Knowles. 2012. Infer.NET 2.5. Microsoft Research Cambridge. http://research.microsoft.com/infernet.

Roshanak Mirzaee, Hossein Rajaby Faghihi, Qiang Ning, and Parisa Kordjamshidi. 2021. Spartqa: A textual question answering benchmark for spatial reasoning. In *Proceedings of the 2021 Conference of the North American Chapter of the Association for Computational Linguistics: Human Language Technologies*, pages 4582–4598.

Nikhil Muralidhar, Mohammad Raihanul Islam, Manish Marwah, Anuj Karpatne, and Naren Ramakrishnan. 2018. Incorporating prior domain knowledge into deep neural networks. In *2018 IEEE International Conference on Big Data (Big Data)*, pages 36–45. IEEE.

Yatin Nandwani, Abhishek Pathak, Mausam, and Parag Singla. 2019a. A primal dual formulation for deep learning with constraints. In *NeurIPS*.

Yatin Nandwani, Abhishek Pathak, Parag Singla, et al. 2019b. A primal dual formulation for deep learning with constraints. In *Advances in Neural Information Processing Systems*, pages 12157–12168.

Anh Nguyen, Jason Yosinski, and Jeff Clune. 2015. Deep neural networks are easily fooled: High confidence predictions for unrecognizable images. In *Proceedings of the IEEE conference on computer vision and pattern recognition*, pages 427–436.

Avi Pfeffer. 2016. *Practical Probabilistic Programming*. Manning Publications.

Alexander Ratner, Stephen H. Bach, Henry Ehrenberg, Jason Fries, Sen Wu, and Christopher Ré. 2017. Snorkel: Rapid training data creation with weak supervision. *Proc. VLDB Endow.*, 11(3):269–282.

N. Rizzolo and D. Roth. 2010. Learning based Java for rapid development of NLP systems. In *Proceedings of the Seventh Conference on International Language Resources and Evaluation*.

D. Roth and W. Yih. 2005. Integer linear programming inference for conditional random fields. In *Proc. of the International Conference on Machine Learning (ICML)*, pages 737–744.

Alexander Rush. 2020. Torch-struct: Deep structured prediction library. In *Proceedings of the 58th Annual Meeting of the Association for Computational Linguistics: System Demonstrations*, pages 335–342, Online. Association for Computational Linguistics.

Erik Tjong Kim Sang and Fien De Meulder. 2003. Introduction to the conll-2003 shared task: Language-independent named entity recognition. In *Proceedings of the Seventh Conference on Natural Language Learning at HLT-NAACL 2003*, pages 142–147.

Taisuke Sato and Yoshitaka Kameya. 1997. Prism: A language for symbolic-statistical modeling. In *Proceedings of the International Joint Conference on Artificial Intelligence (IJCAI)*, pages 1330–1339.

Russell Stewart and Stefano Ermon. 2017. Label-free supervision of neural networks with physics and domain knowledge. In *Proceedings of the AAAI Conference on Artificial Intelligence*, volume 31.

Haitian Sun, Bhuwan Dhingra, Manzil Zaheer, Kathryn Mazaitis, Ruslan Salakhutdinov, and William Cohen. 2018. Open domain question answering using early fusion of knowledge bases and text. In *Proceedings of the 2018 Conference on Empirical Methods in Natural Language Processing*, pages 4231–4242.

Niket Tandon, Bhavana Dalvi, Keisuke Sakaguchi, Peter Clark, and Antoine Bosselut. 2019. WIQA: A dataset for "what if..." reasoning over procedural text. In *Proceedings of the 2019 Conference on Empirical Methods in Natural Language Processing and the 9th International Joint Conference on Natural Language Processing (EMNLP-IJCNLP)*, pages 6076–6085, Hong Kong, China. Association for Computational Linguistics.

Jingyi Xu, Zilu Zhang, Tal Friedman, Yitao Liang, and Guy Van den Broeck. 2018. A semantic loss function for deep learning with symbolic knowledge. In *Proceedings of the 35th International Conference on Machine Learning*, volume 80 of *Proceedings of Machine Learning Research*, pages 5502–5511. PMLR.

Bishan Yang and Tom Mitchell. 2017. Leveraging knowledge bases in lstms for improving machine reading. In *Proceedings of the 55th Annual Meeting of the Association for Computational Linguistics (Volume 1: Long Papers)*, pages 1436–1446.

Xiao Zhang, Maria Leonor Pacheco, Chang Li, and Dan Goldwasser. 2016. Introducing DRAIL – a step towards declarative deep relational learning. In *Proceedings of the Workshop on Structured Prediction for NLP*, pages 54–62, Austin, TX. Association for Computational Linguistics.

Da Zheng, Minjie Wang, Quan Gan, Zheng Zhang, and George Karypis. 2020. Learning graph neural networks with deep graph library. WWW '20, New York, NY, USA. Association for Computing Machinery.

A Global Constraints and Mapping

Following is an example of the mapping between OWL constraint, graph structure and the logic python constraint. The ontology definition in OWL:

```
<owl:ObjectProperty rdf:ID="work_for">
    <rdfs:domain rdf:resource="#people"/>
    <rdfs:range rdf:resource="#organization"/>
</owl:ObjectProperty>
```

or equivalent graph structure definition:

```
work_for.has_a(arg1=people, arg2=organization)
```

DomiKnowS's constrain language representation:

```
ifL(work_for('x'), andL(people(path=('x',arg1)), organization(path='x',arg2)))
```

All three above constraints represent the same knowledge that a *work_for* relationship only holds between *people* and *organization.*

In order to map this logical constrain to ILP, the solver collects sets of candidates for each used in the constrain concepts.

ILP inequalities are created for each of the combinations of candidates sets. The internal nested *andL* logical expression is translated to a set of three algebraic inequalities. The new variable *varAND*) is created to transfer the result of the internal expression into the external one.

```
varAND <= varPhraseIsPeople
varAND <= varPhraseIsOrganization
varPhraseIsPeople + varPhraseIsOrganization <= varAND + 1
```

External *ifL* expression is translated to a single algebraic inequality (refers to the variable *varAND*):

```
varPhraseIsWorkFor <= varAND
```

B Program Composition

The Program instances allow the user to define different training tasks without extra effort to change the underlying models. One can define end-to-end models, pipelines, and two step tuning paradigms just by defining different program instances and calling them one after another. For instance, we can seamlessly switch between the following variations of learning paradigms on the EMR task.
End-To-End training:

```
program = Program(graph, poi=(phrase, sentence, pair))
program.train()
```

Pre-train phrase then just train on the pairs:

```
program_1 = Program(graph, poi=(phrase, sentence))
program_2 = Program(graph, poi=(pair))
program_1.train(); program_2.train()
```

Pre-train phrase and use the result in the end-to-end training:

	Precision			Recall			F1		
	Entity	Relation	All	Entity	Relation	All	Entity	Relation	All
Baseline	0.898	0.960	0.933	0.7619	**0.807**	0.787	0.818	**0.872**	0.848
Baselin + ILP	0.896	**0.986**	**0.946**	**0.816**	0.77	**0.791**	**0.847**	0.86	**0.854**
Baseline + IML	0.8851	0.979	0.937	0.746	0.712	0.727	0.8	0.82	0.811
Baseline + PD	**0.9**	0.952	0.929	0.765	0.789	0.779	0.821	0.859	0.842

Table 1: The results on the 25% of the data on Conll benchmark.

	Precision			Recall			F1		
	Entity	Relation	All	Entity	Relation	All	Entity	Relation	All
Baseline	0.909	0.954	0.934	0.824	0.914	0.874	0.86	0.934	0.901
Baselin + ILP	**0.911**	**0.989**	**0.954**	**0.855**	0.903	**0.882**	**0.877**	**0.944**	**0.914**
Baseline + IML	0.904	**0.989**	0.951	0.831	0.884	0.861	0.86	0.933	0.901
Baseline + PD	0.910	0.934	0.923	0.827	**0.915**	0.876	0.862	0.924	0.897

Table 2: The results on 100% of data on Conll benchmark.

```
program_1 = POIProgram(graph, poi=(phrase, sentence), ...)
program_2 = POIProgram(graph, poi=(phrase, sentence, pair), ...)
program_1.train(...)
program_2.train(...)
```

C Experiments

C.1 EMR

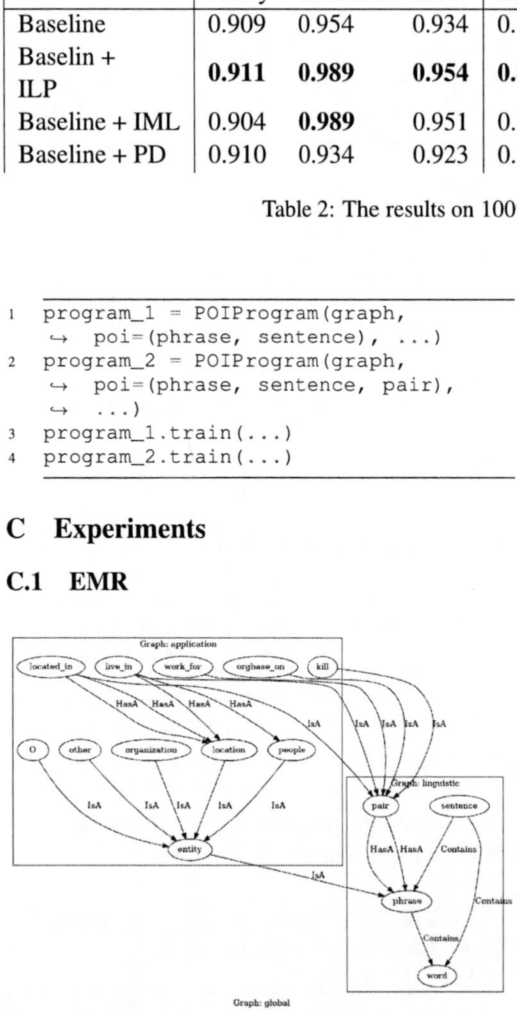

Figure 1: The domain knowledge used for the named entity and relation extraction task expressed as a graph in DomiKnowS

Figure 1 shows the prior structural domain knowledge expressed as a graph and used in this example. It contains the basic concepts such as 'sentence', 'phrase', 'word', and 'pair' and the existing relationships between them alongside the possible output concepts such as 'people' and 'work_for'. Figure 2 also represents a sample DataNode graph populated for a single phrase, alongside its properties and decisions.

Tables 1 and 2 summarize the results of the model applied on only 25% of the training data and the whole 100% of the training data based on the CONLL dataset respectively.

C.2 Question Answering

WIQA dataset contains 39,705 multiple choice questions regarding cause and effects in the context of a procedural paragraph. The answer is always either *is less*, *is more*, or *no effect*. To model this task in DomiKnowS, we define *paragraph*, *question*, *symmetric*, and *transitive* concepts. Each *paragraph* comes with a set of *questions*. As explained by Asai and Hajishirzi, enforcing constraints between different question answers can be beneficial to the models' performance. Here, two questions can be the opposite of each other with a symmetric relationship between their answers, or three questions may introduce a chain of reasoning of cause and effects leading to a transitivity property among their answers. Following is a sample constraint defined in DomiKnowS to represent the symmetric property between questions.

```
symmetric.has_a(arg1=question, arg2=question)
ifL(is_more('x'), is_less(path=('x', arg2))
```

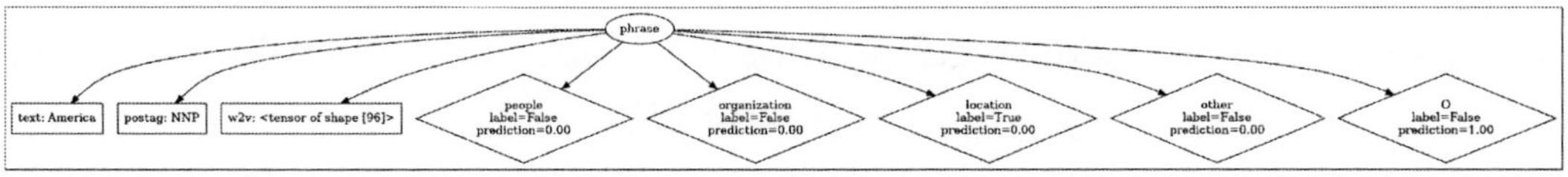

Figure 2: Sample DataNode graph populated for one single phrase from the Named Entity and Relation Extraction task.

Model	Test Accuracy
Baseline	74.22%
Baseline + IML	75.49%
Baseline + PD	76.59%
Baseline + ILP	79.05%
Baseline + PD + ILP	**80.35%**

Table 3: Results of accuracy on WIQA dataset

The results for the WIQA dataset are shown in table 3. Using IML method with this task results in 1.27% improvement while Primal Dual does a better job by improving the accuracy with 2.37%. The best result is achieved with the combination of ILP and Primal Dual with 6.1% improvement over the baseline.

OpenFraming: Open-sourced Tool for Computational Framing Analysis of Multilingual Data

Vibhu Bhatia* **Vidya Akavoor*** **Sejin Paik*** **Lei Guo** **Mona Jalal**
Alyssa Smith[†] **David Tofu** **Edward Halim** **Yimeng Sun** **Margrit Betke**
Prakash Ishwar **Derry Tanti Wijaya**[‡]
Boston University
wijaya@bu.edu

Abstract

When journalists cover a news story, they can cover the story from multiple angles or perspectives. These perspectives are called "frames", and usage of one frame or another may influence public perception and opinion of the issue at hand. We develop a web-based system for analyzing frames in multilingual text documents. We propose and guide users through a five-step end-to-end computational framing analysis framework grounded in media framing theory in communication research. Users can use the framework to analyze multilingual text data, starting from the exploration of frames in user's corpora and through review of previous framing literature (step 1-3) to frame classification (step 4) and prediction (step 5). The framework combines unsupervised and supervised machine learning and leverages a state-of-the-art (SoTA) multilingual language model, which can significantly enhance frame prediction performance while requiring a considerably small sample of manual annotations. Through the interactive website, anyone can perform the proposed computational framing analysis, making advanced computational analysis available to researchers without a programming background and bridging the digital divide within the communication research discipline in particular and the academic community in general. The system is available online at http://www.openframing.org[1], via an API http://www.openframing.org:5000/docs/, or through our GitHub page https://github.com/vibss2397/openFraming.

1 Introduction

We live in a world saturated with media. Any major public issue, such as the ongoing COVID-19 pandemic and the Black Lives Matter protests, attracts tremendous attention from hundreds of thousands of news media outlets — traditional and emerging - around the world. The reporting angles on a single issue are often varied across different media outlets. In covering COVID-19, for example, some media outlets focus on government response and actions while others emphasize the economic consequences. Social science scholars call this process *media framing*. To define, or to *frame*, is "to select some aspects of a perceived reality and make them more salient in a communicating text" (Entman, 1993). When used in news articles, frames can strongly impact public perception of the topics reported and lead to different assessments by readers (Hamborg, 2020), or even reinforce stereotypes and project explicit and implicit social and racial biases (Drakulich, 2015; Sap et al., 2019).

Frame discovery in media text has been traditionally accomplished using methods such as *quantitative content analysis* (Krippendorff, 2018), which is a manual method widely used by social scientists. However, in the emerging media environment, the sheer volume and velocity with which content is generated makes manual labeling increasingly intractable. To overcome this "Big Data" challenge, our cross-disciplinary team, which consists of computer science and communication researchers have employed methods based on SoTA machine learning (ML) techniques to detect frames automatically and robustly (Akyürek et al., 2020; Liu et al., 2019).

However, these SoTA ML models are not readily accessible to social sciences scholars who typically do not have machine learning and programming training. The current ecosystem around "Big Data" creates new digital divides between the Big Data rich and the Big Data poor (Boyd and Crawford, 2012). Among other barriers, the limited access to computational resources and skillsets prevents many communication scholars from taking advantage of a large number of unprecedented ML models of the day and hampers their ability to glean

* Contributed equally
† While at Summer research in Boston University
‡ Corresponding author
[1]Best viewed with Google Chrome browser

Proceedings of the 2021 Conference on Empirical Methods in Natural Language Processing: System Demonstrations, pages 242–250
November 7–11, 2021. ©2021 Association for Computational Linguistics

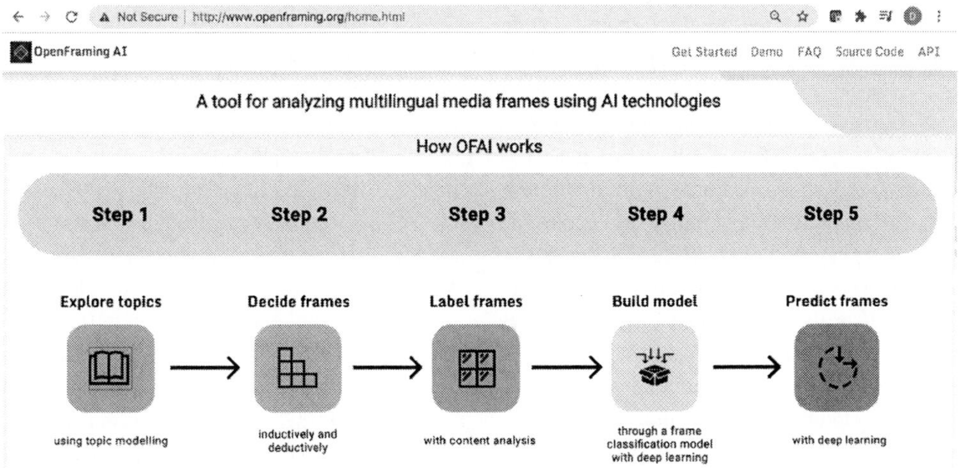

Figure 1: Our proposed five-step computational framing analysis framework that is grounded in media framing theory in communication research. Users can use our framework to analyze frames in text, starting from the *inductive* exploration of frames in user's corpora via topic modeling (step 1) and *deductively* through review of previous framing literature (step 2), to labeling frames for training data with content analysis (step 3), to training the frame classification model (step 4) and to prediction on unlabeled data (step 5).

valuable insights from unprecedentedly large media datasets since framing, especially at scale, defines how news media coverage shapes mass opinion.

Our goal is to make computational framing analysis accessible to researchers from a diverse array of disciplines. We present OpenFraming (www.openframing.org), a free and user-friendly Web-based system that allows researchers to conduct computational framing analysis without having to write and debug complex code. There does, of course, exist click-and-play commercial software, but these tools are often costly and pose issues for researchers due to a lack of transparency into their inner computational mechanisms. This black box problem is present in various applications of data science techniques in communication research (Guo, 2018), thus hindering the open science movement in the field (van Atteveldt and Peng, 2018). In contrast, our system is based on SoTA framing research and our code is publicly available under MIT license.

Specifically, we propose a five-step analytical framework (Figure 1) allowing users to identify frames in large-scale media text by leveraging SoTA computational frame analysis research techniques. Our work is advantageous in at least five aspects. First, the framework is grounded in media framing theory, one of the most established theories in communication research (D'Angelo, 2018; Reese et al., 2001b). Second, we provide a web-based, user-friendly graphic interface where researchers with little or no computational background can perform advanced data analysis through a click-and-play approach. Third, all algorithms used are open to users and the benefits and limitations of the algorithms are explained at each step. Fourth, given the increasing importance of understanding information flow at a global scale, our tool can be used to analyze media content in 23 languages based on a SoTA multilingual language model (Devlin et al., 2018). Lastly, with the support of a research grant, we make our tool entirely free to the academic community.

We will start with a review of the theoretical and methodological backgrounds based on which our system is developed. We will then detail the five-step framing analysis facilitated by the system. The importance of bridging the digital divide in the field of computational communication research will also be discussed.

2 Related Work

To frame is "to select some aspects of a perceived reality and make them more salient in a communicating text" (Entman, 1993). Like any type of communication, news involves framing. The ideology of a society, ownership of a news organization, media routine, as well as individual media worker's preferences all play some role, consciously or not, in shaping the news content (Shoemaker and Reese, 1995). Reese et al. (2001a) defines media frames as "organizing principles that are socially shared and persistent over time, that work symbolically to meaningfully structure the social world". In other words, one can frame an issue in multiple ways, but a frame must be shared by the target audience on some level for it to be communicable and effective. Accordingly, news frame analysis should focus on frames that are "persistent over time". These include generic frames that appear across issues, time, and space, such as human interest, conflict, attribution of responsibility, and economic consequences (Neuman et al., 1992; Nisbet, 2010; Semetko and Valkenburg, 2000). For any particular issue, journalists also apply issue-specific frames e.g., reporters often use peace- and war-oriented frames to help their audience understand the complexity of wars (Neumann and Fahmy, 2012).

Empirically, communication researchers have developed a variety of approaches to analyze frames. There are in general three computational approaches: 1) lexical-based, 2) unsupervised ML, and 3) supervised ML.

The lexical-based approach relies on predefined lists of words, known as lexicons or dictionaries, with each word associated with a certain frame (Field et al., 2018). For example, (Lind et al., 2019) develops keywords to search for frames in the news coverage of immigration. We, however, contend that the lexical-based approach is not ideal for news frame analysis. Unlike the topic-like frames in Lind et al. (2019), many enduring media frames (e.g., conflict, human interest) are abstract and involve complex meanings, which cannot be easily captured by a list of words and terms.

The other two approaches are based on ML models that learn from data. While unsupervised ML models discover patterns of frames from unlabeled data, supervised ML is done by training a model on a sample of documents that are labeled with the "correct" frame. In communication research, the "correct frame" often refers to labels provided by human coders through quantitative content analysis (Krippendorff, 2004).

Several existing news frame studies used an unsupervised ML approach. The Latent Dirichlet Allocation (LDA) topic modeling (Blei et al., 2003) is a popular example (see Maier et al. (2018) for a systematic review). In analyzing news content, the text is observed as a set of latent "topics" and these topics are distributed over words in a probabilistic order. The output of the LDA topic modeling is a "topic matrix" with a list of keywords representing each topic. Researchers will have to review the top keywords and decide on a label to represent the meaning of each topic. Some studies approach media framing by analyzing mainly themes or topics. This approach is problematic because, again, news frame analysis should identify patterns that endure over time, which is different from thematic or topical analyses that describe themes or topics as instances reported in certain stories (Reese, 2007). Given this, the LDA approach is most useful for exploratory analysis. Although the LDA-generated topics are not necessarily equivalent to frames, the information can be used to obtain initial ideas about the data and infer potential frames for the next step of supervised frame analysis (Guo et al., 2016).

Supervised ML also has become increasingly common in communication research (Colleoni et al., 2014; De Grove et al., 2020). Our recent studies use BERT language model (Devlin et al., 2018) and fine-tune it for the task of identifying frames in the news coverage about US gun violence which demonstrate a high level of accuracy for multilingual frame detection (Liu et al., 2019; Akyürek et al., 2020) with a relatively small amount of data: 1.3k English frame-labeled news headlines.

Based on the review of the literature, we propose a five-step end-to-end multilingual framing analysis framework that combines unsupervised and supervised ML. Unsupervised ML can help develop a holistic picture of large-scale text corpora, but is not sufficient for a news frame analysis. Adding a supervised approach to the research framework is essential because the goal is to identify enduring frames—generic and issue-specific frames to contribute to the media framing literature. Furthermore, since developing multilingual ground truth labels through manual content analysis is labor-intensive and time-consuming, to address this challenge in part, our proposed framework incorporates a SoTA multilingual language model such as BERT that allows transfer learning from pretrained models to the task at hand. As a result, it would require relatively fewer labeled documents to fine-tune, while still achieving robust prediction performance.

3 System Description: Five-step Multilingual Framing Analysis

Our analytical framework, available publicly via www.openframing.org, involves five steps that researchers can take to conduct a end-to-end computational framing analysis of multilingual text corpora (Figure 1). To help demonstrate the research procedure, we will accompany the description of our system by a case study that examines frames in the U.S. news coverage of the U.S. gun violence issue–also provided as a demo at http://www.openframing.org/demos.html.

Before using the system, researchers should first collect data related to the issue under consideration. As for the case study, we collect news headlines using the keyword combination (gun OR firearm OR nra OR "2nd amendment" OR "second amendment" OR AR15 OR "assault weapon" OR rifle OR "brady act" OR "brady bill" OR shooting) and collected a total of 42,917 U.S. English news articles from 2018 using Brandwatch Consumer Research[2].

Step 1: Explore Topics with Topic Modeling To analyze how the news media frame an issue, we first suggest users come up with a list of specific "frames" that guide the discussion of the issue. This process of searching for frames should be both inductively—based on an observation of the data—and deductively—based on the review of the previous framing literature. Both steps are essential because the analysis of frames should not just aim for a full capture of the data (inductive), but also to build and further advance the prior knowledge of the media framing theory (deductive).

Step 1 (Figure 2) focuses on the inductive part of the research. The goal of this first step is to preliminarily examine the LDA "topic" information of the data, which helps researchers decide the final frames to be analyzed in Step 2.

While there is some flexibility regarding the format of the input dataset (the system currently supports .xls, .xlsx, .csv, or .tsv), the file must contain a column labeled "example", which contains one document per row. Throughout this paper, we call the unit of analysis a "document", which can be a news headline, a news article, or a tweet. Our system also provides users with a list of data cleaning options (some of them are shown in Figure 2). In particular, we provide the option of running the analysis in multiple languages. The Natural Language Toolkit (NLTK) provides a library of stopwords available in 23 languages, which we use to remove stopwords in text in the language specified by the user. The LDA topic modeling, which is language invariant, is then applied to generate topics from the text when user hits the "submit" button. We use the Mallet LDA implementation (McCallum, 2002). The system then sends the user an e-mail with a link to download the results of the

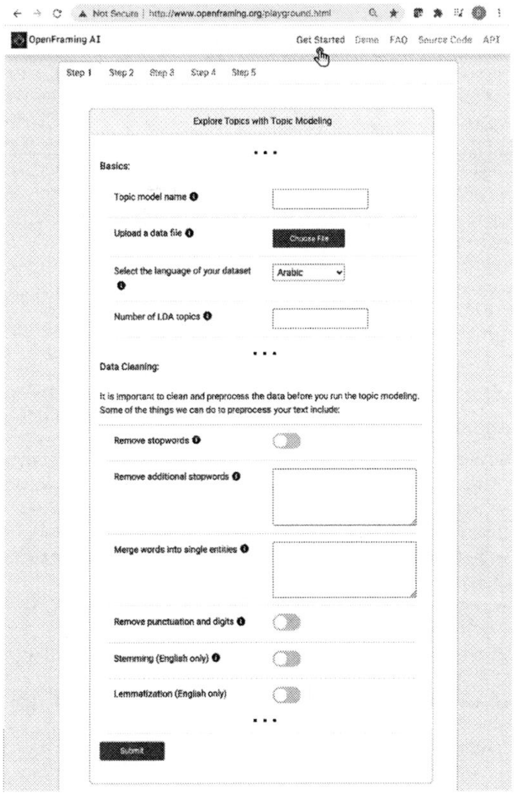

Figure 2: Step 1 of the 5-step framing analysis that allows users to explore topics in their corpora with LDA topic modeling.

analysis–the topics discovered and the keywords per topic.

Although the LDA topic modeling is a computational method, its implementation involves a series of human reasoning. For instance, as mentioned above, researchers should decide the data cleaning procedures, the number of LDA topics, and the number of keywords associated with each topic. Our tool not only allows users to specify their preferred settings but also provides guidance and recommendations for each decision through the information ⓘ buttons on Figure 2. Following previous research, we recommend users try different numbers of topics before making the final decision.

In conducting the gun violence study, we first used the LDA to explore prominent topics in our dataset about the U.S. gun violence issue. For demonstration purposes, we tried 5, 10, and 15 topics. Based on the five-topic LDA output (Figure 3), we can manually assign labels to these topics: 1) mass shootings, 2) police officers, 3) school shootings and demonstrations, 4) gun rights and gun control, and 5) the second amendment. It is recommended that at least two researchers independently review the topics and then decide the labels collec-

[2]https://www.brandwatch.com/

	Topic 1	Topic 2	Topic 3	Topic 4	Topic 5
KW 1	time	police	student	trump	law
KW 2	life	officer	high	president	firearm
KW 3	mass	shot	florida	nra	state
KW 4	victim	man	parkland	house	weapon
KW 5	year	told	douglas	republican	rifle
KW 6	family	county	teacher	state	violence
KW 7	killed	yearold	stoneman	white	company
KW 8	friend	suspect	cruz	democrat	year
KW 9	video	report	march	bill	amendment
KW10	day	department	marjory	control	ban

Figure 3: The LDA topic modeling output for our gun violence news headlines based on five topics.

tively. When we increase the number of topics from five to 10, more information emerges such as mental health. However, when we further increase the number of topics to 15, redundancy occurs—for example, many topics are related to gun control—and certain topics contain words that are not semantically meaningful. This indicates that we may have reached the saturation point, thus further increasing the number of topics would be less likely to generate any new topical information.

After users try a series of numbers and explore the corresponding topic-keyword matrices in datasets of different languages, they will be able to develop a preliminary idea of the multilingual data. This concludes Step 1 of the framing analysis.

Step 2-3: Decide and Label Frames In Step 2, researchers are recommended to consult the LDA topic modeling results from Step 1 (inductive) and previous literature about media framing of the issue under investigation (deductive), and then decide a list of frames to be analyzed.

For our case study, based on the LDA modeling results of the news coverage of U.S. gun violence and the literature review of the media framing of this topic, we decided in Step 2 the following list of frames: 1) Gun/2nd amendment rights; 2) Gun control/regulation; 3) Politics; 4) Mental health; 5) School or public space safety; 6) Race/ethnicity; 7) Public opinion; 8) Society/culture; and 9) Economic consequences. On this list, some frames are issue-specific frames that are unique to the media coverage of gun violence such as "gun/2nd Amendment rights" and "mental health," other frames are generic frames such as "economic consequences" that apply to all kinds of issues. It is also important to note that although the LDA topic modeling results do not have explicit reference to "society/culture," we still include it because it is a media frame discussed in the previous literature about gun violence media coverage (Birkland and Lawrence, 2009; Schnell, 2001).

In Step 3, once the list of frames is decided, the user should draw a sample of the data and apply quantitative content analysis (QCA) (Krippendorff, 2004) to manually label frames. This annotated sample will be used as the ground truth to train an ML model in Step 4. In our case study, we selected a random sample of 1.3k English headlines, and recruited two human coders to annotate the frames of the headlines. Following the QCA procedure, we created a codebook to explain each frame and held multiple training sessions for the coders to understand how to identify the dominant frames of the headlines. To test intercoder reliability, the two coders for each language were instructed to code a sample of news headlines independently and their results were compared. They ultimately reached a robust level of intercoder reliability (0.90 α).

Step 4: Build a Frame Classification Model with Deep Learning The goal of Step 4 is to use the documents the users have labeled from Step 3 to build supervised ML models that can then predict frames in unlabeled documents. Our analytical framework incorporates SoTA language model BERT, which stands for Bidirectional Encoder Representations from Transformers (Devlin et al., 2018). In order to analyze text in multiple languages, we use a recent multilingual extension of BERT: XLM-Roberta (Conneau et al., 2019).

BERT is one of the most successful deep learning language models in natural language processing (NLP). Trained on a large text corpus (i.e., Wikipedia pages and books), the model produces embeddings (i.e., vectors of numbers) to represent the meaning of sentences, taking into consideration the relationships between words and their context. On top of that, XLM-Roberta is further trained on a large corpus of multilingual data, that is, 2.5TB of filtered web data in 100 languages. The vector representations of text in any of the 100 languages the model is pretrained on can then be used to generate insight into any text in the given language. Further discussion of our system's multilingual capability and other recommendations for best practices can be found in the comprehensive FAQ section of our website.[3]

Building a deep learning model from scratch is hard because it requires extensive training data. A common approach is to "transfer" insight from a pretrained deep learning model and use it to perform similar tasks on another dataset. This is called transfer learning. With the capability of transferring knowledge from a pretrained model to the

[3]http://www.openframing.org/faq.html

current task, one can build a model with a high level of accuracy even using a small sample of ground truth labels. In short, our system first obtains some knowledge from XLM-Roberta about how to create meaningful vector representations of text in multiple languages, and fine-tunes these representations using the provided human annotations for frame classification[4]. Our system implements 5-fold cross-validation and provides three evaluation scores—precision, recall, and F-score—to assess the performance of the trained model. These are sent via an email to the user once training is done, together with the ID of the model trained on the user's entire labeled data that the user can use for frame prediction in Step 5. As for our gun violence case study, we use the above-discussed approach. Based on 5-fold cross-validation, the model to predict frames in the English news headlines reached 0.83 accuracy.

Step 5: Predict Frames with Deep Learning Once the user is satisfied with the average model performance from Step 4, they can upload an unlabeled dataset and the user's trained model can be used to predict the frames in the dataset. Our system also provides four English pretrained models on topics of gun violence trained on the gun violence frame corpus (Liu et al., 2019; Akyürek et al., 2020; Guo et al., 2021), and immigration, tobacco, and same-sex marriage trained on the media frame corpus (Card et al., 2015; Field et al., 2018).

We use the gun violence model trained from Step 4–which obtains a 5-fold cross-validation accuracy of 0.83–to predict the frames of the remaining English news headlines about the U.S. gun violence issue from different years. Figure 4 visualize the results, which can also be accessed at the demo part of our website http://www.openframing.org/demos.html. It is clear that the volume of coverage increased after each mass shooting case (Figure 4) and overall, the issue was largely politicized in the media discourse. The demo also allows comparison of conservative and liberal-leaning news coverage in the U.S., where the former emphasized the mental health frame more than so the latter. With results of news frames like the ones demonstrated here, users can run additional statistics to compare news framing strategies across different societies, or different types of news media within a certain society.

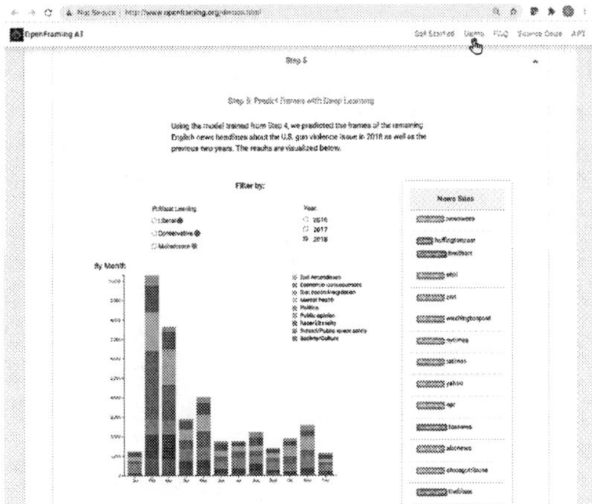

Figure 4: Screenshot of part of the web page for the gun violence study demo, showing 2018 headline frame predictions.

4 Discussion and Conclusion

As we have argued, applying SoTA computational methods to framing analysis can make a significant methodological contribution to the field. However, the implementation involves at least two challenges: the lack of computational resources and skills. Deep learning models such as XLM-Roberta, are extremely large ML models with millions of parameters to train. Even fine-tuning them requires computers with GPU compute capability, which is expensive and not widely available. Some cloud services such as Google Colab provide free but limited access to GPUs. The intensive computational requirements for running large ML models and the unequal access to these computing resources among researchers contribute to the digital and compute divide (Strubell et al., 2019).

For communication researchers, the divide is exacerbated due to the shortage of computational research skills. Implementing and fine-tuning topic modeling or deep learning models such as the ones introduced here requires the understanding and a considerable degree of comfortability with using a deep learning programming framework such as Pytorch, machine learning libraries such as scikit-learn for the training and evaluation setup and analysis, NLP libraries such as NLTK to clean and preprocess the text, as well as Python programming that is required for using these frameworks and libraries. Users with little experience in computer science or programming would find it challenging to run the computational analysis on their own.

With the support of a cross-disciplinary team, our system aims to make the computational fram-

[4]We use one set of training parameters recommended for BERT: a learning rate of 5e-5, 3 epochs of fine-tuning, and a batch size of 8

ing analysis accessible to researchers with no or little prior experience in computer science and programming. Through a click-and-play web-based system, the users can follow the guidance on the website and run the advanced computational analysis step by step. Users with different levels of expertise would know where to start and how to interact with the system. Also unlike many of the similar applications in the market, our system prioritizes transparency in its data processing and algorithms. The tool is entirely open-sourced and users will have access to the raw code on our Github page.

5 Future Directions

In the future, we are extending our system to support multilingual framing analysis on noisy or informal text, such as those present in social media posts, using recent methods such as Wibowo et al. (2021) to convert informal to formal text prior to doing framing analysis. Other interesting future directions include extending our system to support computational multimodal (i.e., text and image) framing analysis. As journalists have been using both text and images to frame news stories (Messaris and Abraham, 2001; Coleman and Wu, 2015; Dan, 2017; Powell et al., 2015), text and images have worked together to create a holistic perception of news and hence must be considered together when analyzing news frames (Wessler et al., 2016). Although such use of multimodal inputs has been explored in many NLP tasks such as multimodal machine translation (Specia et al., 2016; Hewitt et al., 2018; Khani et al., 2021) and vision-language tasks such as multilingual image retrieval or captioning (Kim et al., 2020; Burns et al., 2020; Rasooli et al., 2021), there is not yet a computational tool that can support multimodal framing. Furthermore, in addition to communication scholars benefiting from such tool that can analyze, on large scale, images and headlines in tandem for frames, newsroom editors would also benefit from tools that can identify images that help depict the main thrust of the story's focus (Caple, 2010). Such tools do not yet exist, and a system that can support multimodal framing will be able to address this need.

Acknowledgments

This work is supported in part by the U.S. NSF grant 1838193, DARPA HR001118S0044 (the LwLL program), and the Department of the Air Force FA8750-19-2-3334 (Semi-supervised Learning of Multimodal Representations). The U.S. Government is authorized to reproduce and distribute reprints for Governmental purposes. The views and conclusions contained in this publication are those of the authors and should not be interpreted as representing official policies or endorsements of DARPA, the Air Force, and the U.S. Government.

References

Afra Feyza Akyürek, Lei Guo, Randa Elanwar, Prakash Ishwar, Margrit Betke, and Derry Tanti Wijaya. 2020. Multi-label and multilingual news framing analysis. In *Proceedings of the 58th Annual Meeting of the Association for Computational Linguistics*, pages 8614–8624, Online. Association for Computational Linguistics.

Thomas A Birkland and Regina G Lawrence. 2009. Media framing and policy change after columbine. *American Behavioral Scientist*, 52(10):1405–1425.

David M Blei, Andrew Y Ng, and Michael I Jordan. 2003. Latent dirichlet allocation. *Journal of machine Learning research*, 3(Jan):993–1022.

Danah Boyd and Kate Crawford. 2012. Critical questions for big data: Provocations for a cultural, technological, and scholarly phenomenon. *Information, communication & society*, 15(5):662–679.

Andrea Burns, Donghyun Kim, Derry Wijaya, Kate Saenko, and Bryan A Plummer. 2020. Learning to scale multilingual representations for vision-language tasks. In *European Conference on Computer Vision*, pages 197–213. Springer.

Helen Caple. 2010. What you see and what you get: The evolving role of news photographs in an Australian broadsheet. *Journalism and Meaning-Making: Reading the Newspaper*, pages 199–220.

Dallas Card, Amber Boydstun, Justin H Gross, Philip Resnik, and Noah A Smith. 2015. The media frames corpus: Annotations of frames across issues. In *Proceedings of the 53rd Annual Meeting of the Association for Computational Linguistics and the 7th International Joint Conference on Natural Language Processing (Volume 2: Short Papers)*, pages 438–444.

Renita Coleman and Denis Wu. 2015. *Image and emotion in voter decisions: The affect agenda*. Lexington Books.

Elanor Colleoni, Alessandro Rozza, and Adam Arvidsson. 2014. Echo chamber or public sphere? predicting political orientation and measuring political homophily in twitter using big data. *Journal of communication*, 64(2):317–332.

Alexis Conneau, Kartikay Khandelwal, Naman Goyal, Vishrav Chaudhary, Guillaume Wenzek, Francisco

Guzmán, Edouard Grave, Myle Ott, Luke Zettlemoyer, and Veselin Stoyanov. 2019. Unsupervised cross-lingual representation learning at scale. *arXiv preprint arXiv:1911.02116*.

Viorela Dan. 2017. *Integrative framing analysis: Framing health through words and visuals*. Routledge.

Paul D'Angelo. 2018. *Doing news framing analysis II: Empirical and theoretical perspectives*. Routledge.

Frederik De Grove, Kristof Boghe, and Lieven De Marez. 2020. (what) can journalism studies learn from supervised machine learning? *Journalism Studies*, 21(7):912–927.

Jacob Devlin, Ming-Wei Chang, Kenton Lee, and Kristina Toutanova. 2018. Bert: Pre-training of deep bidirectional transformers for language understanding. *arXiv preprint arXiv:1810.04805*.

Kevin M Drakulich. 2015. Explicit and hidden racial bias in the framing of social problems. *Social Problems*, 62(3):391–418.

Robert M Entman. 1993. Framing: Toward clarification of a fractured paradigm. *Journal of Communication*.

Anjalie Field, Doron Kliger, Shuly Wintner, Jennifer Pan, Dan Jurafsky, and Yulia Tsvetkov. 2018. Framing and agenda-setting in russian news: a computational analysis of intricate political strategies. *arXiv preprint arXiv:1808.09386*.

Lei Guo. 2018. Ignorance or uncertainty: How the "black box" dilemma in big data research may "misinform" political communication. In *Digital Discussions*, pages 50–67. Routledge.

Lei Guo, Kate Mays, Yiyan Zhang, Derry Wijaya, and Margrit Betke. 2021. What makes gun violence a (less) prominent issue? a computational analysis of compelling arguments and selective agenda setting. *Mass communication and society*, pages 1–25.

Lei Guo, Chris J Vargo, Zixuan Pan, Weicong Ding, and Prakash Ishwar. 2016. Big social data analytics in journalism and mass communication: Comparing dictionary-based text analysis and unsupervised topic modeling. *Journalism & Mass Communication Quarterly*, 93(2):332–359.

Felix Hamborg. 2020. Media bias, the social sciences, and nlp: Automating frame analyses to identify bias by word choice and labeling. In *Proceedings of the 58th Annual Meeting of the Association for Computational Linguistics: Student Research Workshop*, pages 79–87.

John Hewitt, Daphne Ippolito, Brendan Callahan, Reno Kriz, Derry Tanti Wijaya, and Chris Callison-Burch. 2018. Learning translations via images with a massively multilingual image dataset. In *Proceedings of the 56th Annual Meeting of the Association for Computational Linguistics (Volume 1: Long Papers)*, pages 2566–2576.

Nikzad Khani, Isidora Tourni, Mohammad Sadegh Rasooli, Chris Callison-Burch, and Derry Tanti Wijaya. 2021. Cultural and geographical influences on image translatability of words across languages. In *Proceedings of the 2021 Conference of the North American Chapter of the Association for Computational Linguistics: Human Language Technologies*, pages 198–209.

Donghyun Kim, Kuniaki Saito, Kate Saenko, Stan Sclaroff, and Bryan Plummer. 2020. Mule: Multimodal universal language embedding. In *Proceedings of the AAAI Conference on Artificial Intelligence*, volume 34, pages 11254–11261.

Klaus Krippendorff. 2004. Content analysis: An introduction to its methodology.

Klaus Krippendorff. 2018. *Content analysis: An introduction to its methodology*. Sage publications.

Fabienne Lind, Jakob-Moritz Eberl, Tobias Heidenreich, and Hajo G Boomgaarden. 2019. Computational communication sciencel when the journey is as important as the goal: A roadmap to multilingual dictionary construction. *International Journal of Communication*, 13:21.

Siyi Liu, Lei Guo, Kate Mays, Margrit Betke, and Derry Tanti Wijaya. 2019. Detecting frames in news headlines and its application to analyzing news framing trends surrounding us gun violence. In *Proceedings of the 23rd Conference on Computational Natural Language Learning (CoNLL)*, pages 504–514.

Daniel Maier, Annie Waldherr, Peter Miltner, Gregor Wiedemann, Andreas Niekler, Alexa Keinert, Barbara Pfetsch, Gerhard Heyer, Ueli Reber, Thomas Häussler, et al. 2018. Applying lda topic modeling in communication research: Toward a valid and reliable methodology. *Communication Methods and Measures*, 12(2-3):93–118.

Andrew Kachites McCallum. 2002. Mallet: A machine learning for language toolkit. Http://mallet.cs.umass.edu.

Paul Messaris and Linus Abraham. 2001. The role of images in framing news stories. In *Framing public life*, pages 231–242. Routledge.

W Russell Neuman, Russell W Neuman, Marion R Just, and Ann N Crigler. 1992. *Common knowledge: News and the construction of political meaning*. University of Chicago Press.

Rico Neumann and Shahira Fahmy. 2012. Analyzing the spell of war: A war/peace framing analysis of the 2009 visual coverage of the sri lankan civil war in western newswires. *Mass Communication and Society*, 15(2):169–200.

Matthew C Nisbet. 2010. Knowledge into action: Framing the debates over climate change and poverty. In *Doing news framing analysis*, pages 59–99. Routledge.

Thomas E Powell, Hajo G Boomgaarden, Knut De Swert, and Claes H de Vreese. 2015. A clearer picture: The contribution of visuals and text to framing effects. *Journal of Communication*, 65(6):997–1017.

Mohammad Sadegh Rasooli, Chris Callison-Burch, and Derry Tanti Wijaya. 2021. " wikily" neural machine translation tailored to cross-lingual tasks. *arXiv preprint arXiv:2104.08384*.

Stephen D Reese. 2007. The framing project: A bridging model for media research revisited. *Journal of communication*, 57(1):148–154.

Stephen D Reese, Jr Gandy, and August E Grant. 2001a. Prologue—framing public life: A bridging model for media research. In *Framing public life*, pages 23–48. Routledge.

Stephen D Reese, Oscar H Gandy Jr, and August E Grant. 2001b. *Framing public life: Perspectives on media and our understanding of the social world*. Routledge.

Maarten Sap, Saadia Gabriel, Lianhui Qin, Dan Jurafsky, Noah A Smith, and Yejin Choi. 2019. Social bias frames: Reasoning about social and power implications of language. *arXiv preprint arXiv:1911.03891*.

Frauke Schnell, Karen Callaghan. 2001. Assessing the democratic debate: How the news media frame elite policy discourse. *Political communication*, 18(2):183–213.

Holli A Semetko and Patti M Valkenburg. 2000. Framing european politics: A content analysis of press and television news. *Journal of communication*, 50(2):93–109.

P. Shoemaker and Stephen D. Reese. 1995. Mediating the message: Theories of influences on mass media content.

Lucia Specia, Stella Frank, Khalil Sima'An, and Desmond Elliott. 2016. A shared task on multimodal machine translation and crosslingual image description. In *Proceedings of the First Conference on Machine Translation: Volume 2, Shared Task Papers*, pages 543–553.

Emma Strubell, Ananya Ganesh, and Andrew McCallum. 2019. Energy and policy considerations for deep learning in nlp. *arXiv preprint arXiv:1906.02243*.

Wouter van Atteveldt and Tai-Quan Peng. 2018. When communication meets computation: Opportunities, challenges, and pitfalls in computational communication science. *Communication Methods and Measures*, 12(2-3):81–92.

Hartmut Wessler, Antal Wozniak, Lutz Hofer, and Julia Lück. 2016. Global multimodal news frames on climate change: A comparison of five democracies around the world. *The International Journal of Press/Politics*, 21(4):423–445.

Haryo Akbarianto Wibowo, Made Nindyatama Nityasya, Afra Feyza Akyürek, Suci Fitriany, Alham Fikri Aji, Radityo Eko Prasojo, and Derry Tanti Wijaya. 2021. Indocollex: A testbed for morphological transformation of indonesian word colloquialism. *Findings of the Association for Computational Linguistics: ACL-IJCNLP 2021*.

IrEne-viz: Visualizing Energy Consumption of Transformer Models

Yash Kumar Lal, Qingqing Cao, Harsh Trivedi, Reetu Singh,
Aruna Balasubramanian, Niranjan Balasubramanian
Department of Computer Science
Stony Brook University
Stony Brook, NY 11794, USA
{ylal,qicao,hjtrivedi,reesingh,arunab,niranjan}@cs.stonybrook.edu

Abstract

IrEne (Cao et al., 2021) is an energy prediction system that accurately predicts the interpretable inference energy consumption of a wide range of Transformer-based NLP models. We present the IrEne-viz tool, an online platform for visualizing and exploring energy consumption of various Transformer-based models easily. Additionally, we release a public API that can be used to access granular information about energy consumption of transformer models and their components. The live demo is available at `http://stonybrooknlp.github.io/irene/demo/`.

1 Introduction

Pretrained transformers have shown strong results on downstream NLP tasks, resulting in wide-spread adoption. With their deployment in large-scale public-facing systems serving hundreds of millions of requests per day, it has become important to study their energy footprint at inference time. Inference energy can incur substantial costs especially for models that are critical for high-volume web services.

Designing energy efficient and cost-effective models requires both accurate and interpretable energy modeling. Current approaches to energy modeling treat the model as a monolithic entity. In our previous work (Cao et al., 2021), we introduced a tree-like abstraction to decompose a model into its components. We designed a multi-level prediction method that predicts energy in all the components of the abstraction tree in a bottom-up fashion using resource utilization and model description features. This system called IrEne is used as the base of this work. IrEne provides more accurate energy prediction than other methods and is designed to be interpretable. However, it is nontrivial to retrieve data from that system, making it difficult to perform analysis or visualization for the same.

In this work, we present IrEne-viz, a user-friendly dashboard that allows visualization of inference energy consumption of a transformer-based model and its various components. Users will be able to interact with the different operations present in a model. Our interface allows people to easily understand the energy bottlenecks during inference. Additionally, we make our pipeline public by exposing it as an API endpoint. Having such data readily available will further research in the area and allow the community to use it for their own purposes, such as analyzing accuracy or latency trade-offs against energy. For instance, Cao et al. (2021) compared accuracy of BERT on a specific task while varying the number of layers and made observations about the energy-accuracy tradeoff. We design IrEne-viz to be:

- **Easy to use** - Our browser interface is intuitive and allows for thorough exploration of a model, its operations, and their energy usage.
- **Easy to access** - The model tree and its features are readily available through a public API in an easy-to-use JSON format.
- **Easy to extend** - New models to be tracked can be included easily.

2 Related Work

There has been increased interest in the energy consumption of NLP models in recent years. Despite some progress in modeling, there is a lack of visualisation and analysis tools for the same.

2.1 Energy Estimation

Schwartz et al. (2019) suggest using metrics like floating point operations (FPO) to measure energy efficiency. However, Henderson (2020) argues such

Proceedings of the 2021 Conference on Empirical Methods in Natural Language Processing: System Demonstrations, pages 251–258
November 7–11, 2021.

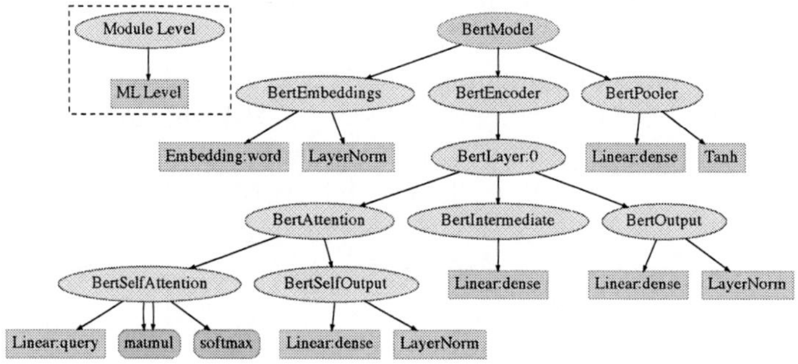

Figure 1: A tree view of a 1-layer BERT model. The yellow rectangle nodes stand for basic machine learning (ML) level operations. The brown rectangle nodes are also ML level which are non-parametric (i.e., has no trainable parameters). The ML level operations are model-agnostic and provided by machine learning software framework. The light blue oval nodes denote model-specific operations that reflect the architectural semantics given by the model developer .

metrics alone cannot accurately reflect energy consumption. Energy prediction of applications on mobile devices is a well-studied topic in the systems community (Pathak et al., 2011, 2012; Yoon et al., 2012; Cao et al., 2017) but they require fine-grained understanding of the application. None of these systems predict energy for NLP models.

Henderson (2020) use the *experiment-impact-tracker* software framework to report the aggregated energy of benchmark programs, built on Strubell et al. (2019). However, Cao et al. (2020) show that this type of resource utilization only modeling can be highly inaccurate. Zhou et al. (2020) presents an energy efficient benchmark for NLP models. However, they only report the time (hours) and cost (dollars) for training and testing NLP models, the actual energy numbers remain unknown.

2.2 Transformer Model Visualization

For NLP, a number of tools exist for investigating specific model classes, such as RNNs (Strobelt et al., 2018), Transformers (Hoover et al., 2020; Vig and Belinkov, 2019), or text generation (Strobelt et al., 2018). More generally, AllenNLP Interpret (Wallace et al., 2019) introduces a modular framework for interpretability components, focused on single-datapoint explanations and integrated tightly with the AllenNLP (Gardner et al., 2017) framework. Lal et al. (2021) present a tool to visualize token embeddings through each layer of a Transformer and highlight distances between certain token embeddings. No such visualization work exists for energy consumption of NLP models.

3 IrEne - Prediction Engine

We briefly review the IrEne system which we use as the energy prediction engine. Please refer to (Cao et al., 2021) for more details. IrEne is an interpretable energy prediction system. It represents transformer models in a tree-based abstraction, and generates energy prediction for each node of the tree, thus directly supporting interpretability. IrEne also comes with data it was trained on – for each tree node, it has associated resource utilization and model-related features, and ground-truth energy measured with a hardware power monitor.

Tree Abstraction

IrEne uses a model tree abstraction that represents the model nodes in three-levels: math level, machine learning (ML) level and module level. Math level nodes are a finite set of mathematical operations (like addition, subtraction, matrix multiplication etc); they form model-agnostic ML level nodes (such as Linear, LayerNorm etc.), which further can be used to construct complex module level nodes. Module level nodes are groups of lower ML level node operations that reflect the logic units of the NLP algorithms defined by model authors. The model tree abstraction is such that each parent node captures computation of all of its children nodes. Figure 1 shows an example tree representation for a 1-layer BERT transformer. This abstraction makes energy calibration more interpretable by allowing us to understand and analyze how the components of a model contribute to its energy usage.

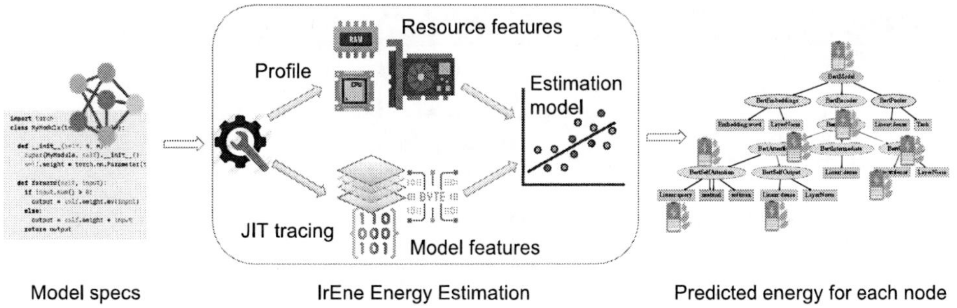

Figure 2: IrEne works by taking model specifications (for example, model code) as inputs and extracting a model tree representation using code instrumentation and run-time tracing. IrEne then runs the model once on a given hardware and feeds resource profiles combined with the model computation features into a regressor to predict the energy of the entire model tree representation. The root of the tree represents the energy of the entire NLP model and each child node represents the energy of different modules/ML operators that make up the model.

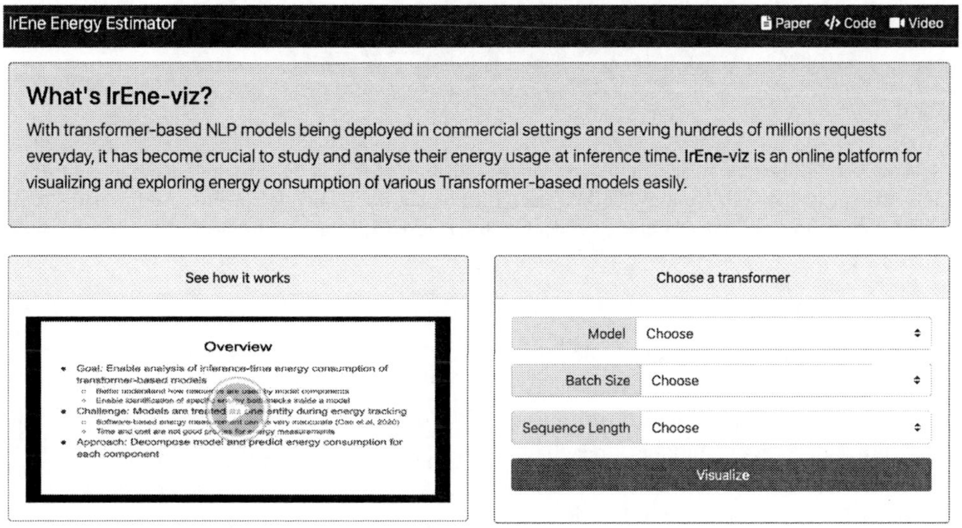

Figure 3: IrEne-viz has a simple input screen where a user can select which Transformer model they want to analyze, and specify the input sequence length and batch size for the model.

Resource Usage Collection

For a given transformer model, IrEne generates a tree representation in the aforementioned abstraction and populates each node with relevant features and ground-truth energy measurement.

To construct the tree, the transformer model[1] is run on the target hardware on randomly generated input for given batch size and input sequence length[2]. This provides execution graph and the JIT trace containing runtime information, which is combined as to form the final tree representation.

Irene uses resource utilization and model-based features. Resource features capture how the models use hardware resources and cause energy activities. Model features like input size and number of parameters are obtained from PyTorch model directly. A list of features, as described in Cao et al. (2021), is shown in Table 1.

Irene collects ground-truth energy for each node using a highly accurate power monitor, and runs it several times to get a reliable estimate. One can use the power monitor to measure energy directly at runtime for visualization. However, this is cumbersome and requires physical access to the device which is not always feasible with cloud-based deployments.

[1]We used HuggingFace Transformers library v4.2.2

[2]The batch size and input sequence length together decide the amount of input data to the model, therefore, they both affect the model energy consumption.

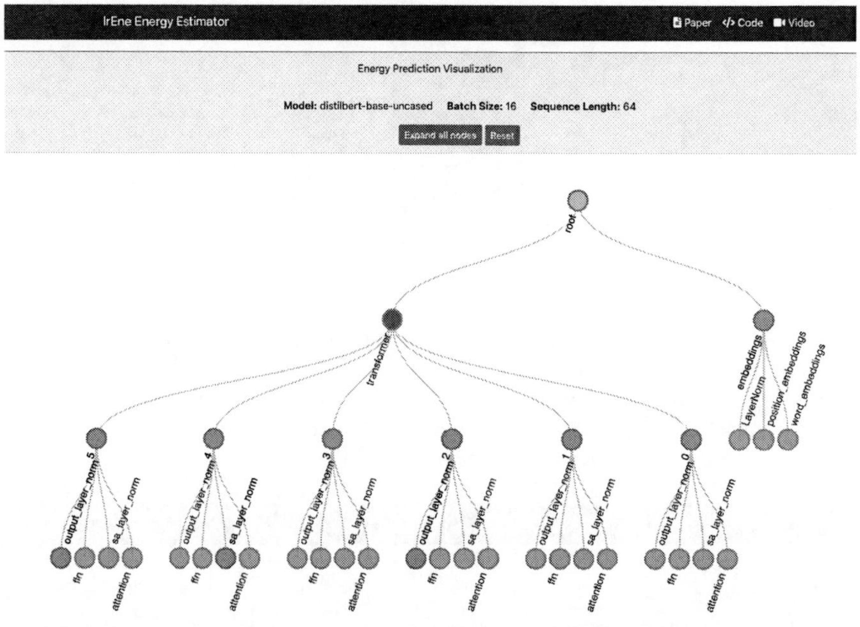

Figure 4: The user will be able to see an interactive visualization of the model components in a tree format. They will be able to expand and collapse it as per their need for granularity in energy analysis. Additionally, to the right, a list of model operations, in order of energy consumption, is provided for easy browsing.

Training and Prediction

IrEne predicts the energy for every node in the model tree in a bottom-up fashion. At the leaves, where the nodes correspond to the ML primitives, IrEne uses separate regression models for each type of ML primitive (e.g., one regressor for Linear Layer, another for LayerNorm etc.). For the intermediate nodes, their energy is predicted recursively using a single regressor that makes a weighted combination of the predicted energy values from its children, and mean squared loss between predicted and ground-truth energy for all tree nodes is jointly minimized. For both types of regressors, IrEne uses features that are derived from resource utilization (e.g. cpu utilization) and generalized node features (e.g. size of inputs) enabling accurate multi-level energy prediction. Using the model tree abstraction and multi-level prediction model makes IrEne generalizable, in the sense that once trained, it can work on unseen NLP models with similar components.

batch_size : batch size
seq_len : # of input tokens
flops : floating point operations (unit: million)
mem_bytes : memory read and write (unit: MiB)
cpu_util : CPU utilization (unit: %)
mem_usg : memory usage (unit: %)
gpu_util : GPU processor utilization (unit: %)
gm_usg : GPU memory usage (unit: %)
g_clk : GPU processor clock speed (unit: MHz)
gm_clk : GPU memory clock speed (unit: MHz)
latency : inference latency (unit: s)
gpu_energy : GPU driver energy (unit: joule)

Table 1: Features used for energy estimation in IrEne.

4 User Interface and Functionality

The goal of IrEne-viz is to provide an easy way for users to analyze the energy of a given Transformer model (for a specified input size). To do so, we design a browser-based user interface (UI) in IrEne-viz that controls the input size and selects the model, as shown in Figure 3. We then estimate the energy consumption of the model and visualize the energy for each part in the Transformer model. Specifically, an user selects a predefined Transformer model[3] via the dropdown menu and enters the batch size and input sequence length. After pressing the visualize button, IrEne-viz backend server will run the energy estimation and send the energy result back to the browser for visualization.

[3]We are adding functionality to support customized models

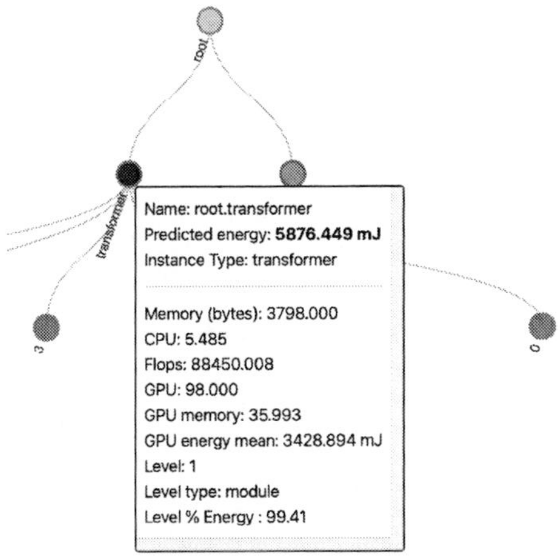

Figure 5: Hovering over any node provides the user with additional information about that node. This includes measurements of memory usage, flops and CPU cycles. Users can select models optimal for their hardware requirements.

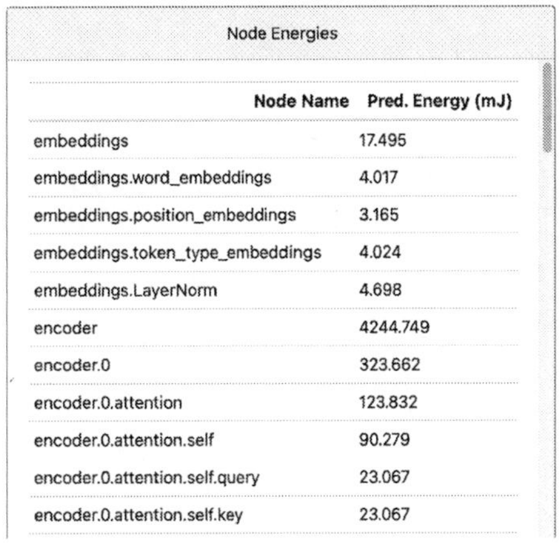
Node Energies

Node Name	Pred. Energy (mJ)
embeddings	17.495
embeddings.word_embeddings	4.017
embeddings.position_embeddings	3.165
embeddings.token_type_embeddings	4.024
embeddings.LayerNorm	4.698
encoder	4244.749
encoder.0	323.662
encoder.0.attention	123.832
encoder.0.attention.self	90.279
encoder.0.attention.self.query	23.067
encoder.0.attention.self.key	23.067

Figure 6: The dashboard also provides a list of all model operations along with their predicted energy consumption for easy identification of bottlenecks.

In IrEne-viz, we support two core functionalities:
Functionality 1 - Explore the energy consumption of the model. Besides the entire model energy, users can interactively explore the energy consumed by any block inside the model, as shown in Figure 4. Additionally, we support inspecting the resource and model features used to estimate the energy, as described in Figure 5.

Functionality 2 - Find energy bottlenecks. At each level of the model, users can easily identify operations that can be improved (or pruned) in terms of their relative energy usage. The visualization dashboard also displays a list of model operations along with their predicted energy usage, as presented in Figure 6.

5 System Implementation

To make IrEne-viz modular and extensible, we design an energy analysis pipeline consisting of three components: a visualization panel that accepts user requests and presents energy results, a prediction engine (IrEne) that predicts energy consumption and a backend server that encapsulates IrEne and serves information through an API endpoint. The API and the prediction engine can be used as individual entities as well. They are also designed to be extensible, so adding new features is easy. The visualization panel is intuitive and informative, allowing easy exploration of data.

Figure 7 shows the full pipeline used for this application. The visualization panel queries the API with the user-desired model name, input sequence length and batch size. This information is passed on to the prediction engine. The engine performs resource collection for the corresponding model specifications and predicts the energy usage of each component. The API sends the visualization panel a full tree representation of the model containing all the model information.

5.1 Visualization Panel

The browser-based UI is built up of HTML webpages using a bootstrap template. The visualization widget is developed using D3.js (Bostock, 2012) embedded in a Flask (Grinberg, 2018) application. A user can decide which model they want to analyze, and provide desired values for batch size and input sequence length. Upon selection, a full tree with information about the model is presented. We also provide an option to display the entire tree at once and, since there are lot of components in a model, collapse it into one root component for easier analysis. Users are able to interact with different components to explore every component in the model. They can click on a component to expand and show all the components in that subtree. When the cursor hovers over it, all the resource information about that component is shown to the user. At any level, the color of the component indicates the percentage of energy consumption it is responsible for. Additionally, we present a list of model components with their predicted energy use on one part of the screen. This frontend applica-

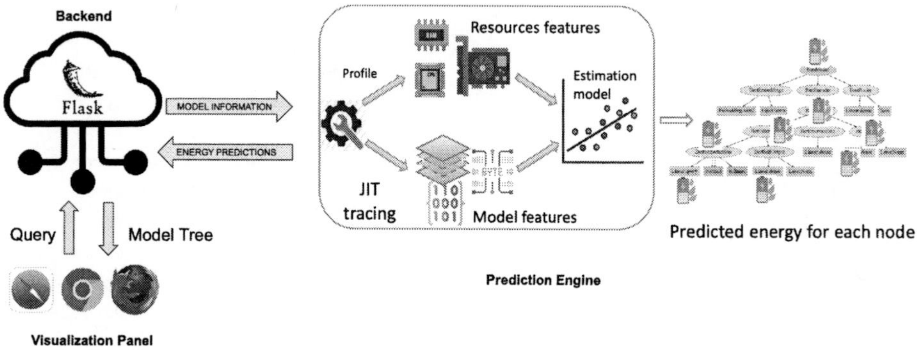

Figure 7: Full system pipeline. The **visualization panel** queries the **backend** with the model name, input sequence length and batch size. This information is passed on to the **prediction engine**, which performs resource collection and predicts the energy usage of each component. The **prediction engine** generates full tree with all the model information and prediction energy back to the **backend**, which in turn passes it to **visualization panel** .

tion is deployed on Heroku and will be available publicly soon.

5.2 Backend

First, we download the configuration of the specified model from Huggingface Hub (Wolf et al., 2020) and use it convert it into a tree object. A model is composed of multiple module-level components, and a module-level component itself is made up of other module-level or ML-level components. Each parent component encapsulates the computation of all of its child components.

First, we run the model to extract the model tree structure. A profiler process is started in the background to monitor usage of various resources. For each type of abstraction described, we find every component in the model.[4] It is run with dummy inputs of the required input size for a fixed number of times so that the profiler can log energy usage reliably (low standard deviation in energy measurements). We reconcile resource usage logs with their respective components using the timestamp at which they were run. Next, we annotate the model tree objects with these features.

To generate energy predictions, we use the Cao et al. (2021) model. We load the saved weights, use the features we just collected to perform inference. The same model tree object is populated with the predicted energy numbers, and can now be used for visualization. The backend encapsulates the prediction engine, which is deployed as a Flask API hosted on a GPU desktop using nginx.

For currently supported models, it takes 15-25 minutes to gather resource usage and make predictions. So, to speed up visualization, we cache results for these models and serve them to the user.

We expose the full end-to-end-pipeline as a Flask API endpoint, and make it available for public use. Querying it for model energy usage information only requires a simple GET request to be made. In addition to this, we plan to expose the model tree abstraction as another API endpoint so that the community can use it for other purposes like runtime analysis.

6 Conclusion and Roadmap

IrEne-viz provides an integrated UI and components for visualizing and exploring the energy consumption of various Transformer models. It is under active development and is being constantly refined for release. We are adding support for live models immediately. For new models, users will be sent an email with a custom link to their requested visualization. As the community uses it, we will cache resource usage and predictions for more intermediate nodes found in various transformer-based models. This optimization will gradually result in lower times for newer models.

Our end-to-end pipeline, served as an API, can be used to build an energy leaderboard. This platform can be extended to compare the energy of architectural modifications (e.g. activation or normalization function) of different models for given input. By extending this work to other harware, we aim to

[4]For the profiler to collect correct energy statistics, we make sure no other significant process is running on the same machine.

provide energy optimization suggestions based on energy profiles of a model on the given hardware. In our previous work, (Cao et al., 2021) we also studied accuracy vs energy trade-offs, which will be integrated into the dashboard.

7 Acknowledgements

This work was supported in part by the National Science Foundation under grants IIS-1815358.

References

Mike Bostock. 2012. D3.js - data-driven documents.

Qingqing Cao, Aruna Balasubramanian, and Niranjan Balasubramanian. 2020. Towards accurate and reliable energy measurement of NLP models. In *Proceedings of SustaiNLP: Workshop on Simple and Efficient Natural Language Processing*, pages 141–148, Online. Association for Computational Linguistics.

Qingqing Cao, Yash Kumar Lal, Harsh Trivedi, Aruna Balasubramanian, and Niranjan Balasubramanian. 2021. IrEne: Interpretable energy prediction for transformers. In *Association for Computational Linguistics: ACL 2021*, Online. Association for Computational Linguistics.

Yi Cao, Javad Nejati, Muhammad Wajahat, Aruna Balasubramanian, and Anshul Gandhi. 2017. Deconstructing the Energy Consumption of the Mobile Page Load. *Proceedings of the ACM on Measurement and Analysis of Computing Systems*, 1(1):6:1–6:25.

Matt Gardner, Joel Grus, Mark Neumann, Oyvind Tafjord, Pradeep Dasigi, Nelson F. Liu, Matthew Peters, Michael Schmitz, and Luke S. Zettlemoyer. 2017. Allennlp: A deep semantic natural language processing platform.

Miguel Grinberg. 2018. *Flask web development: developing web applications with python.* " O'Reilly Media, Inc.".

James Henderson. 2020. The unstoppable rise of computational linguistics in deep learning. In *Proceedings of the 58th Annual Meeting of the Association for Computational Linguistics*, pages 6294–6306, Online. Association for Computational Linguistics.

Benjamin Hoover, Hendrik Strobelt, and Sebastian Gehrmann. 2020. exBERT: A Visual Analysis Tool to Explore Learned Representations in Transformer Models. In *Proceedings of the 58th Annual Meeting of the Association for Computational Linguistics: System Demonstrations*, pages 187–196, Online. Association for Computational Linguistics.

Vasudev Lal, Arden Ma, Estelle Aflalo, Phillip Howard, Ana Simoes, Daniel Korat, Oren Pereg, Gadi Singer, and Moshe Wasserblat. 2021. InterpreT: An interactive visualization tool for interpreting transformers. In *Proceedings of the 16th Conference of the European Chapter of the Association for Computational Linguistics: System Demonstrations*, pages 135–142, Online. Association for Computational Linguistics.

Abhinav Pathak, Y. Charlie Hu, and Ming Zhang. 2012. Where is the energy spent inside my app? fine grained energy accounting on smartphones with Eprof. In *Proceedings of the 7th ACM european conference on Computer Systems*, EuroSys '12, pages 29–42, New York, NY, USA. Association for Computing Machinery.

Abhinav Pathak, Y. Charlie Hu, Ming Zhang, Paramvir Bahl, and Yi-Min Wang. 2011. Fine-grained power modeling for smartphones using system call tracing. In *Proceedings of the sixth conference on Computer systems*, EuroSys '11, pages 153–168, New York, NY, USA. Association for Computing Machinery.

Roy Schwartz, Jesse Dodge, Noah A. Smith, and Oren Etzioni. 2019. Green AI. *CoRR*, abs/1907.10597.

H. Strobelt, S. Gehrmann, M. Behrisch, A. Perer, H. Pfister, and A. M. Rush. 2018. Seq2Seq-Vis: A Visual Debugging Tool for Sequence-to-Sequence Models. *ArXiv e-prints*.

Hendrik Strobelt, Sebastian Gehrmann, Hanspeter Pfister, and Alexander M. Rush. 2018. Lstmvis: A tool for visual analysis of hidden state dynamics in recurrent neural networks. *IEEE Transactions on Visualization and Computer Graphics*, 24(1):667–676.

Emma Strubell, Ananya Ganesh, and Andrew McCallum. 2019. Energy and policy considerations for deep learning in NLP. In *Proceedings of the 57th Annual Meeting of the Association for Computational Linguistics*, pages 3645–3650, Florence, Italy. Association for Computational Linguistics.

Jesse Vig and Yonatan Belinkov. 2019. Analyzing the structure of attention in a transformer language model. In *Proceedings of the 2019 ACL Workshop BlackboxNLP: Analyzing and Interpreting Neural Networks for NLP*, pages 63–76, Florence, Italy. Association for Computational Linguistics.

Eric Wallace, Jens Tuyls, Junlin Wang, Sanjay Subramanian, Matt Gardner, and Sameer Singh. 2019. AllenNLP Interpret: A framework for explaining predictions of NLP models. In *Empirical Methods in Natural Language Processing*.

Thomas Wolf, Lysandre Debut, Victor Sanh, Julien Chaumond, Clement Delangue, Anthony Moi, Pierric Cistac, Tim Rault, Remi Louf, Morgan Funtowicz, Joe Davison, Sam Shleifer, Patrick von Platen, Clara Ma, Yacine Jernite, Julien Plu, Canwen Xu, Teven Le Scao, Sylvain Gugger, Mariama Drame,

Quentin Lhoest, and Alexander Rush. 2020. Transformers: State-of-the-art natural language processing. In *Proceedings of the 2020 Conference on Empirical Methods in Natural Language Processing: System Demonstrations*, pages 38–45, Online. Association for Computational Linguistics.

Chanmin Yoon, Dongwon Kim, Wonwoo Jung, Chulkoo Kang, and Hojung Cha. 2012. AppScope: application energy metering framework for android smartphones using kernel activity monitoring. In *Proceedings of the 2012 USENIX conference on Annual Technical Conference*, USENIX ATC'12, page 36, USA. USENIX Association.

Xiyou Zhou, Zhiyu Chen, Xiaoyong Jin, and William Yang Wang. 2020. HULK: an energy efficiency benchmark platform for responsible natural language processing. *CoRR*, abs/2002.05829.

Open-Domain Question-Answering for COVID-19 and Other Emergent Domains

Sharon Levy§, Kevin Mo¶, Wenhan Xiong§, William Yang Wang§
§University of California, Santa Barbara
¶Princeton University
{sharonlevy,xwhan,william}@cs.ucsb.edu, kevinmo@princeton.edu

Abstract

Since late 2019, COVID-19 has quickly emerged as the newest biomedical domain, resulting in a surge of new information. As with other emergent domains, the discussion surrounding the topic has been rapidly changing, leading to the spread of misinformation. This has created the need for a public space for users to ask questions and receive credible, scientific answers. To fulfill this need, we turn to the task of open-domain question-answering, which we can use to efficiently find answers to free-text questions from a large set of documents. In this work, we present such a system for the emergent domain of COVID-19. Despite the small data size available, we are able to successfully train the system to retrieve answers from a large-scale corpus of published COVID-19 scientific papers. Furthermore, we incorporate effective re-ranking and question-answering techniques, such as document diversity and multiple answer spans. Our open-domain question-answering system can further act as a model for the quick development of similar systems that can be adapted and modified for other developing emergent domains.

1 Introduction

With the rise of social media and other online sources, it is easy to access information from sites without third-party filtering (Allcott and Gentzkow, 2017). As such, it is important in today's society to create systems that can provide credible and reliable information to users. This is especially true in the context of emergent domains which, unlike more established sectors, may contain rapidly changing information. COVID-19 follows this pattern, with over 100,000 related articles published in 2020 and new research findings still frequently reported (Else, 2020).

However, the vast interest and exposure surrounding this topic have consequently generated a rise in misinformation (Kouzy et al., 2020; Medina Serrano et al., 2020). This can lead to lower compliance with various preventative measures such as social distancing, which in turn can continue the spread of the virus (Bridgman et al., 2020; Tasnim et al., 2020). A question-answering system that allows users to ask free-text questions with answers deriving from published articles and reliable scientific sources can help mitigate this spread of misinformation and inform the public at the same time.

The task of open-domain question-answering has risen in prominence in recent years (Chen et al., 2017; Yang et al., 2019; Xiong et al., 2021a). Systems have evolved from keyword-based approaches (Salton and McGill, 1986) to the utilization of neural networks with dense passage retrieval (Xiong et al., 2021b). Furthermore, large-scale datasets have been used to train and test these systems, such as general knowledge datasets (Joshi et al., 2017; Nguyen et al., 2016) and domain-specific datasets[1] (Tsatsaronis et al., 2012). However, many of these systems are evaluated on these established datasets with abundant questions and clearly defined answers. In the case of an emergent domain system, this likely will not be available and the reduced data size can result in lower answer precision.

In this paper, we build an open-domain question-answering system in the emergent domain of COVID-19. We aim to overcome a staple issue with emergent domain question-answering systems: lack of data. While several COVID-19-related datasets have been published since the beginning of the pandemic (Roberts et al., 2020; Tang et al., 2020), they are small in scale and cannot be used for training our models. We tackle the issue of data shortage by fine-tuning pre-trained biomedical language models with a small in-domain dataset. Though these models are not trained on COVID-19 data, they allow our system to warm start with general biomedical terminology. Other COVID-

[1] https://trec.nist.gov/data.html

Proceedings of the 2021 Conference on Empirical Methods in Natural Language Processing: System Demonstrations, pages 259–266
November 7–11, 2021.

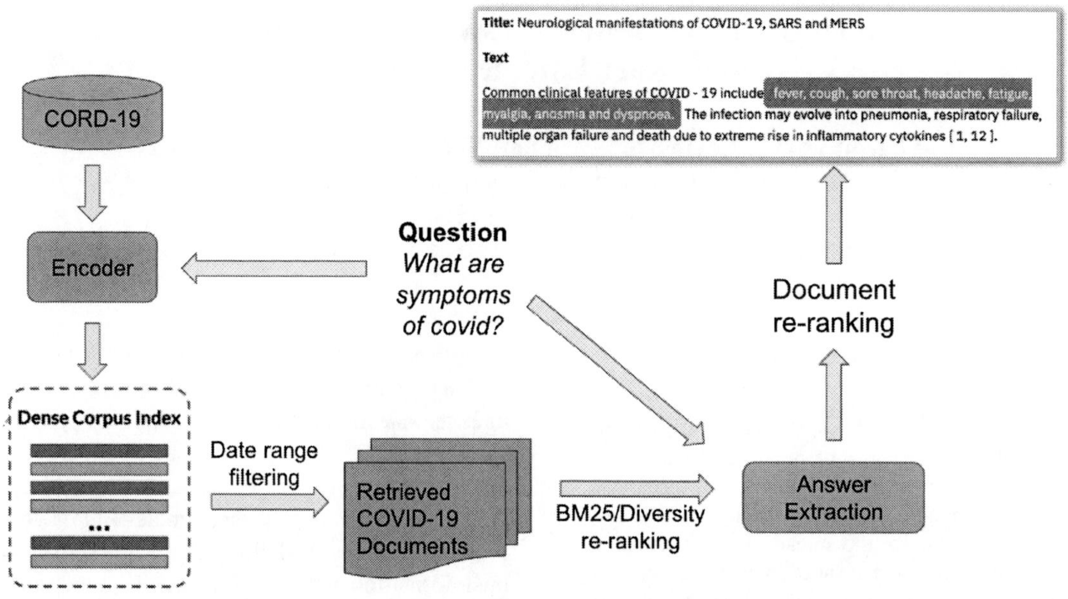

Figure 1: An overview of the COVID-19 open-domain question-answering system. The retrieval component is shown on the left and the reading comprehension/answer extraction component is shown on the right.

19-related question-answering systems have been created in recent months (Bhatia et al., 2020; Yan et al., 2021; Reddy et al., 2020). However, our system incorporates multiple state-of-the-art information retrieval techniques with dense retrieval and BM25 (Robertson and Zaragoza, 2009) and the additional functionality of diversity re-ranking and multiple answer spans.

Our system is comprised of two models: the retrieval model and reading comprehension model. Our system consists of several layers of document and answer re-ranking to increase both quality and diversity in our answers. The overall system can be seen in Figure 1. We additionally provide code[2] to create an online demo site to visualize our system and provide multiple filters for users to further refine their queries.

Our contributions are

1. We set a precedent for quickly creating an effective open-domain question-answering system for an emergent domain.
2. We integrate multiple stages of document re-ranking throughout our pipeline to provide relevant and diverse answers.
3. We create an online demo to allow the public to easily obtain answers to COVID-19-related questions from credible scientific sources.

2 Retrieval

The retrieval model consists of a dense retriever and contains further layers of re-ranking. In the following sections, we describe the data used to train our model, along with the model details and re-ranking strategies.

2.1 Data

As mentioned in Section 1, several COVID-19-related datasets have been published throughout the pandemic. However, there are a limited number of sizable datasets focused on the general areas of information retrieval and question-answering. In order to train on in-domain data, we utilize the COVID-QA (Möller et al., 2020) dataset to fine-tune our model for the document retrieval task. COVID-QA is a COVID-19 question-answering dataset and contains multiple question-answer pairs for each context document (2,019 QA pairs in total), where the documents are COVID-19-related PubMed[3] articles.

In order to transform the question-answering dataset for our retrieval task, we choose to utilize the questions and their related context articles during training. We split each context article into size

[2] https://github.com/sharonlevy/Open_Domain_COVIDQA

[3] https://pubmed.ncbi.nlm.nih.gov/

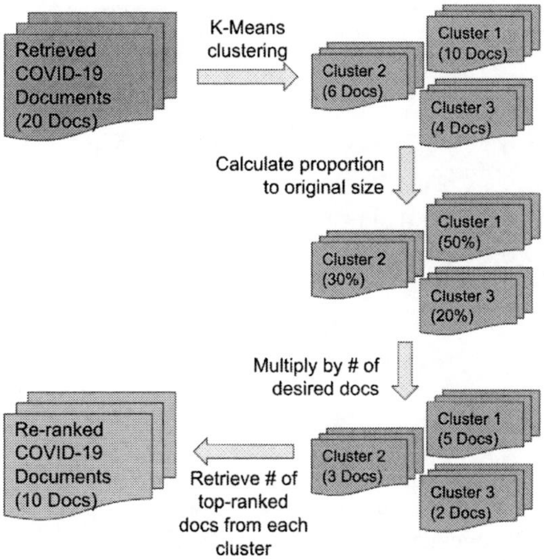

Figure 2: An outline of the diversity re-ranking process discussed in Section 2.4. After the retrieval size for each cluster is calculated, the top-ranking documents (as determined by the hybrid model) are selected from each cluster according to this size and accumulated into the final set of retrieved documents. This final set is also ordered according to the original ranking by the hybrid model.

100-200 tokens. Given the answer for each question and context article pair, we extract only the chunks of text that contain the answer with simple string matching and use this as a positive sample for each question. We further partition the dataset into training, development, and test sets. These splits are made at 70%, 10%, and 20%, respectively. Additionally, we remove any document-specific questions (e.g. How many participants are there in this study?) from the test set for a fair assessment.

We utilize the CORD-19 (Wang et al., 2020) dataset as our document corpus for the open-domain retrieval task. The corpus website is consistently updated with newly published COVID-19-related papers from several sources. Similar to the COVID-QA dataset, we pre-process each article by splitting it into multiple document entries based on paragraph text cutoffs. Paragraphs that are longer than 200 tokens are split further until they reach the desired 100-200 token size.

2.2 Dense Retriever

The dense retriever consists of a unified encoder for encoding both questions and text documents. We utilize the pre-trained PubMedBERT model (Gu et al., 2020) as the encoder and fine-tune on the COVID-QA dataset. We utilize both positive and negative samples during training. Positive samples consist of paragraphs that contain the exact answer span for the current question. Likewise, negative samples consist of paragraphs that do not contain the exact answer.

Model	FM@5	FM@20	FM@50
Dense Retrieval	0.300	0.471	0.556
BM25	0.346	0.486	0.556
Hybrid Model	**0.362**	**0.498**	**0.607**

Table 1: Comparison of dense retriever, BM25, and hybrid models for open-domain retrieval on the test set of COVID-QA. Results are evaluated with fuzzy matching (FM) scores at various retrieval count thresholds. The fuzzy matching process is described in Section 2.5.

During training, the model learns to encode questions and positive paragraphs into similar vectors such that positive paragraphs are ranked higher than negative paragraphs in similarity. After training, the CORD-19 document corpus is passed through the trained encoder and the embeddings are indexed and saved. During test time, the question is used as input to the model. The resulting embedding is used to find similarly embedded documents from the existing dense document embeddings using inner product similarity scores.

2.3 BM25 Re-ranking

While the dense retriever excels in the retrieval of documents with semantic similarity to a query, there may be specific keywords in the query that are important for document retrieval. This is especially true in biomedical domains, such as COVID-19, which heavily rely on particular terminology. As a result, our system includes a second stage during retrieval in which we re-rank the top-n retrieved documents with the BM25 algorithm. Specifically, we use the BM25+ algorithm defined in (Lv and Zhai, 2011). BM25 depends on keyword matching and ranks documents based on the appearance of query terms within the document corpus. We further simplify this by first removing stop words from the top-n documents before re-ranking. We define the combination of our dense retriever with BM25 re-ranking as our hybrid model.

2.4 Retrieval Diversity

Following the re-ranking of retrieved documents with BM25, we aim to increase the diversity of

Model	Datasets	Exact Match	F1
BERT	COVID-QA	12.27	39.07
BERT	SQUAD2.0	29.24	59.34
BioBERT	SQUAD2.0	30.54	59.39
BERT	SQUAD2.0 + COVID-QA	33.68	65.53
BioBERT	SQUAD2.0 + COVID-QA	37.59	66.67
BioBERT w/ multiple answer spans	SQUAD2.0 + COVID-QA	**39.16**	**72.03**

Table 2: Comparison of BERT and BioBERT models fine-tuned on combinations of COVID-QA and SQuAD2.0. The final row includes the BioBERT model with multiple answer spans extracted. Each model was evaluated on a held-out test set from COVID-QA.

these documents so that a user does not view nearly identical texts. To do this, we cluster the top-k re-ranked documents into three clusters with K-Means clustering (MacQueen et al., 1967) and TF-IDF features. For each cluster, we compute its size in proportion to k. This relative size is multiplied by the desired number of documents l (where $l < k$) to be retrieved. Given the resulting size for each cluster, the most relevant (top-ranked) documents are chosen in their current ranking order. This procedure is illustrated in Figure 2. Following this method allows us to present the user with more diverse and relevant documents that would otherwise be ranked lower.

2.5 Retrieval Experiments

We use the test subset of the COVID-QA dataset to evaluate our retrieval model. However, as COVID-QA is intended for the question-answering task, we cannot accurately evaluate our model by simply calculating the retrieval rank of the correct document. This is due to our specific task of open-domain question-answering, in which we are retrieving from the large CORD-19 corpus instead of the much smaller pool of documents in COVID-QA. As a result, we define a fuzzy matching metric to evaluate the quality of our retrieved documents. This is a combination of deep semantic matching and keyword matching. We have varying combinations and thresholds based on respective conditions, such as differing answer lengths. We evaluate the answer in each QA pair in our COVID-QA test set against each retrieved document.

The deep semantic matching is achieved through the Sentence-BERT model (Reimers and Gurevych, 2019) and F1 score is utilized for keyword matching. Each retrieved document is split into a list of sentences and each sentence is evaluated for three conditions:

1. Cosine similarity score that is greater than or equal to threshold a of the sentence/query pair encoded with Sentence-BERT.
2. Cosine similarity score greater than or equal to threshold b, where $b < a$, and F1 score greater than or equal to threshold c.
3. F1 score greater than or equal to threshold d, where $d > c$. This is only calculated if the token count of an answer is less than or equal to 3.

If any of the three conditions are achieved for any sentence within the retrieved document, the document is evaluated as a positive retrieval and containing the answer to the query.

We show the impact of the BM25 re-ranking stage in the hybrid model in Table 1. It can be seen that individually, BM25 and the dense retriever models obtain similar retrieval results. However, the hybrid model of dense retrieval followed by BM25 re-ranking allows the system to obtain more relevant documents for the user.

3 Reading Comprehension

The second stage of our system consists of a reading comprehension model that can answer the original query based on the retrieved documents. We describe the training data, model design, and document re-ranking associated with our model in the following sections.

3.1 Data

We utilize the COVID-QA dataset to train our model for the reading comprehension task. Unlike the retrieval model, the reading comprehension model utilizes both questions and answers, along with their respective context articles for training. As mentioned in Section 2.1, we partition the

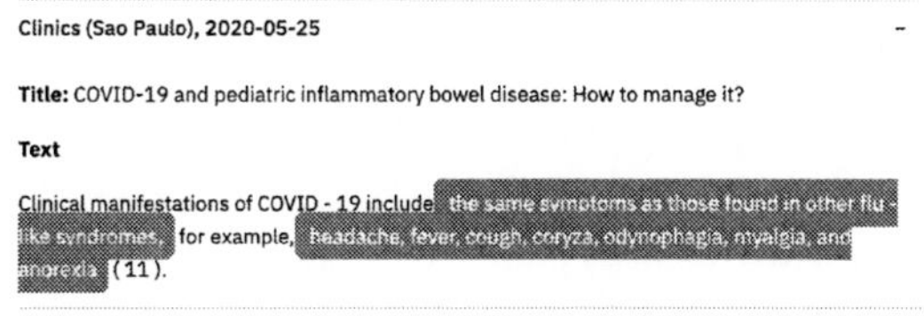

Figure 3: An example of returning multiple answers to a user for the query: "What are symptoms of covid?"

dataset into training, development, and test sets and utilize this to evaluate the model.

3.2 Methodology

The reading comprehension model performs extractive question-answering. Given a question and paragraph pair, the model learns to find start and end tokens to represent the answer span (or spans) in the paragraph text. This is done by choosing the highest-ranked start and end tokens produced by the model where the start token is earlier than the end token in the text sequence. We utilize a variant of BioBERT (Lee et al., 2019) that is fine-tuned on the SQuAD2.0 (Rajpurkar et al., 2018) dataset[4]. We find that fine-tuning this model on COVID-QA allows the model to train on both in-domain (COVID-QA) and out-domain (SQuAD2.0) data and increases results for this task when evaluated on the test set of COVID-QA.

3.3 Multiple Answers

Some retrieved documents may contain answer spans that are not contiguous. In order to accommodate this, we rank the top-m start and end tokens according to confidence scores and select the pairs of tokens that do not overlap with higher-ranked answer spans. This allows each document to highlight up to m answers rather than just one answer and increases evaluation results. We show the effect of adding multiple answer spans in Table 2 in comparison to various model and fine-tuning dataset combinations. An example of multiple answer spans for a given query can be seen in Figure 3.

3.4 Document Re-ranking

When the reading comprehension model is utilized in the overall system, it is used to answer the same question within a set of documents retrieved from the hybrid retriever model. While the documents are already re-ranked by the retriever, we further re-rank these documents again following the answer extraction portion of the system. When answering a question for each document, the reading comprehension model provides a confidence score alongside each start and end token. We utilize these confidence scores and reorder the current set of retrieved documents based on the combination of the start and end scores for the top answer in each document. As a result, if a question is not easily answered in a highly ranked retrieved document, the respective document will subsequently be moved to a lower rank.

[4]https://huggingface.co/ktrapeznikov/biobert_v1.1_pubmed_squad_v2

Figure 4: The side panel in the demo website which allows users to filter the number of documents retrieved and the date range for the publication date of these documents.

4 Open-domain Question Answering

In the previous sections, we describe the retrieval and reading comprehension models. We combine the two models for the end-to-end open-domain question-answering task. The full system overview can be seen in Figure 1. Once the retriever is trained, the CORD-19 corpus is encoded and stored. When a user queries the system with a question, this question is encoded using the unified retriever model and the resulting vector is used to retrieve similar documents from the dense corpus. Once the top documents are retrieved, they are re-ranked with the BM25 algorithm and further clustered/re-ranked to introduce diversity to the results. The top remaining documents are used as input to the reading comprehension model along with the initial question. This model computes the answer span (and potentially spans) for each document. The documents are then re-ranked given the reading comprehension model's confidence score in the top answer span and the answers for each document are highlighted.

5 Demo

We build an online demo that allows users to easily utilize our system. This website is powered through Streamlit[5].

5.1 Query Filters

The input documents for the demo are from the CORD-19 corpus. These documents are pre-encoded by the trained hybrid retrieval model. We include several features for users to filter in order to narrow down their search. A user is able to decide how many documents they would like to be retrieved (in the range from 1 to 5) from the drop-down menu. We include start and end date selection boxes to allow users to further filter the retrieved documents by publication date within the top retrieved documents. These components are shown in Figure 4. If there are no documents available for the date range, we show this as a message and instead retrieve relevant documents from any date range for the user.

5.2 Demo Procedure

The user can enter a free-text question in English into the search bar as seen in Figure 5. This question is encoded by the trained retrieval model and used to find matching documents. The reading comprehension model uses the retrieved documents and query to extract the answer (or answers) and re-rank the documents based on the answer confidence scores. The chosen number of retrieved documents is displayed to the user. Each document is displayed alongside its journal or source name and publication date from its respective CORD-19 article. The user can expand each document heading to view the article title and text snippet. The

[5] https://streamlit.io/

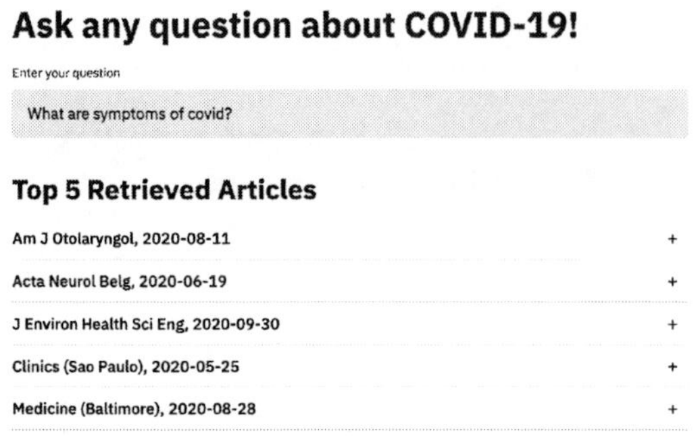

Figure 5: The list of documents returned to a user for a given query. Each document is labeled by its publishing journal and publication date.

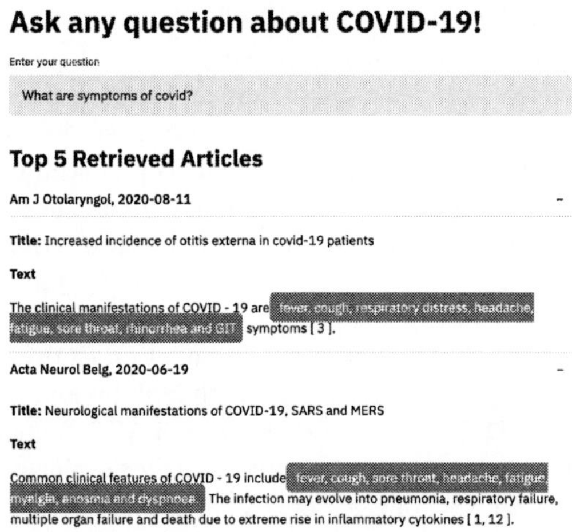

Figure 6: Retrieved documents for a given query can be expanded to show their respective article titles and text snippets. Extracted answers for each document are highlighted in red.

extracted answers are highlighted in red as seen in Figure 6.

6 Conclusion

In this paper, we present an open-domain question answering system for the emergent domain of COVID-19. Our system is comprised of retrieval and reading comprehension components, with several layers of refinement to increase the quality and diversity of responses. The system allows users to quickly search COVID-19-related questions and obtain a set of answers from biomedical publications. Additionally, we provide a demo website that allows users to easily interact with our system and apply additional filters to further refine their search. We hope that amidst the time of a global pandemic, our system can serve as both a resource in finding credible answers to users' COVID-19 questions and a model for future systems in similar emergent domains.

References

Hunt Allcott and Matthew Gentzkow. 2017. Social media and fake news in the 2016 election. *Journal of economic perspectives*, 31(2):211–36.

Parminder Bhatia, Kristjan Arumae, Nima Pourdamghani, Suyog Deshpande, Ben Snively, Mona Mona, Colby Wise, George Price, Shyam Ramaswamy, and T. Kass-Hout. 2020. Aws cord19-search: A scientific literature search engine for covid-19. *ArXiv*, abs/2007.09186.

Aengus Bridgman, Eric Merkley, Peter John Loewen, Taylor Owen, Derek Ruths, Lisa Teichmann, and Oleg Zhilin. 2020. The causes and consequences of covid-19 misperceptions: Understanding the role of news and social media. *Harvard Kennedy School Misinformation Review*, 1(3).

Danqi Chen, Adam Fisch, Jason Weston, and Antoine Bordes. 2017. Reading Wikipedia to answer open-domain questions. In *Proceedings of the 55th Annual Meeting of the Association for Computational Linguistics (Volume 1: Long Papers)*, pages 1870–1879, Vancouver, Canada. Association for Computational Linguistics.

Holly Else. 2020. How a torrent of covid science changed research publishing-in seven charts. *Nature*, pages 553–553.

Yu Gu, Robert Tinn, Hao Cheng, Michael Lucas, Naoto Usuyama, Xiaodong Liu, Tristan Naumann, Jianfeng Gao, and Hoifung Poon. 2020. Domain-specific language model pretraining for biomedical natural language processing. *arXiv preprint arXiv:2007.15779*.

Mandar Joshi, Eunsol Choi, Daniel S Weld, and Luke Zettlemoyer. 2017. Triviaqa: A large scale distantly supervised challenge dataset for reading comprehension. In *Proceedings of the 55th Annual Meeting of the Association for Computational Linguistics (Volume 1: Long Papers)*, pages 1601–1611.

Ramez Kouzy, Joseph Abi Jaoude, Afif Kraitem, Molly B El Alam, Basil Karam, Elio Adib, Jabra Zarka, Cindy Traboulsi, Elie W Akl, and Khalil Baddour. 2020. Coronavirus goes viral: quantifying the covid-19 misinformation epidemic on twitter. *Cureus*, 12(3).

Jinhyuk Lee, Wonjin Yoon, Sungdong Kim, Donghyeon Kim, Sunkyu Kim, Chan Ho So, and Jaewoo Kang. 2019. BioBERT: a pre-trained biomedical language representation model for biomedical text mining. *Bioinformatics*, 36(4):1234–1240.

Yuanhua Lv and ChengXiang Zhai. 2011. Lower-bounding term frequency normalization. In *Proceedings of the 20th ACM International Conference on Information and Knowledge Management*, CIKM '11, page 7–16, New York, NY, USA. Association for Computing Machinery.

James MacQueen et al. 1967. Some methods for classification and analysis of multivariate observations. In *Proceedings of the fifth Berkeley symposium on mathematical statistics and probability*, volume 1, pages 281–297. Oakland, CA, USA.

Juan Carlos Medina Serrano, Orestis Papakyriakopoulos, and Simon Hegelich. 2020. NLP-based feature extraction for the detection of COVID-19 misinformation videos on YouTube. In *Proceedings of the 1st Workshop on NLP for COVID-19 at ACL 2020*, Online. Association for Computational Linguistics.

Timo Möller, Anthony Reina, Raghavan Jayakumar, and Malte Pietsch. 2020. COVID-QA: A question answering dataset for COVID-19. In *Proceedings of the 1st Workshop on NLP for COVID-19 at ACL 2020*, Online. Association for Computational Linguistics.

Tri Nguyen, Mir Rosenberg, Xia Song, Jianfeng Gao, Saurabh Tiwary, Rangan Majumder, and Li Deng. 2016. Ms marco: A human generated machine reading comprehension dataset. In *CoCo@ NIPS*.

Pranav Rajpurkar, Robin Jia, and Percy Liang. 2018. Know what you don't know: Unanswerable questions for SQuAD. In *Proceedings of the 56th Annual Meeting of the Association for Computational Linguistics (Volume 2: Short Papers)*, pages 784–789, Melbourne, Australia. Association for Computational Linguistics.

Revanth Gangi Reddy, Bhavani Iyer, Md Arafat Sultan, Rong Zhang, Avi Sil, Vittorio Castelli, Radu Florian, and Salim Roukos. 2020. End-to-end qa on covid-19: Domain adaptation with synthetic training. *arXiv preprint arXiv:2012.01414*.

Nils Reimers and Iryna Gurevych. 2019. Sentence-BERT: Sentence embeddings using Siamese BERT-networks. In *Proceedings of the 2019 Conference on Empirical Methods in Natural Language Processing and the 9th International Joint Conference on Natural Language Processing (EMNLP-IJCNLP)*, pages 3982–3992, Hong Kong, China. Association for Computational Linguistics.

Kirk Roberts, Tasmeer Alam, Steven Bedrick, Dina Demner-Fushman, Kyle Lo, Ian Soboroff, Ellen Voorhees, Lucy Lu Wang, and William R Hersh. 2020. TREC-COVID: rationale and structure of an information retrieval shared task for COVID-19. *Journal of the American Medical Informatics Association*, 27(9):1431–1436.

Stephen Robertson and Hugo Zaragoza. 2009. *The probabilistic relevance framework: BM25 and beyond*. Now Publishers Inc.

Gerard Salton and Michael J McGill. 1986. Introduction to modern information retrieval.

Raphael Tang, Rodrigo Nogueira, Edwin Zhang, Nikhil Gupta, Phuong Cam, Kyunghyun Cho, and Jimmy Lin. 2020. Rapidly bootstrapping a question answering dataset for covid-19. *arXiv preprint arXiv:2004.11339*.

Samia Tasnim, Md Mahbub Hossain, and Hoimonty Mazumder. 2020. Impact of rumors and misinformation on covid-19 in social media. *Journal of preventive medicine and public health*, 53(3):171–174.

George Tsatsaronis, Michael Schroeder, Georgios Paliouras, Yannis Almirantis, Ion Androutsopoulos, Eric Gaussier, Patrick Gallinari, Thierry Artieres, Michael R Alvers, Matthias Zschunke, et al. 2012. Bioasq: A challenge on large-scale biomedical semantic indexing and question answering. In *2012 AAAI Fall Symposium Series*.

Lucy Lu Wang, Kyle Lo, Yoganand Chandrasekhar, Russell Reas, Jiangjiang Yang, Doug Burdick, Darrin Eide, Kathryn Funk, Yannis Katsis, Rodney Michael Kinney, Yunyao Li, Ziyang Liu, William Merrill, Paul Mooney, Dewey A. Murdick, Devvret Rishi, Jerry Sheehan, Zhihong Shen, Brandon Stilson, Alex D. Wade, Kuansan Wang, Nancy Xin Ru Wang, Christopher Wilhelm, Boya Xie, Douglas M. Raymond, Daniel S. Weld, Oren Etzioni, and Sebastian Kohlmeier. 2020. CORD-19: The COVID-19 open research dataset. In *Proceedings of the 1st Workshop on NLP for COVID-19 at ACL 2020*, Online. Association for Computational Linguistics.

Wenhan Xiong, Xiang Lorraine Li, Srinivasan Iyer, Jingfei Du, Patrick Lewis, William Yang Wang, Yashar Mehdad, Wen-tau Yih, Sebastian Riedel, Douwe Kiela, and Barlas Oğuz. 2021a. Answering complex open-domain questions with multi-hop dense retrieval. *International Conference on Learning Representations*.

Wenhan Xiong, Hong Wang, and William Yang Wang. 2021b. Progressively pretrained dense corpus index for open-domain question answering. In *Proceedings of the 16th Conference of the European Chapter of the Association for Computational Linguistics: Main Volume*, pages 2803–2815, Online. Association for Computational Linguistics.

Rui Yan, Weiheng Liao, Jianwei Cui, Hailei Zhang, Yichuan Hu, and Dongyan Zhao. 2021. *Multilingual COVID-QA: Learning towards Global Information Sharing via Web Question Answering in Multiple Languages*, page 2590–2600. Association for Computing Machinery, New York, NY, USA.

Wei Yang, Yuqing Xie, Aileen Lin, Xingyu Li, Luchen Tan, Kun Xiong, Ming Li, and Jimmy Lin. 2019. End-to-end open-domain question answering with bertserini. In *Proceedings of the 2019 Conference of the North American Chapter of the Association for Computational Linguistics (Demonstrations)*, pages 72–77.

Project Debater APIs: Decomposing the AI Grand Challenge

Roy Bar-Haim, Yoav Kantor, Elad Venezian*, **Yoav Katz, Noam Slonim**
IBM Research
{roybar,yoavka,eladv,katz,noams}@il.ibm.com

Abstract

Project Debater was revealed in 2019 as the first AI system that can debate human experts on complex topics. Engaging in a live debate requires a diverse set of skills, and Project Debater has been developed accordingly as a collection of components, each designed to perform a specific subtask. *Project Debater APIs* provide access to many of these capabilities, as well as to more recently developed ones. This diverse set of web services, publicly available for academic use, includes core NLP services, argument mining and analysis capabilities, and higher-level services for content summarization. We describe these APIs and their performance, and demonstrate how they can be used for building practical solutions. In particular, we will focus on *Key Point Analysis*, a novel technology that identifies the main points and their prevalence in a collection of texts such as survey responses and user reviews.

1 Introduction

Argumentation and debating are fundamental capabilities of human intelligence. They are essential for a wide range of everyday activities that involve reasoning, decision making or persuasion. Over the last few years, there has been growing interest in *Computational Argumentation*, defined as "the application of computational methods for analyzing and synthesizing argumentation and human debate" (Gurevych et al., 2016). A recent milestone in this field is *Project Debater*, which was revealed in 2019 as the first AI system that can debate human experts on complex topics[1]. Project Debater is the third in the series of IBM Research AI's grand challenges, following Deep Blue and Watson. It has been developed for over six years by a large team of researchers and engineers, and its live demonstration in February 2019 received massive media attention. In our recent paper, "An autonomous debating system", published in the Nature magazine (Slonim et al., 2021), we describe Project Debater's architecture and evaluate its performance.

To debate humans, an AI must be equipped with a diverse set of skills. It has to be able to pinpoint relevant arguments for a given debate topic in a massive corpus, detect the stance of arguments and assess their quality. It also has to identify principled, recurring arguments that are relevant for the specific topic, organize the different types of arguments into a compelling narrative, recognize the arguments made by the human opponent, and make a rebuttal. Accordingly, Project Debater has been developed as a collection of components, each designed to perform a specific subtask. Over the years, we published more than 50 papers describing these components and released many related datasets for academic use.

Successfully engaging in a debate requires high level of accuracy from each component. For example, failing to detect the argument's stance may result in arguing in favor of your opponent – a dire situation in a debate. A crucial part of developing highly accurate models was the collection of uniquely large scale, high-quality labeled datasets for training each component. The evidence detection classifier, for instance, was trained using 200K labeled examples, and was able to achieve a remarkable precision of 95% for top 40 candidates (Ein-Dor et al., 2020).

Another major challenge was scalability. One example is applying Wikification (Mihalcea and Csomai, 2007) to our 10 billion sentences corpus, a task that was infeasible for any of the available tools. We therefore developed a novel, fast Wikification algorithm, which can be applied to massive corpora while achieving competitive accuracy (Shnayderman et al., 2019).

Project Debater APIs give access to selected capabilities originally developed for the live debating

*First three authors equally contributed to this work.

[1] `https://www.research.ibm.com/artificial-intelligence/project-debater/`

Proceedings of the 2021 Conference on Empirical Methods in Natural Language Processing: System Demonstrations, pages 267–274
November 7–11, 2021. ©2021 Association for Computational Linguistics

system, as well as related technologies we have developed more recently. We provide free access for academic use to these APIs, as well as trial and licensing options for developers. The APIs can be divided into three main groups:

- *Core NLU services*, including Wikification, semantic relatedness between Wikipedia concepts, short text clustering, and common theme extraction for texts. These general-purpose tools may be useful in many different use cases, and may serve as building blocks in a variety of NLP applications.
- *Argument Mining and Analysis*, including the detection of sentences containing claims and evidence, claim boundaries detection within a sentence, argument quality assessment and stance classification (pro/con). These services are of particular interest to the computational argumentation research community.
- *Content summarization*, including two high-level services: *Narrative Generation* constructs a well-structured speech that supports or contests a given topic, according to the specified polarity. *Key Point Analysis* summarizes a collection of comments as a small set of automatically extracted, human-readable key points, each assigned with a numeric measure of its prominence in the input. These tools may serve data scientists analyzing opinionated texts such as user reviews, survey responses, social media, customer feedback, etc.

Several demonstrations of argument mining capabilities have been previously published (Stab et al., 2018; Wachsmuth et al., 2017; Chernodub et al., 2019), some of which also provide access to their capabilities via APIs. However, Project Debater APIs offer a much broader set of services, trained on unique large-scale, high quality datasets, which have been developed over many years of research.

The next sections describe each of the APIs and their performance assessment, and how they can be accessed and used via the Debater Early Access Program. We then describe several examples of using and combining these APIs in practical applications.

2 Services Overview

In this section we provide a short description for each service, and point to its related publications, and other relevant resources. All the training datasets for these services have been developed as part of Project Debater.

2.1 Core NLU Services

This group of services includes several fundamental natural language processing tasks.

Text wikification. The Wikification service identifies mentions of Wikipedia concepts in the given text. We created our own wikifier, described in (Shnayderman et al., 2019), since existing tools were far too slow to be applied to the Lexis-Nexis corpus we used for argument mining, which contains about 10 billion sentences. We developed a simple rule-based method, which relies on matching the mentions to the Wikipedia title, as well as on Wikipedia redirects. This approach enables very fast Wikification, about 20 times faster than the commonly-used TagMe Wikifier (Ferragina and Scaiella, 2010), while achieving competitive accuracy.

Concept relatedness. This service measures the semantic relatedness between a pair of Wikipedia concepts. We trained a BERT regressor (Devlin et al., 2019) on the WORD dataset (Ein Dor et al., 2018), which includes 13K pairs of Wikipedia concepts manually annotated to determine their level of relatedness. The input to the regressor is the first sentence in the Wikipedia article of each concept.

Text clustering. Our Text clustering service is based the Sequential Information Bottleneck (sIB) algorithm (Slonim et al., 2002). This unsupervised algorithm has been shown to achieve strong results on standard benchmarks. However, sIB has not been as popular as other clustering algorithms such as K-Means, since its run time was significantly higher. Our implementation of sIB is highly optimized, leveraging the sparseness of bag of words representation. With this optimization, the run time of sIB is very fast, and even comparable with K-Means. The python code of this implementation is also available[2].

Common theme extraction. This service gets a clustering partition of sentences and returns Wikipedia concepts representing the main themes in each cluster. These themes aim to represent the subjects that are discussed by the sentences of this cluster, and distinguish it from other clusters. This

[2] https://github.com/IBM/sib

service is based on the hypergeometric test, applied to the concepts mentioned in the sentences of each cluster. The service identifies concepts that are enriched in each cluster compared to the other clusters, taking into account the semantic relatedness of different concepts.

2.2 Argument Mining and Analysis

This group includes classifiers and regressors that aim to identify arguments in input texts, determine their stance, and assess their quality.

Claim Detection. This service identifies whether a sentence contains a claim with respect to a given topic. This task was introduced by Levy et al. (2014). They define a Claim as *"a general, concise statement that directly supports or contests the given Topic"*. The claim detection model is a BERT-based classifier, trained on 90K positive and negative labeled examples from the Lexis-Nexis corpus. The model is similar to the one described in (Ein-Dor et al., 2020).

Claim Boundaries. Given an input sentence that is assumed to contain a claim, this service returns the boundaries of the claim within the sentence (Levy et al., 2014). The Claim Boundaries service may be used to refine the results of the Claim Detection service, which provides sentence-level classification. The service is based on a BERT model, which was fine-tuned on 52K crowd-annotated examples mined from the Lexis-Nexis corpus.

Evidence Detection. Similar to the Claim Detection service, this service gets a sentence and a topic and identifies whether the sentence is an Evidence supporting or contesting the topic. In our context, an Evidence is an argument that contains research results or an expert opinion. This is a BERT based service which was fine-tuned using 200K annotated examples from Lexis-Nexis corpus. This model is based on the work of Ein-Dor et al. (2020).

Argument Quality. This service, based on the work of Gretz et al. (2020), produces a numeric quality score for a given argument. The service is based on a BERT regressor, which was trained on 27K arguments, collected for a variety of topics and annotated with quality scores. Both the arguments and the quality scores were collected via crowdsourcing. The real-valued argument quality scores were derived from a large number of binary labels collected from crowd annotators. Specifically, for each example, the annotators were asked whether the sentence, as is, may fit in a speech supporting or contesting the given topic. High quality scores typically indicate arguments that are grammatically valid, use proper language, make a clear and concise argument, have a clear stance towards the topic, etc.

Pro-Con. This service (Bar-Haim et al., 2017; Toledo-Ronen et al., 2020), gets an argument and a topic and predicts whether the argument supports or contests the topic. This service is a BERT-based classifier, which was trained on 400K stance-labeled examples. It includes arguments extracted from the Lexis-Nexis corpus, as well as arguments collected via crowsourcing. The set of training arguments was automatically expanded by replacing the original debate concept with consistent and contrastive expansions, based on the work of Bar-Haim et al. (2019).

2.3 Content Summarization

This group contains two high-level services that create different types of summaries.

Key Point Analysis. This service summarizes a collection of comments on a given topic as a small set of *key points* (Bar-Haim et al., 2020a,b). The salience of each key point is given by the number of its matching sentences in the given comments. The input for the service is a collection of textual comments, which are split into sentences. The output is a short list of key points and their salience, along with a list of matching sentences per key point. A key point matches a sentence if it captures the gist of the sentence, or is directly supported by a point made in the sentence. The service selects key points from a subset of concise, high-quality sentences (according to the quality service described above), aiming to achieve high coverage of the given comments. Matching sentences to key points is performed by a RoBERTa-large model (Liu et al., 2019), trained on a dataset of 24K (argument, key point) pairs, labeled as matched/unmatched. It is also possible to specify the key points as part of the input, in which case the service matches the sentences to the given key points.

Narrative Generation This service receives a topic, and a list of arguments that support or contest the topic, and constructs a well-structured speech summarizing the relevant input arguments that are compatible with the requested stance (pro or con).

It works as follows: first, we select high-quality arguments with the right stance. Then, the service performs Key Point Analysis over these arguments. Finally, The service selects the most prominent key points, and for each key point, it selects the best arguments to create a corresponding paragraph. Alternatively, paragraphs may be generated based on the output of the text clustering service. Selected arguments are slightly rephrased as required and connecting text is added to improve the fluency of the resulting speech.

2.4 Wikipedia Sentence-Level Index

In addition to the above groups of services, we also provide a sentence-level index of Wikipedia. The index underlying our search service is a data structure that is populated with sentences, enriched with some metadata, such as the Wikipedia concepts mentioned in each sentence (as identified by the Wikification service), named entities, and multiple lexicons. The index facilitates fast retrieval of sentences according to queries that may refer to the text and/or the metadata, with word distance restrictions. For example, retrieve all the sentences that satisfy the template "`<PERSON> ... that ... <CONCEPT> ... <SENTIMENT-WORD>`".

3 Assessment

Table 1 includes assessment results for various services. For each service, we specify the benchmark that was used for testing, the evaluation measure(s) and the results. If the results in the table are quoted from one of our papers, this is indicated by ✓. Unless otherwise mentioned, the results are from the same paper that is cited for the dataset. In cases where the results for the service were not available (this happens, for example, if the current service implementation is different from the one described in the paper), we ran the service on the benchmark and reported the results.

The text clustering assessment is the only one that is not performed over a Project Debater dataset, but over a standard benchmark - the widely-used 20 newsgroups dataset, which contains about 18,000 news posts on 20 topics (Lang, 1995). We clustered these posts into 20 clusters, and compared the results with the original partition. We report Adjusted Mutual Information (AMI) and Adjusted Rand Index (ARI) measures. Our results (AMI=0.595 and ARI=0.466) are considerably better than those obtained with K-Means (AMI=0.228 and ARI=0.071).

Overall, the results confirm the high quality of our services.

4 The Debater Early Access Program

The 12 Project Debater APIs are offered via the *IBM Debater Early Access Program.* The goal of this program is to make core capabilities from Project Debater available as building blocks for a variety of text understanding applications.

The Early Access Program is freely available for academic use on the IBM Cloud, and can also be licensed for commercial use. As part of the program, both Python and Java SDKs are available. All the services are REST-based, which enables their usage by any desired programming language. In order to access these APIs, an API key is required. We supply such API keys freely for non-commercial use.

The early access website, shown in Figure 2, contains various resources[3]. The main tab includes a detailed description of all the services with Python, Java, and CURL code examples. The description also includes links to related publications. In addition, it contains a demo UI, which allows interacting with the APIs online.

The *Examples* tab contains step-by-step tutorials, which demonstrate how the APIs can be applied in complex scenarios, to solve real-world problems. The *Data Sets* tab contains a link to all Project Debater datasets. Finally, there is a tab for the *Speech By Crowd* application. Speech By Crowd is a web application that enables the user to collect and analyze opinions on a desired controversial topic. The application is free for non-commercial use. The application has been demonstrated in several events, as we discuss in the next section.

5 Use Cases

5.1 Analysing Surveys and Reviews

Surveys are commonly used by decision makers to collect opinions from a large audience. However, extracting the key issues that came up in hundreds or thousands of survey responses is a very challenging task.

Existing automated approaches are often limited to identifying key phrases or concepts and the

[3] `https://early-access-program.debater.res.ibm.com/academic_use`

Service	Benchmark	Measure	Result	From Paper?
Evidence Detection	VLD (Ein-Dor et al., 2020)	Precision@40	0.95	✓
Argument Quality	IBM-Rank30k-WA (Gretz et al., 2020)	Pearson / Spearman correlation	0.52 / 0.48	✓
Concepts relatedness	WORD (Ein Dor et al., 2018)	Pearson / Spearman correlations	0.85 / 0.57	
Text wikification	Trans (Shnayderman et al., 2019)	Precision / Recall / F1	0.76 / 0.62 / 0.68	✓
Pro-Con	IBM-Rank30k (Gretz et al., 2020)	Accuracy	0.92	
Text clustering	20 Newsgroups (Lang, 1995)	AMI / ARI	0.595 / 0.466	
Key Point Analysis	ArgKP (Bar-Haim et al., 2020a); Results are from (Bar-Haim et al., 2020b)	F1	0.77	✓

Table 1: Project Debater APIs assessment

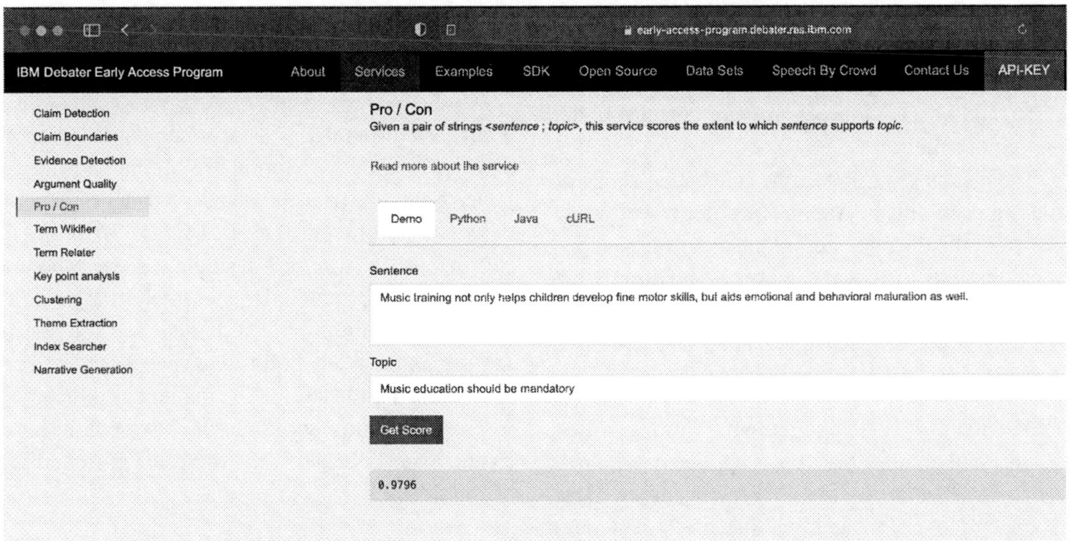

Figure 1: The IBM Debater Early Access Program web page. The list of services is shown on the left. For the selected service - the pro-con service, there is an expandable short description and a demo that allows trying the service online.

overall sentiment toward them, but do not provide detailed, actionable insights. Using Debater APIs, and in particular Key Point Analysis (KPA), we are able to analyze and derive insights from answers to open-ended survey questions.

Austin Municipal Survey Tutorial. To demonstrate this capability, we have prepared a hands-on tutorial, publicly available on GitHub[4]. In this tutorial, we analyze free-text responses for a community survey conducted in the city of Austin in the years 2016 and 2017. In this survey, the citizens of Austin were asked "If there was ONE thing you could share with the Mayor regarding the City of Austin (any comment, suggestion, etc.), what would it be?".

In the tutorial, we first run KPA on 1000 randomly selected sentences from 2016. We then use the Argument Quality (AQ) service and run KPA on 1000 top-quality sentences from 2016. We show that selecting higher-quality sentences for our sample results in a better summary, and higher coverage of the resulting key points. Figure 2 is a screenshot from the Jupyter Notebook of the tutorial. It shows the overall coverage of the extracted key points, and lists the top key points found, and for each key point - the number of its matching sentences and its top-scoring matches.

The tutorial also shows how to compare the 2016

[4]`https://github.com/IBM/debater-eap-tutorial`

```
In [11]: kpa_result_top_aq_1000_2016, kpa_top_aq_1000_2016_job_id = run_kpa(sentences_2016_top_1000_aq,
                                                    {'n_top_kps': 20, 'mapping_threshold': 0.95})
         print_results(kpa_result_top_aq_1000_2016, n_sentences_per_kp=2, title='Top aq 2016')

         Top aq 2016 coverage: 49.89
         Top aq 2016 key points:
         93 - Traffic congestion needs major improvement
                 - Austin need improved transportation infrastructure to alleviate current traffic and
                   accommodate rapid population growth.
                 - Fast population growth is the cities biggest problem in areas such as congestion and
                   expensiveness.
         91 - We need affordable housing.
                 - Affordable housing is crucial, & keeping seniors in their homes is part of that challenge!
                 - We need better housing solutions for low income and homeless individuals.
         53 - Integrated transportation is critical.
                 - a public transit train system is a necessity
                 - Steiner Ranch area needs more access to public transportation (bus, train, etc>) and
                   taxi/ridesharing  to/from downtown and airport
```

Figure 2: A screenshot from the Jupyter Notebook of the tutorial, showing the results for running KPA on the 2016 Austin survey data (1000 top-quality sentences). The coverage, top three key points and top 2 matching sentences per key point are displayed.

responses to those from 2017. This can be done by mapping 1000 top-quality sentences from 2017 to the same set of key points that was extracted for 2016, and observe the year-to-year changes in the key point salience.

The results show that traffic congestion is one of the top problems in Austin. In order to better understand the citizens' complaints and suggestions regarding this topic, we can use two additional services, Wikification and Concept Relatedness, to identify sentences that are related to the *Traffic* concept and run KPA only on this subset.

IBM Employee Engagement Survey. Key Point Analysis has also been applied to analyze the 2020 IBM employee engagement survey. Over 300K employees wrote more than 550K sentences in total. These sentences were automatically classified into positive and negative, and we ran KPA on each set separately to extract positive and negative key points. The HR team reported that these analyses enable them to extract actionable and valuable insights with significantly less effort.

Business Reviews. Similar to surveys, KPA can also be used for effectively summarizing user reviews. In our recent work (Bar-Haim et al., 2021) we demonstrate its application to the Yelp dataset of business reviews.

5.2 Online Debates

In the following public demonstrations, we combined several services to summarize online debates, where hundreds or thousands of participants submit online their pro and con arguments for a controversial topic, using the Speech by Crowd platform. We used the *pro-con* service to split arguments by stance, the *argument quality* service to filter out low quality arguments, the *KPA* service to summarize the data into key points and the *narrative generation* to create a coherent speech.

That's Debateable. "That's Debatable" is a TV show presented by Bloomberg Media and Intelligence Squared. In each episode, a panel of experts debates a controversial topic, such as *"It's time to redistribute the wealth"*. Using the above pipeline, we were able to summarize thousands of arguments submitted online by the audience, and the resulting pro and con key points and speeches were presented during the show. The audience contributed interesting points, some of which were not raised by the expert debaters, and therefore enriched the discussion.[5]

Grammy Music Debates. During the Grammys 2021 event, four music debate topics (e.g., virtual concerts vs. live shows) were published on the event's website. Hundreds of arguments contributed by music fans were collected for each topic, and the same method was applied to analyze and summarize them[6].

6 Conclusion

We introduced *Project Debater APIs*, which provide access to many of the core capabilities of the Project Debater grand challenge, as well as more recent technologies such as Key Point Analysis. The evaluation we presented confirms the high quality of these services. We discussed different use cases for these APIs, in particular for analyzing and summarizing various types of opinionated texts. We

[5] https://www.research.ibm.com/interactive/project-debater/thats-debatable/

[6] https://www.grammy.com/watson

believe that this diverse set of services may be used as building blocks in many text understanding applications, and may be relevant for a broad audience in the NLP community.

Acknowledgements

The authors thank Alon Halfon, Naftali Liberman, Amir Menczel, Guy Moshkowich, Dafna Sheinwald, Ilya Shnayderman and Artem Spector for their contribution to the development of the IBM Debater Early Access Program.

References

Roy Bar-Haim, Indrajit Bhattacharya, Francesco Dinuzzo, Amrita Saha, and Noam Slonim. 2017. Stance classification of context-dependent claims. In *Proceedings of the 15th Conference of the European Chapter of the Association for Computational Linguistics: Volume 1, Long Papers*, pages 251–261. Association for Computational Linguistics.

Roy Bar-Haim, Lilach Eden, Roni Friedman, Yoav Kantor, Dan Lahav, and Noam Slonim. 2020a. From arguments to key points: Towards automatic argument summarization. In *Proceedings of the 58th Annual Meeting of the Association for Computational Linguistics*, pages 4029–4039, Online. Association for Computational Linguistics.

Roy Bar-Haim, Lilach Eden, Yoav Kantor, Roni Friedman, and Noam Slonim. 2021. Every bite is an experience: Key Point Analysis of business reviews. In *Proceedings of the 59th Annual Meeting of the Association for Computational Linguistics and the 11th International Joint Conference on Natural Language Processing (Volume 1: Long Papers)*, pages 3376–3386, Online. Association for Computational Linguistics.

Roy Bar-Haim, Yoav Kantor, Lilach Eden, Roni Friedman, Dan Lahav, and Noam Slonim. 2020b. Quantitative argument summarization and beyond: Cross-domain key point analysis. In *Proceedings of the 2020 Conference on Empirical Methods in Natural Language Processing (EMNLP)*, pages 39–49, Online. Association for Computational Linguistics.

Roy Bar-Haim, Dalia Krieger, Orith Toledo-Ronen, Lilach Edelstein, Yonatan Bilu, Alon Halfon, Yoav Katz, Amir Menczel, Ranit Aharonov, and Noam Slonim. 2019. From surrogacy to adoption; from bitcoin to cryptocurrency: Debate topic expansion. In *Proceedings of the 57th Annual Meeting of the Association for Computational Linguistics*, pages 977–990, Florence, Italy. Association for Computational Linguistics.

Artem Chernodub, Oleksiy Oliynyk, Philipp Heidenreich, Alexander Bondarenko, Matthias Hagen, Chris Biemann, and Alexander Panchenko. 2019. TARGER: Neural argument mining at your fingertips. In *Proceedings of the 57th Annual Meeting of the Association for Computational Linguistics: System Demonstrations*, pages 195–200, Florence, Italy. Association for Computational Linguistics.

Jacob Devlin, Ming-Wei Chang, Kenton Lee, and Kristina Toutanova. 2019. BERT: pre-training of deep bidirectional transformers for language understanding. In *Proceedings of the 2019 Conference of the North American Chapter of the Association for Computational Linguistics: Human Language Technologies, NAACL-HLT 2019, Minneapolis, MN, USA, June 2-7, 2019, Volume 1 (Long and Short Papers)*, pages 4171–4186. Association for Computational Linguistics.

Liat Ein Dor, Alon Halfon, Yoav Kantor, Ran Levy, Yosi Mass, Ruty Rinott, Eyal Shnarch, and Noam Slonim. 2018. Semantic relatedness of wikipedia concepts - benchmark data and a working solution. In *Proceedings of the Eleventh International Conference on Language Resources and Evaluation (LREC-2018)*. European Language Resource Association.

Liat Ein-Dor, Eyal Shnarch, Lena Dankin, Alon Halfon, Benjamin Sznajder, Ariel Gera, Carlos Alzate, Martin Gleize, Leshem Choshen, Yufang Hou, Yonatan Bilu, Ranit Aharonov, and Noam Slonim. 2020. Corpus wide argument mining - A working solution. In *Proceedings of the Thirty-Fourth AAAI Conference on Artificial Intelligence*, pages 7683–7691. AAAI Press.

Paolo Ferragina and Ugo Scaiella. 2010. Tagme: On-the-fly annotation of short text fragments (by wikipedia entities). In *Proceedings of the 19th ACM International Conference on Information and Knowledge Management*, CIKM '10, pages 1625–1628, New York, NY, USA. ACM.

Shai Gretz, Roni Friedman, Edo Cohen-Karlik, Assaf Toledo, Dan Lahav, Ranit Aharonov, and Noam Slonim. 2020. A large-scale dataset for argument quality ranking: Construction and analysis. *Proceedings of the AAAI Conference on Artificial Intelligence*, 34(05):7805–7813.

Iryna Gurevych, Eduard H. Hovy, Noam Slonim, and Benno Stein. 2016. Debating Technologies (Dagstuhl Seminar 15512). *Dagstuhl Reports*, 5(12):18–46.

Ken Lang. 1995. Newsweeder: Learning to filter netnews. In Armand Prieditis and Stuart Russell, editors, *Machine Learning Proceedings 1995*, pages 331–339. Morgan Kaufmann, San Francisco (CA).

Ran Levy, Yonatan Bilu, Daniel Hershcovich, Ehud Aharoni, and Noam Slonim. 2014. Context dependent claim detection. In *Proceedings of COLING 2014, the 25th International Conference on Computational Linguistics: Technical Papers*, pages 1489–1500, Dublin, Ireland. Dublin City University and Association for Computational Linguistics.

Yinhan Liu, Myle Ott, Naman Goyal, Jingfei Du, Mandar Joshi, Danqi Chen, Omer Levy, Mike Lewis, Luke Zettlemoyer, and Veselin Stoyanov. 2019. Roberta: A robustly optimized BERT pretraining approach. *CoRR*, abs/1907.11692.

Rada Mihalcea and Andras Csomai. 2007. Wikify! linking documents to encyclopedic knowledge. In *Proceedings of the Sixteenth ACM Conference on Conference on Information and Knowledge Management*, CIKM '07, page 233–242, New York, NY, USA. Association for Computing Machinery.

Ilya Shnayderman, Liat Ein-Dor, Yosi Mass, Alon Halfon, Benjamin Sznajder, Artem Spector, Yoav Katz, Dafna Sheinwald, Ranit Aharonov, and Noam Slonim. 2019. Fast end-to-end wikification. *arXiv preprint arXiv:1908.06785*.

Noam Slonim, Yonatan Bilu, Carlos Alzate, Roy Bar-Haim, Ben Bogin, Francesca Bonin, Leshem Choshen, Edo Cohen-Karlik, Lena Dankin, Lilach Edelstein, Liat Ein-Dor, Roni Friedman-Melamed, Assaf Gavron, Ariel Gera, Martin Gleize, Shai Gretz, Dan Gutfreund, Alon Halfon, Daniel Hershcovich, Ron Hoory, Yufang Hou, Shay Hummel, Michal Jacovi, Charles Jochim, Yoav Kantor, Yoav Katz, David Konopnicki, Zvi Kons, Lili Kotlerman, Dalia Krieger, Dan Lahav, Tamar Lavee, Ran Levy, Naftali Liberman, Yosi Mass, Amir Menczel, Shachar Mirkin, Guy Moshkowich, Shila Ofek-Koifman, Matan Orbach, Ella Rabinovich, Ruty Rinott, Slava Shechtman, Dafna Sheinwald, Eyal Shnarch, Ilya Shnayderman, Aya Soffer, Artem Spector, Benjamin Sznajder, Assaf Toledo, Orith Toledo-Ronen, Elad Venezian, and Ranit Aharonov. 2021. An autonomous debating system. *Nature*, 591(7850):379–384.

Noam Slonim, Nir Friedman, and Naftali Tishby. 2002. Unsupervised document classification using sequential information maximization. In *Proceedings of the 25th Annual International ACM SIGIR Conference on Research and Development in Information Retrieval*, SIGIR '02, page 129–136, New York, NY, USA. Association for Computing Machinery.

Christian Stab, Johannes Daxenberger, Chris Stahlhut, Tristan Miller, Benjamin Schiller, Christopher Tauchmann, Steffen Eger, and Iryna Gurevych. 2018. ArgumenText: Searching for arguments in heterogeneous sources. In *Proceedings of the 2018 Conference of the North American Chapter of the Association for Computational Linguistics: Demonstrations*, pages 21–25, New Orleans, Louisiana. Association for Computational Linguistics.

Orith Toledo-Ronen, Matan Orbach, Yonatan Bilu, Artem Spector, and Noam Slonim. 2020. Multilingual argument mining: Datasets and analysis. In *Findings of the Association for Computational Linguistics: EMNLP 2020*, pages 303–317, Online. Association for Computational Linguistics.

Henning Wachsmuth, Martin Potthast, Khalid Al-Khatib, Yamen Ajjour, Jana Puschmann, Jiani Qu, Jonas Dorsch, Viorel Morari, Janek Bevendorff, and Benno Stein. 2017. Building an argument search engine for the web. In *Proceedings of the 4th Workshop on Argument Mining*, pages 49–59, Copenhagen, Denmark. Association for Computational Linguistics.

CroAno : A Crowd Annotation Platform for Improving Label Consistency of Chinese NER Dataset

Baoli Zhang[*1], **Zhucong Li**[*1,2], **Zhen Gan**[3], **Yubo Chen**[1,2], **Jing Wan**[3], **Kang Liu**[1,2], **Jun Zhao**[1,2], **Shengping Liu**[4], **Yafei Shi**[4]

[1] National Laboratory of Pattern Recognition, Institute of Automation, Chinese Academy of Sciences, Beijing, China

[2] School of Artificial Intelligence, University of Chinese Academy of Sciences,Beijing, China

[3] Beijing University of Chemical Technology, Beijing, China

[4] Unisound Ai Technology Co,.Ltd, Beijing, China

{baoli.zhang, zhucong.li, yubo.chen, kliu, jzhao}@nlpr.ia.ac.cn, {ganzhen,wanj}@mail.buct.edu.cn, {liushengping, shiyafei}@unisound.com

Abstract

In this paper, we introduce `CroAno`, a web-based crowd annotation platform for the Chinese named entity recognition (NER). Besides some basic features for crowd annotation like fast tagging and data management, `CroAno` provides a systematic solution for improving label consistency of Chinese NER dataset. **1) Disagreement Adjudicator**: `CroAno` uses a multi-dimensional highlight mode to visualize instance-level inconsistent entities and makes the revision process user-friendly. **2) Inconsistency Detector**: `CroAno` employs a detector to locate corpus-level label inconsistency and provides users an interface to correct inconsistent entities in batches. **3) Prediction Error Analyzer**: We deconstruct the entity prediction error of the model to six fine-grained entity error types. Users can employ this error system to detect corpus-level inconsistency from a model perspective. To validate the effectiveness of our platform, we use `CroAno` to revise two public datasets. In the two revised datasets, we get an improvement of +1.96% and +2.57% F1 respectively in model performance.

1 Introduction

Named entity recognition (NER), the task of detecting and classifying named entities in texts, has made significant progress relying on data-driven methods (Lample et al., 2016). Existing supervised approaches to NER require massive high-quality annotated data. Since hiring annotation experts is costly and time-consuming, crowd annotation and non-experts annotators are more generally used, the drawback is a higher proportion of inconsistency in the annotation.

[*] co-first authors, they contributed equally to this work.

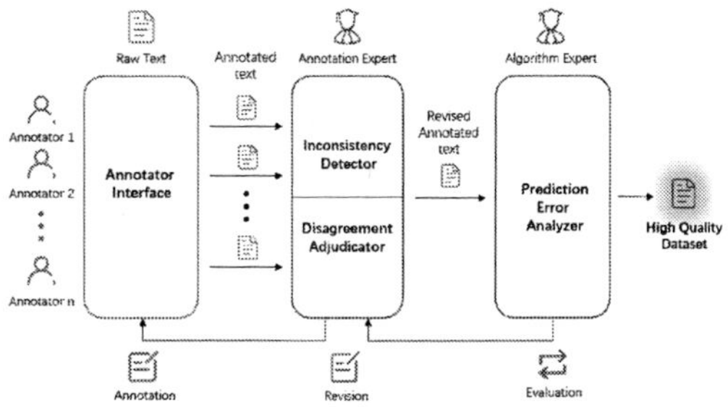

Figure 1: The whole architecture of CroAno.

However, existing NER annotation tools for crowd annotation (Ogren Philip, 2006; Chen and Styler, 2013; Manning et al., 2014; Samih et al., 2016) mainly aim to improve annotating efficiency and rarely consider the dataset's consistency. Label inconsistency is ubiquitous in NER datasets. For example, *OntoNotes 4.0* (Weischedel et al., 2011), which is a classical Chinese NER benchmark, the proportion of label inconsistency is up to 10% according to our estimation. In this dataset, the mention of "中国人民" (Chinese People) appears 36 times, of which the whole mention is marked as entity 23 times, and "中国" (China) is separately labeled as entity 13 times. Such inconsistency may confuse the NER model and cause disastrous results.

In this paper, we propose a web-based **crowd annotation platform** named `CroAno`. As shown in Figure 1, `CroAno` contains three modules to improve label consistency of the Chinese NER dataset.

Disagreement Adjudicator: Crowd annotation tools usually distribute the same instance to different annotators, which would cause disagreement. We call this phenomenon instance-level label incon-

Proceedings of the 2021 Conference on Empirical Methods in Natural Language Processing: System Demonstrations, pages 275–282
November 7–11, 2021.

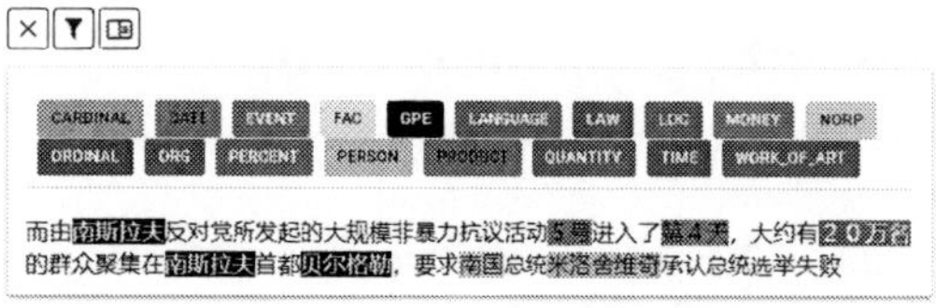

Figure 2: The screenshot of Annotator Interface.

Figure 3: The screenshot of Disagreement Adjudicator.

sistency, because this inconsistency occurs in the same instance. Instance-level label inconsistency is easy to locate but difficult to display and correct. YEDDA (Yang et al., 2018) employs a comparison report to show these inconsistencies to annotation experts. But it failed to display detailed information of inconsistent entities, and annotation experts cannot directly correct these entities through the comparison report. To solve these display and correction issues, CroAno uses a multi-dimensional display mode to show inconsistent instances and employs the "click to correct" method to facilitate correction.

Inconsistency Detector: This module is designed to solve corpus-level label inconsistency, especially corpus-level pre&suffix inconsistency. Corpus-level pre&suffix inconsistency refers to the inconsistency of whether a descriptive string is included in the entity string. In *OntoNotes4.0*, the string "超过"(over) is included as a prefix of *Money* entity in some instances while in other instances the string is excluded as an external prefix. Locating these inconsistent entities is hard because a global perspective is required. CroAno uses a detector to locate potential inconsistency and provides an interface to support users correct these inconsistent entities in batches.

Prediction Error Analyzer: As mentioned above, disagreement adjudicator and inconsistency detector are responsible to solve label inconsistency from a data perspective, while prediction error analyzer can detect label inconsistency from a model perspective. To analyze inconsistency, we deconstruct entity prediction error of the model to a novel error system, which gives entity prediction error more abundant information with six fine-grained error types. CroAno provides a search API, which supports users to employ the error system to locate specific entities and their context. Moreover, CroAno employs an elaborately designed interface to differentiate the model prediction and the annotation.

In summary, the contributions of this paper are as follows:

- We propose a crowd annotation platform, which can promote label consistency of the Chinese NER dataset. The site can be accessed by http://116.62.20.198:3000, and instruction video is provided at https://www.youtube.com/watch?v=wt2ma9FU540. To the best of our knowledge, CroAno is the first crowd annotation platform that aims at promoting label consistency of NER dataset.

- We introduce three novel modules to promote label consistency of the NER dataset. Disagreement Adjudicator provides a multi-dimensional highlight mode to visualize and an interface function to revise instance-level inconsistency. Inconsistency Detector employs locating and revising strategies to correct corpus-level label inconsistency. Prediction Error Analyzer can help algorithm experts detect corpus-level inconsistency from a model perspective.

- To validate the effectiveness of our platform, we use CroAno to revise two public datasets. In the two revised datasets, we get an improvement of +1.96% and +2.57% in F1 respectively. It is worth mentioning that the promotion of data can be inherited by any NER model.

2 User Roles in CroAno

CroAno defines three roles: the crowd annotator, the annotation expert and the algorithm expert. The crowd annotator completes basic annotation tasks. The annotation expert is responsible for guideline formulation, data management, task distribution, and label consistency optimization. The algorithm expert is responsible for providing analyses and

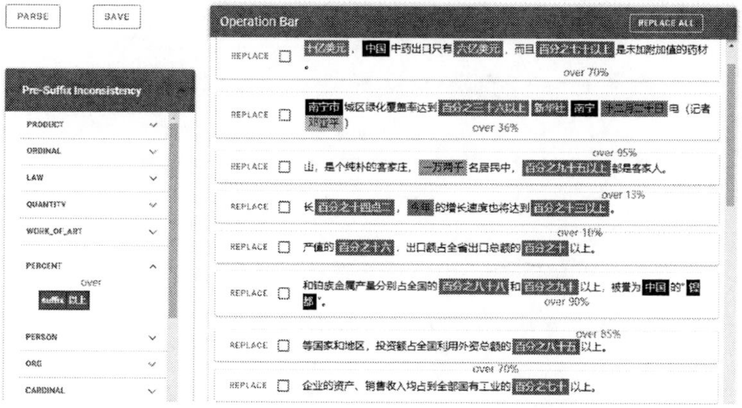

Figure 4: The screenshot of Inconsistency Detector,We provide English translations for inconsistent entities.

suggestions of the annotation result from the perspective of the model.

The crowd annotator uses Annotator Interface for annotation. After preliminary annotation, results are sent to the annotation expert.

The annotation expert uses Disagreement Adjudicator and Inconsistency Detector for revision. Specifically, the annotation expert uses Disagreement Adjudicator to modify instance-level inconsistency from multi-annotators, and then uses Inconsistency Detector to detect and modify corpus-level inconsistency. After that, the promoted dataset is sent to the algorithm expert.

The algorithm expert uses Prediction Error Analyzer for evaluation. The algorithm expert can use Prediction Error Analyzer to detect the difference between model prediction and annotators annotation to get promotion direction of annotation or just revise the annotation.

The following sections will introduce the main modules of `CroAno`.

3 Annotator Interface

This section describes the interface, which is designed for easily annotating. As shown in Figure 2, the interface uses different colors to distinguish the entity categories. Annotators can locate an entity and its span with the left mouse button. And They can choose an entity category by short-cut key or click the corresponding button in the entity label bar.

Except for basic annotating function, they can mark the current instance as "annotated" by clicking the first top-left button, filter "annotated instances" by clicking the second top-left button, and get the guideline by clicking the last top-left button.

4 Disagreement Adjudicator

This section describes Disagreement Adjudicator, which is designed for solving instance-level label inconsistency. Instance-level inconsistency means disagreement annotations between different annotators within the same instance. Apart from annotation errors, different understandings of the guideline can also lead to disagreement. This type of inconsistency needs to be revised by the annotation expert. Difficulties in implementing this operation are to visualize disagreement entities and revise.

`CroAno` uses a novel multi-dimensional highlight mode to visualize disagreement entities. As shown in Figure 3, underlines of text represent annotators annotation, the background represents agreement entities or approved entities. Figure 3 shows an instance annotated by two annotators. The "美国"(America) entity has two black underlines and black background, which means the two annotators consistently annotated this span as GPE.

The revision stage is easy to execute. The annotation expert can click any disagreement entity to get a revision dialog. The dialog will display all corresponding disagreement entities, and the annotation expert can select a proper one.

5 Inconsistency Detector

This section describes Inconsistency Detector, which is designed for reducing corpus-level pre&suffix inconsistency.

5.1 Overview

In NER dataset, some entity types have descriptive words. It is difficult to reach an agreement on a descriptive string that should be included in the entity

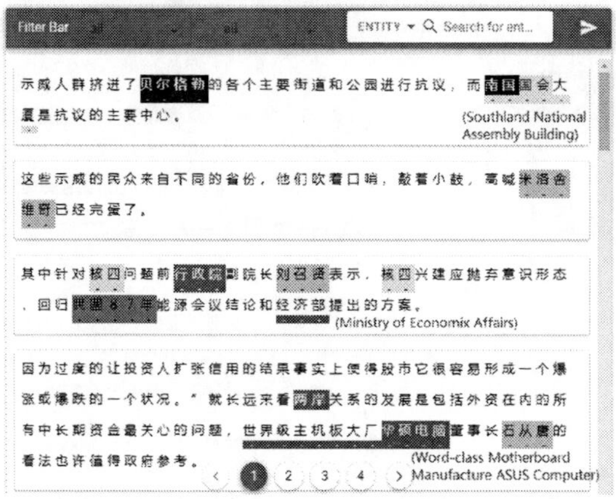

Figure 5: The screenshot of Prediction Error Analyzer. We provide English translations for mistakenly predicted entities in this figure.

string. For example, the *MONEY* entity type has a descriptive word "more than". In some instances the word "more than" is contained inside the entity string as a prefix, while in other instances the word is excluded as an external prefix. Appendix A displays inconsistent pre&suffixes of two NER dataset and some example instances.

Our proposed framework contains a detector algorithm to detect potential inconsistent pre&suffixes and an interface to help users to revise these inconsistencies.

5.2 Pre&Suffix Inconsistency Detector

We denote the dataset as D, the entit set extracted from the dataset as S. We use *entity* denotes a specific entity object from entity set. An entity object has at least four attributes, including *string*, *sentence*, *start*, *end*. *String* denotes the entity string, *sentence* represents the instance text string that contains this entity. Given a specific entity, the expression *sentence[start: end] == string* is always true.

We use p denotes entity prefix, p_i denotes prefix with length i.

$$p_i = \begin{cases} string[:i], & \text{if } len(string) \leq i \\ '', & \text{otherwise} \end{cases} \tag{1}$$

We use e denotes external descriptive word before entity string, e_i denotes external prefix with length i.

$$\mathrm{e}_i = \begin{cases} sentence[start - i : start], & \text{if } start - i \geq 0 \\ '', & \text{otherwise} \end{cases} \tag{2}$$

Take the inconsistent prefix detection algorithm as an example as shown in Algorithm 1. The basic idea of inconsistency detector is that if a descriptive string appears both as a prefix or an external prefix, this string is considered an inconsistent prefix.

Algorithm 1 Inconsistent Prefix Detection Algorithm

Input: Entity set S, Max prefix length: l
Output: Inconsistent prefixes
$I \leftarrow \emptyset$
E$\leftarrow \emptyset$
for entity in S **do**
  for i = 1 to l **do**
    Obtain p_i. (Eq.1)
    Obtain e_i. (Eq.2)
    $I = I \cup p_i$
    $E = E \cup e_i$
  end for
end for
return $I \cap E$

We first construct two empty string sets called prefix_set and external_prefix_set. We then traverse the entity set to add entity prefix and external_prefix respectively to the two string set.

After the traverse, the intersection of two string sets are strings that appearing in both entity prefix or entity external prefix. These strings are potential inconsistent prefixes.

6 Prediction Error Analyzer

This section describes Prediction Error Analyzer, which is designed for detecting label consistency from the model perspective.

6.1 Overview

From an intuitive perspective, The basic idea of this module is that the NER model trained with trainset can learn regulations of this annotation. When an entity gets a wrong prediction compared to annotation result in testset, it has a high proportion that the model has learnt an inconsistent regulation from trainset.

To support the need to detect inconsistent entities with the NER model, CroAno provides a will-designed error system, a search API based on the error system, and a visualization interface for users to compare the differences between model prediction and annotations from the annotator.

6.2 Error System

Existing entity error only measures if an entity is correctly predicted or not, which misses much useful information. `CroAno` deconstruct entity prediction error to a well-designed error system.

The error system consists of six different error types. **Extra Error** and **Missing Error** means that the NER model predicts an extra entity or misses an entity compared with annotators annotation. **Long Error** and **Short Error** means that the NER model predicts an entity that contains or is within an annotated entity. **Tag Error** and **Intersect Error** means different tags and intersect boundary between model prediction and annotation.

6.3 Search and Visualize Instances

The search API is used to filter entities and their context by the error system and other features. For example, if the algorithm expert finds that the *PERSON* entity type has a high proportion to be mistakenly missing in model prediction, they can use the search API to extract these instances.

The visualization interface is designed to make users directly perceive the difference between model prediction and annotations from the annotator. As shown in Figure 5, annotations from the annotator are marked by the background, while the highlighted underline exhibits annotations predicted by the model.

Except for detecting corpus-level inconsistency of the NER dataset, Prediction Error Analyzer can be used to detect annotation errors or catch the model's weakness to decide the improvement direction of the model itself.

Dataset	Type	Train	Dev	Test
2*OntoNotes	Sentence	15.7K	4.3K	4.3K
	Char	491.9K	200.5K	208.1K
2*CCKS	Sentence	1K	-	0.4K
	Char	418.4K	-	132.7K

Table 1: Statistics of dataset.

7 Technical Details

This section introduces some necessary technical details. `CroAno` has a web-based front-end server built on `Vue` in JavaScript and a back-end server built on `Django` in Python. CroAno has an environment decoupled from the operating system, which means it is deployment-free. `CroAno` implement the interface design based on an open-source `Django` framework named doccano [1].

8 Experiments

In this section, we conduct experiments on a standard benchmark and a medical benchmark to verify the effectiveness of Inconsistency Detector.

8.1 Experimental Setting

Dataset. Two Chinese NER datasets are used in this paper, which include *OntoNotes 4.0* (Weischedel et al., 2011) and *CCKS 2019* (Han et al., 2020). *OntoNotes 4.0* is collected from the news domain, while *CCKS 2019* is collected from the medical domain. For *OntoNotes 4.0*, we use the same data split as (Zhang and Yang, 2018). Since the *CCKS 2019* dataset does not have a development set, we randomly select 20% samples from the training set as the development. Statistics of dataset is shown in Table 1.

Dataset Correction. We invite two volunteers to use Inconsistency Detector to correct the two datasets. The correction is for the entire dataset including training set, development set, and test set. It is worth mentioning that to count the learning and mastering time of the function, modify both datasets took less than half an hour.

Model Settings. We appliy two most widely recognized NER baseline models, denoted as BiLSTM-CRF (Ma and Hovy, 2016) and BERT-Tagger (Devlin et al., 2018), respectively. We uniformly use AdamW (Loshchilov and Hutter, 2018) as an optimizer. For (Ma and Hovy, 2016), we use the same character embeddings as (Zhang and Yang, 2018) and set the initial learning rate to 0.01.

[1] `http://doccano.herokuapp.com/`

For (Devlin et al., 2018), we set the initial learning rate to 0.00005.

8.2 Results

The model performance before/after correcting is shown in Table 2 and the statistics of inconsistent entities correction is shown in Table 3.

2*Model	OntoNotes 4.0		CCKS 2019	
	Before	After	Before	After
BiLSTM-CRF	67.9	**69.38**	80.79	**82.88**
BERT-Tagger	74.56	**76.52**	83.31	**85.88**

Table 2: Model performance before/after correcting.

Dataset	Total Entity	Correction	Correction Ratio
OntoNotes	49262	730	1.48%
CCKS	18294	700	3.83%

Table 3: Statistics of inconsistent entities correcting.

OntoNotes 4.0. We correct 730 entities in total, accounting for 1.4% of the total number of entities. After correction, BiLSTM-CRF reachs a 69.38% F1-score, an increase of 1.48%. The improvement of BERT-Tagger is even more significant, an increase of 1.96%, reaching 76.52% F1-score.

CCKS 2019. We correct 700 entities in total, accounting for 4.3% of the total number of entities. After correction, BiLSTM-CRF reached a 82.88% F1-score, an increase of 2.09%. Consistent with Ontonotes, the improvement of BERT-Tagger is more significant, an increase of 2.57%, reaching 85.88% F1-score.

The experiments prove that the annotator expert can use `CroAno` to promote dataset, and this promotion can be inherited by widely recognized BiLSTM-CRF model and BERT-Tagger model.

9 Related Works

Most of the existing crowd annotation tools for NER are dedicated to basic functions such as interface friendliness, the convenience of operation, and annotation prompts, which are all designed for annotators. Next, this section will compare the features of `CroAno` with the following related works:

`BRAT` (Stenetorp et al., 2012) is a web-based general annotation tool that can handle various annotation tasks, including span annotations and the relationship between spans. As an early annotation tool, `BRAT` has great influence. However, compared with crowd annotation platforms such as `CroAno`, it cannot manage crowdsource or reduce the label inconsistency.

`GATE` (Bontcheva et al., 2013) is a web-based collaborative text annotation framework. It enables users to perform complex corpus annotation projects, which involve a distributed team of annotators. Same as `brat`, `GATE` also lacks the ability to reduce the label inconsistency.

`SLATE` (Kummerfeld, 2019) is a lightweight annotation tool with a terminal-based workflow. It is designed for annotation experts, focusing on fast labeling. `SLATE` has a certain visual disagreement adjudication capability. However, due to the limited visualization ability of the terminal-based approach, it can only simply prompt disagreement samples. Besides, the disagreement adjudication cannot be applied at the entity-level.

`AlpacaTag` (Lin et al., 2019) applies the model ensemble mechanism to merge the results of different annotators, thereby realizing disagreement adjudication without relying on annotating experts. It is worth noting that the results of such a black box model are not interpretable for humans. Especially for fields such as clinical diagnosis and drug discovery, black box models often mean potential risks and poor persuasiveness.

`YEDDA` (Yang et al., 2018) provides a systematic solution for text span annotations such as collaborative user annotations, administrator evaluation. `YEDDA` can locate the position of disagreement and display it by generating a Latex file, but it cannot directly adjudicate disagreement like `CroAno`.

To the best of our knowledge, `CroAno` is the first crowd annotation platform providing the tool that can locate and fix inconsistent labels. `CroAno` can also make the full use of the ability of the algorithm expert and the annotation expert.

10 Conclusion and Future Directions

In this paper, we propose a web-based crowd annotation platform, which provides a systematic solution for improving the label consistency of the Chinese NER dataset. To solve instance-level inconsistency, we propose Disagreement Adjudicator. To solve corpus-level inconsistency, we propose Inconsistency Detector and Prediction Error Analyzer from statistic and model perspectives respectively.

The future directions are to extend `CroAno` to a cross-task and multi-language version and implement more prosperous model analysis functions.

Acknowledge

This work is supported by the National Key Research and Development Program of China (No. 2020AAA0106400). This work is supported by the National Natural Science Foundation of China (No.61976211,No.61806201). This work is supported by Beijing Academy of Artificial Intelligence (BAAI2019QN0301) , the Key Research Program of the Chinese Academy of Sciences (Grant NO. ZDBS-SSW-JSC006) and the Youth Innovation Promotion Association CAS.

References

Kalina Bontcheva, Hamish Cunningham, Ian Roberts, Angus Roberts, Valentin Tablan, Niraj Aswani, and Genevieve Gorrell. 2013. Gate teamware: a web-based, collaborative text annotation framework. *Language Resources and Evaluation*, 47(4):1007–1029.

Wei-Te Chen and Will Styler. 2013. Anafora: A web-based general purpose annotation tool. In *Proceedings of the 2013 NAACL HLT Demonstration Session*, pages 14–19.

Jacob Devlin, Ming-Wei Chang, Kenton Lee, and Kristina Toutanova. 2018. Bert: Pre-training of deep bidirectional transformers for language understanding. *arXiv preprint arXiv:1810.04805*.

Xianpei Han, Zhichun Wang, Jiangtao Zhang, Qinghua Wen, Wenqi Li, Buzhou Tang, Qi Wang, Zhifan Feng, Yang Zhang, Yajuan Lu, et al. 2020. Overview of the ccks 2019 knowledge graph evaluation track: Entity, relation, event and qa. *arXiv preprint arXiv:2003.03875*.

Jonathan K Kummerfeld. 2019. Slate: A super-lightweight annotation tool for experts. In *Proceedings of the 57th Annual Meeting of the Association for Computational Linguistics: System Demonstrations*, pages 7–12.

Guillaume Lample, Miguel Ballesteros, Sandeep Subramanian, Kazuya Kawakami, and Chris Dyer. 2016. Neural architectures for named entity recognition. In *Proceedings of the 2016 Conference of the North American Chapter of the Association for Computational Linguistics: Human Language Technologies*, pages 260–270.

Bill Yuchen Lin, Dong-Ho Lee, Frank F Xu, Ouyu Lan, and Xiang Ren. 2019. Alpacatag: An active learning-based crowd annotation framework for sequence tagging. In *Proceedings of the 57th Annual Meeting of the Association for Computational Linguistics: System Demonstrations*, pages 58–63.

Ilya Loshchilov and Frank Hutter. 2018. Fixing weight decay regularization in adam.

Xuezhe Ma and Eduard Hovy. 2016. End-to-end sequence labeling via bi-directional lstm-cnns-crf. In *Proceedings of the 54th Annual Meeting of the Association for Computational Linguistics (Volume 1: Long Papers)*, pages 1064–1074.

Christopher D Manning, Mihai Surdeanu, John Bauer, Jenny Rose Finkel, Steven Bethard, and David McClosky. 2014. The stanford corenlp natural language processing toolkit. In *Proceedings of 52nd annual meeting of the association for computational linguistics: system demonstrations*, pages 55–60.

V Knowtator Ogren Philip. 2006. A protégé plug-in for annotated corpus construction. In *Human language technology conference of the North American chapter of the association of computational linguistics (HLT-NAACL)*.

Younes Samih, Wolfgang Maier, and Laura Kallmeyer. 2016. Sawt: Sequence annotation web tool. In *Proceedings of the Second Workshop on Computational Approaches to Code Switching*, pages 65–70.

Pontus Stenetorp, Sampo Pyysalo, Goran Topić, Tomoko Ohta, Sophia Ananiadou, and Jun'ichi Tsujii. 2012. Brat: a web-based tool for nlp-assisted text annotation. In *Proceedings of the Demonstrations at the 13th Conference of the European Chapter of the Association for Computational Linguistics*, pages 102–107.

Ralph Weischedel, Sameer Pradhan, Lance Ramshaw, Martha Palmer, Nianwen Xue, Mitchell Marcus, Ann Taylor, Craig Greenberg, Eduard Hovy, Robert Belvin, et al. 2011. Ontonotes release 4.0. *LDC2011T03, Philadelphia, Penn.: Linguistic Data Consortium*.

Jie Yang, Yue Zhang, Linwei Li, and Xingxuan Li. 2018. Yedda: A lightweight collaborative text span annotation tool. In *Proceedings of ACL 2018, System Demonstrations*, pages 31–36.

Yue Zhang and Jie Yang. 2018. Chinese ner using lattice lstm. In *Proceedings of the 56th Annual Meeting of the Association for Computational Linguistics (Volume 1: Long Papers)*, pages 1554–1564.

A Inconsistent Pre&Suffix Example

The cause of the inconsistent prefixes and suffixes is divergent perceptions of different annotators on the annotation guideline. For example, some entity categories have specific descriptive strings. Because deleting these additive strings does not change the entity semantics, this leads to opposite annotation strategies.

Some of the inconsistent prefixes or suffixes detected by this algorithm in the Ontonotes dataset and the CCKS medical dataset are shown in Table4 and Table5. Some instances that contain inconsistent pre&suffix in the Ontonotes dataset are shown in Table6.

Entity Type	Inconsistent Prefixes	Inconsistent Suffixes
WORK_OF_ART	《	》、节目(show)
CARDINAL	上(more than)、超过(more than)、近(nearly)	辆、颗、位、个、家、种、项、名、所 (all of these suffixes are Chinese measure word)
DATA	不到(less than)、过去(over the past)、过去的(over the past)	之内(within)、内(within)
LOC		地区(area)
NORP		民族(nation)、人民(people)、人士(person)、民众(the public)
GPE	驻	市区(city)、特区(special administrative region)、政府(government)

Table 4: Some inconsistent prefixes and suffixes in Ontonotes4.0.

Entity Type	Inconsistent Prefixes	Inconsistent Suffixes
Anatomic Site	近端(proximal)、左(left)、双侧(bilateral)、左侧(left side)	上端(upper)、旁(side)、部
Diseases and Diagnoses	轻度(mild)	不能明确(not clear)、可能(possible)、术后(post operation)、化疗(chemotherapy)
Image Examination		增强(enhancement)、检查(examination)、平扫(plain CT scan)
Operation	行(perform)	治疗(therapy)
Medicine		片(tablet)
Laboratory Inspection	血(blood)	百分比(percentage)、数(count)、浓度(concentration)、压积

Table 5: Some inconsistent prefixes and suffixes in CCKS medical dataset.

Entity Type	Prefix or Suffix	Prefix or Suffix in Entity Content	Prefix or Suffix out of Entity Content
WORK OF ART	Prefix: 《	他们想到了哈尔·荷尔布鲁克和电影 [《惊天大阴谋》] WORK_OF_ART They thought of Hal Holbrook and the movie "Plot."	张曼玉、梁朝伟主演的《[花样年华]WORK_OF_ART》 In the Mood for Love staring Maggie Cheung and Tony Leung Chiu-wai
CARDINAL	Suffix: 位	已有[172位]CARDINAL个人和14个机构获奖 172 individuals and 14 institutions have been awarded	参与评证的律师总计约[700]CARDINAL位，评件总案数为7200余件 A total of about 700 lawyers participated in theevaluation, and the total number of cases was more than 7,200
LOC	Suffix: 地区	要求日本自卫队分担[亚太地区]LOC的安全责任 Asking Japan's Self-Defense Forces to share security responsibilities in the Asia-Pacific region	英文[亚洲周刊]发布的[亚太]LOC地区城市排名中，台北和大版并列第二 Taipei and Osaka have tied for second place in a ranking of cities in the Asis-Pacific region released by the English-language magazine Asia Week

Table 6: Pre&Suffix inconsistent instances.

iFACETSUM: Coreference-based Interactive Faceted Summarization for Multi-Document Exploration

Eran Hirsch[1], **Alon Eirew**[1,2*], **Ori Shapira**[1*], **Avi Caciularu**[1], **Arie Cattan**[1], **Ori Ernst**[1], **Ramakanth Pasunuru**[3], **Hadar Ronen**[4], **Mohit Bansal**[3], **Ido Dagan**[1]

[1]Bar-Ilan University [2]Intel Labs, Israel [3]UNC Chapel Hill [4]Peres Academic Center
{hirsch.eran, obspp18}@gmail.com
alon.eirew@intel.com dagan@cs.biu.ac.il

Abstract

We introduce iFACETSUM,[1] a web application for exploring topical document sets. iFACETSUM integrates interactive summarization together with faceted search, by providing a novel faceted navigation scheme that yields abstractive summaries for the user's selections. This approach offers both a comprehensive overview as well as concise details regarding subtopics of choice. Fine-grained facets are automatically produced based on cross-document coreference pipelines, rendering generic concepts, entities and statements surfacing in the source texts. We analyze the effectiveness of our application through small-scale user studies, which suggest the usefulness of our approach.

1 Introduction

An information consumer aspiring to explore a new topic will often be faced with an extensive collection of texts from which to acquire knowledge. Confronted with these texts, the reader would have difficulty determining where to start reading and obtaining details about specific aspects of the topic. Addressing this we present iFACETSUM, illustrated in Figure 1, an *interactive faceted summarization* approach and system for navigating within a large input document-set on a topic. The system initially provides a full high-level overview of the topic at a glance in the form of facets. A user can then dive further into subtopics of interest and obtain concise facet-based summaries, capturing the valuable information of a subtopic.

The challenge of knowledge navigation has been addressed with various solutions, mainly under the umbrella of *exploratory search* (Marchionini, 2006) tasks. For example, in Complex Interactive Question Answering (ciQA) (Kelly and Lin, 2007) and Conversational QA (Reddy et al., 2019), a user interacts with a QA system in order to meet an information need on the source text(s). Interactive information retrieval (Ingwersen, 1992) and conversational search (Radlinski and Craswell, 2017) refine document retrieval through different means of textual interaction. Both tasks do not offer a preliminary outline of the source documents, and hence expect a user to formulate queries or questions without system guidance. Furthermore, short answers, such as those output in conversational QA, may be insufficient, while lists of relevant textual results, such as in conversational search, may be overwhelming and provoke an inefficient navigation process.

As a midpoint solution, interactive summarization provides an initial summary as an overview of the topic, and the ability to inquire, via suggested or free-text queries, for more information in the form of summary expansions (e.g. Shapira et al., 2021; Avinesh et al., 2018). Here still, the initial summary, along with the suggested queries, do not produce the full high-level picture, and therefore hints only partially at the possible subtopics that the user might want to explore.

iFACETSUM builds upon the interactive summarization scheme, extending it via the effective faceted search approach (Hearst, 2006a) (§2.1), coupled with facet-based abstractive summarization (§3.2). The presented facet values provide a comprehensive overview of the input topic, while the abstractive summaries deliver concise fine-grained information on selected facet values (see Figure 1). Furthermore, since facets are hierarchically updated in accordance to facet-value selections, navigating deeper into subtopics becomes seamless. In terms of backend implementation, facets are automatically derived over the input document set in a novel manner, based on cross-document coreference resolution (Cattan et al., 2021) and proposition alignment (Ernst et al.,

* Equal contribution.

[1]Demo at https://biu-nlp.github.io/iFACETSUM/WebApp/client/, and code at https://github.com/BIU-NLP/iFACETSUM.

Proceedings of the 2021 Conference on Empirical Methods in Natural Language Processing: System Demonstrations, pages 283–297
November 7–11, 2021.

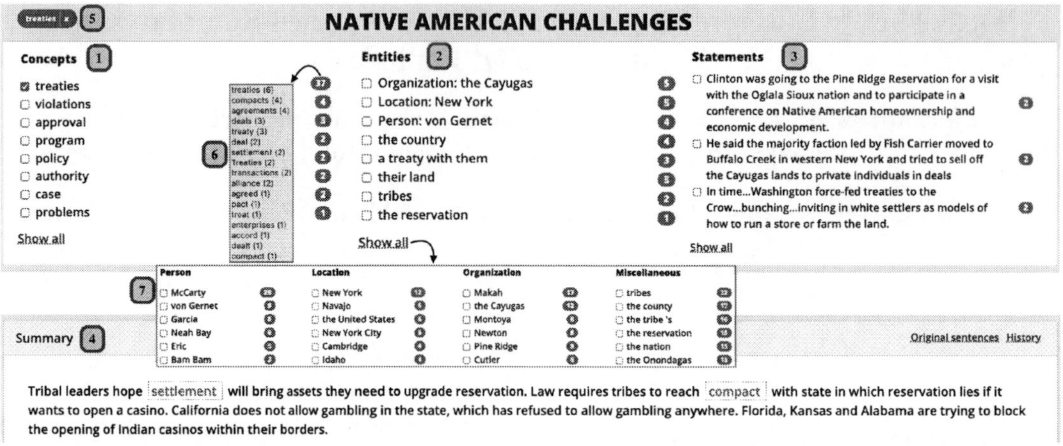

Figure 1: Our iFACETSUM web application over a set of 25 documents about "Native American Challenges". The user gets an overview of the topic as *Concepts* [1], *Entities* [2] and *Statements* [3] facets. The facets are updated in response to the user's choice of the facet-value "treaties" [5]. An abstractive summary is generated for the set of sentences corresponding to the "treaties" semantic cluster [4]. The mentions of a facet-value appear when hovering over its frequency [6]. Clicking "Show all" opens a pop-up with more facet-values. The *Entities* pop-up is categorized into further facets of *Person*, *Location*, *Organization* and *Miscellaneous* [7].

2020), yielding clusters of facet-value mentions (§3). Accordingly, summaries are generated based on the sentences that contain mentions of *all* selected facet-values.

We conduct usability studies on our system, and demonstrate its utility for easy navigation in topical document sets, while enabling deep diving into desired knowledge without losing the context of the exploration process.

We next describe iFACETSUM's interface in §2 and its backend implementation in §3. This is followed by the description and results of our usability investigations in §4, an overview of related work in §5, and finally conclusions and suggestions for future work in §6.

2 iFACETSUM Interface

iFACETSUM is a web application for exploring a document-set on a topic, shown in Figure 1. It generally consists of the *faceted navigation* component (top of figure, described in §2.1) , and the facet-based *summary* component (bottom of figure, §2.2). The former rests upon a faceted-navigation panel that provides orientation on the source topic, while the latter supplies the user with key information about selected facet-values. This flow facilitates guided exploration, over the full scope of the topical information and within subtopics of interest.

2.1 Faceted Navigation

Faceted search is a technique used to provide more effective information-seeking support (Tunkelang, 2009), by allowing users to narrow down results based on rich attributes. A *facet* describes an attribute type, and *facet-terms* or *facet-values* represent attribute values. iFACETSUM's facets are formed using techniques that identify recurring mentions of sub-sentential units in texts, as explained further in §3.1.

The faceted navigation component is laid-out to the user in the form of three general facets (Figure 1, [1], [2] and [3]): (1) *Generic Concepts* facet, e.g., "poverty" and "treaties". (2) *Entities* facet, containing values such as e.g., "Clinton" as a person or "Nebraska" as a location. (3) *Statements* facet, which lists specific statements mentioned several times, such as "Nebraska does not allow casino gambling".

In our data scheme, each facet-value encapsulates a cluster of mentions that semantically refer to a common concept, entity or statement, and, as such, may be lexically diverse (e.g., the "case" concept associates with mentions of "lawsuit", "fight", "battle", "debate"). A *facet-value sentence-set* is defined as the set of sentences pertaining to all of a facet-value's mentions. The *facet-value label* is the facet-value name presented to the user, and is chosen to be the most frequent lexical type in the mention cluster corresponding to that facet-value.

The values under each facet are ordered by their frequencies (number of mentions) in the source document set, as an indication for level of salience. A facet-value is shown with its corresponding frequency, and its various mention forms are revealed by hovering over the frequency meter (e.g., depicted in [6], the cluster "treaties" includes mentions of "agreements", "deals", etc.). Only a few of the top facet-values are shown under each facet, while clicking *Show all* expands the facet in full, in a pop-up. The pop-up for the *Entities* facet partitions the facet-values to particular sub-facets: *Person*, *Location*, *Organization* and *Miscellaneous* ([7]).

By clicking a facet-value, the system generates a summary of its sentence-set. Additionally, the facets update to include only values appearing in that sentence-set. The updated facet view thus gives an overview which is fine-grained for the selected subtopic, while iteratively selecting additional facet-values supports diving deeper into it. When additional facets are gradually selected, a summary is generated over the intersection of the sentence-sets of all selected facets. Any of the selected facet-values can be canceled out, whereby the system updates accordingly.

2.2 Facet-based Summarization

Upon a change in selection of facet-values, the system provides the user with targeted information via an abstractive summary of the selections' sentence-set ([4]). As more facet-values are selected, the generated summary is based on the intersection of the sentence sets of all selected facets, becoming more specific. The user can further view the complete set of source sentences used to generate the summary, and those sentences' full documents (Figures 3 and 4 in Appendix). Additionally, clicking "History" shows all previously generated summaries (Figure 5 in Appendix).

3 Backend Algorithms

As portrayed in §2, iFACETSUM supports two central features: presenting a faceted navigation panel and generating a summary around selected facet-values. We next describe how facet-values are generated using CD coreference resolution (§3.1), and how we apply abstractive summarization, based on a facet-value selection (§3.2). Figure 2 illustrates the entire process.

3.1 Coreference-based Facet Formation

As described in §2.1, there are three main facets. *Concepts* and *Entities* are extracted using cross-document (CD) coreference resolution pipelines, while *Statements* via a proposition alignment pipeline, described next.[2]

Concepts. We found that identifying and grouping together significant co-occurring events within the source document collection helps to expose and emphasize the notable concepts in the topic. To that end, we employ CD **event coreference resolution** which detects these concepts.

CD coreference resolution (Lee et al., 2012) clusters text mentions that refer to the same event or entity across multiple documents. Presently, the Cross-Document Language Model (CDLM) (Caciularu et al., 2021) is the state-of-the-art for CD coreference resolution. This model is pretrained on multiple related documents via cross-document masking, encouraging the model to learn cross-document and long-range relationships. Specifically, we employ the CDLM version fine-tuned for coreference on the ECB+ corpus (Cybulska and Vossen, 2014). This model does not include a mention detection component, but rather expects relevant mentions to be marked within the input texts. We therefore leverage the mention detection ability of the model by Cattan et al. (2021).

Once we have obtained the coreference clusters from CDLM, events whose mentions are predominantly verbs are filtered out,[3] since those usually present specific actions that tend to be less informative compared to nominal types that refer to more generic events (e.g., "said", "found" "increase" compared to "unemployment", "poverty", "crash").

CD event coreference resolution separates specific event instances, hence differentiating between clusters of similar event types with different arguments (e.g., "unemployment" in Navajo vs. "unemployment" in Cayuga). Since generic event types, like "unemployment", are more suitable as facet-values, clusters with the same label (most frequent mention) are merged. Each such merged clusters then constitutes a single facet-value, to be presented to the user as described in §2.1.[4]

[2]Facet extraction runs in a pre-processing step, since it is not fast enough for real-time latency (see Appendix A.2).

[3] Using spaCy (Honnibal et al., 2020).

[4]We observed that the CD event coreference model has a tendency to wrongly collapse events of the same type, effec-

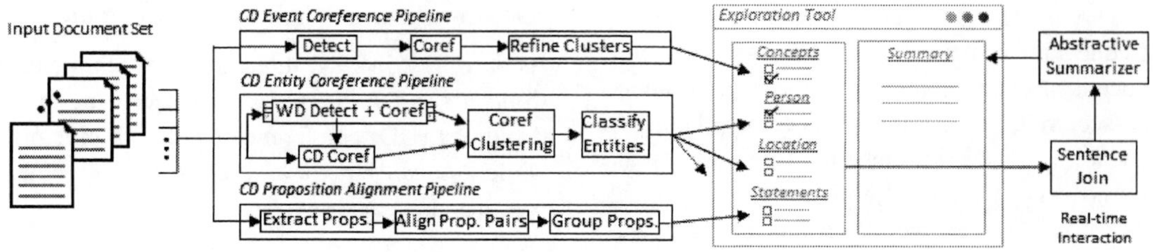

Figure 2: The iFACETSUM architecture. CD = cross-document, WD = within-document.

Entities. The *Entities* facet-values help the user focus on entities such as people (e.g., "Clinton"), locations (e.g., "New York"), organizations (e.g., "FBI") and others (e.g., "the casino"). We created a separate pipeline for CD **entity coreference resolution**, since we observed subpar performance when applying the above CD coreference pipeline for entity coreference.[5]

Unlike event coreference, mostly studied in the CD setting, entity coreference has recently seen impressive progress in the *within*-document (WD) setting (Wu et al., 2020; Joshi et al., 2020). Hence, we leverage WD entity coreference in our entity recognition pipeline, which comprises three main steps. (1) We use SpanBERT[6] (Joshi et al., 2020), a state-of-the-art transformer-based LM for WD entity coreference resolution, to detect and cluster coreferring entity mentions within each separate document. (2) The entity mentions detected in the first step are marked as input for a CD entity coreference reolution model. To overcome ECB+ entity scarcity referred earlier, we use an alternative model that is trained on the WEC-Eng dataset (Eirew et al., 2021).[7] (3) Finally, we apply agglomerative clustering to combine the coreference clusters from steps 1 and 2 (WD and CD), and produce the overall entity coreference clusters (details in Appendix A.2).

Once all entity coreference clusters are extracted, we bin them into more specific categories ("Person", "Location" and "Organization"), as portrayed in §2.1, by invoking a Named Entity Recognition (NER) model.[3] A facet-value cluster is tagged with the majority NER label of the mentions in the cluster, among Person, Organization and Location. If no NER label is assigned to a cluster, it is tagged as "Miscellaneous" (more details in Appendix A.2).

Statements. Key statements benefit a user by presenting information about specific facts. To generate these statements, we group together coreferring propositions (rather than words) that describe the same fact within the source documents, as seen in §2.1.

Following Ernst et al. (2020), our pipeline consists of three steps. (1) Proposition candidates are extracted with OpenIE (Stanovsky et al., 2018). (2) Pairs of propositions expressing the same statement are matched using the SuperPAL model (Ernst et al., 2020), considering proposition pairs whose alignment score is above 0.5 as matched. (3) A propositions graph is created by connecting pairs of nodes that represent similar propositions, and proposition clusters are matched for the connected components in the graph (more details in Appendix A.2).

3.2 Abstractive Facet Summarization

In the standard summarization setting, a system receives a single or multiple documents as input, as well as a query in the query-focused task. In our case, the input is a set of sentences that have one or more selected facet-values in common, effectively providing a *multi-facet* summary. Given the set of sentences that correspond to the facet-value selection(s), these sentences are concatenated, ordered by their position in their source document (more details in Appendix A.2). This text is then given as input to BART (Lewis et al., 2020), a denoising sequence-to-sequence model fine-tuned on the single-document abstractive summarization task.[8]

iFACETSUM presents abstractive rather than extractive summaries due to their enhanced readability, particularly when summarizing a set of related sentences. This choice follows prior work, which

tively aiding our concept formation.

[5]This is in line with previous work (Cattan et al., 2021) which points out that the ECB+ dataset only considers entities that are arguments of event mentions, which is non-exhaustive.

[6]Using AllenNLP (Gardner et al., 2018).

[7]Fine-tuning CDLM on WEC-Eng is computationally infeasible, and therefore we use the model by Eirew et al. (2021).

[8]We use the huggingface model from https://huggingface.co/facebook/bart-large-cnn.

showed that fusing sentences with shared points of coreference potentially facilitates coherence of abstractive summaries (Lebanoff et al., 2020). Indeed, in an internal manual assessment of 30 random individual summaries produced by iFACETSUM, with 5 readability measures (Dang, 2006), testers found overall that the summaries are highly readable. To verify that factuality is not compromised, an additional inspection found that these summaries were also factually consistent to the input text, with 28 out of 30 sampled sentences marked as consistent. See Appendix B.3 for scores and more details on these assessments.

4 System Experiments

iFACETSUM aims to provide an effective means of information seeking in scenarios that require learning or investigating a new topic (Marchionini, 2006). To that end, we tested this goal through two small-scale experiments with human subjects, as a preliminary examination of the system. In the first experiment, we conducted a pilot usability study to inspect whether users felt they were able to satisfactorily complete an information seeking task using our system. In the second, we examined whether iFACETSUM is preferred over a standard document-search system to complete the exploration task.

4.1 Usability Study

Setup. The purpose of this experiment was to get general feedback, from human subjects, on the usability of the system, following established usability study methodologies (Nielsen, 1994). To simulate a realistic use case of topic exploration, we instructed participants to use the system in order to prepare a draft review, given an informational goal, that a reporter could then use to write a report on the topic. We prepared guiding story-lines (Appendix B, Table 1), as informational goals, for two topics from the DUC 2006 MDS dataset (NIST, 2005). To analyze iFACETSUM in different exploratory situations, one topic is broad with higher information variability across the articles ("Native American Challenges"), while the other is more focused on a specific event ("EgyptAir Crash").

In this pilot usability study, six participants[9] explored both topics in random order. During system usage we observed the users' activity, via a "think aloud" technique (Van Someren et al., 1994), to obtain user remarks. After exploring a topic, a user rated, from 1 to 5, the usefulness of different aspects of each component in the interface. After both topics, a System Usability Scale (SUS) questionnaire (Brooke, 1995) was filled, to assess global usability of the system (overall score from 0 to 100). Further details are available in Appendix B.1.

Results. The average SUS score over the 6 participants is 82.9, where 80.3 is considered "excellent" (UIUX-Trend, 2021). From the average component ratings over the 12 sessions, users expressed their satisfaction with the facet view's and summaries' quality for the use of the tasks. The overall facets quality received a score of 4.3 (SD=0.7), summary coherence 4.7 (SD=0.5), summary informativeness 4.2 (SD=1.1), summary non-redundancy 3.8 (SD=1.0), and summary length 4.3 (SD=0.9). General feedback and issues raised by participants are available in Appendix B.1. Overall, participants were pleased with their experience and some voiced their desire to use the tool right away for current event issues, like COVID-19 vaccination.

As expected, users noticed a difference between the two topics, and mentioned that they preferred the *Concepts* facet for "Native American Challenges", while preferring the *Entities* facet for "EgyptAir Crash". Users found the *Statements* facet-values rather lengthy and less useful, and at times considered it a substitute for summarizing the topic. Future improvements of the system may include considering alternative uses of the aligned statements, like linking specific fact mentions across documents.

4.2 Comparative Analysis

To further investigate whether iFACETSUM is an effective tool for exploring a new topic, we conducted a small-scale comparison with a search tool, which roughly simulates common means for learning about a new topic. We asked four new experimentees to carry out the exploration task described in §4.1, once with our system on one topic, and once with the search tool on the other topic (in different orders). The search tool used was DocFetcher,[10] an open source desktop search application, which indexes the given files, enables searching documents with queries, and highlights

[9]The discount usability testing principle contends that six evaluators are sufficient for prototype evaluation (Nielsen, 1993).

[10]`http://docfetcher.sourceforge.net`

query terms within retrieved documents. The participants finished their assignment with iFACETSUM slightly faster than with the search tool. More importantly, they conveyed their satisfaction of using iFACETSUM as a tool for navigating through multiple texts, and learning about a new topic. The participants filled a questionnaire, rating each question on a scale of 1 (DocFetcher is preferred) to 7 (iFACETSUM is preferred). The questions included: (1) Which system was *easier to use* in order to get the desired result? (Avg=5.5, SD=1.73); (2) With which system was it easier for you to *get an overview* of the topic? (Avg=5, SD=2.3); (3) With which system was it easier for you to get *detailed information* about a subtopic of interest? (Avg=5.25, SD=0.9); (4) If you had to learn about or explore a new topic, *which system would you choose*? (Avg=5.25, SD=0.95). Overall, participants favored iFACETSUM in all questions, preferring it for future use (details in Appendix B.2).

5 Related Work

Attaining information of interest from large document sets has been approached with different techniques. A vast amount of research has been conducted on *multi-document summarization*, as a method for presenting the central aspects of a target set of texts (e.g. Barzilay et al., 1999; Haghighi and Vanderwende, 2009; Bing et al., 2015; Yasunaga et al., 2017), where *query-focused summarization* (Dang, 2005) biases the output summary around a given query (e.g. Daumé III and Marcu, 2006; Baumel et al., 2018; Xu and Lapata, 2020).

Recognizing the need for dynamically acquiring a broader or deeper scope of the source texts, *exploratory search* (Marchionini, 2006; White and Roth, 2009) was coined as an umbrella term for allowing more dynamic interactive exploration of information. Adapting the summarization paradigm to the exploratory setting, *interactive summarization* enables a user to refine or expand on a summary via different modes of interaction. For example, Shapira et al. (2021), Avinesh et al. (2018) and Baumel et al. (2014) provide a limited (or no) initial summary on the document set, and support iterative interaction, via queries or preference highlights, to update the summary. However, the succinct initial summary, possibly accompanied by few suggested queries, do not display the *full* scope of the source texts, which limits the user's perception of the many available sub-topics to learn more about.

On the other hand, other exploratory search approaches *do* provide a more elaborate overview of the source data through sophisticated dashboards or facets of extracted information or metadata (e.g. O'Connor et al., 2010; Koren et al., 2008; Hope et al., 2020). Indeed, faceted navigation (Hearst, 2006a; Tunkelang, 2009) is an effective instrument for navigating within a large data source (Hearst et al., 2002; Ruotsalo et al., 2020). While most faceted search systems generate facets from semi- or fully-structured data, as prominently encountered in e-commerce websites and in research (Hearst, 2006b; Ben-Yitzhak et al., 2008), some works generate facet hierarchies from unstructured open-domain texts. For example, from product reviews, Ly et al. (2011) extract product aspects and present several summaries, each focused on a single aspect as a "facet", in a form of single-level faceted search. Hope et al. (2020) devise facet-values from scientific articles by eliciting unstructured textual information (topics, entities) from the articles and their structured metadata (e.g article authors). Although these search tools offer a more comprehensive overview of the source data, they either present raw-text search results or do not allow thorough navigation.

iFACETSUM fully integrates dynamic multi-level faceted navigation into interactive multi-document summarization. The facets serve as an efficient means of grasping the topic, and render an intuitive medium for navigating through the information. The abstractive summaries generated at real-time expose concise details for any combination of sub-topics of choice. Furthermore, we innovatively employ coreference resolution and proposition alignment to generate fine-grained open-domain facets.

6 Conclusion and Future Work

In this paper, we presented iFACETSUM, a novel text exploration approach and tool over large document sets, which incorporates faceted search into interactive summarization. Its faceted navigation design provides a user with an overview of the topic and the ability to gradually investigate subtopics of interest, communicating concise information via multi-facet abstractive summarization. Fine-grained facet-values are generated from the source texts based on cross-document coreference pipelines. Small-scale user studies suggest the utility of our approach for exploring a new topic from multiple documents.

Future work may speed up the coreference-based facet extraction pipeline, allowing for real-time processing of ad-hoc document sets, and may investigate further methods for facet generation. Additional search techniques might be integrated into the exploration scheme, including free text searching as raised in the user study. It would also be appealing to try adapting the system to domains other than news, such as the medical or scientific domains, for which exploration tools would be very useful. Such adaptations would depend on the portability of the underlying technologies of cross-document coreference resolution and proposition alignment. Finally, future work may explore additional ways of leveraging the power of recent proposition alignment methods.

7 Ethical Considerations

Usability Study. We conducted the usability study (§4.1) over Zoom sessions (`https://zoom.us/`), and carried out the "think aloud" technique through screen sharing and a with an open camera. Participants volunteered to take part in the study, and took about 45 minutes of each of their time. An *informed consent* form was signed by the participant before each study.

The comparative study included four NLP doctoral students from our lab who volunteered for the experiment. The summary readability and factual consistency assessments were done by two authors of this paper.

Computation. We ran the three pre-processing pipelines mentioned in §3.1 on 2 to 4 GPUs, where each pipeline ran from a few minutes to 10 hours per topic (25 news articles). Six such topics were prepared for the demo applications. (more details in Appendix A.2).

The summarization model runs in real-time (per user interaction) over a CPU in less than 3 seconds per summary. Summaries are cached to refrain from recomputing summaries for repeated queries.

Dataset. The DUC 2006 data was acquired according to the required NIST guidelines (`duc.nist.gov`).

Multilingualism. All models used within the components of iFACETSUM were trained on English data, thus making the system compatible for English only. Supporting other languages requires replacing the contained models to ones compliant to the desired languages.

Acknowledgments

This work was supported in part by the German Research Foundation through the German-Israeli Project Cooperation (DIP, grant DA 1600/1-1); by the Israel Science Foundation (grant 1951/17); by a grant from the Israel Ministry of Science and Technology; and by grants from Intel Labs. RP and MB were supported by NSF-CAREER Award 1846185 and a Microsoft PhD Fellowship.

References

PVS Avinesh, Benjamin Hättasch, Orkan Ozyurt, Carsten Binnig, and Christian M Meyer. 2018. Sherlock: A System for Interactive Summarization of Large Text Collections. *Proceedings of the VLDB Endowment*, 11(12).

Shany Barhom, Vered Shwartz, Alon Eirew, Michael Bugert, Nils Reimers, and Ido Dagan. 2019. Revisiting joint modeling of cross-document entity and event coreference resolution. In *Proceedings of the 57th Annual Meeting of the Association for Computational Linguistics*, pages 4179–4189, Florence, Italy. Association for Computational Linguistics.

Regina Barzilay, Kathleen R. McKeown, and Michael Elhadad. 1999. Information Fusion in the Context of Multi-Document Summarization. In *Proceedings of the 37th Annual Meeting of the Association for Computational Linguistics*, pages 550–557, College Park, Maryland, USA. Association for Computational Linguistics.

Tal Baumel, Raphael Cohen, and Michael Elhadad. 2014. Query-Chain Focused Summarization. In *Proceedings of the 52nd Annual Meeting of the Association for Computational Linguistics (Volume 1: Long Papers)*, pages 913–922, Baltimore, Maryland. Association for Computational Linguistics.

Tal Baumel, Matan Eyal, and Michael Elhadad. 2018. Query Focused Abstractive Summarization: Incorporating Query Relevance, Multi-Document Coverage, and Summary Length Constraints into seq2seq Models.

Ori Ben-Yitzhak, Nadav Golbandi, Nadav Har'El, Ronny Lempel, Andreas Neumann, Shila Ofek-Koifman, Dafna Sheinwald, Eugene Shekita, Benjamin Sznajder, and Sivan Yogev. 2008. Beyond Basic Faceted Search. In *Proceedings of the 2008 International Conference on Web Search and Data Mining*, WSDM '08, page 33–44, New York, NY, USA. Association for Computing Machinery.

Lidong Bing, Piji Li, Yi Liao, Wai Lam, Weiwei Guo, and Rebecca Passonneau. 2015. Abstractive Multi-Document Summarization via Phrase Selection and

Merging. In *Proceedings of the 53rd Annual Meeting of the Association for Computational Linguistics and the 7th International Joint Conference on Natural Language Processing (Volume 1: Long Papers)*, pages 1587–1597, Beijing, China. Association for Computational Linguistics.

John Brooke. 1995. SUS: A quick and dirty usability scale. *Usability Eval. Ind.*, 189.

Avi Caciularu, Arman Cohan, Iz Beltagy, Matthew E. Peters, Arie Cattan, and Ido Dagan. 2021. CDLM: Cross-Document Language Modeling. In *Findings of the Association for Computational Linguistics: EMNLP 2021*.

Arie Cattan, Alon Eirew, Gabriel Stanovsky, Mandar Joshi, and Ido Dagan. 2021. Cross-document coreference resolution over predicted mentions.

Agata Cybulska and Piek Vossen. 2014. Using a sledgehammer to crack a nut? lexical diversity and event coreference resolution. In *Proceedings of the Ninth International Conference on Language Resources and Evaluation (LREC'14)*, pages 4545–4552, Reykjavik, Iceland. European Language Resources Association (ELRA).

Hoa Trang Dang. 2005. Overview of DUC 2005. In *Proceedings of the document understanding conference*, volume 2005, pages 1–12.

Hoa Trang Dang. 2006. Overview of DUC 2006. In *Document Understanding Conference*.

Hal Daumé III and Daniel Marcu. 2006. Bayesian Query-Focused Summarization. In *Proceedings of the 21st International Conference on Computational Linguistics and 44th Annual Meeting of the Association for Computational Linguistics*, pages 305–312, Sydney, Australia. Association for Computational Linguistics.

Alon Eirew, Arie Cattan, and Ido Dagan. 2021. WEC: Deriving a large-scale cross-document event coreference dataset from Wikipedia. In *Proceedings of the 2021 Conference of the North American Chapter of the Association for Computational Linguistics: Human Language Technologies*, pages 2498–2510, Online. Association for Computational Linguistics.

Ori Ernst, Ori Shapira, Ramakanth Pasunuru, Michael Lepioshkin, Jacob Goldberger, Mohit Bansal, and Ido Dagan. 2020. SuperPAL: Supervised Proposition ALignment for Multi-Document Summarization and Derivative Sub-Tasks.

Matt Gardner, Joel Grus, Mark Neumann, Oyvind Tafjord, Pradeep Dasigi, Nelson F. Liu, Matthew Peters, Michael Schmitz, and Luke Zettlemoyer. 2018. AllenNLP: A deep semantic natural language processing platform. In *Proceedings of Workshop for NLP Open Source Software (NLP-OSS)*, pages 1–6, Melbourne, Australia. Association for Computational Linguistics.

Aria Haghighi and Lucy Vanderwende. 2009. Exploring Content Models for Multi-Document Summarization. In *Proceedings of Human Language Technologies: The 2009 Annual Conference of the North American Chapter of the Association for Computational Linguistics*, pages 362–370, Boulder, Colorado. Association for Computational Linguistics.

Marti Hearst, Ame Elliott, Jennifer English, Rashmi Sinha, Kirsten Swearingen, and Ka-Ping Yee. 2002. Finding the flow in web site search. *Communications of the ACM*, 45(9):42–49.

Marti A. Hearst. 2006a. Clustering Versus Faceted Categories for Information Exploration. *Communications of the ACM*, 49(4):59–61.

Marti A. Hearst. 2006b. Design recommendations for hierarchical faceted search interfaces. In *ACM SIGIR workshop on faceted search*, pages 1–5.

Matthew Honnibal, Ines Montani, Sofie Van Landeghem, and Adriane Boyd. 2020. spaCy: Industrial-strength Natural Language Processing in Python.

Tom Hope, Jason Portenoy, Kishore Vasan, Jonathan Borchardt, Eric Horvitz, Daniel Weld, Marti Hearst, and Jevin West. 2020. SciSight: Combining faceted navigation and research group detection for COVID-19 exploratory scientific search. In *Proceedings of the 2020 Conference on Empirical Methods in Natural Language Processing: System Demonstrations*, pages 135–143, Online. Association for Computational Linguistics.

Peter Ingwersen. 1992. *Information retrieval interaction*, volume 246. Taylor Graham London.

Mandar Joshi, Danqi Chen, Yinhan Liu, Daniel S. Weld, Luke Zettlemoyer, and Omer Levy. 2020. SpanBERT: Improving pre-training by representing and predicting spans. *Transactions of the Association for Computational Linguistics*, 8:64–77.

Diane Kelly and Jimmy Lin. 2007. Overview of the TREC 2006 ciQA task. In *ACM SIGIR Forum*, volume 41, pages 107–116. ACM New York, NY, USA.

Kian Kenyon-Dean, Jackie Chi Kit Cheung, and Doina Precup. 2018. Resolving Event Coreference with Supervised Representation Learning and Clustering-Oriented Regularization. In *Proceedings of the Seventh Joint Conference on Lexical and Computational Semantics*, pages 1–10, New Orleans, Louisiana. Association for Computational Linguistics.

Jonathan Koren, Yi Zhang, and Xue Liu. 2008. Personalized Interactive Faceted Search. In *Proceedings of the 17th International Conference on World Wide Web*, WWW '08, page 477–486, New York, NY, USA. Association for Computing Machinery.

Logan Lebanoff, John Muchovej, Franck Dernoncourt, Doo Soon Kim, Lidan Wang, Walter Chang, and Fei Liu. 2020. Understanding Points of Correspondence between Sentences for Abstractive Summarization. In *Proceedings of the 58th Annual Meeting of the Association for Computational Linguistics: Student Research Workshop*, pages 191–198, Online. Association for Computational Linguistics.

Heeyoung Lee, Marta Recasens, Angel Chang, Mihai Surdeanu, and Dan Jurafsky. 2012. Joint Entity and Event Coreference Resolution across Documents. In *Proceedings of the 2012 Joint Conference on Empirical Methods in Natural Language Processing and Computational Natural Language Learning*, pages 489–500, Jeju Island, Korea. Association for Computational Linguistics.

Mike Lewis, Yinhan Liu, Naman Goyal, Marjan Ghazvininejad, Abdelrahman Mohamed, Omer Levy, Veselin Stoyanov, and Luke Zettlemoyer. 2020. {BART}: Denoising Sequence-to-Sequence Pre-training for Natural Language Generation, Translation, and Comprehension. In *Proceedings of the 58th Annual Meeting of the Association for Computational Linguistics*, pages 7871–7880, Online. Association for Computational Linguistics.

Duy Khang Ly, Kazunari Sugiyama, Ziheng Lin, and Min-Yen Kan. 2011. Product Review Summarization based on Facet Identification and Sentence Clustering.

Gary Marchionini. 2006. Exploratory Search: from Finding to Understanding. *Communications of the ACM*, 49(4):41–46.

Yehudit Meged, Avi Caciularu, Vered Shwartz, and Ido Dagan. 2020. Paraphrasing vs coreferring: Two sides of the same coin. In *Findings of the Association for Computational Linguistics: EMNLP 2020*, pages 4897–4907, Online. Association for Computational Linguistics.

Jakob Nielsen. 1993. *Usability engineering*. Academic Press.

Jakob Nielsen. 1994. *Usability engineering*, page 165. Morgan Kaufmann.

NIST. 2005. DUC 2006: Task, Documents, and Measures. `https://duc.nist.gov/duc2006/tasks.html`. Accessed: 2020-05-19.

Brendan O'Connor, Michel Krieger, and David Ahn. 2010. TweetMotif: Exploratory Search and Topic Summarization for Twitter. *Proceedings of the International AAAI Conference on Web and Social Media*, 4(1).

Filip Radlinski and Nick Craswell. 2017. A Theoretical Framework for Conversational Search. In *Proceedings of the 2017 Conference on Conference Human Information Interaction and Retrieval*, CHIIR '17, page 117–126, New York, NY, USA. Association for Computing Machinery.

Siva Reddy, Danqi Chen, and Christopher D. Manning. 2019. {C}o{QA}: A Conversational Question Answering Challenge. *Transactions of the Association for Computational Linguistics*, 7:249–266.

Tuukka Ruotsalo, Giulio Jacucci, and Samuel Kaski. 2020. Interactive faceted query suggestion for exploratory search: Whole-session effectiveness and interaction engagement. *Journal of the Association for Information Science and Technology*, 71(7):742–756.

Ori Shapira, Ramakanth Pasunuru, Hadar Ronen, Mohit Bansal, Yael Amsterdamer, and Ido Dagan. 2021. Extending Multi-Document Summarization Evaluation to the Interactive Setting. In *Proceedings of the 2021 Conference of the North American Chapter of the Association for Computational Linguistics: Human Language Technologies*, pages 657–677, Online. Association for Computational Linguistics.

Gabriel Stanovsky, Julian Michael, Luke Zettlemoyer, and Ido Dagan. 2018. Supervised Open Information Extraction. In *Proceedings of the 2018 Conference of the North American Chapter of the Association for Computational Linguistics: Human Language Technologies, Volume 1 (Long Papers)*, pages 885–895, New Orleans, Louisiana. Association for Computational Linguistics.

Daniel Tunkelang. 2009. Faceted Search. *Synthesis lectures on information concepts, retrieval, and services*, 1(1):1–80.

UIUX-Trend. 2021. Measuring and Interpreting System Usability Scale - UIUX Trend. `https://uiuxtrend.com/measuring-system-usability-scale-sus/`. Accessed: 2021-06-28.

MW Van Someren, YF Barnard, and JAC Sandberg. 1994. The think aloud method: a practical approach to modelling cognitive. *London: AcademicPress*.

Ryen W White and Resa A Roth. 2009. Exploratory search: Beyond the query-response paradigm. *Synthesis lectures on information concepts, retrieval, and services*, 1(1):1–98.

Wei Wu, Fei Wang, Arianna Yuan, Fei Wu, and Jiwei Li. 2020. CorefQA: Coreference resolution as query-based span prediction. In *Proceedings of the 58th Annual Meeting of the Association for Computational Linguistics*, pages 6953–6963, Online. Association for Computational Linguistics.

Yumo Xu and Mirella Lapata. 2020. Coarse-to-Fine Query Focused Multi-Document Summarization. In *Proceedings of the 2020 Conference on Empirical Methods in Natural Language Processing (EMNLP)*, pages 3632–3645, Online. Association for Computational Linguistics.

Michihiro Yasunaga, Rui Zhang, Kshitijh Meelu, Ayush Pareek, Krishnan Srinivasan, and Dragomir Radev. 2017. Graph-based Neural Multi-Document

Summarization. In *Proceedings of the 21st Conference on Computational Natural Language Learning (CoNLL 2017)*, pages 452–462, Vancouver, Canada. Association for Computational Linguistics.

A Implementation Details

A.1 Interface

The frontend uses the reactjs library (`https://reactjs.org/`) and the bootstrap library (`https://getbootstrap.com/`).

A.2 Backend

The backend service is written in python, using the tornado web server library (`https://www.tornadoweb.org`). The summarization model was downloaded from huggingface (`https://huggingface.co/facebook/bart-large-cnn`). The service is deployed on a Linux server with CPU only.

All coreference and proposition alignment models described in §3.1 are previously trained models. Links to these trained models are available in the project's GitHub.

For creating the CD coreference clusters for events with the fine-tuned CDLM model, we used two 32GB V100-SMX2 GPUs, for about 6 hours per topic. For creating the CD coreference clusters for entities, we used one 12GB TITAN Xp GPU, for about 5 minutes per topic. For creating the proposition alignment clusters we used four GeForce GTX 1080 Ti GPUs, for about 10 hours per topic.

CD entity coreference merging step. As described in §3.1, our final CD entity coreference step merges WD and CD predictions. The SpanBERT WD model outputs clusters of coreferring mentions, while the CD entity model (Eirew et al., 2021) outputs a pairwise score for each pair of mentions. We therefore convert SpanBERT clusters to mention-pair scores, by scoring pairs that are clustered together as 1, and 0 otherwise. Then, following common practice (Kenyon-Dean et al., 2018; Barhom et al., 2019; Meged et al., 2020; Eirew et al., 2021), we apply agglomerative clustering over all mention-pairs (both WD and CD) and produce the final entity coreference clusters. Since WD coreference quality is superior to that of CD coreference, the high *WD* coreferring mention-pair scores of 1 causes the clustering algorithm to favor those pairs for overall coreference clusters.

Proposition-level similarity threshold. The proposition alignment model computes a pairwise similarity between pairs of propositions, and we only consider pairs with a score above 0.5 (as a standard binary classification heuristic). We then create a similarity graph, where each proposition is a node, and paired propositions are linked with an edge. The final clusters are the connected components in the graph. For example, if for propositions P_1, P_2 and P_3, there exist pairs (P_1, P_2) and (P_1, P_3), then P_1, P_2 and P_3 will be clustered together.

Facet-value label. As mentioned in §3.1, each facet-value is linked to a coreference cluster (a set of mentions) and has a label which is displayed to the user. For concepts and entities, this label is the text of the cluster's most frequent mention. For statements, there is no repetition of mention texts in the cluster. There, we use the text of the longest mention, under the assumption that it has more context for the user to understand the statement.

Entities sub-facet categorization. After computing the *Entities* facet-values with entity coreference resolution, we categorize each facet-value to a specific entity type. For this, we first calculated the named entity class, with NER, for each mention in the facet-value cluster. All tokens of a mention were to be classified with the same NER class in order for the mention to be considered classified. Then, the class repeating the most times in a cluster was chosen as the class of the cluster. If all mentions of a cluster were not classified, we categorized the facet-value as *Miscellaneous*.

We mapped spaCy's NER classes to names that we found are more friendly to non NLP-practitioners (e.g., "GPE" is named "Location").

Facet-value filters. After generating the potential facet-values (coreference clusters), we filter out:

- Clusters with more than 50 mentions, under the assumption that they are too noisy for the user.
- Singleton clusters, i.e. a cluster with one mention or one linked sentence (coreferring in the same sentence), under the assumption that they are uninformative.
- Clusters whose label is 2 characters or less (e.g., "'s", "AP").

- Clusters whose label has a verb part-of-speech tag.

Summarization model input. As described in §3.2, BART is used to summarize the set of input sentences relevant to the facet-value selections. Since BART has an input-length limit of 1024 tokens, ordering the sentences based on their sentence index raises the likelihood that summaries will be based on sentences from multiple documents. The documents were ordered by their alphanumeric file system order based on their document ID.

A.3 Data

DUC 2006 MDS dataset is used for demonstrating the application, specifically with 6 topics: D0601, D0602, D0606, D0608, D0617, D0629.

B Experiment Details

We carried out a usability study and a system comparison experiment (§4), as well as a summary quality evaluation (§3.2).

B.1 Usability Study

For the usability study, six participants were gathered based on prior acquaintance. Each user had a 45 minutes Zoom session with an experienced experiment overseer. The participants first filled an experiment participation consent form. Before starting the actual experiment, the users were presented with another topic for experimenting with the system, followed by instructions of the experiment overseer, to reduce the learning curve of using the system for the first time.

Table 1 shows the two tasks that each user received. Participants conducted the experiments on the two topics in different orders.

SUS questionnaire. The SUS questionnaire (Brooke, 1995) was filled once by each user after both topics, with the following 10 questions:

1. I think that I would like to use this system frequently.
2. I found the system unnecessarily complex.
3. I thought the system was easy to use.
4. I think that I would need the support of a technical person to be able to use this system.
5. I found the various functions in this system were well integrated.

Topic	Task
Native American Challenges (D0601)	As a junior reporter, you were assigned a task to read 25 documents about Native American Challenge and hand out a draft to a reporter who will write the actual report. For your draft, describe two / three challenges that Native American communities face. For each challenge, explain any possible causes, difficulties that arise, and things being done for or against.
EgyptAir Crash (D0617)	As a junior reporter, you were assigned a task to read 25 documents about the EgyptAir Crash and hand out a draft to a reporter who will write the actual report. Describe the crash and two theories around it. For each theory, describe who stands behind it, who opposes it and what are the claims supporting it.

Table 1: The tasks that each user received in both usability study and comparison study. The tasks order was shuffled among the users.

6. I thought there was too much inconsistency in this system.
7. I would imagine that most people would learn to use this system very quickly.
8. I found the system very cumbersome to use.
9. I felt very confident using the system.
10. I needed to learn a lot of things before I could get going with this system.

To calculate the SUS score, the following procedure is taken (Brooke, 1995): First sum the score contributions from each item. Each item's score contribution will range from 0 to 4. For items 1,3,5,7,and 9 the score contribution is the scale position minus 1. For items 2,4,6,8 and 10, the contribution is 5 minus the scale position. Multiply the sum of the scores by 2.5 to obtain the overall value of SU. SUS scores have a range of 0 to 100.

The final scores of the six participants are:

User	1	2	3	4	5	6
Score	82.5	85	50	97.5	100	82.5

Usefulness questionnaire. After exploring each topic, the participants filled a questionnaire as follows:

- For the requirements of the given task, how useful was the Facets component between 1 (not useful at all) and 5 (very useful)?
- Overall, the summaries output by the system were: between 1 (I disagree) and 5 (I agree)
  - Coherent
  - Informative
  - Non-Redundant
  - Length was about right

The average and (StD) results on the 12 sessions (2 topic for 6 participants) are:

System Aspect	Score
Facets quality	4.3 (0.7)
Summ. coherence	4.7 (0.5)
Summ. informativeness	4.2 (1.1)
Summ. non-redundancy	3.8 (1.0)
Summ. length is about right	4.3 (0.9)

Comments raised by participants. During the sessions, the experiment overseer collected comments and ideas for improvements raised by the participants. The consensus was that the summaries were very impressive, especially when realizing that they summarize many sentences from multiple documents, and that the *Concepts* and *Entities* facets were useful for navigating through the vast information. For improvement, suggestions included to reverse the order of the history list, to add a reset button of all filters and to move the facet-value frequency meter closer to the facet-value label. Some mentioned that the *Statements* facet was less useful, since it acts like a summary that is unnecessary with respect to the navigation process.

B.2 System Comparison Experiment

For the comparative experiment, we gathered 4 graduate students from our NLP lab and gave them offline assignments which took about 45 minutes. At the beginning, each student was given a document of instructions describing iFACETSUM and DocFetcher, and were told to take a few minutes to play with each system on a third topic. Then each student was given a document with an assignment, with the same tasks as the usability study (Table 1). The participants were told to stop the exploration process once they felt satisfied with their outcome. There were 4 variants of the assignment document (one for each student), for all combinations of 2 systems and 2 topics, where a participant does not repeat the topic on both systems.

Questionnaire. After both topics, the users answered a comparative usability questionnaire, as mentioned in §4.2.

The average time for completing the assignment with DocFetcher was 16 minutes and the average for iFACETSUM was 15 minutes. We found that drafts written by participants using the two systems were comparable in informativeness, and importantly that the participants preferred iFACETSUM over the standard search approach (from questionnaire results and general comments).

B.3 Summary Quality Assessment

To assess the quality of the summaries output by our system (using BART fine-tuned on a summarization task), we collected 5 output summaries from each of the 6 supported topics (30 summaries overall) by submitting random facet-value selections (one or more selections per summary). These selections yielded sentence sets (summarizer inputs) of varying sizes (2 to 47 sentences).

The summaries were rated for five standard summary readability criteria, as defined in (Dang, 2006), on a 1-to-5 Likert scale. Two of the authors rated all summaries, and then reconciliated on scores with a large (3 or more points) difference, in which case scores may have been slightly revised. In addition, we added a sixth aspect - "Factuality", which was assessed by binary scoring. For each of the 30 summaries, a single sampled summary sentence was scored 0 if any fact in it did not have evidence in the source text, and 1 otherwise (30 sentences tested). We found that many sentences were lightly paraphrased or were fusions of two sub-sentential extractions, yielding high factuality scores. Results appear in Table 2.

C iFACETSUM Features and Sample Session

Feature Explanations. Some of the features of iFACETSUM, presented in §2, are further explained here:

Summary Aspect	Score
Grammatically	4.20 (0.94)
Non-redundancy	4.58 (0.77)
Referential clarity	4.10 (1.02)
Focus	3.93 (1.12)
Structure & Coherence	3.55 (1.14)
Factuality	93.3%

Table 2: Average and (StD.) scores of the summary evaluation ratings over 30 random summaries generated by the system, with a 1 (worst) to 5 (best) scale. For Factuality, the score is the percent of factual sentences (out of 30 sentences).

- Clicking "Original sentences" for a summary opens a pop-up window with the set of sentences used to generate the summary. The sentences are marked with mentions pertaining to the selected facet-values. They are grouped by their parent document and then listed in order of their position in their corresponding document. (Figure 3)
- Clicking a document title in the sentences pop-up opens another pop-up window with that document in full. The sentences from the parent pop-up are marked in red. (Figure 4)
- Clicking "History" opens a pop-up window with all the facet-value selections and resulting summaries from the current exploration session. (Figure 5)
- If a complete sentence from the summary has already been seen in a previous one, that sentence is tinted in purple. We found this useful given the summarization model's occasional extractiveness. (Figure 6)

Facet-value examples. We show in Table 3 some examples of facet-values and their mention clusters.

Sample session. In Table 4 we show the facet selections and resulting summaries from part of a session in the usability study.

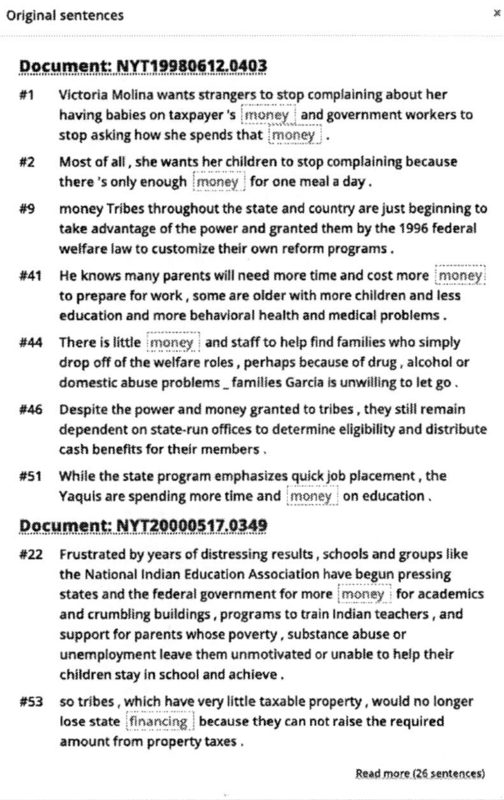

Figure 3: The original sentences popup, which lists the sentences used to create the inquired summary.

Facet	Facet-Value Examples
Concepts	"treaties" ("agreements", "deals", "treaty", "deal", "settlements", ...) "revenues" ("incomes", "profit")
Entities	"Makah" ("The Makah tribe", "The Olympic Peninsula tribe", ...) "the plane" ("the jet", "767", "EgyptAir Flight 990")
Statements	"Native Americans are leaving reservations and relocating in urbans areas" ("Indians now living in urban areas", "migration from the reseravtions continues", ...)

Table 3: Examples of facet-values.

Query	Summary
treaties (34 sentences)	Tribal leaders hope **settlement** will bring assets they need to upgrade reservation. Law requires tribes to reach **compact** with state in which reservation lies if it wants to open a casino. California does not allow gambling in the state, which has not allowed gambling in Nebraska. Florida, Kansas and Alabama have sued the U.S. Interior Department.
treaties, New York (5 sentences)	McCurn previously ruled that **New York** illegally acquired the Cayugas reservation land in 1795 and 1807. The state purchased it in violation of the 1790 Indian Trade and Intercourse Act, which required Congressional approval for all Indian land **transactions**. It was long-standing New York policy to assume authority over Indian land **deals** within its borders.
treaties, Florida (1 sentence)	In addition, **Florida**, Kansas and Alabama, trying to block the opening of Indian casinos within their borders, have sued the U.S. Interior Department with the aim of overturning new rules that allow the federal government to license tribal casinos in cases where states are reluctant to negotiate **compacts**.

Table 4: A snippet of a sample iFACETSUM session. Words in bold are mentions of the selected facet-value(s) (e.g., "compact" is a mention of "treaties").

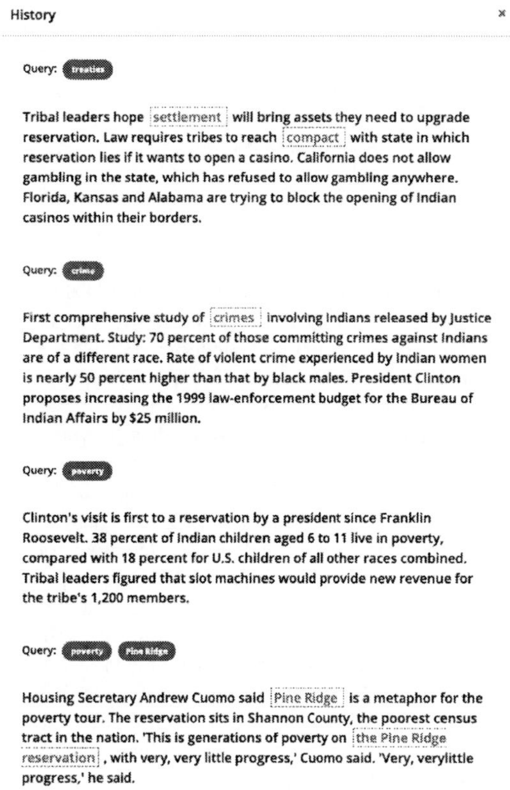

Figure 5: The history popup, containing all interactions from the current session. For each interaction, the facet selections and corresponding summary are shown.

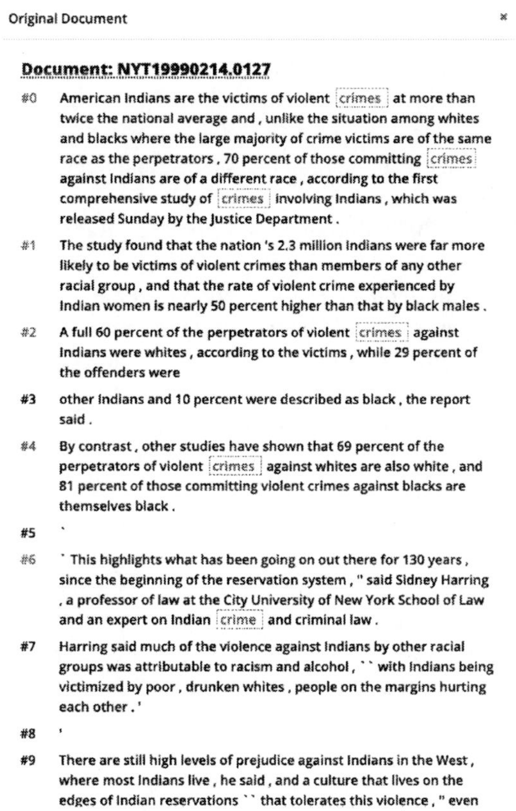

Figure 4: The original document popup, marking the sentences and mentions relevant to the *sentences popup* from which this document was requested. A document enables the user to get more context on the summary.

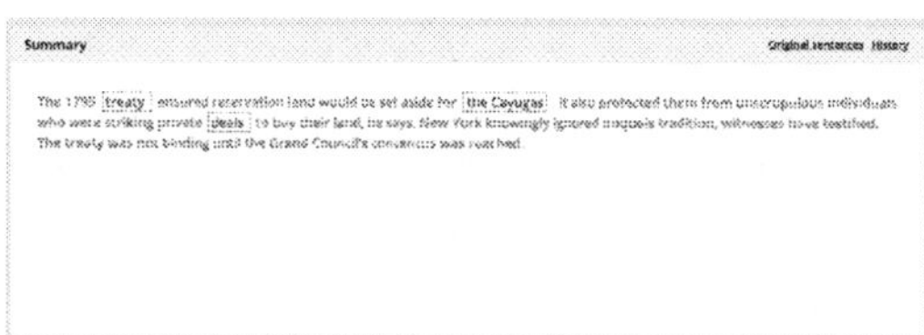

Figure 6: The sentence is tinted purple, indicating it was already extracted as part of a previous summary, relieving the user from reading it again.

AMuSE-WSD: An All-in-one Multilingual System for Easy Word Sense Disambiguation

Riccardo Orlando
Babelscape, Italy
orlando@babelscape.com

Simone Conia
Sapienza University of Rome
conia@di.uniroma1.it

Fabrizio Brignone
Babelscape, Italy
brignone@babelscape.com

Francesco Cecconi
Babelscape, Italy
cecconi@babelscape.com

Roberto Navigli
Sapienza University of Rome
navigli@diag.uniroma1.it

Abstract

Over the past few years, Word Sense Disambiguation (WSD) has received renewed interest: recently proposed systems have shown the remarkable effectiveness of deep learning techniques in this task, especially when aided by modern pretrained language models. Unfortunately, such systems are still not available as ready-to-use end-to-end packages, making it difficult for researchers to take advantage of their performance. The only alternative for a user interested in applying WSD to downstream tasks is to use currently available end-to-end WSD systems, which, however, still rely on graph-based heuristics or non-neural machine learning algorithms. In this paper, we fill this gap and propose AMuSE-WSD, the first end-to-end system to offer high-quality sense information in 40 languages through a state-of-the-art neural model for WSD. We hope that AMuSE-WSD will provide a stepping stone for the integration of meaning into real-world applications and encourage further studies in lexical semantics. AMuSE-WSD is available online at `http://nlp.uniroma1.it/amuse-wsd`.

1 Introduction

Word Sense Disambiguation (WSD) is the task of associating a word in context with its most appropriate sense from a predefined sense inventory (Bevilacqua et al., 2021). Learning the meaning of a word in context is often considered to be a fundamental step in enabling machine understanding of text (Navigli, 2018): indeed, a word can be polysemous, that is, it can refer to different meanings depending on the context. Over the past few years, WSD has received growing attention and has been proven to be useful in an increasing range of applications, such as machine translation (Liu et al., 2018; Pu et al., 2018; Raganato et al., 2019), information extraction (Zhong and Ng, 2012; Delli Bovi et al., 2015), information retrieval (Blloshmi et al., 2021), text categorization (Shimura et al., 2019) and question answering (Ramakrishnan et al., 2003).

WSD approaches usually fall into two categories: knowledge-based (Moro et al., 2014; Agirre et al., 2014; Chaplot and Salakhutdinov, 2018), which leverage computational lexicons, and supervised (Bevilacqua and Navigli, 2020; Blevins and Zettlemoyer, 2020; Conia and Navigli, 2021; Barba et al., 2021; ElSheikh et al., 2021), which train machine learning models on sense-annotated data. While early work mainly belongs to the former category (Navigli, 2009), recent studies have shown the superiority in performance of the latter category, especially thanks to complex neural networks (Bevilacqua et al., 2021). However, as WSD systems become more and more reliant on increasingly complex input representations – pretrained language models are becoming the *de facto* representation method in several NLP tasks – and involve neural architectures, the entry requirements for end users have also become higher. Indeed, the implementation of state-of-the-art WSD systems is frequently anything but straightforward. What is more, such systems are often not ready to be used off-the-shelf and require additional preprocessing and postprocessing modules for document splitting, tokenization, lemmatization and part-of-speech tagging. These complications may make the use of recent high-performing WSD systems unattractive, or even out of reach, for researchers who want to take advantage of explicit semantic information in other areas of research, but who are not experts in WSD.

In order to make WSD more accessible, there have been several attempts at providing ready-to-use WSD systems that can be easily integrated into other systems (Navigli and Ponzetto, 2012b; Moro et al., 2014; Agirre et al., 2014; Scozzafava et al., 2020). Nevertheless, current ready-to-use WSD systems are either English-only or based on approaches that now lag behind state-of-the-art mod-

Proceedings of the 2021 Conference on Empirical Methods in Natural Language Processing: System Demonstrations, pages 298–307
November 7–11, 2021. ©2021 Association for Computational Linguistics

els in terms of performance.

In this paper, we fill the gap and present AMuSE-WSD, an easy-to-use, off-the-shelf WSD package that provides sense annotations in multiple languages through a state-of-the-art neural-based model. The main features of AMuSE-WSD can be summarized as follows:

- We propose the first ready-to-use WSD package to offer a multilingual WSD system built on top of modern pretrained language models;
- AMuSE-WSD offers an easy-to-use REST API that can be queried either online for ease of use, or offline to minimize inference times;
- Our system comes with a Web interface to let users disambiguate short documents on the fly without a single line of code;
- We support 40 languages offline and 10 languages online.

We hope that AMuSE-WSD will facilitate the integration of semantic information into tasks that may benefit from high-quality sense information, enabling the exploitation of WSD in multiple languages.[1]

2 System Description

AMuSE-WSD is the first all-in-one multilingual system for WSD based on a state-of-the-art neural model. Our system encapsulates this model in a pipeline which provides word-level semantic information in an end-to-end fashion so that a user is not required to provide anything more than raw text as input. In this Section, we provide a description of the various components of our model, focusing on its preprocessing pipeline (Section 2.1) and our WSD system (Section 2.2), which is the core of AMuSE-WSD. Furthermore, we provide an overview of its performance on several standard benchmarks for WSD (Section 2.3).

2.1 Preprocessing

Preprocessing is one important aspect that is often overlooked by state-of-the-art models built for research purposes, as they often rely on pre-parsed documents that are already split into sentences, tokenized, lemmatized and PoS-tagged. However, a good preprocessing pipeline is a necessary condition for a high-quality WSD system. Indeed, the most popular sense inventories for WSD, e.g. WordNet (Miller, 1992) and BabelNet (Navigli and Ponzetto, 2012a; Navigli et al., 2021), define the possible meanings of a word with respect to its lemma and PoS tag. Therefore, an accurate preprocessing pipeline is fundamental in order to generate the correct candidate set of possible meanings.

AMuSE-WSD's preprocessing pipeline takes advantage of two popular toolkits, spaCy (Honnibal et al., 2020) and Stanza (Qi et al., 2020), to provide high-quality document splitting, tokenization, lemmatization and PoS tags to the core WSD model. We provide more technical details about the features of our preprocessing pipeline in Section 3.

2.2 Model Architecture

The core of AMuSE-WSD is its WSD model. Since the main objective of our system is to provide the best possible automatic annotations for WSD, our package features a reimplementation of the state-of-the-art WSD model proposed recently by Conia and Navigli (2021). Differently from other ready-to-use WSD packages which are based on graph-based heuristics (Moro et al., 2014; Scozzafava et al., 2020) or non-neural models (Papandrea et al., 2017), this neural architecture is built on top of a Transformer encoder (Vaswani et al., 2017). More specifically, given a word w in context, the WSD model i) builds a contextualized representation $\mathbf{e}_w \in \mathbb{R}^{d_L}$ of the word w as the average of the hidden states of the last four layers of a pretrained Transformer encoder L, ii) applies a non-linear transformation to obtain a sense-specific hidden representation $\mathbf{h}_w \in \mathbb{R}^{d_h}$, and finally iii) computes the output score distribution $\mathbf{o}_w \in \mathbb{R}^{|S|}$ over all the possible senses of a sense inventory S. More formally:

$$\begin{aligned}\mathbf{e}_w &= \mathrm{BatchNorm}\left(\frac{1}{4}\sum_{i=1}^{4}\mathbf{l}_w^{-k}\right)\\ \mathbf{h}_w &= \mathrm{Swish}(\mathbf{W}_h\mathbf{e}_w + \mathbf{b}_h)\\ \mathbf{o}_w &= \mathbf{W}_o\mathbf{h}_w + \mathbf{b}_o\end{aligned}$$

where $\mathbf{l}_w^{-k}$ is the hidden state of the k-th layer of L from its topmost layer, $\mathrm{BatchNorm}(\cdot)$ is the batch normalization operation, and $\mathrm{Swish}(x) = x \cdot \mathrm{sigmoid}(x)$ is the Swish activation function (Ramachandran et al., 2018).

We follow Conia and Navigli (2021) in framing WSD as a multi-label classification problem in

[1]AMuSE-WSD can be downloaded for offline use upon request at http://nlp.uniroma1.it/resources. It is licensed under Creative Commons Attribution-NonCommercial-ShareAlike 4.0 International.

		English datasets						Multilingual datasets		
		SE2	SE3	SE07	SE13	SE15	ALL	SE13	SE15	XL-WSD
WSD Modules	BERT-large	76.3	73.2	66.2	71.7	74.1	73.5	–	–	–
	Conia and Navigli (2020)	77.1	76.4	70.3	76.2	77.2	76.4	–	–	–
	Scarlini et al. (2020)	78.0	77.1	71.0	77.3	83.2	77.9	78.3	70.8	–
	Blevins and Zettlemoyer (2020)	79.4	77.4	74.5	79.7	81.7	79.0	–	–	–
	Bevilacqua and Navigli (2020)	80.8	79.0	75.2	80.7	81.8	80.1	80.3	70.7	–
	Conia and Navigli (2021)	80.4	77.8	76.2	81.8	83.3	80.2	–	–	–
End-to-End Systems	Moro et al. (2014)	67.0	63.5	51.6	66.4	70.3	65.5	65.6	–	52.9
	Papandrea et al. (2017)	73.8	70.8	64.2	67.2	71.5	–	–	–	–
	Scozzafava et al. (2020)	71.6	72.0	59.3	72.2	75.8	71.7	73.2	66.2	57.7
	AMuSE-WSD$_{\text{BERT-large}}$	**80.6**	**78.4**	**76.5**	**81.0**	82.7	**80.2**	–	–	–
	AMuSE-WSD$_{\text{XMLR-large}}$	79.5	77.6	74.1	79.9	**83.4**	79.3	**80.0**	**73.0**	**67.3**
	AMuSE-WSD$_{\text{XMLR-base}}$	77.8	76.0	72.1	77.7	81.5	77.5	76.8	73.0	66.2
	AMuSE-WSD$_{\text{m-MiniLM}}$	76.3	72.4	69.5	76.1	77.8	75.1	74.5	69.6	63.9

Table 1: English WSD results in F_1 scores on Senseval-2 (SE2), Senseval-3 (SE3), SemEval-2007 (SE07), SemEval-2013 (SE13), SemEval-2015 (SE15), and the concatenation of all the datasets (ALL). We also include results on multilingual WSD in SemEval-2013 (DE, ES, FR, IT), SemEval-2015 (IT, ES), and XL-WSD (average over 17 languages, English excluded). We distinguish between *WSD Modules*, that is, research systems that need to be inserted into a pipeline, and *End-to-End WSD Systems*. Best results among end-to-end systems in **bold**.

which the model can learn to assign multiple valid senses to each target word. Indeed, the "boundaries" between different senses of a polysemous word are not always clear cut or well defined (Erk and McCarthy, 2009), often leading to cases in which, given a word in context, more than one meaning is deemed appropriate by human annotators. Framing WSD as a multi-label classification problem allows the model to take advantage of such cases. In particular, this means that the model is trained to predict whether a sense $s \in S_w$ is appropriate for a word w in a given context, independently of the other senses in S_w.

2.3 Evaluation

Datasets. We compare the performance of our model against currently available end-to-end WSD systems on the unified evaluation framework for English all-words WSD proposed by Raganato et al. (2017). This evaluation includes five gold datasets, namely, Senseval-2 (Edmonds and Cotton, 2001), Senseval-3 (Mihalcea et al., 2004), SemEval-2007 (Agirre and Soroa, 2007), SemEval-2013 (Navigli et al., 2013), and SemEval-2015 (Moro and Navigli, 2015). We also evaluate our model in multilingual WSD using the French, German, Italian and Spanish datasets provided as part of SemEval-2013, and the Italian and Spanish datasets of SemEval-2015. Finally, we evaluate AMuSE-WSD on XL-WSD (Pasini et al., 2021), a new multilingual dataset which comprises 17 languages.

Experimental setup. We evaluate how the performance of AMuSE-WSD varies when using four different pretrained language models to represent input sentences: a high-performing English-only version based on BERT-large-cased (Devlin et al., 2019), a high-performing multilingual version based on XLM-RoBERTa-large (Conneau et al., 2020), a multilingual version that relies on the smaller XLM-RoBERTa-base to balance quality and inference time, and a multilingual version based on Multilingual-MiniLM (Wang et al., 2020) that minimizes inference time while still providing good results. In any case, the weights of the underlying language model are left frozen, that is, they are not updated during training. Each model is trained for 25 epochs using Adam (Kingma and Ba, 2015) with a learning rate of 10^{-4}. We train each model configuration on the union of SemCor (Miller et al., 1994) and the WordNet Gloss Corpus. Following standard practice, we perform model selection choosing the checkpoint with highest F1 score on SemEval-2007, the smallest evaluation dataset.

Results. Table 1 shows how AMuSE-WSD performs in comparison to currently available end-to-end WSD systems, that is, systems that only require raw text in input. AMuSE-WSD (XLMR-large) offers a very significant improvement over SyntagRank (Scozzafava et al., 2020), the previous best end-to-end system, both in English WSD (+7.6 in F_1 score on the concatenation of all the English test sets) and multilingual WSD (+6.8, +6.8 and +9.6 in F_1 score on SemEval-2013, SemEval-2015 and XL-WSD, respectively). It is worth noting that even the lightest – and therefore faster – configuration of AMuSE-WSD (m-MiniLM) still shows significant improvements over SyntagRank (+3.4 and +6.2 in F_1 score on ALL and XL-WSD, respectively). For completeness, Table 1 also reports the performance of recently proposed, non end-to-end modules for WSD.

3 AMuSE-WSD API

AMuSE-WSD can easily be used to integrate sense information into downstream tasks. Indeed, AMuSE-WSD is a simple solution for out-of-the-box sense disambiguation as it offers a RESTful API that provides access to a full end-to-end state-of-the-art pretrained model for multilingual WSD. The main advantage of our system is that it is fully self-contained as it takes care of the preprocessing information usually needed by a WSD system, namely, document splitting, tokenization, lemmatization and part-of-speech tagging (see Section 2.1). This means that AMuSE-WSD takes just raw text as input, freeing the user from the burden of having to compose complex preprocessing pipelines. Furthermore, our system is optimized to speed up inference, especially on CPU, which makes AMuSE-WSD accessible to a broader audience with smaller hardware budgets. Finally, the API is available both as a Web API, so as to obtain sense annotations without installing any software, and offline API, so that a user can host AMuSE-WSD locally and minimize inference times. In the following, we provide more details on the main set of functionalities offered by AMuSE-WSD.

Document-level preprocessing. The AMuSE-WSD API lets the user obtain disambiguated text for batches of sentences in a single query to the service, reducing the load on the network and the latency of the responses. On top of this, one common use case for end users is the disambiguation of long texts. In order to assist users in such cases, AMuSE-WSD supports the disambiguation of documents of arbitrary length, performing document splitting to enable faster inference by transparently batching text segments.

Sentence-level preprocessing. The only piece of information the end user needs to provide to AMuSE-WSD is raw text. Nonetheless, the underlying model needs lemmas and part-of-speech tags in order to select the proper sense for a word (see Section 2.1). To this end, AMuSE-WSD integrates a preprocessing pipeline, transparent to the user, that performs tokenization, lemmatization and part-of-speech tagging. In the search for the optimal compromise between latency and accuracy of the preprocessing, AMuSE-WSD employs two different preprocessing pipelines depending on the language of the input document, built around spaCy and Stanza. For each of the 40 supported languages, our system selects one of the preprocessing models available in either spaCy or Stanza, prioritizing the former for its high inference speed and falling back to Stanza for lower-resource languages where the performance of the former is suboptimal.

Usage. The AMuSE-WSD API exposes an endpoint named `/api/model`. The endpoint accepts `POST` requests with a `JSON` body, containing a list of documents. For each document, two parameters must be specified:

- `text`: the text of the document.
- `lang`: the language of the document.

Each request returns a `JSON` response containing a list of objects, one for each input document. Each object in the response provides the tokenization, lemmatization, PoS-tagging and sense information of the corresponding input document. The AMuSE-WSD API returns labels that are easily usable for users interested in WordNet, BabelNet and the NLTK WordNet API, making it simple to switch from one resource/tool to another. For example, the response to a request that contains only one sentence will have the following structure:

```
[{
    "tokens": [
        ...
        {
            "index": 5,
            "text": "river",
            "pos": "NOUN",
            "lemma": "river",
            "bnSynsetId": "bn:00067948n",
            "wnSynsetOffset": "9411430n",
            "nltkSynset": "river.n.01"
        },
        ...
    ]
}]
```

We refer to the online documentation for more details, including the full list of supported languages.[2]

3.1 Offline API

To further promote the integration of WSD into large-scale applications, AMuSE-WSD is also distributed as a Docker[3] image that can be deployed locally on the user's own hardware. We provide several ready-to-use images suitable for different configurations and use cases, depending on whether a user is constrained by hardware requirements or prefers the highest quality over shorter inference times. The images are differentiated based on their size in parameters and on the hardware they are optimized for, that is, CPU or GPU. In the following, we provide more details on the Docker images.

Model configurations. With AMuSE-WSD, an end user can choose between four different types of pre-built Docker images which differ in the pretrained language model used to compute contextualized word representations:

- `amuse-large` uses BERT-large and provides state-of-the-art results in English WSD.
- `amuse-large-multilingual` employs XLM-RoBERTa-large and thus offers the best results in multilingual WSD. However, it is also the most demanding in terms of hardware requirements.
- `amuse-medium-multilingual` adopts XLM-RoBERTa-base which provides outputs that in 98% of cases are the same as those of its larger counterpart, but taking half the time.
- `amuse-small-multilingual` uses the multilingual version of MiniLM, a language model distilled from XLM-RoBERTa-base. It is three times faster and three times smaller, while still achieving remarkable results.

Inference times. In order to further promote its accessibility, AMuSE-WSD is also available in Docker images optimized to run on CPU thanks to ONNX. The ONNX Runtime[4] is an engine built with the aim of significantly improving inference times while, at the same time, reducing system footprint. With ONNX, our system is up to 2.5 times faster on CPU while also being 1.2 times smaller compared to its vanilla PyTorch implementation. We evaluate the inference speed of AMuSE-WSD on two sets of documents: the concatenation of all the sentences of the unified evaluation framework for WSD by Raganato et al. (2017) and a set of 300 documents whose lengths range from 1500 to 3500 characters. Table 2 compares the inference times of our system in several configurations, showing the gains of ONNX on CPU.

AMUSE-WSD			**ALL**		**Long**	
CONFIGURATIONS			Δ (ms)	$\uparrow$	Δ (ms)	$\uparrow$
English	large	PLAIN	163	1.0×	1610	1.0×
	large	ONNX	93	1.7×	1230	1.3×
	large	CUDA	12	13.6×	170	9.5×
Multilingual	large	PLAIN	190	1.0×	2940	1.0×
	large	ONNX	128	1.5×	2170	1.3×
	large	CUDA	13	14.6×	180	16.3×
	medium	PLAIN	136	1.0×	1050	1.0×
	medium	ONNX	61	2.2×	880	1.2×
	medium	CUDA	11	12.4×	150	7.0×
	small	PLAIN	96	1.0×	600	1.0×
	small	ONNX	39	2.5×	460	1.3×
	small	CUDA	9	10.7×	90	6.7×

Table 2: Inference time for several configurations over two sets of documents: the concatenation of all the test sets of the unified evaluation framework for WSD (**ALL**), and a set of 300 documents whose lengths are between 1500 and 3500 characters (**Long**). Δ: latency or median time in milliseconds AMuSE-WSD takes to serve one inference request. $\uparrow$: Inference speed-up provided by the ONNX and CUDA implementations over vanilla PyTorch.

4 Web Interface

AMuSE-WSD comes with a Web interface which allows users to disambiguate text on the fly without having to write a single line of code. Figure 1 shows the home page of AMuSE-WSD in which a user can type a short text (up to 3000 characters) and indicate the language of the inserted text. Figure 2 shows, instead, how the Web interface displays the senses for the input sentence *"the quick brown fox jumps over the lazy dog"*, while Figures 3 and 4 show a correctly disambiguated word, that is, *bank*, which is ambiguous both in English and Italian. For each content word (nouns, adjectives, adverbs and verbs), the interface shows the corresponding sense predicted by the underlying WSD model, including its definition from WordNet and an image, if available. Each meaning is linked

[2] `http://nlp.uniroma1.it/amuse-wsd/api-documentation`

[3] `https://www.docker.com`

[4] `https://www.onnxruntime.ai`

Figure 1: The home page of the Web interface of AMuSE-WSD. Users can write (or paste) text in the text area. The dropdown menu allows users to select the language of the input text from among the 10 available in the online interface.

to its corresponding Web page in BabelNet 5,[5] a multilingual encyclopedic dictionary that includes WordNet, Open Multilingual WordNet, Wikipedia, Wikidata and Wiktionary, *inter alia*. Users can click on a meaning to obtain further information about it, ranging from other definitions to its translation in other languages, from its hypernyms (generalizations) to its hyponyms (specializations).

We believe that this interface will be especially useful for researchers, teachers, students and curious people who may be interested in understanding how WSD can be taken advantage of in other fields. Moreover, we also believe that an easy-to-use interface will attract the attention of more researchers on the task of WSD itself, encouraging future developments in this area.

5 Conclusion

Over the past few years, WSD has witnessed an increasing rate of development, especially thanks to the renewed interest in neural networks and the advent of modern pretrained language models. However, research implementations are often far from being ready-to-use as they either take as input pre-parsed documents or require setting up a preprocessing pipeline to take care, at least, of document splitting, tokenization, lemmatization and PoS tagging. Unfortunately, currently available ready-to-use WSD systems now lag behind the state of the art and offer solutions based on non-neural approaches.

In this paper, we addressed this issue and presented AMuSE-WSD, an All-in-one Multilingual System for Easy Word Sense Disambiguation. To the best of our knowledge, AMuSE-WSD is the first system for end-to-end WSD to encapsulate a state-of-the-art neural model for sense disambiguation in multiple languages. Our system makes it easy to obtain and use word-level semantic information about word meanings through a RESTful API. This API is available both online, that is, a user can disambiguate text through HTTP requests to our server, and offline, that is, a user can download prepackaged Docker images and run them locally to minimize inference times on large bulks of documents. We provide different configurations to satisfy different needs, from images that are optimized to run on constrained hardware to high-performing

[5] https://babelnet.org

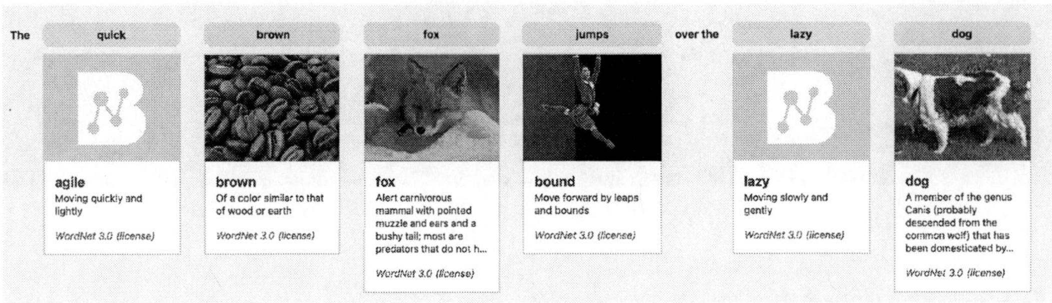

Figure 2: Overview of the Web interface of AMuSE-WSD. The WSD model tags each content word with a WordNet sense, its definition and an image, if available. Each sense is linked to BabelNet which provides more information about senses, from their translation into other languages to their related meanings.

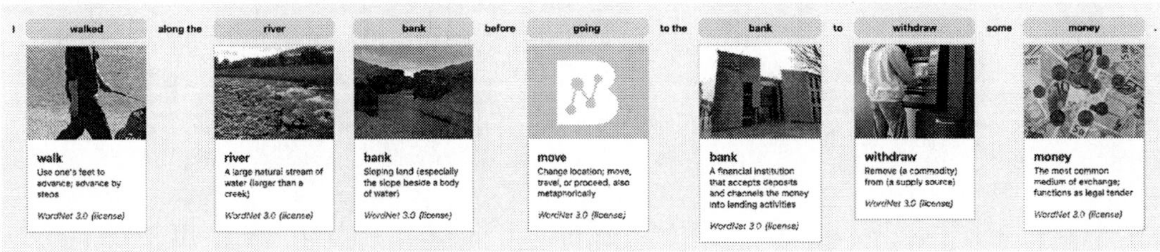

Figure 3: An example in which AMuSE-WSD correctly distinguishes between two different senses of the word *bank* (its geographical and financial senses).

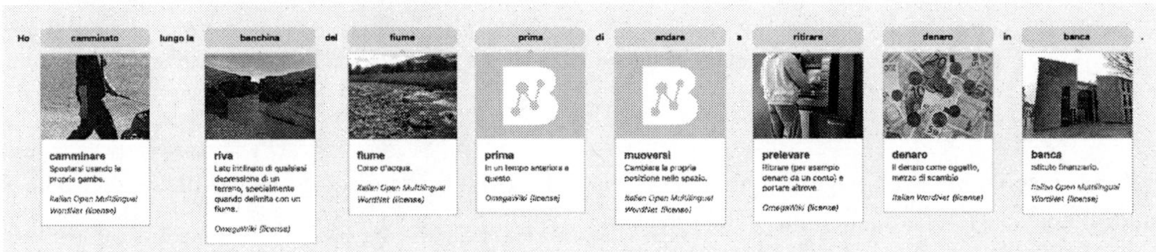

Figure 4: The output of AMuSE-WSD for the Italian translation of the sentence shown in Figure 3.

images. Last but not least, AMuSE-WSD comes with an intuitive Web interface that lets users disambiguate short documents on the fly without writing a single line of code. Not only does this interface showcase the capabilities of our system, but we also hope it will attract the interest of new researchers to the field of lexical semantics.

Acknowledgments

The authors gratefully acknowledge the support of the ERC Consolidator Grant MOUSSE No. 726487 and the European Language Grid project No. 825627 (Universal Semantic Annotator, USeA) under the European Union's Horizon 2020 research and innovation programme.

References

Eneko Agirre, Oier López de Lacalle, and Aitor Soroa. 2014. Random walks for Knowledge-Based Word Sense Disambiguation. *Computational Linguistics*, 40(1):57–84.

Eneko Agirre and Aitor Soroa. 2007. SemEval-2007 task 02: Evaluating Word Sense Induction and Discrimination Systems. In *Proceedings of the Fourth International Workshop on Semantic Evaluations (SemEval-2007)*, pages 7–12, Prague, Czech Republic.

Edoardo Barba, Luigi Procopio, and Roberto Navigli. 2021. ConSeC: Word Sense Disambiguation as Continuous Sense Comprehension. In *Proceedings of the 2021 Conference on Empirical Methods in Natural Language Processing (EMNLP)*, Punta Cana, Dominican Republic.

Michele Bevilacqua and Roberto Navigli. 2020. Breaking through the 80% glass ceiling: Raising the state of the art in Word Sense Disambiguation by incorporating knowledge graph information. In *Pro-*

ceedings of the 58th Annual Meeting of the Association for Computational Linguistics, pages 2854–2864, Online.

Michele Bevilacqua, Tommaso Pasini, Alessandro Raganato, and Roberto Navigli. 2021. Recent trends in Word Sense Disambiguation: A survey. In *Proceedings of the Thirtieth International Joint Conference on Artificial Intelligence, IJCAI-21*, pages 4330–4338. Survey Track.

Terra Blevins and Luke Zettlemoyer. 2020. Moving down the long tail of Word Sense Disambiguation with gloss informed bi-encoders. In *Proceedings of the 58th Annual Meeting of the Association for Computational Linguistics*, pages 1006–1017, Online.

Rexhina Blloshmi, Tommaso Pasini, Niccolò Campolungo, Somnath Banarjee, Roberto Navigli, and Gabriella Pasi. 2021. IR like a SIR: Sense-enhanced Information Retrieval for Multiple Languages. In *Proceedings of the 2021 Conference on Empirical Methods in Natural Language Processing (EMNLP)*, Punta Cana, Dominican Republic.

Devendra Singh Chaplot and Ruslan Salakhutdinov. 2018. Knowledge-Based Word Sense Disambiguation using topic models. In *Proceedings of the Thirty-Second AAAI Conference on Artificial Intelligence, (AAAI-18), the 30th innovative Applications of Artificial Intelligence (IAAI-18), and the 8th AAAI Symposium on Educational Advances in Artificial Intelligence (EAAI-18), New Orleans, Louisiana, USA, February 2-7, 2018*, pages 5062–5069.

Simone Conia and Roberto Navigli. 2020. Conception: Multilingually-enhanced, human-readable concept vector representations. In *Proceedings of the 28th International Conference on Computational Linguistics*, pages 3268–3284, Barcelona, Spain (Online).

Simone Conia and Roberto Navigli. 2021. Framing Word Sense Disambiguation as a multi-label problem for model-agnostic knowledge integration. In *Proceedings of the 16th Conference of the European Chapter of the Association for Computational Linguistics: Main Volume*, pages 3269–3275, Online.

Alexis Conneau, Kartikay Khandelwal, Naman Goyal, Vishrav Chaudhary, Guillaume Wenzek, Francisco Guzmán, Edouard Grave, Myle Ott, Luke Zettlemoyer, and Veselin Stoyanov. 2020. Unsupervised cross-lingual representation learning at scale. In *Proceedings of the 58th Annual Meeting of the Association for Computational Linguistics*, pages 8440–8451, Online.

Claudio Delli Bovi, Luca Telesca, and Roberto Navigli. 2015. Large-scale Information Extraction from textual definitions through deep syntactic and semantic analysis. *Transactions of the Association for Computational Linguistics*, 3:529–543.

Jacob Devlin, Ming-Wei Chang, Kenton Lee, and Kristina Toutanova. 2019. BERT: Pre-training of Deep Bidirectional Transformers for Language Understanding. In *Proceedings of the 2019 Conference of the North American Chapter of the Association for Computational Linguistics: Human Language Technologies, Volume 1 (Long and Short Papers)*, pages 4171–4186, Minneapolis, Minnesota.

Philip Edmonds and Scott Cotton. 2001. SENSEVAL-2: Overview. In *Proceedings of SENSEVAL-2 Second International Workshop on Evaluating Word Sense Disambiguation Systems*, pages 1–5, Toulouse, France.

Ahmed ElSheikh, Michele Bevilacqua, and Roberto Navigli. 2021. Integrating personalized PageRank into neural Word Sense Disambiguation. In *Proceedings of the 2021 Conference on Empirical Methods in Natural Language Processing (EMNLP)*, Punta Cana, Dominican Republic.

Katrin Erk and Diana McCarthy. 2009. Graded Word Sense Assignment. In *Proceedings of the 2009 Conference on Empirical Methods in Natural Language Processing*, pages 440–449, Singapore.

Matthew Honnibal, Ines Montani, Sofie Van Landeghem, and Adriane Boyd. 2020. spaCy: Industrial-strength Natural Language Processing in Python.

Diederik P. Kingma and Jimmy Ba. 2015. Adam: A method for stochastic optimization. In *3rd International Conference on Learning Representations, ICLR 2015, San Diego, CA, USA, May 7-9, 2015, Conference Track Proceedings*.

Frederick Liu, Han Lu, and Graham Neubig. 2018. Handling homographs in Neural Machine Translation. In *Proceedings of the 2018 Conference of the North American Chapter of the Association for Computational Linguistics: Human Language Technologies, Volume 1 (Long Papers)*, pages 1336–1345, New Orleans, Louisiana.

Rada Mihalcea, Timothy Chklovski, and Adam Kilgarriff. 2004. The senseval-3 English lexical sample task. In *Proceedings of SENSEVAL-3, the Third International Workshop on the Evaluation of Systems for the Semantic Analysis of Text*, pages 25–28, Barcelona, Spain.

George A. Miller. 1992. WordNet: A lexical database for English. In *Speech and Natural Language: Proceedings of a Workshop Held at Harriman, New York, February 23-26, 1992*.

George A. Miller, Martin Chodorow, Shari Landes, Claudia Leacock, and Robert G. Thomas. 1994. Using a semantic concordance for sense identification. In *Human Language Technology: Proceedings of a Workshop held at Plainsboro, New Jersey, March 8-11, 1994*.

Andrea Moro and Roberto Navigli. 2015. SemEval-2015 task 13: Multilingual All-Words Sense Disambiguation and Entity Linking. In *Proceedings of the*

9th International Workshop on Semantic Evaluation (SemEval 2015), pages 288–297, Denver, Colorado.

Andrea Moro, Alessandro Raganato, and Roberto Navigli. 2014. Entity Linking meets Word Sense Disambiguation: A unified approach. *Transactions of the Association for Computational Linguistics*, 2:231–244.

Roberto Navigli. 2009. Word Sense Disambiguation: A survey. *ACM Comput. Surv.*, 41(2).

Roberto Navigli. 2018. Natural Language Understanding: Instructions for (present and future) use. In *Proceedings of the Twenty-Seventh International Joint Conference on Artificial Intelligence, IJCAI 2018, July 13-19, 2018, Stockholm, Sweden*, pages 5697–5702.

Roberto Navigli, Michele Bevilacqua, Simone Conia, Dario Montagnini, and Francesco Cecconi. 2021. Ten years of BabelNet: A survey. In *Proceedings of the Thirtieth International Joint Conference on Artificial Intelligence, IJCAI-21*, pages 4559–4567. Survey Track.

Roberto Navigli, David Jurgens, and Daniele Vannella. 2013. SemEval-2013 task 12: Multilingual Word Sense Disambiguation. In *Second Joint Conference on Lexical and Computational Semantics (*SEM), Volume 2: Proceedings of the Seventh International Workshop on Semantic Evaluation (SemEval 2013)*, pages 222–231, Atlanta, Georgia, USA.

Roberto Navigli and Simone Paolo Ponzetto. 2012a. BabelNet: The automatic construction, evaluation and application of a wide-coverage multilingual semantic network. *Artif. Intell.*, 193:217–250.

Roberto Navigli and Simone Paolo Ponzetto. 2012b. Multilingual WSD with just a few lines of code: the BabelNet API. In *Proceedings of the ACL 2012 System Demonstrations*, pages 67–72, Jeju Island, Korea. Association for Computational Linguistics.

Simone Papandrea, Alessandro Raganato, and Claudio Delli Bovi. 2017. SupWSD: A flexible toolkit for supervised Word Sense Disambiguation. In *Proceedings of the 2017 Conference on Empirical Methods in Natural Language Processing: System Demonstrations*, pages 103–108, Copenhagen, Denmark.

Tommaso Pasini, Alessandro Raganato, and Roberto Navigli. 2021. XL-WSD: An extra-large and cross-lingual evaluation framework for Word Sense Disambiguation. *Proceedings of the AAAI Conference on Artificial Intelligence*, 35(15):13648–13656.

Xiao Pu, Nikolaos Pappas, James Henderson, and Andrei Popescu-Belis. 2018. Integrating weakly supervised Word Sense Disambiguation into Neural Machine Translation. *Transactions of the Association for Computational Linguistics*, 6:635–649.

Peng Qi, Yuhao Zhang, Yuhui Zhang, Jason Bolton, and Christopher D. Manning. 2020. Stanza: A python natural language processing toolkit for many human languages. In *Proceedings of the 58th Annual Meeting of the Association for Computational Linguistics: System Demonstrations*, pages 101–108, Online.

Alessandro Raganato, Jose Camacho-Collados, and Roberto Navigli. 2017. Word Sense Disambiguation: A unified evaluation framework and empirical comparison. In *Proceedings of the 15th Conference of the European Chapter of the Association for Computational Linguistics: Volume 1, Long Papers*, pages 99–110, Valencia, Spain.

Alessandro Raganato, Yves Scherrer, and Jörg Tiedemann. 2019. The MuCoW test suite at WMT 2019: Automatically harvested multilingual contrastive Word Sense Disambiguation test sets for machine translation. In *Proceedings of the Fourth Conference on Machine Translation (Volume 2: Shared Task Papers, Day 1)*, pages 470–480, Florence, Italy.

Prajit Ramachandran, Barret Zoph, and Quoc V. Le. 2018. Searching for activation functions. In *6th International Conference on Learning Representations, ICLR 2018, Vancouver, BC, Canada, April 30 - May 3, 2018, Workshop Track Proceedings*.

Ganesh Ramakrishnan, Apurva Jadhav, Ashutosh Joshi, Soumen Chakrabarti, and Pushpak Bhattacharyya. 2003. Question Answering via Bayesian inference on lexical relations. In *Proceedings of the ACL 2003 Workshop on Multilingual Summarization and Question Answering*, pages 1–10, Sapporo, Japan.

Bianca Scarlini, Tommaso Pasini, and Roberto Navigli. 2020. With more contexts comes better performance: Contextualized Sense Embeddings for all-round Word Sense Disambiguation. In *Proceedings of the 2020 Conference on Empirical Methods in Natural Language Processing (EMNLP)*, pages 3528–3539, Online.

Federico Scozzafava, Marco Maru, Fabrizio Brignone, Giovanni Torrisi, and Roberto Navigli. 2020. Personalized PageRank with syntagmatic information for multilingual Word Sense Disambiguation. In *Proceedings of the 58th Annual Meeting of the Association for Computational Linguistics: System Demonstrations*, pages 37–46, Online.

Kazuya Shimura, Jiyi Li, and Fumiyo Fukumoto. 2019. Text Categorization by learning predominant sense of words as auxiliary task. In *Proceedings of the 57th Annual Meeting of the Association for Computational Linguistics*, pages 1109–1119, Florence, Italy.

Ashish Vaswani, Noam Shazeer, Niki Parmar, Jakob Uszkoreit, Llion Jones, Aidan N. Gomez, Lukasz Kaiser, and Illia Polosukhin. 2017. Attention is all you need. In *Advances in Neural Information Processing Systems 30: Annual Conference on Neural*

Information Processing Systems 2017, December 4-9, 2017, Long Beach, CA, USA, pages 5998–6008.

Wenhui Wang, Furu Wei, Li Dong, Hangbo Bao, Nan Yang, and Ming Zhou. 2020. Minilm: Deep self-attention distillation for task-agnostic compression of pre-trained transformers. In *Advances in Neural Information Processing Systems 33: Annual Conference on Neural Information Processing Systems 2020, NeurIPS 2020, December 6-12, 2020, virtual.*

Zhi Zhong and Hwee Tou Ng. 2012. Word Sense Disambiguation improves Information Retrieval. In *Proceedings of the 50th Annual Meeting of the Association for Computational Linguistics (Volume 1: Long Papers)*, pages 273–282, Jeju Island, Korea.

SeqAttack: On Adversarial Attacks for Named Entity Recognition

Walter Simoncini and **Gerasimos Spanakis**
Maastricht University
{w.simoncini@student., jerry.spanakis@}maastrichtuniversity.nl

Abstract

Named Entity Recognition is a fundamental task in information extraction and is an essential element for various Natural Language Processing pipelines. Adversarial attacks have been shown to greatly affect the performance of text classification systems but knowledge about their effectiveness against named entity recognition models is limited. This paper investigates the effectiveness and portability of adversarial attacks from text classification to named entity recognition and the ability of adversarial training to counteract these attacks. We find that character-level and word-level attacks are the most effective, but adversarial training can grant significant protection at little to no expense of standard performance. Alongside our results, we also release SeqAttack, a framework to conduct adversarial attacks against token classification models (used in this work for named entity recognition) and a companion web application to inspect and cherry pick adversarial examples.

1 Introduction

Named Entity Recognition (NER) is the task of recognizing named entities in a chunk of text. Named entities are words (one or more) belonging to a particular semantic category, such as location, person or organization. NER is used both as a standalone tool and as an essential component in several Natural Language Processing (NLP) pipelines, such as Information Retrieval (Petkova and Croft, 2007) and Machine Translation (Babych and Hartley, 2003). Traditionally, NER has been attempted with rule-based approaches, Hidden Markov Models and Conditional Random Fields (Li et al., 2020a). In recent years, deep learning has outperformed these methods (Li et al., 2017) (Liu et al., 2019a), especially with the introduction of general-purpose language models such as BERT (Devlin et al., 2019).

Neural networks are vulnerable to adversarial attacks, which can be defined as processes that craft incorrectly-predicted samples from correctly-predicted inputs by applying small perturbations, an example of which can be seen in Figure 1. This shows that deep learning models are fragile and might not be ready for deployment in a critical scenario. The most popular technique to overcome this issue is adversarial training, which uses adversarial attacks to craft additional training samples and retrains the model from scratch (Li et al., 2020b) (Li et al., 2021). Adversarial attacks and training were largely explored with regards to text classification, but current research on NER has only explored attacks based on adversarial typos (Araujo et al., 2020) and the effectiveness of more complex attacks (at the word and sentence levels) is unknown. Word-level attacks are particularly important because they generate adversarial examples highly likely to appear in the real world, providing valuable additional training data (an example can be seen in Figure 1). This paper aims to tackle this problem by investigating the following research questions:

- **RQ1**: How robust are named entity recognition models against adversarial attacks at the character, word and sentence level? In particular, this paper focuses on a $\text{BERT}_{\text{base}}$ cased model trained on CoNLL2003 (Tjong Kim Sang and De Meulder, 2003) in order to maintain consistency across the paper.

Figure 1: Word-level adversarial example for NER from CoNLL2003 (Tjong Kim Sang and De Meulder, 2003). Changing *standings* to *ranking* induces an incorrect classification of *Super G* as a non-entity.

Proceedings of the 2021 Conference on Empirical Methods in Natural Language Processing: System Demonstrations, pages 308–318
November 7–11, 2021. ©2021 Association for Computational Linguistics

- **RQ2**: How do word and character level adversarial training affect a named entity recognition model's robustness?

2 Related Work

2.1 Adversarial attacks

Several attack strategies are available to fool text classification models. In this paper, we follow the taxonomy by (Yuan et al., 2019), focusing on the properties in the list below, with the addition of granularity (Zhang et al., 2020):

- **Model knowledge:** if all the model information is known, attacks are defined as *white box*. *Black box* attacks instead have access only to the confidence scores. This paper focuses on *black box* attacks.

- **Specificity:** attacks which aim to change the model's prediction to a specific class are called *targeted*, whereas *untargeted attacks* consider any incorrect prediction valid.

- **Granularity:** adversarial examples can be crafted by applying perturbations at the character (e.g. swap, insertion), word (e.g. word replacement, insertion) or sentence level (e.g. paraphrasing).

Some popular attack strategies organized by *granularity* are presented below.

2.2 Attack strategies

At the **character-level** DeepWordBug (Gao et al., 2018) generates at each step candidate adversaries by swapping adjacent characters, substituting a character with a random one, deleting or inserting a character. At the **word-level** TextFooler (Jin et al., 2020) ranks the words in a sample by prediction relevance and replaces the most important ones using a word embedding optimized for synonyms (Mrkšić et al., 2016). BERT-Attack (Li et al., 2020b) and CLARE (Li et al., 2021) operate similarly, but they respectively use BERT and DistillRoBERTa (Sanh et al., 2019) (Liu et al., 2019b) as language models to suggest potential candidates. CLARE supports token replacements, insertions, and merges. Meanwhile, BERT-Attack and TextFooler only support token replacements. All word-level attacks enforce a semantic similarity constraint using the Universal Sentence Encoder (Cer et al., 2018). Finally, at the **sentence-level**, SCPN (Iyyer et al., 2018) generates paraphrases that match one of its built-in syntactic forms.

In comparison to text classification, to the authors' knowledge, adversarial attacks (and training) for NER only appears in two work (Araujo et al., 2020) and (Wang et al., 2020). The former tackles biomedical NER, showing that BERT-based models are susceptible to character swaps, keyboard typo noise and synonym-based entity-word substitutions. The latter integrates adversarial training in the train loop of an LSTM-CNN: at each training step adversarial examples are obtained by perturbing the word embeddings directly. This paper contributes by evaluating a larger number of attack strategies and the portability of adversarial attacks for text classification to token classification problems. Moreover, we provide new insights and a comparison of the samples generated by the different attack strategies.

2.3 Adversarial training

Adversarial training aims to improve a model's robustness using adversarial examples. This task can be achieved mainly in two ways: via data augmentation and by integrating adversarial training within the model train loop.

The first method attacks the victim model using the training set as the attack input and, once obtained enough samples, retrains the model from scratch. One of the first work to use this technique is (Alzantot et al., 2018), in which the authors adversarially train a sentiment classification model on the IMDB dataset without success. Later work, such as (Li et al., 2020b) and (Li et al., 2021) show more interesting results: the former uses adversarial training to make a natural language inference model more robust, gaining 15% after-attack accuracy at the expense of a minimal test accuracy loss. The latter adversarially trains BERT and TextCNN models on the AG news dataset obtaining similar improvements: without loss of test accuracy the authors manage to reduce the attack rate by 12.3% and 3.5% for BERT and TextCNN respectively. The second method is used by (Wang et al., 2020), where adversarial training is integrated in the training loop using a loss function that takes into account adversarial perturbations. Using this technique, the authors improve the model's generalizability by reducing overfitting.

3 The SeqAttack framework

The most popular frameworks for conducting adversarial attacks are `TextAttack` (Morris et al., 2020) and `OpenAttack` (Zeng et al., 2021), but they do not support token classification problems such as named entity recognition, in which each token is either classified as being the beginning of (B), inside (I) or outside an entity (O) according to the inside-outside-beginning (IOB) schema (Ramshaw and Marcus, 1995). In order to attack NER models we developed `SeqAttack`, a framework for conducting adversarial attacks against token classification models. The framework extends `TextAttack` and inherits its design, where attacks are composed of a goal function (the objective to optimize), transformations (how the input text is perturbed), constraints which limit the candidate perturbations and a search method. The framework can be used by NLP practitioners to attack models, for data augmentation and to quickly prototype attack strategies. Inheriting the structure of `TextAttack` also means that its attack strategies can be easily ported and used against NER models. In `TextAttack`, every attack optimizes a goal function, which in the case of text classification is defined as $1 - p_{\hat{y}}$. Where $\hat{y}$ is the ground truth and $p_{\hat{y}}$ is the normalized confidence score for the ground truth. In `SeqAttack`, in order to support NER, the goal function is reformulated as follows:

$$y_{\text{adv}} = \frac{\sum_{i=0}^{N} \text{goal}(y_i, \hat{y_i})}{\text{countEntities}(x)}$$

$$\text{goal}(y, \hat{y}) = \begin{cases} 0 & \text{if } \hat{y} = 0 \\ 1 - p_{\hat{y}} & \text{if } \hat{y} \neq 0 \land \hat{y} = y \\ 1 & \text{if } \hat{y} \neq 0 \land \hat{y} \neq y \end{cases}$$

Where y is the model prediction, N the number of tokens in the sample and x the attacked sample. countEntities(x) returns the number of entity tokens in a sample. We call this function the **untargeted NER** goal function. goal$(y, \hat{y})$ considers valid any incorrect classification of an entity token. It's important to note that this function assigns no score to newly introduced entities. This is due to the fact that the CoNLL2003 metrics consider only the classification of ground truth named entities. We also define the **untargeted-strict NER** goal function, which assigns no score to flips between I-CLS and B-CLS. Figure 3 highlights the difference between the two goal functions.

3.1 Adversarial attacks

This paper employs attack strategies implemented in `TextAttack` that proved to be successful for text classification to attack NER models with minor adaptations. In particular the following modifications were applied:

3.1.1 DeepWordBug

We use two different versions of this attack strategy: **DeepWordBug-I**, true to the original implementation and **DeepWordBug-II**, which is not allowed to modify named entities. Both attacks have a Levenshtein distance constraint, whose maximum allowed distance is specified with a subscript, as in DeepWordBug-I_5.

3.1.2 BERT-Attack

The sentence similarity constraint was set to 0.4 and the replacement of numeric tokens with alphanumeric ones was forbidden (i.e. "4" cannot be replaced by "car"). Only non-entity tokens are allowed to be replaced (to avoid the generation of trivial examples, e.g. swapping a location with a person's name) and candidate replacements which are named entities are also rejected (e.g. the candidate replacement "Amsterdam" will be rejected). The attack can perturb up to 40% of the words in a sample.

3.1.3 CLARE

The implementation of CLARE used in this paper only supports replacements and insertions. Similarly to BERT-Attack, the replacement of entity tokens is forbidden and candidate replacements which are named entities are rejected. When a new token is inserted, it is automatically labelled as being outside an entity (O). If a token insertion splits a named entity the beginning/inside labels will be adjusted accordingly.

3.1.4 SCPN

Using the `OpenAttack` implementation, the algorithm iteratively generates candidate paraphrases, using the original sample or a paraphrase as the starting point. The candidates are processed to remove identical consecutive unigrams and bigrams, and only the candidates which preserve at least one named entity are kept. Every token which is not an entity in the original sample is labelled as being outside an entity (O). An example can be seen in Figure 2.

Figure 2: A paraphrase generated by SCPN (bottom) and its original counterpart (top). Named entities in the paraphrase were re-labelled with the corresponding ground truth and the other tokens were labelled as non-entities. Original sample from CoNLL2003 (Tjong Kim Sang and De Meulder, 2003).

Figure 3: Changing two numbers causes *Caen*'s label to flip from B-ORG to I-ORG. The untargeted goal function would consider *Caen* to be an incorrect classification (and thus a success) meanwhile the untargeted-strict goal function would not. Example from CoNLL2003 (Tjong Kim Sang and De Meulder, 2003).

3.2 Adversarial training

This paper approaches adversarial training using the training dataset augmentation strategy: we attack the model using its training set as the input, generating at most one adversarial example per train sample, and we retrain the model with the augmented dataset. DeepWordBug-I_5 and BERT-Attack were chosen as the attack strategies so as to investigate the different effect of word-level and character-level adversarial training.

4 Experiments

4.1 Adversarial attacks

The attack techniques in section 3 were evaluated on a $\text{BERT}_{\text{base}}$ cased model (Devlin et al., 2019), fine tuned on the CoNLL2003 dataset for three epochs using the `transformers` library (Wolf et al., 2020). All attacks use the **untargeted-strict** goal function and target a subset of 256 samples from the test set, selected such that the model incorrectly predicts up to 10% of the entities contained in each sample. For each sample, the attack is allowed up to 120 seconds and a maximum of 512 model invocations (queries).

4.1.1 Evaluation metrics

The attacks are evaluated following previous work (Li et al., 2021), (Jin et al., 2020), (Morris et al., 2020), which employ the following automated metrics (in addition to accuracy, recall and F1 score as in the CoNLL2003 task):

- **Attack Rate (A-Rate)**: percentage of adversarial examples that can fool the model. An adversarial example is considered successful when at least one entity is incorrectly classified.
- **Modification Rate (Mod)**: percentage of modified tokens. Insert operations increase by one the modified tokens count (Li et al., 2021).
- **Δ Grammar Errors (ΔGErr)**: difference in the number of grammar errors between the adversarial example and its original counterpart, calculated with LanguageTool (Naber et al., 2003).
- **Textual similarity (Sim)**: cosine similarity between the adversarial example and the original input calculated via the Universal Sentence Encoder.

We also define the **Labels Score** (L-Score) metric as the percentage of incorrectly classified entities in a sample. All metrics defined above are averaged over the successful samples (with the exception of the attack rate). Table 1 lists the metrics for the original and attacked datasets.

4.2 Adversarial training

Table 1 shows that our victim model is vulnerable to adversarial attacks, which raises the question: is it possible to exploit attacks to make the model more robust while maintaining a reasonable performance on standard data? And what is the difference in model performance between models adversarially trained with word-level and character-level adversarial examples, both in normal conditions and when under attack?

To answer this question we trained a $\text{BERT}_{\text{base}}$ cased model, named $\text{NER}_{\text{small}}$, on $1/3$ of the CoNLL2003 dataset, equivalent to 5000 examples. A smaller dataset simulates a low-resource scenario

Attack	Acc	Recall	F1	A-Rate ↑	Mod ↓	L-Score ↑	Sim ↑	ΔGErr ↓
Bert-Attack	72%	88%	79%	44%	22%	20%	84%	0.26
CLARE	78%	81%	79%	37%	70%	56%	86%	0.33
DeepWordBug-II$_5$	86%	92%	89%	27%	18%	24%	86%	1.6
DeepWordBug-II$_{30}$	82%	93%	87%	30%	21%	23%	83%	3.05
DeepWordBug-I$_5$	48%	49%	49%	78%	24%	64%	77%	1.4
SCPN	90%	92%	91%	18%	66%	58%	59%	0.92
Original	98%	99%	98%					

Table 1: Comparison of attack strategies on the CoNLL2003 test set using the **untargeted strict** goal function. The metrics were calculated using `seqeval` (Nakayama, 2018). ↑ (↓) indicate whether the higher (or lower) the better from the attack perspective.

Model	Acc	Recall	F1	A-Rate ↑	Mod ↓	L-Score ↑	Sim ↑	ΔGErr ↓
NER$_{small}$ 500	73%	71%	72%	84%	26%	71%	73%	1.5
NER$_{small}$ 1000	78%	77%	77%	82%	27%	70%	73%	1.54
NER$_{small}$ 1500	77%	77%	77%	84%	26%	68%	73%	1.47
NER$_{small}$ 2000	79%	79%	79%	82%	28%	67%	72%	1.48
NER$_{small}$ (baseline)	52%	50%	51%	89%	24%	78%	75%	3.83

Table 2: Comparison of CoNLL2003 models against DeepWordBug-I$_5$, trained using a different amount of adversarial examples generated by DeepWordBug (specified next to the model) and the **untargeted** goal function. The attack had up to 45 seconds to successfully attack an input sample. ↑ (↓) indicate whether the higher (or lower) the better from the attack perspective.

and highlights the differences between the two adversarial training strategies. The model achieves a reasonable performance on the test set (Table 4, last row) but it can be fooled by both DeepWordBug-I$_5$ (Table 2) and BERT-Attack (Table 3). The adversarial data augmentation was done by attacking NER$_{small}$ using its own training set as the attack input. We respectively generated 2000 and 1000 adversarial examples for DeepWordBug-I$_5$ and BERT-Attack, which were then used to train robust models, whose performance on CoNLL2003 is listed in Tables 4 and 5.

4.2.1 Model evaluation

To evaluate the effectiveness of adversarial training we ran the same attacks against NER$_{small}$ and its robust counterparts, using the same CoNLL2003 subset used for evaluating attack strategies. Both attack strategies were allowed up to 512 model invocations. DeepWordBug-I$_5$ and BERT-Attack were respectively allowed up to 45 and 60 seconds to attack each sample.

5 Results and discussion

5.1 Adversarial attacks

Table 1 lists the after-attack metrics for the various attack strategies. By observing the metrics we can notice that DeepWordBug-I$_5$ is the most effective. Its success is most likely due to the fact that it can modify named entities. In fact, when named entities are preserved as in DeepWordBug-II$_5$, the attack rate drops to 27% and increasing the Levenshtein distance constraint to 30 has little effectiveness. Word-level attacks are less effective than unconstrained character-level attacks, but perform better than similarly constrained character-level attacks, decreasing a model's accuracy by up to 26% in the case of BERT-Attack. Even if less effective, word-level attack strategies may be useful for adversarial training since the generated samples are highly grammatical (introducing less than 0.5 grammar errors per sample), have a low percentage of modified words (except when insertions are used) and maintain a high sentence similarity: 84-86% for BERT-Attack and CLARE versus 77% for DeepWordBug-I$_5$. Some adversarial examples generated respectively by BERT-attack and CLARE can be seen in the appendix (Figures 8 and 9). Future work may attempt to apply word-level attacks also on the entities themselves, making sure to preserve the entity class. This would both speed up the adversarial examples generation (due to the higher sensitivity) and uncover examples highly likely to appear in the real world.

Model	Acc	Recall	F1	A-Rate ↑	Mod ↓	L-Score ↑	Sim ↑	ΔGErr ↓
NER_{small} 500	94%	95%	94%	16%	19%	52%	89%	0.08
NER_{small} 1000	94%	95%	94%	12%	19%	50%	89%	0.2
NER_{small} (baseline)	88%	89%	89%	20%	18%	55%	88%	0.17

Table 3: Comparison of CoNLL2003 models against BERT-Attack, trained using a different amount of adversarial examples generated by BERT-Attack (specified next to the model) and the **untargeted** goal function. The attack had up to 60 seconds to successfully attack an input sample. ↑ (↓) indicate whether the higher (or lower) the better from the attack perspective.

5.2 Adversarial training

Tables 2 and 3 respectively summarize the attack metrics for DeepWordBug-I_5 and BERT-Attack. In line with the adversarial attacks results, DeepWordBug-I_5 obtains a largely better success than BERT-Attack, reducing the model's after-attack accuracy to 52%, where BERT-Attack only manages to reduce the accuracy to 88%.

Adversarial training grants a significant protection from both attacks: in the case of DeepWordBug-I_5 (Table 2) adding only 500 samples to the training set already increases the after attack accuracy by 21%, without affecting the test set metrics, causing at the same time an increase in the modification rate and a decrease in the similarity score. The improvement is statistically significant: a paired t-test with regards to the modification rate and the labels score respectively yields p-values of 0.0086 and 2.42e-09, confirming the added robustness of the adversarially trained model. The improvement is also visible in Figure 4, where the labels score distribution of the attacked dataset for the normal model is more skewed towards the right than its robust counterpart, showing a smaller attack success on individual samples for the robust model. Similarly, the modification rate distribution for the normal model is more skewed towards the left, thus more words need to be perturbed to fool the robust model. Adding more samples further improves the after attack scores at a small cost of the standard metrics (Table 4), but the improvement over the robust model with 500 samples is statistically significant only when 2000 adversarial examples are used, and only in regards to the labels score (p = 0.017).

Similarly, the robust models trained with BERT-attack have a performance similar to NER_{small} on the test set, even improving the model's F1 score by 1% (Table 5). Using only 500 samples the after-attack accuracy increases by 6% and the attack-rate drops by 4%. Adding more samples further reduces the attack rate (Table 3). Using only 500 samples causes a significant improvement in the modification rate needed to break the model, yielding a p-value of 2.66e-05, but does not grant significant improvement in the labels score (p = 0.4). The latter improves significantly only when 1000 samples are used, where the p-value for the labels score is 0.011. These results are very encouraging, since the added robustness does not affect the test-set metrics and even improves it, suggesting that this attack method could be used for data augmentation in low-resource scenarios, a potential direction for future research. The difference in the number of samples needed to grant a significant robustness against DeepWordBug-I_5 and BERT-Attack may be explained by the initial effectiveness of the attack strategy: the former reduces the baseline accuracy to 52%, meanwhile the latter only reduces it to 88%.

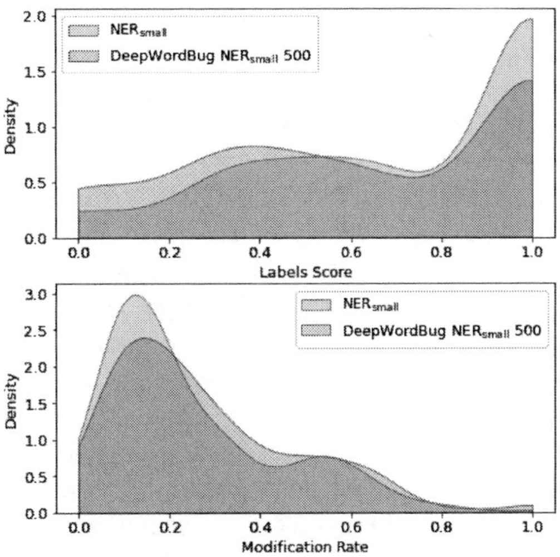

Figure 4: KDE plots for the labels score and modification rate distributions for NER_{small} and its robust counterpart, when attacked with DeepWordBug-I_5. To be successful, the attack needs to alter more words for the robust model, and nonetheless achieves a lower labels score on average.

Examples	Acc	Recall	F1
500 examples	91%	90%	90%
1000 examples	90%	89%	90%
1500 examples	90%	90%	90%
2000 examples	90%	89%	90%
$\text{NER}_{\text{small}}$	91%	90%	90%

Table 4: CoNLL2003 test set metrics for the adversarially trained models against DeepWordBug. Adding adversarial examples slightly worsens the metrics due to overfitting.

Examples	Acc	Recall	F1
500 examples	91%	90%	91%
1000 examples	91%	90%	91%
$\text{NER}_{\text{small}}$	91%	90%	90%

Table 5: CoNLL2003 test set metrics for the adversarially trained models against BERT-Attack. Adversarial examples slightly improve the metrics, potentially covering blind spots in the training set.

6 Conclusion

In this paper we showed that NER models are vulnerable to adversarial attacks at the character, word and sentence level. When allowed to alter named entities, DeepWordBug is the most effective, but it produces highly ungrammatical samples (appendix Figures 6, 7). Thus, character-level attacks are not recommended for adversarial training or data augmentation since the produced samples are unlikely to appear in a real-world setting. Word-level attacks instead produce more fluent adversarial examples (appendix Figures 8, 9), which can be used both for adversarial training and for data augmentation. Finally, with regards to sentence-level attacks, this paper finds that they often produce low-quality samples for this particular dataset (appendix Figure 5). This is probably due to the fact that SCPN paraphrases are generated following a small set of target syntactic forms, which are incompatible with CoNLL2003. Further research in this direction is recommended, as paraphrasing methods produce a richer variety of samples and may reveal weaknesses in a model which cannot be discovered by character-level or word-level attacks.

To help NLP practitioners evaluate and improve their models' robustness and to foster research on adversarial attacks in token classification (and named entity recognition) we release `SeqAttack`[1], a Python library for conducting adversarial attacks against token classification models. The library is accompanied by a web application[2] to inspect the generated adversarial examples and cherry pick them for adversarial training.

References

Moustafa Alzantot, Yash Sharma, Ahmed Elgohary, Bo-Jhang Ho, Mani Srivastava, and Kai-Wei Chang. 2018. Generating natural language adversarial examples. In *Proceedings of the 2018 Conference on Empirical Methods in Natural Language Processing*, pages 2890–2896, Brussels, Belgium. Association for Computational Linguistics.

Vladimir Araujo, Andres Carvallo, Carlos Aspillaga, and Denis Parra. 2020. On adversarial examples for biomedical nlp tasks. *arXiv preprint arXiv:2004.11157*.

Bogdan Babych and Anthony Hartley. 2003. Improving machine translation quality with automatic named entity recognition. In *Proceedings of the 7th International EAMT workshop on MT and other language technology tools, Improving MT through other language technology tools, Resource and tools for building MT at EACL 2003*.

Daniel Cer, Yinfei Yang, Sheng-yi Kong, Nan Hua, Nicole Limtiaco, Rhomni St. John, Noah Constant, Mario Guajardo-Cespedes, Steve Yuan, Chris Tar, Brian Strope, and Ray Kurzweil. 2018. Universal sentence encoder for English. In *Proceedings of the 2018 Conference on Empirical Methods in Natural Language Processing: System Demonstrations*, pages 169–174, Brussels, Belgium. Association for Computational Linguistics.

Jacob Devlin, Ming-Wei Chang, Kenton Lee, and Kristina Toutanova. 2019. BERT: Pre-training of deep bidirectional transformers for language understanding. In *Proceedings of the 2019 Conference of the North American Chapter of the Association for Computational Linguistics: Human Language Technologies, Volume 1 (Long and Short Papers)*, pages 4171–4186, Minneapolis, Minnesota. Association for Computational Linguistics.

Ji Gao, Jack Lanchantin, Mary Lou Soffa, and Yanjun Qi. 2018. Black-box generation of adversarial text sequences to evade deep learning classifiers. In *2018 IEEE Security and Privacy Workshops (SPW)*, pages 50–56. IEEE.

Mohit Iyyer, John Wieting, Kevin Gimpel, and Luke Zettlemoyer. 2018. Adversarial example generation with syntactically controlled paraphrase networks.

[1] `https://github.com/WalterSimoncini/SeqAttack`

[2] Application available at `https://ner-attack.ashita.nl/`

In *Proceedings of the 2018 Conference of the North American Chapter of the Association for Computational Linguistics: Human Language Technologies, Volume 1 (Long Papers)*, pages 1875–1885, New Orleans, Louisiana. Association for Computational Linguistics.

Di Jin, Zhijing Jin, Joey Tianyi Zhou, and Peter Szolovits. 2020. Is BERT really robust? A strong baseline for natural language attack on text classification and entailment. In *The Thirty-Fourth AAAI Conference on Artificial Intelligence, AAAI 2020, The Thirty-Second Innovative Applications of Artificial Intelligence Conference, IAAI 2020, The Tenth AAAI Symposium on Educational Advances in Artificial Intelligence, EAAI 2020, New York, NY, USA, February 7-12, 2020*, pages 8018–8025. AAAI Press.

Dianqi Li, Yizhe Zhang, Hao Peng, Liqun Chen, Chris Brockett, Ming-Ting Sun, and Bill Dolan. 2021. Contextualized perturbation for textual adversarial attack. In *Proceedings of the 2021 Conference of the North American Chapter of the Association for Computational Linguistics: Human Language Technologies*, pages 5053–5069, Online. Association for Computational Linguistics.

Jing Li, Aixin Sun, Jianglei Han, and Chenliang Li. 2020a. A survey on deep learning for named entity recognition. *IEEE Transactions on Knowledge and Data Engineering*.

Linyang Li, Ruotian Ma, Qipeng Guo, Xiangyang Xue, and Xipeng Qiu. 2020b. BERT-ATTACK: Adversarial attack against BERT using BERT. In *Proceedings of the 2020 Conference on Empirical Methods in Natural Language Processing (EMNLP)*, pages 6193–6202, Online. Association for Computational Linguistics.

Peng-Hsuan Li, Ruo-Ping Dong, Yu-Siang Wang, Ju-Chieh Chou, and Wei-Yun Ma. 2017. Leveraging linguistic structures for named entity recognition with bidirectional recursive neural networks. In *Proceedings of the 2017 Conference on Empirical Methods in Natural Language Processing*, pages 2664–2669, Copenhagen, Denmark. Association for Computational Linguistics.

Yijin Liu, Fandong Meng, Jinchao Zhang, Jinan Xu, Yufeng Chen, and Jie Zhou. 2019a. GCDT: A global context enhanced deep transition architecture for sequence labeling. In *Proceedings of the 57th Annual Meeting of the Association for Computational Linguistics*, pages 2431–2441, Florence, Italy. Association for Computational Linguistics.

Yinhan Liu, Myle Ott, Naman Goyal, Jingfei Du, Mandar Joshi, Danqi Chen, Omer Levy, Mike Lewis, Luke Zettlemoyer, and Veselin Stoyanov. 2019b. Roberta: A robustly optimized bert pretraining approach. *arXiv preprint arXiv:1907.11692*.

John Morris, Eli Lifland, Jin Yong Yoo, Jake Grigsby, Di Jin, and Yanjun Qi. 2020. TextAttack: A framework for adversarial attacks, data augmentation, and adversarial training in NLP. In *Proceedings of the 2020 Conference on Empirical Methods in Natural Language Processing: System Demonstrations*, pages 119–126, Online. Association for Computational Linguistics.

Nikola Mrkšić, Diarmuid Ó Séaghdha, Blaise Thomson, Milica Gašić, Lina M. Rojas-Barahona, Pei-Hao Su, David Vandyke, Tsung-Hsien Wen, and Steve Young. 2016. Counter-fitting word vectors to linguistic constraints. In *Proceedings of the 2016 Conference of the North American Chapter of the Association for Computational Linguistics: Human Language Technologies*, pages 142–148, San Diego, California. Association for Computational Linguistics.

Daniel Naber et al. 2003. A rule-based style and grammar checker.

Hiroki Nakayama. 2018. seqeval: A python framework for sequence labeling evaluation. Software available from https://github.com/chakki-works/seqeval.

Desislava Petkova and W Bruce Croft. 2007. Proximity-based document representation for named entity retrieval. In *Proceedings of the sixteenth ACM conference on Conference on information and knowledge management*, pages 731–740.

Lance Ramshaw and Mitch Marcus. 1995. Text chunking using transformation-based learning. In *Third Workshop on Very Large Corpora*.

Victor Sanh, Lysandre Debut, Julien Chaumond, and Thomas Wolf. 2019. Distilbert, a distilled version of bert: smaller, faster, cheaper and lighter. *ArXiv*, abs/1910.01108.

Erik F. Tjong Kim Sang and Fien De Meulder. 2003. Introduction to the CoNLL-2003 shared task: Language-independent named entity recognition. In *Proceedings of the Seventh Conference on Natural Language Learning at HLT-NAACL 2003*, pages 142–147.

Jiuniu Wang, Wenjia Xu, Xingyu Fu, Guangluan Xu, and Yirong Wu. 2020. Astral: adversarial trained lstm-cnn for named entity recognition. *Knowledge-Based Systems*, 197:105842.

Thomas Wolf, Lysandre Debut, Victor Sanh, Julien Chaumond, Clement Delangue, Anthony Moi, Pierric Cistac, Tim Rault, Remi Louf, Morgan Funtowicz, Joe Davison, Sam Shleifer, Patrick von Platen, Clara Ma, Yacine Jernite, Julien Plu, Canwen Xu, Teven Le Scao, Sylvain Gugger, Mariama Drame, Quentin Lhoest, and Alexander Rush. 2020. Transformers: State-of-the-art natural language processing. In *Proceedings of the 2020 Conference on Empirical Methods in Natural Language Processing:*

System Demonstrations, pages 38–45, Online. Association for Computational Linguistics.

Xiaoyong Yuan, Pan He, Qile Zhu, and Xiaolin Li. 2019. Adversarial examples: Attacks and defenses for deep learning. *IEEE transactions on neural networks and learning systems*, 30(9):2805–2824.

Guoyang Zeng, Fanchao Qi, Qianrui Zhou, Tingji Zhang, Zixian Ma, Bairu Hou, Yuan Zang, Zhiyuan Liu, and Maosong Sun. 2021. OpenAttack: An open-source textual adversarial attack toolkit. In *Proceedings of the 59th Annual Meeting of the Association for Computational Linguistics and the 11th International Joint Conference on Natural Language Processing: System Demonstrations*, pages 363–371, Online. Association for Computational Linguistics.

Wei Emma Zhang, Quan Z Sheng, Ahoud Alhazmi, and Chenliang Li. 2020. Adversarial attacks on deep-learning models in natural language processing: A survey. *ACM Transactions on Intelligent Systems and Technology (TIST)*, 11(3):1–41.

Figure 5: Adversarial examples generated by SCPN, when attacking a BERT-based model trained on CoNLL2003. For each pair the top row represents the original sample and the bottom row its attacked counterpart. The modified words are underlined in red.

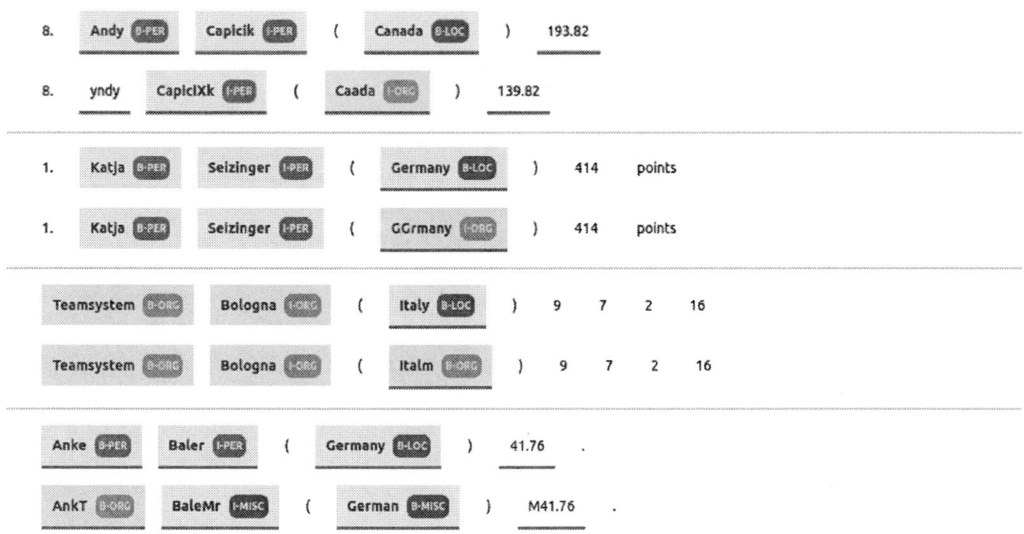

Figure 6: Adversarial examples generated by DeepWordBug-I, when attacking a BERT-based model trained on CoNLL2003. For each pair the top row represents the original sample and the bottom row its attacked counterpart. The modified words are underlined in red.

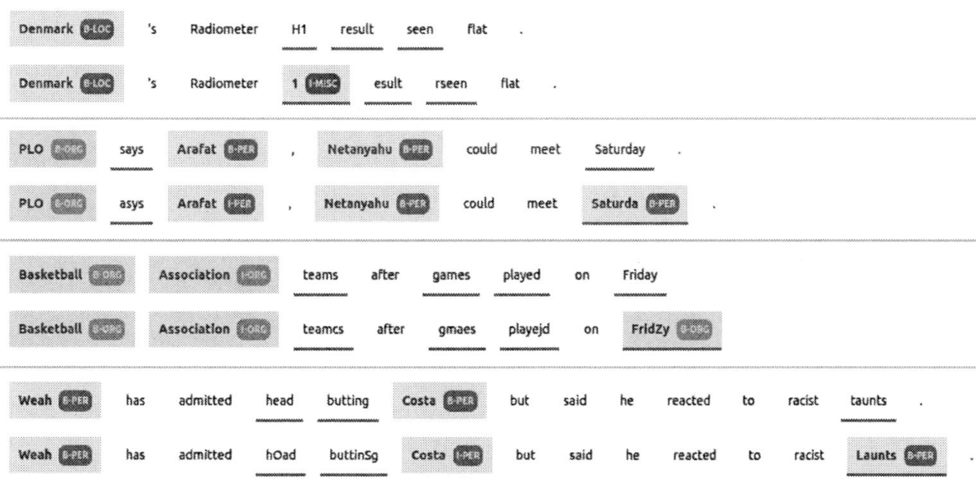

Figure 7: Adversarial examples generated by DeepWordBug-II, when attacking a BERT-based model trained on CoNLL2003. For each pair the top row represents the original sample and the bottom row its attacked counterpart. The modified words are underlined in red.

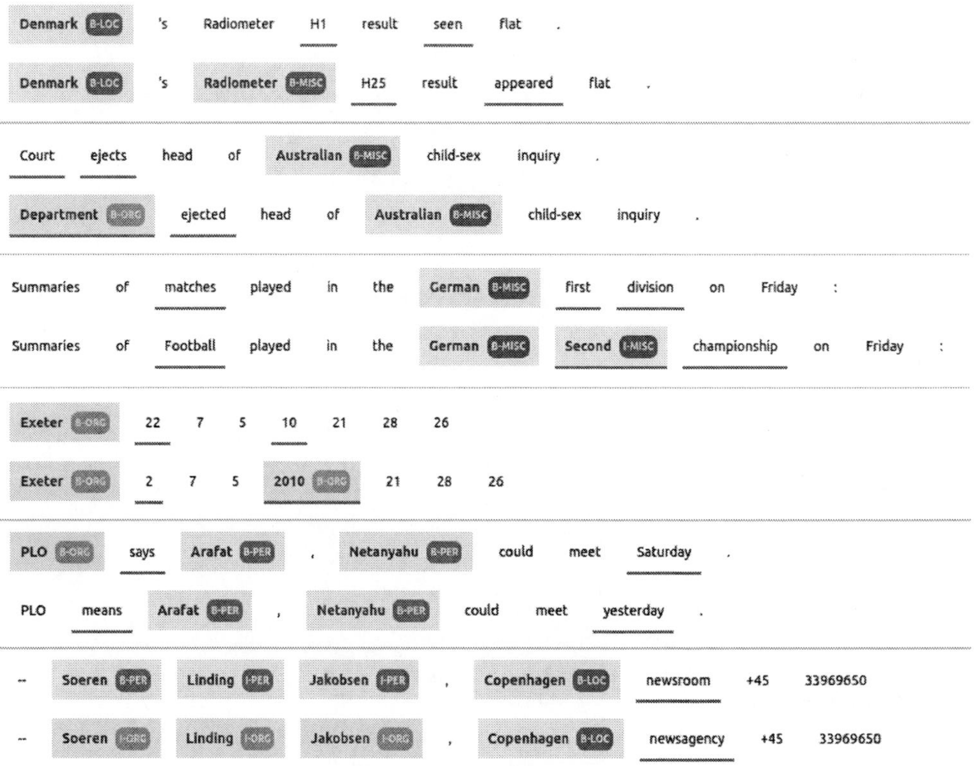

Figure 8: Adversarial examples generated by BERT-Attack, when attacking a BERT-based model trained on CoNLL2003. For each pair the top row represents the original sample and the bottom row its attacked counterpart. The modified words are underlined in red.

Figure 9: Adversarial examples generated by CLARE, when attacking a BERT-based model trained on CoNLL2003. For each pair the top row represents the original sample and the bottom row its attacked counterpart. The modified words are underlined in red.

InVeRo-XL: Making Cross-Lingual Semantic Role Labeling Accessible with Intelligible Verbs and Roles

Simone Conia
Sapienza University of Rome
conia@di.uniroma1.it

Riccardo Orlando
Babelscape, Italy
orlando@babelscape.com

Fabrizio Brignone
Babelscape, Italy
brignone@babelscape.com

Francesco Cecconi
Babelscape, Italy
cecconi@babelscape.com

Roberto Navigli
Sapienza University of Rome
navigli@diag.uniroma1.it

Abstract

Notwithstanding the growing interest in cross-lingual techniques for Natural Language Processing, there has been a surprisingly small number of efforts aimed at the development of easy-to-use tools for cross-lingual Semantic Role Labeling. In this paper, we fill this gap and present InVeRo-XL, an off-the-shelf state-of-the-art system capable of annotating text with predicate sense and semantic role labels from 7 predicate-argument structure inventories in more than 40 languages. We hope that our system – with its easy-to-use RESTful API and Web interface – will become a valuable tool for the research community, encouraging the integration of sentence-level semantics into cross-lingual downstream tasks. InVeRo-XL is available online at http://nlp.uniroma1.it/invero.

1 Introduction

Informally, Semantic Role Labeling (SRL) is often defined as the task of automatically answering the question *"Who did What, to Whom, Where, When, and How?"* (Màrquez et al., 2008). More precisely, SRL aims at recovering the predicate-argument structures within a sentence, providing an explicit overlay that uncovers the underlying semantics of text. For this reason, SRL is thought to be key in enabling Natural Language Understanding (Navigli, 2018). Today SRL is still an open problem, with several research papers being published each year at top-tier conferences, revealing novel insights and proposing better approaches. Over the years, thanks to this active development, SRL has been successfully exploited in a wide array of downstream tasks that span across different areas of Artificial Intelligence, from Natural Language Processing (NLP) with Information Retrieval (Christensen et al., 2010), Question Answering (He et al., 2015), Machine Translation (Marcheggiani et al., 2018) and Semantic Parsing (Banarescu et al., 2013), to Computer Vision with Visual Semantic Role Labeling (Gupta and Malik, 2015) and Situation Recognition (Yatskar et al., 2016).

Recently, the growing interest in cross-lingual NLP, supported by the increasingly wide availability of pretrained multilingual language models such as BERT (Devlin et al., 2019) and XLM-RoBERTa (Conneau et al., 2020), has sparked renewed interest in multilingual and cross-lingual SRL. In just a few years, researchers have found ways to design fully-neural end-to-end systems for SRL (Cai et al., 2018), to take advantage of contextual word representations (Peters et al., 2018; Li et al., 2019), to achieve high performance on multiple languages (He et al., 2019a; Conia and Navigli, 2020), to generate sense and role labels with sequence-to-sequence models (Blloshmi et al., 2021) and to perform SRL jointly across heterogeneous inventories (Conia et al., 2021).

Since SRL is a task that involves complex linguistic theories, inventories and techniques, there have been efforts to develop easy-to-use tools that offer automatic predicate sense and semantic role annotations to users interested in the integration of sentence-level semantics into downstream tasks. Some notable examples include SENNA[1] (Collobert et al., 2011), which uses an ensemble of feature-based classifiers (Koomen et al., 2005), AllenNLP's SRL demo[2], which provides a reimplementation of a BERT-based model (Shi and Lin, 2019), and InVeRo (Conia et al., 2020), which offers annotations according to two different linguistic inventories, PropBank (Palmer et al., 2005) and

[1] https://ronan.collobert.com/senna
[2] https://demo.allennlp.org/semantic-role-labeling

Proceedings of the 2021 Conference on Empirical Methods in Natural Language Processing: System Demonstrations, pages 319–328
November 7–11, 2021.

VerbAtlas (Di Fabio et al., 2019). However, one important drawback of the above-mentioned tools is that they are able to perform SRL only in English, which hinders the exploitation of their annotations in multilingual and cross-lingual NLP.

In order to fill this gap, we build upon InVeRo and propose its next major release, InVeRo-XL, with the objective of making SRL accessible in multiple languages. We rebuild InVeRo-XL from the ground up to offer:

- The first end-to-end system to tackle the whole SRL pipeline in over 40 languages;
- The first off-the-shelf system to provide SRL annotations for 7 linguistic inventories;
- A RESTful API service that can be queried either online, so as not to install any software, or offline, to maximize throughput;
- A Web interface that provides a visualization of the system output which can be useful for teaching purposes, comparing linguistic theories, and prototyping new ideas.

We believe that InVeRo-XL can provide a stepping stone for the integration of explicit sentence-level semantics into cross-lingual tasks, attracting new researchers to the field of SRL and its applications.[3]

1.1 What's New in InVeRo-XL

As previously mentioned, InVeRo-XL is the successor of InVeRo. Although its main new feature is the ability to provide predicate sense and semantic role annotations in over 40 languages with 7 different inventories, InVeRo-XL has been overhauled to also improve several other important aspects. In particular:

- **Preprocessing:** while its predecessor used a very limited set of rules to preprocess English text, InVeRo-XL features a multilingual preprocessing module based on spaCy and Stanza;
- **SRL model:** the English-only model has been replaced by a cross-lingual model that is able to perform not only span-based SRL, but also dependency-based SRL;
- **API:** the service is now able to handle batched requests and documents of arbitrary length;
- **Offline usage:** InVeRo-XL is now available for download, free for research purposes, allowing users to host their own instance locally.

2 System Overview

In this Section, we provide an overview of the main components of InVeRo-XL and how they interact, describing in detail the preprocessing module (Section 2.1) and the SRL model (Section 2.2).

2.1 Preprocessing

The previous version of InVeRo-XL preprocessed an English sentence using a very limited and simple set of rules. In order to correctly support more languages, InVeRo-XL now relies on both spaCy (Honnibal et al., 2020) and Stanza (Qi et al., 2020) to deal transparently with document splitting and tokenization. An automatic language detector based on fastText[4] (Joulin et al., 2017) is used to dynamically choose between the two preprocessing tools, depending on the language detected: spaCy is faster for high-resource languages, e.g. English, but also less reliable on lower-resource languages, e.g. Catalan, for which our system falls back to Stanza.

2.2 Model Architecture

In line with its predecessor, InVeRo-XL encapsulates an SRL model that falls within the broad category of end-to-end systems, tackling the whole SRL pipeline – predicate identification, predicate sense disambiguation, argument identification and argument classification – in a single forward pass. However, the design of the SRL model itself has been completely revamped and now follows the architecture recently proposed by Conia et al. (2021), which is capable of performing cross-lingual SRL with heterogeneous linguistic inventories. In the following, we describe the main components of the SRL model architecture provided by InVeRo-XL.

Multilingual word encoder. The first component of our model is a multilingual word encoder that takes advantage of a pretrained language model, XLM-RoBERTa (Conneau et al., 2020), to provide rich contextualized word representations.

[3] InVeRo-XL can be downloaded upon request at `http://nlp.uniroma1.it/resources`. InVeRo-XL is licensed under Creative Commons Attribution-NonCommercial-ShareAlike 4.0 International.

[4] `https://fasttext.cc`

More formally, for each word w_i in an input sentence $\mathbf{w} = \langle w_1, w_2, \dots, w_n \rangle$ of length n, it computes an encoding $\mathbf{e}_i = \text{Swish}(\mathbf{W}^w \mathbf{h}_i + \mathbf{b}^w)$ as a non-linear projection of the concatenation $\mathbf{h}_i$ of the corresponding hidden states of the four topmost layers of the language model.

Universal word encoder. The resulting sequence of multilingual word encodings $\mathbf{E} = \langle \mathbf{e}_1, \mathbf{e}_2, \dots, \mathbf{e}_n \rangle$ is then given to a "universal" word encoder that computes a sequence of task-specific timestep encodings $\mathbf{T} = \langle \mathbf{t}_1, \mathbf{t}_2, \dots, \mathbf{t}_n \rangle$ as follows:

$$\mathbf{t}_i^j = \begin{cases} \mathbf{e}_i & \text{if } \; j = 0 \\ \mathbf{t}_i^{j-1} \oplus \text{BiLSTM}_i^j(\mathbf{t}^{j-1}) & \text{otherwise} \end{cases}$$
$$\mathbf{T} = \langle \mathbf{t}_1^K, \mathbf{t}_2^K, \dots, \mathbf{t}_n^K \rangle$$

where $\text{BiLSTM}_i^j(\cdot)$ is the i-th timestep of the j-th BiLSTM layer and K is the total number of BiLSTM layers. The purpose of this encoder is to create representations that are shared across languages and inventories and are, therefore, "universal".

Universal predicate-argument encoder. Similarly to the encoder above, the objective of the universal predicate-argument encoder is to build predicate-specific argument representations that lie in a vector space shared across languages and inventories. Assuming that w_p is a predicate in the input sentence $\mathbf{w}$, this encoder builds a sequence $\mathbf{A}$ of predicate-specific argument encodings as follows:

$$\mathbf{a}_i^j = \begin{cases} \mathbf{t}_p \oplus \mathbf{t}_i & \text{if } \; j = 0 \\ \mathbf{a}_i^{j-1} \oplus \text{BiLSTM}_i^j(\mathbf{a}^{j-1}) & \text{otherwise} \end{cases}$$
$$\mathbf{A} = \langle \mathbf{a}_1^{K'}, \mathbf{a}_2^{K'}, \dots, \mathbf{a}_n^{K'} \rangle$$

where $\mathbf{t}_i$ is the i-th timestep encoding from the universal sentence encoder, $\mathbf{a}_i^j$ is the argument encoding for w_i with respect to w_p produced after the j-th BiLSTM layer, and K' is the total number of BiLSTM layers.

Inventory-specific decoders. Finally, the universal encodings are given to a set of classifiers in order to obtain the desired output labels. More specifically, for each inventory, we need three types of output: i) whether a word w_i is a predicate w_p; ii) the most appropriate sense s for a predicate w_p; iii) which semantic role r, possibly the null role, exists between a word w_i and a predicate w_p. More formally, our model features three classifiers for each inventory I as follows:

$$\sigma^p(w_i|I) = \mathbf{W}^{p|I}\,\text{Swish}(\mathbf{W}^p \mathbf{t}_i + \mathbf{b}^p) + \mathbf{b}^{p|I}$$
$$\sigma^s(w_p|I) = \mathbf{W}^{s|I}\,\text{Swish}(\mathbf{W}^s \mathbf{t}_p + \mathbf{b}^s) + \mathbf{b}^{s|I}$$
$$\sigma^r(w_r|w_p, I) = \mathbf{W}^{r|I}\,\text{Swish}(\mathbf{W}^r \mathbf{a}_i + \mathbf{b}^r) + \mathbf{b}^{r|I}$$

where each $\sigma^{\cdot}(\cdot)$ provides a score distribution over the possible output classes, i.e. two (true or false) for predicate identification, the number of senses of an inventory for predicate sense disambiguation, and the number of semantic roles (including the null role) of an inventory for argument labeling.

Miscellanea. While we follow the architecture proposed by Conia et al. (2021), the SRL model of InVeRo-XL also comes with a small but significant number of enhancements. One such enhancement is that, while Conia et al. (2021) propose a model for dependency-based SRL, our model is also able to perform span-based SRL by treating spans as sequences of BIO tags. In order to correctly decode valid spans at inference time, InVeRo-XL makes use of a Viterbi decoder. Other improvements include training the model with the RAdam optimizer (Liu et al., 2020), ensuring that each training batch features a balanced number of instances for each language in the training set, and searching randomly for better hyperparameter values.

2.3 Evaluation

Datasets. We report the performance of InVeRo-XL on two gold standard benchmarks for SRL: CoNLL-2009 (Hajič et al., 2009) for dependency-based SRL and CoNLL-2012 (Pradhan et al., 2012) for span-based SRL. To the best of our knowledge, CoNLL-2009 is the largest benchmark for multilingual SRL as it comprises six languages, namely, Catalan, Chinese, Czech, English, German and Spanish.[5] The main challenge of this benchmark is that each language was annotated with a different predicate-argument structure inventory, e.g. the English PropBank (Palmer et al., 2005) for English, AnCora (Taulé et al., 2008) for Spanish/Catalan and PDT-Vallex (Hajic et al., 2003) for Czech. While CoNLL-2009 is an ideal test bed for evaluating the multilingual capabilities of an SRL system, dependency-based annotations may look unfamiliar to end users who are not used to the

[5]Japanese is not available anymore from LDC due to licensing issues.

		Catalan	Czech	German	English	Spanish	Chinese
Span	AllenNLP's SRL demo	–	–	–	86.5	–	–
	InVeRo	–	–	–	86.2	–	–
	InVeRo-XL$_{\text{span-based}}$	**83.3**	**85.9**	**87.0**	**86.8**	**81.8**	**84.9**
Dependency	Marcheggiani et al. (2017)	—	86.0	—	87.7	80.3	81.2
	Chen et al. (2019)	81.7	88.1	76.4	91.1	81.3	81.7
	Cai and Lapata (2019b)	—	—	82.7	90.0	81.8	83.6
	Cai and Lapata (2019a)	—	—	83.8	91.2	82.9	85.0
	Lyu et al. (2019)	80.9	87.5	75.8	90.1	80.5	83.3
	He et al. (2019b)	86.0	89.7	81.1	90.9	85.2	86.9
	Conia and Navigli (2020)	88.3	**92.1**	89.1	**92.4**	86.9	**89.1**
	Conia et al. (2021)	88.0	91.5	88.0	91.8	86.3	87.7
	InVeRo-XL$_{\text{dependency-based}}$	**88.7**	**92.1**	**89.9**	92.1	**87.2**	**89.1**

Table 1: Comparison between InVeRo-XL and other recent systems for SRL. **Top:** F_1 scores on argument labeling with pre-identified predicates using the official CoNLL-2005 scoring script on the CoNLL-2012 English test set for span-based SRL and the CoNLL-2009 test sets converted from dependency-based to span-based as described in Section 2.3. **Bottom:** F_1 scores on argument labeling and sense disambiguation with pre-identified predicates using the official CoNLL-2009 scoring script on the test sets of the CoNLL-2009 shared task for dependency-based multilingual SRL.

notion of syntactic/semantic heads. Therefore, differently from Conia et al. (2021), we also adapt the system to perform span-based SRL and evaluate its effectiveness on the standard English datasets of CoNLL-2012 and on CoNLL-2009, converting dependency-based annotations to span-based annotations. We convert an argument head to an argument span by considering all those words that fall in the syntactic subtree whose root is the argument head and discarding all those predicates for which this conversion produces overlapping spans.

Experimental setup. We train the dependency-based SRL model on the standard training splits of CoNLL-2009, making the model learn from all six languages jointly. Instead, we train the span-based SRL model on the union of the English training split of CoNLL-2012 and the Catalan, Chinese, Czech, German and Spanish training sets converted from dependency-based to span-based, as explained above. Each model configuration is trained for 30 epochs using the RAdam optimizer with learning rates of 10^{-5} for the weights of XLM-RoBERTa and 10^{-3} for the other weights. Following standard practice, we select the model checkpoint with highest F_1 score on the development set.

Results. Table 1 (top) shows how InVeRo-XL performs on the English test set of CoNLL-2012 for span-based SRL compared to its previous release (InVeRo) and the previously best-performing online system for SRL (AllenNLP's SRL demo). Not only does InVeRo-XL achieve better results, but it is also the only system that is capable of performing span-based cross-lingual SRL, showing strong results on each of the non-English test sets of CoNLL-2009 converted from dependency-based to span-based as described in Section 2.3. Furthermore, Table 1 (bottom) shows that InVeRo-XL achieves results that are comparable to or better than those of current state-of-the-art models on 5 of the 6 languages of CoNLL-2009 for dependency-based SRL, the key advantages being that our model is part of a prepackaged tool with additional user-friendly features (see Sections 3 and 4).

3 The InVeRo-XL API

In order to facilitate the integration of predicate-argument structure information into downstream tasks, InVeRo-XL exposes its fully self-contained end-to-end multilingual SRL pipeline through an easy-to-use RESTful API. In the following, we provide an overview of the main functionalities of the InVeRo-XL API, from its Resource API (Section 3.1) to its Model API (Section 3.2) and how to host InVeRo-XL locally on a user's own hardware (Section 3.3). We refer users to the online documentation for the complete list of supported languages and inventories, together with other details.[6]

3.1 Resource API

The Resource API is a simple way for obtaining semantic information about predicates using the intelligible verb senses and semantic roles defined by VerbAtlas, a large-scale predicate-argument structure inventory which clusters WordNet synsets (Miller, 1992) that share similar semantic behavior. The Resource API of InVeRo-XL builds upon the functionalities provided by its predecessor with the key difference that it now supports multiple languages thanks to BabelNet 5.0[7] (Navigli and Ponzetto, 2012; Navigli et al., 2021), a multilingual encyclopedic dictionary that provides unified access to several knowledge bases including WordNet.

More specifically, the Resource API defines two endpoints:

- `/api/verbatlas/predicate`: given a predicate p, this endpoint retrieves the set of VerbAtlas frames which include at least one sense of p.
- `/api/verbatlas/frame`: given a VerbAtlas frame f, this endpoint retrieves its predicate-argument structure, i.e., the semantic roles, and the WordNet/BabelNet synsets that belong to f.

3.2 Model API

The Model API of InVeRo-XL has been updated to not only take advantage of the new multilingual SRL system but also to provide quality-of-life improvements. The Model API now accepts requests in over 40 languages and returns semantic annotations according to 7 linguistic inventories. On top of this, the Model API is now able to process documents of arbitrary length and to handle batches of documents in a single request.

More specifically, the Model API exposes an endpoint named `/api/model`. This endpoint accepts `POST` requests with a `JSON` body containing a list of input objects, one for each document the user wishes to annotate. Each input object shall specify the following fields:

- `text`: a mandatory field that contains the text of the document.


```
[{
    "tokens": [
        ...
        { "index": 2, "text": "volpe" },
        { "index": 3, "text": "salta" },
        { "index": 4, "text": "sul" },
        ...
    ],
    "annotations": [
        {
            "tokenIndex": 3,
            "verbatlas": {
                "sense": "GO-FORWARD",
                "arguments": [
                    {
                        "role": "Agent",
                        "score": 1.0,
                        "span": [0, 3]
                    },{
                        "role": "Destination",
                        "score": 1.0,
                        "span": [4, 6]
                    },
                    ...
                ]
            },
            "englishPropbank": {...},
            "chinesePropbank": {...},
            "germanPropbank": {...},
            "pdtVallex": {...},
            "catalanAncora": {...},
            "spanishAncora": {...}
        }
        ...
    ]
}]
```


Figure 1: An example of a response from the Model API for an input Italian sentence. The response contains the tokenized input sentence and the automatic SRL annotations according to 7 different linguistic inventories.

- `lang`: an optional field that indicates the language of the document. If omitted, InVeRo-XL will use an automatic language detector (see Section 2.1).

Each request to the Model API returns a `JSON` response containing a list of output objects, one for each input document, containing the automatic annotations according to each of the 7 linguistic inventories, as shown in Figure 1.

[6] http://nlp.uniroma1.it/invero/api-documentation

[7] https://babelnet.org

Figure 2: The home page of the Web interface of InVeRo-XL. Users can search for predicate information (e.g. the VerbAtlas frames a verb belongs to) and tag sentences in multiple languages with different linguistic inventories (see Figure 3).

3.3 Offline Usage

One of the most requested features that is currently missing from InVeRo is the possibility of running an offline instance of the service so as to annotate large quantities of text in a shorter time, independently of the latency of the network and the volume of requests being processed by our Web server. To address this issue, InVeRo-XL is also distributed as a Docker[8] image that can be deployed locally on a user's own hardware.[9] While network latency is often a bottleneck for processing a request, an offline instance of InVeRo-XL does not suffer from such a constraint and can therefore benefit greatly from running on better hardware, e.g. on GPU. We distribute InVeRo-XL in two configurations:

- `invero-xl-span` is the configuration that performs multilingual span-based SRL and is the one used by InVeRo-XL's Web server;
- `invero-xl-dependency` is an alternative configuration built to perform multilingual dependency-based SRL.

Running a local instance of InVeRo-XL is also simple. First, users are required to perform a one-time setup to load one of the available images:

```
#!/bin/bash
docker load -i invero-xl-span_2.0.0.tar
```

After that, InVeRo-XL can be started with:

```
#!/bin/bash
PORT=12345
LANGUAGES="EN IT FR ZH"

docker run \
  --name invero-xl-span-en \
  -p $PORT:80 \
  -e LANGUAGES=$LANGUAGES
  invero-xl-span:2.0.0
```

Once started, users can forward their requests locally. We refer the reader to the online documentation for further details.[10]

4 Web Interface

Similarly to its predecessor, InVeRo-XL includes a public-facing Web interface (Figures 2 and 3) that provides a visual environment for both the Resource API and the Model API, allowing users to explore the main functionalities while also providing an intuitive overview of how an SRL system annotates a sentence or a short document. Most importantly, the Web interface of InVeRo-XL has been updated to reflect the changes in the Model API and the underlying SRL model; now users can annotate text in 12 languages[11] and visualize predicate senses and semantic roles in 7 linguistic inventories on the fly, without having to write code.

Figure 3 shows an example sentence in Italian with its corresponding predicate senses and seman-

[8] `https://www.docker.com`

[9] Docker images for InVeRo-XL are freely available for research purposes at `http://nlp.uniroma1.it/resources`.

[10] `http://nlp.uniroma1.it/invero/api-documentation`

[11] We limit the number of languages available on the Web interface due to hardware constraints as Stanza and spaCy use one preprocessing model for each language.

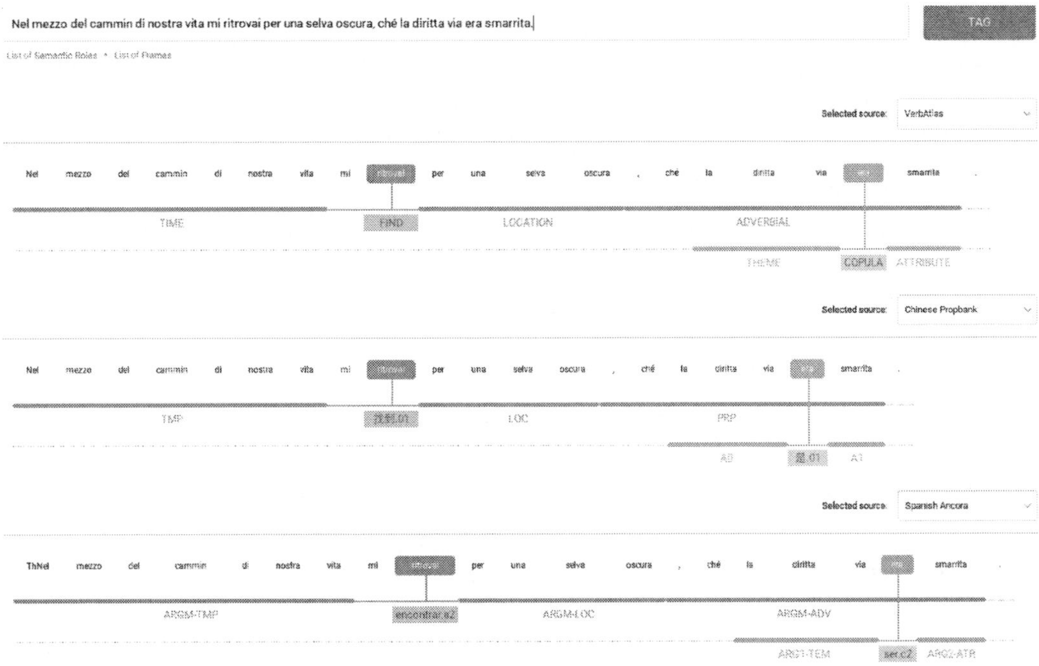

Figure 3: The beginning of the Divine Comedy by Dante Alighieri in Italian as tagged by InVeRo-XL with three predicate-argument structure inventories – VerbAtlas, the Chinese PropBank and the Spanish AnCora. "Nel mezzo del cammin di nostra vista mi ritrovai per una selva oscura, ché la diritta via era smarrita" translates into "Midway upon the journey of our life I found myself within a forest dark, for the straightforward pathway had been lost".

tic roles as provided by InVeRo-XL. Thanks to a dropdown menu, users can immediately switch from the labels of one inventory to those of another, independently of the input language, without reloading the Web page. We argue that this Web interface should help teachers explain SRL to their students, allow linguists to compare linguistic inventories on particular case studies, attract new researchers to the field, and inspire others to exploit SRL in downstream tasks or even real-world scenarios.

5 Conclusion and Future Work

Over the years, the research community has greatly advanced the field of SRL, proposing ever more complex approaches to tackle the task more effectively. However, despite the growing interest in cross-lingual NLP, there have been very few efforts to develop automatic tools to perform SRL in multiple languages. Our objective with InVeRo-XL is to fill this gap and equip researchers with an easy-to-use, high-performing system capable of providing predicate sense and semantic role annotations in over 40 languages with 7 linguistic inventories. Users can take advantage of our state-of-the-art system for cross-lingual SRL through a RESTful API that relieves them from the need to reimplement complex neural models and/or to build an efficient preprocessing/postprocessing pipeline.

Although InVeRo-XL is a major step forward compared to its predecessor, we intend to further improve our system by adopting future and more advanced SRL model architectures and by including new training datasets, such as UniteD-SRL (Tripodi et al., 2021). We strongly believe that InVeRo-XL will facilitate the integration of SRL into downstream cross-lingual tasks, hopefully aiding further advancements in cross-lingual Natural Language Understanding.

Acknowledgments

The authors gratefully acknowledge the support of the ERC Consolidator Grant MOUSSE No. 726487 and the European Language Grid project No. 825627 (Universal Semantic Annotator, USeA) under the European Union's Horizon 2020 research and innovation programme.

References

Laura Banarescu, Claire Bonial, Shu Cai, Madalina Georgescu, Kira Griffitt, Ulf Hermjakob, Kevin Knight, Philipp Koehn, Martha Palmer, and Nathan Schneider. 2013. Abstract Meaning Representation for sembanking. In *Proceedings of the 7th Linguistic Annotation Workshop and Interoperability with Discourse*, pages 178–186, Sofia, Bulgaria.

Rexhina Blloshmi, Simone Conia, Rocco Tripodi, and Roberto Navigli. 2021. Generating Senses and RoLes: An end-to-end model for dependency- and span-based Semantic Role Labeling. In *Proceedings of the Thirtieth International Joint Conference on Artificial Intelligence, IJCAI-21*, pages 3786–3793. Main Track.

Jiaxun Cai, Shexia He, Zuchao Li, and Hai Zhao. 2018. A full end-to-end semantic role labeler, syntactic-agnostic over syntactic-aware? In *Proceedings of the 27th International Conference on Computational Linguistics*, pages 2753–2765, Santa Fe, New Mexico, USA.

Rui Cai and Mirella Lapata. 2019a. Semi-supervised Semantic Role Labeling with cross-view training. In *Proceedings of the 2019 Conference on Empirical Methods in Natural Language Processing and the 9th International Joint Conference on Natural Language Processing (EMNLP-IJCNLP)*, pages 1018–1027, Hong Kong, China.

Rui Cai and Mirella Lapata. 2019b. Syntax-aware Semantic Role Labeling without parsing. *Trans. Assoc. Comput. Linguistics*, 7:343–356.

Xinchi Chen, Chunchuan Lyu, and Ivan Titov. 2019. Capturing argument interaction in Semantic Role Labeling with capsule networks. In *Proceedings of the 2019 Conference on Empirical Methods in Natural Language Processing and the 9th International Joint Conference on Natural Language Processing (EMNLP-IJCNLP)*, pages 5415–5425, Hong Kong, China.

Janara Christensen, Mausam, Stephen Soderland, and Oren Etzioni. 2010. Semantic Role Labeling for open information extraction. In *Proceedings of the NAACL HLT 2010 First International Workshop on Formalisms and Methodology for Learning by Reading*, pages 52–60, Los Angeles, California.

Ronan Collobert, Jason Weston, Léon Bottou, Michael Karlen, Koray Kavukcuoglu, and Pavel P. Kuksa. 2011. Natural language processing (almost) from scratch. *J. Mach. Learn. Res.*, 12:2493–2537.

Simone Conia, Andrea Bacciu, and Roberto Navigli. 2021. Unifying cross-lingual Semantic Role Labeling with heterogeneous linguistic resources. In *Proceedings of the 2021 Conference of the North American Chapter of the Association for Computational Linguistics: Human Language Technologies*, pages 338–351, Online.

Simone Conia, Fabrizio Brignone, Davide Zanfardino, and Roberto Navigli. 2020. InVeRo: Making Semantic Role Labeling accessible with intelligible verbs and roles. In *Proceedings of the 2020 Conference on Empirical Methods in Natural Language Processing: System Demonstrations*, pages 77–84, Online.

Simone Conia and Roberto Navigli. 2020. Bridging the gap in multilingual Semantic Role Labeling: A language-agnostic approach. In *Proceedings of the 28th International Conference on Computational Linguistics*, pages 1396–1410, Barcelona, Spain (Online).

Alexis Conneau, Kartikay Khandelwal, Naman Goyal, Vishrav Chaudhary, Guillaume Wenzek, Francisco Guzmán, Edouard Grave, Myle Ott, Luke Zettlemoyer, and Veselin Stoyanov. 2020. Unsupervised cross-lingual representation learning at scale. In *Proceedings of the 58th Annual Meeting of the Association for Computational Linguistics*, pages 8440–8451, Online.

Jacob Devlin, Ming-Wei Chang, Kenton Lee, and Kristina Toutanova. 2019. BERT: Pre-training of deep bidirectional transformers for language understanding. In *Proceedings of the 2019 Conference of the North American Chapter of the Association for Computational Linguistics: Human Language Technologies, Volume 1 (Long and Short Papers)*, pages 4171–4186, Minneapolis, Minnesota.

Andrea Di Fabio, Simone Conia, and Roberto Navigli. 2019. VerbAtlas: A novel large-scale verbal semantic resource and its application to Semantic Role Labeling. In *Proceedings of the 2019 Conference on Empirical Methods in Natural Language Processing and the 9th International Joint Conference on Natural Language Processing (EMNLP-IJCNLP)*, pages 627–637, Hong Kong, China.

Saurabh Gupta and Jitendra Malik. 2015. Visual Semantic Role Labeling. *arXiv*, abs/1505.04474.

Jan Hajič, Massimiliano Ciaramita, Richard Johansson, Daisuke Kawahara, Maria Antònia Martí, Lluís Màrquez, Adam Meyers, Joakim Nivre, Sebastian Padó, Jan Štěpánek, Pavel Straňák, Mihai Surdeanu, Nianwen Xue, and Yi Zhang. 2009. The CoNLL-2009 shared task: Syntactic and semantic dependencies in multiple languages. In *Proceedings of the Thirteenth Conference on Computational Natural Language Learning (CoNLL 2009): Shared Task*, pages 1–18, Boulder, Colorado.

Jan Hajic, Jarmila Panevová, Zdenka Urešová, Alevtina Bémová, Veronika Kolárová, and Petr Pajas. 2003. PDT-VALLEX: Creating a large-coverage valency lexicon for treebank annotation. In *Proceedings of the second workshop on treebanks and linguistic theories*, volume 9, pages 57–68.

Luheng He, Mike Lewis, and Luke Zettlemoyer. 2015. Question-answer driven Semantic Role Labeling:

Using natural language to annotate natural language. In *Proceedings of the 2015 Conference on Empirical Methods in Natural Language Processing*, pages 643–653, Lisbon, Portugal.

Shexia He, Zuchao Li, and Hai Zhao. 2019a. Syntax-aware multilingual Semantic Role Labeling. In *Proceedings of the 2019 Conference on Empirical Methods in Natural Language Processing and the 9th International Joint Conference on Natural Language Processing (EMNLP-IJCNLP)*, pages 5350–5359, Hong Kong, China.

Shexia He, Zuchao Li, and Hai Zhao. 2019b. Syntax-aware multilingual Semantic Role Labeling. In *Proceedings of the 2019 Conference on Empirical Methods in Natural Language Processing and the 9th International Joint Conference on Natural Language Processing, EMNLP-IJCNLP 2019, Hong Kong, China, November 3-7, 2019*, pages 5349–5358.

Matthew Honnibal, Ines Montani, Sofie Van Landeghem, and Adriane Boyd. 2020. spaCy: Industrial-strength Natural Language Processing in Python.

Armand Joulin, Edouard Grave, Piotr Bojanowski, and Tomas Mikolov. 2017. Bag of tricks for efficient text classification. In *Proceedings of the 15th Conference of the European Chapter of the Association for Computational Linguistics: Volume 2, Short Papers*, pages 427–431, Valencia, Spain.

Peter Koomen, Vasin Punyakanok, Dan Roth, and Wen-tau Yih. 2005. Generalized inference with multiple Semantic Role Labeling systems. In *Proceedings of the Ninth Conference on Computational Natural Language Learning (CoNLL-2005)*, pages 181–184, Ann Arbor, Michigan.

Zuchao Li, Shexia He, Hai Zhao, Yiqing Zhang, Zhuosheng Zhang, Xi Zhou, and Xiang Zhou. 2019. Dependency or span, end-to-end uniform Semantic Role Labeling. In *The Thirty-Third AAAI Conference on Artificial Intelligence, AAAI 2019, The Thirty-First Innovative Applications of Artificial Intelligence Conference, IAAI 2019, The Ninth AAAI Symposium on Educational Advances in Artificial Intelligence, EAAI 2019, Honolulu, Hawaii, USA, January 27 - February 1, 2019*, pages 6730–6737.

Liyuan Liu, Haoming Jiang, Pengcheng He, Weizhu Chen, Xiaodong Liu, Jianfeng Gao, and Jiawei Han. 2020. On the variance of the adaptive learning rate and beyond. In *8th International Conference on Learning Representations, ICLR 2020, Addis Ababa, Ethiopia, April 26-30, 2020*.

Chunchuan Lyu, Shay B. Cohen, and Ivan Titov. 2019. Semantic Role Labeling with iterative structure refinement. In *Proceedings of the 2019 Conference on Empirical Methods in Natural Language Processing and the 9th International Joint Conference on Natural Language Processing (EMNLP-IJCNLP)*, pages 1071–1082, Hong Kong, China.

Diego Marcheggiani, Jasmijn Bastings, and Ivan Titov. 2018. Exploiting semantics in Neural Machine Translation with graph convolutional networks. In *Proceedings of the 2018 Conference of the North American Chapter of the Association for Computational Linguistics: Human Language Technologies, Volume 2 (Short Papers)*, pages 486–492, New Orleans, Louisiana.

Diego Marcheggiani, Anton Frolov, and Ivan Titov. 2017. A simple and accurate syntax-agnostic neural model for dependency-based Semantic Role Labeling. In *Proceedings of the 21st Conference on Computational Natural Language Learning (CoNLL 2017)*, pages 411–420, Vancouver, Canada.

Lluís Màrquez, Xavier Carreras, Kenneth C. Litkowski, and Suzanne Stevenson. 2008. Special issue introduction: Semantic Role Labeling: An introduction to the special issue. *Computational Linguistics*, 34(2):145–159.

George A. Miller. 1992. WordNet: A lexical database for English. In *Speech and Natural Language: Proceedings of a Workshop Held at Harriman, New York, February 23-26, 1992*.

Roberto Navigli. 2018. Natural Language Understanding: Instructions for (present and future) use. In *Proceedings of the Twenty-Seventh International Joint Conference on Artificial Intelligence, IJCAI 2018, July 13-19, 2018, Stockholm, Sweden*, pages 5697–5702.

Roberto Navigli, Michele Bevilacqua, Simone Conia, Dario Montagnini, and Francesco Cecconi. 2021. Ten years of BabelNet: A survey. In *Proceedings of the Thirtieth International Joint Conference on Artificial Intelligence, IJCAI-21*, pages 4559–4567. Survey Track.

Roberto Navigli and Simone Paolo Ponzetto. 2012. BabelNet: The automatic construction, evaluation and application of a wide-coverage multilingual semantic network. *Artif. Intell.*, 193:217–250.

Martha Palmer, Daniel Gildea, and Paul Kingsbury. 2005. The Proposition Bank: An annotated corpus of semantic roles. *Computational Linguistics*, 31(1):71–106.

Matthew E. Peters, Mark Neumann, Mohit Iyyer, Matt Gardner, Christopher Clark, Kenton Lee, and Luke Zettlemoyer. 2018. Deep contextualized word representations. In *Proceedings of the 2018 Conference of the North American Chapter of the Association for Computational Linguistics: Human Language Technologies, Volume 1 (Long Papers)*, pages 2227–2237, New Orleans, Louisiana.

Sameer Pradhan, Alessandro Moschitti, Nianwen Xue, Olga Uryupina, and Yuchen Zhang. 2012. CoNLL-2012 shared task: Modeling multilingual unrestricted coreference in OntoNotes. In *Joint Conference on EMNLP and CoNLL - Shared Task*, pages 1–40, Jeju Island, Korea.

Peng Qi, Yuhao Zhang, Yuhui Zhang, Jason Bolton, and Christopher D. Manning. 2020. Stanza: A Python Natural Language Processing toolkit for many human languages. In *Proceedings of the 58th Annual Meeting of the Association for Computational Linguistics: System Demonstrations*, pages 101–108, Online.

Peng Shi and Jimmy Lin. 2019. Simple BERT models for relation extraction and semantic role labeling. *CoRR*, abs/1904.05255.

Mariona Taulé, M. Antònia Martí, and Marta Recasens. 2008. AnCora: Multilevel annotated corpora for Catalan and Spanish. In *Proceedings of the Sixth International Conference on Language Resources and Evaluation (LREC'08)*, Marrakech, Morocco.

Rocco Tripodi, Simone Conia, and Roberto Navigli. 2021. UniteD-SRL: A unified dataset for span- and dependency-based multilingual and cross-lingual Semantic Role Labeling. In *Proceedings of the 2021 Conference on Empirical Methods in Natural Language Processing (EMNLP)*.

Mark Yatskar, Luke S. Zettlemoyer, and Ali Farhadi. 2016. Situation Recognition: Visual Semantic Role Labeling for image understanding. In *2016 IEEE Conference on Computer Vision and Pattern Recognition, CVPR 2016, Las Vegas, NV, USA, June 27-30, 2016*, pages 5534–5542.

SummerTime: Text Summarization Toolkit for Non-experts

Ansong Ni[†] **Zhangir Azerbayev**[†] **Mutethia Mutuma**[†] **Troy Feng**[†]
Yusen Zhang[♣] **Tao Yu**[†] **Ahmed Hassan Awadallah**[◇] **Dragomir Radev**[†]
[†]Yale University [♣]Penn State University [◇]Microsoft Research
{ansong.ni, tao.yu, dragomir.radev}@yale.edu

Abstract

Recent advances in summarization provide models that can generate summaries of higher quality. Such models now exist for a number of summarization tasks, including query-based summarization, dialogue summarization, and multi-document summarization. While such models and tasks are rapidly growing in the research field, it has also become challenging for non-experts to keep track of them. To make summarization methods more accessible to a wider audience, we develop SummerTime by rethinking the summarization task from the perspective of an NLP non-expert. SummerTime is a complete toolkit for text summarization, including various models, datasets and evaluation metrics, for a full spectrum of summarization-related tasks. SummerTime integrates with libraries designed for NLP researchers, and enables users with easy-to-use APIs. With SummerTime, users can locate pipeline solutions and search for the best model with their own data, and visualize the differences, all with a few lines of code. We also provide explanations for models and evaluation metrics to help users understand the model behaviors and select models that best suit their needs. Our library, along with a notebook demo, is available at `https://github.com/Yale-LILY/SummerTime`.

1 Introduction

The goal of text summarization is to generate short and fluent summaries from longer textual sources, while preserving the most salient information in them. Benefiting from recent advances of deep neural networks, in particular sequence to sequence models, with or without attention (Sutskever et al., 2014; Bahdanau et al., 2014; Vaswani et al., 2017), current state-of-the-art summarization models produce high quality summaries that can be useful in practice cases (Zhang et al., 2020a; Lewis et al., 2020). Moreover, neural summarization

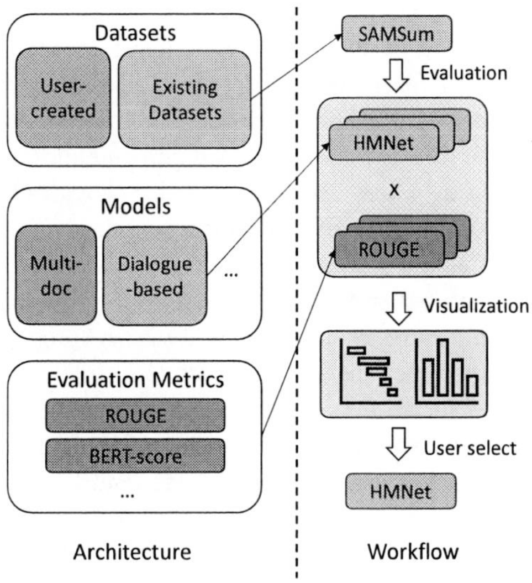

Figure 1: SummerTime is a toolkit for helping non-expert users to find the best summarization models for their own data and use cases.

has broadened its scope with the introduction of more summarization tasks, such as query-based summarization (Dang, 2005; Zhong et al., 2021), long-document summarization (Cohan et al., 2018), multi-document summarization (Ganesan et al., 2010; Fabbri et al., 2019), dialogue summarization (Gliwa et al., 2019; Zhong et al., 2021). Such summarization tasks can also be from different domains (Hermann et al., 2015; Zhang et al., 2019; Cohan et al., 2018).

However, as the field rapidly grows, it is often hard for NLP non-experts to follow all relevant new models, datasets, and evaluation metrics. Moreover, those models and datasets are often from different sources, making it a non-trivial effort for the users to directly compare the performance of such models side-by-side. This makes it hard for them to decide which models to use. The development of libraries such as *Transformers* (Wolf et al., 2020) alleviate such problems to some extent, but they only

Proceedings of the 2021 Conference on Empirical Methods in Natural Language Processing: System Demonstrations, pages 329–338
November 7–11, 2021.

cover a narrow range of summarization models and tasks and assume certain proficiency in NLP from the users, thus the target audience is still largely the research community.

To address those challenges for non-expert users and make state-of-the-art summarizers more accessible as a tool, we introduce SummerTime, a text summarization toolkit intended for users with no NLP background. We build this library from this perspective, and provide an integration of different summarization models, datasets and evaluation metrics, all in one place. We allow the users to view a side-by-side comparison of all classic and state-of-the-art summarization models we support, on their own data and combined into pipelines that fit their own task. SummerTime also provides the functionality for automatic model selection, by constructing pipelines for specific tasks first and iteratively evaluation to find the best working solutions. Assuming no background in NLP, we list "pros and cons" for each model, and provide simple explanations for all the evaluation metrics we support. Moreover, we go beyond pure numbers and provide visualization of the performance and output of different models, to facilitate users in making decisions about which models or pipelines to finally adopt.

The purpose of SummerTime is not to replace any previous work, on the contrary, we integrate existing libraries and place them in the same framework. We provide wrappers around such libraries intended for expert users, maintaining the user-friendly and easy-to-use APIs.

2 Related Work

2.1 Text Summarization

Text summarization has been a long-standing task for natural language processing. Early systems for summarization had been focusing on extractive summarization (Mihalcea and Tarau, 2004; Erkan and Radev, 2004), by finding the most salient sentences from source documents. With the advancement of neural networks (Bahdanau et al., 2014; Sutskever et al., 2014), the task of abstractive summarization has been receiving more attention (Rush et al., 2015; Chopra et al., 2016; Nallapati et al., 2016; Celikyilmaz et al., 2018; Chen and Bansal, 2018; Lebanoff et al., 2019) while neural-based methods have also been developed for extractive summarization (Zhong et al., 2019b,a; Xu and Durrett, 2019; Cho et al., 2019; Zhong et al., 2020; Jia et al., 2020). Moreover, the field of text summarization has also been broadening into several subcategories, such as multi-document summarization (McKeown and Radev, 1995; Carbonell and Goldstein, 1998; Ganesan et al., 2010; Fabbri et al., 2019), query-based summarization (Daumé III and Marcu, 2006; Otterbacher et al., 2009; Wang et al., 2016; Litvak and Vanetik, 2017; Nema et al., 2017; Baumel et al., 2018; Kulkarni et al., 2020) and dialogue summarization (Zhong et al., 2021; Chen et al., 2021a,b; Gliwa et al., 2019; Chen and Yang, 2020; Zhu et al., 2020). The proposed tasks, along with the datasets can also be classified by domain, such as news (Hermann et al., 2015; Fabbri et al., 2019; Narayan et al., 2018), meetings (Zhong et al., 2021; Carletta et al., 2005; Janin et al., 2003), scientifc literature (Cohan et al., 2018; Yasunaga et al., 2019), and medical records (DeYoung et al., 2021; Zhang et al., 2019; Portet et al., 2009).

2.2 Existing Systems for Summarization

Transformers (Wolf et al., 2020) includes a large number of transformer-based models in its *Modelhub*[1], including BART (Lewis et al., 2020) and Pegasus (Zhang et al., 2020a), two strong neural summarizers we also use in SummerTime. It also hosts datasets for various NLP tasks in its *Datasets*[2] library (Lhoest et al., 2021). Despite the wide coverage in transformer-based models, *Transformers* do not natively support models or pipelines that can handle aforementioned subcategories of summarization tasks. Moreover, it assumes certain NLP proficiency in its users, thus is harder for non-expert users to use. We integrate with *Transformers* and *Datasets* to import the state-of-the-art models, as well as summarization datasets into SummerTime, under the same easy-to-use framework.

Another library that we integrate with is *SummEval* (Fabbri et al., 2020), which is a collection of evaluation metrics for text summarization. SummerTime adopts a subset of such metrics in *SummEval* that are more popular and easier to understand. SummerTime also works well with *SummVis* (Vig et al., 2021), which provides an interactive way of analysing summarization results on the token-level. We also allow SummerTime to store output in a format that can be directly used by *SummVis* and its UI.

Other systems also exist for text summarization.

[1]https://huggingface.co/models
[2]https://huggingface.co/datasets

MEAD[3] is a platform for multi-lingual summarization. *Sumy*[4] can produce extractive summaries from HTML pages or plain texts, using several traditional summarization methods including Mihalcea and Tarau (2004) and Erkan and Radev (2004). *OpenNMT*[5] is mostly for machine translation, but it also hosts several summarization models such as Gehrmann et al. (2018).

3 SummerTime

The main purpose of SummerTime is to help non-expert users navigate through various summarization models, datasets and evaluation metrics, and provide simple yet comprehensive information for them to select the models that best suit their needs. Figure 1 shows how SummerTime is split into different modules to help users achieve such goal.

We will describe in detail each component of SummerTime in the following sections. With Section 3.1, we introduce the models we support in all subcategories of summarization; in Section 3.2 we list all the existing datasets we support and how users can create their own evaluation set. Finally in Section 3.3, we explain the evaluation metrics included with SummerTime and how they can help users find the most suitable model for their task.

3.1 Summarization Models

Here we introduce the summarization tasks SummerTime covers and the models we include to support these tasks. We first introduce the single-document summarization models (*i.e.,* "base models") in SummerTime, and then we show how those models can be used in a pipeline with other methods to complete more complex tasks such as query-based summarization and multi-document summarization.

Single-document Summarization

The following base summarization models are used in SummerTime. They all take a single document and generate a short summary.

TextRank (Mihalcea and Tarau, 2004) is a graph-based ranking model that can be used to perform extractive summarization;

LexRank (Erkan and Radev, 2004) is also a graph-based extractive summarization model, which is originally developed for multi-document summarization, but can also be applied to a single document. It uses centrality in a graph representation of sentences to measure their relative importance;

BART (Lewis et al., 2020) is an autoencoder model trained with denoising objectives during training. This seq2seq model is constructed with a bidirectional transformer encoder and a left-to-right transformer decoder, which can be fine-tuned to perform abstractive summarization;

Pegasus (Zhang et al., 2020a) proposes a new self-supervised pretraining objective for abstractive summarization, by reconstructing the target sentence with the remaining sentences in the document, it also shows strong results in low-resource settings;

Longformer (Beltagy et al., 2020) addresses the problem of memory need for self-attention models by using a combination of sliding window attention and global attention to approximate standard self-attention. It is able to support input length of 16K tokens, a large improvement over previous transformer-based models.

Multi-document Summarization

For multi-document summarization, we adopt two popular single-document summarizers to complete the task, as this is shown to be effective in previous work (Fabbri et al., 2019).

Combine-then-summarize is a pipeline method to handle multiple source documents, where the documents are concatenated and then a single document summarizer is used to produce the summary. Note that the length of the combined documents may exceed the input length limit for typical transformer-based models;

Summarize-then-combine first summarizes each source document independently, then merges the resulting summaries. Compared to the combine-then-summarize method, it is not affected by overlong inputs. However, since each document is summarized separately, the final summary may contain redundant information (Carbonell and Goldstein, 1998).

Query-based Summarization

For summarization tasks based on queries, we adopt a pipeline method and first use retrieval methods to identify salient sentences or utterances in the original document or dialogue, then generate summaries with a single-document summarization model.

TF-IDF retrieval is used in a pipeline to first retrieve the sentences that are most similar to the

[3] http://www.summarization.com/mead/

[4] https://github.com/miso-belica/sumy

[5] https://github.com/OpenNMT/OpenNMT-py

Pegasus:
Introduced in 2019, a large neural abstractive summarization model trained on web crawl and news data.
Strengths:
- High accuracy;
- Performs well on almost all kinds of non-literary written text;

Weaknesses:
- High memory usage

Initialization arguments:
- `device = 'cpu'` specifies the device the model is stored on and uses for computation. Use `device='gpu'` to run on an Nvidia GPU.

Figure 2: A short description of the Pegasus model, SummerTime includes such short descriptions for each supported models to help user making choices.

query based on the TF-IDF metric;
BM25 retrieval is used in the same pipeline, but BM25 is used as the similarity metric for retrieving the top-k relevant sentences.

Dialogue Summarization

Dialogue summarization is used to extract salient information from a dialogue. SummerTime includes two methods for dialogue summarization.
Flatten-then-summarize first flattens the dialogue data while preserving the speaker information, then a summarizer is used to generate the summary. Zhong et al. (2021) found that this presents a strong baseline for dialogue summarization.
HMNet (Zhu et al., 2020) explores the semantic structure of dialogues and develops a hierarchical architecture to first encode each utterance then aggregate with another encoder in modeling the long dialogue script. It also exploits role vectors to perform better speaker modeling.

Since we assume no NLP background of our target users, we provide a short description for every model to illustrate the strengths and weaknesses for each model. Such manually written descriptions are displayed when calling a static `get_description()` method on the model class. A sample description is shown in Figure 2.

3.2 Datasets

With SummerTime, users can easily create or convert their own summarization datasets and evaluate all the supporting models within the framework. However, in the case that no such datasets are available, SummerTime also provides access to a list of existing summarization datasets. This way, users can select models that perform the best on one or more datasets that are similar to their task.
CNN/DM (Hermann et al., 2015) contains news articles from CNN and Daily Mail. Version 1.0.0 of it was originally developed for reading comprehension and abstractive question answering, then the extractive and abstractive summarization annotations were added in version 2.0.0 and 3.0.0, respectively;
Multi-News (Fabbri et al., 2019) is a large-scale multi-document summarization dataset which contains news articles from the site newser.com with corresponding human-written summaries. Over 1,500 sites, i.e. news sources, appear as source documents, which is higher than the other common news datasets.
SAMSum (Gliwa et al., 2019) is a dataset with chat dialogues corpus, and human-annotated abstractive summarizations. In the SAMSum corpus, each dialogue is written by one person. After collecting all the dialogues, experts write a single summary for each dialogue.
XSum (Narayan et al., 2018) is a news summarization dataset for generating a one-sentence summary aiming to answer the question "What is the article about?". It consists of real-world articles and corresponding one-sentence summarization from British Broadcasting Corporation (BBC).
ScisummNet (Yasunaga et al., 2019) is a human-annotated dataset made for citation-aware scientific paper summarization (Scisumm). It contains over 1,000 papers in the ACL anthology network as well as their citation networks and their manually labeled summaries.
QMSum (Zhong et al., 2021) is designed for query-based multi-domain meeting summarization. It collects the meetings from AMI and ICSI dataset, as well as the committee meetings of the Welsh Parliament and Parliament of Canada. Experts manually wrote summaries for each meeting.
ArXiv (Cohan et al., 2018) is a dataset extracted from research papers for abstractive summarization of single, longer-form documents. For each research paper from arxiv.org, its abstract is used as ground-truth summaries.
PubMedQA (Jin et al., 2019) is a question answering dataset on the biomedical domain. Every QA instance contains a short answer and a long answer, latter of which can also be used for query-based summarization.
SummScreen (Chen et al., 2021a) consists of community contributed transcripts of television show episodes from The TVMegaSite, Inc. (TMS) and ForeverDream (FD). The summary of each tran-

Dataset	Domain	Size	Src. length	Tgt. length	Query	Multi-doc	Dial.	Lang.
CNN/DM(3.0.0)	News	300k	781	56	✗	✗	✗	En
Multi-News	News	56k	2.1k	263.8	✗	✓	✗	En
SAMSum	Open-domain	16k	94	20	✗	✗	✓	En
XSum	News	226k	431	23.3	✗	✗	✗	En
ScisummNet	Scientific articles	1k	4.7k	150	✗	✗	✗	En
QMSum	Meetings	1k	9.0k	69.6	✓	✗	✓	En
ArXiv	Scientific papers	215k	4.9k	220	✗	✗	✗	En
PubMedQA	Biomedial	273.5k	239	43	✓	✗	✗	En
SummScreen	TV shows	26.9k	6.6k	337.4	✗	✗	✓	En
MLSum	News	1.5M	635	31.8	✗	✗	✗	Fr, De, Es, Ru, Tr

Table 1: The summarization datasets included in SummerTime. "Dial." is short for "Dialogue" while "Lang." denotes the languages of each of the datasets.

script is the recap from TMS, or a recap of the FD shows from Wikipedia and TVMaze.

MLSum (Scialom et al., 2020) is a large-scale multilingual summarization dataset. It contains over 1.5M news articles in five languages, namely French, German, Spanish, Russian, and Turkish.

A summary of all datasets included in SummerTime is shown as Table 1, it is worth noticing that the fields in this table (*i.e.,* domain, query-based, multi-doc, etc) are also incorporated in each of the dataset classes (*e.g.,* `SAMSumDataset`) as class variables, so that such labels can later be used to identify applicable models. Similar with the models classes, we include a short description for each of the datasets. Note that the datasets, either existing ones or user created are mainly for evaluation purposes. We leave the important task of finetuning the models on these datasets for future work, for which we describe in more detail in Section 5.

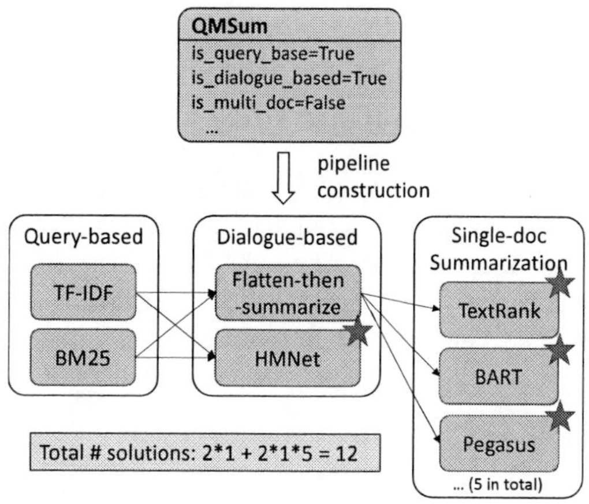

Figure 3: An illustration of how SummerTime finds solutions to a specific tasks defined by a dataset. The red star denotes that an ending point is reached.

3.3 Evaluation Metrics

To evaluate the performance of each supported model on certain dataset, SummerTime integrates with *SummEval* (Fabbri et al., 2020) and provides the following evaluation metrics for the users to understand model performance:

ROUGE (Lin, 2004) is a recall-oriented method based on overlapping n-grams, word sequences, and word pairs between the generated output and the gold summary;

BLEU (Papineni et al., 2002) measures n-gram precision and employs a penalty for brevity, BLEU is often used as an evaluation metric for machine translation;

ROUGE-WE (Ng and Abrecht, 2015) aims to go beyond surface lexical similarity and uses pretrained word embeddings to measure the similarity between different words and presents a better correlation with human judgements;

METEOR (Lavie and Agarwal, 2007) is based on word-to-word matches between generated and reference summaries, it consider two words as "aligned" based on a Porter stemmer (Porter, 2001) or synonyms in WordNet (Miller, 1995);

BERTScore (Zhang et al., 2020b) computes token-level similarity between sentences with the contextualized embeddings of each tokens.

Since we assume no NLP background from our target users, we make sure that SummerTime provides a short explanation for each evaluation metric as well as a clarification whether high or low scores are better for a given evaluation metric, to help the non-expert users understand the meaning of the metrics and use them to make decisions.

Algorithm 1 SELECT($\mathcal{M}, \mathcal{D}, \mathcal{E}$)

Input: $\mathcal{M}$: a pool of models to choose from, $\mathcal{D}$: a set of examples from a dataset, $\mathcal{T}$: a set of evaluation metrics, d: initial resource number, k: increase resource factor
Output: $M \subseteq \mathcal{M}$: a subset of models;

1: Initialize $M = \mathcal{M}, M' = \emptyset$
2: **while** $M' \neq M$ **do**
3:     $D = sample(\mathcal{D}, d)$
4:     **for each** $m \in M, e \in \mathcal{E}$ **do**
5:         $r_m^e = eval(m, D, e)$
6:     **end for**
7:     $M' = M$
8:     **for each** $m \in M$ **do**
9:         **if** $\exists m'$ s.t. $r_{m'}^e > r_m^e, \forall e \in \mathcal{E}$ **then**
10:             $M = M \backslash m$
11:         **end if**
12:     **end for**
13:     $d = d * k$
14: **end while**

```
import dataset
import model
import evaluation

# load a supported dataset
dataset.list_all_dataset()
dataset.CnndmDataset.show_description()
cnn_dataset = dataset.CnndmDataset()

# OPTION 1: user manually select and evaluate
model.list_all_models()
model.BartModel.show_capability()
exp_model = model.BartModel()

summaries = exp_model.summarize(articles)
targets = [instance.summary for instance in
            cnn_dataset.test_set]

bert_metric = evaluation.BertScore()
bert_metric.evaluate(summaries, targets)

# OPTION 2: automatic pipeline assembly
# Here we use a more complex task: query-
# based + dialogue-based summarization
qmsum_dataset = dataset.QMsumDataset()
assembled_models =
      assemble_model_pipeline(QMsumDataset)

# AND automatic model selection
model_selector = evaluation.ModelSelector(
                    models=assembled_models,
                    dataset=qmsum_dataset,
                    metrics=[bert_metric])
eval_table = model_selector.run()
model_selector.visualize()
```

Figure 4: Example code for using SummerTime. Additionally, we show two ways for performing model selection and evaluation.

4 Model Selection

In this section, we describe in detail about the workflow of SummerTime and how it can help our non-expert users find the best models for their use cases, which is one of the main functionalities that makes SummerTime stands out from similar libraries. A concrete code example of this is shown in Figure 4.

Create/select datasets The user would first load a dataset with the APIs we provide. During the process, the users also need to specify some Boolean attributes (*e.g.,* `is_query_based`, `is_dialogue_based`) to facilitate next steps. Alternatively, the user can also choose to use one of the datasets that are included in SummerTime, where such attributes are already specified in Table 1.

Construct pipelines After identifying the potential pipeline modules (*e.g.,* query-based module, dialogue-based module) that are applicable to the task, SummerTime automatically constructs solutions to a specific dataset by combining the pipelines and summarization models specified in Section 3.1. It further places all such constructed solutions in a pool for further evaluation and selection purposes. An example of this process in shown in Figure 3.

Search for the best models As shown in Figure 3, there can be a large pool of solutions to be evaluated. To save time and resources in searching for best models, SummerTime adopts the idea of successive halving (Li et al., 2017; Jamieson and Talwalkar, 2016). More specifically, SummerTime first uses a small number of examples from the dataset to evaluate all the candidates and eliminate models that are surpassed by at least one other model on every evaluation metric, then it does so iteratively and gradually increases the evaluation set size to reduce the variance. As shown in Algorithm 1, the final output is a set of competing models M that are better[6] than one another on at least one metric.

Visualization In addition to showing the numerical results as tables, SummerTime also allows the users to visualize the differences between different models with different charts and *SummVis* (Vig et al., 2021). Figure 5 shows some examples of such visualization methods SummerTime provides. A scatter plot can help the users understand the distribution of the model's performance over each example, while the radar chart is an intuitive way of comparing different models over various metrics.

[6]Note that in line 9 of the algorithm, the symbol ">" is conceptual and should be interpreted as "better than"

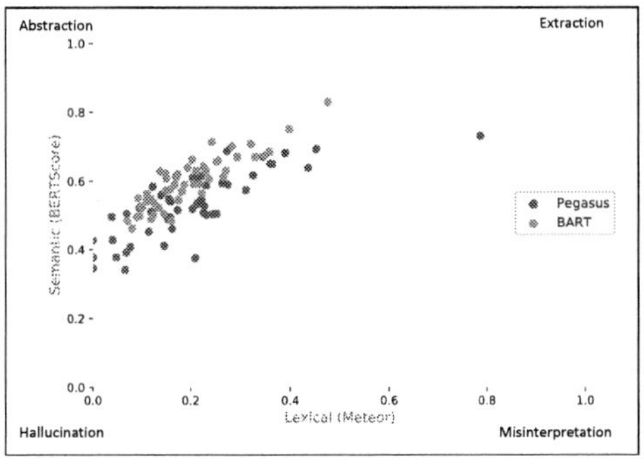

(a) Visualize the performance distribution of the models over the examples.

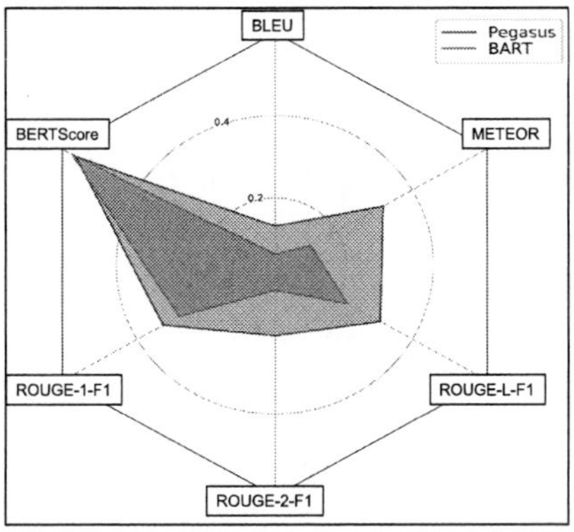

(b) Visualize the performance of models over different evaluation metrics.

Figure 5: Examples of the visualization SummerTime provides for the users to better compare the performance between different models.

SummerTime can also output the generated summaries to file formats that are directly compatible with *SummVis* (Vig et al., 2021), so that the users can easily use it to visualize the per-instance output differences on the token level.

5 Future Work

An important piece of future work for SummerTime is to include more summarization models (*e.g.*, multilingual, query-aware, etc) to enlarge the number of choices for the users, and more datasets to increase the chance of users finding similar tasks or domain for evaluation when they do not have a dataset of their own. We also plan to add more visualization methods for the users to better understand the differences between the outputs of various models and the behavior of each individual model itself. Moreover, we would like to enable fine-tuning for a subset of smaller models we support, to enable better performance on some domains or tasks for which no pretrained models are available. With all such potential improvements in the near future, we plan to supply SummerTime not only as a way for non-expert users to access state-of-art summarization models, but also as a go-to choice to quickly establishing baseline results for researchers as well.

6 Conclusion

We introduce SummerTime, a text summarization toolkit designed for non-expert users. SummerTime includes various summarization datasets, models and evaluation metrics and covers a wide range of summarization tasks. It can also automatically identify the best models or pipelines for a specific dataset and task, and visualize the differences between the model outputs and performances. SummerTime is open source under the Apache-2.0 license and is available online.

Acknowledgements

The authors would like to thank Rui Zhang, Alexander Fabbri, Chenguang Zhu, Budhaditya Deb, Asli Celikyilmaz and Rahul Jha for their advice for this work. This work is supported in part by a grant from Microsoft Research.

References

Dzmitry Bahdanau, Kyunghyun Cho, and Yoshua Bengio. 2014. Neural machine translation by jointly learning to align and translate. *arXiv preprint arXiv:1409.0473*.

Tal Baumel, Matan Eyal, and Michael Elhadad. 2018. Query focused abstractive summarization: Incorporating query relevance, multi-document coverage, and summary length constraints into seq2seq models. *arXiv preprint arXiv:1801.07704*.

Iz Beltagy, Matthew E. Peters, and Arman Cohan. 2020. Longformer: The long-document transformer. *arXiv:2004.05150*.

Jaime Carbonell and Jade Goldstein. 1998. The use of mmr, diversity-based reranking for reordering documents and producing summaries. In *Proceedings of the 21st annual international ACM SIGIR conference on Research and development in information retrieval*, pages 335–336.

Jean Carletta, Simone Ashby, Sebastien Bourban, Mike Flynn, Mael Guillemot, Thomas Hain, Jaroslav Kadlec, Vasilis Karaiskos, Wessel Kraaij, Melissa Kronenthal, et al. 2005. The ami meeting corpus: A pre-announcement. In *International workshop on machine learning for multimodal interaction*, pages 28–39. Springer.

Asli Celikyilmaz, Antoine Bosselut, Xiaodong He, and Yejin Choi. 2018. Deep communicating agents for abstractive summarization. In *Proceedings of the 2018 Conference of the North American Chapter of the Association for Computational Linguistics: Human Language Technologies, Volume 1 (Long Papers)*, volume 1, pages 1662–1675.

Jiaao Chen and Diyi Yang. 2020. Multi-view sequence-to-sequence models with conversational structure for abstractive dialogue summarization. In *Proceedings of the 2020 Conference on Empirical Methods in Natural Language Processing (EMNLP)*, pages 4106–4118, Online. Association for Computational Linguistics.

Mingda Chen, Zewei Chu, Sam Wiseman, and Kevin Gimpel. 2021a. Summscreen: A dataset for abstractive screenplay summarization. *arXiv preprint arXiv:2104.07091*.

Yen-Chun Chen and Mohit Bansal. 2018. Fast abstractive summarization with reinforce-selected sentence rewriting. In *Proceedings of the 56th Annual Meeting of the Association for Computational Linguistics (Volume 1: Long Papers)*, volume 1, pages 675–686.

Yulong Chen, Yang Liu, Liang Chen, and Yue Zhang. 2021b. Dialsumm: A real-life scenario dialogue summarization dataset. *arXiv preprint arXiv:2105.06762*.

Sangwoo Cho, Logan Lebanoff, Hassan Foroosh, and Fei Liu. 2019. Improving the similarity measure of determinantal point processes for extractive multi-document summarization. In *Proceedings of the 57th Annual Meeting of the Association for Computational Linguistics*, pages 1027–1038.

Sumit Chopra, Michael Auli, and Alexander M Rush. 2016. Abstractive sentence summarization with attentive recurrent neural networks. In *Proceedings of the 2016 Conference of the North American Chapter of the Association for Computational Linguistics: Human Language Technologies*, pages 93–98.

Arman Cohan, Franck Dernoncourt, Doo Soon Kim, Trung Bui, Seokhwan Kim, Walter Chang, and Nazli Goharian. 2018. A discourse-aware attention model for abstractive summarization of long documents. In *Proceedings of the 2018 Conference of the North American Chapter of the Association for Computational Linguistics: Human Language Technologies, Volume 2 (Short Papers)*, pages 615–621, New Orleans, Louisiana. Association for Computational Linguistics.

Hoa Trang Dang. 2005. Overview of duc 2005. In *Proceedings of the document understanding conference*, volume 2005, pages 1–12.

Hal Daumé III and Daniel Marcu. 2006. Bayesian query-focused summarization. In *Proceedings of the 21st International Conference on Computational Linguistics and 44th Annual Meeting of the Association for Computational Linguistics*, pages 305–312, Sydney, Australia. Association for Computational Linguistics.

Jay DeYoung, Iz Beltagy, Madeleine van Zuylen, Bailey Kuehl, and Lucy Lu Wang. 2021. Ms2: Multi-document summarization of medical studies.

Günes Erkan and Dragomir R Radev. 2004. Lexrank: Graph-based lexical centrality as salience in text summarization. *Journal of artificial intelligence research*, 22:457–479.

Alexander Fabbri, Irene Li, Tianwei She, Suyi Li, and Dragomir Radev. 2019. Multi-news: A large-scale multi-document summarization dataset and abstractive hierarchical model. In *Proceedings of the 57th Annual Meeting of the Association for Computational Linguistics*, pages 1074–1084, Florence, Italy. Association for Computational Linguistics.

Alexander R Fabbri, Wojciech Kryściński, Bryan McCann, Caiming Xiong, Richard Socher, and Dragomir Radev. 2020. Summeval: Re-evaluating summarization evaluation. *arXiv preprint arXiv:2007.12626*.

Kavita Ganesan, ChengXiang Zhai, and Jiawei Han. 2010. Opinosis: a graph-based approach to abstractive summarization of highly redundant opinions. In *Proceedings of the 23rd International Conference on Computational Linguistics*, pages 340–348.

Sebastian Gehrmann, Yuntian Deng, and Alexander Rush. 2018. Bottom-up abstractive summarization. In *Proceedings of the 2018 Conference on Empirical Methods in Natural Language Processing*, pages 4098–4109.

Bogdan Gliwa, Iwona Mochol, Maciej Biesek, and Aleksander Wawer. 2019. SAMSum corpus: A human-annotated dialogue dataset for abstractive summarization. In *Proceedings of the 2nd Workshop on New Frontiers in Summarization*, pages 70–79, Hong Kong, China. Association for Computational Linguistics.

Karl Moritz Hermann, Tomáš Kočiský, Edward Grefenstette, Lasse Espeholt, Will Kay, Mustafa Suleyman, and Phil Blunsom. 2015. Teaching machines to read and comprehend. In *Proceedings of the 28th International Conference on Neural Information Processing Systems-Volume 1*, pages 1693–1701.

Kevin Jamieson and Ameet Talwalkar. 2016. Non-stochastic best arm identification and hyperparameter optimization. In *Artificial Intelligence and Statistics*, pages 240–248. PMLR.

Adam Janin, Don Baron, Jane Edwards, Dan Ellis, David Gelbart, Nelson Morgan, Barbara Peskin, Thilo Pfau, Elizabeth Shriberg, Andreas Stolcke, et al. 2003. The icsi meeting corpus. In *2003 IEEE International Conference on Acoustics, Speech, and Signal Processing, 2003. Proceedings.(ICASSP'03).*, volume 1, pages I–I. IEEE.

Ruipeng Jia, Yanan Cao, Hengzhu Tang, Fang Fang, Cong Cao, and Shi Wang. 2020. Neural extractive summarization with hierarchical attentive heterogeneous graph network. In *Proceedings of the 2020 Conference on Empirical Methods in Natural Language Processing (EMNLP)*, pages 3622–3631.

Qiao Jin, Bhuwan Dhingra, Zhengping Liu, William Cohen, and Xinghua Lu. 2019. PubMedQA: A dataset for biomedical research question answering. In *Proceedings of the 2019 Conference on Empirical Methods in Natural Language Processing and the 9th International Joint Conference on Natural Language Processing (EMNLP-IJCNLP)*, pages 2567–2577, Hong Kong, China. Association for Computational Linguistics.

Sayali Kulkarni, Sheide Chammas, Wan Zhu, Fei Sha, and Eugene Ie. 2020. Aquamuse: Automatically generating datasets for query-based multi-document summarization. *arXiv preprint arXiv:2010.12694*.

Alon Lavie and Abhaya Agarwal. 2007. Meteor: An automatic metric for mt evaluation with high levels of correlation with human judgments. In *Proceedings of the second workshop on statistical machine translation*, pages 228–231.

Logan Lebanoff, Kaiqiang Song, Franck Dernoncourt, Doo Soon Kim, Seokhwan Kim, Walter Chang, and Fei Liu. 2019. Scoring sentence singletons and pairs for abstractive summarization. In *Proceedings of the 57th Annual Meeting of the Association for Computational Linguistics*, pages 2175–2189.

Mike Lewis, Yinhan Liu, Naman Goyal, Marjan Ghazvininejad, Abdelrahman Mohamed, Omer Levy, Veselin Stoyanov, and Luke Zettlemoyer. 2020. BART: Denoising sequence-to-sequence pre-training for natural language generation, translation, and comprehension. In *Proceedings of the 58th Annual Meeting of the Association for Computational Linguistics*, pages 7871–7880, Online. Association for Computational Linguistics.

Quentin Lhoest, Albert Villanova del Moral, Yacine Jernite, Abhishek Thakur, Patrick von Platen, Suraj Patil, Julien Chaumond, Mariama Drame, Julien Plu, Lewis Tunstall, Joe Davison, Mario Šaško, Gunjan Chhablani, Bhavitvya Malik, Simon Brandeis, Teven Le Scao, Victor Sanh, Canwen Xu, Nicolas Patry, Angelina McMillan-Major, Philipp Schmid, Sylvain Gugger, Clément Delangue, Théo Matussière, Lysandre Debut, Stas Bekman, Pierric Cistac, Thibault Goehringer, Victor Mustar, François Lagunas, Alexander M. Rush, and Thomas Wolf. 2021. Datasets: A community library for natural language processing.

Lisha Li, Kevin Jamieson, Giulia DeSalvo, Afshin Rostamizadeh, and Ameet Talwalkar. 2017. Hyperband: A novel bandit-based approach to hyperparameter optimization. *The Journal of Machine Learning Research*, 18(1):6765–6816.

Chin-Yew Lin. 2004. Rouge: A package for automatic evaluation of summaries. In *Text summarization branches out*, pages 74–81.

Marina Litvak and Natalia Vanetik. 2017. Query-based summarization using MDL principle. In *Proceedings of the MultiLing 2017 Workshop on Summarization and Summary Evaluation Across Source Types and Genres*, pages 22–31, Valencia, Spain. Association for Computational Linguistics.

Kathleen McKeown and Dragomir R Radev. 1995. Generating summaries of multiple news articles. In *Proceedings of the 18th annual international ACM SIGIR conference on Research and development in information retrieval*, pages 74–82.

Rada Mihalcea and Paul Tarau. 2004. TextRank: Bringing order into text. In *Proceedings of the 2004 Conference on Empirical Methods in Natural Language Processing*, pages 404–411, Barcelona, Spain. Association for Computational Linguistics.

George A Miller. 1995. Wordnet: a lexical database for english. *Communications of the ACM*, 38(11):39–41.

Ramesh Nallapati, Bowen Zhou, Cicero dos Santos, Ça glar Gulçehre, and Bing Xiang. 2016. Abstractive text summarization using sequence-to-sequence rnns and beyond. *CoNLL 2016*, page 280.

Shashi Narayan, Shay B. Cohen, and Mirella Lapata. 2018. Don't give me the details, just the summary! Topic-aware convolutional neural networks for extreme summarization. In *Proceedings of the 2018 Conference on Empirical Methods in Natural Language Processing*, Brussels, Belgium.

Preksha Nema, Mitesh M. Khapra, Anirban Laha, and Balaraman Ravindran. 2017. Diversity driven attention model for query-based abstractive summarization. In *Proceedings of the 55th Annual Meeting of the Association for Computational Linguistics (Volume 1: Long Papers)*, pages 1063–1072, Vancouver, Canada. Association for Computational Linguistics.

Jun-Ping Ng and Viktoria Abrecht. 2015. Better summarization evaluation with word embeddings for ROUGE. In *Proceedings of the 2015 Conference on Empirical Methods in Natural Language Processing*, pages 1925–1930, Lisbon, Portugal. Association for Computational Linguistics.

Jahna Otterbacher, Gunes Erkan, and Dragomir R Radev. 2009. Biased lexrank: Passage retrieval using random walks with question-based priors. *Information Processing & Management*, 45(1):42–54.

Kishore Papineni, Salim Roukos, Todd Ward, and Wei-Jing Zhu. 2002. Bleu: a method for automatic evaluation of machine translation. In *Proceedings of the 40th annual meeting of the Association for Computational Linguistics*, pages 311–318.

Martin F Porter. 2001. Snowball: A language for stemming algorithms.

François Portet, Ehud Reiter, Albert Gatt, Jim Hunter, Somayajulu Sripada, Yvonne Freer, and Cindy Sykes. 2009. Automatic generation of textual summaries from neonatal intensive care data. *Artificial Intelligence*, 173(7-8):789–816.

Alexander M Rush, Sumit Chopra, and Jason Weston. 2015. A neural attention model for abstractive sentence summarization. In *Proceedings of the 2015 Conference on Empirical Methods in Natural Language Processing*, pages 379–389.

Thomas Scialom, Paul-Alexis Dray, Sylvain Lamprier, Benjamin Piwowarski, and Jacopo Staiano. 2020. MLSUM: The multilingual summarization corpus. In *Proceedings of the 2020 Conference on Empirical Methods in Natural Language Processing (EMNLP)*, pages 8051–8067, Online. Association for Computational Linguistics.

Ilya Sutskever, Oriol Vinyals, and Quoc V Le. 2014. Sequence to sequence learning with neural networks. *Advances in Neural Information Processing Systems*, 27:3104–3112.

Ashish Vaswani, Noam Shazeer, Niki Parmar, Jakob Uszkoreit, Llion Jones, Aidan N Gomez, Łukasz Kaiser, and Illia Polosukhin. 2017. Attention is all you need. *Advances in Neural Information Processing Systems*, 30:5998–6008.

Jesse Vig, Wojciech Kryscinski, Karan Goel, and Nazneen Fatema Rajani. 2021. Summvis: Interactive visual analysis of models, data, and evaluation for text summarization. *arXiv preprint arXiv:2104.07605*.

Lu Wang, Hema Raghavan, Vittorio Castelli, Radu Florian, and Claire Cardie. 2016. A sentence compression based framework to query-focused multi-document summarization. *arXiv preprint arXiv:1606.07548*.

Thomas Wolf, Lysandre Debut, Victor Sanh, Julien Chaumond, Clement Delangue, Anthony Moi, Pierric Cistac, Tim Rault, Remi Louf, Morgan Funtowicz, Joe Davison, Sam Shleifer, Patrick von Platen, Clara Ma, Yacine Jernite, Julien Plu, Canwen Xu, Teven Le Scao, Sylvain Gugger, Mariama Drame, Quentin Lhoest, and Alexander Rush. 2020. Transformers: State-of-the-art natural language processing. In *Proceedings of the 2020 Conference on Empirical Methods in Natural Language Processing: System Demonstrations*, pages 38–45, Online. Association for Computational Linguistics.

Jiacheng Xu and Greg Durrett. 2019. Neural extractive text summarization with syntactic compression. In *Proceedings of the 2019 Conference on Empirical Methods in Natural Language Processing*, Hong Kong, China. Association for Computational Linguistics.

Michihiro Yasunaga, Jungo Kasai, Rui Zhang, Alexander R Fabbri, Irene Li, Dan Friedman, and Dragomir R Radev. 2019. Scisummnet: A large annotated corpus and content-impact models for scientific paper summarization with citation networks. In *Proceedings of the AAAI Conference on Artificial Intelligence*, volume 33, pages 7386–7393.

Jingqing Zhang, Yao Zhao, Mohammad Saleh, and Peter Liu. 2020a. Pegasus: Pre-training with extracted gap-sentences for abstractive summarization. In *International Conference on Machine Learning*, pages 11328–11339. PMLR.

Tianyi Zhang, Varsha Kishore, Felix Wu, Kilian Q. Weinberger, and Yoav Artzi. 2020b. Bertscore: Evaluating text generation with bert. In *International Conference on Learning Representations*.

Yuhao Zhang, Derek Merck, Emily Bao Tsai, Christopher D Manning, and Curtis P Langlotz. 2019. Optimizing the factual correctness of a summary: A study of summarizing radiology reports. *arXiv preprint arXiv:1911.02541*.

Ming Zhong, Pengfei Liu, Yiran Chen, Danqing Wang, Xipeng Qiu, and Xuanjing Huang. 2020. Extractive summarization as text matching. In *Proceedings of the 58th Annual Meeting of the Association for Computational Linguistics, ACL 2020, Online, July 5-10, 2020*, pages 6197–6208. Association for Computational Linguistics.

Ming Zhong, Pengfei Liu, Danqing Wang, Xipeng Qiu, and Xuan-Jing Huang. 2019a. Searching for effective neural extractive summarization: What works and what's next. In *Proceedings of the 57th Annual Meeting of the Association for Computational Linguistics*, pages 1049–1058.

Ming Zhong, Danqing Wang, Pengfei Liu, Xipeng Qiu, and Xuanjing Huang. 2019b. A closer look at data bias in neural extractive summarization models. *EMNLP-IJCNLP 2019*, page 80.

Ming Zhong, Da Yin, Tao Yu, Ahmad Zaidi, Mutethia Mutuma, Rahul Jha, Ahmed Hassan Awadallah, Asli Celikyilmaz, Yang Liu, Xipeng Qiu, and Dragomir Radev. 2021. QMSum: A new benchmark for query-based multi-domain meeting summarization. In *Proceedings of the 2021 Conference of the North American Chapter of the Association for Computational Linguistics: Human Language Technologies*, pages 5905–5921, Online. Association for Computational Linguistics.

Chenguang Zhu, Ruochen Xu, Michael Zeng, and Xuedong Huang. 2020. A hierarchical network for abstractive meeting summarization with cross-domain pretraining. In *Findings of the Association for Computational Linguistics: EMNLP 2020*, pages 194–203, Online. Association for Computational Linguistics.

Chandler: An Explainable Sarcastic Response Generator

Silviu Vlad Oprea[1], **Steven R. Wilson**[1,2], **Walid Magdy**[1]
[1]School of Informatics, University of Edinburgh, Edinburgh, United Kingdom
[2]School of Engineering and Computer Science, Oakland University, Rochester, MI, USA
{silviu.oprea,steven.wilson}@ed.ac.uk,wmagdy@inf.ed.ac.uk

Abstract

We introduce Chandler, a system that generates sarcastic responses to a given utterance. Previous sarcasm generators assume the intended meaning that sarcasm conceals is the opposite of the literal meaning. We argue that this traditional theory of sarcasm provides a grounding that is neither necessary, nor sufficient, for sarcasm to occur. Instead, we ground our generation process on a formal theory that specifies conditions that unambiguously differentiate sarcasm from non-sarcasm. Furthermore, Chandler not only generates sarcastic responses, but also *explanations* for why each response is sarcastic. This provides accountability, crucial for avoiding miscommunication between humans and conversational agents, particularly considering that sarcastic communication can be offensive. In human evaluation, Chandler achieves comparable or higher sarcasm scores, compared to state-of-the-art generators, while generating more diverse responses, that are more specific and more coherent to the input.

1 Introduction

The prevalence of sarcasm on the social web (Khodak et al., 2018; Sykora et al., 2020) has motivated more and more computational investigations across the research community. Most focus on textual sarcasm detection (Riloff et al., 2013; Joshi et al., 2016; Wallace et al., 2015; Rajadesingan et al., 2015; Bamman and Smith, 2015; Amir et al., 2016; Hazarika et al., 2018; Oprea and Magdy, 2019): the task of classifying whether or not a given text is sarcastic.

Recently, a new research direction considers sarcasm generation. This is motivated by the potential to create approachable conversational agents. These would be more effective at emulating a human correspondent, considering that sarcasm is a natural part of human discourse (Mishra et al., 2019). The limited amount of work on sarcasm generation is spread across two variants of the task: generating a *sarcastic response* to an input utterance (Joshi et al., 2015); and generating a *sarcastic paraphrase* of an input utterance (Mishra et al., 2019; Chakrabarty et al., 2020).

A major limitation of existing sarcasm generation systems is that they rely on variants of the traditional theory of sarcasm: that the intended meaning concealed by sarcasm is the opposite of the literal meaning. Driven by this assumption, their aim is to generate phrases that either express two incongruous propositions (Joshi et al., 2015; Mishra et al., 2019; Chakrabarty et al., 2020), or express a proposition that is incongruous to the discourse setting (Joshi et al., 2015). However, the traditional theory provides a grounding that is neither necessary, nor sufficient, for sarcasm to occur, as discussed in Section 3. Furthermore, it is less obvious how previous systems that consider the task of generating sarcastic paraphrases, rather than responses, could be used for enabling conversational agents to generate sarcasm.

To overcome these limitations, we first select a formal theory that, from a linguistic-theoretical perspective, specifies devices whose presence is both necessary and sufficient to identify sarcasm, unambiguously differentiating it from non-sarcasm. Grounded on this theory, we propose our sarcasm generation system, *Chandler*[1]. Being grounded in a theory, Chandler is also explainable. That is, we are able to generate not only sarcastic responses, but also *explanations* for why each response is sarcastic. We believe this kind of accountability is crucial for avoiding miscommunication between humans and conversational agents, particularly considering the potentially offensive nature of sarcastic communication (Wilson, 2006).

We employ human annotators on a crowdsourcing platform to evaluate Chandler against state-of-the-art generators, across multiple dimensions.

[1]Inspired by the popular TV sitcom.

Proceedings of the 2021 Conference on Empirical Methods in Natural Language Processing: System Demonstrations, pages 339–349
November 7–11, 2021.

Chandler achieves comparable or higher sarcasm scores, while generating responses that are more diverse, and are perceived as more specific and coherent than those of previous sarcasm generators.

A live demo of the system, allowing users to input an utterance and view sarcastic responses, along with their explanations, is available at `https://bit.ly/ChandlerEMNLP`. We will also release, along with the camera ready version, all inputs, responses, model checkpoints, and the code that implements Chandler, our explainable sarcasm generator, under a Creative Commons CC BY-NC license.

2 Related Work

The earliest work on sarcasm generation is that of Joshi et al. (2015), who introduce SarcasmBot, a sarcastic response generation system. SarcasmBot generates a response based on one of eight possible generators, each containing a set of predefined patterns. The generators do not in fact account for the meaning of the input, rather, they only focus on aspects such as the overall sentiment or presence of swear words.

Mishra et al. (2019) suggest a sarcastic paraphrase generator. They assume that the input is always of negative polarity, and use an unsupervised pipeline of four modules to convert such an input $u^{(-)}$ to a sarcastic version. In the Sentiment Neutralisation module, they filter out negative sentiment words from $u^{(-)}$ to produce $u^{(0)}$. In the Positive Sentiment Induction module, they modify $u^{(0)}$ to convey positive sentiment, producing $u^{(+)}$. Next, in the Negative Situation Retrieval module, they mine a phrase $v^{(-)}$ that expresses a negative situation. $v^{(-)}$ is selected from a set of predefined phrases, based on the similarity to the original input. Finally, the Sarcasm Synthesis module constructs the sarcastic paraphrase from $u^{(+)}$ and $v^{(-)}$.

Chakrabarty et al. (2020) present a similar pipeline. Their R^3 system first employs a Reversal of Valence module, which replaces input words of negative valence with their lexical antonyms using WordNet (Miller, 1995) to produce $u^{(+)}$. Next, it builds an utterance v that is incongruous to $u^{(+)}$, and generates sarcasm from $u^{(+)}$ and v.

Second, they all rely on variants of the traditional theory of sarcasm, which provides a grounding that is neither necessary, nor sufficient, for sarcasm to occur, as discussed in Section 3. Third, the systems of Mishra et al. (2019) and Chakrabarty et al. (2020) are only designed to work with negative inputs. However, sarcastic communication can have many communicative goals, including to praise (Bruntsch and Ruch, 2017), or strengthen friendships (Jorgensen, 1996; Pexman and Zvaigzne, 2004)

3 Linguistic Grounding

The goal of this section is to select a linguistic theory on which to ground the sarcasm generation process.

Gricean Theory In the traditional theory, sarcasm is a form of figurative language that is created by literally saying one thing but meaning the opposite. As Sperber and Wilson (1981) point out, a semantic theory of sarcasm that provides such an explanation would need to provide (a) a mechanism of deriving figurative meaning, (b) and an explanation of why figurative meaning exists in the first place. The traditional theory is incomplete because it does not provide answers to such questions. Moving further Grice (Grice, 1975) sees sarcasm as a blatant flouting of the first maxim of quality ("do not say what you believe is false"), giving rise to a conversational implicature that ensures the cooperative principle is observed. That is, the sarcastic speaker does not figuratively mean, but conversationally implicates the opposite of what they say. A main limitation of the Gricean view is that the flouting is not necessary for sarcasm to occur. For instance, consider sarcastic understatements such as saying "This was not the best movie ever" to mean the movie was bad. Violation is also not sufficient. For instance, it also occurs in the construction of certain stylistic devices, such as metaphors.

Echoic Theories Consider the following scenario:

> [Scenario 1] Alice and Bob go for a walk. Despite Alice's requests, Bob refuses to bring along an umbrella, assuring her it would not rain. Momentarily after leaving the house, it starts raining. Alice to Bob:
>
> (1) a. It's definitely not raining.

Sperber and Wilson (1981) invite us to reconsider the goal of sarcastic utterances. According to the theories discussed so far, Alice's goal is to sarcastically convey her belief about the weather—a belief that is the opposite of what she says. Note, however, that especially when prosodic or other contextual cues are missing, knowing her belief is a prerequisite for, not a consequence of, recognising her sarcasm. Sperber and Wilson (1981) suggest a different goal that she might have, mainly that of conveying a belief not about the weather, but about the content of 1a itself. In their view, the utterance is not *used*[2] by Alice, but is an echoic *mention* of a previous proposition, mainly the one expressed by Bob's claim that it would not rain. Through the mention, Alice expresses a dissociative attitude towards Bob's claim, perhaps suggesting it was ridiculous of him to expect a dry weather. This *echoic mention theory* offers an explanation for why sarcasm exists in the first place. However, it does not cover all instances of sarcasm. An example of a non-echoic sarcastic utterance is Alice saying:

(1) b. Thanks for leaving the umbrella at home.

The echoic mention theory is also unable to differentiate between sarcastic and non-sarcastic echoic mentions. Several variants of the echoic mention theory have been suggested (Kreuz and Glucksberg, 1989; Wilson and Sperber, 1992; Sperber and Wilson, 1998), however they all suffer from similar limitations. We invite the interested reader to further consult Giora (1995), Kumon-Nakamura et al. (1995), and Utsumi (2000).

Pretense Theories Clark and Gerrig (1984) introduce the *pretense theory* of sarcasm which claims that a sarcastic speaker pretends to be an injudicious person speaking to an imaginary uninitiated audience who would accept the literal interpretation of the speaker's utterance. This way, the speaker expresses a negative attitude towards the pretended person, the imaginary audience, and the situation portrayed through their acting. A variant of the pretense theory is viewing sarcasm as a *joint pretense* of the speaker and the listener (Clark, 1996). That is, instead of the speaker pretending to be an imaginary person, both interlocutors pretend to be in an imaginary situation in which they are performing a serious communicative act directed at the listener. Sarcasm is caused by the joint pretense of the speaker and the listener that the imaginary situation is taking place. Both theories fail to distinguish sarcasm from non-sarcastic pretense, such as parody. Their assumptions are, therefore, not sufficient to explain sarcasm. They are also not necessary. An argument in this direction is provided by Utsumi (2000, p. 1782).

3.1 Implicit Display Theory

The theories reviewed so far make assumptions about the nature of sarcasm that are neither necessary, nor sufficient, for sarcasm to occur. We now introduce the Implicit Display Theory (IDT) (Utsumi, 1996), which focuses specifically on making the distinction between sarcasm and non-sarcasm. Because of this, we chose it to serve as a grounding for our generation process. We provide a brief introduction here, but invite the interested reader to consult (Utsumi, 2000) for an overview of how it overcomes the limitations of previous theories.

The IDT first defines the concept of an ironic environment. We say a situation in which an utterance occurs is surrounded by an ironic environment if the discourse context includes the following components:

1. The speaker has expectation Q at time t_0;
2. Q fails at time $t_1 > t_0$;
3. The speaker has a negative attitude towards the failure of Q.

In Utsumi (1996)'s view, such a situation within the discourse context facilitates the use of sarcasm. Note that the negative attitude could have several intensities, could be serious, or joking. Note also that the idea of linking sarcasm to an expectation is not new to Utsumi (1996), rather it is supported by previous work (Kreuz and Glucksberg, 1989; Kumon-Nakamura et al., 1995).

From here, according to the IDT, an utterance is sarcastic if and only if it is given in a situation surrounded by an ironic environment and it implicitly displays all three components of the ironic environment. Implicit display is realised if the utterance:

1. alludes to the speaker's failed expectation Q;
2. includes pragmatic insincerity, by intentionally violating one of the pragmatic principles;
3. implies (indirectly expresses) the speaker's negative attitude towards the failure of Q.

The pragmatic principles that we are referring to include, among others, Grice's maxims (Grice, 1975), and the felicity conditions for well-formed speech acts (Searle and Searle, 1969).

A final claim of the theory is that sarcasm is a prototype-based category characterised by implicit display. That is, the degree of sarcasm of an utter-

[2]See Sperber and Wilson (1981) for a discussion on the use–mention distinction.

ance is proportional to how many implicit display conditions the utterance meets.

4 Methodology

The IDT directly suggests an algorithm for sarcasm generation that identifies an ironic environment, then creates an utterance that implicitly displays it. We now discuss how we implement each step.

Ironic Environment Let U_{in} be an input text to our system. Herein, we assume the expectation Q that is part of the ironic environment negates what U_{in} proposes. For instance, say U_{in} expresses the event $P =$ [<user> wins the marathon]. We assume $Q = \neg P =$ [<user> does not win the marathon]. As we shall see, the algorithm we suggest will not, in fact, require us to formulate Q, but it relies on the above assumption.

Allusion to Q Following Utsumi (2000), we define allusion in terms of coherence relations, similar to the relations of rhetorical structure theory (RST) (Mann and Thompson, 1987). That is, if U is an utterance that expresses proposition α, we say U alludes to the expectation Q if and only if there is a chain of coherence relations from α to Q. So, we need to first select a proposition α to either start or end the coherence chain, then specify the chain between α and Q, and formulate U such that it expresses α. We suggest defining such α as objects of if-then relations, where the subject is P, the proposition expressed by input text U_{in}. That is, relations of the form "if P then α" should hold. To infer α given U_{in}, we use COMET (Bosselut et al., 2019), an adaptation framework for constructing commonsense knowledge. Specifically, we use the COMET variant fine-tuned on ATOMIC (Sap et al., 2019), a dataset of typed if-then relations. [3]. COMET inputs the subject of the relation, along with the relation type, and outputs the relation object. In our case, the subject is U_{in}, and we set α to the output.

We leverage four relation types. In the examples that follow, assume the input text is $U_{\text{in}} =$'<user> won the marathon': (1) **xNeed**: the object α of a relation of this type specifies an action that the user needed to perform before the event took place, e.g. "if U_{in} then $\alpha =$ [*xNeed* to train hard]"; (2) **xAttr**: the object α specifies how a user that would perform such an action is seen, e.g. "if P then $\alpha =$ [*xAttr* competitive]"; (3) **xReact**: the object α specifies how the user could feel as a result of the event, e.g. "if P then $\alpha =$ [*xReact* happy]"; and (4) **xEffect**: the object specifies a possible effect that the action has on the user, e.g. "if P then $\alpha =$ [*xEffect* gets congratulated]". In Table 1 we show, for each relation type, the coherence chains between the relation object α and the failed expectation Q. Under these conditions, to generate an utterance U that alludes to Q, we simply need to choose U to expresses α.

[3]We use the COMET checkpoint published at `http://bit.ly/comet-checkpoints`.

Algorithm 1: Generate sarcastic response

input: utterance U_{in};
ironic environment
  Let $Q := \neg P$ be the failed expectation;
implicit display
  Choose an if-then relation type τ from *xNeed*, *xAttr*, *xReact*, and *xEffect*;
  Let $\alpha = \text{COMET}(U_{\text{in}}, \tau)$;
return response U that expresses *emotion*$(\neg\alpha)$;

Pragmatic insincerity The second requirement for implicit display is that the utterance generated U should include pragmatic insincerity. In this paper, we focus on violating Grice's maxim of quality (Grice, 1975), where we aim for the propositional contents of U (generated utterance) and U_{in} (input text) to be incongruous. To achieve this, we first choose an if-then relation type, then infer the relation object α from U_{in} using COMET, and construct U to express $\neg\alpha$. For instance, if $U_{\text{in}} =$'<user> won the marathon', and we have chosen the *xAttr* relation type, U could be chose to express $\neg\alpha =$ [<user> is not competitive].

Negative attitude To fulfill the last requirement of implicit display, the utterance generated should imply a negative attitude towards the failure of the expectation Q. As pointed out by Utsumi (1996), this can be achieved by embedding verbal cues usually associated with such attitudes, including hyperbole and interjections.

Logical form and explainability At this point we formulate Algorithm 1 for generating a sarcastic response U, given an input utterance U_{in} that expresses proposition P. We refer to *emotion*$(\neg\alpha)$ as the *logical form* of the sarcastic response we generate. Here, *emotion* is a function that augments $\neg\alpha$ to express a negative attitude. Note that the logical form, together with the coherence chain between α and the failed expectation Q, provide a complete explanation for *how* and *why* sarcasm occurs. The explanation is $\epsilon = (\text{emotion}(\neg\alpha), \mathcal{C})$, where is the coherence chain from α to Q. The co-

relation type	example relation	coherence chain
xNeed	if P then $\alpha =$ [xNeed to train hard]	volitional-cause(α, P) and contrast(P, Q)
xAttr	if P then $\alpha =$ [xAttr competitive]	condition(α, I_P) $\wedge$ purpose(I_P, P) $\wedge$ contrast(P, Q)
xReact	if P then $\alpha =$ [xReact happy]	contrast(Q, P) $\wedge$ volitional-result(P, α)
xEffect	if P then $\alpha =$ [xEffect gets congratulated]	contrast(Q, P) $\wedge$ non-volitional-result(P, α)

Table 1: Coherence chains between the object α of an if-then relation and the failed expectation Q, for each relation type, as discussed in Section 4. Here, P is the proposition expressed by the input text U_{in}. In the examples, U_{in} ='<user> won the marathon'.

herence chain for each relation type can be selected from Table 1. This makes our sarcasm generation process accountable.

Logical Form to Text To convert the logical form to text, we rely on predefined patterns for each if-then relation type. As a running example, assume the input utterance U_{in} ='<user> won the marathon' and the chosen relation type is *xAttr*. Say α = COMET(U_{in}, *xAttr*) = [*xAttr* competitive]. The logical form is *emotion*($\neg$[*xAttr* competitive]). We construct an intermediate utterance U^0_{out} using the rule *<user> <verb> competitive*, where *<verb>* is a verb specific to each relation type. In our example, U^0_{out} could be '<user> is competitive'. From U^0_{out}, we generate a sarcastic response U_{out} to U_{in} as follows. We first apply a rule-based algorithm to generate the negation of U^0_{out} in a manner similar to Chakrabarty et al. (2020), discussed in Section 2. The result could be '<user> is not competitive', expressing $\neg$[*xAttr* competitive]. Next, in a pattern-based manner, we augment this with hyperbole and interjections, as indicated by Utsumi (2000), to get U_{out}, expressing *emotion*($\neg$[*xAttr* competitive]). This could be '<user> is definitely not competitive, yay!'. A full list of patterns is shown in the Appendix A.

In the running example we focused on the *xAttr* relation type. Recall there are four relation types that we consider, *xNeed*, *xAttr*, *xReact*, and *xEffect*. As such, for each input text U_{in}, we generate 4 responses, one for each relation type. We use the pattern Ch-<relation > to refer to each response of our system, *Chandler*. For instance, Ch-xAttr refers to U_{out} built considering the *xAttr* relation, while Ch-xNeed refers to U_{out} built considering the *xNeed* relation.

Note that other strategies for converting the logical form of sarcasm to text are possible. For instance, using policy-based generation with external rewards (Mishra et al., 2019) might have lead to higher perceived sarcasticness of our generated responses. We leave this to future work. Our goal was to provide a theory-based, explainable, generation framework.

5 Experiments

5.1 Setup

To evaluate Chandler, we built a survey[4] that we published on the Prolific Academic[5] crowdsourcing platform. In the survey, we presented annotators with the input text U_{in}, along with the responses produced by Chandler-xNeed, Chandler-xAttr, Chandler-xReact, and Chandler-xEffect.

We also included a response from DialoGPT (Zhang et al., 2020), a recent dialogue system that is not built to be sarcastic; a response produced by SarcasmBot, the sarcastic response generator of Joshi et al. (2015); and a response produced by R^3, the state-of-the-art sarcastic paraphrase generator of Chakrabarty et al. (2020). While not designed to produce responses, we applied R^3 to the output of DialoGPT to get a sarcastic rephrase of a response to the input.

As inputs, we selected texts from the corpus published by Wilson and Mihalcea (2019). The corpus contains short texts (extracted from tweets) where users describe actions they performed. We compute the sentiment polarity of each text using the classifier of Barbieri et al. (2020), a RoBERTa model (Liu et al., 2019) fine-tuned on the tweet sentiment dataset of Rosenthal et al. (2017). Next, we form five partitions of 50 texts each: *very negative* and *very positive*, containing the top 50 texts based on their negative and positive probabilities, respectively; *negative*, containing random texts for which the probability of being negative was higher that the probabilities of being positive or neutral; and *positive* and *neutral*, partitions that we formed analogously to how we formed the *negative* partition. Our final input dataset contains 250 texts. For each input, we collected 3 annotations for its

[4]Participant information sheet is shown in Appendix C.
[5]https://prolific.co

system	response
DialoGPT	I'm not sure if you're being sarcastic or not.
DialoGPT+R^3	I'm sure if you're being sarcastic or not. No one has yet been hurt.
SarcasmBot	That is a very useful piece of information! LMAO
Ch-xNeed	Yay! Good job not knowing how to write.
Ch-xAttr	Yay! You're not a very unintelligent person, that's for sure.
Ch-xReact	You're not feeling very embarrassed right now, that's for sure. Yay!
Ch-xEffect	You're not really going to sigh in frustration right now, that's for sure. Brilliant!

Table 2: Responses generated by all systems to the utterance "I ran out of characters :drooling_face:", as discussed in Section 5.1.

System	sarc.	hum.	coh.	spec.	diversity
DialoGPT (non-sarcastic)	0.6	0.3	2.3	2.0	0.92
DialoGPT+R^3	0.8	0.3	0.9	1.3	0.92
SarcasmBot	2.5	0.8	1.4	0.9	0.14
Ch-xNeed	1.9	0.6	1.3	1.6	0.80
Ch-xAttr	2.1	0.6	1.3	1.4	0.80
Ch-xReact	1.7	0.4	1.0	1.0	0.35
Ch-xEffect	1.6	0.5	1.1	1.3	0.67

Table 3: Means of the sarcasm, humour, specificity, and coherence scores provided by annotators, for each variant of Chandler (Ch), as discussed in Section 5.2. Diversity is the ratio of unique responses generated for our 250 inputs.

responses.

Table 2 shows an example input utterance, along with responses from all systems.

All in all, each survey instance contained a specific input text, and seven responses generated as mentioned above and presented in a random order. In the survey, we asked annotators to evaluate each response across four dimensions: (1) Sarcasm: How sarcastic is the response? (2) Humour: How funny is the remark? (3) Coherence: How coherent is the remark to the input? It is coherent if it sounds like sensible response that a person might give in a real conversation; and (4) Specificity: How specific is the remark to the input? It is not specific if it can be used as a response to many other inputs. Each dimension ranged from 0 to 4, in line with previous work (Chakrabarty et al., 2020).

5.2 Results

In Table 3 we show mean sarcasm, humour, specificity, and coherence scores provided by annotators for each variant of Chandler, across all inputs.

We have four strategies for alluding to the failed expectation, depending on the relation type considered. We notice the highest sarcasm score is achieved by Ch-xAttr, followed by Ch-xNeed, Ch-xReact and Ch-xEffect. Out of the allusion strategies selected, the responses perceived as most sarcastic are those that mention attributes of the user. Similarly, we notice that, among variants of Chandler, those that use the xAttr and xNeed relations are perceived and the most coherent and specific to the input, and achieve the highest humour score.

Chandler achieves lower specificity and coherence scores compared to DialoGPT, which is to be expected considering that DialoGPT is not designed to conceal the intended meaning using sarcasm. The sarcasm score, however, for all variants of Chandler, is considerably higher compared to DialoGPT. The situation is similar when comparing Chandler to DialoGPT+R^3.

When comparing to SarcasmBot, while specificity is considerably higher for most variants of Chandler, and coherence is similar, sarcasm score is slightly lower. In particular, the most sarcastic variant of Chandler, Ch-xAttr, achieves a sarcasm score of 2.1, compared 2.5 achieved by SarcasmBot. This is expected, considering that SarcasmBot provides responses from a fixed set of responses that were carefully curated for sarcasm. However, using SarcasmBot in the real world is not practical, as the original authors point out (Joshi et al., 2015). When analysing its outputs, we noticed a very low diversity, as shown in Table 3, where we define diversity as ratio of unique responses generated across our 250 inputs. In particular, SarcasmBot produced a total of only 28 unique responses[6]. In a real scenario of a user interacting with a conversational agent, the user might not appreciate repeatedly receiving the same response, that is not even specific to the meaning of the input. Indeed, in our experiments, we noticed that most of the time a fallback generator of SarcasmBot was employed, returning the simple concatenation of a random positive phrase to a random negative one, from a set of predefined phrases that have no specific connection to the input.

6 Conclusion

We have presented Chandler, a linguistically informed framework for generating sarcastic responses to an input utterance. Chandler is the first such system that does not rely exclusively on predefined patterns, and focuses on explainable generation, grounded on a linguistic theory of sarcasm that overcomes the limitations of previous theories assumed by previous sarcasm generators.

[6]All 28 responses are listed in the Appendix B.

Acknowledgments

This work was supported in part by the EPSRC Centre for Doctoral Training in Data Science, funded by the UK Engineering and Physical Sciences Research Council (grant EP/L016427/1); the University of Edinburgh; and The Financial Times.

References

Silvio Amir, Byron C. Wallace, Hao Lyu, Paula Carvalho, and Mario J. Silva. 2016. Modelling context with user embeddings for sarcasm detection in social media. In *CoNLL*, pages 167–177. ACL.

David Bamman and Noah A. Smith. 2015. Contextualized sarcasm detection on twitter. In *ICWSM*, pages 574–577. AAAI Press.

Francesco Barbieri, Jose Camacho-Collados, Luis Espinosa Anke, and Leonardo Neves. 2020. TweetEval: Unified benchmark and comparative evaluation for tweet classification. In *Findings of the Association for Computational Linguistics: EMNLP 2020*, pages 1644–1650, Online. ACL.

Antoine Bosselut, Hannah Rashkin, Maarten Sap, Chaitanya Malaviya, Asli Celikyilmaz, and Yejin Choi. 2019. COMET: Commonsense transformers for automatic knowledge graph construction. In *ACL*, pages 4762–4779. ACL.

Richard Bruntsch and Willibald Ruch. 2017. Studying irony detection beyond ironic criticism: Let's include ironic praise. *Frontiers in Psychology*, 8:606.

Tuhin Chakrabarty, Debanjan Ghosh, Smaranda Muresan, and Nanyun Peng. 2020. R^3: Reverse, retrieve, and rank for sarcasm generation with commonsense knowledge. In *ACL*, pages 7976–7986. ACL.

Herbert H. Clark. 1996. *Using Language*. Cambridge University Press.

Herbert H. Clark and Richard J. Gerrig. 1984. On the pretense theory of irony. *Journal of Experimental Psychology: General*, 113(1):121–126.

Rachel Giora. 1995. On irony and negation. *Discourse Processes*, 19(2):239–264.

H. P. Grice. 1975. Logic and conversation. In Peter Cole and Jerry L. Morgan, editors, *Syntax and Semantics: Vol. 3: Speech Acts*, pages 41–58. Academic Press, Cambridge, UK.

Devamanyu Hazarika, Soujanya Poria, Sruthi Gorantla, Erik Cambria, Roger Zimmermann, and Rada Mihalcea. 2018. Cascade: Contextual sarcasm detection in online discussion forums. In *COLING*, pages 1837–1848. ACL.

Julia Jorgensen. 1996. The functions of sarcastic irony in speech. *Journal of Pragmatics*, 26(5):613–634.

Aditya Joshi, Anoop Kunchukuttan, Mark James Carman, and Pushpak Bhattacharyya. 2015. Sarcasmbot: An open-source sarcasm-generation module for chatbots. In *WISDOM at KDD*. ACM.

Aditya Joshi, Vaibhav Tripathi, Kevin Patel, Pushpak Bhattacharyya, and Mark Carman. 2016. Are word embedding-based features useful for sarcasm detection? In *EMNLP*, pages 1006–1011. ACL.

Mikhail Khodak, Nikunj Saunshi, and Kiran Vodrahalli. 2018. A large self-annotated corpus for sarcasm. In *LREC*. ELRA.

Roger J. Kreuz and Sam Glucksberg. 1989. How to Be Sarcastic: The Echoic Reminder Theory of Verbal Irony. *Journal of Experimental Psychology: General*, 118(4):374–386.

Sachi Kumon-Nakamura, Sam Glucksberg, and Mary Brown. 1995. How about another piece of pie: The allusional pretense theory of discourse irony.

Yinhan Liu, Myle Ott, Naman Goyal, Jingfei Du, Mandar Joshi, Danqi Chen, Omer Levy, Mike Lewis, Luke Zettlemoyer, and Veselin Stoyanov. 2019. Roberta: A robustly optimized bert pretraining approach. *arXiv preprint arXiv:1907.11692*.

William C. Mann and Sandra A. Thompson. 1987. *Rhetorical Structure Theory: Description and Construction of Text Structures*, pages 85–95. Springer Netherlands, Dordrecht.

George A. Miller. 1995. Wordnet: A lexical database for english. *Communications of the ACM*, 38(11):39–41.

Abhijit Mishra, Tarun Tater, and Karthik Sankaranarayanan. 2019. A modular architecture for unsupervised sarcasm generation. In *EMNLP-IJCNLP*, pages 6144–6154. ACL.

Silviu Oprea and Walid Magdy. 2019. Exploring author context for detecting intended vs perceived sarcasm. In *Proceedings of the 57th Annual Meeting of the Association for Computational Linguistics*, pages 2854–2859, Florence, Italy. Association for Computational Linguistics.

Penny M. Pexman and Meghan T. Zvaigzne. 2004. Does irony go better with friends? *Metaphor and Symbol*, 19(2):143–163.

Ashwin Rajadesingan, Reza Zafarani, and Huan Liu. 2015. Sarcasm detection on twitter: A behavioral modeling approach. In *WSDM*, pages 97–106. ACM.

Ellen Riloff, Ashequl Qadir, Prafulla Surve, Lalindra De Silva, Nathan Gilbert, and Ruihong Huang. 2013. Sarcasm as contrast between a positive sentiment and negative situation. In *EMNLP*, pages 704–714. ACL.

Sara Rosenthal, Noura Farra, and Preslav Nakov. 2017. SemEval-2017 task 4: Sentiment analysis in Twitter. In *Proceedings of the 11th International Workshop on Semantic Evaluation (SemEval-2017)*, pages 502–518, Vancouver, Canada. ACL.

Maarten Sap, Ronan Le Bras, Emily Allaway, Chandra Bhagavatula, Nicholas Lourie, Hannah Rashkin, Brendan Roof, Noah A. Smith, and Yejin Choi. 2019. Atomic: An atlas of machine commonsense for if-then reasoning. *Proceedings of the AAAI Conference on Artificial Intelligence*, 33(01):3027–3035.

John R Searle and John Rogers Searle. 1969. *Speech acts: An essay in the philosophy of language*, volume 626. Cambridge University Press, Cambridge, UK.

Dan Sperber and Deirdre Wilson. 1981. Irony and the use-mention distinction. *Philosophy*, 3:143–184.

Dan Sperber and Deirdre Wilson. 1998. Irony and relevance: A reply to seto, hamamoto and yamanashi. In R. Carston and S. Uchida, editors, *Relevance theory: Applications and implications*, pages 289–293. Benjamins, Amsterdam.

Martin Sykora, Suzanne Elayan, and Thomas W Jackson. 2020. A qualitative analysis of sarcasm, irony and related #hashtags on twitter. *Big Data & Society*, 7(2):2053951720972735.

Akira Utsumi. 1996. Implicit display theory of verbal irony: Towards a computational model of irony. In *Proceedings of the International Workshop on Computational Humor (IWCH'96)*.

Akira Utsumi. 2000. Verbal irony as implicit display of ironic environment: Distinguishing ironic utterances from nonirony. *Journal of Pragmatics*, 32(12):1777–1806.

Byron C. Wallace, Do Kook Choe, and Eugene Charniak. 2015. Sparse, contextually informed models for irony detection: Exploiting user communities, entities and sentiment. In *ACL*, pages 1035–1044. ACL.

Deirdre Wilson. 2006. The pragmatics of verbal irony: Echo or pretence? *Lingua*, 116(10):1722–1743.

Deirdre Wilson and Dan Sperber. 1992. On verbal irony. *Lingua*, 87(1):53–76.

Steven Wilson and Rada Mihalcea. 2019. Predicting human activities from user-generated content. In *Proceedings of the 57th Annual Meeting of the Association for Computational Linguistics*, pages 2572–2582, Florence, Italy. Association for Computational Linguistics.

Yizhe Zhang, Siqi Sun, Michel Galley, Yen-Chun Chen, Chris Brockett, Xiang Gao, Jianfeng Gao, Jingjing Liu, and Bill Dolan. 2020. DialoGPT : Large-scale generative pre-training for conversational response generation. In *Proceedings of the 58th Annual Meeting of the Association for Computational Linguistics: System Demonstrations*, pages 270–278. ACL.

A Logical Form to Text Patterns

In this Section we show the patterns used by Chandler to convert the logical form of sarcasm to text, as discussed in Section 4. We show patterns for each if-then relation type, *xNeed*, *xAttr*, *xReact*, and *xEffect*.

In the patterns below, <inten> is an intensifier, <suff_inten> is an intensifier added at the end of a phrase, <pos> is a positive emotion word, and <interj> an interjection. Inspired by (Utsumi, 2000) and (Joshi et al., 2015), each of these were randomly chosen from the following sets:

- <inten> : [very]
- <suff_inten> : [for sure]
- <pos> : [Good job, Well done]
- <intrj> : [Yay!, Brilliant!]

<obt> below is the object of the corresponding if-then relation object, as provided by COMET when taking in the input tweet.

A.1 Patterns for the Complete Version of Chandler

xNeed patterns:

- You didn't <obt> , that's <suff_inten> . <pos> !

xAttr patterns:

- <interj> You're not <inten> <obt> , that's <suff_inten> .
- <interj> <pos> not being <obt> .
- <interj> You're not a very <obt> person that's <suff_inten> ."

xReact patterns:

- You're not feeling <inten> <obt> right now, that's <suff_inten> . <interj>

xEffect patterns:

- You're not <inten> going to obt_inf right now, that's <suff_inten> . <interj>

B SarcasmBot Responses

As discussed in Section 5.2, we noticed SarcasmBot produced a total of only 28 unique responses to our set of 250 inputs. Here they are:

1. Unbelievable that you just said 'sucky'! You are really very classy!
2. Awesome!
3. Brilliant!
4. Let's party!
5. Oh you poor thing!
6. You owe me a drink for that awesome piece of news!

7. Wow, you said 'sucks', didn't you? Your mom will be really proud of you!
8. Wow, you said 'suck', didn't you? Your mom will be really proud of you!
9. I'd feel terrible if I were you!
10. You are such a simple person!
11. Aww!! That's so adorable!
12. That deserves an applause.
13. I am so sorry for you!
14. Yay! Yawn!
15. How exciting! Yawn!
16. How exciting! *rolls eyes*
17. Wow! *rolls eyes*
18. Yay! *rolls eyes*
19. Yay! LMAO
20. Wow! Yawn!
21. How exciting! LMAO
22. Wow! LMAO
23. That is a very useful piece of information! *rolls eyes*
24. That is a very useful piece of information! LMAO
25. That is a very useful piece of information! Yawn!
26. Unbelievable that you just said 'sobbing'! You are really very classy!
27. Unbelievable that you just said 'sucks'! You are really very classy!
28. Unbelievable that you just said 'bloody'! You are really very classy!

C Participant Information Sheet

C.1 What will I do?

Imagine someone (we'll call them PersonX), makes a statement. You will be shown a few responses to that statement. The responses were generated by chatbots (computer programs). Some sentences talk about sensitive topics, such as tragic life events. Responses to such sentences could be potentially inappropriate, or even offensive or harmful. Unfortunately, chatbots do not understand whether or not a topic is sensitive for a human. Please be fully aware of this when accepting to take part in our study.

For each response, you will be asked:

1. How sarcastic you find the response? (0 - not sarcastic, 3 - very sarcastic)

2. How funny you find the response? (0 - not funny, 3 - very funny)

3. How specific is the response to PersonX's statement? The response is specific if it mentions details that show a good understanding of PersonX's statement and its implications. Otherwise it's general. (0 - very general, 3 - very specific).

4. How coherent is the response to PersonX's statement? The response is coherent if it makes sense as a response. That is, it's a clear and sensible response that someone might actually give. It does not matter if it's specific or general. (0 - not coherent, 3 - very coherent).

Let's take a quick example. In this example, imagine that PersonX's statement is "I went to the grocery store". Here are some responses about this statement.

About being specific:

- "That's great." - Very general response. You can say this as a response to pretty much anything.

- "Nice to hear you are enjoying this sunny day." - General response. It does provides some details about the day (that it's sunny). However, those details are not uniquely related to PersonX's statement.

- "You must be tired." - More specific response. It shows an understanding that going somewhere (anywhere at all) may cause tiredness.

- "You probably bought a lot of vegetables." - Specific response. It shows an understanding of what a grocery store is. That is, a place where you can probably buy vegetables.

- "You must have been quite hungry for carrots." - Very specific response. It shows an understanding of what a grocery store is, about what carrots are, and about the link between carrots and the store (mainly, that carrots are sold there).

About being coherent:

- "I'm cold." - Not coherent. It has nothing to do with PersonX's statement

- "I went to the grocery store". It's not a suitable response that someone would normally give.

- "I had such a wonderful dream last night, there were a lot of awesome cars painted blue." - Not coherent. It does not make sense as a response to PersonX's statement.

- "I sometimes dream about eating carrots." - More coherent response. Someone might sometimes say this as a response, although it's not a common response.

- "OK thanks." - Very coherent. One might actually say this as a response. Notice it's not specific to PersonX's statement. You can say it as a response to many other statements. Still, it's coherent to PersonX's statement. Thanks a lot for getting me those carrots, I'll pay you back next week. - Very coherent and very specific to PersonX's statement.

C.2 Participant Information Sheet and Consent Form

- Principal investigator: Prof. Walid Magdy

- Researcher collecting data: Silviu Oprea

- Funder (if applicable): EPSRC, Financial Times

This study is in the process of being certified according to the Informatics Research Ethics Process, RT number 2019/87618. Please take time to read the following information carefully. You should keep this page for your records.

C.3 Who are the researchers?

We are the Social Media Analysis and Support for Humanity (SMASH) group, a research group that brings together a range of researchers from the University of Edinburgh in order to build on our existing strengths in social media research. This research group focuses on mining structures and behaviours in social networks. The principal investigator is Prof. Walid Magdy.

C.4 What is the purpose of the study?

This study aims to understand what linguistic style people associate with sarcasm.

C.5 Why have I been asked to take part?

We target everyone registered as living in the United Kingdom on the Prolific Academic platform.

C.6 Do I have to take part?

No—participation in this study is entirely up to you. You can withdraw from the study at any time, without giving a reason. Your rights will not be affected. If you wish to withdraw, contact the PI. We will stop using your data in any publications or presentations submitted after you have withdrawn consent. However, we will keep copies of your original consent, and of your withdrawal request.

C.7 What will happen if I decide to take part?

You will be asked to fill in a survey. The flow of the survey is the following:

- You will be shown a short text (originating from a tweet) and asked whether it is, in your view, appropriate to respond sarcastically to that text.

- If you say "no", you will be shown another text. The process will repeat until you say "yes" or 10 texts have been shown.

- If you say "yes":
  - You will be shown 7 responses to the text that you selected;
  - For each response, you will be asked to specify, on a scale from 1 to 5: (a) How sarcastic it is; (b) How funny it is; (c) How coherent it is to the original text; It is coherent if it sounds like a reasonable response that a person might give. (d) How specific it is to the original text; It is specific if it mentions details about the original text, or its implications, that make this response not appropriate as a response to many other texts.

We estimate it will take around 3 minutes to complete the survey.

C.8 Compensation

You will be paid £0.38 for your participation in this study.

C.9 Are there any risks associated with taking part?

Please note: some of the texts that you will see include content that you might consider sensitive, or might trigger unwanted memories. For instance, they might mention losing a family member, losing friends, break-ups, failure in exams, or health issues.

C.10 Are there any benefits associated with taking part?

Financial compensation of £0.38.

C.11 What will happen to the results of this study?

The results of this study may be summarised in published articles, reports and presentations. Quotes or key findings will be anonymized: We will remove any information that could, in our assessment, allow anyone to identify you. With your consent, information can also be used for future research. Your data may be archived for a minimum of 2 years.

C.12 Data protection and confidentiality

Your data will be processed in accordance with Data Protection Law. Throughout your entire interaction with us, the only information collected about you specifically is your Prolific Academic identification number. This data will only be viewed by the team members of the SMASH group, listed here: `http://smash.inf.ed.ac.uk`. All other data, including the responses you provide, and the amount of time you took to fill in the survey, will be made public on the internet as part of Open Science, available to be indexed by search engines. The Open Science initiative is described here: `https://en.wikipedia.org/wiki/Open_science`.

C.13 What are my data protection rights?

The University of Edinburgh is a Data Controller for the information you provide. You have the right to access information held about you. Your right of access can be exercised in accordance Data Protection Law. You also have other rights including rights of correction, erasure and objection. However, we will have no control for the data that will be made public, as specific in the previous section. For more details, including the right to lodge a complaint with the Information Commissioner's Office, please visit `www.ico.org.uk`. Questions, comments and requests about your personal data can also be sent to the University Data Protection Officer at `dpo@ed.ac.uk`. For general information about how we use your data, go to: `edin.ac/privacy-research`.

C.14 Who can I contact?

If you have any further questions about the study, please contact the lead researcher, Silviu Oprea, `silviu.oprea@ed.ac.uk`. If you wish to make a complaint about the study, please contact `inf-ethics@inf.ed.ac.uk`. When you contact us, please provide the study title and detail the nature of your complaint.

C.15 Updated information

If the research project changes in any way, an updated Participant Information Sheet will be made available on `http://web.inf.ed.ac.uk/infweb/research/study-updates`.

C.16 Consent

By proceeding with the study, you agree to all of the following statements:

- I have read and understood the above information.
- I understand that my participation is voluntary, and I can withdraw at any time.
- I consent to my anonymised data being used in academic publications and presentations, as well as published publicly on the internet, as part of Open Science.
- I am aware that I will see potentially offensive, harmful, or hurtful content.
- I allow my data to be used in future ethically approved research.

TABPERT: An Effective Platform for Tabular Perturbation

Nupur Jain
IIT Kanpur
nupurj@iitk.ac.in

Vivek Gupta
University of Utah
vgupta@cs.utah.edu

Anshul Rai
IIT Kanpur
anshulra@iitk.ac.in

Gaurav Kumar
IIT Kanpur
gauravkg@iitk.ac.in

Abstract

To truly grasp reasoning ability, a Natural Language Inference model should be evaluated on counterfactual data. TABPERT facilitates this by assisting in the generation of such counterfactual data for assessing model tabular reasoning issues. TABPERT allows a user to update a table, change its associated hypotheses, change their labels, and highlight rows that are relevant for the hypothesis classification. TABPERT also captures information about the techniques used to automatically produce the table, as well as the strategies employed to generate the challenging hypotheses. These counterfactual tables and hypotheses, as well as the metadata, can then be used to explore an existing model's shortcomings methodically and quantitatively.

New York Stock Exchange	
Type	Stock exchange
Location	New York City, New York, U.S.
Founded	May 17, 1792; 226 years ago
Currency	United States dollar
No. of listings	2,400
Volume	US$20.161 trillion (2011)

H1: NYSE has fewer than 3,000 stocks listed.
H2: Over 2,500 stocks are listed in the NYSE.
H3: S&P 500 stock trading volume is over $10 trillion.

Figure 1: A tabular premise example. The table's first and second columns correspond to the keys and their associated values, respectively. The hypothesis H1 is entailed by the data in the table, H2 is a contradiction, and H3 is neutral, i.e., neither entailed nor contradictory.

1 Introduction

Given factual evidence, a crucial part of NLP model reasoning capacity is evaluating whether a given hypothesis is an entailment (true), a contradiction (false), or is neutral (cannot be determined). Current transformers-based models have been shown to outperform humans on these tasks when the evidence is presented as simple unstructured text (Wang et al., 2018, 2019); however, when tested with semi-structured evidence (Gupta et al., 2020; Chen et al., 2019), such as tables, as shown in Figure 1, the very same models struggle to match human accuracy (Neeraja et al., 2021; Wang et al., 2021; Aly et al., 2021).

Furthermore, there can be several reasons for a model's correct predictions on a particular example. For example, Poliak et al. (2018); Gururangan et al. (2018) show that multiple NLI datasets such as the SNLI and MNLI datasets (Bowman et al., 2015; Williams et al., 2018) exhibit hypothesis bias, i.e., the hypothesis-only model performs significantly better than the majority label baseline. In the context of tables, Gupta et al. (2020); Neeraja et al. (2021); Gupta et al. (2021) show that the right prediction does not always imply reasoning: there can be dataset biases in semi-structured datasets too, such as hypothesis or premise artefacts (spurious patterns) which can wrongly support a particular label.

Additionally, a model can also ignore the ground evidence and use its pre-trained knowledge for making predictions (Gupta et al., 2021). When deployed in the real world on out-of-domain (different category) or counterfactual (stories tables) examples, these models fail embarrassingly. One way to avoid this inflated performance projection is to test models on several challenging sets before deployment. For example, Gupta et al. (2020); Neeraja et al. (2021) evaluate the RoBERTa$_{Large}$ (Liu et al., 2019) models on two additional adversarial sets (hypothesis-perturbed and out-of-domain) and observe a significant performance drop. However, manually creating such challenge sets can be tricky, both in terms of the annotation cost involved and the actual annotation process, especially with tabular data of semi-structured nature.

Recently, Ribeiro et al. (2020a) have shown that one can deploy simple tricks to semi-automate

Proceedings of the 2021 Conference on Empirical Methods in Natural Language Processing: System Demonstrations, pages 350–360
November 7–11, 2021. ©2021 Association for Computational Linguistics

this process of altering existing data. This semi-automated approach can then generate difficult adversarial counterfactual contrast sets, which can subsequently be utilised to perform behavioural testing of existing NLP models. However, such methods are currently only applicable to unstructured data and cannot be directly used for semi-structured text such as tables.

To fill this gap, in this work, we present TABPERT. TABPERT is an annotation platform specifically designed to work on semi-structured tabular data. For example, TABPERT can support the semi-automatic creation of tabular counterfactual data. Through TABPERT, annotators can modify tables in several ways, such as (a) *deleting information*: deleting an attribute-value pair or an existing row completely, (b) *inserting information*: inserting an attribute-value pair for an existing row or creating a fresh row, (c) *modifying information*: editing the attribute or values cells of an existing row, and (d) *modifying hypotheses or labels*: modifying an existing hypothesis and its inference label. Furthermore, each component of TABPERT can be customized to meet the individual needs of a project that necessitates tabular perturbations.

TABPERT additionally logs the strategy used to modify each attribute-value of the table. In addition to the gold label, users can manually log information about the technique used for perturbing a table-hypothesis pair and the rows relevant to the hypothesis. This information is crucial in understanding the challenges annotated data poses to the existing model, and therefore, can be utilized to probe a model's yet-unknown shortcomings systematically.

The contributions of our work can be summarised as below:

1. TABPERT can help delete, modify, and insert information in semi-structured tabular data for creating counterfactual examples.

2. TABPERT auto-logs table perturbation metadata and supports manual hypothesis modification and inference labels annotation.

3. TABPERT assists users in logging metadata, including hypothesis-related table rows and the perturbation strategy used, which is crucial for model performance analysis.

4. We present a case study for TABPERT via the generation and evaluation of a counterfactual INFOTABS dataset and RoBERTa$_{Large}$ model, respectively.

The TABPERT source code, the annotated counterfactual INFOTABS dataset, the NLI RoBERTa$_{Large}$ model, the annotation instructions with examples set, and all other associated scripts, are available at `https://tabpert.github.io`. The annotator instruction video describing TABPERT usage is accessible at `https://www.youtube.com/watch?v=sbCH_zD53Kg`.

2 Tables are Challenging

One might argue that creating a counterfactual dataset for tables is not a challenging task and that table modification can be fully automated by merely *'shuffling'* or *'inserting'* attribute values of one table row into another table row (with the same attribute) as long as they are from similar categories, e.g. shuffle *'Producer'* of one movie with *'Producer'* of another movie). One can extend this further by shuffling rows with different attributes in the same as well as different tables (same category) as long as the name-entity type for values is similar, e.g. shuffle *'Producer'* with the *'Director'* of the same or a different movie with each other.

This method, however, does not automate the updation of associated hypotheses and inference labels. Furthermore, such automated shuffling quite often flagrantly violates common-sense logical constraints. For example, a person's *'Birth Date'* must be before their *'Died Date'*, a person's *'Marriage Date'* should be after their *'Birth Date'* and before their *'Died Date'*, an album's *'Released Date'* should be after its *'Recording date'* and so on. The updated table may be self-contradictory if these constraints are not enforced. While some of these constraints can be automatically met and therefore not violated, the vast majority of them inevitably sneak through due to their enormous diversity and variance[1]. Furthermore, due to the domain-specific nature of these constraints, enforcing them automatically during perturbation is a challenging task. Keeping this in mind, automated perturbations like these are only appropriate for table initialization. Human annotators can then manually analyze and modify the initialized tables for self-consistency, i.e., no logical common sense constraint violation.

[1] In real data, these constraints are naturally satisfied.

3 TABPERT Functions, Aspects, and Usability

TABPERT is currently supported on common web browsers such as Google Chrome and can be installed to run locally[2]. We start with a dataset of tables along with already annotated labelled hypotheses. We utilize the INFOTABS dataset for the case study provided in this research. INFOTABS is a semi-structured natural language inference dataset that consists of entity tables and human-written hypotheses. We create three counterfactual tables (labelled A, B, and C) for each original table in the dataset. There are three main steps required for successful annotation, as described below.

3.1 Automatic Initialization

First, we initialise TABPERT with original tables and counterfactual tables generated via automatic random 'shuffling' of table rows or attribute values[3]. Automatic initialization is beneficial as manual table creation is both time-consuming and highly error-plausible.

The values used for shuffling (referred to as the '*shuffle source*') can be taken from one of several possible locations. Table 1 explains how these values can be picked from these locations. The location of the *shuffle source* that is used is recorded in the metadata of the attribute-value in the first 4 bits of a 7-bit string, as described in Table 1. For example, suppose the value *'The Coca-Cola Company'* in the *'Manufacturer'* key in a table in the *'Food'* category is replaced with the value *'Hood River Distillers'* which is a value in the *'Distributor'* key of a table in the *'Food'* category of the external split. Then, *'Hood River Distillers'* will have the metadata *'1011000'* after initialization[4]. These bits can be used to determine which way of shuffling was more effective, i.e., generate counterfactual data which have a greater impact on model performance, as demonstrated in the performance analysis (Section 4). The last 3 bits are explained in Section 3.2.

The initialization for the hypotheses and their labels is done by copying them exactly from the original dataset, and they are modified by human annotators using the TABPERT platform.

[2]https://github.com/utahnlp/tabpert

[3]Only a subset of all values are shuffled at random. The location of the shuffle source (described later) is likewise picked at random among this subset.

[4]Values taken from different keys, must have the same entity-type, as explained in Section 3.2.

Bit	Location	Same	Different
1	Split	0	1
2	Category	0	1
3	Table	0	1
4	Key	0	1

Table 1: First Four Bits of Table Value Metadata. These bits represent the location of the *shuffle source*. The 1st bit indicates whether is an external set (1) or the same set (0), the 2nd bit indicates whether it is a different (1) or the same (0) table category, the 3rd bit represents if it is the same (0) or a different (1) table, and the 4th represents whether it is the same (0) or a different (1) key. For values that do not change, the initial four bits are '0000'. Also, when the 3rd bit is 0, then the first two bits are necessarily 0.

3.2 Modifying Tables

Annotators can now modify these automatically-perturbed tables from initialization to remove self-contradictions and inconsistency to create valid counterfactual examples. All the cells (attributes and values) in the three counterfactual tables (A, B, and C) can be edited[5]. Table rows can be modified via the dragging and dropping of a value cell from (a) same counterfactual table (cut-paste effect), (b) from another counterfactual table (cut-paste effect), or (c) from the original table (copy-paste effect). To minimise errors during this drag-and-drop operation, a type validation check runs in the background, which prevents drag and drop between different key categories (for example, it is forbidden to drag a *Person's Name* into *Date of Birth*). To achieve such type validation, key 'entity type' must be provided before beginning the annotation procedure[6]. Keys for which this information is missing can be dropped anywhere without restriction.

TABPERT also supports five additional functions for more challenging edits. The *'Add Value'* box allows annotators to add new values by dragging and dropping a new cell to the correct location and inputting the desired new value. Additionally, one can utilise the *'Add Section'* button for inserting an entirely new row. For deleting a value, drag and drop the desired cell to the *'Delete Vaue'* Box. A complete row can also be deleted with the *'Edit Section Name or Delete Section'* option. To edit the text, 'click' on the value and then edit it. These modification details are recorded automatically in the last 3 bits of the 7-bit metadata: the 5th bit represents a copy-paste from the original table, the

[5]The original table cannot be changed. This is done to prevent inadvertent edits.

[6]This can be done manually or using NER tagging.

6th represents a value update operation, and the 7th bit represents a new cell or row addition.

Figure 3a shows the main parts of the TABPERT platform for counterfactual table perturbation.

3.3 Hypothesis Modification and Metadata

The text of a hypothesis of a counterfactual table can be edited directly, and its corresponding label can also be selected from drop-down menu options. In addition, the annotator enters the following metadata information:

1. The strategies used by the annotator to modify the hypothesis. The five main strategies can be selected using check-boxes (selecting multiple values is allowed), as shown in Figure 3c. The *'Other'* option corresponds to hypothesis changes that do not fall into the five main strategies.

2. All the relevant rows of the table which are necessary for deciding the inference label.

Figure 3b shows the main TABPERT view for hypothesis modification, with hypothesis and inference label. The annotator inserts metadata by clicking the '+' symbol on the left side of each counterfactual hypothesis (below label drop-down), as shown in Figure 3b. This opens a metadata collection window, as shown in Figure 3c. We use 6 bits to store this metadata information: each of the initial 5 bits represents a strategy (the order of the bits is the same as the order in which the strategies are mentioned on TABPERT as shown in Figure 3c). The last bit represents the 'Other' option. Additionally, the relevant rows' 'attribute keys' are stored in a list (array) along with each modified hypothesis.

3.4 TABPERT Aspects

The TABPERT web-app's core tech stack consists of ReactJS[7] and Flask[8]. Here, Flask is used as the main back-end Python web framework, and Javascript library ReactJS is used for the front-end. We used Flask because it is easy to extend, giving us the ability to easily integrate Python libraries to manipulate JSON and TSV files quickly. We used ReactJS because of the *react-beautiful-dnd* library[9] essential for simulating the drag-and-drop function.

[7]https://reactjs.org/

[8]https://flask.palletsprojects.com/en/2.0.x/

[9]https://www.npmjs.com/package/react-beautiful-dnd

4 Case Study on INFOTABS

We used TABPERT to create counterfactual data for the INFOTABS dataset. Each table is saved as a JSON file with keys and values as attributes in INFOTABS. We sampled 47 tables with 423 table-hypothesis pairs taken from the α_1 set of INFOTABS. For initialization, we shuffled the entities in this sampled α_1 set with those in the tables from both the $Train$ set (the 'external' set) and the complete α_1 set (the 'internal' set). Including both sets creates more diversity in automatic initialization[10].

Annotation Guidelines Following a similar line as earlier works by Ribeiro et al. (2020b) and Sakaguchi et al. (2020) for creating challenging adversarial test sets, we guided the annotators in annotating three counterfactual tables (A, B, C) for each original α_1 table. This ensures enough diversity and coverage in the collected counterfactual data. For each counterfactual table, we encouraged annotators to use the following strategies: (a) For *Table A*: change the table such that the *entailment* (E) and *contradiction* (C) labels are flipped, but the hypothesis remains unchanged, (b) For *Table B*: change the hypothesis so that the *entailment* (E) and *contradiction* (C) labels are flipped; make any necessary changes to the table, and (c) For *Table C*: write a new but related hypothesis with similar reasoning; the table can be modified as needed. We also recommend that annotators modify the *neutrals* (N) by adding more *'true'* information from the table to the hypotheses to make them more challenging. The above-discussed procedure ensures that (a) the final labels are balanced, (b) the reversed label eliminates hypothesis bias (Gupta et al., 2020; Chen et al., 2019), and (c) due to lexical overlap, *neutrals* (N) are closer to *entailments* (E) (Glockner et al., 2018). Finally, after annotation, we have 109 counterfactual tables with a total of 982 table-hypothesis pairs, with Table A having 423, Table B having 405, and Table C having 154 pairs.

Experiment and Analysis To check if the annotated counterfactual data is challenging for existing models, we use RoBERTa$_{Large}$ to obtain prediction labels for the original and counterfactual data. We also obtain hypothesis-only baseline predictions using the RoBERTa$_{Large}$ model on the two sets. Table 2 shows the performance results in the form

[10]As discussed earlier, annotators manually fix the constraint violations during annotation.

(a) **Table Perturbation:** ❶ Table Title ❷ a Key (Section Name) ❸ the Values associated with a Key ❹ Add Value ❺ Add Section ❻ Delete Value ❼ Edit Section Name or Delete Section

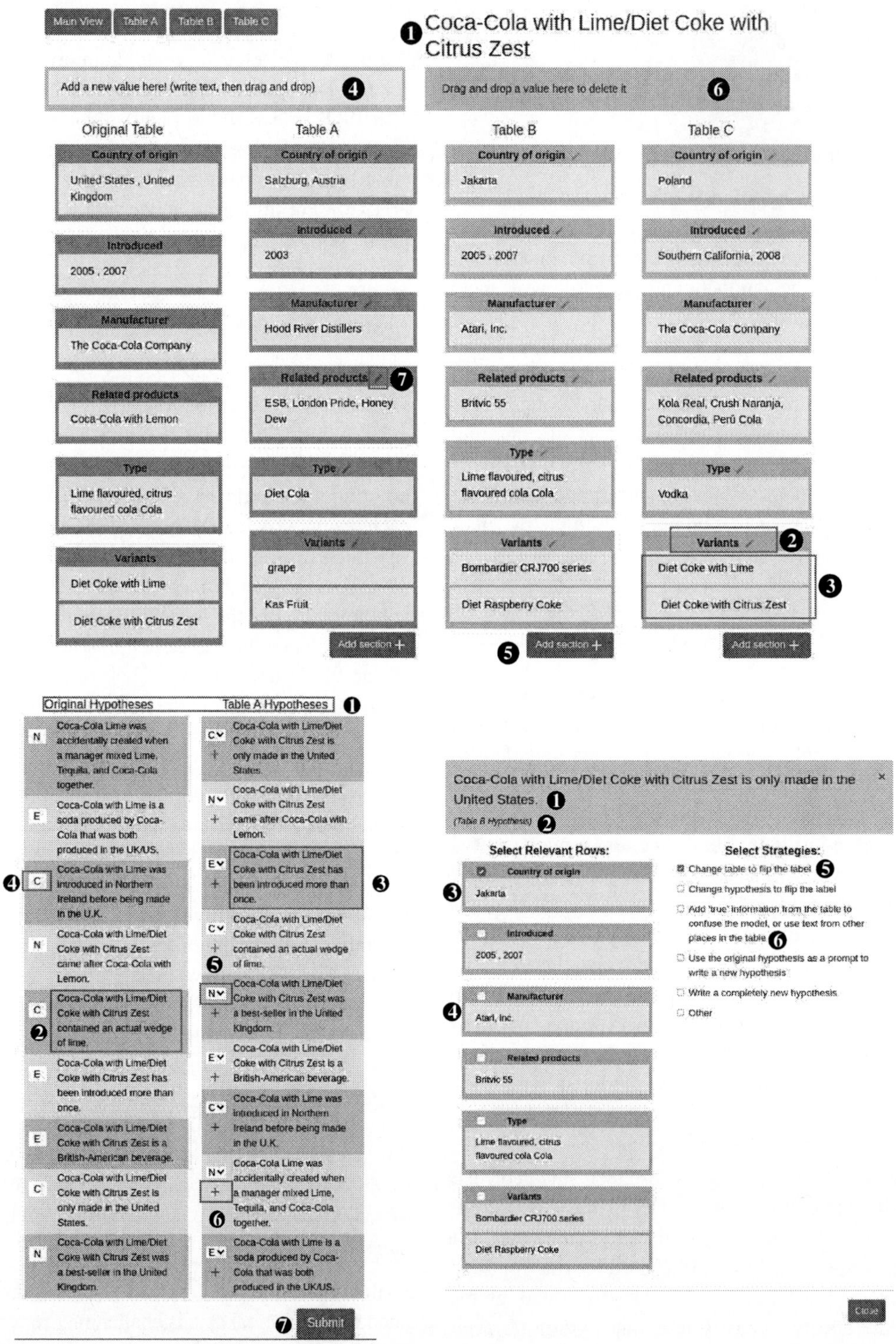

(b) **Hypotheses Perturbation:** ❶ Tables corresponding to the hypothesis sets ❷ an Original Hypothesis ❸ a Counterfactual Hypothesis of Table A ❹ the NLI Label corresponding to an Original Hypothesis ❺ the NLI Label corresponding to a Table A Counterfactual Hypothesis ❻ Open Modal for Hypothesis Metadata (Figure 3c) ❼ Save Option

(c) **Hypothesis Metadata:** (Select Relevant Rows and Hypothesis Perturbation Strategies) ❶ the Hypothesis ❷ Table Name ❸ a Relevant Row (checkbox selected) ❹ an Irrelevant Row (checkbox unselected) ❺ a Used Strategy (checkbox selected) ❻ an Unused Strategy (checkbox unselected)

Figure 2: Main Features of the TABPERT Platform

of accuracy. The table-sentence data was represented in *'para'* form (Gupta et al., 2020) in two ways: (a) with all table rows, (b) using only the relevant rows (obtained via annotated metadata) (Gupta et al., 2021).

Performance Analysis It is evident from Table 2 that RoBERTa$_{Large}$ has difficulty in predicting labels correctly for counterfactual data. Furthermore, the model's higher performance with relevant rows indicates that it most likely utilises irrelevant rows as artefacts when making predictions (Neeraja et al., 2021). On counterfactual data, the hypothesis-only model's performance is close to majority-label baselines, confirming a reduction in hypothesis bias. Humans, on the other hand, find both datasets equally difficult and obtain an accuracy of $\approx 85\%$ on each[11].

Model Type	Original	Counterfactual
Majority	33.33	33.33
Hypo Only	64.32	44.85
All Rows	78.91	61.26
Relevant Rows	74.11	65.85
Human	84.8	85.8

Table 2: Performance (accuracy %) of the INFOTABS RoBERTa$_{Large}$ model on original and counterfactual annotated data.

Perturbation Analysis We also study the hypothesis annotation metadata to see which hypothesis modification strategies are more effective. From Figure 4, it is evident that manual *Table Change* with *Label Flip* (*TC* + *LF*) is more effective than manual *Hypothesis Change* with *Label Flip* (*HC* + *LF*). Furthermore, all *Label Flip* methods are typically more effective than *Hypothesis Prompt* (*HypoPrompt*) and *Text Overlap* (*Overlap*). This, we believe, is due to the ineffectiveness of hypothesis bias with flipped labels. Surprisingly, there is a modest performance increase on new hypotheses, showing that simple data generation is an unsuccessful method. Furthermore, no *Other* perturbation techniques result in any substantial performance drop.

We also did a similar analysis on the table perturbation metadata; refer to Section A of the Appendix for details. Refer to Section C of the Appendix examples of counterfactual perturbation using each strategy.

[11]There is no difference in performance between A, B, and C type counterfactual table-example pairs. See Figure 5 in the Appendix.

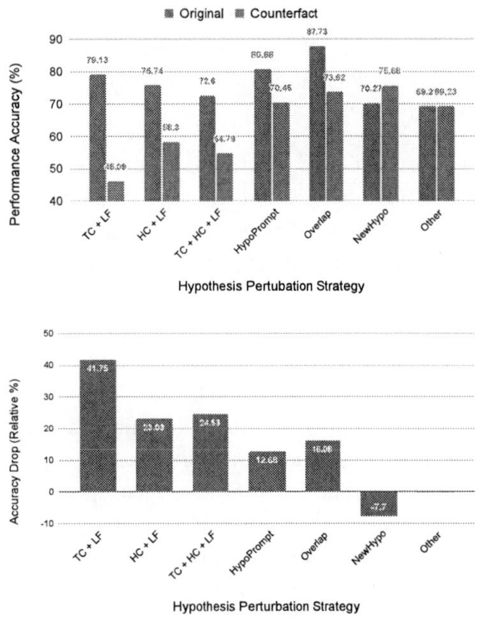

Figure 4: Performance drop after counterfactual perturbation with various strategies.

5 TABPERT Utility

Main Platform TABPERT is a tool designed for efficient and accurate table perturbation. One such case is creating tabular data for tabular inference tasks, as demonstrated through this paper. TABPERT supports several features which aid in the creation of effective counterfactual tabular data. It has numerous optimizations with a friendly user interface to ensure fast annotation of data. This ensures huge data collection, leading to scalability. TABPERT enables a larger range of services compared to using spreadsheets or the MTurk platform. For example, the drag-and-drop functionality simplifies annotation and helps easily visualise a complicated job. All the tabular data can be examined in a single view. The automatic type validation during initialisation and modification reduces the chances of unintended errors.

Customizing TABPERT **Functionality** The initialization source code, as well as the platform, are designed to be modular. This facilitates component addition, deletion, and updation. For example, the ability to reorganize table parts, copy values across table triplets (in addition to cut-paste), auto-save work[12], and an undo option, as well as checkpoints

[12]Currently, the Save button must be pressed manually to save work. However, even semi-completed work can be saved

added to reverse mistakes, may all be readily implemented. The augmentation initialization code can also be configured to suit the requirements of the task.

Metadata Counterfactual data can be utilized as a difficult adversarial test set to assess tabular model reasoning. For example, as demonstrated in Section 4, The model performs poorly on counterfactual hypotheses with flipped labels on tables with relevant rows drawn from the external set (in our case, the $Train$ set), indicating model overfitting on pre-trained knowledge. The recorded metadata can also be utilized to guide annotators in creating increasingly difficult data. For example, annotators can be encouraged to focus more on *Label Flip* methods with external set-initialised tables rows to generate more challenging counterfactual data. Label flipping techniques can also be used to test a model for hypothesis bias. The metadata associated with hypotheses-specific relevant rows assists in pruning premise tables, which improves inference model reasoning and interpretability, as shown in Section 4. These are only a handful of the countless possible application scenarios.

In Section B of the Appendix, we also compare and contrast TABPERT with spreadsheets on effectiveness, visual benefits, and metadata aspects.

6 TABPERT Limitations and Future

During our pilot study, the platform was run locally by three annotators. This was not an issue because the number of annotators was limited, and the tables were divided among them manually. If we want numerous annotators to be able to make simultaneous modifications for large-scale distribution, we must host our platform on a centralized server. This is something we intend to accomplish in the not-too-distant future.

Finally, the counterfactual data generated by modifications has to be manually stored by pressing a button. This was done so that if the user made a mistake, the original data would not be erased, and the user may save the data after they are satisfied with the modifications. To accommodate both of these circumstances, we would like to include an auto-save function along with an undo option.

7 Conclusions

TABPERT is an effective platform for examining semi-structured tabular data and generating counterfactual tabular perturbations. Annotators can use the platform to alter tables and hypothesis phrases, as well as collect related metadata information, in order to produce tabular counterfactual data. The metadata collected can be utilised to analyze the unknown vulnerabilities with existing NLP systems quantitatively and methodically. We believe that TABPERT will be helpful to academics that work with semi-structured data such as tables. Many non-academic industrial scenarios that require table modification, such as e-commerce product specification tables, financial and tax statements tables, and so on, may also leverage TABPERT.

by pressing the button several times at regular intervals.

8 Acknowledgements

We appreciate the Utah NLP group members' valuable suggestions at various phases of the project, as well as the reviewers' helpful remarks. We also acknowledge NSF grants #1801446 (SATC) and #1822877 (Cyberlearning), as well as a kind donation from Verisk Inc. We also like to thank Alokit Innovations for providing a mentoring platform.

References

Rami Aly, Zhijiang Guo, Michael Schlichtkrull, James Thorne, Andreas Vlachos, Christos Christodoulopoulos, Oana Cocarascu, and Arpit Mittal. 2021. FEVEROUS: Fact extraction and VERification over unstructured and structured information. *arXiv preprint arXiv:2106.05707*.

Samuel R. Bowman, Gabor Angeli, Christopher Potts, and Christopher D. Manning. 2015. A Large Annotated Corpus for Learning Natural Language Inference. In *Proceedings of the 2015 Conference on Empirical Methods in Natural Language Processing*.

Wenhu Chen, Hongmin Wang, Jianshu Chen, Yunkai Zhang, Hong Wang, Shiyang Li, Xiyou Zhou, and William Yang Wang. 2019. TabFact: A large-scale dataset for table-based fact verification. In *International Conference on Learning Representations*.

Max Glockner, Vered Shwartz, and Yoav Goldberg. 2018. Breaking NLI systems with sentences that require simple lexical inferences. In *The 56th Annual Meeting of the Association for Computational Linguistics (ACL)*, Melbourne, Australia.

Vivek Gupta, Riyaz A. Bhat, Atreya Ghosal, Manish Srivastava, Maneesh Singh, and Vivek Srikumar. 2021. Is my model using the right evidence? systematic probes for examining evidence-based tabular reasoning. *CoRR*, abs/2108.00578.

Vivek Gupta, Maitrey Mehta, Pegah Nokhiz, and Vivek Srikumar. 2020. INFOTABS: Inference on tables as semi-structured data. In *Proceedings of the 58th Annual Meeting of the Association for Computational Linguistics*, pages 2309–2324, Online. Association for Computational Linguistics.

Suchin Gururangan, Swabha Swayamdipta, Omer Levy, Roy Schwartz, Samuel Bowman, and Noah A. Smith. 2018. Annotation artifacts in natural language inference data. In *Proceedings of the 2018 Conference of the North American Chapter of the Association for Computational Linguistics: Human Language Technologies, Volume 2 (Short Papers)*, pages 107–112, New Orleans, Louisiana. Association for Computational Linguistics.

Yinhan Liu, Myle Ott, Naman Goyal, Jingfei Du, Mandar Joshi, Danqi Chen, Omer Levy, Mike Lewis, Luke Zettlemoyer, and Veselin Stoyanov. 2019. Roberta: A Robustly Optimized BERT Pretraining Approach. *arXiv preprint arXiv:1907.11692*.

J. Neeraja, Vivek Gupta, and Vivek Srikumar. 2021. Incorporating external knowledge to enhance tabular reasoning. In *Proceedings of the 2021 Conference of the North American Chapter of the Association for Computational Linguistics: Human Language Technologies*, pages 2799–2809, Online. Association for Computational Linguistics.

Adam Poliak, Jason Naradowsky, Aparajita Haldar, Rachel Rudinger, and Benjamin Van Durme. 2018. Hypothesis only baselines in natural language inference. In *Proceedings of the Seventh Joint Conference on Lexical and Computational Semantics*, pages 180–191, New Orleans, Louisiana. Association for Computational Linguistics.

Marco Tulio Ribeiro, Tongshuang Wu, Carlos Guestrin, and Sameer Singh. 2020a. Beyond Accuracy: Behavioral testing of NLP models with CheckList. In *Proceedings of the 58th Annual Meeting of the Association for Computational Linguistics*, pages 4902–4912.

Marco Tulio Ribeiro, Tongshuang Wu, Carlos Guestrin, and Sameer Singh. 2020b. Beyond accuracy: Behavioral testing of NLP models with CheckList. In *Proceedings of the 58th Annual Meeting of the Association for Computational Linguistics*, pages 4902–4912, Online. Association for Computational Linguistics.

Keisuke Sakaguchi, Ronan Le Bras, Chandra Bhagavatula, and Yejin Choi. 2020. WINOGRANDE: An adversarial winograd schema challenge at scale. In *AAAI*.

Alex Wang, Yada Pruksachatkun, Nikita Nangia, Amanpreet Singh, Julian Michael, Felix Hill, Omer Levy, and Samuel R Bowman. 2019. SuperGLUE: a stickier benchmark for general-purpose language understanding systems. In *Proceedings of the 33rd International Conference on Neural Information Processing Systems*, pages 3266–3280.

Alex Wang, Amanpreet Singh, Julian Michael, Felix Hill, Omer Levy, and Samuel Bowman. 2018. GLUE: A multi-task benchmark and analysis platform for natural language understanding. In *Proceedings of the 2018 EMNLP Workshop BlackboxNLP: Analyzing and Interpreting Neural Networks for NLP*, pages 353–355.

Nancy XR Wang, Diwakar Mahajan, Marina Danilevsk Rosenthal, et al. 2021. SemEval-2021 task 9: Fact verification and evidence finding for tabular data in scientific documents (SEM-TAB-FACTS). *arXiv preprint arXiv:2105.13995*.

Adina Williams, Nikita Nangia, and Samuel Bowman. 2018. A broad-coverage challenge corpus for sentence understanding through inference. In *Proceedings of the 2018 Conference of the North American Chapter of the Association for Computational Linguistics: Human Language Technologies, Volume 1 (Long Papers)*, pages 1112–1122, New Orleans, Louisiana. Association for Computational Linguistics.

A Appendix: Performance vs Perturbation

Figure 5 shows the relative accuracy drop of the model performance for each table perturbation strategy. There is no significant difference in the average accuracy across the A, B, and C counterfactual types. Figure 6 shows the number of examples for each hypothesis perturbation strategy. *Label Flip* (*LF*) is frequently used by the annotators with either the hypothesis or the table changes. Annotators also regularly use the *HypoPrompt* and Hypothesis overlap strategy for creating counterfactuals. Annotators avoid making new hypotheses.

B Appendix: TABPERT vs Spreadsheets

Effectiveness When utilizing spreadsheets for annotation, it becomes quite difficult and time-consuming to cut/copy-paste cells. The efficient drag-drop feature with automatic type restrictions in TABPERT makes it a much easier and faster procedure. Editing and altering text in TABPERT is also easier compare to that on a spreadsheet. Our study found that it takes around 7 minutes on average to annotate a new table with 9 statements using TABPERT, but the same work done using a spreadsheet takes more than 30 minutes.

Visualization Benefits TABPERT's table visualisation provides a view of the entire data on a single screen. Seeing the entire picture (tables and hypotheses) is incredibly helpful for assessing the quality of annotations. It also allows the

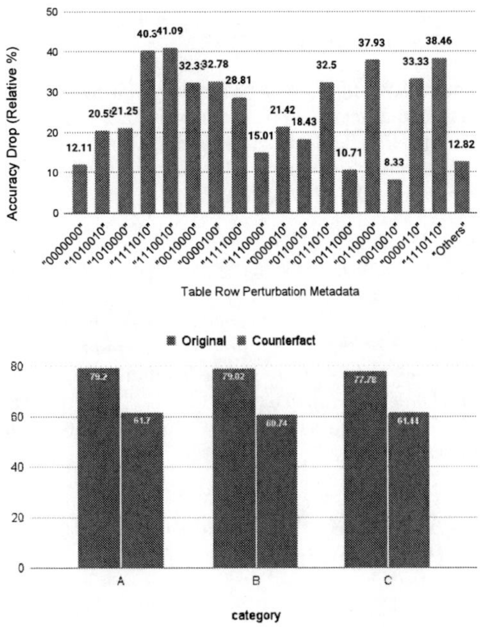

Figure 5: (Top) Performance drop with counterfactual perturbation with several perturbation strategies (using Table 1 for interpreting the analysis). (Bottom) Performance on A,B and C counterfactual tables.

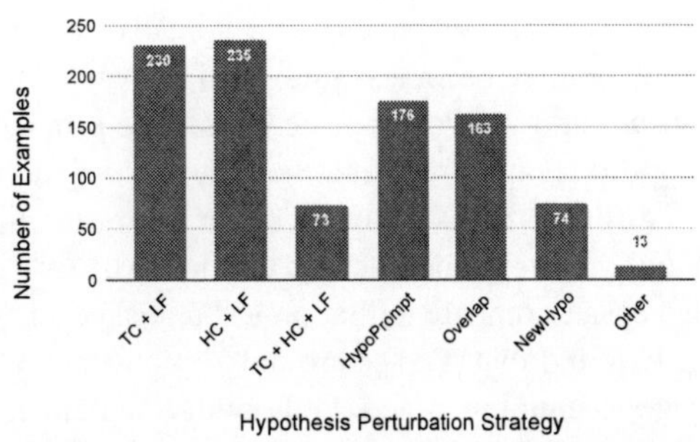

si

Figure 6: Number of examples of each hypothesis perturbation strategy.

annotator to quickly follow label and hypothesis changes, which is not feasible in a cumbersome spreadsheet's view.

Furthermore, having a single screen 'Focus View' on a single counterfactual table makes altering hypotheses even easier. Using this focus feature, updating the labels or adding new information to the hypothesis is straightforward. This focus view is not viable with a spreadsheet; to make appropriate alterations, one must search and navigate to each spreadsheet cell.

In addition to this, the lack of scrolling required while dragging and dropping on our platform saves annotators time. To discover the relevant cells in a spreadsheet, one must execute numerous scrolling operations to the up, down, left, or right.

Finally, in TABPERT, the cell size is set to exactly fit its contents, but in a spreadsheet, cells in each row and columns have the same height and width, making it quite problematic to view text properly.

Metadata Collection TABPERT makes it simple to gather information such as methods used to change a hypothesis and rows utilized to answer each hypothesis, using checkboxes. In a spreadsheet, this would require 9 columns of checkboxes for each table or manually writing the metadata, which is now automatically done with a single click, thus making the process simple and efficient. Moreover, automatic metadata collection about a drag and drop location is not possible in a spreadsheet.

C Appendix: Qualitative Counterfactual Perturbation Examples

Tables 3, 4, 5, 6, 7 illustrate the five strategies used for counterfactual table-hypothesis perturbation. Here, *Before* and *After* row represent hypothesis and corresponding relevant table rows[13] before and after counterfactual perturbation. In the *After* row, we also provide the 7-bit meta-data associated with each row value. Finally, the *Automatic Initialisation* row explains the meaning of the first four bits of this meta-data, and the *Manual Editing* row explains the last three bits, for all the value in concern.

[13]For simplicity, we only include the rows of the table relevant to the hypotheses.

	Premise	Hypothesis	Label	Predicted
Before (T14)	Box Office 1. $61.3 million Budget 1. $26 million	Flatliners made over double what it cost to make at the box office.	E	E
After (T14A)	Box Office 1. $ 140.7 million (1010 010) Budget 1. $85 million (0111 010)	Flatliners made over double what it cost to make at the box office.	C	E
Automatic Initialisation Manual Editing	1010: different dataset, same category, different table, same key 0111: same dataset, different category, different table, different key 010: value text edited			

Table 3: Example using Strategy 1
Strategy: Change table to flip label (TC+LF)

	Premise	Hypothesis	Label	Predicted
Before (T14)	Box Office 1. $61.3 million Budget 1. $26 million	Flatliners made over double what it cost to make at the box office	E	E
After (T14B)	Box Office 1. $ 13.3 million (1010 010) Budget 1. $5.9 million (0110 010)	Flatliners made over triple what it cost to make at the box office.	C	E
Automatic Initialisation Manual Editing	0110: same dataset, different category, different table, same key 1010: different dataset, same category, different table, same key 010: value text edited			

Table 4: Example using Strategy 2
Strategy: Change hypothesis to flip label (HC+LF)

	Premise	Hypothesis	Label	Predicted
Before (T14)	Produced by 1. Michael Douglas 2. Rick Bieber Directed by 1. Joel Schumacher	Rick Bieber put more money into Flatliners than Michael Douglas did.	N	N
After (T14A)	Produced by 1. Rick Bieber (0000 100) 2. Michael Douglas (0000 100) Directed by 1. Empress Teimei (1111 000)	Rick Bieber put more money into Flatliners directed by Empress Teimei, than Michael Douglas did	N	N
Automatic Initialisation Manual Editing	0000: same dataset, same category, same table, same key 1111: different dataset, different category, different table, different key 000: no change 100: copied from the original table			

Table 5: Example using Strategy 3
Strategy: Add 'true' information from the table to confuse the model (Overlap)

	Premise	Hypothesis	Label	Predicted
Before (T14)	Edited by 1. Robert Brown Written by 1. Peter Filardi	Flatliners was Peter Filardi's first writing credit.	N	N
After (T14B)	Edited by 1. James Newton Howard (0000 100) 2. Robert Brown (0000 000) Written by 1. Lee Beom-seon (1110 000)	Flatliners was mostly edited by Robert Brown.	N	E.
Automatic Initialisation Manual Editing	0000: same dataset, same category, same table, same key 1110: different dataset, different category, different table, same key 000: no change 100: copied from the original table			

Table 6: Example using Strategy 4
Strategy: Use the original hypothesis to write a new hypothesis (HypoPrompt)

	Premise	Hypothesis	Label	Predicted
Before (T14)	Box Office 1. $61.3 million Budget 1. $26 million	Flatliners made 50 million over it's budget at the box office.	C	E
After (T14C)	Box Office 1. US$85.4 million (December 2017) (0111 000) Budget 1. $26 million (0000 000)	Flatliners costed around $25 million in making and was a hit.	E	C
Automatic Initialisation Manual Editing	0000: same dataset, same category, same table, same key 0111: same dataset, different category, different table, different key 000 : no change			

Table 7: Example using Strategy 5
Strategy: Write a completely new hypothesis (NewHypo)

DRIFT: A Toolkit for Diachronic Analysis of Scientific Literature

Abheesht Sharma*
Dept. of CS&IS
BITS Pilani, Goa Campus
f20171014@goa.bits-pilani.ac.in

Gunjan Chhablani*
Dept. of CS&IS
BITS Pilani, Goa Campus
chhablani.gunjan@gmail.com

Harshit Pandey*
Dept. of Computer Science
Pune University
hp2pandey1@gmail.com

Rajaswa Patil
Dept. of E & E Engineering
BITS Pilani, Goa Campus
f20170334@goa.bits-pilani.ac.in

Abstract

In this work, we present to the NLP community, and to the wider research community as a whole, an application for the diachronic analysis of research corpora. We open source an easy-to-use tool coined *DRIFT*, which allows researchers to track research trends and development over the years. The analysis methods are collated from well-cited research works, with a few of our own methods added for good measure. Succinctly put, some of the analysis methods are: keyword extraction, word clouds, predicting declining/stagnant/growing trends using Productivity, tracking bi-grams using Acceleration plots, finding the Semantic Drift of words, tracking trends using similarity, etc. To demonstrate the utility and efficacy of our tool, we perform a case study on the *cs.CL* corpus of the arXiv repository and draw inferences from the analysis methods. The toolkit and the associated code are available here.

1 Introduction

Historians perform comparative studies between the past and the present to explain certain phenomena. Studying the past also helps us in making plausible predictions about the future. Major sources of information about the past are old-age texts, tomes and manuscripts. Language changes and shifts with changes in society and culture. For example, words such as *curglaff* and *lunting* have become obsolete, the word *gay*'s meaning has changed entirely and new words such as *LOL* and *ROFL* have gained prominence with the emergence of the "texting generation".

In the research world, analysis of old articles and papers is gaining importance. Analysing old documents can revive research topics which have been forgotten over the decades; removing the cobwebs on these topics can inspire path-breaking research. Explanations of why we arrived at certain conclusions can also be gleaned by peeping into the past. Performing such diachronic analysis of text has become easy because of the rapid growth of NLP. Temporal word embeddings such as TWEC (Di Carlo et al., 2019) enable us to do so.

In this paper, we introduce a hassle-free application for the diachronic analysis of research corpora. We name our application *DRIFT*, an acronym for **D**iach**R**onic Analysis of Scient**IF**ic Li**T**erature. *DRIFT* provides researchers a one-click way to perform various diachronic analyses.

Our contribution is two-fold: 1) We assemble (and propose) different methods for diachronic analysis of research corpora; 2) We make it extremely convenient for researchers to analyse research trends; this, in turn, will encourage researchers to find latent, quiescent topics which may have huge research potential in the near future. The main principles behind the design for *DRIFT* are **ease of usage** and **flexibility**.

The rest of the paper is organised as follows. In Section 2, we perform an extensive literature survey. Section 3 describes the research corpora and the methods for crawling the corpora. In Section 4, we explain the training methodology for obtaining diachronic embeddings and our easy-to-use application's dashboard and layout in detail. Section 5 elucidates the various analysis methods which researchers can employ with a mere click of a button.

2 Related Works

2.1 Diachronic Embeddings

Savants have attempted to leverage word embeddings to study semantic changes of words over time (Hamilton et al., 2016; Kulkarni et al., 2014).

* Equal contribution. Author ordering determined by coin flip.

Proceedings of the 2021 Conference on Empirical Methods in Natural Language Processing: System Demonstrations, pages 361–371
November 7–11, 2021.

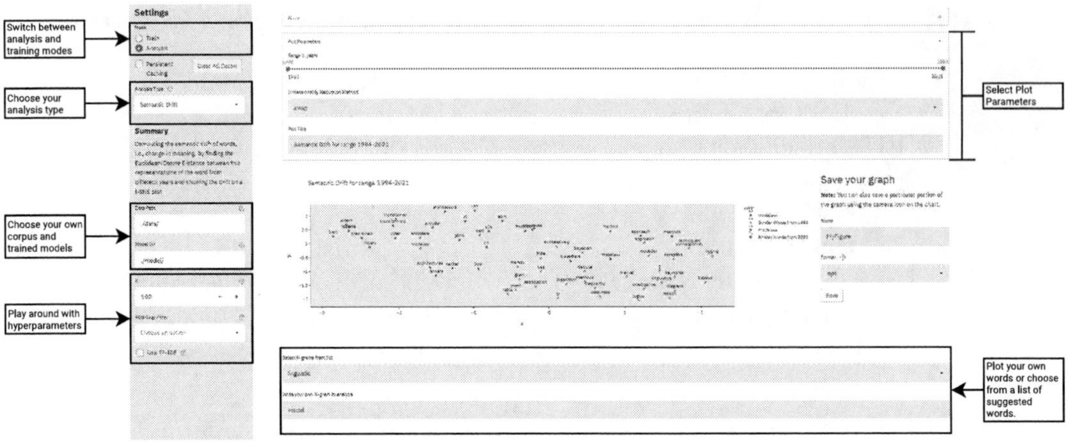

Figure 1: Snapshot for the application dashboard.

The major issue has been the inability to compare word vectors of two different time periods since word embedding algorithms are stochastic in nature and invariant under rotation, i.e., they belong to different coordinate systems (Kutuzov et al., 2018). Therefore, attempts have been made to align these vectors (Szymanski, 2017; Schlechtweg et al., 2019; Bamman et al., 2014). The most recent attempt to resolve this issue is TWEC (Di Carlo et al., 2019), which implicitly aligns the word vectors. We use TWEC in our work.

2.2 Analysis Attempts and Tools for Research Corpora

Many researchers have devoted their time to analysing different research corpora with respect to time. Most of the analysis is citation-based, or the researchers analyse the diversity of the research world (age-based, gender-based analysis) (Mohammad, 2019). In some, authors have introduced new research corpora such as the NLP4NLP Corpus (Mariani et al., 2019). Gollapalli and Li (2015) perform comparative analyses between two conferences such as EMNLP and ACL by expressing both venues as a probability distribution over time. A good amount of research has also focused on statistical techniques. For example, Schumann (2016) uses frequency and productivity to identify emerging/stagnant/falling topics. Others have devised Machine Learning/Deep Learning methods to identify future trends (Francopoulo et al., 2016).

NLP Scholar (Mohammad, 2020) is an interactive, visual tool which makes it simpler for researchers to find impactful scientific articles in bygone years from the ACL Anthology based on the number of citations, searching for relevant related works, study the changes in the number of articles and citations, etc.

While significant effort has gone into procuring research corpora and in devising different analysis methods, not much work has been done in building a user-friendly, convenient application which ties up statistical, learning-based analysis and temporal embedding-based methods and makes it easy for the research community to draw inferences and identify research trends.

3 Datasets

arXiv[1] is a free-access repository of e-prints of scientific papers, articles, essays and studies, launched in 1991 by Cornell University. arXiv covers a vast array of disciplines such as Computer Science, Mathematics, Physics, Chemistry, etc. We perform our experiments and analysis on a burgeoning subdomain of Computer Science, namely, Computation and Language (*cs.CL*).

Moreover, we perform our analyses on abstracts. The rationale behind this is: 1) The abstract of a paper condenses and encapsulates the whole paper and conveys its major contributions; 2) The rest of the paper may have tables, figures, arcane mathematical equations, intricacies and esoteric jargon which are difficult to work with.

We restrict our analysis to the 1994-2021 period for the following reasons: 1) arXiv has cs.CL and cs.CV papers from 1994 onwards; 2) We considered crawling the abstracts of papers published prior to 1994 from their PDFs (we obtained the

[1] `https://arxiv.org/`

URLs from the ACL Anthology[2]). However, this proved to be no mean feat, considering that the old PDFs used different font styles, unselectable texts, etc. The procured abstracts had grammatical flaws.

We use the arXiv API to obtain the metadata of the papers (specifically, URL, date of submission, title, authors, and abstract). To ensure that low quality articles are not included, we sort the papers by their relevance. In total, we analyse 27,384 abstracts.

4 Methodology

4.1 Diachronic Embeddings

As mentioned earlier, we use TWEC (Di Carlo et al., 2019) (Temporal Word Embeddings with Compass) to create dynamic word embeddings for each time slice. TWEC uses Word2Vec (Mikolov et al., 2013) and trains it on data for all the years to learn atemporal embeddings. Then, the "pre-trained" target embeddings are frozen, which serves as the "compass" and temporal embeddings are learned for each year as context embeddings. We use this method because it scales well with large corpora, and it also makes the training simple and efficient.

4.2 Application

We build our application using Streamlit[3], a framework in Python for making data applications. An overview of the application dashboard is shown in Figure 1. The dashboard has two modes: *Train* and *Analysis*. The general workflow of the application is shown in Figure 2 and described as follows:

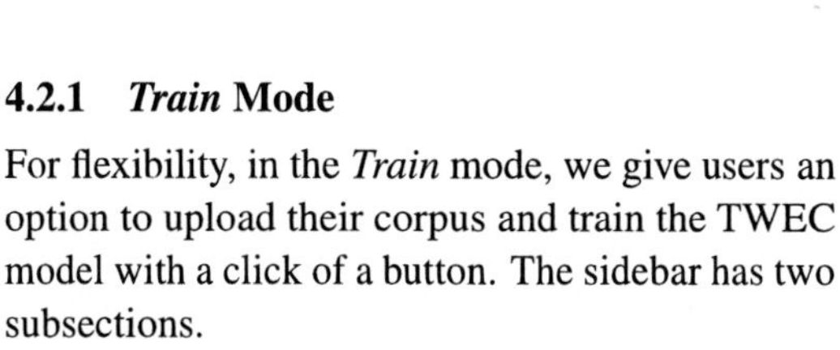

Figure 2: System design for the application.

4.2.1 *Train* Mode

For flexibility, in the *Train* mode, we give users an option to upload their corpus and train the TWEC model with a click of a button. The sidebar has two subsections.

[2]https://github.com/acl-org/acl-anthology
[3]https://streamlit.io/

Preprocessing Before training TWEC, the dataset has to be preprocessed. The preprocessing pipeline we employ comprises simple steps: convert to lower-case, lemmatisation, remove punctuation and stopwords, remove non-alphanumerics, etc. We also remove words which frequently appear in research papers such as *paper*, *systems*, *result*, *approach*, etc. This subsection has three input text boxes: *JSON Path* for the input dataset/corpus, *Text Key* for the key whose corresponding value contains raw text, *Data Path*, where the preprocessed data is to be stored. On clicking the button *Preprocess*, the raw text is preprocessed.

Training TWEC hyperparameters such as embedding size, number of static iterations, dynamic iterations, negative samples, window size are presented as text boxes/drop-down menus here. On clicking the button *Train*, the TWEC model is trained on the corpus. Options/hyperparameters/input paths for preprocessing and TWEC training are presented as text boxes/drop-down menus in the sidebar.

4.2.2 *Analysis* Mode

The *Analysis* mode is the most vital component of the application. The analysis method can be chosen from a drop-down menu. Once an analysis method is chosen, the sidebar displays several parameters which generally include data path, K (number of keywords to choose from compass), whether to use TF-IDF or use particular Parts-of-Speech, etc. As an example, method-specific parameters for *Semantic Drift* include: model path, K(sim.) (top-k most similar words to be shown around chosen words), K(drift) (allows user to select from top-k most drifted words), and distance metric (euclidean/cosine distance).

The page for every analysis method contains an expander, i.e., a collapsible section which has options such as a slider to decide the range of years to be considered for analysis, or a text box for a particular word to be analysed. Below the expander, interactive graphs, t-SNE (Maaten and Hinton, 2008)/UMAP (McInnes et al., 2020)/PCA plots and tables are displayed, based upon user's selection. Every button, text box, drop-down menu has a "help" option to guide users on its usage and purpose.

On the right-hand side, there is an option to export graphs in different formats such as PDF, SVG, etc. for easy integration with research papers.

5 Analysis Methods and Discussion

5.1 Word Cloud

A Word Cloud is a graphical representation of the keywords of a corpus, i.e., words which have higher frequency are given more importance. This importance is translated in terms of size and colour in the visualisation. We give the user an option to choose the year for which the analysis is to be done. Other options in the sidebar include minimum and maximum font size, number of words to be displayed, colour, width and height of the word cloud. The user can select the year from the expander. On the main page, we display the word cloud. An example is shown in Figure 7.

5.2 Productivity/Frequency Plot

Schumann (2016) uses normalized term frequency and term productivity as measures for identifying growing/consolidated/declining terms. Term productivity is a measure of the ability of a concept to produce new multi-word terms. In our case, we use bigrams. For each year y and single-word term t, and associated n multi-word terms m, the productivity is given by the entropy:

$$e(t, y) = -\sum_{i=1}^{n} \log_2(p_{m_i,y}).p_{m_i,y} \tag{1}$$

where

$$p_{m,y} = \frac{f(m)}{\sum_{i=1}^{n} f(m_i)} \tag{2}$$

and $f(m)$ is frequency of the term. Based on these two measures (over the years), words are clustered into three categories:

- **Growing Terms**: Those which have increasing frequency and productivity in the recent years.
- **Consolidated Terms**: Those that are growing in frequency, but not in productivity.
- **Terms in Decline**: Those which have reached an upper bound of productivity and have low frequency.

In the sidebar, the user can choose the N in N-gram and the K in Top-K. The default for keyword extraction in all the methods is normalised frequency, but the user can opt for frequency or TF-IDF. Alternatively, the user can also choose the POS tag for filtering the keywords.

In the expander, the user can select words from the suggested keywords or add their own words for analysis. In the main section, the productivity and normalised frequency graphs are displayed. Below these graphs, we have a dataframe which displays which clusters the words belong to. An example is shown in Figure 10.

5.3 Acceleration Plot

Inspired by Dridi et al. (2019), we analyse the semantic shift of a pair of words with respect to each other. We aim to identify fast converging keywords using "acceleration". The acceleration matrix is calculated as the difference between similarity matrices of two different time periods, where each entry is:

$$acc(w_i, w_j)^{t \to (t+1)} = sim(w_i, w_j)^{(t+1)} - sim(w_i, w_j)^{t} \tag{3}$$

where (w_i, w_j) is the word pair being analysed, $sim(w_i, w_j)$ is the cosine similarity between words w_i and w_j, and $(t, t+1)$ is the time range. If the words w_i and w_j converge, the cosine similarity value between them will increase, or in other words, $acc(w_i, w_j)^{t \to (t+1)} > 0$. We pick the word pairs with the highest acceleration values.

To demonstrate the convergence of a pair of words, we plot the pair on a two-dimensional plot, along with the top-K most similar words around them. An example is shown in Figure 4.

In addition to K, POS Tag Filters and an option to opt for TF-IDF, we also have $K(acc.)$ and $K(sim.)$. The parameter, $K(sim.)$, is for deciding how many words to plot around the two chosen words. $K(acc.)$ is for finding the top-K most accelerated pair of words.

The expander has a slider for selecting the range of years, below which there is a dataframe, listing the top-K most accelerated keywords. There are two drop-downs for selecting the pair of words to be analysed.

The main section has the graph of the embedding space, showing the convergence/divergence of the chosen pair of words.

5.4 Semantic Drift

The semantics of words perpetually change over time, i.e., words drift from one point to another. This incessant *semantic drift* is a product of changing social and cultural norms, transition in linguistic usage, amongst other factors. Since we use

	$model_{2010}$	$gmms_{2011}$	$markov_{2014}$	hmm_{2016}	asr_{2017}	$acoustic_{2019}$
0	$gmms_{2011}$ (0.6)	$subspace_{2014}$ (0.78)	hmm_{2016} (0.68)	$markov_{2017}$ (0.61)	$e2e_{2020}$ (0.5)	$phonetic_{2021}$ (0.5)
1	$gaussian_{2011}$ (0.51)	$mixture_{2014}$ (0.71)	$hmms_{2016}$ (0.66)	dnn_{2017} (0.59)	hmm_{2020} (0.49)	$spectrograms_{2020}$ (0.47)
2	$hide_{2011}$ (0.51)	$gaussian_{2014}$ (0.69)	dnn_{2016} (0.55)	gmm_{2017} (0.58)	$acoustic_{2019}$ (0.48)	$audio_{2021}$ (0.46)
3	$mixture_{2011}$ (0.5)	$markov_{2014}$ (0.67)	$conditional_{2016}$ (0.55)	$hmms_{2017}$ (0.56)	$transcription_{2018}$ (0.47)	$ppgs_{2020}$ (0.46)
4	$allocation_{2013}$ (0.47)	$factorial_{2013}$ (0.66)	cd_{2015} (0.53)	asr_{2017} (0.52)	$transcriptions_{2019}$ (0.47)	$mfcc_{2020}$ (0.45)

Figure 3: Tracking the word *"model"* from the year 2010 to the year 2019 with stride=3.

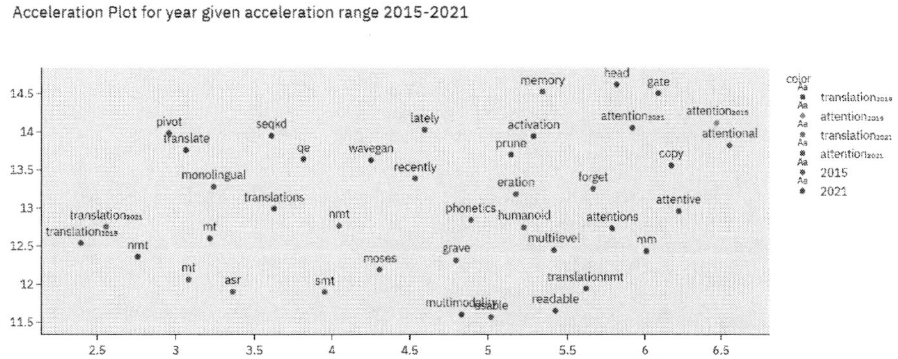

Figure 4: Convergence of the words: *"Translation"* and *"Attention"* (2015-2021).

TWEC embeddings, the representations of a word across time periods are implicitly aligned and we can directly compute the shift as the distance between the two representations.

We compute the drift as the Euclidean Distance or the Cosine Distance between the first year embedding of the word and the last year embedding of the word. We sort the words according to their drift (in descending order). For more details on the algorithm, refer to Subsection A.1 in the Appendix.

In order to visualise the drift, we plot the two representations of the word on a UMAP/tSNE/PCA plot, along with the most similar words in the respective years which are clumped around the two representations. Plotting the top-k most similar words helps the user in analysing the shift in meaning.

Other than the usual parameters - K, POS Tag Filters, TF-IDF, the sidebar has options to choose $K(sim.)$ and $K(drift)$. The expander has a slider for selecting the range of years. Below the graphs, a drop-down menu has the top-K(drift) most drifted words as suggestions. The user can also input a custom word.

A couple of examples are shown in Figure 5. Clearly, the word "model" has drifted from the vicinity of *bayesian, markov, bag, gram, logics* in 2017 to *albert, roberta, xlnet, mbert, bart* in 2021. This makes sense, because back in 1994, a conventional NLP model was related to bag-of-words, and Markov/HMM-based (Fosler-Lussier, 1998)/Bayesian methods, while in 2021, the focus has shifted to RoBERTa (Liu et al., 2020), XLNet (Yang et al., 2019), BART (Lewis et al., 2020) and other transformer models.

5.5 Tracking Clusters

Word meanings change over time. They come closer or drift apart. In any given year, certain words are clumped together, i.e., they belong to one cluster. But over time, clusters can break into two/coalesce together to form one. Unlike the previous module which tracks movement of one word at a time, here, we track the movement of clusters.

Our implementation is simple. Given a range of years, and some common keywords, we cluster the words for every year, and display the UMAP/tSNE/PCA graph (with clusters) for every year separately. We use the KMeans Clustering Algorithm. A visualisation is shown in Figure 9.

The additional options in the sidebar include number of clusters and max. number of clusters. If number of clusters is set to 0, the application finds the optimal number by searching between $[3, Max.\ Number\ of\ Clusters]$ using Silhouette score. Additionally, we have an option to choose the library of implementation: faiss[4]/scikit-learn[5]. Faiss is up to 10 times faster than sklearn.

[4] https://github.com/facebookresearch/faiss

[5] https://github.com/scikit-learn/scikit-learn

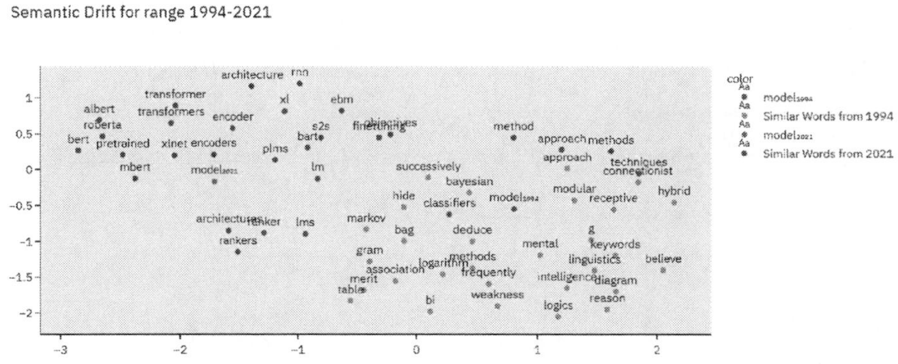

Figure 5: Semantic Drift of the word *"model"* (1994-2021).

5.6 Acceleration Heatmap

We use the same *acceleration* measure as in Section 5.3. Instead of listing the top-K pairs based on acceleration, we plot a heatmap of the acceleration between two years. This can be useful in analysing how different word-pairs are converging at different rates between two years. This heatmap can be used in combination with the Acceleration Plot, where a representation of the word-pairs selected based on the heatmap can be explored. Refer to Figure 6 to get an idea of the visualisation.

5.7 Track Trends with Similarity

We wish to chart the trajectory of a word/topic from *year 1* to *year 2*. To accomplish this, we allow the user to pick a word from *year 1*. At the same time, we ask the user to provide the desired *stride*. We search for the most similar word in the next $stride$ years. We keep doing this iteratively till we reach *year 2*, updating the word at each step via user input from the top-K similar words. An overview of the algorithm is given in Subsection A.2. An example is given in Figure 3. The trajectory we follow is model, gmms, markov, hmm, asr, phonetic. This makes sense, because HMMs, GMMs were used for ASR in the past.

5.8 Keyword Visualisation

Here, we use the YAKE Keyword Extraction method (Campos et al., 2020) to extract keywords. Yake Score is indirectly proportional to the keyword importance. Hence, we report the scores differently[6].

The user can select $Max.\ N-gram$ in the sidebar. The year can be selected from the slider in the expander. The main section has a bar graph, with n-grams on the y-axis and their importance scores on the x-axis. A visualisation is shown in Figure 11.

5.9 LDA Topic Modelling

Latent Dirichlet Allocation (LDA) (Blei et al., 2003) is a generative probabilistic model for an assortment of documents, generally used for topic modelling and extraction. LDA clusters the text data into imaginary topics. Every topic can be represented as a probability distribution over n-grams and every document can be represented as a probability distribution over these generated topics.

We train LDA on a corpus where each document contains the abstracts of a particular year. We express every year as a probability distribution of topics. An example is shown in Figure 8.

6 Accessibility

The code for the toolkit is open-sourced, and is distributed under a MIT License. The latest stable code release is available here. An online demo of the application is hosted here. A set of short video demonstrations can be found here.

7 Conclusion and Future Work

In this paper, we present *DRIFT*, a hassle-free, user-friendly application for diachronic analysis of scientific literature. We compile well-cited research works and provide an interactive and intuitive user-interface using Streamlit. We perform a case-study on *cs.CL* corpus from arXiv repository, and demonstrate the effectiveness and utility of our application in analysing such corpora. As an extension of our work, apart from adding upcoming analysis methods (citation-based/statistical/knowledge graphs), we also intend to make our application

[6] $new\_score = \frac{1}{10^5 \times yake\_score}$

modular to make it easier for users to add their own methods, provide semi-automated inference from the graphs/tables, and allow easy integration with LaTeX.

References

David Bamman, Chris Dyer, and Noah A. Smith. 2014. Distributed representations of geographically situated language. In *Proceedings of the 52nd Annual Meeting of the Association for Computational Linguistics (Volume 2: Short Papers)*, pages 828–834, Baltimore, Maryland. Association for Computational Linguistics.

David M. Blei, Andrew Y. Ng, and Michael I. Jordan. 2003. Latent dirichlet allocation. *J. Mach. Learn. Res.*, 3(null):993–1022.

Ricardo Campos, Vítor Mangaravite, Arian Pasquali, Alípio Jorge, Célia Nunes, and Adam Jatowt. 2020. Yake! keyword extraction from single documents using multiple local features. *Information Sciences*, 509:257–289.

Valerio Di Carlo, Federico Bianchi, and Matteo Palmonari. 2019. Training temporal word embeddings with a compass. *Proceedings of the AAAI Conference on Artificial Intelligence*, 33(01):6326–6334.

Amna Dridi, Mohamed Medhat Gaber, R. Muhammad Atif Azad, and Jagdev Bhogal. 2019. Deephist: Towards a deep learning-based computational history of trends in the nips. In *2019 International Joint Conference on Neural Networks (IJCNN)*, pages 1–8.

Eric Fosler-Lussier. 1998. Markov models and hidden markov models: A brief tutorial. *International Computer Science Institute*.

Gil Francopoulo, Joseph Mariani, and Patrick Paroubek. 2016. Predictive modeling: Guessing the NLP terms of tomorrow. In *Proceedings of the Tenth International Conference on Language Resources and Evaluation (LREC'16)*, pages 336–343, Portorož, Slovenia. European Language Resources Association (ELRA).

Sujatha Das Gollapalli and Xiaoli Li. 2015. EMNLP versus ACL: Analyzing NLP research over time. In *Proceedings of the 2015 Conference on Empirical Methods in Natural Language Processing*, pages 2002–2006, Lisbon, Portugal. Association for Computational Linguistics.

William L. Hamilton, Jure Leskovec, and Dan Jurafsky. 2016. Diachronic word embeddings reveal statistical laws of semantic change. In *Proceedings of the 54th Annual Meeting of the Association for Computational Linguistics (Volume 1: Long Papers)*, pages 1489–1501, Berlin, Germany. Association for Computational Linguistics.

Vivek Kulkarni, Rami Al-Rfou, Bryan Perozzi, and Steven Skiena. 2014. Statistically significant detection of linguistic change.

Andrey Kutuzov, Lilja Øvrelid, Terrence Szymanski, and Erik Velldal. 2018. Diachronic word embeddings and semantic shifts: a survey. In *Proceedings of the 27th International Conference on Computational Linguistics*, pages 1384–1397, Santa Fe, New Mexico, USA. Association for Computational Linguistics.

Mike Lewis, Yinhan Liu, Naman Goyal, Marjan Ghazvininejad, Abdelrahman Mohamed, Omer Levy, Veselin Stoyanov, and Luke Zettlemoyer. 2020. BART: Denoising sequence-to-sequence pretraining for natural language generation, translation, and comprehension. In *Proceedings of the 58th Annual Meeting of the Association for Computational Linguistics*, pages 7871–7880, Online. Association for Computational Linguistics.

Yinhan Liu, Myle Ott, Naman Goyal, Jingfei Du, Mandar Joshi, Danqi Chen, Omer Levy, Mike Lewis, Luke Zettlemoyer, and Veselin Stoyanov. 2020. Ro{bert}a: A robustly optimized {bert} pretraining approach.

L. V. D. Maaten and Geoffrey E. Hinton. 2008. Visualizing data using t-sne. *Journal of Machine Learning Research*, 9:2579–2605.

Joseph Mariani, Gil Francopoulo, and Patrick Paroubek. 2019. The nlp4nlp corpus (i): 50 years of publication, collaboration and citation in speech and language processing. *Frontiers in Research Metrics and Analytics*, 3:36.

Leland McInnes, John Healy, and James Melville. 2020. Umap: Uniform manifold approximation and projection for dimension reduction.

Tomas Mikolov, Kai Chen, Greg Corrado, and Jeffrey Dean. 2013. Efficient estimation of word representations in vector space. *arXiv preprint arXiv:1301.3781*.

Saif M. Mohammad. 2019. The state of nlp literature: A diachronic analysis of the acl anthology.

Saif M. Mohammad. 2020. NLP scholar: An interactive visual explorer for natural language processing literature. In *Proceedings of the 58th Annual Meeting of the Association for Computational Linguistics: System Demonstrations*, pages 232–255, Online. Association for Computational Linguistics.

Dominik Schlechtweg, Anna Hätty, Marco Del Tredici, and Sabine Schulte im Walde. 2019. A wind of change: Detecting and evaluating lexical semantic change across times and domains. In *Proceedings of the 57th Annual Meeting of the Association for Computational Linguistics*, pages 732–746, Florence, Italy. Association for Computational Linguistics.

Anne-Kathrin Schumann. 2016. Brave new world: Uncovering topical dynamics in the ACL Anthology reference corpus using term life cycle information. In *Proceedings of the 10th SIGHUM Workshop on Language Technology for Cultural Heritage, Social Sciences, and Humanities*, pages 1–11, Berlin, Germany. Association for Computational Linguistics.

Terrence Szymanski. 2017. Temporal word analogies: Identifying lexical replacement with diachronic word embeddings. In *Proceedings of the 55th Annual Meeting of the Association for Computational Linguistics (Volume 2: Short Papers)*, pages 448–453, Vancouver, Canada. Association for Computational Linguistics.

Zhilin Yang, Zihang Dai, Yiming Yang, Jaime Carbonell, Russ R Salakhutdinov, and Quoc V Le. 2019. Xlnet: Generalized autoregressive pretraining for language understanding. In *Advances in Neural Information Processing Systems*, volume 32. Curran Associates, Inc.

A Algorithms

A.1 Semantic Shift

An overview of the approach is given in Algorithm 1. The $dist(x, y)$ function can either be the Euclidean Distance or Cosine Distance. In the algorithm, we find the most drifted words from a given list of words by sorting them according to the distance. $year\_x\_model$ is the aligned TWEC Model for year x.

Algorithm 1: Semantic Shift

```
Data: words, year_1, year_2
Result: word_dist
word_dist ← {}
for word in words do
    year_1_emb ← year_1_model(word)
    year_2_emb ← year_2_model(word)
    word_dist[word] ←
      dist(year_1_emb, year_2_emb)
end
word_dist ← sort_by_value(word_dist, "desc")
```

A.2 Track Trends with Similarity

Algorithm 2 gives an overview of our approach. $MSW(word, range = [year+1, year+stride])$ finds the most similar word to $word$ in the years $year + 1, year + 2, ..., year + stride$. Here, we have demonstrated (for the sake of simplicity) that the most similar word is chosen at every step. In the actual implementation, we allow the user to choose from the top-K most similar words at every step. $stride$ is available as an argument in the sidebar, along with $K(sim.)$. In the main section, a table (which is dynamically updated) displays the trajectory taken by the initial word.

Algorithm 2: Track Trends with Similarity

```
Data: word, year_1, year_2
Result: word_traj
year ← year_1
word_iter ← word
word_traj ← [(word, year_1)]
while year ≤ year_2 do
    word_iter ← MSW(word_iter, range =
      [year + 1, year + stride])
    year ← get_year(word_iter)
    word_traj.append((word_iter, year))
end
```

B Additional Demonstrative Analyses

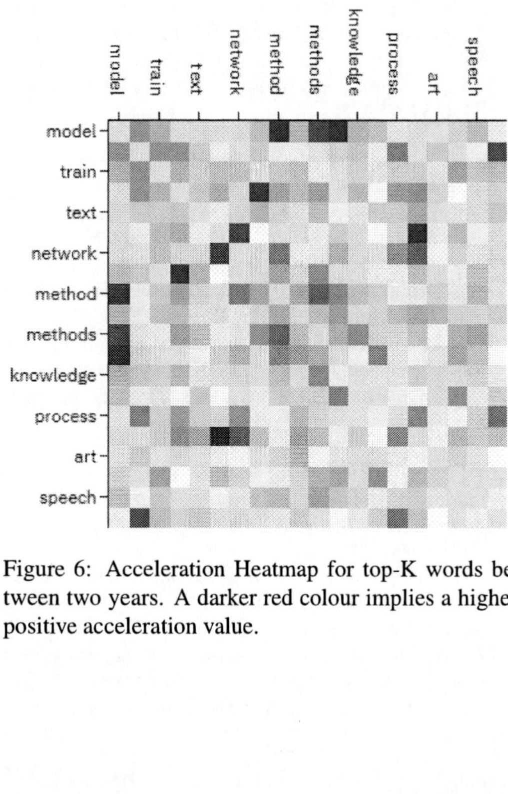

Figure 6: Acceleration Heatmap for top-K words between two years. A darker red colour implies a higher positive acceleration value.

(a) Word Cloud for the year 2000.

(b) Word Cloud for the year 2018.

Figure 7: Word Cloud Demonstrations.

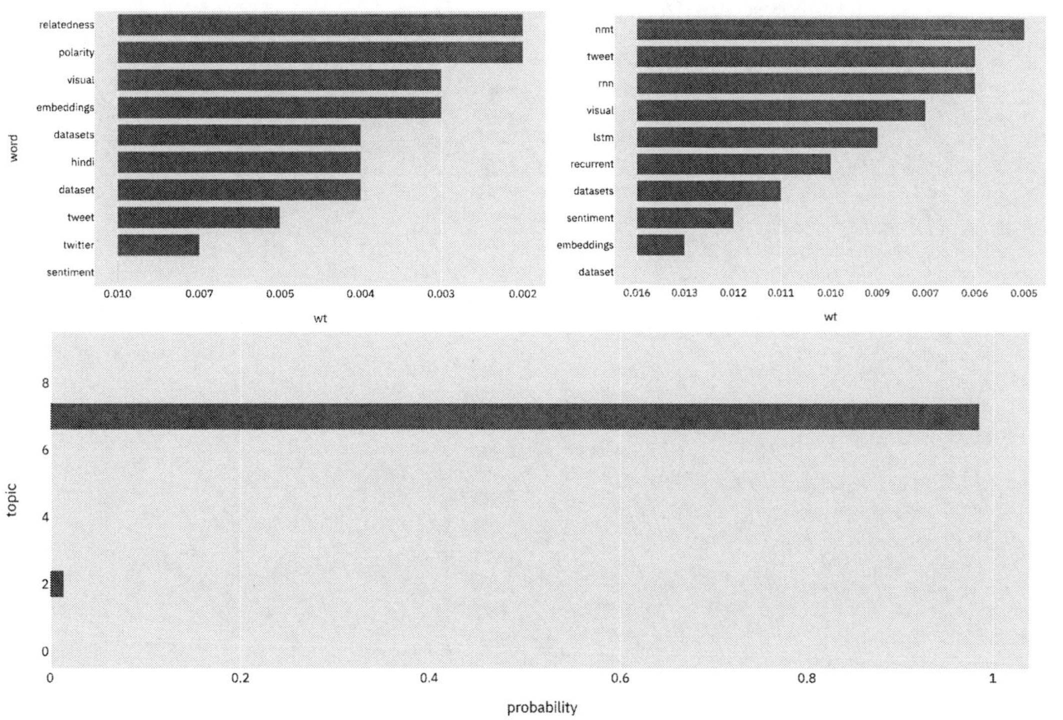

Figure 8: LDA Topic Modeling for the year 2014. The major topics in 2014 are 2 and 7. Topic 2 is primarily composed of "visual", "embeddings", etc. and Topic 7 is composed of "nmt", "tweet", "rnn", etc.

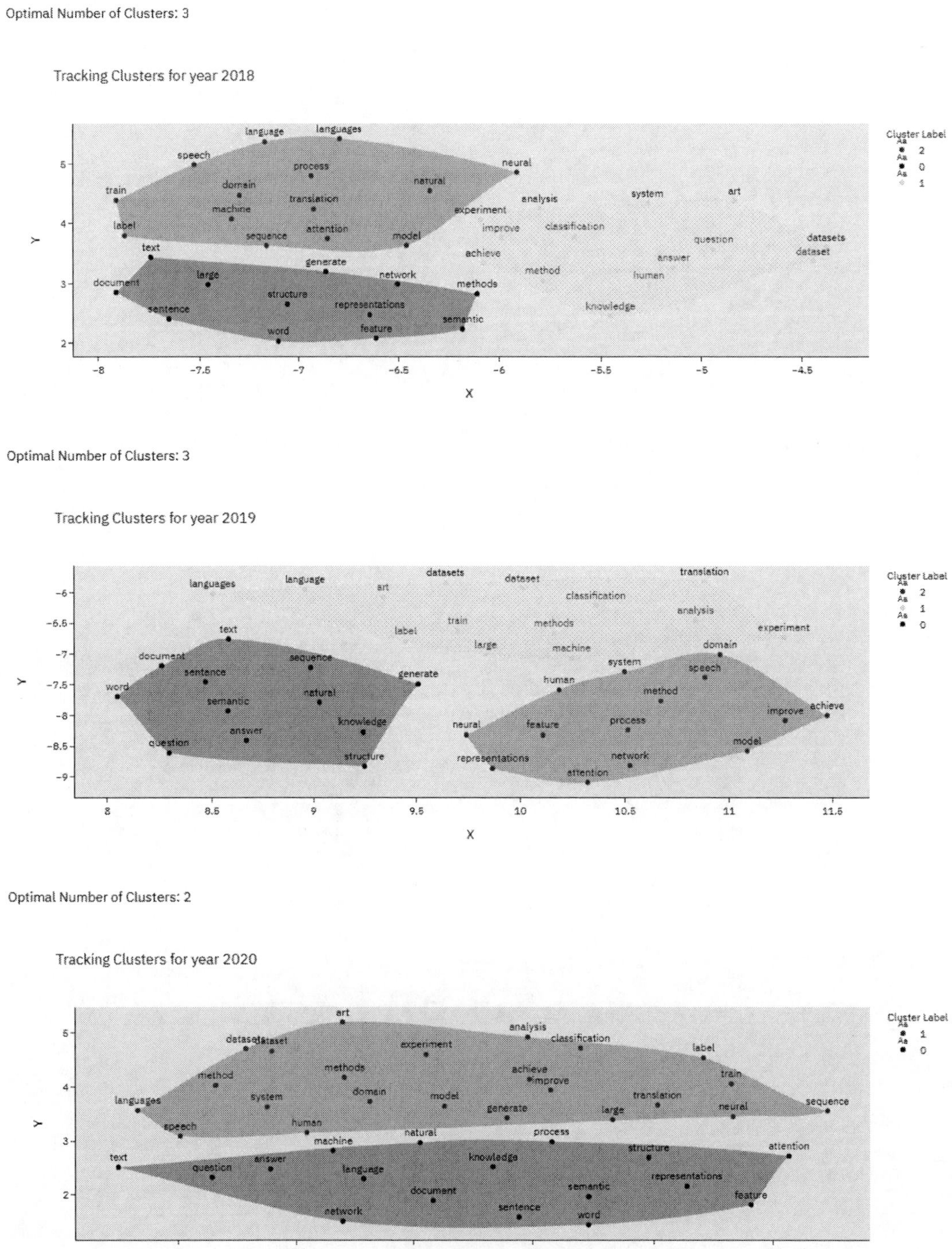

Figure 9: Tracking Clusters from 2018 to 2020.

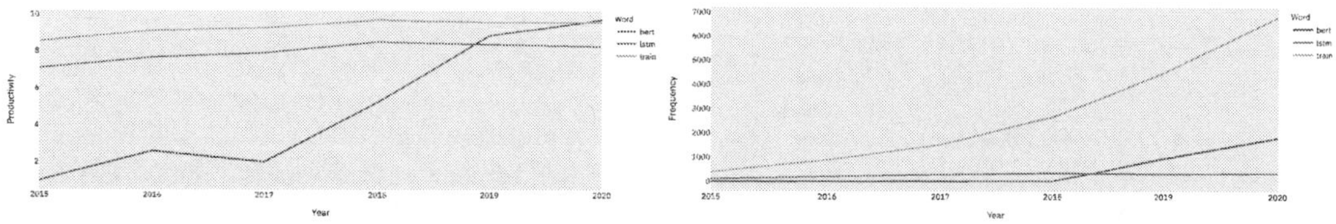

Figure 10: Productivity and Normalised Frequency Plots for the words "BERT", "LSTM", "train" (2015-2020). We can classify "BERT" as a growing term, "train" as a consolidated term and "LSTM", a declining term.

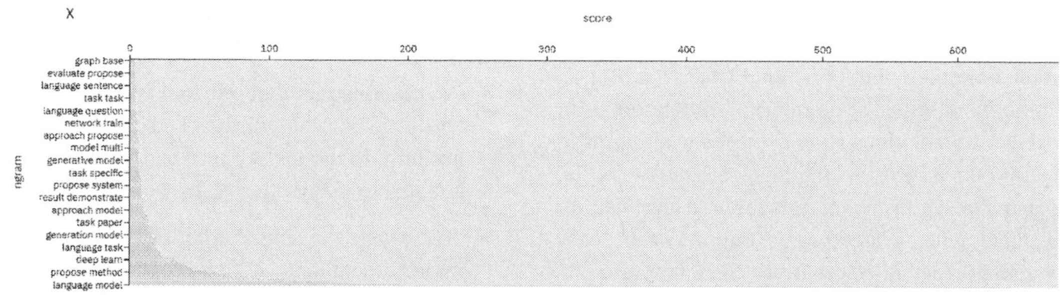

Figure 11: Keyword Visualisation using the YAKE keyword extraction method for the year 2019. Top keywords with $n = 2$ include "language model", "deep learn", "generative model", etc.

FAST: Fast Annotation tool for SmarT devices

Shunyo Kawamoto, Yu Sawai,* Kohei Wakimoto,* Peinan Zhang*
CyberAgent, Inc.
{kawamoto_shunyo,sawai_yu,wakimoto_kohei,zhang_peinan}@cyberagent.co.jp

Abstract

Working with a wide range of annotators with the same attributes is crucial, as in real-world applications. Although such application cases often use crowd-sourcing mechanisms to gather a variety of annotators, most real-world users use mobile devices. In this paper, we propose "FAST," an annotation tool for application tasks that focuses on the user experience of mobile devices, which has not yet been focused on thus far. We designed FAST as a web application for use on any device with a flexible interface that can be customized to fit various tasks. In our experiments, we conducted crowd-sourced annotation for a sentiment analysis task with several annotators and evaluated annotation metrics such as speed, quality, and ease of use from the tool's logs and user surveys. Based on the results of our experiments, we conclude that our system can annotate faster than existing methods while maintaining the annotation quality.

1 Introduction

In the annotation of application tasks, it is important to work with a wide range of annotators as in real-world situations such as in the evaluation of the outputs of natural language generation (NLG) systems or sentiment analysis for user reviews. For instance, when evaluating the outputs of an NLG system for textual-ad creatives, the annotators, often called workers in a crowd-sourcing context, are usually required to annotate whether the generated text is fluent or not[1].

Although such applications often use crowd-sourcing to gather a wide variety of annotators, statistics have shown that a large percentage of real-world users currently use mobile devices such as smartphones (Economic Research Office, 2020). The application task itself, such as sentiment annotation and fluency assessment of the NLG system outputs, is simple. However, it is important to improve the operation interface and evaluate its contribution in detail. This is because a large amount of data is annotated by annotators with various operation proficiency levels.

In addition to the level of proficiency, mobile devices are more likely than desktop devices to be used on the go, during spare time, and in parallel with other tasks (Economic Research Office, 2020). Annotation using mobile devices is expected to collect more data as the time available for work is increased and the effort is reduced.

We propose a novel annotation tool called "FAST"[2], and its contributions are summarized below.

- We propose and develop an annotation tool for the tasks that focuses on the user experience (UX) on mobile devices, which is important but has not yet been addressed in previous studies.
- We demonstrate that our tool is scalable, extensible, and customizable, and can be applied not only to the tasks described in this paper, but also to many other tasks.
- To evaluate the contribution of the tool to the improvement in the UX, we conducted an evaluation experiment with multiple annotators in a setting close to the practical use and obtained the metrics of annotation efficiency. We also conducted quantitative evaluations, such as inter-annotator agreement and subjective evaluations of UX.

*These authors contributed equally.

[1] We use the term "annotation" to refer to the procedure of labeling a single instance.

[2] A short introduction video and the source codes are available at https://github.com/CyberAgent/fast-annotation-tool

Proceedings of the 2021 Conference on Empirical Methods in Natural Language Processing: System Demonstrations, pages 372–381
November 7–11, 2021. ©2021 Association for Computational Linguistics

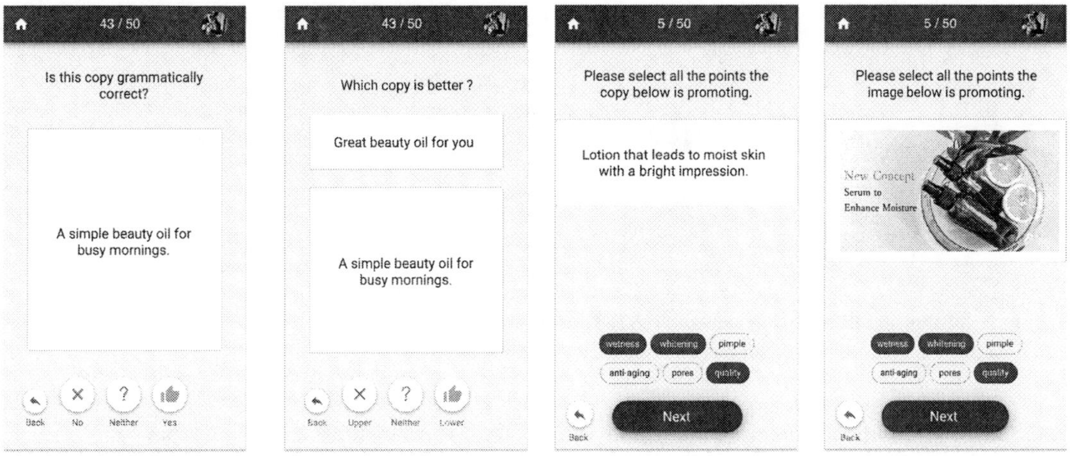

Figure 1: Use-case examples of FAST. In FAST, both texts and images are supported, and users can freely set questions and answers.

2 Related Work

In this section, we review the work related to the issues addressed by FAST. First, we note that FAST is not aimed at performing complete linguistic annotations; rather it focuses on applied tasks such as quality assessment of NLG systems. More specifically, FAST is designed for the annotation of individual tokens and sentences and not for the annotation of relations between tokens and sentences. In addition, we expect the annotators to be users with a wide range of attributes, such as those employed in crowd-sourcing.

Examples of tools that support extensive and detailed linguistic annotation are Brat (Stenetorp et al., 2012), MAE (Rim, 2016), INCEpTION (Klie et al., 2018), and Anafora (Chen and Styler, 2013). Recently, there have also been open-source software (OSS) tools such as doccano (Nakayama et al., 2018) that are suitable for applied tasks such as multi-label classification. Doccano is an OSS tool with mobile support and is currently one of the most popular annotation tools, with more than 4,000 stars on GitHub. This tool is focused on industrial targets such as sentiment analysis done by general users, rather than inter-entity structural annotation done by experts e.g. dependency structure annotations or coreference annotations. In this respect, Doccano and FAST have been developed based on the same motivation, and the target tasks are also similar. Although Doccano supports mobile devices, it essentially has the same UI structure as its desktop version and thus implementing extensible UI system on the top of it requires efforts. Therefore, we developed FAST from scratch and introduced user interfaces dedicated to mobile devices and mechanisms for the easy custom annotation of interface elements which are required for simulating end-users' environment as close as possible.

User Interface and Experience

There are several studies on improving the efficiency of annotation tasks. As a prominent example, SLATE (Kummerfeld, 2019) aims to improve the efficiency of workers who are skilled in keyboard input by focusing on the command line interface. Conversely, in a crowd-sourcing situation, there is a large variation in the operating skills of the workers; therefore, FAST adopts a graphical user interface (UI) and aims to improve efficiency by devising a new UI.

In application tasks, manual evaluation by a large number of non-domain experts is crucial. For example, in the evaluation of the generation quality of NLG systems, which is one of the tasks envisioned by the proposed tool, it is vital to have a group of evaluators similar to the user population that will see the generated sentences (van der Lee et al., 2019). To accommodate a wide variety of workers, the environment in which the tool operates must be versatile; in other words, it must have a web-based interface or a mobile interface. Although there are tools that support mobile devices, such as Doccano mentioned earlier, tools that have a user interface for mobile devices as their primary focus are scarce. In particular, the mobile UIs of the existing tools are the same as those of their PC versions;

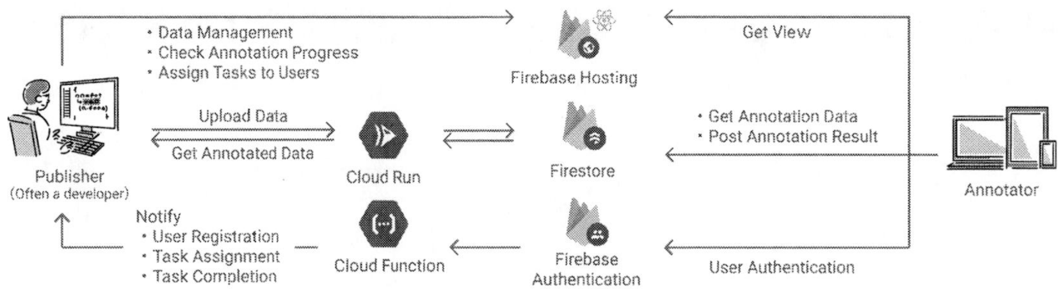

Figure 2: System architecture overview of FAST. The tool consists of serverless backend services and a user-facing interface for annotators, which can run on both PC and mobile devices.

thus, there is significant room for improving the efficiency of mobile interfaces. The proposed tool, FAST, aims to enable users who are not confident in operating PC terminals or those who are familiar with the mobile environment to work comfortably using a standard UI for mobile software.

Evaluation for Annotation Tools

We conclude this chapter with related work on methods to evaluate the contribution of annotation tools. A comparison at the functional level is often performed for tools with a large feature set, such as RedCoat (Stewart et al., 2019). Conversely, there are situations in which the performance of actual tasks are directly evaluated.

TALEN (Mayhew and Roth, 2018) is a tool specialized for creating Named Entity Recognition (NER) datasets in "low-resource" languages, which in some cases the annotators are not aware of. To assist annotators in this task, it includes "entity-propagation" where tagging an entity spills over to others similar to it, and there exists a mechanism to display the vocabulary of known languages. To evaluate these contributions, we adopted a method of comparing the NER task performance of the "low-resource" language with that of the baseline tool. In FAST, as in TALEN, we employ metrics such as the performance in the assumed real task and the time spent for annotation work as quantitative evaluation indicators.

3 System Description

3.1 Supported Annotation Methods

FAST supports Card UI annotations and Multi-label UI annotations. Figure 1 shows the screenshots of each UI.

As can be observed from the figure 1, FAST is highly customizable. By flexibly designing questions and answers, issuers can create annotations for a variety of tasks, ranging from simple binary classification to pairwise comparisons and element selection.

For example, if a set of generated sentences have to be ranked, we simply need to create pairwise sentences and then annotate them. Based on the results, using methods such as TrueSkill(Herbrich et al., 2007), the score and ranking of the sentences can be obtained. In addition, since HTML/CSS can be set as the evaluation target, it is possible to annotate the UI and the multimodal support close to the actual application, such as for evaluation combining images and text.

Card UI In FAST, we adopted the Card UI, which has been adopted by several mobile applications such as Tinder[3] and Grabble[4], as a UI suitable for mobile environments. In the Card UI, the user is presented with a card containing text and a question. The annotator responds with two choices: whether the content of the card matches the question. The annotator can answer by swiping the card or tapping the button at the bottom of the screen. One feature of the Card UI is that the actions to perform are few. Although ordinary tools require at least two actions, selection and decision, the card system allows these actions to be executed with a single action. In addition, because swiping a card in either the left or right direction is a very familiar action in mobile devices, it is intuitive and requires little time for the user to get used to; it is therefore expected to provide fast and comfortable annotation while ensuring quality.

Multi-label UI The UI of the multi-label is depicted on the right side of Figure 1. In the Multi-label UI, multiple buttons are presented to a question. Annotators tap one or more buttons to answer this question. The multi-label method is an anno-

[3] `https://tinder.com/`

[4] `https://www.grabble.com/`

tation method that assumes multiple choices, and several evaluation tools implement it. Compared to the Card UI, the Multi-label UI can handle a wider range of annotations; however, the annotation efficiency is expected to decrease owing to the difference in the number of actions.

3.2 Architecture and Features

As shown in Figure 2, FAST adopts an architecture comprising Google Cloud Platform and Firebase. We adopted such a serverless design instead of hosting it on our own servers to reduce the management cost. Once FAST is deployed, there is no requirement to augment the DB or update the OS subsequently and can be therefore be conveniently operated. Additionally, since Firebase is a pay-per-use system, server costs can be kept very low for low-frequency access applications such as annotation tools. For example, 100,000 annotations cost only approximately \$0.4. which is significantly cheaper than purchasing a new machine.

Detailed logs It is important to keep accurate and detailed logs during an annotation. For example, when we want to estimate the difficulty of an annotation, it is useful to know how long it took the annotator to complete each question, how many times the annotator pressed the back button to revise the answer, which device was used to annotate, and so on. For this reason, FAST collects detailed logs, for example, the timestamp of the user's action (view, select, submit), the user agent, and the size of the screen.

In addition, because FAST can be linked to Google Analytics[5], it is possible to know the location, device, and event information of annotators in real time.

Device dependency As FAST is a web application, it can be run as long as there is an accessible Internet environment and a browser. In other words, there is no device dependency, such as being limited to PCs or mobile devices, and it is possible to work with a wide range of annotators with attributes closer to those of real applications.

Data communication via API We expect that the annotation issuers will have a certain level of developer skills; for example, they could be researchers or machine learning (ML) model developers.

Data communication via APIs allows such developers to perform the entire process from issuing annotations to analyzing the results at a lower cost compared to that in the case of a file format. Therefore, it can reduce the burden on the issuer in the use case, where the annotation is performed several times.

3.3 Overall Flow

The overall flow of the system can be described as follows:

Step 1. Deploying the app and sharing the URL As FAST is a web application, it has to be deployed by the annotation issuer. Then, the URL of the application has to be shared with the annotator.

Step 2. Creating accounts The annotation issuer and the annotator must sign up for a Google account on the web application in order to create an account.

Step 3. Creating tasks and assignment The annotation issuer is then required to create a task using the annotation API. The data to be sent here includes not only the ones to be evaluated but also meta-information, such as the title and format of the task. After the task is created, the issuer allocates the task to the registered annotators in the application.

Step 4. Conducting annotations The annotator confirms that the assigned task has been added to the home screen and executes the annotation.

Step 5. Checking progress and data retrieval Annotation issuers can check the progress of each annotator on the application and receive completion notifications via Slack. After the annotation is completed, the issuer retrieves the data via the API and performs the aggregation process.

4 Experiment

4.1 Metrics

We define some metrics that should be considered when measuring the effectiveness of annotation tools and explain what numbers should be tracked for each metric.

Annotation Efficiency One of the most important metrics in annotation tools is annotation efficiency. Additional data could be collected using a high-efficiency tool within a short period. To track efficiency, we measured the annotation time for the application using a fixed number of annotation questions. In practice, annotators may leave during the annotation process; therefore, in our experiments, logs that took more than 60 seconds were considered dropped annotations and were excluded.

[5]https://analytics.google.com

Annotation Quality The annotated data should be of high quality. The difficulty of the task and the ease of use of the tool are considered to contribute to the quality. We evaluated the correctness rate of the annotation results and the inter-annotator agreement rate to examine the influence of the UI/UX of the tool on the performance.

Qualitative Usability In addition to the aforementioned two metrics, usability as perceived by the annotators is another key metric. To measure this, we requested each annotator to perform the following six annotation tasks and rank them in terms of usability. We also collected qualitative impressions of each task through a user survey in the form of free descriptions. We calculated the average rankings for each task and evaluated them based on the annotators' comments in the experimental results.

4.2 Experiment Setting

We conducted the following three comparative experiments of the evaluation metrics described in Section 4.1.

PC vs. Mobile As mobile devices are more portable and convenient to use than PC devices, people often use them in their spare time. Thus, we assume that mobile device applications are more customary and easier to use than that of PC devices. We conducted a comparison experiment with each device to verify this assumption.

FAST vs. Existing Tool We compare our proposed tool, FAST, with doccano, which is widely used in existing annotation tasks, as described in Section 2.

Card UI vs. Multi-label UI In the proposed tool, FAST, we compare the Multi-label UI, which is commonly used in evaluation annotation, with the Card UI adopted in this study.

Based on the aforementioned scheme, we conducted six annotation tasks through crowd-sourcing via Lancers, Inc.[6] for a total of about 40,000 annotations were worked by 18 annotators in five days. To avoid device mismatch during annotation, the app acquires the UserAgent and only accepts mobile annotations for mobile devices and PC annotations for PC devices. The annotation fee was set at \$0.045 per annotation, taking into account the pre-measured work speed.

In the experiment, we used the product review data crawled from the e-commerce site, which consisted of text with 50 or less Japanese characters and a five-point rating score. As mentioned in 3.1, FAST can be used for a variety of tasks, but in the current study, we simplified the problem for the sake of evaluation and experiment using a task in which whether the review was satisfactory or unsatisfactory has to be selected.

In this study, we removed the data with an intermediate evaluation score of 3 and assigned scores 1 and 2 to "dissatisfied" and scores 4 and 5 to "satisfied." In the actual annotation, the annotator reads the content of the review and selects whether the content is satisfactory or unsatisfactory.

We used a task with binary labels for simplicity, but the Card UI can be applied to tasks with more labels than binary labels depending on the design. Hu (Hu et al., 2020) reduced the multiclass problem to binary labels using pseudo-labels based on a classification model.

4.3 Experiment Flow

The experiment consisted of five phases: two annotation phases and a user survey phase before and after each annotation phase. Each phase can proceed to the next phase only when it is completed.

Phase 1. Tutorial and Pre-Survey Before starting the annotations, we provided each annotator with a tutorial on the entire process and how each tool needs to be used. A user survey questionnaire was also given to the annotators, to collect information on their attributes, their level of skill with PC and mobile devices, and the amount of time they spend out of the office per day. Based on the collected information, we assigned the tasks to the annotators.

Phase 2. General Annotation We requested all the annotators to perform all the annotations described in Section 4.2 on a small set of 50 data points. This was done to allow each annotator to know and experience all the annotation methods to facilitate a fair comparison.

Phase 3. Interim Survey The annotator was asked to sort the six annotation methods in the order of their perceived ease of use through the General Annotation of Phase 2. They were also asked to describe the reasons why the methods were good or bad.

Phase 4. Specific Annotation In the General Annotation of Phase 2, the annotators were familiarized with all the annotation methods. Each annotator was asked to perform a large number of 2,000 annotations using one method in this phase. Ac-

[6] https://www.lancers.jp

Table 1: Experiment results consist of Annotation Efficiency, Annotation Quality, and Qualitative Usability.

Tool	Device	UI	Annotation Efficiency		Annotation Quality		Qualitative Usability
			Total Time (m) (↓ better)	**Average Time (s) (↓ better)**	**Accuracy (↑ better)**	**α (↑ better)**	**Average Rankings (↓ better)**
doccano	PC		5.9	7.3	0.95	0.87	4.91
	Mobile		6.7	8.3	0.98	0.96	5.82
FAST	PC	Multi-label	4.8	5.4	0.97	0.93	2.91
		Card	**4.0**	**4.4**	0.97	0.94	2.12
	Mobile	Multi-label	4.9	5.2	0.97	0.95	3.15
		Card	4.6	4.7	0.97	0.96	**2.03**

cording to the interim user survey results in Phase 1, we assigned three annotators to each annotation method to be equally distributed in terms of attributes and skill level.

Phase 5. Post-Survey To check whether there was any change of opinion regarding a Specific Annotation, we asked the annotators to rank the ease of use of the six annotation methods again, as in the interim user survey of Phase 3. In addition, each annotator was asked to comment on what was good or bad about the Specific Annotation he or she was in charge of.

5 Results and Discussion

The experiment results are presented in Table 1. Annotation Efficiency is the total time required to complete all the tasks (Total Time) and average time per task (Average Time). Annotation Quality that refers to the accuracy and ratings on the inter-annotator agreement is derived from Krippendorff's α. Qualitative Usability is calculated from the average rankings of the Post-Survey ratings.

Notably, we excluded two annotators while calculating the result because they had a markedly low accuracy compared to others as shown in Figure 3. In addition, the annotation speeds varied significantly among the annotators in the experiment. For the Specific Annotation, the annotators were divided into groups. To reduce user bias between the groups, we aggregated the annotation efficiencies from the General Annotation results.

PC vs. Mobile Table 1 shows that the performance of PC and mobile devices is almost the same in terms of the annotation speed and quality. This suggests that the same level of annotation can be performed on a mobile device as on a PC. On the other hand, we could not confirm the superiority of mobile devices in terms of efficiency because the experiment was conducted for only five days. For a more appropriate verification, a comparison based on the measurement of user's working speed and fatigue over a longer period and with regular annotations is necessary. In terms of usability, the mobile device with the Card UI received the most first-place votes in both the interim and post-user surveys, and its average ranking was 0.23 higher than that of the PC with the Card UI. The superiority of the mobile devices in terms of usability was therefore confirmed. Additionally, three out of nine annotators assigned to mobile devices in the Specific Annotation performed their annotations during their spare time, such as in trains, cars, and cafes, confirming the superiority of mobile devices that allow work to be performed in any location.

FAST vs. Existing tool Table 1 shows that the average annotation time for the FAST Card UI is 4.7 seconds on mobile devices, compared to 8.3 seconds for existing tools; therefore, approximately 43% of the annotation time can be reduced using FAST. One of the reasons for this is the number of actions required to select and decide. Doccano requires at least three actions for each annotation, that is, display of the options, selection, and decision, but the Card UI of FAST requires only one action for selection and decision. It is thought that this difference affects the speed and usability of the system. Another reason is whether the UI is designed for mobile devices or not. In the user survey, we confirmed the following opinions about the mobile devices of the existing tools: "I could not operate it with one hand" and "I felt stressed because I had to scroll because the screen size did not fit the device." As for the annotation quality, the agreement rate of the existing tool on PC was 0.87, which was lower than the other patterns. In the annotator's opinion, "errors occurred" and "sometimes the tool does not respond to button presses" were confirmed, which is considered to be due to a problem in the application.

Card UI vs. Multi-label UI Table 1 shows that

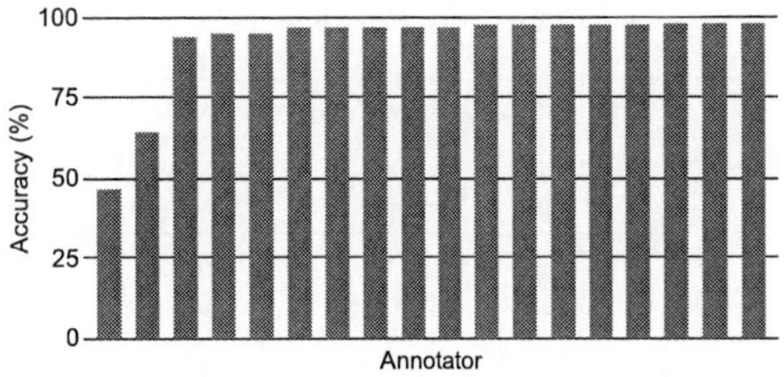

Figure 3: Sorted annotators' accuracy in the Phase 4 Specific Annotation.

the Card UI is 18% faster on mobile devices and 25% faster on PCs than the Multi-label UI. The Card UI is also superior in terms of usability.

For the same reason as in the comparison with the existing tools, the difference in the number of actions is considered to have affected the speed and ease of use.

6 Conclusion

In this study, we proposed and developed FAST, an annotation tool for application tasks that emphasize the impact of UI/UX on mobile devices, which is a crucial topic, although not investigated thus far.

FAST is a web application designed for use on any device, including mobiles and PCs. This web application is highly customizable in that the issuers can create views that are optimized for their tasks utilizing two types of UI: Card UI and Multi-label UI. We compared the devices and UIs, as well as an existing tool with FAST, in an experiment involving a sentiment analysis task; we also evaluated their efficiency, quality, and usability.

The results showed that the mobile operation of FAST provides annotators with a more user-friendly experience while maintaining the efficiency and quality of the PC. Furthermore, in comparison with the existing tools, FAST was able to reduce the annotation time by 43% and an improvement in work efficiency was also confirmed.

In the future, we plan to conduct quantitative evaluations using additional detailed indicators such as the trajectory of user operations, and task load metrics measured using NASA TLX. Moreover, we aim to increase the number of supported task types, enhance the management functions, and support on-premise environments to strengthen its usefulness as a general-purpose annotation tool.

References

Wei-Te Chen and Will Styler. 2013. Anafora: A web-based general purpose annotation tool. In *Proceedings of the 2013 NAACL HLT Demonstration Session*, pages 14–19, Atlanta, Georgia. Association for Computational Linguistics.

Economic Research Office. 2020. Information and Communications in Japan 2020. *White Paper 2020 by The Ministry of Internal Affairs and Communications of Japan.*

Ralf Herbrich, Tom Minka, and Thore Graepel. 2007. TrueSkill™ : A Bayesian Skill Rating System. In *Advances in Neural Information Processing Systems 19*, pages 569–576. MIT Press.

Hengtong Hu, Lingxi Xie, Zewei Du, Richang Hong, and Qi Tian. 2020. One-bit supervision for image classification. In *Advances in Neural Information Processing Systems 33: Annual Conference on Neural Information Processing Systems 2020, NeurIPS 2020, December 6-12, 2020, virtual.*

Jan-Christoph Klie, Michael Bugert, Beto Boullosa, Richard Eckart de Castilho, and Iryna Gurevych. 2018. The INCEpTION platform: Machine-assisted and knowledge-oriented interactive annotation. In *Proceedings of the 27th International Conference on Computational Linguistics: System Demonstrations*, pages 5–9, Santa Fe, New Mexico. Association for Computational Linguistics.

Jonathan K. Kummerfeld. 2019. SLATE: A super-lightweight annotation tool for experts. In *Proceedings of the 57th Annual Meeting of the Association for Computational Linguistics: System Demonstrations*, pages 7–12, Florence, Italy. Association for Computational Linguistics.

Stephen Mayhew and Dan Roth. 2018. TALEN: Tool for annotation of low-resource ENtities. In *Proceedings of ACL 2018, System Demonstrations*, pages 80–86, Melbourne, Australia. Association for Computational Linguistics.

Hiroki Nakayama, Takahiro Kubo, Junya Kamura, Yasufumi Taniguchi, and Xu Liang. 2018. doccano: Text Annotation Tool for Human.

Kyeongmin Rim. 2016. MAE2: Portable Annotation Tool for General Natural Language Use. In *Proc 12th Joint ACL-ISO Workshop on Interoperable Semantic Annotation*, pages 75–80.

Pontus Stenetorp, Sampo Pyysalo, Goran Topić, Tomoko Ohta, Sophia Ananiadou, and Jun'ichi Tsujii. 2012. brat: a web-based tool for NLP-assisted text annotation. In *Proceedings of the Demonstrations at the 13th Conference of the European Chapter of the Association for Computational Linguistics*, pages 102–107, Avignon, France. Association for Computational Linguistics.

Michael Stewart, Wei Liu, and Rachel Cardell-Oliver. 2019. Redcoat: A collaborative annotation tool for hierarchical entity typing. In *Proceedings of the 2019 Conference on Empirical Methods in Natural Language Processing and the 9th International Joint Conference on Natural Language Processing (EMNLP-IJCNLP): System Demonstrations*, pages 193–198, Hong Kong, China. Association for Computational Linguistics.

Chris van der Lee, Albert Gatt, Emiel van Miltenburg, Sander Wubben, and Emiel Krahmer. 2019. Best practices for the human evaluation of automatically generated text. In *Proceedings of the 12th International Conference on Natural Language Generation*, pages 355–368, Tokyo, Japan. Association for Computational Linguistics.

A System Details

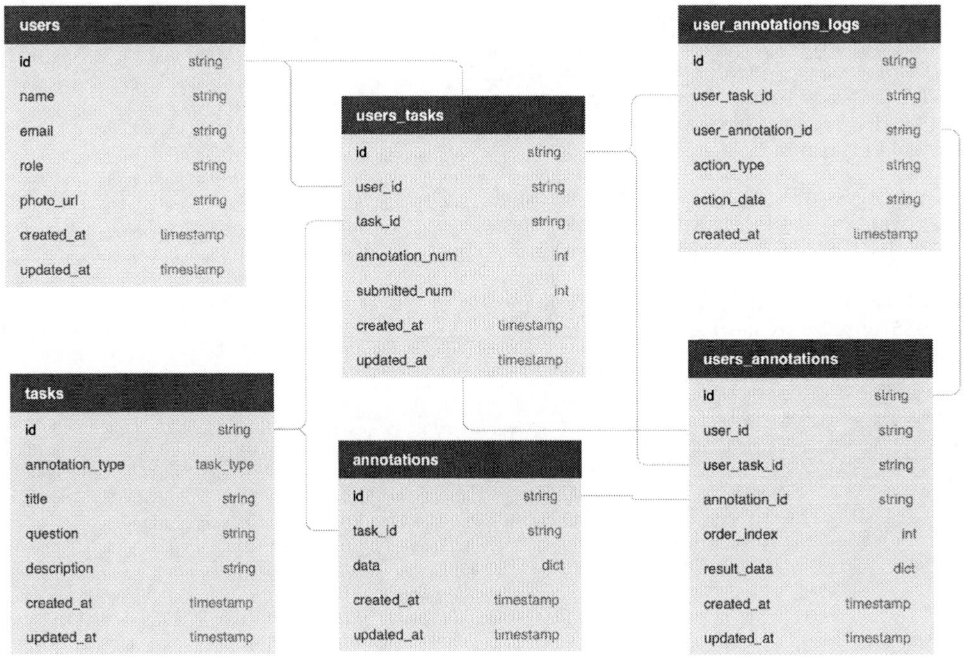

Figure 4: DB Diagram

Listing 1: Sample of annotated data to be fetched via API


```
{
  "task": {
    "id": "card-demo-202000601",
    "annotation_type": "card",
    "title": "Card Demo",
    "question": "This is card demo",
    "description": "This is a card demo, so feel free to annotate it as you wish.",
    "created_at": "2021-06-01T07:39:38.916473+00:00",
    "updated_at": "2021-06-01T07:39:38.916490+00:00"
  },
  "annotations": [
    {
      "id": "0V7KGVUs3cijjr1HG6J6",
      "name": "Shunyo Kawamoto",
      "email": "kawamoto_shunyo@cyberagent.co.jp",
      "data": {
        "text": "This is a annotation.",
        "show_ambiguous_button": true,
        "hidden_data": {
          "desc": "Data for aggregation. It can be a dictionary or a string."
        },
        "yes_button_label": null,
        "question_overwrite": null,
        "no_button_label": null,
        "baseline_text": null
      },
      "result_data": {
        "result": "No",
      },
      "order_index": 44,
      "user_id": "enTz0ydWPXfYyXF9v0huu38a5DA2",
      "user_task_id": "TG9Evly0UQ43hBYlAM8b",
      "annotation_id": "tVl0rySSTMV2m0JEIr1s",
      "created_at": "2021-06-01T08:00:54.099000+00:00",
      "updated_at": "2021-06-01T08:00:54.099000+00:00"
    },
    ...
  ]
}
```

B Survey Details

Table 2: Questions in the Pre-Survey

Question	Format	Options
Email address	Free text	
Gender	Selection	Male, Female, Other
Age	Selection	10s, 20s, ..., Over 70s
Current address (prefecture)	Free text	
Occupation	Free text	
Number of days per week that you go out for more than one hour	Selection	1day, 2day, ..., 7day
Hours away from home per day	Selection	Almost none, 1hour, 2hour, ..., Over 10hour
Model name of mobile device	Free text	
Time spent on the PC per day	Selection	Almost none, 1hour, 2hour, ..., Over 10hour
Time spent on mobile devices per day	Selection	Almost none, 1hour, 2hour, ..., Over 10hour
PC, Mobile proficiency	5-point Likert scale	

Table 3: Questions in the Interim Survey

Question	Format	Options
Email address	Free text	
Ranking of ease of use for each pattern	Selection	1st, 2nd, ..., 6th
Reasons for the patterns that were easiest to use	Free text	
Reasons for the most difficult patterns to use	Free text	
Other problems during annotation, etc.	Free text	

Table 4: Questions in the Post-Survey

Question	Format	Options
Email address	Free text	
Ranking of ease of use for each pattern	Selection	1st, 2nd, ..., 6th
Good points about the tool you were responsible for in Specific Annotation	Free text	
Bad points about the tool you were responsible for in Specific Annotation	Free text	
(Mobile annotators only) The location where you annotated	Free text	

deepQuest-py: Large and Distilled Models for Quality Estimation

Fernando Alva-Manchego,[1] Abiola Obamuyide,[1] Amit Gajbhiye,[1] Frédéric Blain,[1,2] Marina Fomicheva,[1] Lucia Specia[1,3]

[1]University of Sheffield, [2]University of Wolverhampton, [3]Imperial College London

{f.alva,a.obamuyide,a.gajbhiye,m.fomicheva}@sheffield.ac.uk
f.blain@wlv.ac.uk, l.specia@imperial.ac.uk

Abstract

We introduce deepQuest-py, a framework for training and evaluation of large and light-weight models for Quality Estimation (QE). deepQuest-py provides access to (1) state-of-the-art models based on pre-trained Transformers for sentence-level and word-level QE; (2) light-weight and efficient sentence-level models implemented via knowledge distillation; and (3) a web interface for testing models and visualising their predictions. deepQuest-py is available at https://github.com/sheffieldnlp/deepQuest-py under a CC BY-NC-SA licence.

1 Introduction

Quality Estimation (QE) for Machine Translation (MT) aims to predict how good automatic translations are without comparing them to gold-standard references (Specia et al., 2009). This is useful in real-world scenarios (e.g. computer-aided translation or online translation of social media content), where users would benefit from knowing how confident they should be of the generated translations. QE has received increased attention in the MT community, with Shared Tasks being organised yearly since 2012 as part of WMT, the main conference in MT research (Callison-Burch et al., 2012; Bojar et al., 2013, 2014, 2015, 2016, 2017; Specia et al., 2018a; Fonseca et al., 2019; Specia et al., 2020).

Given an original-translation sentence pair, QE scores can be computed in different granularities (Specia et al., 2018b). At the **word-level**, each word in the original and/or translation sentence receives a tag indicating whether it was correctly translated or not (e.g. OK or BAD). Gaps in the translation could also receive labels to indicate when a word is missing. At the **sentence-level**, a single continuous score is predicted for each original-translation pair. For example, 0-100 for direct assessments (DA, Graham et al., 2017), or 0-1 for human-targeted translation error rate (HTER, Snover et al., 2006).

Few open-source software is available for implementing QE models. QuEst (Specia et al., 2013) and QuEst++ (Specia et al., 2015) were the first ones, and included methods that relied on extracting linguistically-motivated features to train traditional machine learning models (e.g. support vector machines). With the advent of neural-based approaches, deepQuest (Ive et al., 2018) provided a TensorFlow-based framework for RNN-based sentence-level and document-level QE models, inspired by the Predictor-Estimator approach (Kim et al., 2017). OpenKiwi (Kepler et al., 2019) implements a common API for experimenting with several feature-based and neural-based QE models. More recently, TransQuest (Ranasinghe et al., 2020b) released state-of-the-art models for sentence-level QE based on pre-trained Transformer architectures.

As shown in the latest WMT20 QE Shared Task (Specia et al., 2020), systems are increasingly relying on large pre-trained models to achieve impressive results in the different proposed tasks. However, their considerable size could prevent their application in scenarios where fast inference is required and small disk space is available. To overcome this limitation, Gajbhiye et al. (2021) propose to use Knowledge Distillation (KD, Hinton et al., 2015) to transfer knowledge from a large top-performing *teacher* model into a smaller (in terms of memory print, computational power and prediction latency) yet well-performing *student* model. The authors applied this framework to QE, and effectively trained light-weight QE models with similar performance to SoTA architectures trained on distilled yet large pre-trained representations.

In this paper, we introduce deepQuest-py, a new version of deepQuest that covers both large and light-weight neural QE models, with a particular emphasis on knowledge distillation. The main fea-

Proceedings of the 2021 Conference on Empirical Methods in Natural Language Processing: System Demonstrations, pages 382–389
November 7–11, 2021. ©2021 Association for Computational Linguistics

tures of deepQuest-py are:

- Implementation of state-of-the-art models for sentence-level (Ranasinghe et al., 2020a) and word-level (Lee, 2020) QE;
- The first implementation of light-weight sentence-level QE models using knowledge distillation (Gajbhiye et al., 2021);
- Easy-to-use command-line interface and API to train and test QE models in custom datasets, as well as those from several WMT QE Shared Tasks thanks to its integration with HuggingFace Datasets (Lhoest et al., 2021); and
- An online tool to try out trained models, evaluate them and visualise their predictions.

Different from existing open-source toolkits in the area, our aim is to provide access to neural QE models for both researchers (via a command-line interface and python library) and end-users (via a web-based tool). Additionally, this is the only tool to provide implementation of knowledge distillation for QE. In the following sections, we detail the main functionalities offered by deepQuest-py: implementation of state-of-the-art sentence-level and word-level models (Sec. 2); implementation of light-weight sentence-level models through knowledge distillation (Sec. 3); and evaluation and visualisation of models' predictions via a web interface (Sec. 4). We expect that deepQuest-py facilitates the implementation of QE models, allows useful analysis of their capabilities, and promotes their adoption by end-users.

2 Large State-of-the-Art Models

In the WMT20 QE Shared Task (Specia et al., 2020), the top performing models were based on fine-tuning pre-trained Transformers (Vaswani et al., 2017), such as BERT (Devlin et al., 2019) or XLM-R (Conneau et al., 2020). deepQuest-py provides access to this type of approaches by building on the HuggingFace Transformers (Wolf et al., 2020)[1] library. We provide implementations for sentence-level and word-level QE.

Sentence-Level. deepQuest-py implements the MonoTransQuest architecture from TransQuest (Ranasinghe et al., 2020a,b), the overall winner in Task 1 (sentence-level direct assessment) of the WMT20 QE Shared Task. In this approach, the original sentence and its translation are concatenated using the [SEP] token, and passed through XLM-R to obtain a joint representation via the [CLS] token. This serves as input to a softmax layer that is used to predict translation quality. In order to boost performance, the authors incorporate two strategies: (1) to use an ensemble of two models: one that fine-tunes XLM-R-base and one that fine-tunes XLM-R-large; and (2) to augment the training data of the QE models with (subsets of) the training data of the NMT models, considering their quality scores as perfect. These extensions are not currently available in deepQuest-py, but the API is flexible-enough to incorporate them in the future.

Word-Level. deepQuest-py implements the model proposed by BeringLab (Lee, 2020), the winner of Task 2 Word-level QE for En-De in the WMT20 QE Shared Task. Similar to the sentence-level models described before, the original sentence and its translation are fed to XLM-R to get contextualised word embeddings. In this approach, both token-level (hidden states) and instance-level ([CLS] token) representations are used as input to dedicated linear layers that predict word-level and sentence-level quality estimates, respectively. The model is trained jointly in these two tasks. In order to boost performance, this approach creates artificial data in a similar fashion to Negri et al. (2018). Given a dataset of parallel source-target sentences, an NMT model is trained using 90% of the data. Then, the NMT model translates source sentences in the remaining 10% of the data. After that, HTER word labels are generated for this 10% of the data, leveraging their manual references as if they were post-edits of the translations generated by the NMT model.deepQuest-py includes scripts and examples for executing this training pipeline, provided that the user has access to automatic translations. For obtaining word-level tags, in particular, deepQuest-py leverages publicly-available scripts.[2]

3 Light-Weight Distilled Models

The most distinctive contribution in deepQuest-py is the **ability to train light-weight and efficient QE models through knowledge distillation**. We

[1]https://github.com/huggingface/transformers

[2]https://github.com/deep-spin/qe-corpus-builder

Name	Training data	Et-En	Ro-En	Si-En	Ne-En	En-Zh
TQ$_{\text{TEACHER}}$	MLQE-gold	0.77	0.88	0.60	0.75	0.44
BiRNN$_{\text{STUDENT}}$	MLQE-dist	0.45	0.62	0.44	0.46	**0.18**
BiRNN$_{\text{STUDENT+AUG}}$	Wiki-dist	**0.50**	**0.69**	**0.45**	**0.54**	0.17
BiRNN	MLQE-gold	0.37	0.60	0.40	0.42	0.15
Predictor-Estimator	MLQE-gold	0.48	0.69	0.37	0.39	0.19
TQ$_{\text{DistilBERT}}$	MLQE-gold	0.62	0.78	0.51	0.61	0.36

Table 1: Pearson correlation with human judgments on the MLQE test set. MLQE-gold: training partition of MLQE dataset; MLQE-dist: distilled version of the MLQE training set with teacher predictions used as labels; Wiki-dist: the Wikipedia dataset produced by data augmentation. Boldface results indicate our best student models.

implement the approach proposed by Gajbhiye et al. (2021) to directly distil **sentence-level** QE models, where the student architecture can be completely different from that of the teacher. Namely, they distill large and powerful QE models based on XLM-R into small bidirectional RNN-based models.

3.1 BiRNN-based Architecture

deepQuest-py implements sentence-level models following the architecture proposed by Ive et al. (2018). In this approach, the original sentence and its translation are encoded independently using dedicated BiRNNs. To obtain predictions, these two representations are concatenated as the weighted sum of their word vectors, generated by an attention mechanism. Then, this joint representation is passed through a dense layer with sigmoid activation to generate the quality estimates. deepQuest-py uses AllenNLP (Gardner et al., 2018)[3] as its backbone for the BiRNN model.

3.2 Knowledge Distillation

For cases where large size SotA QE models are not deployable, Gajbhiye et al. (2021) propose to use a KD approach to train more efficient and well-performing models for sentence-level QE. The approach (illustrated in Figure 1) consists of three steps described below.

Teacher-Student Training. A large SotA QE model generates predictions on a gold training dataset, and these are directly used to train a light-weight model. Gajbhiye et al. (2021) employs pre-trained Transformer models (such as those from Sec. 2) as teachers, and BiRNN models (such as those from Sec. 3.1) as students. Table 2 shows the number of parameters, memory and disk space requirements, as well as inference speed for the teacher model (TQ$_{\text{XLM-R-Large}}$),

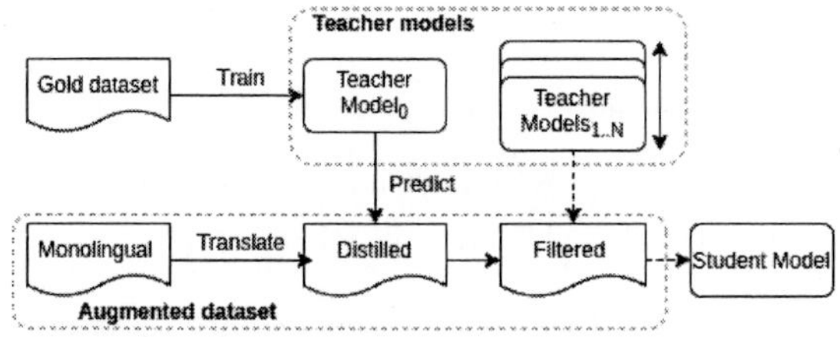

Figure 1: Knowledge distillation with data augmentation and noise filtering based on teacher uncertainty (Gajbhiye et al., 2021).

Name	#params	Inference		Disk
		Speed (secs.)	RAM (MiB)	(M)
TQ$_{\text{XLM-R-Large}}$	561M	0.82	9,263.5	2140
TQ$_{\text{DistilBERT}}$	135M	1.09	1,979.2	517
BiRNN	18M	0.39	155.6	132

Table 2: Efficiency. Inference speed and RAM for prediction are for 1 sentence on CPU (Intel Xeon Silver 4114 CPU @ 2.20GHz).

student model (BiRNN) and a MonoTransQuest model built on DistilBERT (TQ$_{\text{DistilBERT}}$), using data in the MLQE Et-En dataset.

Data Augmentation. Teacher predictions on the gold training dataset may prove insufficient to train the student. Therefore, Gajbhiye et al. (2021) collect additional monolingual data and: (1) translate it with the same MT models used for the gold data, and (2) generate QE scores with the teacher model.

Noise Filtering. Teacher predictions can be noisy and degrade student performance. To overcome this, Gajbhiye et al. (2021) propose a filtering approach based on uncertainty quantification over predictions from an ensemble of teacher models. Concretely, they propose to: (1) train several teacher models on the same dataset with different random initialisations; (2) generate several teacher

[3]https://allennlp.org/

Figure 2: Submission form for the web tool.

predictions for each instance in the student training data; and (3) filter out instances for which the predictions show high variance (i.e. the variance is more than one standard deviation away from its mean).

On experiments performed using the MLQE dataset (Fomicheva et al., 2020), Gajbhiye et al. (2021) show that their approach results in QE models that are 4x smaller in disk space with 8x fewer parameters, and 3x faster in inference speed than large SotA Transformer-based models. In particular, as shown in Table 1, distilled models with augmented data achieved comparable performances to training a large model on DistilBERT ($TQ_{DistilBERT}$), but with a lighter BiRNN-based architecture. In addition, this approach allows for substantial improvements over shallow models trained on gold data (BiRNN and Predictor-Estimator) for all of the language pairs. For further details, we refer the reader to (Gajbhiye et al., 2021).

deepQuest-py provides command-line functionalities for all steps in the KD pipeline.

4 Web Tool for Analysis and Visualisation

deepQuest-py offers a demo web-service with visualization for sentence-level and word-level QE models. The user fills in a simple submission form (Figure 2) indicating: the languages of the original sentences and their translations, the sentences to analyse (either typing them directly or through a .tsv file), the type of model to use for prediction (e.g. Transformer or BiRNN), and the level of granularity for the scores (sentence-level or word-level). After pressing the *score* button, the user is presented with varied results for their analysis:

Scores per Instance. For sentence-level predictions, each submitted original-translation pair is shown alongside its estimated quality score (Figure 3). The value for this score and its interpretation depends on the data that the QE model was trained on. For example, models trained on HTER scores will output values between 0 and 1, with lower scores indicating better quality. On the other hand, models trained on normalised DA scores will output negative and positive values – the higher the better.[4] Two additional metrics are included: the proportion of repeated n-grams in the source/target (named source/target n-grams), and the proportion of words in the target sentence that are copies of words in the source (i.e. untranslated words). The user can navigate through the analysed sentences

[4]While raw DA scores have a 0-100 value range, their normalised values will depend on the actual minimum and maximum scores in the training data.

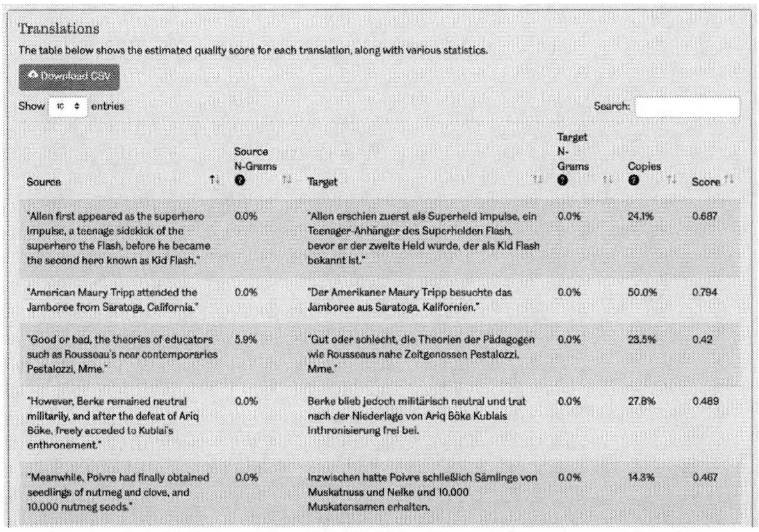

Translations

The table below shows the estimated quality score for each translation, along with various statistics.

Download CSV

Show 10 entries Search:

Source	Source N-Grams	Target	Target N-Grams	Copies	Score
"Allen first appeared as the superhero Impulse, a teenage sidekick of the superhero the Flash, before he became the second hero known as Kid Flash."	0.0%	"Allen erschien zuerst als Superheld Impulse, ein Teenager-Anhänger des Superhelden Flash, bevor er der zweite Held wurde, der als Kid Flash bekannt ist."	0.0%	24.1%	0.687
"American Maury Tripp attended the Jamboree from Saratoga, California."	0.0%	"Der Amerikaner Maury Tripp besuchte das Jamboree aus Saratoga, Kalifornien."	0.0%	50.0%	0.794
"Good or bad, the theories of educators such as Rousseau's near contemporaries Pestalozzi, Mme."	5.9%	"Gut oder schlecht, die Theorien der Pädagogen wie Rousseaus nahe Zeitgenossen Pestalozzi, Mme."	0.0%	23.5%	0.42
"However, Berke remained neutral militarily, and after the defeat of Ariq Böke, freely acceded to Kublai's enthronement."	0.0%	Berke blieb jedoch militärisch neutral und trat nach der Niederlage von Ariq Böke Kublais Inthronisierung frei bei.	0.0%	27.8%	0.489
"Meanwhile, Poivre had finally obtained seedlings of nutmeg and clove, and 10,000 nutmeg seeds."	0.0%	Inzwischen hatte Poivre schließlich Sämlinge von Muskatnuss und Nelke und 10.000 Muskatensamen erhalten.	0.0%	14.3%	0.467

Figure 3: Scores per instance.

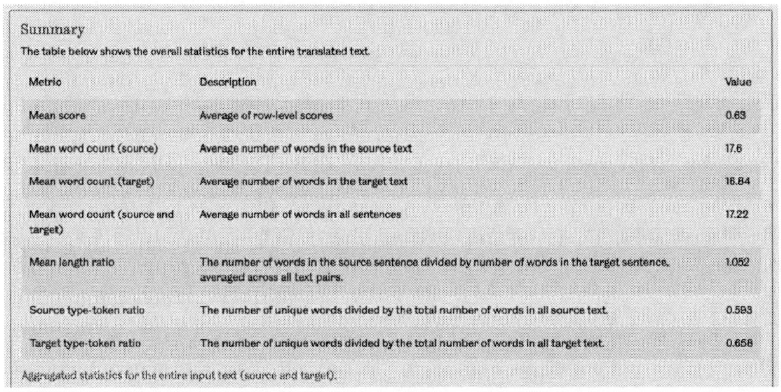

Summary

The table below shows the overall statistics for the entire translated text.

Metric	Description	Value
Mean score	Average of row-level scores	0.63
Mean word count (source)	Average number of words in the source text	17.6
Mean word count (target)	Average number of words in the target text	16.84
Mean word count (source and target)	Average number of words in all sentences	17.22
Mean length ratio	The number of words in the source sentence divided by number of words in the target sentence, averaged across all text pairs.	1.052
Source type-token ratio	The number of unique words divided by the total number of words in all source text.	0.593
Target type-token ratio	The number of unique words divided by the total number of words in all target text.	0.658

Aggregated statistics for the entire input text (source and target).

Figure 4: Statistics summarising the scores for all submitted sentences.

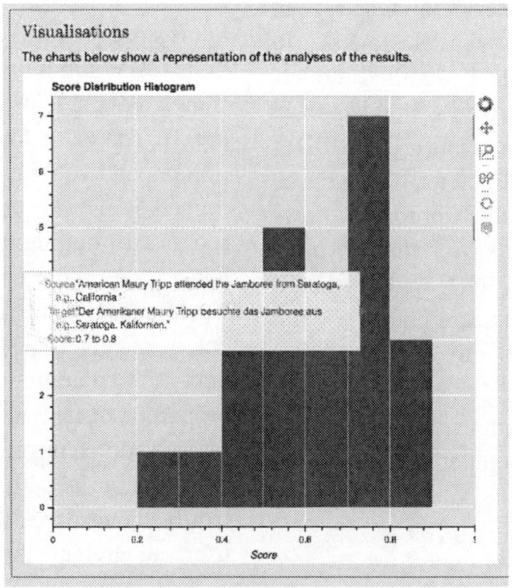

Figure 5: Histogram with the distribution of predicted scores in the dataset.

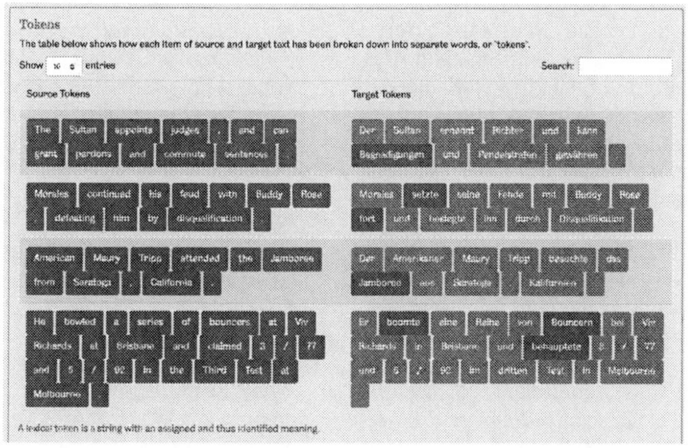

Figure 6: Visualisation of tokens in original (source) and translation (target) sentences. For the translation side, tokens in green are predicted to have an 'OK' label, while tokens in grey, a 'BAD' label. In this example, the model did not produce word-level predictions for the original sentences.

using the form shown (including searching for instances with specific words), or download all the information to a .csv file.

Scores Summary. A table summarises the scores for all the submitted sentences providing some simple statistics. See Figure 4 for the names and descriptions of the metrics considered.

Scores Distribution. The web tool also shows a histogram with the distribution of the sentence-level scores over all submitted instances (Figure 5). The user can hover over the bars in the plot to see examples of original-translation pairs whose scores correspond to the selected range.

Token Annotations. The web tool shows the tokenisation of each original-translation pair (Figure 6). For word-level predictions, in particular, the predicted quality label for each token is shown in different colours: green for 'OK' and grey for 'BAD'. The user can also search within the instances looking for sentences with specific words.

The demo web tool includes Transformer-based sentence-level models for all language pairs in the MLQE dataset: English-German, English-Chinese, Romanian-English, Estonian-English, Nepalese-English, Sinhala-English, and Russian-English. There is also the option to use a multilingual model. For Transformer-based word-level predictions, only an English-German model is available. BiRNN-based (distilled) models for sentence-level QE are available for a subset of languages. We note that our purpose with this paper is not to provide prediction models for multiple languages, but rather to demonstrate the functionalities of the back- and front-end in deepQuest-py.

The demo showcasing all the functionalities offered by deepQuest-py is available at `https://github.com/sheffieldnlp/deepQuest-py/tree/main/demo`.

5 Conclusions

We have presented deepQuest-py, a new framework for implementation and evaluation of QE models. On top of large state-of-art models based on pre-trained Transformer architectures, deepQuest-py targets the development of light-weight and efficient models around the teacher-student framework for knowledge distillation. In addition, deepQuest-py encourages end-user adoption of QE technologies by providing a web application to obtain quality predictions and analyse model performance.

Acknowledgements

This work was supported by funding from the Bergamot project (EU H2020 Grant No. 825303).

References

Ondřej Bojar, Christian Buck, Chris Callison-Burch, Christian Federmann, Barry Haddow, Philipp Koehn, Christof Monz, Matt Post, Radu Soricut, and Lucia Specia. 2013. Findings of the 2013 Workshop on Statistical Machine Translation. In *Proceedings of the Eighth Workshop on Statistical Machine Translation*, pages 1–44, Sofia, Bulgaria. Association for Computational Linguistics.

Ondřej Bojar, Christian Buck, Christian Federmann, Barry Haddow, Philipp Koehn, Johannes Leveling,

Christof Monz, Pavel Pecina, Matt Post, Herve Saint-Amand, Radu Soricut, Lucia Specia, and Aleš Tamchyna. 2014. Findings of the 2014 workshop on statistical machine translation. In *Proceedings of the Ninth Workshop on Statistical Machine Translation*, pages 12–58, Baltimore, Maryland, USA. Association for Computational Linguistics.

Ondřej Bojar, Rajen Chatterjee, Christian Federmann, Yvette Graham, Barry Haddow, Shujian Huang, Matthias Huck, Philipp Koehn, Qun Liu, Varvara Logacheva, Christof Monz, Matteo Negri, Matt Post, Raphael Rubino, Lucia Specia, and Marco Turchi. 2017. Findings of the 2017 conference on machine translation (WMT17). In *Proceedings of the Second Conference on Machine Translation*, pages 169–214, Copenhagen, Denmark. Association for Computational Linguistics.

Ondřej Bojar, Rajen Chatterjee, Christian Federmann, Yvette Graham, Barry Haddow, Matthias Huck, Antonio Jimeno Yepes, Philipp Koehn, Varvara Logacheva, Christof Monz, Matteo Negri, Aurélie Névéol, Mariana Neves, Martin Popel, Matt Post, Raphael Rubino, Carolina Scarton, Lucia Specia, Marco Turchi, Karin Verspoor, and Marcos Zampieri. 2016. Findings of the 2016 conference on machine translation. In *Proceedings of the First Conference on Machine Translation: Volume 2, Shared Task Papers*, pages 131–198, Berlin, Germany. Association for Computational Linguistics.

Ondřej Bojar, Rajen Chatterjee, Christian Federmann, Barry Haddow, Matthias Huck, Chris Hokamp, Philipp Koehn, Varvara Logacheva, Christof Monz, Matteo Negri, Matt Post, Carolina Scarton, Lucia Specia, and Marco Turchi. 2015. Findings of the 2015 workshop on statistical machine translation. In *Proceedings of the Tenth Workshop on Statistical Machine Translation*, pages 1–46, Lisbon, Portugal. Association for Computational Linguistics.

Chris Callison-Burch, Philipp Koehn, Christof Monz, Matt Post, Radu Soricut, and Lucia Specia. 2012. Findings of the 2012 workshop on statistical machine translation. In *Proceedings of the Seventh Workshop on Statistical Machine Translation*, pages 10–51, Montréal, Canada. Association for Computational Linguistics.

Alexis Conneau, Kartikay Khandelwal, Naman Goyal, Vishrav Chaudhary, Guillaume Wenzek, Francisco Guzmán, Edouard Grave, Myle Ott, Luke Zettlemoyer, and Veselin Stoyanov. 2020. Unsupervised cross-lingual representation learning at scale. In *Proceedings of the 58th Annual Meeting of the Association for Computational Linguistics*, pages 8440–8451, Online. Association for Computational Linguistics.

Jacob Devlin, Ming-Wei Chang, Kenton Lee, and Kristina Toutanova. 2019. BERT: Pre-training of deep bidirectional transformers for language understanding. In *Proceedings of the 2019 Conference of the North American Chapter of the Association for Computational Linguistics: Human Language Technologies, Volume 1 (Long and Short Papers)*, pages 4171–4186, Minneapolis, Minnesota. Association for Computational Linguistics.

Marina Fomicheva, Shuo Sun, Lisa Yankovskaya, Frédéric Blain, Francisco Guzmán, Mark Fishel, Nikolaos Aletras, Vishrav Chaudhary, and Lucia Specia. 2020. Unsupervised quality estimation for neural machine translation. *Transactions of the Association for Computational Linguistics*, 8:539–555.

Erick Fonseca, Lisa Yankovskaya, André F. T. Martins, Mark Fishel, and Christian Federmann. 2019. Findings of the WMT 2019 shared tasks on quality estimation. In *Proceedings of the Fourth Conference on Machine Translation (Volume 3: Shared Task Papers, Day 2)*, pages 1–10, Florence, Italy. Association for Computational Linguistics.

Amit Gajbhiye, Marina Fomicheva, Fernando Alva-Manchego, Frédéric Blain, Abiola Obamuyide, Nikolaos Aletras, and Lucia Specia. 2021. Knowledge distillation for quality estimation. In *Findings of the Association for Computational Linguistics: ACL 2021*. Association for Computational Linguistics.

Matt Gardner, Joel Grus, Mark Neumann, Oyvind Tafjord, Pradeep Dasigi, Nelson F. Liu, Matthew Peters, Michael Schmitz, and Luke Zettlemoyer. 2018. AllenNLP: A deep semantic natural language processing platform. In *Proceedings of Workshop for NLP Open Source Software (NLP-OSS)*, pages 1–6, Melbourne, Australia. Association for Computational Linguistics.

Yvette Graham, Timothy Baldwin, Alistair Moffat, and Justin Zobel. 2017. Can machine translation systems be evaluated by the crowd alone. *Natural Language Engineering*, 23(1):3–30.

Geoffrey Hinton, Oriol Vinyals, and Jeffrey Dean. 2015. Distilling the knowledge in a neural network. In *NIPS Deep Learning and Representation Learning Workshop*.

Julia Ive, Frédéric Blain, and Lucia Specia. 2018. deepQuest: A framework for neural-based quality estimation. In *Proceedings of the 27th International Conference on Computational Linguistics*, pages 3146–3157, Santa Fe, New Mexico, USA. Association for Computational Linguistics.

Fabio Kepler, Jonay Trénous, Marcos Treviso, Miguel Vera, and André F. T. Martins. 2019. OpenKiwi: An open source framework for quality estimation. In *Proceedings of the 57th Annual Meeting of the Association for Computational Linguistics: System Demonstrations*, pages 117–122, Florence, Italy. Association for Computational Linguistics.

Hyun Kim, Jong-Hyeok Lee, and Seung-Hoon Na. 2017. Predictor-estimator using multilevel task learning with stack propagation for neural quality estimation. In *Proceedings of the Second Conference on Machine Translation*, pages 562–568, Copenhagen, Denmark. Association for Computational Linguistics.

Dongjun Lee. 2020. Two-phase cross-lingual language model fine-tuning for machine translation quality estimation. In *Proceedings of the Fifth Conference on Machine Translation*, pages 1024–1028, Online. Association for Computational Linguistics.

Quentin Lhoest, Albert Villanova del Moral, Patrick von Platen, Thomas Wolf, Yacine Jernite, Abhishek Thakur, Lewis Tunstall, Suraj Patil, Mariama Drame, Julien Chaumond, Julien Plu, Joe Davison, Simon Brandeis, Teven Le Scao, Victor Sanh, Kevin Canwen Xu, Nicolas Patry, Angelina McMillan-Major, Philipp Schmid, Sylvain Gugger, Steven Liu, Sylvain Lesage, Lysandre Debut, Théo Matussière, Clément Delangue, and Stas Bekman. 2021. huggingface/datasets: 1.11.0.

Matteo Negri, Marco Turchi, Rajen Chatterjee, and Nicola Bertoldi. 2018. ESCAPE: a large-scale synthetic corpus for automatic post-editing. In *Proceedings of the Eleventh International Conference on Language Resources and Evaluation (LREC 2018)*, Miyazaki, Japan. European Language Resources Association (ELRA).

Tharindu Ranasinghe, Constantin Orasan, and Ruslan Mitkov. 2020a. TransQuest at WMT2020: Sentence-level direct assessment. In *Proceedings of the Fifth Conference on Machine Translation*, pages 1049–1055, Online. Association for Computational Linguistics.

Tharindu Ranasinghe, Constantin Orasan, and Ruslan Mitkov. 2020b. TransQuest: Translation quality estimation with cross-lingual transformers. In *Proceedings of the 28th International Conference on Computational Linguistics*, pages 5070–5081, Barcelona, Spain (Online). International Committee on Computational Linguistics.

Matthew Snover, Bonnie Dorr, Rich Schwartz, Linnea Micciulla, and John Makhoul. 2006. A study of translation edit rate with targeted human annotation. In *Proceedings of the 7th Conference of the Association for Machine Translation in the Americas: Technical Papers*, pages 223–231, Cambridge, Massachusetts, USA. Association for Machine Translation in the Americas.

Lucia Specia, Frédéric Blain, Marina Fomicheva, Erick Fonseca, Vishrav Chaudhary, Francisco Guzmán, and André F. T. Martins. 2020. Findings of the WMT 2020 shared task on quality estimation. In *Proceedings of the Fifth Conference on Machine Translation*, pages 743–764, Online. Association for Computational Linguistics.

Lucia Specia, Frédéric Blain, Varvara Logacheva, Ramón F. Astudillo, and André F. T. Martins. 2018a. Findings of the WMT 2018 shared task on quality estimation. In *Proceedings of the Third Conference on Machine Translation: Shared Task Papers*, pages 689–709, Belgium, Brussels. Association for Computational Linguistics.

Lucia Specia, Gustavo Paetzold, and Carolina Scarton. 2015. Multi-level translation quality prediction with QuEst++. In *Proceedings of ACL-IJCNLP 2015 System Demonstrations*, pages 115–120, Beijing, China. Association for Computational Linguistics and The Asian Federation of Natural Language Processing.

Lucia Specia, Carolina Scarton, and Gustavo Henrique Paetzold. 2018b. Quality estimation for machine translation. *Synthesis Lectures on Human Language Technologies*, 11(1):1–162.

Lucia Specia, Kashif Shah, Jose G.C. de Souza, and Trevor Cohn. 2013. QuEst - a translation quality estimation framework. In *Proceedings of the 51st Annual Meeting of the Association for Computational Linguistics: System Demonstrations*, pages 79–84, Sofia, Bulgaria. Association for Computational Linguistics.

Lucia Specia, Marco Turchi, Nicola Cancedda, Nello Cristianini, and Marc Dymetman. 2009. Estimating the sentence-level quality of machine translation systems. In *Proceedings of the 13th Annual conference of the European Association for Machine Translation*, Barcelona, Spain. European Association for Machine Translation.

Ashish Vaswani, Noam Shazeer, Niki Parmar, Jakob Uszkoreit, Llion Jones, Aidan N. Gomez, Łukasz Kaiser, and Illia Polosukhin. 2017. Attention is all you need. In *Proceedings of the 31st International Conference on Neural Information Processing Systems*, NIPS'17, page 6000–6010, Red Hook, NY, USA. Curran Associates Inc.

Thomas Wolf, Lysandre Debut, Victor Sanh, Julien Chaumond, Clement Delangue, Anthony Moi, Pierric Cistac, Tim Rault, Remi Louf, Morgan Funtowicz, Joe Davison, Sam Shleifer, Patrick von Platen, Clara Ma, Yacine Jernite, Julien Plu, Canwen Xu, Teven Le Scao, Sylvain Gugger, Mariama Drame, Quentin Lhoest, and Alexander Rush. 2020. Transformers: State-of-the-art natural language processing. In *Proceedings of the 2020 Conference on Empirical Methods in Natural Language Processing: System Demonstrations*, pages 38–45, Online. Association for Computational Linguistics.

Author Index

Association for Computational Linguistics
209 N. Eighth Street
Stroudsburg, Pennsylvania 18360

ISBN 978-1-7138-9162-8

CURRAN ASSOCIATES INC.
proceedings.com